MY PAST AND THOUGHTS

The Memoirs of Alexander Herzen

TRANSLATED BY Constance Garnett

REVISED BY Humphrey Higgens

INTRODUCTION by Isaiah Berlin

ABRIDGED, WITH A PREFACE AND NOTES

by *Dwight Macdonald*

MY PAST AND THOUGHTS

*The Memoirs of
Alexander Herzen*

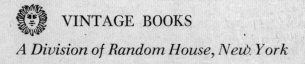 VINTAGE BOOKS

A Division of Random House, New York

Library of Congress Cataloging in Publication Data
Hertzen, Aleksandr Ivnovich, 1812–1870.
   My past and thoughts.
   Reprint of the 1968 ed., published by Knopf,
New York.
   1. Hertzen, Aleksandr Ivanovich, 1812–1870.
I. Title.
[DK209.6.H4A35 1974] 947'.07'0924 [B] 73–15933
ISBN 0–394–71979–4
Manufactured in the United States of America

Who is entitled to write his reminiscences?

Everyone.

Because no one is obliged to read them.

In order to write one's reminiscences it is not at all necessary to be a great man, nor a notorious criminal, nor a celebrated artist, nor a statesman—it is quite enough to be simply a human being, to have something to tell, and not merely to desire to tell it but at least have some little ability to do so.

Every life is interesting; if not the personality, then the environment, the country are interesting, the life itself is interesting. Man likes to enter into another existence, he likes to touch the subtlest fibres of another's heart, and to listen to its beating . . . he compares, he checks it by his own, he seeks for himself confirmation, sympathy, justification. . . .

But may not memoirs be tedious, may not the life described be colourless and commonplace?

Then we shall not read it—there is no worse punishment for a book than that.

Moreover, the right to indite one's memoirs is no relief for the chagrin of this. Benvenuto Cellini's *Diary* is not interesting because he was an excellent worker in gold but because it is in itself as interesting as any novel.

The fact is that the very word 'entitled' to this or that form of composition does not belong to our epoch, but dates from an era of intellectual immaturity, from an era of poet-laureates, doctors' caps, corporations of savants, certificated philosophers, diploma'ed metaphysicians and other Pharisees of the Christian world. Then the act of writing was regarded as something sacred, a man writing for the public used a high-flown, unnatural, choice language; he 'expounded' or 'sang'.

We simply talk; for us writing is the same sort of secular pursuit, the same sort of work or amusement as any other. In this connection it is difficult to dispute 'the right to work'. Whether the work will find recognition and approval is quite a different matter.

A year ago I published in Russian part of my memoirs under the title of *Prison and Exile*. I published it in London at the beginning of the [Crimean] war. I did not reckon upon readers nor upon any attention outside Russia. The success of that book exceeded all expectations: the *Revue des Deux Mondes*, the most chaste and conceited of journals, published half the book in a French translation; the clever and learned *Athenaeum* printed · extracts in English; the whole book has appeared in German and is being published in English.

That is why I have decided to print extracts from other parts.

In another place I speak of the immense importance my memoirs have for me personally, and the object with which I began writing them. I confine myself now to the general remark that the publication of contemporary memoirs is particularly useful for us Russians. Thanks to the censorship we are not accustomed to anything being made public, and the slightest publicity frightens, checks, and surprises us. In England any man who appears on any public stage, whether as a huckster of letters or a guardian of the press, is liable to the same critical examination, to the same hisses and applause as the actor in the lowest theatre in Islington or Paddington. Neither the Queen nor her husband are excluded. It is a mighty curb!

Let our imperial *actors* of the secret and open police, who have been so well protected from publicity by the censorship and paternal punishments, know that sooner or later their deeds will come into the light of day.

ALEXANDER HERZEN, The Pole Star, 1855

CONTENTS

PREFACE

by Dwight Macdonald

ALTHOUGH THE INDEFATIGABLE Constance Garnett translated
Herzen's memoirs fifty years ago, they have never caught on
with American readers. Most people to whom I mention Herzen
have either never heard of him or confuse him with another
nineteenth-century founding father, Herzl, or with the physicist
Hertz, he of the waves. In Russia, *My Past and Thoughts* has
always been standard reading, like *War and Peace;*[1] nor is
Herzen unfamiliar to Western European readers. But like certain wines, he doesn't "travel" well. So far, he hasn't crossed the
Atlantic.

This is strange because *My Past and Thoughts* is, when it's
not great political writing, a classic of autobiography that stands
with Rousseau, Stendhal, Gibbon, Tolstoy, and Henry Adams;
one might add Trotsky and Churchill, who, like Herzen, knew
how to assimilate the personal to the historical. It is also strange
because, unlike some classics, Herzen is extremely readable.[2]
Finally, our neglect is odd because Herzen—though a friend of

---

[1] The opening section of *My Past and Thoughts*, "Nursery and University," reminds me of *War and Peace* in many ways: same period; simple,
classical prose; and large, varied cast of characters from every stratum
of Russian society. The first ten pages, on the burning of Moscow, sound
like an early draft of Tolstoy's novel, right from the first sentence: " 'Vera
Artamonovna, come tell me once more how the French came to Moscow,'
I used to say, rolling myself up in the quilt and stretching in my crib,
which was sewn round with canvas that I might not fall out."
[2] For example—also an instance of personal/historical mixture—there
is the paragraph in which he disposes of the great de Tocqueville.
(Herzen and a friend have just been arrested as suspicious foreigners during the "June Days" that drowned in blood the 1848 revolution.)
　　We were taken away by two soldiers with rifles in front, two behind, and one on each side. The first man we met was a *représentant du peuple* with a silly badge in his buttonhole; it was
Tocqueville, who had written about America. I addressed myself to
him and told him what had happened; it was not a joking matter;
they kept people in prison without any sort of trial, threw them
into the cellars of the Tuileries, and shot them. Tocqueville did not
even ask who we were; he very politely bowed himself off, delivering himself of the following banality: "The legislative authority has

Bakunin and an enemy of Marx—was the founding father of revolutionary socialism in Russia (Lenin revered him) and because, after 1917, our intelligentsia have often seemed more interested in Russian politics than in their own.

There were, of course, reasons why in the thirties we didn't respond to Herzen. In those innocent days, the outrages against rationality and human feeling that we read about in the daily papers were stimulating rather than depressing, since they revealed how absurd and hateful (therefore intolerable, therefore soon to be shattered by the revolutionary masses) was the capitalist status quo. (And we knew just the kind of society that should replace it and how to go about the job.) Marx was our man then, the scholarly genius whose titanic labors in the British Museum had discovered History's "laws of motion"—the prophet of the proletariat as savior and redeemer. (Marx did all right as John the Baptist, but his Jesus wasn't up to the part.) Now we are a world war and a few aborted revolutions the wiser and have come to be suspicious even of the Laws of History. We are, in fact, in much the same state of mind as Herzen after the failure of the 1848 revolution: despair and doubt ravage us, the Marxian dream has turned into the Russian nightmare (or the British doze), and so now we should be able to appreciate Herzen's unsystematic, skeptical, and free-thinking (also free-feeling) approach. His disenchantment, shot through with irony and rooted in his lifelong habit of judging abstract ideas by their concrete results—these qualities now seem to us (or rather, to me: an emendation Herzen would have approved; his political thinking was always personal) more attractive, and more useful, than Marx's optimistic, humorless, and somewhat inhuman doctrine of inevitable (a word Herzen would never have used) progress via historical/materialistical/dialectical necessity (another un-Herzenian word).

It may be objected that Herzen has no "message" for us today. True enough, if a positive program is meant: Herzen was a critic, a reflective observer, and usually a "negativist." All we

---

no right to interfere with the executive." How could he have helped being a minister under Napoleon III!

Fair comment, except for the last sentence, which is a polemical quarter-truth. De Tocqueville was indeed, briefly (June–October, 1849), Minister of Foreign Affairs, but Louis Napoleon was then merely the duly elected President of the Second Republic. He didn't become "Napoleon III" until three years later (long after de Tocqueville had shifted to open and vigorous opposition), when a coup d'état made him the plebiscitary "Emperor of the French."

can learn from him is what a certain historical event meant to his mind and heart, not what to do about it. But this objection shows why Herzen is our man today. In a period like this, when mankind seems to be in an impasse, such a thinker precisely because he is uncommitted to solutions is more useful to us than a thinker like Marx. Herzen's reactions to 1848, for instance, are more to the point today than Marx's. The tragi-comedy of 1848 was the turning point in the intellectual development of both revolutionaries. 1848 stimulated Marx to a mighty effort at system building which now seems—"to me" understood—ethically repulsive, politically ambiguous, and, in its nineteenth-century optimism of progress, intellectually absurd. (How much more creative, usable, and simpatico the pre-1848 young Marx now appears than the mature Marx of *Das Kapital!*) 1848 threw Herzen into a permanent state of disenchantment (his discovery of his wife's infidelity was also an important factor—typically). But now that we can see what the failure of the working class to make a revolution in 1848 meant, both about the working class and Western society, Herzen's despair seems less self-indulgent and more realistic than Marx's optimistic faith. (This system have I shored up against my ruin.) Certainly it is more interesting and—that great cant word of our time—"relevant," because in it we can recognize ourselves and our historical situation as we can't in Marx. *De te fabula narratur—mon semblable, mon frère!*

The above paragraphs were written twenty-five years ago as a preface to some excerpts from *My Past and Thoughts* that I ran in the Winter 1948 number of my then magazine, *Politics*. I reprint them here (with cuts and additions which don't change the general argument) because I'm a thrifty writer and can't see why I should go to the trouble of reformulating what I've already expressed well enough, especially since a quarter-century of American political experience hasn't (alas) "dated" my 1948 remarks. And the last eight years of Johnsonnixonesque Vietnamization of the republic (as Rosa Luxemburg observed, imperialism brutalizes the "mother," or rather "stepmother," country as damagingly as it does the colonies) have depressed me to a political mood which makes my old postwar state of mind look positively euphoric. I am "ravaged by doubt and despair" more virulently and am more skeptical about political programs, radical or bourgeois. My suspicions about Progress, Laws of History, and the Proletariat have long since vanished, to be replaced by bleak certainties. Had anybody predicted in 1948

that I would come to look back on the Roosevelt-Truman period
—those liblab fakers!—as a golden age relative to what we got
later, I'd have been more amused than angry. But so has it come
to pass. And even the Age of Ike now looks to me, if not golden,
at least silver compared to the leaden catastrophes of our last two
presidencies. "In short, if Marx was our man in the thirties,
Herzen may be our man in the forties" is a sentence I deleted
from my old text because it would have blown the gaff on the
spoof. But it now works well enough if "forties" is changed to
"sixties." Or maybe it's not too early to make it "seventies"—the
decade hasn't gotten off to an encouraging start.

My 1948 observations about Herzen's strange failure to catch on
over here are also still (alas) relevant. Just this week—to cite
the most recent findings of a one-man (me), one-question ("Who
was Alexander Herzen?") poll I've been unsystematically con-
ducting for years—I drew the normal blank from two friends I
really thought might know: a sixtyish professor of English, free-
wheeling in his interests and an accomplished parodist, and the
clever, knowledgeable (I thought) youngish editor of a sociocul-
tural "little magazine" I admire. The professor was able to
connect Herzen with politics but ran out of gas on when, where,
and, indeed, who. The editor—just the sort of free-thinker
Herzen would appeal to (I'm sure I've done for him what Meyer
Schapiro did for me when he introduced me to the memoirs in
1943)—was completely blank.[3]

In one way, *My Past and Thoughts* is a hard book to prune
because it's alive all through, remarkably sustained in style and
thought, very few *longueurs*. But, in another way, it's an easy
book to cut because it's not really a book. Herzen was a tempera-
mental anarchist—his adherence to Proudhon and Bakunin and
his rejection of Marx had much deeper roots than politics.
Therefore, he planned his masterpiece according to the best
anarchist principles; i.e., he didn't. Like Topsy, and unlike *Das
Kapital*, it just growed. The architecture is in the most irregular
Gothic style with all sorts of outbuildings—some elegant, some
grotesque—proliferating around the central mass (if there can

---

[3] At least neither mixed him up with Herzl or Hertz. (A little learning
is a dangerous thing.) Checking up about those waves, I ran across
further evidence of Herzen's American invisibility. On my desk I have
four "college-size" dictionaries: *The American College* (Random House,
1947–55), *The Standard College* (Funk & Wagnalls, 1963), *Webster's
New World* (World, 1953–70), and *American Heritage* (Houghton
Mifflin, 1969). All list Herzl, three Hertz, none Herzen.

be a center to so amorphous an assemblage), which itself is constantly pushing up spires, adding lady chapels, breaking out rose windows, and extruding semi-detached cloisters and refectories—always just where you least expect them. Like Sterne in *Tristram Shandy*, Herzen made digression a formal principle, backing into or out of the subject or, when pressed, escaping crabwise with a scuttle to the side. As he remarked in the fourth letter of *Ends and Beginnings* (1862), that extraordinary series of super-Gothic articles disguised as letters to Turgenev, his old friend and comrade in long midnight arguments *à la Russe*:

> Please don't be angry with me for so continually wandering from the point. Parentheses are my joy and my misfortune. A French literary man of the days of the Restoration, a classic and a purist, more than once said to me, taking a pinch of snuff in that prolonged Academy way which will soon have passed away altogether: *"Notre ami abuse de la parenthèse avec intempérance!"* It is for the sake of digressions and parentheses that I prefer writing in the form of letters to friends; one can then write without embarrassment whatever comes into one's head.

My Past and Thoughts began as a series of reminiscences of his childhood and youth which he ran in the Russian-language magazines—*The Pole Star* and, later, *The Bell*—he published and edited from London, where he was a political refugee for the last twenty years of his life.[4] They were an immediate success,

---

[4] *The Bell* (*Kolokol*) was perhaps the most effective muckraking magazine in radical history. Its influence reached its apogee, 1857–62, after the liberal Alexander II had succeeded the despotic Nicholas I. *Kolokol* was widely distributed inside Russia, through underground channels, and was read in the highest offices of the state bureaucracy, including the study of the Tsar himself. "It seemed as if Herzen's *Kolokol* had as many contributors as readers," William Jackson Armstrong observed in *Siberia and the Nihilists* (Pacific Press, Oakland, Cal., 1890). "State secrets of which not ten persons in the empire dreamed were treated by him as things of common knowledge. . . . He kept track as accurately of the corruption and cruelties of the most insignificant police officer as he did of the transactions in the Senate and Council chamber. The dread of appearing in *Kolokol* soon paralyzed the hand of the boldest and most hardened officials in the service." Herzen explains why in the preface to the 1855 English edition of *My Exile in Siberia:* "There is no country in which memoirs can be more useful than in ours. We Russians, thanks to the censorship, are little accustomed to publicity; it frightens, astonishes and offends us. It is time the Imperial artists of the police of St. Petersburg should know that sooner or later their actions, so well hidden by

and so to this nucleus he added from time to time the variegated
products of his prolific journalism, finally giving the medley a
title which covers anything and everything.

The four volumes of the recent Garnett-Higgens version
(Knopf, 1968), from which I have quarried the present abridgment, are structurally an anthology which includes a variety of
subjects in a variety of prose styles. THE NOVEL: "Nursery and
University," whose 150 pages begin Volume I (they are here
given nearly complete), and in Volume II the 100 pages of "A
Family Drama" plus two short stories, "The Engelsons" and
"N. I. Sazonov" (all regretfully omitted here). THE MEMOIR: his
political life and hard times from his first arrest in 1834 to his
arrival in London as an exile for the rest of his life, in 1852
(these occupy the rest of Volumes I and II). THE "PROFILE":
mini and major, of the myriad characters of every class, nation
and politics he met in his active and gregarious life—most are
vignettes, some are full-length portraits (Mazzini, Garibaldi,
Kossuth, Owen, Bakunin, Proudhon, Vitberg, Belinsky, Ketscher),
all are executed with verve, wit, psychological acuity and a
novelist's flair for detail. REPORTAGE that would have made his
fortune—not that he needed another one—had there been a
nineteenth-century *New Yorker*: "The Tsarevich's Visit" in
Volume I; "Money and the Police" in Volume II, with the vivid,
and admiring, sketch of Rothschild at work in his bank (Herzen
was the least snobbish of radicals—like Gandhi, he treated the
rich as social equals); the superb chapters in Volume III on the
national idiosyncrasies of the post-1848 French, Italian, Polish,
Russian and German refugees in London, with whom as the only
comrade in town with ready cash (and a reputation as a soft
touch not completely deserved—his brain was always working)
he became widely acquainted; and his story of Prince Golitsyn
and his serf musicians (see pp. 539–49), a Gogolian comedy
Herzen does full justice to. HISTORY: the chief examples are "The
Emperor Alexander and Karazin" and "Princess Dashkov,"
which are magnificent but also 107 pages, and not even so fat an
abridged edition as this could contain them; they are in Volume

---

prisons, handcuffs and graves, will be revealed in the full glare of day."
Turgenev once told Herzen that when the actors of the Imperial Theater
in Moscow had a row with the director and were getting nowhere, one
of them finally exclaimed: "We will write to *Kolokol*!" The director
caved in at once. . . . Tangentially but profoundly to the present point
is an anecdote from an earlier period of tsarism. Peter the Great asked
an old hitherto faithful manservant why he had conspired to kill him.
"Because the mind loves space," was the reply, "and you cramp me."

IV, along with letters to and from Herzen and a rich variety of political, social and cultural speculations from his last decade— some of his most important writings. Herzen didn't peter out. Nor did he abandon his anarchist belief in creative disorder. Structural coherence, which has begun to erode by the end of Volume I, has by IV yielded completely to Chaos and Old Night. But a night with many stars in it.[5]

A note on the text: Constance Garnett made the first English translation of *My Past and Thoughts.* She worked from the most complete Russian text then available, Slovo's five-volume edition (Berlin, 1921). Her translation was published in six small (duodecimo) and attractive volumes between 1922 and 1927 by Chatto and Windus (London) and Alfred A. Knopf (New York). In 1968 the same publishers put out a new edition, in four large (and attractive) volumes—a revision of the Garnett translation by Humphrey Higgens. Mr. Higgens also added additional material, lacking in Slovo (and hence in Garnett), from the *Collected Works* recently published by the Academy of Sciences of the Soviet Union (Moscow, 30 vols., 1954–64). The present volume is based on Mr. Higgens's edition.

Footnotes: They come in five varieties. (*Tr.*) indicates Miss Garnett's notes (*A.S.*) the Soviet Academy of Sciences', (*R.*) Mr. Higgens's, and (*D.M.*) mine. Herzen's own, or those condensed from Herzen's text, are unmarked.

Omissions: Cuts of a page or more are indicated by ornaments between paragraphs or, when one or more following chapters are omitted, by ornaments at the end of the preceding chapter. Lesser cuts are not indicated—i.e., all dots (. . . .) were in the original. I've made very few lesser cuts because (a) I think they

---

[5] The most discerning appreciation of Herzen as a writer I know is V. S. Pritchett's in *The New Statesman & Nation* for June 12 and 19, 1943. Some excerpts: "His power of observation is extraordinary. . . . Herzen's memory particularizes and generalizes. . . . His most important quality is his sense of situation. . . . his gift for knowing not only what people are but how they are [historically] situated. How rare is the capacity to locate character in its time. . . . His memoirs are the autobiography of a European. . . . He tells a story with the economy of a great reporter. . . . Herzen hardened into a man who could record his experience with an uncommon mixture of nostalgia and scorn. One tempers the other. . . . He is interesting because he is, in many ways, writing our own history, but in that stringent and speculative manner which has disappeared since the decline of philosophic education. Somewhere in the pages of this hard, honest observer of what movements do to men, we shall find ourselves."

distort an author's style more than the big ones do, and (b)
Herzen is too good a writer, his prose is too close-knit and
texturally harmonious to need, or deserve, retail editing. That's
for *patzers*, not for grand masters like Herzen, who is articulate
but not verbose, explicit but never otiose.

Supplementary reading: There are two important books in
English. For Herzen's political-intellectual development in the
context of his period and for a critical psychobiography (the
book's range is wider than its title suggests), read Martin
Malia's *Alexander Herzen and the Birth of Russian Socialism,
1812–1855* (Harvard University Press, 1961). For Herzen's personal life after he left Russia in 1847 up to his death in 1870, see
E. H. Carr's *The Romantic Exiles* (London 1933; Penguin paper-
back, 1968), a fascinating piece of scholarly detective work like
A. J. A. Symons's *The Quest for Corvo*. Mr. Carr has turned up
new material from Herzen's daughter, Herwegh's son, and other
primary sources that supplements, or corrects, factually at least,
the more intimate sections of the memoirs such as "A Family
Drama," Herzen's story of the liaison between his wife and the
German revolutionary poetaster, Georg Herwegh. Carr's book is
subtitled "A 19th-Century Portrait Gallery," which is accurate.
Mr. Carr throws new light on many other figures in the memoirs, notably N. P. Ogarëv ("Poor Nick"), Herzen's lifelong
friend and collaborator, whose wife, Natalie, became in the
London years Herzen's mistress without breaking up, or even
straining, their friendship.

INTRODUCTION

by Isaiah Berlin

ALEXANDER HERZEN, like Diderot, was an amateur of genius whose opinions and activities changed the direction of social thought in his country. Like Diderot, too, he was a brilliant and irrepressible talker: he talked equally well in Russian and in French to his intimate friends and in the Moscow salons—always in an overwhelming flow of ideas and images; the waste, from the point of view of posterity (just as with Diderot) is probably immense: he had no Boswell and no Eckermann to record his conversation, nor was he a man who would have suffered such a relationship. His prose is essentially a form of talk, with the vices and virtues of talk: eloquent, spontaneous, liable to the heightened tones and exaggerations of the born story-teller, unable to resist long digressions which themselves carry him into a network of intersecting tributaries of memory or speculation, but always returning to the main stream of the story or the argument; but above all, his prose has the vitality of spoken words—it appears to owe nothing to the carefully composed formal sentences of the French *'philosophes'* whom he admired or to the terrible philosophical style of the Germans from whom he learnt; we hear his voice almost too much—in the essays, the pamphlets, the autobiography, as much as in the letters and scraps of notes to his friends.

Civilised, imaginative, self-critical, Herzen was a marvellously gifted social observer; the record of what he saw is unique even in the articulate nineteenth century. He had an acute, easily stirred and ironical mind, a fiery and poetical temperament, and a capacity for vivid, often lyrical, writing—qualities that combined and reinforced each other in the succession of sharp vignettes of men, events, ideas, personal relationships, political situations and descriptions of entire forms of life in which his writings abound. He was a man of extreme refinement and sensibility, great intellectual energy and biting wit, easily irritated *amour propre* and a taste for polemical writing; he was addicted to analysis, investigation, exposure; he saw himself as an expert 'unmasker' of appearances and conventions, and dramatised himself as a devastating discoverer of their social and moral core. Tolstoy, who had little sympathy with Herzen's opinions, and was not given to excessive praise of his contempo-

raries among men of letters, especially when they belonged to
his own class and country, said towards the end of his life that
he had never met anyone with 'so rare a combination of scintil-
lating brilliance and depth.' These gifts make a good many of
Herzen's essays, political articles, day-to-day journalism, casual
notes and reviews, and especially letters written to intimates or
to political correspondents, irresistibly readable even to-day,
when the issues with which they were concerned are for the
most part dead and of interest mainly to historians.

Although much has been written about Herzen—and not only
in Russian—the task of his biographers has not been made easier
by the fact that he left an incomparable memorial to himself in
his own greatest work—translated by Constance Garnett as *My
Past and Thoughts*—a literary masterpiece worthy to be placed
by the side of the novels of his contemporaries and countrymen,
Tolstoy, Turgenev, Dostoyevsky. Nor were they altogether unaware of this. Turgenev, an intimate and life-long friend (the
fluctuations of their personal relationship were important in the
life of both; this complex and interesting story has never been
adequately told) admired him as a writer as well as a revolutionary journalist. The celebrated critic Vissarion Belinsky discovered, described and acclaimed his extraordinary literary gift
when they were both young and relatively unknown. Even the
angry and suspicious Dostoyevsky excepted him from the virulent hatred with which he regarded the pro-Western Russian
revolutionaries, recognised the poetry of his writing, and remained well-disposed towards him until the end of his life. As
for Tolstoy, he delighted both in his society and his writings:
half a century after their first meeting in London he still remembered the scene vividly.[1]

It is strange that this remarkable writer, in his lifetime a
celebrated European figure, the admired friend of Michelet,
Mazzini, Garibaldi and Victor Hugo, long canonised in his own
country not only as a revolutionary but as one of its greatest men

---

[1] P. Sergeyenko, in his book on Tolstoy, says that Tolstoy told him in
1908 that he had a very clear recollection of his visit to Herzen in his
London house in March 1861. 'Lev Nikolaevich remembered him as a
not very large, plump little man, who generated electric energy. "Lively,
responsive, intelligent, interesting", Lev Nikolaevich explained (as usual
illustrating every shade of meaning by appropriate movements of his
hands), "Herzen at once began talking to me as if we had known each
other for a long time. I found his personality enchanting. I have never
met a more attractive man. He stood head and shoulders above all the
politicians of his own and of our time."' (P. Sergeyenko, *Tolstoi i ego
sovremenniki*, Moscow, 1911, pp. 13–14.)

of letters, is, even to-day, not much more than a name in the West. The enjoyment to be obtained from reading his prose—for the most part still untranslated—makes this a strange and gratuitous loss.

Alexander Herzen was born in Moscow on the 6th April, 1812, some months before the great fire that destroyed the city during Napoleon's occupation after the battle of Borodino. His father, Ivan Alexandrovich Yakovlev, came of an ancient family distantly related to the Romanov dynasty. Like other rich and well-born members of the Russian gentry, he had spent some years abroad, and, during one of his journeys, met, and took back to Moscow with him, the daughter of a minor Württemberg official, Luiza Haag, a gentle, submissive, somewhat colourless girl, a good deal younger than himself. For some reason, perhaps owing to the disparity in their social positions, he never married her according to the rites of the Church. Yakovlev was a member of the Orthodox Church; she remained a Lutheran.[2] He was a proud, independent, disdainful man, and had grown increasingly morose and misanthropic. He retired before the war of 1812, and at the time of the French invasion was living in bitter and resentful idleness in his house in Moscow. During the occupation he was recognised by Marshal Mortier, whom he had known in Paris, and agreed—in return for a safe conduct enabling him to take his family out of the devastated city—to carry a message from Napoleon to the Emperor Alexander. For this indiscretion he was sent back to his estates and only allowed to return to Moscow somewhat later. In his large and gloomy house on the Arbat he brought up his son, Alexander, to whom he had given the surname Herzen, as if to stress the fact that he was the child of an irregular liaison, an affair of the heart. Luiza Haag was never accorded the full status of a wife, but the boy had every attention lavished upon him. He received the normal education of a young Russian nobleman of his time, that is to say, he was looked after by a host of nurses and serfs, and taught by private tutors, German and French, carefully chosen by his neurotic, irritable, devoted, suspicious father. Every care was taken to develop his gifts. He was a lively and imaginative child and absorbed knowledge easily and eagerly. His father loved him after his fashion: more, certainly, than his other son, also illegitimate, born ten years earlier, whom he had christened Yegor (George). But he was, by the eighteen-twenties, a defeated and

---

[2] There is evidence, although it is not conclusive, that she was married to him according to the Lutheran rite, not recognised by the Orthodox Church.

gloomy man, unable to communicate with his family or indeed anyone else. Shrewd, honourable, and neither unfeeling nor unjust, a 'difficult' character like old Prince Bolkonsky in Tolstoy's *War and Peace*, Ivan Yakovlev emerges from his son's recollections a self-lacerating, grim, shut-in, half-frozen human being, who terrorised his household with his whims and his sarcasm. He kept all doors and windows locked, the blinds permanently drawn, and, apart from a few old friends and his own brothers, saw virtually nobody. In later years his son described him as the product of 'the encounter of two such incompatible things as the eighteenth century and Russian life'—a collision of cultures that had destroyed a good many among the more sensitive members of the Russian gentry in the reigns of Catherine II and her successors. The boy escaped with relief from his father's oppressive and frightening company to the rooms occupied by his mother and the servants; she was kind and unassuming, crushed by her husband, frightened by her foreign surroundings, and seemed to accept her almost Oriental status in the household with uncomplaining resignation. As for the servants, they were serfs from the Yakovlev estates, trained to behave obsequiously to the son and probable heir of their master. Herzen himself, in later years, attributed the deepest of all his social feelings (which his friend, the critic Belinsky, diagnosed so accurately), concern for the freedom and dignity of human individuals, to the barbarous conditions that surrounded him in childhood. He was a favourite child, and much spoiled; but the facts of his irregular birth and of his mother's status were brought home to him by listening to the servants' gossip and, on at least one occasion, by overhearing a conversation about himself between his father and one of his old army comrades. The shock was, according to his own testimony, profound: it was probably one of the determining factors of his life.

He was taught Russian literature and history by a young university student, an enthusiastic follower of the new Romantic movement, which, particularly in its German form, had then begun to dominate Russian intellectual life. He learned French (which his father wrote more easily than Russian) and German (which he spoke with his mother) and European, rather than Russian, history—his tutor was a French refugee who had emigrated to Russia after the French Revolution. The Frenchman did not reveal his political opinions, so Herzen tells us, until one day, when his pupil asked him why Louis XVI had been executed; to this he replied in an altered voice, 'Because he was a traitor to his country', and finding the boy responsive, threw off his reserve and spoke to him openly about the liberty and equality of men. Herzen was a lonely child, at once pampered and cramped, lively and bored; he read voraciously in his father's large library, especially French books of the Enlightenment. He was fourteen when the leaders of the Decembrist conspiracy were hanged by the Emperor Nicholas I. He later declared that this event was the critical turning point of his life; whether this was so or not, the memory of these aristocratic martyrs in the cause of Russian constitutional liberty later became a sacred symbol to him, as to many others of his class and generation, and affected him for the rest of his days. He tells us that a few years after this, he and his intimate friend Nick Ogarëv, standing on the Sparrow Hills above Moscow, took a solemn 'Hannibalic' oath to avenge these fighters for the rights of man, and to dedicate their own lives to the cause for which they had died.

In due course he became a student in the University of Moscow, read Schiller and Goethe, and somewhat later the French utopian socialists, Saint-Simon, Fourier and other social prophets smuggled into Russia in defiance of the censorship, and became a convinced and passionate radical. He and Ogarëv belonged to a group of students who read forbidden books and discussed dangerous ideas; for this he was, together with most other 'unreliable' students, duly arrested and, probably because he declined to repudiate the views imputed to him, condemned to imprisonment. His father used all his influence to get the sentence mitigated, but could not save his son from being exiled to the provincial city of Vyatka, near the borders of Asia, where he was not indeed kept in prison, but put to work in the local administration. To his astonishment, he enjoyed this new test of his powers; he displayed administrative gifts and became a far more competent and perhaps even enthusiastic official than he was later prepared to admit, and helped to expose the corrupt and brutal governor, whom he detested and despised. In Vyatka he became involved in a passionate love affair with a married woman, behaved badly, and suffered agonies of contrition. He read Dante, went through a religious phase, and began a long and passionate correspondence with his first cousin Natalie, who, like himself, was illegitimate, and lived as a companion in the house of a rich and despotic aunt. As a result of his father's ceaseless efforts, he was transferred to the city of Vladimir, and with the help of his young Moscow friends, arranged the elopement of Natalie. They were married in Vladimir against their relations' wishes. He was in due course allowed to return to

Moscow and was appointed to a government post in Petersburg. Whatever his ambitions at the time, he remained indomitably independent and committed to the radical cause. As a result of an indiscreet letter, opened by the censors, in which he had criticised the behaviour of the police, he was again sentenced to a period of exile, this time in Novgorod. Two years later, in 1842, he was once more permitted to return to Moscow. He was by then regarded as an established member of the new radical intelligentsia, and, indeed, as an honoured martyr in its cause, and began to write in the progressive periodicals of the time. He always dealt with the same central theme: the oppression of the individual; the humiliation and degradation of men by political and personal tyranny; the yoke of social custom, the dark ignorance, and savage, arbitrary misgovernment which maimed and destroyed human beings in the brutal and odious Russian Empire.

Like the other members of his circle, the young poet and novelist Turgenev, the critic Belinsky, the future political agitators Bakunin and Katkov (the first in the cause of revolution, the second of reaction), the literary essayist Annenkov, his own intimate friend Ogarëv, Herzen plunged into the study of German metaphysics and French sociological theory and history—the works of Kant, Schelling, and above all, Hegel; also Saint-Simon, Augustin Thierry, Leroux, Mignet and Guizot. He composed arresting historical and philosophical essays, and stories dealing with social issues; they were published, widely read and discussed, and created a considerable reputation for their author. He adopted an uncompromising position. A leading representative of the dissident Russian gentry, his socialist beliefs were caused less by a reaction against the cruelty and chaos of the *laissez-faire* economy of the bourgeois West—for Russia, then in its early industrial beginnings, was still a semi-feudal, socially and economically primitive society—than as a direct response to the agonising social problems in his native land: the poverty of the masses, serfdom and lack of individual freedom at all levels, and a lawless and brutal autocracy.[3] In addition, there was the wounded national pride of a powerful and semi-barbarous society, whose leaders were aware of its backwardness,

---

[3] The historical and sociological explanation of the origins of Russian socialism and of Herzen's part in it cannot be attempted here. It has been treated in a number of (untranslated) Russian monographs, both pre- and post-revolutionary. The most detailed and original study of this topic to date is *Alexander Herzen and the Birth of Russian Socialism, 1812–1855* (1961) by Professor Martin Malia.

and suffered from mingled admiration, envy and resentment of the civilised West. The radicals believed in reform along democratic, secular, Western lines; the Slavophils retreated into mystical nationalism, and preached the need for return to native 'organic' forms of life and faith that, according to them, had been all but ruined by Peter I's reforms, which had merely encouraged a sedulous and humiliating aping of the soulless, and, in any case, hopelessly decadent West. Herzen was an extreme 'Westerner', but he preserved his links with the Slavophil adversaries—he regarded the best among them as romantic reactionaries, misguided nationalists, but honourable allies against the Tsarist bureaucracy—and later tended systematically to minimise his differences with them, perhaps from a desire to see all Russians who were not dead to human feeling ranged in a single vast protest against the evil régime.

In 1847 Ivan Yakovlev died. He left the greater part of his fortune to Luiza Haag and her son, Alexander Herzen. With immense faith in his own powers, and burning with a desire (in Fichte's words that expressed the attitude of a generation) 'to be and do something in the world,' Herzen decided to emigrate. Whether he wished or expected to remain abroad during the rest of his life is uncertain, but so it turned out to be. He left in the same year, and travelled in considerable state, accompanied by his wife, his mother, two friends, as well as servants, and, crossing Germany, towards the end of 1847 reached the coveted city of Paris, the capital of the civilised world. He plunged at once into the life of the exiled radicals and socialists of many nationalities who played a central role in the fermenting intellectual and artistic activity of that city. By 1848, when a series of revolutions broke out in country after country in Europe, he found himself with Bakunin and Proudhon on the extreme left wing of revolutionary socialism. When rumours of his activities reached the Russian government, he was ordered to return immediately. He refused. His fortune in Russia and that of his mother were declared confiscated. Aided by the efforts of the banker James Rothschild who had conceived a liking for the young Russian 'baron' and was in a position to bring pressure on the Russian government, Herzen recovered the major portion of his resources, and thereafter experienced no financial want. This gave him a degree of independence not then enjoyed by many exiles, as well as the financial means for supporting other refugees and radical causes.

Shortly after his arrival in Paris, before the revolution, he contributed a series of impassioned articles to a Moscow periodical controlled by his friends, in which he gave an eloquent and violently critical account of the conditions of life and culture in Paris, and, in particular, a devastating analysis of the degradation of the French bourgeoisie, an indictment not surpassed even in the works of his contemporaries Marx and Heine. His Moscow friends for the most part received this with disfavour: they regarded his analyses as characteristic flights of a highly rhetorical fancy, irresponsible extremism, ill suited to the needs of a misgoverned and backward country compared to which the progress of the middle classes in the West, whatever its shortcomings, was a notable step forward towards universal enlightenment. These early works—*The Letters from Avenue Marigny* and the Italian sketches that followed—possess qualities which became characteristic of all his writings: a rapid torrent of descriptive sentences, fresh, lucid, direct, interspersed with vivid and never irrelevant digressions, variations on the same theme in many keys, puns, neologisms, quotations real and imaginary, verbal inventions, gallicisms which irritated his nationalistic Russian friends, mordant personal observations and cascades of vivid images and incomparable epigrams, which, so far from either tiring or distracting the reader by their virtuosity, add to the force and swiftness of the narrative. The effect is one of spontaneous improvisation: exhilarating conversation by an intellectually gay and exceptionally clever and honest man endowed with singular powers of observation and expression. The mood is one of ardent political radicalism imbued with a typically aristocratic (and even more typically Muscovite) contempt for everything narrow, calculating, self-satisfied, commercial, anything cautious, petty or tending towards compromise and the *juste milieu*, of which Louis Philippe and Guizot are held up to view as particularly repulsive incarnations. Herzen's outlook in these essays is a combination of optimistic idealism—a vision of a socially, intellectually and morally free society, the beginnings of which, like Proudhon, Marx, and Louis Blanc, he saw in the French working class; faith in the radical revolution which alone could create the conditions for their liberation; but with this, a deep distrust (something that most of his allies did not share) of all general formulae as such, of the programmes and battle cries of all the political parties, of the great, official historical goals—progress, liberty, equality, national unity, historic rights, human solidarity—principles and slogans in the name of which men had been, and doubtless would soon again be, violated and slaughtered, and their forms of life condemned and destroyed. Like the more extreme of the left wing disciples of

Hegel, in particular like the anarchist Max Stirner, Herzen saw danger in the great magnificent abstractions the mere sound of which precipitated men into violent and meaningless slaughter—new idols, it seemed to him, on whose altars human blood was to be shed tomorrow as irrationally and uselessly as the blood of the victims of yesterday or the day before, sacrificed in honour of older divinities—church or monarchy or the feudal order or the sacred customs of the tribe, that were now discredited as obstacles to the progress of mankind. Together with this scepticism about the meaning and value of abstract ideals as such, in contrast with the concrete, short-term, immediate goals of identifiable living individuals—specific freedoms, reward for the day's work—Herzen spoke of something even more disquieting—a haunting sense of the ever widening and unbridgeable gulf between the humane values of the relatively free and civilised élites (to which he knew himself to belong) and the actual needs, desires and tastes of the vast voiceless masses of mankind, barbarous enough in the West, wilder still in Russia or the plains of Asia beyond. The old world was crumbling visibly, and it deserved to fall. It would be destroyed by its victims—the slaves who cared nothing for the art and the science of their masters; and indeed, Herzen asks, why should they care? Was it not erected on their suffering and degradation? Young and vigorous, filled with a just hatred of the old world built on their fathers' bones, the new barbarians will raze to the ground the edifices of their oppressors, and with them all that is most sublime and beautiful in Western civilisation; such a cataclysm might be not only inevitable but justified, since this civilisation, noble and valuable in the eyes of its beneficiaries, has offered nothing but suffering, a life without meaning, to the vast majority of mankind. Yet he does not pretend that this makes the prospect, to those who, like him, have tasted the riper fruits of civilisation, any less dreadful.

It has often been asserted by both Russian and Western critics that Herzen arrived in Paris a passionate, even utopian idealist, and that it was the failure of the Revolution of 1848 which brought about his disillusionment and a new, more pessimistic realism. This is not sufficiently borne out by the evidence.[4] Even in 1847, the sceptical note, in particular pessimism about the degree to which human beings can be transformed, and the still deeper scepticism about whether such changes, even if they were

---

[4] The clearest formulation of this well-worn and almost universal thesis is to be found in Mr E. H. Carr's lively and well documented treatment of Herzen in his *The Romantic Exiles* and elsewhere. Mr Malia's book avoids this error.

achieved by fearless and intelligent revolutionaries or reformers, ideal images of whom floated before the eyes of his Westernising friends in Russia, would in fact lead to a juster and freer order, or on the contrary to the rule of new masters over new slaves— that ominous note is sounded before the great débâcle. Yet, despite this, he remained a convinced, ultimately optimistic revolutionary. The spectacle of the workers' revolt and its brutal suppression in Italy and in France, haunted Herzen all his life. His first-hand description of the events of 1848–9, in particular of the drowning in blood of the July revolt in Paris, is a masterpiece of 'committed' historical and sociological writing. So, too, are his sketches of the personalities involved in these upheavals, and his reflections upon them. Most of these essays and letters remain untranslated.

Herzen could not and would not return to Russia. He became a Swiss citizen, and to the disasters of the revolution was added a personal tragedy—the seduction of his adored wife by the most intimate of his new friends, the radical German poet Georg Herwegh, a friend of Marx and Wagner, the 'iron lark' of the German Revolution, as Heine half ironically called him. Herzen's progressive, somewhat Shelleyan, views on love, friendship, equality of the sexes, and the irrationality of bourgeois morality, were tested by this crisis and broken by it. He went almost mad with grief and jealousy: his love, his vanity, his deeper assumptions about the basis of all human relationships, suffered a traumatic shock from which he was never fully to recover. He did what few others have ever done: described every detail of his own agony, every step of his altering relationship with his wife, with Herwegh and Herwegh's wife, as they seemed to him in retrospect; he noted every communication that occurred between them, every moment of anger, despair, affection, love, hope, hatred, contempt and agonised, suicidal self-contempt. Every tone and *nuance* in his own moral and psychological condition are raised to high relief against the background of his public life in the world of exiles and conspirators, French, Italian, German, Russian, Austrian, Hungarian, Polish, who move on and off the stage on which he himself is always the central, self-absorbed, tragic hero. The account is not unbalanced —there is no obvious distortion—but it is wholly egocentric. All his life Herzen perceived the external world clearly, and in proportion, but through the medium of his own self-romanticising personality, with his own impressionable, ill-organised self at the centre of his universe. No matter how violent his torment, he retains full artistic control of the tragedy which he is living through, but also writing. It is, perhaps, this artistic egotism, which all his work exhibits, that was in part responsible both for Natalie's suffocation and for the lack of reticence in his description of what took place: Herzen takes wholly for granted the reader's understanding, and still more, his undivided interest in every detail of his own, the writer's, mental and emotional life. Natalie's letters and desperate flight to Herwegh show the measure of the increasingly destructive effect of Herzen's self-absorbed blindness upon her frail and *exalté* temperament. We know comparatively little of Natalie's relationship with Herwegh: she may well have been physically in love with him, and he with her: the inflated literary language of the letters conceals more than it reveals; what is clear is that she felt unhappy, trapped and irresistibly attracted to her lover. If Herzen sensed this, he perceived it very dimly. He appropriated the feelings of those nearest him as he did the ideas of Hegel or George Sand: that is, he took what he needed, and poured it into the vehement torrent of his own experience. He gave generously, if fitfully, to others; he put his own life into them, but for all his deep and life-long belief in individual liberty and the absolute value of personal life and personal relationships, scarcely understood or tolerated wholly independent lives by the side of his own; his description of his agony is scrupulously and bitterly detailed and accurate, never self-sparing, eloquent but not sentimental, and remorselessly self-absorbed. It is a harrowing document. He did not publish the story in full during his lifetime, but now it forms part of his Memoirs.

Self-expression—the need to say his own word—and perhaps the craving for recognition by others, by Russia, by Europe, were primary needs of Herzen's nature. Consequently, even during this, the darkest period of his life, he continued to pour out a stream of letters and articles in various languages on political and social topics; he helped to keep Proudhon going, kept up a correspondence with Swiss radicals and Russian *émigrés*, read widely, made notes, conceived ideas, argued, worked unremittingly both as a publicist and as an active supporter of left wing and revolutionary causes. After a short while Natalie returned to him in Nice, only to die in his arms. Shortly before her death, a ship on which his mother and one of his children, a deaf-mute, were travelling from Marseilles, sank in a storm. Their bodies were not found. Herzen's life had reached its lowest ebb. He left Nice and the circle of Italian, French and Polish revolutionaries to many of whom he was bound by ties of warm friendship, and with his three surviving children went to England. America was

too far away and, besides, seemed to him too dull. England was
no less remote from the scene of his defeats, political and personal, and yet still a part of Europe. It was then the country
most hospitable to political refugees, civilised, tolerant of eccentricities or indifferent to them, proud of its civil liberties and its
sympathy with the victims of foreign oppression. He arrived in
London in 1851.

He and his children wandered from home to home in London
and its suburbs, and there, after the death of Nicholas I had
made it possible for him to leave Russia, his most intimate
friend, Nicholay Ogarëv, joined them. Together they set up a
printing press, and began to publish a periodical in Russian
called *The Pole Star*—the first organ wholly dedicated to uncompromising agitation against the Imperial Russian régime.
The earliest chapters of *My Past and Thoughts* appeared in its
pages. The memory of the terrible years 1848–51 obsessed
Herzen's thoughts and poisoned his blood stream: it became an
inescapable psychological necessity for him to seek relief by
setting down this bitter history. This was the first section of his
Memoirs to be written. It was an opiate against the appalling
loneliness of a life lived among uninterested strangers[5] while
political reaction seemed to envelop the entire world, leaving no
room for hope. Insensibly he was drawn into the past. He moved
further and further into it and found it a source of liberty and
strength. This is how the book which he conceived on the anal-
ogy of *David Copperfield* came to be composed.[6] He began to

---

[5] Herzen had no close English friends, although he had associates, allies,
and admirers. One of these, the radical journalist W. J. Linton, to whose
English Republic Herzen had contributed articles, described him as
'short of stature, stoutly built, in his last days inclined to corpulence, with
a grand head, long chestnut hair and beard, small luminous eyes, and
rather ruddy complexion. Suave in his manner, courteous, but with an
intense power of irony, witty, . . . clear, concise and impressive, he was
a subtle and profound thinker, with all the passionate nature of the
"barbarian," yet generous and humane.' (*Memories*, London, 1895, pp.
146–7.) And in his *European Republicans*, published two years earlier,
he spoke of him as 'hospitable and taking pleasure in society, . . . a good
conversationalist, with a frank and pleasing manner,' and said that the
Spanish radical Castelar declared that Herzen, with his fair hair and
beard, looked like a Goth, but possessed the warmth, vivacity, 'verve
and inimitable grace' and 'marvellous variety' of a Southerner. Turgenev
and Herzen were the first Russians to move freely in European society.
The impression that they made did a good deal, though perhaps not
enough, to dispel the myth of the dark 'Slav soul,' which took a long
time to die; perhaps it is not altogether dead yet.
[6] 'Copperfield is Dickens's *Past and Thoughts*,' he said in one of his
letters in the early sixties; humility was not among his virtues.

write it in the last months of 1852. He wrote by fits and starts. The first two parts were probably finished by the end of 1853. In 1854 a selection which he called *Prison and Exile*—a title perhaps inspired by Silvio Pellico's celebrated *Le Mie Prigioni*, was published in English. It was an immediate success; encouraged by this, he continued. By the spring of 1855, the first five parts of the work were completed; they were all published by 1857. He revised part IV, added new chapters to it and composed part V; he completed the bulk of part VI by 1858. The sections dealing with his intimate life—his love and the early years of his marriage—were composed in 1857: he could not bring himself to touch upon them until then. This was followed by an interval of seven years. Independent essays such as those on Robert Owen, the actor Shchepkin, the painter Ivanov, Garibaldi (*Camicia Rossa*), were published in London between 1860 and 1864; but these, although usually included in the Memoirs, were not intended for them. The first complete edition of the first four parts appeared in 1861. The final section—part VIII and almost the whole of part VII—were written, in that order, in 1865–7. Herzen deliberately left some sections unpublished: the most intimate details of his personal tragedy appeared posthumously—only a part of the chapter entitled *Oceano Nox* was printed in his lifetime. He omitted also the story of his affairs with Medvedeva in Vyatka and with the serf girl Katerina in Moscow—his confession of them to Natalie cast the first shadow over their relationship, a shadow that never lifted; he could not bear to see it in print while he lived. He suppressed, too, a chapter on 'The German Emigrants' which contains his unflattering comments on Marx and his followers, and some characteristically entertaining and ironical sketches of some of his old friends among the Russian radicals. He genuinely detested the practice of washing the revolutionaries' dirty linen in public, and made it clear that he did not intend to make fun of allies for the entertainment of the common enemy. The first authoritative edition of the Memoirs was compiled by Mikhail Lemke in the first complete edition of Herzen's works, which was begun before, and completed some years after, the Russian Revolution of 1917. It has since been revised in successive Soviet editions. The fullest version is that published in the new exhaustive edition of Herzen's works, a handsome monument of Soviet scholarship—which at the time of writing is still incomplete.

The Memoirs formed a vivid and broken background accompaniment to Herzen's central activity: revolutionary journalism, to which he dedicated his life. The bulk of it is contained in the

most celebrated of all Russian periodicals published abroad—
Kolokol—*The Bell*—edited by Herzen and Ogarëv in London
and then in Geneva from 1857 until 1867, with the motto (taken
from Schiller) *Vivos voco. The Bell* had an immense success. It
was the first systematic instrument of revolutionary propaganda
directed against the Russian autocracy, written with knowledge,
sincerity and mordant eloquence; it gathered round itself all
that was uncowed not only in Russia and the Russian colonies
abroad, but also among Poles and other oppressed nationalities.
It began to penetrate into Russia by secret routes and was regularly read by high officials of State, including, it was rumoured,
the Emperor himself. Herzen used the copious information that
reached him in clandestine letters and personal messages, describing various misdeeds of the Russian bureaucracy to expose
specific scandals—cases of bribery, miscarriage of justice,
tyranny and dishonesty by officials and influential persons. *The
Bell* named names, offered documentary evidence, asked awkward questions and exposed hideous aspects of Russian life.
Russian travellers visited London in order to meet the mysterious leader of the mounting opposition to the Tsar. Generals, high
officials and other loyal subjects of the Empire were among the
many visitors who thronged to see him, some out of curiosity,
others to shake his hand, to express sympathy or admiration. He
reached the peak of his fame, both political and literary, after
the defeat of Russia in the Crimean War and the death of
Nicholas I. The open appeal by Herzen to the new Emperor to
free the serfs and initiate bold and radical reforms 'from above,'
and, after the first concrete steps towards this had been taken in
1859, his paean of praise to Alexander II under the title of 'Thou
hast Conquered, O Galilean,' created the illusion on both sides of
the Russian frontier that a new liberal era was at last dawning,
in which a degree of understanding—perhaps of actual co-
operation—could be achieved between Tsardom and its opponents. This state of mind did not last long. But Herzen's credit
stood very high—higher than that of any other Russian in the
West: in the late fifties and early sixties, he was the acknowledged leader of all that was generous, enlightened, civilised,
humane in Russia. More than Bakunin and even Turgenev,
whose novels formed a central source of knowledge about Russia
in the West, Herzen counteracted the legend, ingrained in the
minds of progressive Europeans (of whom Michelet was perhaps
the most representative), that Russia consisted of nothing save
only the government jack-boot on the one hand, and the dark,

silent, sullen mass of brutalised peasants on the other—an image that was the by-product of the widespread sympathy for the principal victim of Russian despotism, the martyred nation, Poland. Some among the Polish exiles spontaneously conceded this service to the truth on Herzen's part, if only because he was one of the rare Russians who genuinely liked and admired individual Poles, worked in close sympathy with them, and identified the cause of Russian liberation with that of all her oppressed subject nationalities. It was, indeed, this unswerving avoidance of chauvinism that was among the principal causes of the ultimate collapse of *The Bell* and of Herzen's own political undoing.

After Russia, Herzen's deepest love was for Italy and the Italians. The closest ties bound him to the Italian exiles, Mazzini, Garibaldi, Saffi and Orsini. Although he supported every liberal beginning in France, his attitude towards her was more ambiguous. For this there were many reasons. Like Tocqueville (whom he personally disliked), he had a distaste for all that was centralised, bureaucratic, hierarchical, subject to rigid forms or rules; France was to him the incarnation of order, discipline, the worship of the state, of unity, and of despotic, abstract formulae that flattened all things to the same rule and pattern—something that had a family resemblance to the great slave states—Prussia, Austria, Russia; with this he constantly contrasts the decentralised, uncrushed, untidy, 'truly democratic' Italians, whom he believed to possess a deep affinity with the free Russian spirit embodied in the peasant commune with its sense of natural justice and human worth. To this ideal even England seemed to him to be far less hostile than legalistic, calculating France: in such moods he comes close to his romantic Slavophil opponents. Moreover, he could not forget the betrayal of the revolution in Paris by the bourgeois parties in 1848, the execution of the workers, the suppression of the Roman Revolution by the troops of the French Republic, the vanity, weakness and rhetoric of the French radical politicians—Lamartine, Marrast, Ledru-Rollin, Félix Pyat. His sketches of the lives and behaviour of leading French exiles in England are masterpieces of amused, half-sympathetic, half-contemptuous description of the grotesque and futile aspects of every political emigration condemned to sterility, intrigue and a constant flow of self-justifying eloquence before a foreign audience too remote or bored to listen. Yet he thought well of individual members of it: he had for a time been a close ally of Proudhon, and despite their differences, he continued to respect him; he regarded Louis Blanc as an honest and fearless democrat, he was on good terms with Victor Hugo, he liked and admired Michelet. In later years he visited at least one Paris political salon—admittedly, it was that of a Pole—with evident enjoyment: the Goncourts met him there and left a vivid description in their journal of his appearance and his conversation.[7] Although he was half German himself, or perhaps because of it, he felt, like his friend Bakunin, a strong aversion from what he regarded as the incurable philistinism of the Germans, and what seemed to him a peculiarly unattractive combination of craving for blind authority with a tendency to squalid internecine recriminations in public, more pronounced than among other émigrés. Perhaps his hatred of Herwegh, whom he knew to be a friend both of Marx and of Wagner, as well as Marx's onslaughts on Karl Vogt, the Swiss naturalist to whom Herzen was devoted, played some part in this. At least three of his most intimate friends were pure Germans. Goethe and Schiller meant more to him than any Russian writers. Yet there is something genuinely venomous in his account of the German exiles, quite different from the high-spirited sense of comedy with which he describes the idiosyncrasies of the other foreign colonies gathered in London in the fifties and sixties—a city, if we are to believe Herzen, equally unconcerned with their absurdities and

---

[7] See entry in the *Journal* under *8th February* 1865—'Dinner at Charles Edmond's (Chojecki) . . . A Socratic mask with the warm and transparent flesh of a Rubens portrait, a red mark between the eyebrows as from a branding iron, greying beard and hair. As he talks there is a constant ironical chuckle which rises and falls in his throat. His voice is soft and slow, without any of the coarseness one might have expected from the huge neck; the ideas are fine, delicate, pungent, at times subtle, always definite, illuminated by words that take time to arrive, but which always possess the felicitous quality of French as it is spoken by a civilised and witty foreigner.

'He speaks of Bakunin, of his eleven months in prison, chained to a wall, of his escape from Siberia by the Amur River, of his return by way of California, of his arrival in London, where, after a stormy, moist embrace, his first words to Herzen were "Can one get oysters here?".'

Herzen delighted the Goncourts with stories about the Emperor Nicholas walking in the night in his empty palace, after the fall of Eupatoria during the Crimean War, with the heavy, unearthly steps of the stone statue of the Commander in 'Don Juan.' This was followed by anecdotes about English habits and manners—'a country which he loves as the land of liberty'—to illustrate its absurd, class conscious, unyielding traditionalism, particularly noticeable in the relations of masters and servants. The Goncourts quote a characteristic epigram made by Herzen to illustrate the difference between the French and English characters. They faithfully report the story of how James Rothschild managed to save Herzen's property in Russia.

their martyrdoms. As for his hosts, the English, they seldom
appear in his pages. Herzen had met Mill, Carlyle and Owen.
His first night in England was spent with English hosts. He was
on reasonably good terms with one or two editors of radical
papers (some of whom, like Linton and Cowen, helped him to
propagate his views, and to preserve contact with revolutionaries
on the continent as well with clandestine traffic of propaganda to
Russia), and several radically inclined Members of Parliament,
including minor ministers. In general, however, he seems to
have had even less contact with Englishmen than his contemporary and fellow exile, Karl Marx. He admired England. He
admired her constitution; the wild and tangled wood of her
unwritten laws and customs brought the full resources of his
romantic imagination into play. The entertaining passages of
My Past and Thoughts in which he compared the French and
the English, or the English and the Germans, display acute and
amused insight into the national characteristics of the English.
But he could not altogether like them: they remained for him too
insular, too indifferent, too unimaginative, too remote from the
moral, social and aesthetic issues which lay closest to his own
heart, too materialistic and self-satisfied. His judgments about
them, always intelligent and sometimes penetrating, are distant
and tend to be conventional. A description of the trial in London
of a French radical who had killed a political opponent in a duel
in Windsor Great Park is wonderfully executed, but remains a
piece of *genre* painting, a gay and brilliant caricature. The
French, the Swiss, the Italians, even the Germans, certainly the
Poles, are closer to him. He cannot establish any genuine personal relationship with the English. When he thinks of mankind
he does not think of them.

Apart from his central preoccupations, he devoted himself to
the education of his children, which he entrusted in part to an
idealistic German lady, Malwida von Meysenbug, afterwards a
friend of Nietzsche and Romain Rolland. His personal life was
intertwined with that of his intimate friend Ogarëv, and of
Ogarëv's wife who became his mistress; in spite of this the
mutual devotion of the two friends remained unaltered—the
Memoirs reveal little of the curious emotional consequences of
this relationship.[8]

---

[8] See chapters 8 and 12 of E. H. Carr's *The Romantic Exiles* for what
the Memoirs don't reveal, which is a lot. Carr's account draws largely
on Natalie Ogarëv's unpublished diaries. Similarly, Carr uses papers

For the rest, he lived the life of an affluent, well born man of letters, a member of the Russian, and more specifically, Moscow gentry, uprooted from his native soil, unable to achieve a settled existence or even the semblance of inward or outward peace, a life filled with occasional moments of hope and even exultation, followed by long periods of misery, corrosive self-criticism, and most of all overwhelming, omnivorous, bitter nostalgia. It may be this, as much as objective reasons, that caused him to idealise the Russian peasant, and to dream that the answer to the central 'social' question of his time—that of growing inequality, exploitation, dehumanisation of both the oppressor and the oppressed—lay in the preservation of the Russian peasant commune. He perceived in it the seeds of the development of a non-industrial, semi-anarchist socialism. Only such a solution, plainly influenced by the views of Fourier, Proudhon and George Sand, seemed to him free from the crushing, barrack-room discipline demanded by Western communists from Cabet to Marx; and from the equally suffocating, and, it seemed to him, far more vulgar and philistine ideals contained in moderate, half-socialist doctrines, with their faith in the progressive role of developing industrialism preached by the forerunners of social democracy in Germany and France and of the Fabians in England. At times he modified his view: towards the end of his life he began to recognise the historical significance of the organised urban workers. But all in all, he remained faithful to his belief in the Russian peasant commune as an embryonic form of a life in which the quest for individual freedom was reconciled with the need for collective activity and responsibility. He retained to the end a romantic vision of the inevitable coming of a new, just, all-transforming social order.

Herzen is neither consistent nor systematic. His style during his middle years has lost the confident touch of his youth, and conveys the consuming nostalgia that never leaves him. He is obsessed by a sense of blind accident, although his faith in the values of life remains unshaken. Almost all traces of Hegelian influence are gone. 'The absurdity of facts offends us . . . it is as

---

made available to him by Herwegh's son—his fascinating little book is in the Herzen style: as much novel as history—"to correct the serious omission and inaccuracies of the Herzen version" of the liaison between the German radical poet and Herzen's wife. For the Herzen version, see pp. 840–920 and 932–50 of the complete Garnett-Higgens edition (Knopf, 1968), which unhappily had to be omitted in this politically oriented abridgment. I think, myself, that the Herzen version is closer to the truth, and farther from the facts, than the Carr version. (*D.M.*)

though someone had promised that everything in the world will be exquisitely beautiful, just and harmonious. We have marvelled enough at the deep abstract wisdom of nature and history; it is time to realise that nature and history are full of the accidental and senseless, of muddle and bungling.' This is highly characteristic of his mood in the sixties; and it is no accident that his exposition is not ordered, but is a succession of fragments, episodes, isolated vignettes, a mingling of *Dichtung* and *Wahrheit*, facts and poetic licence. His moods alternate sharply. Sometimes he believes in the need for a great, cleansing, revolutionary storm, even were it to take the form of a barbarian invasion likely to destroy all the values that he himself holds dear. At other times he reproaches his old friend Bakunin, who joined him in London after escaping from his Russian prisons, for wanting to make the revolution too soon; for not understanding that dwellings for free men cannot be constructed out of the stones of a prison; that the average European of the nineteenth century is too deeply marked by the slavery of the old order to be capable of conceiving true freedom, that it is not the liberated slaves who will build the new order, but new men brought up in liberty. History has her own tempo. Patience and gradualism— not the haste and violence of a Peter the Great—can alone bring about a permanent transformation. At such moments he wonders whether the future belongs to the free, anarchic peasant, or to the bold and ruthless planner; perhaps it is the industrial worker who is to be the heir to the new, unavoidable, collectivist economic order.[9] Then again he returns to his early moods of disillusionment and wonders whether men in general really desire freedom: perhaps only a few do so in each generation, while most human beings only want good government, no matter at whose hands; and he echoes de Maistre's bitter epigram about Rousseau: 'Monsieur Rousseau has asked why it is that men who are born free are nevertheless everywhere in chains; it is as if one were to ask why sheep, who are born carnivorous, nevertheless everywhere nibble grass.' Herzen develops this theme. Men desire freedom no more than fish desire to fly. The fact that a few flying fish exist does not demonstrate that fish in general were created to fly, or are not fundamentally quite content to stay below the surface of the water, for ever away from the sun and the light. Then he returns to his earlier optimism and the thought that somewhere—in Russia—there lives the unbroken

---

[9] This is the thesis in which orthodox Soviet scholars claim to discern a belated approach to those of Marx.

human being, the peasant with his faculties intact, untainted by the corruption and sophistication of the West. But this Rousseau-inspired faith, as he grows older, grows less secure. His sense of reality is too strong. For all his efforts, and the efforts of his socialist friends, he cannot deceive himself entirely. He oscillates between pessimism and optimism, scepticism and suspicion of his own scepticism, and is kept morally alive only by his hatred of all injustice, all arbitrariness, all mediocrity as such—in particular by his inability to compromise in any degree with either the brutality of reactionaries or the hypocrisy of bourgeois liberals. He is preserved by this, buoyed up by his belief that such evils will destroy themselves, and by his love for his children and his devoted friends, and by his unquenchable delight in the variety of life and the comedy of human character.

On the whole, he grew more pessimistic. He began with an ideal vision of human life, largely ignored the chasm which divided it from the present—whether the Russia of Nicholas, or the corrupt constitutionalism in the West. In his youth he glorified Jacobin radicalism and condemned its opponents in Russia—blind conservatism, Slavophil nostalgia, the cautious gradualism of his friends Granovsky and Turgenev, as well as Hegelian appeals to patience and rational conformity to the inescapable rhythms of history, which seemed to him designed to ensure the triumph of the new bourgeois class. His attitude, before he went abroad, was boldly optimistic. There followed, not indeed a change of view, but a cooling-off, a tendency to a more sober and critical outlook. All genuine change, he began to think in 1847, is necessarily slow; the power of tradition (which he at once mocks at and admires in England) is very great; men are less malleable than was believed in the eighteenth century, nor do they truly seek liberty, only security and contentment; communism is but Tsarism stood on its head, the replacement of one yoke by another; the ideals and watchwords of politics turn out, on examination, to be empty formulae to which devout fanatics happily slaughter hecatombs of their fellows. He no longer feels certain that the gap between the enlightened élite and the masses can ever, in principle, be bridged (this becomes an obsessive refrain in later Russian thought), since the awakened people may, for unalterable psychological or sociological reasons, despise and reject the gifts of a civilisation which will never mean enough to them. But if all this is even in small part true, is radical transformation either practicable or desirable? From this follows Herzen's growing sense of obstacles that may be insurmountable, limits that may be impassable, his empiricism, scepticism, the latent pessimism and despair of the middle sixties. This is the attitude which some Soviet scholars interpret as the beginning of an approach on his part towards a quasi-Marxist recognition of the inexorable laws of social development—in particular the inevitability of industrialism, above all of the central role to be played by the proletariat. This is not how Herzen's Russian left wing critics interpreted his views in his lifetime, or for the half century that followed. To them, rightly or wrongly, these doctrines seemed symptomatic of conservatism and betrayal. For in the fifties and sixties, a new generation of radicals grew up in Russia, then a backward country in the painful process of the earliest, most rudimentary beginnings of slow, sporadic, inefficient industrialisation. These were men of mixed social origins, filled with contempt for the feeble liberal compromises of 1848, with no illusions about the prospects of freedom in the West, determined on more ruthless methods; accepting as true only what the sciences can prove, prepared to be hard, and if need be, unscrupulous and cruel, in order to break the power of their equally ruthless oppressors; bitterly hostile to the aestheticism, the devotion to civilised values, of the 'soft' generation of the forties. Herzen realised that the criticism and abuse showered upon him as an obsolete aristocratic dilet-tante by these 'nihilists' (as they came to be called after Turgenev's novel *Fathers and Sons,* in which this conflict is vividly presented for the first time) was not altogether different from the disdain that he had himself felt in his own youth for the elegant and ineffective reformers of Alexander I's reign; but this did not make his position easier to bear. What was ill-received by the tough-minded revolutionaries pleased Tolstoy, who said more than once that the censorship of Herzen's works in Russia was a characteristic blunder on the part of the govern-ment; the government, in its anxiety to stop young men from marching towards the revolutionary morass, seized them and swept them off to Siberia or prison long before they were even in sight of it, while they were still on the broad highway; Herzen had trodden this very path, he had seen the chasm, and warned against it, particularly in his 'Letters to an Old Comrade.' Nothing, Tolstoy argued, would have proved a better antidote to the 'revolutionary nihilism' which Tolstoy condemned, than Herzen's brilliant analyses. 'Our young generation would not have been the same if Herzen had been read by them during the last twenty years.' Suppression of his books, Tolstoy went on, was both a criminal, and from the point of view of those who did not desire a violent revolution, an idiotic policy. At other times,

Tolstoy was less generous. In 1860, six months before they met, he had been reading Herzen's writings with mingled admiration and irritation: 'Herzen is a man of scattered intellect, and morbid *amour-propre*,' he wrote in a letter, 'but his breadth, ability, goodness, elegance of mind are Russian.' From time to time various correspondents record the fact that Tolstoy read Herzen, at times aloud to his family, with the greatest admiration. In 1896, during one of his angriest, most anti-rationalist moods, he said, 'What has Herzen said that is of the slightest use?'—as for the argument that the generation of the forties could not say what it wanted to say because of the rigid Russian censorship, Herzen wrote in perfect freedom in Paris and yet managed to say 'nothing useful.' What irritated Tolstoy most was Herzen's socialism. In 1908 he complained that Herzen was 'a narrow socialist,' even if he was 'head and shoulders above the other politicians of his age and ours.' The fact that he believed in politics as a weapon was sufficient to condemn him in Tolstoy's eyes. From 1862 onwards, Tolstoy had declared his hostility to faith in liberal reform and improvement of human life by legal or institutional change. Herzen fell under this general ban. Moreover, Tolstoy seems to have felt a certain lack of personal sympathy for Herzen and his public position—even a kind of jealousy. When, in moments of acute discouragement and irritation, Tolstoy spoke (perhaps not very seriously) of leaving Russia forever, he would say that whatever he did, he would not join Herzen or march under his banner: 'he goes his way, I shall go mine.' He seriously underrated Herzen's revolutionary temperament and instincts. However sceptical Herzen may have been of specific revolutionary doctrines or plans in Russia—and no-one was more so—he believed to the end of his life in the moral and social need and the inevitability, sooner or later, of a revolution in Russia—a violent transformation followed by a just, that is a socialist, order. He did not, it is true, close his eyes to the possibility, even the probability, that the great rebellion would extinguish values to which he was himself dedicated—in particular, the freedoms without which he and others like him could not breathe. Nevertheless, he recognised not only the inevitability but the historic justice of the coming cataclysm. His moral tastes, his respect for human values, his entire style of life, divided him from the tough-minded younger radicals of the sixties, but he did not, despite all his distrust of political fanaticism, whether on the right or on the left, turn into a cautious, reformist liberal constitutionalist. Even in his gradualist phase he remained an agitator, an egalitarian and a socialist to the

end. It is this in him that both the Russian populists and the
Russian Marxists—Mikhaylovsky and Lenin—recognised and
saluted.

It was not prudence or moderation that led him to his un-
wavering support of Poland in her insurrection against Russia in
1863. The wave of passionate Russian nationalism which accompanied its suppression, robbed him of sympathy even among
Russian liberals. *The Bell* declined in circulation.[10] The new,
'hard' revolutionaries needed his money, but made it plain that
they looked upon him as a liberal dinosaur, the preacher of
antiquated humanistic views, useless in the violent social
struggle to come. He left London in the late sixties and attempted to produce a French edition of *The Bell* in Geneva.
When that too failed, he visited his friends in Florence, returning to Paris early in 1870, before the outbreak of the Franco-
Prussian War. There he died of pleurisy, broken both morally
and physically, but not disillusioned; still writing with concentrated intelligence and force. His body was taken to Nice, where
he is buried beside his wife. A life-size statue still marks his
grave.

Herzen's ideas have long since entered into the general tex-
ture of Russian political thought—liberals and radicals, populists
and anarchists, socialists and communists, have all claimed him
as an ancestor. But what survives to-day of all that unceasing
and feverish activity, even in his native country, is not a system
or a doctrine but a handful of essays, some remarkable letters,
and the extraordinary amalgam of memory, observation, moral
passion, psychological analysis and political description, wedded
to a major literary talent, which has immortalised his name.
What remains is, above all, a passionate and inextinguishable
temperament and a sense of the movement of nature and of its
unpredictable possibilities, which he felt with an intensity
which not even his uniquely rich and flexible prose could fully
express. He believed that the ultimate goal of life was life itself;

---

[10] Herzen's lifelong enemy, the reactionary Pan-Slavic journalist, M. N.
Katkov, came out strongly for "national unity" against the Polish rebels
—and against Herzen. Russian opinion was overwhelmingly on his side.
A public subscription was raised for Katkov. "He has rendered us great
service!" exclaimed a Moscow nobleman. "He has crushed the serpent's
head! He has broken Herzen's authority!" When a rash of incendiary
fires broke out (cf. Dostoevsky's *The Possessed*), Katkov charged they
were the work of a vast conspiracy organized by the Polish rebels,
"Herzen and his scoundrels," and various persons in Paris, London, and
Geneva including the Duc d'Harcourt. . . . By the end of that year *Kolokol*'s circulation had dropped from 2500 to 500. (*D.M.*)

that the day and the hour were ends in themselves, not a means
to another day or another experience. He believed that remote
ends were a dream, that faith in them was a fatal illusion; that
to sacrifice the present, or the immediate and foreseeable future
to these distant ends must always lead to cruel and futile forms
of human sacrifice. He believed that values were not found in an
impersonal, objective realm, but were created by human beings,
changed with the generations of men, but were nonetheless
binding upon those who lived in their light; that suffering was
inescapable, and infallible knowledge neither attainable nor
needed. He believed in reason, scientific methods, individual
action, empirically discovered truths; but he tended to suspect
that faith in general formulae, laws, prescription in human
affairs was an attempt, sometimes catastrophic, always irrational, to escape from the uncertainty and unpredictable variety
of life to the false security of our own symmetrical fantasies. He
was fully conscious of what he believed. He had obtained this
knowledge at the cost of painful, and, at times, unintended, self-
analysis, and he described what he saw in language of exceptional vitality, precision and poetry. His purely personal credo
remained unaltered from his earliest days: 'Art, and the summer
lightning of individual happiness: these are the only real goods
we have,' he declared in a self-revealing passage of the kind that
so deeply shocked the stern young Russian revolutionaries in the
sixties. Yet even they and their descendants did not and do not
reject his artistic and intellectual achievement.

Herzen was not, and had no desire to be, an impartial observer. No less than the poets and the novelists of his nation, he
created a style, an outlook, and, in the words of Gorky's tribute
to him, 'an entire province, a country astonishingly rich in
ideas,[11] where everything is immediately recognisable as being
his and his alone, a country into which he transplants all that he
touches, in which things, sensations, feelings, persons, ideas,
private and public events, institutions, entire cultures, are given
shape and life by his powerful and coherent historical imagination, and have stood up against the forces of decay in the solid
world which his memory, his intelligence and his artistic genius
recovered and reconstructed. *My Past and Thoughts* is the
Noah's ark in which he saved himself, and not himself alone,
from the destructive flood in which many idealistic radicals of
the forties were drowned. Genuine art survives and transcends
its immediate purpose. The structure that Herzen built in the

---

[11] *Istoriya Russkoy Literatury*, p. 206 (Moscow, 1939).

first place, perhaps, for his own personal salvation, built out of material provided by his own predicament—out of exile, solitude, despair—survives intact. Written abroad, concerned largely with European issues and figures, these reminiscences are a great permanent monument to the civilised, sensitive, morally preoccupied and gifted Russian society to which Herzen belonged; their vitality and fascination have not declined in the hundred years that have passed since the first chapters saw the light.

DEDICATION

(to Nicholay Platonovich Ogarëv[1])

This book speaks chiefly of two persons. One of them is no more:[2] you are still left, and therefore it is to you, my friend, that it rightly belongs.

ISKANDER[3]

1st July, 1860
Eagle's Nest, Bournemouth

MANY OF MY FRIENDS have advised me to begin a complete edition of *My Past and Thoughts*, and there is no difficulty about this, at least so far as Parts I and II are concerned. But they say that the fragments which appeared in *The Pole Star* are rhapsodical and lacking in unity, are broken off at haphazard, sometimes anticipate, sometimes lag behind. I feel that this is true, but I cannot put it right. To make additions, to arrange the chapters in chronological order, would not be a difficult matter; but to recast entirely, *d'un jet*—that I will not undertake.

My Past and Thoughts was not written consecutively: between some chapters there lie whole years. Therefore the whole of it retains the colour of its own time and of varying moods—I should not care to rub this off.

These are not so much notes as a confession, round which, *à propos* of which, have been assembled memories snatched from here and there in the *Past*, and ideas from my *Thoughts*, which here and there have remained behind. Moreover, in these annexes, superstructures, extensions, there *is* a unity: at least I think so.

These notes are not a first experiment. I was twenty-five when I first began to write something in the way of reminiscences. This is how it happened: I had been transferred from Vyatka to Vladimir, and I was horribly bored. I found the stop before Moscow tantalizing, outrageous. I was in the situation of a man who is kept at the last coach-stage for want of horses.

---

[1] For Nikolay Platonovich Ogarëv see E. H. Carr: *The Romantic Exiles* (Gollancz, 1933), Chapters VII, XVI. (*R.*)
[2] Natalya Alexandrovna, Herzen's first cousin and wife. (*R.*)
[3] "Iskander," the Turkish form of "Alexander," was sometimes used by Herzen as a pen name. (*D.M.*)

In reality this was very nearly the most 'pure, most earnest period of a youth which had begun to come to an end.' And my boredom was lucid and contented, as with children on the day before a holiday or a birthday. Every day letters arrived, written in a fine hand;[4] I was proud of them and happy, and they helped me to grow. None the less separation was a torment, and I did not know how to set about pushing aside that eternity—some four months![5] I listened to the advice that was given me and began at leisure to makes notes of my memories of Krutitsky and Vyatka. Three note-books were filled . . . and then the past was flooded by the light of the present.

Belinsky read them in 1840 and liked them, and he printed two of the note-books in *Otechestvenniye Zapiski* (*Notes of the Fatherland*), the first and third; the other must be still lying about somewhere in our house in Moscow, if it has not been used to light the fire.

Fifteen years went by; 'I was living a lonely life in London, near Primrose Hill, cut off from the whole world by distance, by the fog and by my own desire.

'I had not a single close friend in London. There were people for whom I had a regard, and who had the same for me, but no one who was my intimate. All of them, as they came and went and met each other, were interested only in general matters, in the business of the whole of humanity, or at least of a whole people; their acquaintance, one might say, was impersonal. Months would pass and there would **not** be a single word of what I wanted to talk about.

'. . . Meanwhile I was hardly beginning at that time to come to myself, to recover from a series of fearful events, misfortunes, mistakes.[6] The history of the recent years of my life presented itself to me with greater and greater clarity, and I perceived

---

4 The letters were from his cousin, Natalya Alexandrovna Zakharin, whom he shortly married. (*A.S.*)

5 From 2nd January (when Herzen arrived at Vladimir) to 9th May (when he married N. A. Zakharin), 1838. (*A.S.*)

6 Herzen is speaking of his experiences after the defeat of the revolution of 1848, and also of the misfortunes which befell his family: the loss of his mother and son in a shipwreck in 1851, and the death of his wife on 2nd May, 1852. (*A.S.*) The infidelity of his wife with the German revolutionary poetaster, Herwegh, may be presumed to have also weighed on Herzen's mind, judging by his devoting over a hundred pages of Volume II to "A Family Drama"—pages of novelistic poignancy I was sorry to omit from this one-volume selection. For a cool British view of the Herzen–Herwegh affair, ironic and amusing, see E. H. Carr's *The Romantic Exiles*. (*D.M.*)

with dismay that no one but myself was aware of it, and that the truth would die with me.

'I determined to write: but one memory summoned up hundreds of others; all the old, the half-forgotten, rose again: boyhood's dreams, the hopes of youth, a young man's intrepidity, prison and exile—those early misfortunes that had left no bitterness in my heart but had passed like thunderstorms in Spring, refreshing and strengthening my young life with their impact.'

Now I was not writing to gain time: there was nowhere I was in a hurry to go to.

When I began this new work I absolutely forgot the existence of *Notes of a Young Man*,[7] and came upon them by chance in the British Museum when I was going through some Russian magazines. I had copies made and read them through. The feeling they aroused was a strange one: I perceived so palpably how much older I had grown in those fifteen years that at first I was amazed. At that time I had still been playing with life, and with my very happiness, as though there was to be no end to it. The tints of *Notes of a Young Man* were so rosy that I could take nothing from it: it belonged to the time of my youth, and it must be left as it was. Its morning's light was not suited to my evening's labour. There was much truth in it, but also much that was mischievous; more than that, there remained upon it the mark, quite evident to me, of Heine, whom I had read with admiration at Vyatka. In *My Past and Thoughts* the marks of life are visible, and no others are to be seen.

My work progressed slowly. . . . Much time is needed for any event to settle into a perspicuous thought—not a comforting one: melancholy, perhaps, but one that can be reconciled with one's intelligence. Without this there may be sincerity, but truth there cannot be!

Several attempts were unsuccessful and I threw them away. Finally, when this year I was reading my latest note-books to a friend of my youth, I myself recognized the familiar features, and I stopped. My labour was over.

It is very possible that I have greatly overestimated it, that in

---

[7] First translated into English by Humphrey Higgens, this early work occupies pp. 1799–1857 of Volume IV of Mr Higgens's edition. I have had to omit it for space but readers curious about Herzen's literary development, which was remarkable—and sustained—should look it up. His 1840 reconstruction of his childhood is lively and detailed but rather a jumble that quite lacks the Proustian depth of focus, the ordering and enriching of experience in unhurried restrospection that characterizes his treatment, fifteen years later, of the same memories. (*D.M.*)

these rough sketches there is much that is hidden away, but only for me; perhaps I read into it much more than was written; what I have said inspires me with dreams and works like hiero-glyphs to which I hold the key. Perhaps I alone hear spirits knocking beneath these lines . . . perhaps: but the book is no less dear to me for that. For a long time it had taken the place for me both of people and of what I had lost. The time had come to part with the book, too.

All that is personal soon crumbles away, and to this destitu-tion one has to submit. This is not despair, not senility, not coldness and not indifference: it is grey-haired youth, one of the forms of convalescence or, better, that process itself. Only by this means is it humanly possible to survive certain wounds.

In a monk, of whatever age he may be, one is continually meeting both an old man and a young man. By burying every-thing personal he has returned to his youth. He has begun to live easily, on a grand scale—sometimes too grand. . . . In reality a man now and again has a feeling of futility and loneliness among impersonal generalities, the elements of history, and the shapes of the future which pass across their surface like the shadows of clouds. But what follows from this? People would like to preserve everything, both the roses and the snow; they would like the clusters of ripe grapes to be lapped round with May flowers. The monks used to escape from the temptation to murmur by means of prayer. We have no prayers: we have work. Work is our prayer. It is possible that the fruit of both will be the same, but for the moment that is not what I am talking about.

Yes, in life there is a predilection for a recurring rhythm, for the repetition of a *motif*. Who does not know how close old age is to childhood? Look closely, and you will see that on both sides of the full climax of life, with its crowns of flowers and thorns, with its cradles and its graves, epochs often repeat themselves which are similar in their chief features. What youth has not had is already lost; what youth has dreamt of, without an actual sight of it, comes out brighter and more composed, likewise without being actually seen, from behind the clouds and the red glow in the sky.

. . . When I think how we two, now when we are nearly fifty, are standing at the first machine for the manufacture of free speech in Russia,[8] it seems that our childish Grütli[9] on the

---

[8] H.'s printing press in London, with a fount of Russian type. (R.)
[9] According to tradition representatives of the Uri, Schwyz and Unter-walden cantons took an oath in 1307, in Grütli Meadow in Uri canton,

Sparrow Hills were not thirty-three years ago. Even three seems a lot!

Life . . . lives, peoples, revolutions, beloved faces have appeared, changed and vanished between the Sparrow Hills and Primrose Hill; already their traces have almost been swept away by the pitiless whirlwind of events. Everything round me is changed: the Thames flows instead of the Moscow River, and I am surrounded by a strange people . . . and there is no more a way for us back to our country . . . only the dream of two boys, one of thirteen, the other of eleven, has remained intact!

May *My Past and Thoughts* settle my account with my personal life and be its summary. My remaining thoughts belong to my work: my remaining powers, to the struggle!

> *Thus have we kept, we two, our [lofty] league:*
> *We two again will tread the cheerless track,*
> *Tell of the truth, unconscious of fatigue,*
> *On fancies and on persons turn our back.*[10]

---

to fight for the liberation of their country. The alliance of the three cantons laid the foundation of the actual independence of the Swiss State. Herzen is comparing this legendary oath with the oath taken by himself and N. P. Ogarëv on the Sparrow Hills at Moscow. (*A.S.*)

[10] The final lines of Ogarëv's poem, *To Iskander:* the word 'lofty' is omitted from the first line. (*A.S.*)

NURSERY

AND

UNIVERSITY

(1812-1834)

When memories of the past return
And the old road again we tread,
Slowly the feelings of old days
Come back to life within the soul;
Old griefs and joys are here unchanged,
Again the once familiar thrill
Stirs echoes in the troubled heart;
And for remembered woes we sigh.

N. P. OGARËV, *Humorous Verse*

Childhood

'VERA ARTAMONOVNA, come tell me once more how the French
came to Moscow,' I used to say, rolling myself up in the quilt
and stretching in my crib, which was sewn round with canvas
that I might not fall out.

'Oh! what's the use of telling you? You've heard it so many
times; besides it's time to go to sleep. You had better get up a
little earlier to-morrow,' the old woman would usually answer,
although she was as eager to repeat her favourite story as I was to
hear it.

'But do tell me a little bit. How did you find out? How did it
begin?'

'This was how it began. You know what your papa[1] is—he is
always putting things off; he was getting ready and getting
ready, and all of a sudden he was ready! Everyone was saying
"It's time to set off; what is there to wait for? There's almost no
one left in the town." But no: Pavel Ivanovich[2] and he kept talking of how they would go together, and first one wasn't ready
and then the other. At last we were packed and the carriage was
ready; the family sat down to lunch, when all at once our head
cook ran into the dining-room as pale as a sheet, and announced:
"The enemy has marched in at the Dragomilovsky Gate." How
all hearts did sink! "The power of the Cross be with us!" we
cried. What a panic there was! While we were bustling about,
sighing and groaning, we looked and down the street came
galloping dragoons in those helmets with horses' tails streaming
behind. The gates had all been shut, and here was your papa left
behind, and a fine party there was going to be, and you with
him; your wet nurse Darya still had you at the breast, you were
so weak and delicate.'

---

[1] Herzen's father, Ivan Alexeyevich Yakovlev (1767–1846), was a very
wealthy nobleman belonging to one of the most aristocratic families of
Russia. In 1811, at the age of forty-two, he married at Stuttgart a girl of
sixteen, Luiza Haag—though in Russia she was always called Luiza
Ivanovna as easier to pronounce. [She was the daughter of a minor
Württemberg official. (*D.M.*)] As he neglected to repeat the marriage
ceremony in Russia, their son was there illegitimate. Yakovlev is said to
have given him the surname Herzen because he was the 'child of his
heart.' (*Tr.*)

[2] Golokhvastov, the husband of my father's younger sister, Yelizaveta.

3

And I smiled with pride, pleased that I had taken part in the war.

'At the beginning we got along somehow, for the first few days, that is; it was only that two or three soldiers would come in and ask by signs whether there wasn't anything to drink; we would take them a glass each, of course, and they would go away, and touch their caps to us, too. But then, you see, when fires began and kept getting worse and worse, there was such disorder, plundering and all sorts of horrors. At that time we were living in the lodge at the princess's[3] and the house caught fire; then Pavel Ivanovich said, "Let's go to my house: it is built of stone; it stands far back in the courtyard and the outer walls are properly built."

'So we went, masters and servants all together—there was no difference made; we went out into the Tverskoy Boulevard and the trees were beginning to burn—we made our way at last to the Golokhvastovs' house and it was simply blazing, flames from every window. Pavel Ivanovich was dumbfounded, he couldn't believe his eyes. Behind the house there is a big garden, you know; we went into it thinking we would be safe there. We sat there on the seats grieving, when, all at once, a mob of drunken soldiers were upon us; one set about trying to pull off Pavel Ivanovich's sheepskin travelling coat; the old man would not give it up, and the soldier pulled out his sword and struck him smack in the face with it so that he kept the scar to the end of his days; the others set upon us: one soldier tore you from your nurse, opened your baby-clothes to see if there were any money-notes or diamonds hidden among them, saw there was nothing there, and so in a rage he deliberately tore your clothes to pieces and flung them down. As soon as they had gone away, we were in trouble again. Do you remember our Platon who was sent for a soldier? He was dreadfully fond of drink and that day he was very full of courage; he tied on a sabre and walked about like that. The day before the enemy entered, Count Rostopchin[4] had distributed all sorts of weapons at the arsenal; so that was how he had got hold of a sabre. Towards the evening he saw a dragoon ride into the yard; there was a horse standing near the stable, the dragoon wanted to take it, but Platon rushed head-

---

[3] Anna Borisovna Meshchersky. (*A.S.*)

[4] Rostopchin, Fëdor Vasilevich, Count (1763–1826), Governor of Moscow in 1812. Believed to have set fire to the city when the French entered. (*Tr.*)

long at him and, catching hold of the bridle, said: "The horse is ours, I won't give it to you." The dragoon threatened him with a pistol, but seemingly it was not loaded; the master himself saw what was happening and shouted to Platon: "Let the horse alone, it's not your business." But not a bit of it! Platon pulled out his sabre and struck him again and again. "Well," thought we, "now the hour of our death is come; when his comrades see him, it will be the end of us." But when the dragoon fell off Platon seized him by the feet and dragged him to a pit full of lime and threw him in, poor fellow, and he was still alive; his horse stood there and did not stir from the place, but stamped its foot on the ground as though it understood; our servants shut it in the stable; it must have been burnt there. We all hurried out of the courtyard, the fire was more and more dreadful; worn out and with nothing to eat, we got into a house that was still untouched, and set about getting some rest; in less than an hour, our people were shouting from the street: "Come out, come out! Fire! Fire!" Then I took a piece of green baize from the billiard table and wrapped you in it to keep you from the night air; and so we made our way as far as the Tverskoy Square. There the French were trying to put the fire out, because some great man of theirs was living in the governor's house; we simply sat in the street; sentries were walking everywhere, others were riding by on horseback. And you were screaming, straining yourself with crying, your nurse had no more milk, no one had a bit of bread. Natalya Konstantinovna was with us then, a bold wench, you know; she saw that some soldiers were eating something in a corner, took you and went straight to them, showed you and said *"manger* for the little one"; at first they looked at her so sternly and said *"allez, allez,"* but she fell to scolding them. "Ah, you cursed brutes," she said, "You this and that"; the soldiers did not understand a word, but they burst out laughing and gave her some bread soaked in water for you and a crust for herself. Early in the morning an officer came up and gathered together all the men and your papa with them, leaving only the women and Pavel Ivanovich who was wounded, and took them to put out the fire in the houses nearby, so we remained alone till evening; we sat and cried and that was all. When it was dusk, the master came back and with him some sort of officer. . . .'

Allow me to take the old woman's place and continue her narrative. When my father had finished his duties as a fire-brigade man, he met by the Strastny monastery a squadron of Italian cavalry; he went up to their officer and told him in Italian the situation his family was in. When the Italian heard *la sua dolce favella* he promised to speak to the Duke of Treviso,[5] and as a preliminary measure to put a sentry to guard us and prevent barbarous scenes such as had taken place in the Golokhvastovs' garden. He sent an officer to accompany my father with these instructions. Hearing that the whole party had eaten nothing for two days, the officer led us all to a shop that had been broken into; the choicest tea, with the buds in it, and Levant coffee had been thrown about on the floor, together with a great number of dates, figs, and almonds; our servants stuffed their pockets full: there was no lack of dessert. The sentry turned out to be of the greatest use to us: a dozen times gangs of soldiers began molesting the luckless group of women and servants encamped in the corner of Tverskoy Square, but they moved off immediately at his command.

Mortier remembered that he had known my father in Paris and informed Napoleon; Napoleon ordered him to be presented next morning. In a shabby, dark blue, short coat with bronze buttons, intended for sporting wear, without his wig, in high boots that had not been cleaned for several days, with dirty linen and unshaven chin, my father—who worshipped decorum and strict etiquette—made his appearance in the throne room of the Kremlin Palace at the summons of the Emperor of the French.

Their conversation which I have heard many times is fairly correctly given in Baron Fain's[6] *History* and in that of Mik-haylovsky-Danilevsky.

After the usual phrases, abrupt words and laconic remarks, to which a deep meaning was ascribed for thirty-five years, till men realised that their meaning was often quite trivial, Napoleon blamed Rostopchin for the fire, said that it was vandalism, declared as usual his invincible love of peace, maintained that his war was against England and not against Russia, boasted that he had set a guard on the Foundling Hospital and the Uspensky Cathedral, complained of Alexander, and said that he was surrounded by bad advisers and that his (Napoleon's) peaceful inclinations were not known to the Emperor.

My father observed that it was rather for the victor to make offers of peace.

---

[5] Mortier, Edouard Adolphe (1768–1835), Duke of Treviso, general under the Revolution and Napoleon, Marshal of France. Killed, 1835, by the infernal machine of Fieschi. (*Tr.*)
[6] Fain, François, Baron (1778–1837), French historian and secretary of Napoleon. (*Tr.*)

'I have done what I could; I have sent to Kutuzov:[7] he will not enter into negotiations and does not bring my proposals to the cognisance of the Tsar. If they want war, it is not my fault— they shall have war.'

After all this comedy my father asked him for a pass to leave Moscow.

'I have ordered no passes to be given to any one; why are you going? What are you afraid of? I have ordered the markets to be opened.'

The Emperor of the French apparently forgot at that moment that, in addition to open markets, it is as well to have a house with a roof, and that life in the Tverskoy Square in the midst of enemy soldiers was anything but agreeable.

My father pointed this out to him; Napoleon thought a moment and suddenly asked:

'Will you undertake to convey a letter from me to the Emperor? On that condition I will command them to give you a permit to leave the town with all your household.'

'I would accept your Majesty's offer,' my father observed, 'but it is difficult for me to guarantee that it will reach him.'

'Will you give me your word of honour that you will make every effort to deliver the letter in person?'

'*Je m'engage sur mon honneur, Sire.*'

'That is enough. I will send for you. Are you in need of anything?'

'Of a roof for my family while I am here. Nothing else.'

'The Duc de Trévise will do what he can.'

Mortier did, in fact, give us a room in the Governor-General's house, and gave orders that we should be furnished with provisions; his *maître d'hôtel* even sent us wine. A few days passed in this way, after which Mortier sent an adjutant, at four o'clock one morning, to summon my father to the Kremlin.

The fire had attained terrific dimensions during those days; the scorched air, opaque with smoke, was becoming insufferably hot. Napoleon was dressed and was walking about the room, looking careworn and out of temper; he was beginning to feel that his singed laurels would before long be frozen, and there would be no getting out of it here with a jest, as in Egypt. The plan of the campaign was absurd; except Napoleon, everybody knew it: Ney, Narbonne, Berthier, and officers of lower rank; to

---

[7] Kutuzov, Mikhail Illarionovich (1745–1813), Commander-in-Chief of the Russian army in 1812. (*Tr.*)

all objections he had replied with the cabbalistic word 'Moscow'; in Moscow even he guessed the truth.

When my father went in, Napoleon took a sealed letter that was lying on the table, handed it to him and said, bowing him out: 'I rely on your word of honour.' On the envelope was written: '*A mon frère l'Empereur Alexandre.*'

The permit given to my father has survived; it is signed by the Duke of Treviso and countersigned by the *oberpolitsmeyster* of Moscow, Lesseps. A few outsiders, hearing of our permit, joined us, begging my father to take them in the guise of servants or relations. An open wagonette was given us for the wounded old man, my mother and my nurse; the others walked. A few Uhlans escorted us on horseback as far as the Russian rearguard, at the sight of which they wished us a good journey and galloped back. A minute later the Cossacks surrounded the strange refugees and led them to the headquarters of the rearguard. There Wintsengerode and Ilovaysky the Fourth were in command.

Wintsengerode, hearing of the letter, told my father that he would send him on immediately, with two dragoons, to the Tsar in Petersburg.

'What's to be done with your people?' asked the Cossack general, Ilovaysky. 'It is impossible for them to stay here. They are not out of musket-shot, and a real action may be expected any day.'

My father begged that we should, if possible, be taken to his Yaroslavl estate, but incidentally observed that he had not a kopeck with him.

'We will settle up afterwards,' said Ilovaysky, 'and do not worry yourself: I give you my word to send them.'

My father was taken by the military courier system along a road made of fascines in the style of those days. For us Ilovaysky procured some sort of an old conveyance and sent us to the nearest town with a party of French prisoners and an escort of Cossacks; he provided us with money for our expenses until we reached Yaroslavl, and altogether did everything he possibly could in the bustle and apprehension of wartime.

My father was taken straight to Count Arakcheyev[8] and detained in his house. The Count asked for the letter, but my father told him he had given his word of honour to deliver it in

---

[8] Arakcheyev, Aleksey Andreyevich, Count (1769–1834), Minister of War and the most powerful and influential man of the reign of Alexander I, whose intimate friend he was, hated and dreaded for his cruelty. (*Tr.*)

person; Arakcheyev promised to ask the Tsar, and, next day, informed him by letter that the Tsar had charged him to take the letter and to deliver it immediately. He gave a receipt for the letter: that, too, has survived. For a month my father remained under arrest in Arakcheyev's house; no one was allowed to see him except S. S. Shishkov, who came at the Tsar's command to question him concerning the details of the fire, of the enemy's entry into Moscow, and his interview with Napoleon; he was the first eye-witness to arrive in Petersburg. At last Arakcheyev informed my father that the Tsar had ordered his release, and did not hold him to blame for accepting a permit from the enemy in consideration of the extremity in which he was placed. On setting him free Arakcheyev commanded him to leave Petersburg immediately without seeing anybody except his elder brother, to whom he was allowed to say good-bye.

On reaching at nightfall the little Yaroslavl village, my father found us in a peasant's hut (he had no house on that estate). I was asleep on a bench under the window; the window did not close properly, and the snow, drifting through the crack, covered part of the bench and lay, not thawing, on the window-sill.

Everyone was in a state of great perturbation, especially mother. A few days before my father's arrival, the village elder and some of the house-serfs had run hastily in the morning into the hut where she was living, trying to explain something by gestures and insisting on her following them. At that time my mother did not speak a word of Russian; all she could make out was that the matter concerned Pavel Ivanovich; she did not know what to think; the idea occurred to her that they had killed him, or that they meant to kill him and afterwards her. She took me in her arms, and trembling all over, more dead than alive, followed the elder. Golokhvastov was in another hut and they went into it; the old man really was lying dead beside the table at which he had been about to shave; a sudden stroke of paralysis had cut short his life instantaneously.

My mother's position may well be imagined (she was then seventeen), in the midst of these *half-savage* bearded men, dressed in bare sheepskins, talking in a completely unknown language, in a little smoke-blackened hut; and all this in November of the terrible winter of 1812. Her one support had been Golokhvastov; she wept day and night after his death. But these *savages* pitied her from the bottom of their hearts, in all their kindness and simplicity; and the village elder sent his son several times to the town to get raisins, cakes, apples, and bread-rings for her.

Fifteen years later the elder was still living and used sometimes, grey with age and somewhat bald, to come to Moscow. My
mother used customarily to regale him with tea and to talk to
him about the winter of 1812, saying how she had been so afraid
of him and how, without understanding each other, they had
made the arrangements for the funeral of Pavel Ivanovich. The
old man used still to call my mother—as he had then—Yuliza
Ivanovna, instead of Luiza, and used to tell how I was not at all
afraid of his beard and would readily let him take me into his
arms.

From the province of Yaroslavl we moved to that of Tver, and
at last, a year later, made our way back to Moscow. By that time
my father's brother,[9] who had been ambassador to Westphalia
and had afterwards gone on some commission to Bernadotte, had
returned from Sweden; he settled in the same house with us.

I still remember, as in a dream, the traces of the fire, which
remained until early in the 'twenties: great burnt-out houses
without window frames or roofs, tumble-down walls, empty
spaces fenced in, with remains of stoves with chimneys on them.

Tales of the fire of Moscow, of the battle of Borodino, of the
Berezina, of the taking of Paris were my cradle-songs, my nursery
stories, my Iliad and my Odyssey. My mother and our servants,
my father and Vera Artamonovna were continually going back
to the terrible time which had impressed them so recently, so
intimately, and so acutely. Then the returning generals and
officers began crowding into Moscow. My father's old comrades
of the Izmaylovsky regiment, now the heroes of a bloody war
scarcely ended, were often at our house. They found relief from
their fatigues and battles in describing them. This was in reality
the most brilliant moment of the Petersburg period; the consciousness of strength gave new life, and all practical affairs and
troubles seemed to be put off till the morrow when work would
begin again: now all that was wanted was to revel in the joys of
victory.

From these gentlemen my eager ears heard even more about
the war than from Vera Artamonovna. I was particularly fond of
the stories told by Count Miloradovich;[10] he spoke with the

---

[9] Yakovlev, Lev Alexeyevich (1764–1839), 'the Senator.' (A.S.)
[10] One of the generals of the campaign of 1812. Military Governor-
General of Petersburg at the accession of Nicholas in 1825, and killed in
the rising of December 14th. (Tr.)

greatest vivacity, with lively mimicry, with roars of laughter, and more than once I fell asleep, on the sofa behind him, to the sound of them.

Of course, in such surroundings I was a desperate patriot and intended to go into the army; but an exclusive sentiment of nationality never leads to any good; it led me to the following incident. Among others who used to visit us was the Comte de Quinsonaas, a French *émigré* and a lieutenant-general in the Russian service. A desperate royalist, he took part in the celebrated fête of Versailles, at which the King's life-guards trampled underfoot the popular cockade and at which Marie Antoinette drank to the destruction of the revolution. This French count, a tall, thin, graceful old man with grey hair, was the very model of politeness and elegant manners. There was a peerage awaiting him in Paris, where he had already been to congratulate Louis XVIII on getting his situation. He had returned to Russia to dispose of his estate. Unluckily for me this most courteous of the generals of all the Russian armies had to begin speaking of the war in my presence.

'But surely you must have been fighting against us?' I remarked with extreme naïveté.

'*Non, mon petit, non; j'étais dans l'armée russe.*'

'What?' said I, 'you, a Frenchman, and fighting in our army? That's impossible!'

My father glanced sternly at me and changed the subject. The Count heroically set things right by saying to my father that 'he liked such *patriotic* sentiments.' My father had not liked them, and when the Count had gone away he gave me a terrible scolding. 'This is what comes of rushing headlong into conversation about all sorts of things you don't understand and can't understand; it was out of fidelity to *his* king that the Count served under *our* emperor.'

I certainly did not understand that.

My father had spent twelve years abroad and his brother still longer; they tried to arrange their life in the foreign style while avoiding great expense and retaining all Russian comforts. Their life never was so arranged, either because they did not know how to manage or because the nature of a Russian landowner was stronger in them than their foreign habits. The management of their land and house was in common, the estate was undivided, an immense crowd of house-serfs peopled the ground floor, and consequently all conditions for disorder were present.

Two nurses looked after me, one Russian and one German. Vera Artamonovna and Madame Proveau were very kind women, but it bored me to watch them all day long knitting stockings and bickering together, and so at every favourable opportunity I ran away to the half of the house occupied by my uncle, the Senator (the one who had been an ambassador), to see my one friend, his valet Calot.

I have rarely met a kinder, gentler, milder man; utterly alone in Russia, parted from all his own people, with difficulty speaking broken Russian, his devotion to me was like a woman's. I spent whole hours in his room, worried him, got in his way, played pranks—he bore it all with a good-natured smile; cut all sorts of marvels out of cardboard for me and carved various trifles out of wood (and how I loved him for it!). In the evenings he used to bring me up picture-books from the library—the Travels of Gmelin[11] and of Pallas,[12] and a fat book of *The World in Pictures*,[13] which I liked so much that I looked at it until the binding, although of leather, gave way; for a couple of hours at a time Calot would show me the same pictures, repeating the same explanation for the thousandth time.

Before my birthday and my name-day Calot would lock himself up in his room, from which came the sounds of a hammer and other tools; often he would pass along the corridor with rapid steps, locking his door after him every time, sometimes carrying a little sauce-pan of glue, sometimes a parcel with things wrapped up. It may well be imagined how much I longed to know what he was making; I used to send the house-serf boys to try and find out, but Calot kept a sharp look-out. We somehow discovered, on the staircase, a little crack which looked straight into his room, but it was of no help to us; all we could see was the upper part of the window and the portrait of Frederick II with a huge nose and huge star and the expression of an emaciated hawk. Two days before the event the noise would cease and the room would be opened—everything in it was as usual, except for scraps of coloured and gold paper here and there; I would

---

[11] Gmelin, Johann Georg (1709–55), a learned German who travelled in the East. (*Tr.*)

[12] Pallas, Peter Simon (1741–1811), German traveller and naturalist who explored the Urals, Kirghiz Steppes, Altai Mountains, and parts of Siberia. (*Tr.*)

[13] *Orbis sensualium pictus* by Yan Amos Komensky (1592–1670), a Czech pedagogue and humanist. (*R.*)

flush crimson, devoured with curiosity, but Calot, with an air of strained gravity, refused to approach the delicate subject.

I lived in agonies until the momentous day. At five o'clock in the morning I was awake and thinking of Calot's preparations; at eight o'clock he would himself appear in a white cravat, a white waistcoat and a dark-blue tail-coat—with empty hands. When would it end? Had he spoiled it? And time passed and the ordinary presents came, and Yelizaveta Alexeyevna Golokhavastov's footman had already appeared with a costly toy, wrapped up in a napkin, and the Senator had already brought me some marvel, but the uneasy expectation of the surprise troubled my joy.

All at once, as it were casually, after dinner or after tea, Nurse would say to me:

'Go downstairs just a minute; there is somebody asking for you.'

At last, I thought, and went down, sliding on my arms down the banisters of the staircase. The doors into the ball-room were thrown open noisily, music was playing. A transparency with my monogram was lit up, serf-boys dressed up as Turks offered me sweetmeats, then followed a puppet show or indoor fireworks. Calot, perspiring with his efforts, was with his own hands setting everything in motion, and was no less enraptured than I was.

What presents could be compared with such an entertainment! I have never been fond of *things*, the bump of ownership and acquisitiveness has never been developed in me at any age, and now, after the prolonged suspense, the numbers of candles, the tinsel and the smell of gunpowder! Only one thing was lacking—a comrade of my own age, but I spent all my childhood in solitude,[14] and certainly was not over-indulged in that respect.

---

[14] My father had, besides me, another son ten years older.* I was always fond of him, but he could not be a companion to me. From his twelfth to his thirtieth year he was always in the hands of the surgeons. After a series of tortures, endured with extreme fortitude and rendering his whole existence one intermittent operation, the doctors declared his disease incurable. His health was shattered; circumstances and character contributed to the complete ruin of his life. The pages in which I speak of his lonely and melancholy existence have been omitted. I do not wish to print them without his consent.

* Yegor Ivanovich Herzen (1803–82). (*A.S.*)

My father and the Senator had an elder brother,[15] between whom and the two younger brothers there was an open feud, in spite of which they managed their estate in common or rather ruined it in common. The triple control and the quarrel together led to glaring disorganisation. My father and the Senator did everything to thwart the elder brother, who did the same by them. The village elders and peasants lost their heads: one brother was demanding wagons; another, hay; a third, firewood; each gave orders, each sent his authorised agents. The elder brother would appoint a village elder, the younger ones would remove him in a month, upon some nonsensical pretext, and appoint another whom their senior would not recognise. With all this, of course, backbiting, slander, spies and favourites were naturally plentiful, and under it all the poor peasants, who found neither justice nor defence, were harassed on all sides and oppressed with the double burden of work and the disorganisation caused by the capricious demands of their owners.

The first consequence of the feud between the brothers that made some impression upon them, was the loss of their great lawsuit with the Counts Devier, though justice was on their side. Though their interests were the same, they could never agree on a course of action; their opponents naturally profited by this. In addition to the loss of a large and fine estate, the Senate sentenced each of the brothers to pay costs and damages to the amount of thirty thousand paper roubles. This lesson opened their eyes and they made up their minds to divide their property. The preliminary negotiations lasted for about a year, the estate was carved into three fairly equal parts and they were to decide by casting lots which was to come to which. The Senator and my father visited their elder brother, whom they had not seen for several years, to negotiate and be reconciled; then there was a rumour that he would visit us to complete the arrangements. The rumour of the visit of this elder brother[16] excited horror and anxiety in our household.

---

[15] There were originally four brothers: Pëtr, the grandfather of 'the cousin from Korcheva' mentioned in Chapter 3; Alexander, the elder brother here described, who is believed to have been the model from whom Dostoevsky drew the character of Fëdor Pavlovich in *The Brothers Karamazov;* Lev, always referred to as 'the Senator,' and Ivan, Herzen's father. Of the sisters one was Yelizaveta Alexeyevna Golokhvastov and one was Marya Alexeyevna Khovansky. The family of the Yakovlevs was one of the oldest and most aristocratic in Russia. (*Tr.*)

[16] This brother, Alexander, had an illegitimate daughter, Natalya, who became the wife of her first cousin, the author of this book. (*R.*)

He was one of those grotesquely odd creatures who are only possible in Russia, where life is so odd as to be grotesque. He was a man gifted by nature, yet he spent his whole life in absurd actions, often almost crimes. He had received a sound education in the French style, was very well read—and spent his time in debauchery and empty idleness up to the day of his death. He, too, had served at first in the Izmaylovsky regiment, had been something like an aide-de-camp in attendance on Potëmkin, then served in some mission, and returning to Petersburg was made Procurator of the Synod. Neither diplomatic nor monastic surroundings could restain his unbridled character. For his quarrels with the heads of the Church he was removed from his post; for a slap in the face, which he either tried to give, or gave, to a gentleman at an official dinner at the Governor-General's, he was banished from Petersburg. He went to his Tambov estate; there the peasants nearly murdered him for his brutality and amorous propensities; he was indebted to his coachman and his horses for his life.

After that he settled in Moscow. Deserted by all his relations and also by his acquaintances, he lived in solitude in his big house in the Tverskoy Boulevard, oppressing his house-serfs and ruining his peasants. He amassed a great library of books and collected a regular harem of serf-girls, both of which he kept under lock and key. Deprived of every occupation and concealing a passionate vanity, often extremely naïve, he amused himself by buying unnecessary things, and bringing unnecessary lawsuits, which he pursued with great bitterness. His lawsuit concerning an Amati violin lasted *thirty* years, and ended in his winning it. After another lawsuit he succeeded by extraordinary efforts in winning a wall which was common to two houses, the possession of which was of no use to him whatever. Being himself on the retired list, he used, on reading in the newspapers of the promotions of his fellow-soldiers, to buy such orders as had been given to them, and lay them on his table as a mournful reminder of the decorations he might have received!

His brothers and sisters were afraid of him and had nothing to do with him; our servants would go a long way round to avoid his house for fear of meeting him, and would turn pale at the sight of him; women went in terror of his impudent persecution; the house-serfs paid for special services of prayer that they might not come into his possession.

So this was the terrible man who was to visit us. Extraordinary excitement prevailed throughout the house from early morning; I had never seen this legendary 'enemy-brother,' though I was born in his house, where my father stayed when he came back from foreign parts; I longed to see him and at the same time I was frightened—I do not know why, but I was terribly frightened.

Two hours before his arrival, my father's eldest nephew, two intimate acquaintances and a good-natured stout and flabby official who was in charge of the legal business arrived. They were all sitting in silent expectation, when suddenly the butler came in, and, in a voice unlike his own, announced that the brother 'had graciously pleased to arrive.'

'Show him up,' said the Senator, with perceptible agitation, while my father began taking snuff, the nephew straightened his cravat, and the official hawked and coughed. I had been ordered to go upstairs but, trembling all over, I stayed in the next room.

Slowly and majestically the 'brother' advanced, and the Senator and my father went to meet him. He was holding an ikon with both hands before his chest, as people do at weddings and funerals, and in a drawling voice, a little through his nose, he addressed his brothers in the following words:

'With this ikon our father blessed me before his end, charging me and our late brother Pëtr to watch over you and to be a father to you in his place . . . if our father knew of your conduct to your elder brother! . . .'

'Come, *mon cher frère*,' observed my father in his studiously indifferent voice, 'you have carried out our father's last wish well indeed. It would be better to forget these memories, painful to you as well as to us.'

'How? What?' shouted the devout brother. 'Is this what you have summoned me for? . . .' and he flung down the ikon, so that the silver setting gave a metallic clink. At this point the Senator shouted in a voice still more terrifying. I rushed headlong upstairs and only had time to see the official and the nephew, no less scared, retreating to the balcony.

What was done and how it was done, I cannot say; the frightened servants huddled into corners out of sight, no one knew anything of what happened, and neither the Senator nor my father ever spoke of this scene before me. Little by little the noise subsided and the partition of the estate was carried out, whether then or on another day I do not remember.

My father received Vasilevskoye, a big estate in the Ruzsky district, near Moscow. We spent the whole summer there the following year; meanwhile the Senator bought himself a house on the Arbat, and we went to live alone in our great house, deserted and deathlike. Soon afterwards my father too bought a house in Old Konyushennaya Street.

With the Senator there departed first Calot, and secondly the source of all animation in our house. The Senator alone had prevented the hypochondriacal disposition of my father from prevailing; now it had full sway. The new house was gloomy; it suggested a prison or a hospital; the ground floor was vaulted and the thick walls made the windows look like the embrasures of a fortress. The house was surrounded on all sides by a court-yard unnecessarily large.

To tell the truth, it is more of a wonder that the Senator managed to live so long under the same roof as my father than that they parted. I have rarely seen two men so complete a contrast as they were.

The Senator was of a kindly disposition, and fond of amuse-ments; he had spent his whole life in the world of artificial light and of official diplomacy, the world that surrounded the court, without a notion that there was another more serious world, although he had been not merely in contact with but intimately connected with all the great events from 1789 to 1815. Count Vorontsov had sent him to Lord Grenville[17] to find out what General Bonaparte was going to undertake after abandoning the Egyptian army. He had been in Paris at the coronation of Napoleon. In 1811 Napoleon had ordered him to be detained in Cassel, where he was ambassador 'at the court of King Jerome,'[18] as my father used to say in moments of vexation. In fact, he took part in all the great events of his time, but in a queer way, irregularly.

When a captain in the Life Guards of the Izmaylovsky regi-ment, he was sent on a mission to London; Paul, seeing this in the muster-roll, ordered him to return at once to Petersburg. The soldier-diplomat set off by the first ship and appeared on parade.

'Do you want to remain in London?' Paul asked in his hoarse voice.

'If it should please your Majesty to permit me,' answered the captain-diplomat.

'Go back and lose no time,' said Paul in his hoarse voice, and he did go back, without even seeing his relations, who lived in Moscow.

---

[17] British Foreign Secretary in 1791, and Prime Minister, 1806 and 1807, when the Act for the abolition of the slave trade was passed. (*Tr.*)
[18] *I.e.*, of Jérôme Bonaparte, King of Westphalia from 1807 to 1813. (*Tr.*)

While diplomatic questions were being settled by bayonets and grape-shot, he was an ambassador and concluded his diplomatic career at the time of the Congress of Vienna, that bright festival of all the diplomats. Returning to Russia he was appointed court chamberlain in Moscow, where there is no court. Though he knew nothing of Russian law and legal procedure, he got into the Senate, became a member of the Council of Guardians, a director of the Mariinsky Hospital, and of the Alexandriinsky Institute, and he performed all his duties with a zeal that was hardly necessary, with a censoriousness that only did harm and with an honesty that no one noticed.

He was never at home, he tired out two teams of four strong horses in the course of the day, one set in the morning, the other after dinner. Besides the Senate, the sittings of which he never neglected, and the Council of Guardians, which he attended twice a week, besides the Hospital and the Institute, he hardly missed a single French play, and visited the English Club three times a week. He had no time to be bored: he was always busy and interested. He was always going somewhere, and his life rolled lightly on good springs through a world of official papers and red tape.

Moreover, up to the age of seventy-five he was as strong as a young man, was present at all the great balls and dinners, took part in every ceremonial assembly and annual function, whether it was of an agricultural or medical or fire insurance society or of the Society of Natural Philosophy . . . and, on the top of it all, perhaps because of it, preserved to old age some degree of human feeling and a certain warmth of heart.

No greater contrast to the sanguine Senator, who was always in motion and only occasionally visited his home, can possibly be imagined than my father, who hardly ever went out of his courtyard, hated the whole official world and was everlastingly freakish and discontented. We also had eight horses (very poor ones), but our stable was something like an almshouse for broken-down nags; my father kept them partly for the sake of appearances and partly so that the two coachmen and the two postillions should have something to do, besides fetching the *Moscow News* and getting up cock-fights, which they did very successfully between the coachhouse and the neighbour's yard.

My father had scarcely been in the service at all; educated by a French tutor, in the house of a devoutly religious aunt, he entered the Izmaylovsky regiment as a sergeant at sixteen, served until the accession of Paul, and retired with the rank of

captain in the Guards. In 1801 he went abroad and remained
until the end of 1811, wandering from one country to another.
He returned with my mother three months before my birth, and
after the fire of Moscow he spent a year on his estate in the
province of Tver, and then returned to live in Moscow, trying to
order his life so as to be as solitary and dreary as possible. His
brother's liveliness hindered him in this.

After the Senator left us, everything in the house began to
assume a more and more gloomy aspect. The walls, the furniture, the servants, everything bore a look of discontent and
suspicion, and I need hardly say that my father himself was of
all the most discontented. The unnatural stillness, the whispers
and cautious footsteps of the servants, did not suggest attentive
solicitude, but oppression and terror. In the rooms everything
was stationary; for five or six years the same books would lie in
the very same places with the same markers in them. In my
father's bedroom and study the furniture was not moved nor the
windows opened for years together. When he went away into the
country he took the key of his room in his pocket, that they
might not venture to scrub the floor or wash the walls in his
absence.

Youth

UNTIL I WAS ten years old I noticed nothing strange or special in
my position; it seemed to me simple and natural that I should be
living in my father's house; that in his part of it I should be on
my best behaviour, while my mother lived in another part of the
house, in which I could be as noisy and mischievous as I liked.
The Senator spoiled me and gave me presents, Calot carried me
about in his arms, Vera Artamonovna dressed me, put me to bed,
and gave me my bath, Madame Proveau took me out for walks
and talked to me in German; everything went on in its regular
way, yet I began pondering on things.

Stray remarks, carelessly uttered words, began to attract my
attention. Old Madame Proveau and all the servants were devoted to my mother, while they feared and disliked my father.
The scenes which sometimes took place between them were often

the subject of conversation between Madame Proveau and Vera Artamonovna, both of whom always took my mother's side.

My mother certainly had a good deal to put up with. Being an extremely kind-hearted woman, with no strength of will, she was completely crushed by my father, and, as always happens with weak characters, put up a desperate opposition in trifling matters and things of no consequence. Unhappily, in these trifling matters my father was nearly always in the right, and the dispute always ended for him in triumph.

'If I were in the mistress's place,' Madame Proveau would say, for instance, 'I would simply go straight back to Stuttgart; much comfort she gets—nothing but fads and unpleasantness, and deadly dullness.'

'To be sure,' Vera Artamonovna would assent, 'but that's what ties her, hand and foot,' and she would point with her knitting-needle towards me. 'How can she take him with her—what to? And as for leaving him here alone, with the way we live—why, even if one was no relation, one would have pity on him!'

Children in general have far more insight than is supposed; they are quickly distracted and forget for a time what has struck them, but they go back to it persistently, especially if it is anything mysterious or frightening and with wonderful persever-ance and ingenuity they go on probing until they reach the truth.

Once I became curious, within a few weeks I had found out all the details of my father's meeting with my mother, had heard how she had brought herself to leave her parents' home, how she had been hidden at the Senator's in the Russian Embassy at Cassel, and had crossed the frontier dressed as a boy; all this I found out without putting a single question to anyone.

The first result of these discoveries was to estrange me from my father because of the scenes of which I have spoken. I had seen them before, but I used to think all that quite normal—part of the regular order of things; for I was so accustomed to the fact that everyone in the house, not excepting the Senator, was afraid of my father, and that he was given to scolding everyone, that I saw nothing strange in it. Now I began to think so no longer, and the thought that some of it was endured on my account sometimes threw a dark, oppressive cloud over my bright, child-ish imagination.

A second idea that took root in me from that time was that I was far less dependent on my father than children are as a rule. I liked this feeling of independence which I imagined for myself.

Two or three years later two of my father's old comrades in the regiment, P. K. Essen, the Governor-General of Orenburg, and A. N. Bakhmetev, formerly Governor in Bessarabia, a general who had lost his leg at Borodino, were sitting with my father. My room was next to the ballroom in which they were. Among other things my father told them that he had been speaking to Prince Yusupov about putting me into the civil service.

'There's no time to be lost,' he added; 'you know that it will take him years to reach any kind of decent rank in the service.'

'What a strange idea, dear friend, to make him a clerk,' Essen said, good-naturedly. 'Leave it to me, and I will get him into the Ural Cossacks. We'll get him a commission, that's all that matters: after that he will make his way, like the rest of us.'

My father did not agree and said that he had grown to dislike everything military, and that he hoped in time to get me a post on some mission to a warm country, where he would go to end his days.

Bakhmetev, who had taken little part in the conversation, got up on his crutches and said:

'It seems to me that you ought to think very seriously over Pëtr Kirillovich's advice. If you don't want to put his name down at Orenburg, you might put him down here. We are old friends, and it's my habit to say openly what I think; if you put him into the civil service and the university you will do no good to *your young man*, nor to society either. He is quite obviously *in a false position*; only the military service can open a career for him and put him right. Before he gets command of a company, all dangerous ideas will have subsided. Military discipline is a grand schooling, and after that it all depends on him. You say that he has abilities, but you don't mean to say that none but fools go into the army, do you? What about us and all our set? There's only one objection you can make—that he will have to serve longer before he gets a commission, but it's just over that that we can help you.'

This conversation had as much effect as the remarks of Madame Proveau and Vera Artamonovna. By that time I was thirteen[1] and such lessons, turned over and over, and analysed from every point of view during weeks and months of complete solitude, bore their fruit. The result of this conversation was that, although I had till then, like all boys, dreamed of the army and a uniform, and had been ready to cry at my father's wanting me to go into the civil service, my enthusiasm for soldiering suddenly cooled, and my craving and weakness for epaulettes, aiguillettes and striped trousers, were by degrees completely

---

[1] Herzen was not more than eight at this time. (*A.S.*)

eradicated. My dying passion for a uniform had, however, one last flicker. A cousin of ours, who had been at a boarding-school in Moscow and used sometimes to spend a holiday with us, had entered the Yamburgsky regiment of Uhlans. In 1825 he came to Moscow as an ensign and stayed a few days with us. My heart throbbed when I saw him with all his little cords and laces, with a sword, and a four-cornered shako worn a little on one side and fastened with a chin-strap. He was a boy of seventeen and short for his age. Next morning I dressed up in his uniform, put on his sword and shako and looked at myself in the glass. Goodness! how handsome I thought myself in the short dark-blue jacket with red braid! And the tassels and the pompon, and the pouch . . . what were the yellow nankeen breeches and the short camlet jacket which I used to wear at home, in comparison with these?

The cousin's visit might have destroyed the effect of the generals' talk, but soon circumstances turned me against the army again, and this time for good.

The spiritual result of my meditations on my 'false position' was much the same as that which I had deduced from the talk of my two nurses. I felt myself more independent of society, of which I knew absolutely nothing, felt that in reality I was thrown on my own resources, and with somewhat childish conceit thought I would show the old generals what I was made of.

With all this it may well be imagined how drearily and monotonously the time passed in the strange convent-like seclusion of my father's house. I had neither encouragement nor distraction; my father had spoilt me until I was ten, and now he was almost always dissatisfied with me; I had no companions, my teachers called to give lessons and went away, and, seeing them out of the yard, I used to run off on the sly, to play with the house-serf boys, which was strictly forbidden. The rest of my time I spent wandering aimlessly about the big, dark rooms, which had their windows shut all day and were only dimly lit in the evening, doing nothing or reading anything that turned up.

The servants' hall and the maids' room provided the only keen enjoyment left me. There I had complete liberty; I took the side of one party against another, discussed their business with my friends, and gave my opinion upon them, knew all their intimate affairs, and never dropped a word in the drawing-room about the secrets of the servants' hall.

I must pause upon this subject. Indeed, I do not intend to

avoid digressions and episodes; that is part of every conversation; indeed of life itself.

Children as a rule are fond of servants; their parents forbid them, especially in Russia, to associate with servants; the children do not obey them because in the drawing-room it is dull, while in the maids' room it is lively. In this case, as in thousands of others, parents do not know what they are about. I do not imagine that our hall was a less wholesome place for children than our 'tea-room' or 'sitting-room.' In the servants' hall children pick up coarse expressions and bad manners, that is true; but in the drawing-room they pick up coarse ideas and bad feelings.

The very orders to children to keep away from those with whom they are continually in contact is immoral.

A great deal is said among us about the complete depravity of servants, especially when they are serfs. They certainly are not distinguished by exemplary strictness of conduct, and their moral degradation can be seen from the fact that they put up with too much and are too rarely moved to indignation and resistance. But that is not the point. I should like to know what class in Russia is less depraved? The nobility or the officials? The clergy, perhaps?

Why do you laugh?

The peasants, perhaps, are the only ones who could put up some kind of claim to be different. . . .

The difference between the nobleman and the serving man is very small. I hate the demagogues' flattery of the mob, particularly since the troubles of 1848, but the aristocrats' slander of the people I hate even more. By picturing servants and slaves as degraded animals, the slave-owners throw dust in people's eyes and stifle the voice of conscience in themselves. We are not often better than the lower classes, but we express ourselves more gently and conceal our egoism and our passions more adroitly; our desires are not so coarse, and the ease with which they are satisfied and our habit of not controlling them make them less conspicuous; we are simply wealthier and better fed and consequently more fastidious. When Count Almaviva recited to the Barber of Seville the catalogue of the qualities he expected from a servant, Figaro observed with a sigh: 'If a servant must have all these virtues, are there many gentlemen fit to be lackeys?'

Dissoluteness in Russia as a rule does not go deep; it is more savage and dirty, noisy and coarse, dishevelled and shameless than profound. The clergy, shut up at home, drink and overeat themselves with the merchants. The nobility get drunk in public, play cards until they are ruined, thrash their servants, seduce their housemaids, manage their business affairs badly and their family life still worse. The officials do the same, but in a dirtier way, and in addition are guilty of grovelling before their superiors and pilfering. As far as stealing in the literal sense goes, the nobility are less guilty: they take openly what belongs to others; besides, when it suits them they are just as grasping as other people.

All these amiable weaknesses are to be met with in a still coarser form in officials who stand below the fourteenth grade,[2] and in gentlefolk who are dependent not on the Tsar but on the landowners. But in what way they are worse than others as a class, I do not know.

Going over my recollections, not only of the serfs in our house and in the Senator's, but also of two or three households with which we were intimate for twenty-five years, I do not remember anything particularly vicious in their behaviour. Petty thefts, perhaps, . . . but on that matter all ideas are so dulled by the serfs' position, that it is difficult to judge; *human property* does not stand on much ceremony with its kith and kin, and is pretty cavalier with the master's goods. It would be only fair to exclude from this generalisation the confidential servants, the favourites of both sexes, masters' mistresses and tale-bearers; but in the first place they are an exception—these Kleinmikhels of the stable[3] and Benckendorfs[4] from the cellar, Perekusikhins[5] in striped linen gowns, and barefoot Pompadours; moreover, they do behave better than any of the rest: they only get drunk at night and do not pawn their clothes at the gin-shop.

The simple-minded immorality of the rest revolves round a glass of vodka and a bottle of beer, a merry talk and a pipe, absences from home without leave, quarrels which sometimes end in fights, and cunning tricks played on masters who expect of them something inhuman and impossible. Of course, the lack of all education on the one hand, and on the other the simplicity

---

2 Peter I's Table of Ranks, 24th January, 1722, was drawn up in three parallel columns, civil, military and court, each divided into fourteen ranks or classes, most of which were given Latin or German names. It established a bureaucratic hierarchy based on ability rather than birth. (*R.*)

3 Kleinmikhel, Pëtr Andreyevich, Minister of Means of Communication under Nicholas I. (*Tr.*)

4 Benckendorf, Alexander Khristoforovich, Chief of Gendarmes, and favourite of Nicholas I. (*Tr.*)

5 Perekusikhin, Marya Savvishna, favourite of Catherine II. (*Tr.*)

of the peasant serfs have introduced into their manners much that is ugly and distorted, but for all that, like the negroes in America, they have remained half infantile; trifles amuse them, trifles distress them; their desires are limited, and are rather naïve and human than vicious.

Alcohol and tea, the tavern and the eating-house, are the two permanent passions of the Russian servant; for their sake he steals, for their sake he is poor, on their account he endures persecution and punishment and leaves his family in poverty. Nothing is easier than for a Father Mathew,[6] from the height of his teetotal intoxication, to condemn drunkenness and, while sitting at the tea-table, to wonder why it is that servants go for their tea to the eating-house, instead of drinking it at home, although at home it is cheaper.

Alcohol stupefies a man, it enables him to forget himself, stimulates him and induces an artificial gaiety; this stupefaction and stimulation are the more agreeable the less the man is developed and the more he is bound to a narrow, empty life. How can a servant not drink when he is condemned to the everlasting waiting in the hall, to perpetual poverty, to being a slave, to being sold? He drinks to excess—when he can—because he cannot drink every day. In Italy and the South of France there are no drunkards, because there is plenty of wine. The savage drunkenness of the English working man is to be explained in exactly the same way. These men are broken in the helpless and unequal conflict with hunger and poverty; however hard they have struggled they have met everywhere a leaden legal code and harsh resistance that has flung them back into the dark depths of common life, and condemned them to the never-ending, aimless toil that eats away mind and body alike. It is not surprising that a man who spends six days as a lever, a cog, a spring, a screw, on Saturday afternoon breaks savagely out of the penal servitude of factory work, and drinks himself silly in half an hour, the more so since his exhaustion cannot stand much. The moralists would do better to drink Irish or Scotch whisky themselves and hold their tongues, or their inhuman philanthropy may call down terrible retribution on them.

Drinking tea at the eating-house means something quite different to servants. Tea at home is not the same thing for the

---

[6] Father Mathew (1790–1856), an Irish priest, who had remarkable success in a great temperance campaign based on the religious appeal. (*Tr.*)

house-serf; at home everything reminds him that he is a servant; at home he is in the dirty servants' room, he must get the samovar himself; at home he has a cup with a broken handle, and any minute his master may ring for him. At the eating-house he is a free man, he is a gentleman; for him the table is laid and the lamps are lit; for him the waiter runs with the tray; the cup shines, the tea-pot glitters, he gives orders and is obeyed, he enjoys himself and gaily calls for pressed caviare or a turnover with his tea.

In all this there is more childish simplicity than dissoluteness. Impressions quickly take possession of them but do not send down roots; their minds are continually occupied, or rather distracted, by casual subjects, small desires, trivial aims. A childish belief in everything marvellous turns a grown-up man into a coward, and the same childish belief comforts him at the most difficult moments. I was filled with wonder when I was present at the death of two or three of my father's servants; it was then that one could judge of the simple-hearted carelessness with which their lives had passed, of the absence of great sins upon their conscience; if there was anything, it had all been settled at confession with the priest.

This resemblance between servants and children accounts for their mutual attraction. Children hate the aristocratic ideas of the grown-ups and their benevolently condescending manners, because they are clever and understand that in the eyes of grown-up people they are children, while in the eyes of servants they are people. Consequently they are much fonder of playing cards or lotto with the maids than with visitors. Visitors play for the children's benefit with condescension, give way to them, tease them and stop playing whenever they feel like it; the maids, as a rule, play as much for their own sakes as for the children's; and that gives the game interest.

Servants are extremely devoted to children, and this is not the devotion of a slave, but the mutual affection of the *weak* and the *simple*.

In old days there used to be a patriarchal dynastic affection between landowners and their house-servants, such as exists now in Turkey. To-day there are in Russia no more of those devoted servants, attached to the line and the family of their masters. And that is easy to understand. The landowner no longer believes in his power, he does not believe that he will have to answer for his serfs at the terrible Day of Judgment, but simply makes use of his power for his own advantage. The servant does not believe in his subjection and endures violence not as a

chastisement and trial from God, but simply because he is defenceless; the big fish swallows the little ones.

I used to know in my youth two or three examples of those
zealots of slavery, of whom eighty-year-old landowners speak
with a sigh, telling stories of their unflagging service and their
great diligence, and forgetting to add in what way their fathers
and themselves repaid such self-sacrifice.

On one of the Senator's estates a feeble old man called Andrey
Stepanov was living in peace, that is, on free rations.

He had been valet to the Senator and my father when they
were serving in the Guards, and was a good, honest, and sober
man, who looked into his young masters' eyes, and, to use their
own words, 'guessed from them what they wanted,' which, I
imagine, was not an easy task. Afterwards he looked after the
estate near Moscow. Cut off from the beginning of the war of
1812 from all communication, and afterwards left alone, without
money, on the ashes of a village which had been burnt to the
ground, he sold some beams to escape starvation. The Senator, on
his return to Russia, proceeded to set his estate in order, and at
last came to the beams. He punished his former valet by sending
him away in disgrace, depriving him of his duties. The old man,
burdened with a family, trudged off to pick up what food he
could. We sometimes had to drive through the village where
Andrey Stepanov lived, and stay there for a day or two. The
feeble old man, crippled by paralysis, used to come every time
leaning on his crutch, to pay his respects to my father and to
have a talk with him.

The devotion and the gentleness with which he talked, his
sorrowful appearance, the locks of yellowish grey hair on each
side of his bald pate, touched me deeply.

'I have heard, sir,' he said on one occasion, 'that your brother
has thought proper to receive another decoration. I am getting
old, your honour, I shall soon give up my soul to God, and yet
the Lord has not vouchsafed to me to see your brother in his
decorations: if only I might once before my end behold his
honour in his ribbons and all his insignia!'

I looked at the old man: his face was so childishly candid, his
bent figure, his painfully twisted face, lustreless eyes, and weak
voice—all inspired confidence; he was not lying, he was not
flattering, he really longed before his death to see, in 'his decorations and insignia,' the man who for fifteen years could not
forgive him the loss of a few beams. Was this a saint, or a
madman? But perhaps it is only madmen who attain saintliness?

The new generation has not this idolatrous worship, and if

there are cases of serfs not caring for freedom, that is simply due
to indolence and material considerations. It is more depraved,
there is no doubt, but it is a sign that it is nearer to its ending; if
they want to see anything on their master's neck, it is certainly
not the Vladimir ribbon.

Here I will say something of the situation of our own servants.

Neither the Senator nor my father oppressed the house-serfs
particularly: that is, they did not ill-treat them physically. The
Senator was hasty and impatient, and consequently often rough
and unjust, but he had so little contact with the house-serfs and
took so little notice of them that they scarcely knew each other.
My father wearied them with his caprices, never let pass a look,
a word or a movement, and was everlastingly lecturing them; to
a Russian this is often worse than blows and abuse.

Corporal punishment was almost unknown in our house, and
the two or three cases in which the Senator and my father
resorted to the revolting method of the police station were so
exceptional that all the servants talked about it for months afterwards; and it was only provoked by glaring offences.

More frequently house-serfs were sent for soldiers, and this
punishment was a terror to all the young men; without kith or
kin, they still preferred to remain house-serfs, rather than to be
in harness for twenty years. I was greatly affected by those
terrible scenes. . . . Two soldiers of the police would appear at
the summons of the landowner: they would stealthily, in a
casual, sudden way, seize the appointed victim. The village elder
commonly announced at this point that the master had the evening before ordered that he was to be produced at the recruiting-
office, and the man would try through his tears to put a brave
face on it, while the women wept: everyone made him presents
and I gave him everything I could, that is, perhaps a neckerchief
worth twenty kopecks.

I remember, too, my father's ordering some village elder's
beard to be shaved off, because he had spent the *obrok*[7] which
he had collected. I did not understand this punishment, but was
struck by the appearance of this old man of sixty; he was in
floods of tears, and kept bowing to the ground and begging for a
fine of a hundred silver roubles in addition to the *obrok* if only
he might be spared this disgrace.

When the Senator was living with us, the common household

---

[7] Payment in money or kind by a serf in lieu of labour for his master.
(*Tr.*)

consisted of thirty men and almost as many women; the married
women, however, performed no service: they looked after their
own families; there were five or six maids and laundresses, who
never came upstairs. To these must be added the *boys and girls*
who were being trained in their duties, that is, in sloth and
idleness, in lying and the use of corn-spirit.

To give an idea of the life in Russia of those days, I think it
will not be out of place to say a few words on the maintenance of
the house-serfs. At first they used to be given five paper roubles a
month for victuals, and afterwards six. The women had a rouble
a month less, and children under ten had half the full allowance.
The servants made up 'artels'[8] and did not complain of the
allowance being too small, which shows how extraordinarily
cheap provisions were. The highest wage was a hundred roubles
a year, while others received half that amount and some only
thirty roubles. Boys under eighteen got no wages at all. In addition to their wages, servants were given clothes, greatcoats,
shirts, sheets, blankets, towels and mattresses made of canvas;
boys, who did not get wages, were allowed money for their
physical and moral purification, that is, for the bath-house and
for preparing for communion. Taking everything into account, a
servant cost about three hundred paper roubles a year; if to this
we add a share of medicine, of a doctor and of the surplus stores
brought from the country, even then it is not over 350 roubles.
This is only a *quarter* of the cost of a servant in Paris or London.

Slave-owners usually take into account the *insurance* premium
of slavery, that is, the maintenance of wife and children by the
owner, and a meagre crust of bread somewhere in the village for
the slave in old age. Of course this must be taken into account;
but the cost is greatly lessened by the *fear* of corporal punishment, the impossibility of changing their condition, and a much
lower scale of maintenance.

I have seen enough of the way in which the terrible consciousness of serfdom destroys and poisons the existence of house-serfs,
the way in which it oppresses and stupefies their souls. Peasants,
especially those who pay a fixed sum in lieu of labour, have less
feeling of their personal bondage; they somehow succeed in not
believing in their complete slavery. But for the house-serf, sitting on a dirty locker in the hall from morning till night, or
standing with a plate at table, there is no room for doubt.

Of course there are people who live in the hall like fish in
water, people whose souls have never awakened, who have

---

[8] *I.e.*, clubs or guilds for messing or working together. (*Tr.*)

acquired a taste for their manner of life and who perform their duties with a sort of artistic relish.

Of that class we had one extremely interesting specimen, our footman Bakay, a man of tall figure and athletic build, with solid, dignified features and an air of the greatest profundity; he lived to an advanced age, imagining that the position of a footman was one of the greatest consequence.

This worthy old man was perpetually angry or a little drunk, or angry and a little drunk at once. He took an exalted view of his duties and ascribed a solemn importance to them: with a peculiar bang and crash he would throw up the steps of the carriage and slam the carriage door with a report like a musket-shot. With a gloomy air he stood up stiff and rigid behind the carriage, and every time there was a jolt over a rut he would shout in a thick and displeased voice to the coachman: 'Steady!' regardless of the fact that the rut was already five paces behind.

Apart from going out with the carriage, his chief occupation, a duty he had voluntarily undertaken, consisted of training the serf-boys in the aristocratic manners to be employed in the hall. When he was sober, things went fairly well, but when his head was a little dizzy, he became incredibly pedantic and tyrannical. I sometimes stood up for my friends, but my authority had little influence on Bakay, whose temper was of a Roman severity; he would open the door into the *salon* for me and say:

'This is not the place for you; be pleased to leave the room or I shall carry you out.'

He lost no opportunity of abusing the boys, and often added a cuff to his words, or 'beat butter,' that is, with his thumb and little finger dexterously gave them a sly flip on the head with the sharpness and force of a spring.

When at last he had chased the boys out and was left alone, he transferred his persecution to his one friend, Macbeth, a big Newfoundland dog, whom he used to feed, comb and fondle. After sitting in solitude for two or three minutes he would go out into the yard, call Macbeth to join him on the locker, and begin a conversation.

'What are you sitting out there in the yard in the frost for, stupid, when there is a warm room for you? What a beast! What are you staring for, eh? Have you nothing to say?'

Usually a slap would follow these words. Macbeth would sometimes growl at his benefactor; and then Bakay would upbraid him in earnest:

'You may go on feeding a dog, but he will still remain a dog;

he will show his teeth at anyone, without caring who it is . . . the fleas would have eaten him up if it had not been for me!'

And offended by his friend's ingratitude he would wrathfully take a pinch of snuff and fling what was left between his fingers on Macbeth's nose. Then the dog would sneeze, clumsily wipe out of his eyes with his paw the snuff that had fallen on his nose, and, leaving the locker indignantly, would scratch at the door; Bakay would open it with the word 'rascal' and give him a kick as he went. . . . Then the boys would come back, and he would set to flipping them on the head again.

Before Macbeth we had a setter called Berta; she fell very ill and Bakay took her on to his mattress and looked after her for two or three weeks. Early one morning I went out into the hall. Bakay tried to say something to me, but his voice broke and a big tear rolled down his cheek—the dog was dead. There is a fact for the student of human nature! I do not for a moment suppose that he disliked the boys; it was simply a case of a severe character, accentuated by drink and unconsciously grown accustomed to the spirit that prevailed in the hall.

But besides these amateurs of slavery, what gloomy images of martyrs, of hopeless victims, pass mournfully before my memory!

The Senator had a cook, Alexey, a sober, industrious man of exceptional talent who made his way in the world. The Senator himself got him taken into the Tsar's kitchen, where there was at that time a celebrated French cook. After being trained there he got a post in the English Club, grew rich, married and lived like a gentleman; but the strings which tied him to serfdom would not let him sleep soundly at night, nor take pleasure in his situation.

After having a service celebrated to the Iversky Madonna, Alexey plucked up his courage and presented himself before the Senator to ask for his freedom for five thousand paper roubles. The Senator was proud of *his* cook, just as he was proud of *his* painter, and so he would not take the money, but told the cook that he should be set free for nothing at his master's death.

The cook was thunderstruck; he grieved, grew thin and worn, turned grey and . . . being a Russian, took to drink. He neglected his work; the English Club dismissed him. He was engaged by the Princess Trubetskoy, who worried him by her petty niggardliness. Being on one occasion extremely offended by her, Alexey, who was fond of expressing himself eloquently, said, speaking though his nose with his air of dignity:

'What an opaque soul dwells in your luminous body!'

The princess was furious; she turned the cook away, and, as might be expected from a Russian lady, wrote a complaint to the Senator. The Senator would have done nothing to him, but, as a courteous gentleman, he felt bound to send for the cook, gave him a good cursing and told him to go and beg the princess's pardon.

The cook did not go to the princess but went to the pot-house. Within a year he had lost everything, from the capital he had saved up for his ransom to the last of his aprons. His wife struggled and struggled on with him, but at last went off and took a place as a nurse. Nothing was heard of him for a long time. Then the police brought Alexey, wild-looking and in tatters; he had been picked up in the street, he had no lodging, he migrated from tavern to tavern. The police insisted that his master should take him. The Senator was distressed and perhaps conscience-stricken, too; he received him rather mildly and gave him a room. Alexey went on drinking, was noisy when he was drunk and imagined that he was composing verses; he certainly had some imagination of an incoherent sort. We were at that time at Vasilevskoye. The Senator, not knowing what to do with the cook, sent him there, thinking that my father would bring him to reason. But the man was too completely shattered. I saw in his case the concentrated anger and hatred against the masters which lies in the heart of the serf: he would talk with a grinding of the teeth and with gesticulations which, especially in a cook, might have been dangerous. He was not afraid to give full rein to his tongue in my presence; he was fond of me and would often, patting me familiarly on the shoulders, say that I was:

'A good branch of a rotten tree.'

After the Senator's death my father gave him his freedom at once. It was too late and simply meant getting rid of him; he just disappeared.

❖   ❖   ❖

I will say only one thing more, to conclude this gloomy subject: the hall had no really bad influence upon me at all. On the contrary, it awakened in me from my earliest years an invincible hatred for every form of slavery and every form of tyranny. At times, when I was a child, Vera Artamonovna would say by way of the greatest rebuke for some naughtiness: 'Wait a bit, you

will grow up and turn into just such another master as the rest.'
I felt this a horrible insult. The old woman need not have worried herself—just such another as the rest, anyway, I have not
become.

Besides the hall and the maids' room I had one other distraction, and in that I was not hindered in any way. I loved reading
as much as I hated lessons. My passion for unsystematic reading
was, indeed, one of the chief obstacles to serious study. I never
could, for instance, then or later, endure the theoretical study of
languages, but I very soon learnt to understand and gabble them
incorrectly, and at that stage I remained, because it was sufficient for my reading.

My father and the Senator had between them a fairly large
library, consisting of French books of the eighteenth century.
The books lay about in heaps in a damp, unused room on the
ground floor of the Senator's house. Calot had the key. I was
allowed to rummage in these literary granaries as I liked, and I
read and read to my heart's content. My father saw two advantages in it, that I should learn French more quickly and that I
was occupied—that is, I was sitting quiet and in my own room.
Besides, I did not show him all the books I read, nor lay them on
the table; some of them were hidden in a bureau.

What did I read? Novels and plays, of course. I read fifty
volumes of the French *Répertoire* and the Russian *Theatre*; in
every volume there were three or four plays. Besides French
novels my mother had the tales of La Fontaine and the comedies
of Kotzebue, and I read them two or three times. I cannot say
that the novels had much influence on me; and though like all
boys I pounced eagerly on all equivocal or somewhat improper
scenes, they did not interest me particularly. A play which I
liked beyond all measure and read over twenty times, (and
moreover in the Russian translation in *Theatre*) the *Marriage of
Figaro*,[9] had much greater influence on me. I was in love with
Cherubino and the Countess, and what is more, I was myself
Cherubino; my heart throbbed as I read it and without clearly
recognising it I was conscious of a new sensation. How enchanting I thought the scene in which the page is dressed up as a girl,
how intensely I longed to hide somebody's ribbon in my bosom
and kiss it in secret. In reality I had in those years no feminine
society.

---

[9] *Le Mariage de Figaro*, a satirical comedy by Beaumarchais (*né* Caron,
1732–99), a watchmaker's son who rose to wealth and influence and by
his writings helped to bring about the Revolution. (*Tr.*)

I only remember that occasionally on Sundays Bakhmetev's two daughters used to come from their boarding-school to visit us. The younger, a girl of sixteen, was strikingly beautiful. I was overwhelmed when she entered the room and never ventured to address a word to her, but kept stealing looks at her lovely dark eyes and dark curls. I never dropped a hint to any one on the subject and the first breath of love passed unknown to any one, even to her.

Years afterwards, when I met her, my heart throbbed violently and I remembered how at twelve years old I had worshipped her beauty.

I forgot to say that *Werther* interested me almost as much as the *Marriage of Figaro;* half the novel was beyond me and I skipped it, and hurried on to the terrible *dénouement,* over which I wept like a madman. In 1839 *Werther* happened to come into my hands again; this was when I was at Vladimir and I told my wife how as a boy I had cried over it and began reading her the last letters . . . and when I came to the same passage, my tears began flowing again and I had to stop.

Up to the age of fourteen I cannot say that my father greatly restricted my liberty, but the whole atmosphere of our house was oppressive for a lively boy. The persistent and unnecessary fussiness concerning my physical health, together with complete indifference to my moral well-being, was horribly wearisome. There were ever-lasting precautions against my taking a chill, or eating anything indigestible, and anxious solicitude over the slightest cough or cold in the head. In the winter I was kept indoors for weeks at a time and, when I was allowed to go out, it was only wearing warm high boots, thick scarves and such things. At home it was always insufferably hot from the stoves. All this would inevitably have made me a frail and delicate child but for the iron health I inherited from my mother. She by no means shared my father's prejudices, and in her half of the house allowed me everything which was forbidden in his.

My education made slow progress without competition, encouragement, or approval; I did my lessons lazily, without method or supervision, and thought to make a good memory and lively imagination take the place of hard work. I need hardly say that there was no supervision over my teachers either; once the terms upon which they were engaged were settled, they might, so long as they turned up at the proper time and sat through their hour, go on for years without rendering any account to any one.

◈   ◈   ◈

At twelve years old I was transferred from feminine to masculine hands. About that time my father made two unsuccessful
attempts to engage a German to look after me.

A German who looks after children is neither a tutor nor a
dyadka;[10] it is quite a special profession. He does not teach the
children and he does not dress them, but sees that they are
taught and dressed, takes care of their health, goes out for walks
with them and talks any nonsense to them so long as it is in
German. If there is a tutor in the house, the German is under his
orders; if there is a *dyadka,* he takes his orders from the German.
The visiting teachers who come late owing to unforeseen causes
and leave early owing to circumstances over which they have no
control, do their best to win the German's favour, and in spite of
his complete illiteracy he begins to regard himself as a man of
learning. Governesses employ the German in shopping for them
and on all sorts of errands, but only allow him to pay his court to
them if they suffer from striking physical defects or a complete
lack of other admirers. Boys of fourteen will go, without their
parents' knowledge, to the German's room to smoke, and he puts
up with it because he must have powerful auxiliary resources in
order to remain in the house. In fact what mostly happens is that
at this time the German is thanked, presented with a watch and
discharged. If he is tired of sauntering about the streets with
children and receiving reprimands for their having colds, or
stains on their clothes, the 'children's German' becomes simply a
German, sets up a little shop, sells amber cigarette-holders, eau-
de-Cologne and cigars to his former nurslings and carries out for
them *secret* commissions of another kind.

The first German who was engaged to look after me was a
native of Silesia and was called Jokisch; to my mind the surname was more than sufficient reason not to have engaged him.
He was a tall, bald man, distinguished by an extreme lack of
cleanliness; he used to boast of his knowledge of agricultural
science, and I imagine .it must have been on that account that
my father engaged him. I looked on the Silesian giant with
aversion, and the only thing that reconciled me to him was that
he used, as we walked about the Devichy grounds and to the

---

[10] A man, usually a serf, whose duties resembled those of the *paedagogus*
in a household in ancient Rome. (*R.*)

Presnensky ponds, to tell me smutty stories which I passed on to the hall. He stayed no more than a year; he did something disgraceful at our country place and the gardener tried to kill him with a scythe, so my father told him to take himself off.

He was succeeded by a Brunswick-Wolfenbüttel soldier (probably a deserter) called Fëdor Karlovich, who was distinguished by his fine handwriting and extreme stupidity. He had been in the same position in two families before and had acquired some experience, so adopted the tone of a tutor; moreover, when he spoke French he would say 'sh' for 'zh', and invariably put the accent on the wrong syllable.[11]

I had not a particle of respect for him and poisoned every moment of his existence, especially after I had convinced myself that he was incapable of understanding decimal fractions and the rule of three. As a rule there is a great deal of ruthlessness and even cruelty in boys' hearts; with positive ferocity I persecuted the poor Wolfenbüttel *Jäger* with proportion sums; this so interested me that I triumphantly informed my father of Fëdor Karlovich's stupidity, though I was not given to discussing such subjects with him.

Moreover, Fëdor Karlovich boasted to me that he had a new swallow-tail coat, dark blue with gold buttons, and I actually did see him on one occasion setting off to attend a wedding in a swallow-tail coat which was too big for him but had gold buttons. The boy whose duty it was to wait upon him informed me that he had borrowed the coat from a friend who served at the counter of a perfumery shop. Without the slightest sympathy I pestered the poor fellow to tell me where his blue dress-coat was.

'There are so many moths in your house,' he said, 'that I have left it with a tailor I know, to be taken care of.'

'Where does that tailor live?'

'What is that to you?'

'Why not tell me?'

'You needn't poke your nose into other people's business.'

'Well, perhaps not, but it is my name-day in a week, so please do get the blue coat from the tailor for that day.'

'No, I won't. You don't deserve it because you are so impertinent.'

And I would threaten him with my finger.

For his final discomfiture Fëdor Karlovich must needs one day

---

[11] The English speak French worse than the Germans, but they only distort the language, while the Germans *degrade* it.

brag before Bouchot, my French teacher, of having been a recruit at Waterloo, and of the Germans having given the French a terrible thrashing. Bouchot merely stared at him and took a pinch of snuff with such a terrible air that the conqueror of Napoleon was a good deal disconcerted. Bouchot walked off leaning angrily on his gnarled stick and never referred to him afterwards except as '*le soldat de Vilain-ton.*' I did not know at the time that this pun was perpetrated by Béranger and could not boast of having sprung from Bouchot's fertile fancy.

At last Blücher's companion in arms had some quarrel with my father and left our house; after that my father did not worry me with any more Germans.

While our Brunswick-Wolfenbüttel friend held the field I sometimes used to visit some boys with whom a friend of his lived, also in the capacity of a 'German'; and with these boys we used to take long walks; after his departure I was left again in complete solitude. I was bored, struggled to get out of it, and found no means of escape. As I had no chance of overriding my father's will I might perhaps have been broken in to this existence if a new intellectual interest and two meetings, of which I will speak in the following chapter, had not soon afterwards saved me. I am quite certain that my father had not the faintest notion what sort of life he was forcing upon me, or he would not have thwarted me in the most innocent desires nor have refused my most natural requests.

Sometimes he allowed me to go with the Senator to the French theatre, and this was the greatest enjoyment for me; I was passionately fond of seeing acting, but this pleasure brought me as much pain as joy. The Senator used to arrive with me when the play was half over and, as he invariably had an invitation for the evening, would take me away before the end. The theatre was in Apraxin's house, at the Arbatsky Gate, and we lived in Old Konyushennaya Street, that is very close by, but my father sternly forbade my returning without the Senator.

I was about fifteen when my father engaged a priest to give me Divinity lessons, so far as was necessary for entering the University. The Catechism came into my hands after I had read Voltaire. Nowhere does religion play so modest a part in education as in Russia, and that, of course, is a great piece of good fortune. A priest is always paid half-price for lessons in religion, and, indeed, if the same priest gives Latin lessons also, he is paid more for them than for teaching the Catechism.

My father regarded religion as among the essential belongings of a well-bred man; he used to say that one must believe in the

Holy Scriptures without criticism, because one could do nothing in that domain with reason, and all intellectual considerations merely obscured the subject; that one must observe the rites of the religion in which one was born, without, however, giving way to excessive devoutness, which was all right for old women, but not proper in men. Did he himself believe? I imagine that he did believe a little, from habit, from regard for propriety, and from a desire to be on the safe side. He did not himself, however, take part in any church observances, sheltering himself behind the delicate state of his health. He scarcely ever received a priest; at most he would ask him to perform a service in the empty *salon* and would send him out there a five-rouble note. In the winter he excused himself on the plea that the priest and the deacon always brought such chilliness with them that he invariably caught cold. In the country he used to go to church and have the priest to his house, but with an eye more to the considerations of society and authority than to God-fearing ones.

My mother was a Lutheran and therefore one degree more religious; on one or two Sundays in every month she would drive to her church, or as Bakay persisted in calling it, to 'her *Kirche*,' and, having nothing better to do, I went with her. There I learned to mimic the German pastors, their declamation and verbosity, with artistic finish, and I retained the talent in riper years.

Every year my father commanded me to take the sacrament. I was afraid of confession, and the church *mise en scène* altogether impressed and alarmed me. With genuine awe I went up to take the sacrament, but I cannot call it a religious feeling; it was the awe which is inspired by everything incomprehensible and mysterious, especially when a grave and solemn significance is attributed to it; casting spells and telling fortunes affect one in the same way. I took the sacrament after the early service in Holy Week, and, after devouring eggs coloured red, *paskha* and Easter cakes, I thought no more of religion for the rest of the year.

But I used to read the Gospel a great deal and with love, both in the Slavonic and in the Lutheran translation. I read it without any guidance, and, though I did not understand everything, I felt a deep and genuine respect for what I read. In my early youth I was often influenced by Voltairianism, and was fond of irony and mockery, but I do not remember that I ever took the Gospel in my hand with a cold feeling; and it has been the same with me all my life; at all ages and under various circumstances

I have gone back to reading the Gospel, and every time its words have brought peace and meekness to my soul.

When the priest began giving me lessons he was surprised to find not only that I had a general knowledge of the Gospel but that I could quote texts, word for word. 'But the Lord God,' he said, 'though He has opened his mind, had not yet opened his heart.' And my theologian, shrugging his shoulders, marvelled at my 'double nature,' but was pleased with me, thinking that I should be able to pass my examination.

Soon a religion of a different sort took possession of my soul.

Political Awakening

ONE WINTER MORNING the Senator arrived not at the time he usually visited us; looking anxious, he went with hurried footsteps into my father's study and closed the door, motioning me to remain in the *salon*.

Luckily I had not long to rack my brains guessing what was the matter. The door from the hall opened a little way and a red face, half-hidden in the wolf-fur of a livery overcoat, called me in a whisper; it was the Senator's footman. I rushed to the door.

'Haven't you heard?' he asked.

'What?'

'The Tsar has just died at Taganrog.'

The news impressed me; I had never thought of the possibility of the Tsar's death; I had grown up with a great respect for Alexander, and recalled mournfully how I had seen him not long before in Moscow. When we were out walking, we had mét him beyond the Tverskoy Gate; he was slowly riding along with two or three generals, returning from Khodynki, where there had been a review. His face was gracious, his features soft and rounded, his expression tired and melancholy. When he was on a level with us I raised my hat, and he bowed to me, smiling. What a contrast to Nicholas, who always looked like a slightly bald Medusa with cropped hair and moustaches. In the street, at the court, with his children and ministers, with his courtiers and maids of honour, Nicholas was always trying whether his eyes

had the power of a rattlesnake, of freezing blood in the veins.[1]
If Alexander's external gentleness was assumed, surely such
hypocrisy is better than the naked candour of autocracy.

While vague ideas floated through my mind, while portraits of
the new Emperor Constantine were sold in the shops, while
appeals to take the oath of allegiance were being delivered, and
good people were hastening to do so, rumours were suddenly
afloat that the Tsarevich had refused the crown. Then that
same footman of the Senator's who was greatly interested in
political news and had a fine field for gathering it—in all the
public offices and vestibules of senators, to one or other of which
he was always driving from morning to night, for he did not
share the privilege of the horses, who were changed after dinner—informed me that there had been rioting in Petersburg and
that cannon were being fired in Galernaya Street.

On the following evening Count Komarovsky, a general of the
gendarmes, was with us: he told us of the square formed in St.
Isaac's Square, of the Horse Guards' attack, of the death of Count
Miloradovich.

Then followed arrests; 'So-and-so has been taken,' 'So-and-so
has been seized,' 'So-and-so has been brought up from the
country,' terrified parents trembled for their children. The sky
was overcast with gloomy storm-clouds.

In the reign of Alexander political oppression was rare; the
Tsar did, it is true, banish Pushkin for his verses and Labzin for
having, when he was secretary, proposed to elect the coachman,
Ilya Baykov, a member of the Academy of Arts;[2] but there was no
systematic persecution. The secret police had not yet grown into

---

[1] The story is told that on one occasion in his own household, in the
presence, that is, of two or three heads of the secret police, two or three
maids of honour and generals in waiting, he tried his Medusa glance
on his daughter Marya Nikolayevna. She is like her father, and her eyes
really do recall the terrible look in his. The daughter boldly endured
her father's stare. The Tsar turned pale, his cheeks twitched, and his
eyes grew still more ferocious; his daughter met him with the same look
in hers. Everyone turned pale and trembled; the maids of honour and the
generals in waiting dared not breathe, so panic-stricken were they at
this cannibalistic imperial duel with the eyes, in the style of that
described by Byron in *Don Juan*.* Nicholas got up: he felt that he had
met his match.

[2] The President of the Academy proposed Arakcheyev as honorary member. Alexander Fëdorovich Labzin (1766–1825), asked in what the

* 'Her father's blood before her father's face
Boiled up, and proved her truly of his race.'
Don Juan, canto IV, stanza 44

an independent body of gendarmes, but consisted of a department under the control of de Sanglain, an old Voltairian, a wit, a great talker, and a humorist in the style of Jouy.[3] Under Nicholas this gentleman himself was under the supervision of the police and he was considered a liberal, though he was exactly what he had always been; from this fact alone, it is easy to judge of the difference between the two reigns.

Nicholas was completely unknown until he came to the throne; in the reign of Alexander he was of no consequence, and no one was interested in him. Now everyone rushed to inquire about him; no one could answer questions but the officers of the Guards; they hated him for his cold cruelty, his petty fussiness and his vindictiveness. One of the first anecdotes that went the round of the town confirmed the officers' opinion of him. The story was that at some drill or other the Grand Duke had so far forgotten himself as to try and take an officer by the collar. The officer responded with the words: 'Your Highness, my sword is in my hand.' Nicholas drew back, said nothing, but never forgot the answer. After the Fourteenth of December he made inquiries on two occasions as to whether this officer was implicated. Fortunately he was not.[4]

Count's services to the arts consisted. The President was at a loss and answered that Arakcheyev was the man who was closest to the Tsar. 'If that is sufficient reason, then I propose his coachman, Ilya Baykov,' observed the secretary; 'he not only is close to the Tsar, but sits in front of him.' Labzin was a mystic and the editor of the *Messenger of Zion*; Alexander himself was a mystic of the same sort, but with the fall of Golitsyn's ministry he handed over his former 'brethren of Christ and of the inner man' to Arakcheyev to do with as he pleased. Labzin was banished to Simbirsk.

[3] Victor Joseph Étienne de Jouy, a popular French writer (1764–1846). (*Tr.*)

[4] The officer, if I am not mistaken, Count Samoylov, had left the army and was living quietly in Moscow. Nicholas recognised him at the theatre, fancied that he was dressed with rather elaborate originality, and expressed the royal desire that such costumes should be ridiculed on the stage. The theatre director and *patriot*, Zagoskin, commissioned one of his actors to represent Samoylov in some vaudeville. The rumour of this was soon all over the town. When the performance was over, the real Samoylov went into the director's box and asked permission to say a few words to his double. The director was frightened but, afraid of a scene, summoned the actor. 'You have acted me very well,' the count said to him, 'and the only thing wanting to complete the likeness is this diamond which I always wear; allow me to hand it to you; you will wear it next time you are ordered to represent me.' After this Samoylov calmly returned to his seat. The stupid jest at his expense fell as flat as the proclamation that Chaadayev was mad and other august pranks.

The tone of society changed before one's eyes; the rapid deterioration in morals was a melancholy proof of how little the sense of personal dignity was developed among Russian aristocrats. Nobody (except women) dared utter a warm word about relations or friends, whose hands they had shaken only the day before they had been carried off at night by the police. On the contrary, there were savage fanatics for slavery, some from abjectness, others, worse still, from disinterested motives.

Women alone did not take part in this shameful abandonment of those who were near and dear . . . and women alone stood at the Cross too, and at the blood-stained guillotine there stood, first, Lucile Desmoulins,[5] that Ophelia of the revolution, always beside the axe, waiting for her turn, and later, George Sand, who gave the hand of sympathy and friendship on the scaffold to the youthful fanatic Alibaud.[6]

The wives of men exiled to hard labour lost their civil rights, abandoned wealth and social position, and went to a lifetime of bondage in the terrible climate of Eastern Siberia, under the still more terrible oppression of the police there.[7] Sisters, who had not the right to go with their brothers, withdrew from court, and many left Russia; almost all of them kept a feeling of love for the victims alive in their hearts; but there was no such love in the men: terror consumed it in their hearts, and not one of them dared mention the *unfortunates*.

◈   ◈   ◈

The accounts of the rising and of the trial of the leaders, and the horror in Moscow, made a deep impression on me; a new world was revealed to me which became more and more the centre of my moral existence. I do not know how it came to pass, but, though I had no understanding, or only a very dim one, of what it all meant, I felt that I was not on the same side as the grape-shot and victory, prisons and chains. The execution of Pestel[8] and his associates finally dissipated the childish dream of my soul.

---

[5] Wife of Camille Desmoulins, who at his execution appealed to the crowd, was arrested and also executed in 1794. (*Tr.*)

[6] Alibaud, Louis (1810–36), attempted to assassinate Louis Philippe in 1836. (*Tr.*)

[7] See *Russian Women* (1871–2) by Nikolay Alexeyevich Nekrasov (1821–78). (*R.*)

[8] Pestel, Pavel Ivanovich (1793–1826), leader of the officers in the Southern Army who supported the attempt to overthrow the autocracy and

Everyone expected some mitigation of the sentence on the condemned men, since the coronation was about to take place. Even my father, in spite of his caution and his scepticism, said that the death penalty would not be carried out, and that all this was done merely to impress people. But, like everyone else, he knew little of the youthful monarch. Nicholas left Petersburg, and, without visiting Moscow, stopped at the Petrovsky Palace. . . . The inhabitants of Moscow could scarcely believe their eyes when they read in the *Moscow News* the terrible news of the fourteenth of July.

The Russian people had become unaccustomed to the death penalty; since the days of Mirovich,[9] who was executed instead of Catherine II, and of Pugachëv[10] and his companions, there had been no executions; men had died under the knout, soldiers had run the gauntlet (contrary to the law) until they fell dead, but the death penalty *de jure* did not exist.[11] The story is told that in the reign of Paul there was some partial rising of the Cossacks on the Don in which two officers were implicated. Paul ordered them to be tried by court-martial, and gave the hetman or general full authority. The court condemned them to death,

---

establish constitutional government. The other four who were hanged were Ryleyev, Kakhovsky, Bestuzhev-Ryumin, and Muravëv-Apostol. (*Tr.*)

[9] Mirovich, Vasily Yakovlevich (1740–64), in 1762 tried to rescue from the Schlüsselburg the legitimate heir to the Russian throne, known as Ivan VI, who perished in the attempt. It is said that Catherine had given orders that he was to be murdered if any attempt were made to release him. Mirovich was beheaded. (*Tr.*)

[10] Pugachëv, Emelyan Ivanovich (*c.* 1742–75), the Cossack leader of the great rising of the serfs in 1775. (*Tr.*)

[11] By an *ukaz* of Yelizaveta Petrovna of 30th September, 1754, the death penalty (in case of the award of it) was commuted to another punishment (penal servitude, branding, etc.). Catherine II confirmed, by an *ukaz* of 6th April, 1775, the legality of the *ukaz* of 1754; but the *ukaz* of Yelizaveta Petrovna was interpreted as not being applicable to state (extraordinary) crimes (hence the executions of Mirovich and Pugachëv). The question of capital punishment in Russia was put before the State Council in 1823, in connection with the forming of a scheme for a universal code. Some members of the Council interpreted the *ukaz* of 1754 as having abolished capital punishment for all crimes, including state crimes; but the majority of the members, relying upon the fact that in the text of the *ukaz* of 1754 only common crimes were spoken of, and finding support in the practice of Catherine II, pronounced that capital punishment in cases of state crimes was juridically valid. Nicholas I availed himself of this later in awarding the sentences for the Decembrist affair. (*A.S.*)

but no one dared to confirm the sentence; the hetman submitted the matter to the Tsar. 'They are a pack of women,' said Paul; 'they want to throw the execution on me: very much obliged to them,' and he commuted the sentence to penal servitude.

Nicholas reintroduced the death penalty into our criminal proceedings, at first illegally, but afterwards he legitimised it into his Code.[12]

The day after receiving the terrible news there was a religious service in the Kremlin.[13] After celebrating the execution Nicholas made his triumphal entry into Moscow. I saw him then for the first time; he was on horseback, riding beside a carriage in which the two empresses, his wife and Alexander's widow, were sitting. He was handsome, but there was a coldness about his looks; no face could have more mercilessly betrayed the character of the man than his. The sharply retreating forehead and the lower jaw developed at the expense of the skull were expressive of iron will and feeble intelligence, rather of cruelty than of sensuality; but the chief point in the face was the eyes, which were entirely without warmth, without a trace of mercy, wintry eyes. I do not believe that he ever passionately loved any woman, as Paul loved Anna Lopukhin,[14] and as Alexander loved all women except his wife; 'he was favourably disposed to them,' nothing more.

In the Vatican there is a new gallery in which Pius VII, I

---

[12] By the Code of Laws published in 1832 the death penalty was prescribed for political crimes, military crimes (in time of military operations) and crimes against quarantine regulations. (A.S.)

[13] Nicholas's victory over the Five was celebrated by a religious service in Moscow. In the midst of the Kremlin the Metropolitan Filaret thanked God for the murders. The whole of the Royal Family took part in the service,* near them the Senate and the ministers and in the immense space around, packed masses of the Guards knelt bareheaded, and also took part in the prayers; cannon thundered from the heights of the Kremlin. Never have the gallows been celebrated with such pomp; Nicholas knew the importance of the victory!

I was present at that service, a boy of fourteen lost in the crowd, and on the spot, before that altar defiled by bloody rites, I swore to avenge the murdered men, and dedicated myself to the struggle with that throne, with that altar, with those cannon. I have not avenged them: the Guards and the throne, the altar and the cannon all remain, but for thirty years I have stood under that flag and have never once deserted it. (The Pole Star, 1855.)

[14] Paul's mistress, the daughter of Lopukhin, the chief of the Moscow police, better known under her married name as Princess Gagarin. (Tr.)

* Nicholas I was not present. (A.S.)

believe, placed an immense number of statues, busts, and statuettes, dug up in Rome and its environs. The whole history of the decline of Rome is there expressed in eyebrows, lips, foreheads; from the daughter of Augustus down to Poppaea the matrons have succeeded in transforming themselves into cocottes, and the type of cocotte is predominant and persists; the masculine type, surpassing itself, so to speak, in Antinous and Hermaphroditus, divides into two. On one hand there is sensual and moral degradation, low brows and features defiled by vice and gluttony, bloodshed and every wickedness in the world, petty as in the *hetaira* Heliogabalus, or with pendulous cheeks like Galba; the last type is wonderfully reproduced in the King of Naples. . . . But there is another—the type of military commander in whom everything that makes a good citizen, everything human, has died out, and there is left nothing but the passion for domination; the mind is narrow and there is no heart at all; they are the monks of the love of power; strength and harshness of will are manifest in their features. Such were the Emperors of the Praetorian Guard and of the army, whom mutinous legionaries raised to power for an hour. Among their number I found many heads that recalled Nicholas before he wore a moustache. I understand the necessity for these grim and inflexible guards beside one who is dying in frenzy, but what use are they to one who is young, whose career is just starting?

In spite of the fact that political dreams absorbed me day and night, my ideas were not distinguished by any peculiar insight; they were so confused that I actually imagined that the object of the Petersburg rising was, among other things, to put the Tsarevich Constantine on the throne, while limiting his power. This led to my being devoted for a whole year to that eccentric creature. He was at that time more popular than Nicholas; for what reason I do not know, but the masses, for whom he had never done anything good, and the soldiers, to whom he had done nothing but harm, loved him. I well remember how during the coronation he walked beside the pale-faced Nicholas with puckered, light-yellow, bristling eyebrows, a bent figure with the shoulders hunched up to the ears, wearing the uniform of the Lettish Guards with a yellow collar. After giving away the bride at the wedding of Nicholas with Russia, he went away to complete the disaffection of Warsaw. Nothing more was heard of him until the 29th of November, 1830.[15]

---

[15] The date when the Polish rebellion broke out. (*Tr.*)

My hero was not handsome and you could not find such a type in the Vatican. I should have called it the *Gatchina*[16] type, if I had not seen the King of Sardinia.

I need hardly say that now loneliness weighed upon me more than ever, for I longed to communicate my ideas and my dreams to someone, to test them and to hear them confirmed; I was too proudly conscious of being 'ill-intentioned' to say nothing about it, or to speak of it indiscriminately.

My first choice of a confidant was my Russian tutor.

I. E. Protopopov was full of that vague and generous liberalism which often passes away with the first grey hair, with marriage and a post, but yet does ennoble a man. My teacher was touched, and as he was taking leave embraced me with the words: 'God grant that these feelings may ripen and grow stronger in you.' His sympathy was a great comfort to me. After this he began bringing me much-soiled manuscript copies, in small handwriting, of poems: 'An Ode to Freedom' and 'The Dagger' by Pushkin, and Ryleyev's 'Thoughts'. I used to copy them in secret . . . (*and now* I print them openly!).

Of course my reading, too, took a different turn. Politics was now in the foreground, and above all the history of the Revolution, of which I knew nothing except from Madame Proveau's tales. In the library in the basement I discovered a history of the 'nineties written by a Royalist. It was so partial that even at fourteen I did not believe it. I happened to hear from old Bouchot that he had been in Paris during the Revolution, and I longed to question him; but Bouchot was a stern and forbidding man with an immense nose and spectacles; he never indulged in superfluous conversation with me; he conjugated verbs, dictated copies, scolded me and went away, leaning on his thick gnarled stick.

'Why did they execute Louis XVI?' I asked him in the middle of a lesson.

The old man looked at me, frowning with one grey eyebrow and lifting the other, pushed his spectacles up on his forehead like a visor, pulled out a large blue handkerchief and, wiping his nose with dignity, said:

'*Parce qu'il a été traître à la patrie.*'

---

[16] Gatchina was an estate which had belonged to Grigory Orlov. Catherine II bought it from his executors and presented it to Paul. He ran it like a barracks and drilled his battalions there, which were largely composed of criminals and runaways. (*R.*)

'If you had been one of the judges, would you have signed the death sentence?'

'With both hands.'

This lesson was of more value to me than all the subjunctives; it was enough for me; it was clear that the King had deserved to be executed.

Old Bouchot did not like me and thought me empty-headed and mischievous because I did not prepare my lessons properly, and he often used to say, 'You'll come to no good,' but when he noticed my sympathy with his regicide ideas, he began to be gracious instead of being cross, forgave my mistakes and used to tell me episodes of the year '93 and how he had left France, when 'the dissolute and the dishonest' got the upper hand. He would finish the lesson with the same dignity, without a smile, but now he would say indulgently:

'I really did think that you were coming to no good, but your generous feelings will be your salvation.'

To this encouragement and sympathy from my teacher was soon added a warmer sympathy which had more influence on me.

The granddaughter[17] of my father's eldest brother was living in a little town in the province of Tver. I had known her from my earliest childhood, but we rarely met; she used to come once a year for Christmas or for carnival to stay at Moscow with her aunt. Nevertheless, we became friends. She was five years older than I, but so small and young-looking that she might have been taken for the same age. What I particularly liked her for was that she was the first person who treated me as a human being, that is, did not continually express surprise at my having grown, ask me what lessons I was doing, and whether I was good at them, and whether I wanted to go into the army and into what regiment, but talked to me as people in general talk to each other—though she did retain that tone of authority which girls like to assume with boys who are a little younger than themselves.

We had been writing to each other since 1824, and frequently, but letters again mean pens and paper, again the schoolroom table with its blots and pictures carved with a penknife; I longed to see her, to talk to her about my new ideas, and so it may be imagined with what joy I heard that my cousin was coming in

---

[17] Tatyana Kuchin, known in Russian literature under her married name, Passek. She wrote memoirs, which throw interesting sidelights on Herzen's narrative. (*Tr.*)

February (1826), and would stay with us for some months. I scratched on my table the days of the month until her arrival and blotted them out as they passed, sometimes intentionally forgetting three days so as to have the pleasure of blotting out rather more at once, and yet the time dragged on very slowly; then the time fixed had passed and another was fixed, and that passed, as always happens.

I was sitting one evening with my tutor Protopopov in my schoolroom, and he, as usual, taking a sip of fizzing *kvas* after every sentence, was talking of the hexameter, horribly chopping up, with voice and hand, every line of Gnedich's *Iliad* into feet, when all of a sudden the snow in the yard crunched with a different sound from that made by town sledges, the tied-up bell gave the relic of a tinkle, there were voices in the courtyard . . . I flushed crimson, I had no more thought for the wrath of 'Achilles, son of Peleus'; I rushed headlong to the hall and my cousin from Tver, wrapped in fur coats, shawls, and scarves, wearing a hood and high, white fur boots, flushed with the frost and, perhaps, with joy, rushed to kiss me.

People usually recall their early childhood, its griefs and joys, with a smile of condescension, as though like Sofya Pavlovna in *Woe from Wit*,[18] they would say, looking prim: 'Childishness!' As though they had grown better in later years, as though their feelings were keener or deeper. Within three years children are ashamed of their playthings—let them: they long to be grown-up, they grow and change so rapidly, they see *that* from their jackets and the pages of their schoolbooks. But one would have thought grown-up people might understand that childhood together with two or three years of youth is the fullest, most exquisite part of life, the part that is most our own, and, indeed, almost the most important, for it imperceptibly shapes our future.

So long as a man is advancing with swift footsteps without stopping or taking thought, so long as he does not come to a precipice or break his neck, he imagines that his life lies before him, looks down on the past and does not know how to appreciate the present. But when experience has crushed the flowers of spring and has chilled the glow on the cheeks of summer, when he begins to suspect that life, properly speaking, is over, and what remains is its continuation, then he returns with different feelings to the bright, warm, lovely memories of early youth.

---

[18] By A. S. Griboyedov. (Act I, scene 7.) (*A.S.*)

Nature with her everlasting snares and economic devices *gives* man youth, but *takes* the formed man for herself; she draws him on, entangles him in a web of social and family relations, three-fourths of which are independent of his will; he, of course, gives his personal character to his actions but he belongs to himself far less than in youth; the lyrical element in the personality is feebler and therefore also his senses and his power of enjoyment—everything—is weaker, except the mind and the will.

My cousin's life was not a bed of roses. Her mother she lost when she was a child. Her father was a desperate gambler, and, like all who have gambling in their blood, he was a dozen times reduced to poverty and a dozen times rich again, and ended all the same by completely ruining himself. *Les beaux restes* of his property he devoted to a stud-farm on which he concentrated all his thoughts and feelings. His son, an ensign in the Uhlans, my cousin's only brother and a very good-natured youth, was going the straight road to ruin; at nineteen he was already a more passionate gambler than his father.

At fifty the father, for no reason at all, married an old maid who had been a pupil in the Smolny Convent.[19] Such a complete, perfect type of the Petersburg boarding-school mistress it has never been my lot to meet. She had been one of the best pupils, and afterwards had become *dame de classe* in the school; thin, fair, and short-sighted, there was something didactic and edifying in her very appearance. Not at all stupid, she was full of an icy exaltation in her speech, talked in hackneyed phrases of virtue and devotion, knew chronology and geography by heart, spoke French with a revolting correctness and concealed within her an egotism that bordered on the factitious modesty of a Jesuit. In addition to these traits of the 'seminarists in yellow shawls'[20] she had others which were purely Nevsky or Smolny characteristics. She used to raise to heaven eyes full of tears as she spoke of the visits of their common mother (the Empress Marya Fëdorovna), was in love with the Emperor Alexander and, I remember, used to wear a locket, or a signet ring, with an extract in it of a letter from the Empress Elizabeth, *'Il a repris son sourire de bienveillance!'*

The reader can picture the harmonious trio: the father a gam-

---

[19] Originally a convent, this was a famous girls' school founded by Catherine II. (*Tr.*) The Bolsheviks gave "Smolny" an incongruous historical resonance when they commandeered the school buildings for their putsch, sometimes called a revolution, in October 1917. (*D.M.*)

[20] A. S. Pushkin: *Yevgeny Onegin*, III, 28. (*A.S.*)

bler, passionately devoted to horses, gypsies, noise, carousals, races and trotting matches; the daughter brought up in a complete independence, accustomed to do what she liked in the house; and the learned lady who, from an elderly schoolmistress, had been turned into a young wife. Of course, she did not like her stepdaughter, and of course her stepdaughter did not like her; as a rule great affection can only exist between women of five-and-thirty and girls of seventeen when the former, with resolute self-sacrifice, determine to have no sex.

I am not at all surprised at the usual hostility between stepdaughters and stepmothers: it is natural and it is morally right. The new person put into the mother's place excites aversion in the children; the second marriage is for them like a second funeral. The children's love is vividly expressed in this feeling and it whispers to the orphans: 'Your father's wife is not your mother at all.' At first Christianity understood that with the conception of marriage which it developed, with the immortality of the soul which it preached, a second marriage was altogether incongruous; but, making continual concessions to the world, the Church was too artful by half and was confronted with the implacable logic of life, with the simple childish heart that in practice revolts against the pious absurdity of regarding its father's companion as its mother.

On her side, too, the woman, who comes to her new home from her wedding and finds a ready-made family awaiting her, is in an awkward position; she has nothing to do with them, she must affect feelings which she cannot have, she must persuade herself and others that another woman's children are as dear to her as if they were her own.

And therefore I do not in the least blame the lady from the convent nor my cousin for their mutual dislike, but I understand how the young girl, unaccustomed to discipline, was fretting to escape to freedom, wherever that might be, out of the parental home. Her father was beginning to get old and was more and more under the thumb of his learned wife. Her brother, the Uhlan, was going from bad to worse and, in fact, life was not pleasant at home; at last she persuaded her stepmother to let her come for some months, possibly even for a year, to us.

The day after her arrival my cousin turned the whole order of my life, except my lessons, upside down, arbitrarily fixed hours for our reading together, advised me not to read novels, but recommended Ségur's *Universal History* and the *Travels of Anacharsis*. Her stoical ideals led her to oppose my marked inclination for smoking in secret, which I did by rolling the tobacco in paper (cigarettes did not exist in those days); in general, she liked preaching morality to me, and if I did not obey her teaching at least I listened meekly. Luckily she could not keep up to her own standards and, forgetting her rules, she read Zschokke's[21] tales with me instead of an archaeological novel, and secretly sent a boy out to buy, in winter, buckwheat cakes and pease-pudding with vegetable oil, and in summer gooseberries and currants.

I think my cousin's influence over me was very good; a warm element came with her into the cell-like seclusion of my youth; it fostered and perhaps, indeed, preserved the scarcely developed feelings which might very well have been completely crushed by my father's irony. I learnt to be observant, to be wounded by a word, to care about my friends, to love; I learnt to talk about my feelings. She supported my political aspirations, predicted for me an unusual future and fame, and I, with childish vanity, believed her that I was a future 'Brutus or Fabricius.'

To me alone she confided the secret of her love for an officer in the Alexandriinsky Regiment of Hussars, in a black pelisse and black dolman; it was a genuine secret, for the hussar himself, as he commanded his squadron, never suspected what a pure flame was glowing for him in the bosom of a girl of eighteen. I do not know whether I envied his lot—probably I did a little—but I was proud of having been chosen as her confidant, and imagined (after Werther) that this was one of those tragic passions, which would have a great *dénouement* accompanied by suicide, poison, and a dagger, and the idea even occurred to me that I might go to him and tell him all about it.

My cousin had brought shuttlecocks from Korcheva, and in one of the shuttlecocks there was a pin; she would never play with any other, and whenever it fell to me or anyone else she would take it, saying she was used to playing with it. The demon of mischief, which was always my evil tempter, prompted me to change the pin, that is, to stick it in another shuttlecock. The trick succeeded perfectly: my cousin always took the one with the pin in it. A fortnight later I told her; her face changed, she dissolved into tears and went off to her own room. I was frightened and unhappy and, after waiting for half an hour,

---

[21] Heinrich Zschokke (1771–1848) wrote in German *Tales of Swiss Life*, in five vols., and also dramas—as well as a religious work *Stunden der Andacht*, in eight vols., which was widely read up to the middle of the nineteenth century and was attacked for ascribing more importance to religious feeling than to orthodox belief. (*Tr.*)

went to see her; her door was locked. I begged her to open it; she refused to let me in and said that she was ill, that I was no friend of hers, but a heartless boy. I wrote her a note and besought her to forgive me; after tea we made it up, I kissed her hand, she embraced me and at once explained the full importance of the matter. A year before the hussar had dined with them and after dinner played battledore and shuttlecock with her —it was his shuttlecock that had been marked with a pin. I had pangs of conscience: I thought that I had committed a real sacrilege.

My cousin stayed until October. Her father sent for her to come home, promising to let her come to us at Vasilevskoye the following year. We were horrified at the idea of parting, but so it was: one autumn day a *brichka* came for her; her maid carried off boxes and baskets to pack in it, and our servants put in all sorts of provisions for a full week's journey, and crowded at the entrance to say good-bye. We hugged each other hard, she wept and I wept—the *brichka* drove out into the street, turned into a side-street near the very place where the buckwheat cakes and pease-pudding were sold, and vanished. I walked about in the courtyard: and there it was rather cold and nasty; I went up into my room—and there it seemed cold and empty. I set to work on my lesson for Protopopov, while I wondered where the *brichka* was now, and whether it had passed the town-gate or not.

My only comfort was the thought of our being together again at Vasilevskoye the following June!

For me the country was always a time of renewal; I was passionately fond of country life. The forest, the fields, and the freedom—it was all so new for me who had been brought up in cotton-wool, within brick walls, not daring on any pretext to go out beyond the gate without asking leave and being accompanied by a footman. . . .

'Are we going to Vasilevskoye or not?' From early spring I was quite engrossed by this question. My father invariably said that this year he was going away early, that he longed to see the leaves come out; but he could never be ready before July. Some years he was so much behind that we never went at all. He wrote to the country every winter that the house was to be ready and thoroughly warmed, but this was done from deep considerations of policy rather than quite seriously, in order that the village head-man and the clerk to the *Zemstvo* might be afraid he would soon be coming and look after their work more carefully.

It seemed that we were going. My father told the Senator that he was longing to rest in the country and that the estate needed his inspection, but again weeks went by.

Little by little there seemed more ground for hope: provisions began to be sent off, sugar, tea, all sorts of cereals, and wine —and again there was a pause; then at last an order was despatched to the village elder to send so many peasants' horses by such a day—and so we were going, we were going!

I did not think then how onerous the loss of four or five days, when work in the fields was at its height, must have been to the peasants, but rejoiced with all my heart and hastened to pack my lesson-books and exercise books. The horses were brought, and with inward satisfaction I heard their munching and snorting in the courtyard, and took great interest in the bustle of the coachmen, and the wrangling of the servants as to who should sit in which cart and where each should put his belongings. In the servants' quarters lights were burning until daybreak, and all were packing, dragging sacks and bags from place to place, and dressing for the journey (which was fifty miles at most!). My father's valet was the most exasperated of all, for he realised how important it was to stow things properly; with intense irritation he fiercely ejected everything which had been put in by others, tore his hair with vexation and was quite unapproachable.

My father did not get up a bit earlier next day; in fact I think he got up later than usual, and drank his coffee just as slowly, but at last, at eleven o'clock, he ordered the horses to be put to. Behind the carriage, which had four seats and was drawn by six of my father's own horses, there came three and sometimes four conveyances—a barouche, a *brichka*, a wagon or, instead of it, two carts; all these were filled with the house-serfs and their belongings and, although wagon-loads had been sent on beforehand, everything was so tightly packed that no one could sit with comfort.

We stopped half-way to have dinner and to feed the horses in the big village of Perkhushkovo, the name of which occurs in Napoleon's bulletins. This village belonged to the son of that elder brother of my father's of whom I have spoken in connection with the division of the property. The neglected house of the owner stood on the high-road, surrounded by flat, cheerless-looking fields; but even this dusty vista delighted me after the cramped life of town. In the house the warped floors and stairs shook, noises and footsteps resounded loudly, and the walls echoed them as it were with astonishment. The old-fashioned furniture from the former owner's cabinet of curiosities was living out its day here in exile; I wandered with curiosity from room to room, went upstairs and downstairs and finally into the kitchen. There our man-cook, with a cross and ironical expression, was preparing a hasty dinner. The steward, a grey-haired old man with a swelling on his head, was usually sitting in the kitchen; the cook addressed his remarks to him and criticised the stove and the hearth, while the steward listened to him and from time to time answered laconically: 'May-be; perhaps it's so,' and looked disconsolately at all the upset, wondering when the devil would carry us off again.

The dinner was served on a special English service, made of tin or some composition, bought *ad hoc*. Meanwhile the horses had been put in; in the hall and vestibule people who were fond of watching meetings and leave-takings of the gentry were gathering together: footmen who were finishing their lives on bread and pure country air, old women who had been prepossessing maids thirty years before, all the locusts of a landowner's household who through no fault of their own eat up the peasants' labour like real locusts. With them came children with flaxen hair; barefooted and dirty, they kept poking forward while the old women pulled them back. The children screamed and the old women screamed at them; and they caught me at every opportunity, and marvelled every year that I had grown so much. My father said a few words to them; some went up to kiss his hand, which he never gave them, others bowed, and we set off.

A few miles from Prince Golitsyn's estate of Vyazma the headman of Vasilevskoye was waiting for us on horseback at the edge of the forest, and he escorted us on a by-road. In the village by the big house, approached by a long avenue of limes, we were met by the priest, his wife, the church servitors, the house-serfs, several peasants, and Pronka, the fool, the only one with any feeling of human dignity, for he did not take off his greasy hat, but stood smiling at a little distance and took to his heels as soon as anyone from the town servants tried to come near him.

I have seen few palaces more pleasant to look at than Vasilevskoye. For anyone who knows Kuntsevo and Yusupov's Arkhangelskoye, or Lopukhin's estate facing the Savva monastery, it is enough to say that Vasilevskoye lies on a continuation of the same bank of the Moskva, twenty miles from the monastery. On the sloping side of the river lie the village, the church, and the old manor house. On the other side there is a hill and a small village, and there my father had built a new house. The view

from it embraced the country within a radius of ten miles; far
and wide rolled seas of quivering corn; homesteads and villages
with white churches could be seen here and there; forests of
various hues made a semi-circular setting, and the Moskva like a
pale blue ribbon ran through it all. Early in the morning I
opened the window in my room upstairs and looked and listened
and breathed.

And yet I regretted the old stone house, perhaps because it was
in it that I first made acquaintance with the country; I so loved
the long, shady avenue leading up to it and the garden that had
run wild; the house was falling into ruins and a slender, graceful birch tree was growing out of a crack in the wall of the
vestibule. On the left an avenue of willows ran along the river-
side, beyond it there were reeds and the white sand down to the
river; on that sand and among those reeds I used at eleven and
twelve years old to play for a whole morning. A bent old man,
the gardener, used nearly always to be sitting before the house;
he used to triple-distil peppermint liquor, cook berries, and
secretly regale me with all sorts of vegetables. There were great
numbers of crows in the garden: the tops of the trees were
covered with their nests, and they used to circle round them,
cawing; sometimes, especially towards the evening, they used to
take wing, hundreds at a time, racing after one another with a
great clamour; sometimes one would fly hurriedly from tree to
tree and then all would be still. . . . And towards night an owl
would wail somewhere in the distance like a child, or go off into
a peal of laughter. . . . I was afraid of these wild wailing
sounds and yet I went to listen to them.

Every year, or, at least, every other year, we used to go to
Vasilevskoye. As I went away I used to measure my height on
the wall by the balcony, and I went at once on arriving to find
how much I had grown. But in the country I could measure not
only my physical growth: these periodical returns to the same
objects showed me plainly the difference in my inner development. Other books were brought, other objects interested me. In
1823 I was still quite a child; I had children's books with me,
and even those I did not read, but was much more interested in a
hare and a squirrel which lived in the loft near my room.
One of my principal enjoyments consisted in my father's permission to fire a small cannon every evening, an operation which of
course entertained all the servants, and grey-haired old men of
fifty were as much diverted as I was. In 1827 I brought with me
Plutarch and Schiller; early in the morning I used to go out into

the forest, as far as I could into the thickest part of it and, imagining that I was in the Bohemian forests,[22] read aloud to myself. Nevertheless, I was greatly interested also in a dam which I was making in a small stream with the help of a serf-boy, and would run a dozen times a day to look at it and repair it. In 1829 and 1830 I was writing a philosophical article on Schiller's *Wallenstein*, and of my old toys none but the cannon retained its charm.

Besides firing the cannon there was, however, another enjoyment for which I retained an unalterable passion—watching the evenings in the country; now as then such evenings are for me still times of devoutness, peace, and poetry. One of the last serenely bright moments in my life reminds me also of those village evenings. The sun was sinking majestically, brilliantly, into an ocean of fire, was dissolving into it. . . . All at once the rich purple was followed by deep blue dusk, and everything was covered with a smoky mist: in Italy the darkness falls quickly. We mounted our mules; on the way from Frascati to Rome we had to ride through a little village; here and there lights were already twinkling; everything was still, the hoofs of the mules rang on the stone, a fresh and rather damp wind was blowing from the Apennines. As we came out of the village, there was a little Madonna standing in a niche with a lamp burning before her; some peasant girls as they came from work with white kerchiefs on their heads sank on their knees and chanted a prayer; they were joined by some needy *pifferari* who were passing by. I was deeply affected, deeply touched. We looked at each other . . . and rode on at a slow pace to the inn where a carriage was waiting for us. As we drove homewards I talked of the evenings at Vasilevskoye. But what was there to tell?

> *In silence stood the garden trees,*
> *Among the hills the village lay,*
> *And thither at the fall of night*
> *The lingering cattle wend their way.*

N. P. Ogarëv, *Humorous Verse*

. . . The shepherd cracks his long whip and plays on his birch-bark pipe; there is the lowing and bleating and stamping of the herds returning over the bridge, the dog with a bark chases a straying sheep while she runs with a sort of wooden gallop; and then the songs of the peasant girls, on their way home from the

---

[22] The scene of Schiller's *Die Räuber*. (*A.S.*)

fields, come closer and closer; but the path turns off to the right
and the sounds recede again. From the houses children, little
girls, run out at the creaking gates to meet their cows and sheep;
work is over. The children are playing in the street and on the
river-bank, their voices ring out with shrill clarity over the river
in the evening glow; the scorched smell of barns mingles with
the air, the dew begins little by little to spread like smoke over
the fields, the wind moves over the forest with a sound as though
the leaves were boiling, the summer lightning, quivering, lights
up the landscape with a dying, tremulous azure, and Vera
Artamonovna, grumbling rather than cross, says, coming upon
me under a lime tree:

'How is it there's no finding you anywhere? And tea has been
served long ago and everyone is at table. Here I have been
looking and looking for you until my legs are tired. I can't go
running about at my age; and why are you lying on the damp
grass like that? . . . you'll have a cold to-morrow, I'll be
bound.'

'Oh, that'll do, that'll do,' I say to the old woman with a
laugh; 'I shan't have a cold and I don't want any tea, but you
steal me the best of the cream from the very top.'

'Well, you really are a boy, there's no being angry with you
. . . what a sweet tooth you've got! I have got the cream ready
for you without your asking. Look at the lightning . . . well,
that's right! It brings the corn on.'

And I go home skipping and whistling.

We did not go to Vasilevskoye after 1832. My father sold it
while I was in exile. In 1843 we stayed at another estate in the
Moscow province, in the district of Zvenigorod, about fourteen
miles from Vasilevskoye. I could not help going over to visit my
old home. And here we were again riding along the same by-
road; the familiar fir-wood and the hill covered with nut trees
came into view, and then the ford over the river, the ford that
had so delighted me twenty years before, the gurgling of the
water, the crunching of the pebbles, the shouting coachman and
the struggling horses . . . and here was the village and the
priest's house where he used to sit on a bench in a dark-brown
cassock, simple-hearted, good-natured, red-haired, always in a
sweat, always nibbling something and always afflicted with a
hiccup; and here was the counting-house where the clerk Vasily
Yepifanov, who was never sober, used to write his accounts,
huddled up over the paper, holding the pen by the very end with
his third finger bent tightly under it. The priest is dead and
Vasily Yepifanov is keeping accounts and getting drunk in

another village. We stopped at the village head-man's hut, but found only the wife at home, for her husband was in the fields.

A strange element had crept in during those ten years; instead of our house on the hill there was a new one, and a new garden was laid out beside it. As we turned by the church and the graveyard we met a deformed-looking creature, dragging itself along almost on all fours; it was trying to show me something, and I went up; it was a hunchbacked, paralytic old woman, half-crazy, who used to live on charity and work in the former priest's garden. She had been about seventy then and death had just passed by her. She recognised me, shed tears, shook her head and kept saying:

'Ough! why even you are getting old. I only knew you from your walk, while I—there, there, ough! ough! don't talk of it!'

As we were driving back, I saw in the fields in the distance the village head-man, the same as in our time. At first he did not know me, but when we had driven by, as though suddenly coming to himself with a start, he took off his hat and bowed low. When we had driven a little farther I turned round; the head-man, Grigory Gorsky, was still standing in the same place, looking after us; his tall, bearded figure, bowing in the midst of the cornfield, gave us a friendly send-off from the home which had passed into the hands of strangers.

Nick and the Sparrow Hills

'Write then how in this place [the Sparrow Hills] the story of our lives, yours and mine, began to unfold. . . .'

A Letter, 1833

THREE YEARS before the time I am speaking of we were walking on the banks of the Moskva at Luzhniki, that is, on the other side of the Sparrow Hills. At the river's edge we met a French tutor of our acquaintance in nothing but his shirt; he was panic-stricken and was shouting, 'He is drowning, he is drowning!' But before our friend had time to take off his shirt or put on his trousers a Ural Cossack ran down from the Sparrow Hills, dashed into the water, vanished, and a minute later reappeared with a frail man, whose head and arms were flopping about like clothes hung out in the wind. He laid him on the bank, saying, 'He'll still recover if we roll him about.'

The people standing round collected fifty roubles and offered it to the Cossack. The latter, without making faces over it, said very simply: 'It's a sin to take money for such a thing, and it was no trouble; come to think of it, he weighs no more than a cat. We are poor people, though,' he added. 'Ask, we don't; but there, if people give, why not take? We are humbly thankful.' Then tying up the money in a handkerchief he went to graze his horses on the hill. My father asked his name and wrote about the incident next day to Essen. Essen promoted him to be a non-commissioned officer. A few months later the Cossack came to see us and with him a pock-marked, bald German, smelling of scent and wearing a curled, fair wig; he came to thank us on behalf of the Cossack—it was the drowned man. From that time he took to coming to see us.

Karl Ivanovich Sonnenberg, that was his name, was at that time completing the German part of the education of two young rascals; from them he went to a landowner of Simbirsk, and from him to a distant relative of my father's. The boy, the care of whose health and German accent had been entrusted to him, and whom Sonnenberg called Nick, attracted me. There was something kind, gentle and pensive about him; he was not at all like the other boys it had been my luck to meet. We became close friends. He was silent and pensive: I was high-spirited but afraid to rag him.

About the time when my cousin went back to Korcheva, Nick's grandmother died; his mother he had lost in early childhood. There was a great upset in the house and Sonnenberg, who really had nothing to do, fussed about too, and imagined that he was run off his legs; he brought Nick in the morning and asked that he might remain with us for the rest of the day. Nick was sad and frightened; I suppose he had been fond of his grandmother.

. . . After we had been sitting still a little I suggested reading Schiller. I was surprised at the similarity of our tastes; he knew far more by heart than I did and knew precisely the passages I liked best; we closed the book and, so to speak, began sounding each other's sympathies.

From Möros who went with a dagger in his sleeve 'to free the city from the tyrant,' from Wilhelm Tell who waited for Vogt on the narrow path at Küsznacht, the transition to Nicholas and the Fourteenth of December was easy. These thoughts and these comparisons were not new to Nick; he, too, knew Pushkin's and Ryleyev's[1] unpublished poems. The contrast between him and the empty-headed boys I had occasionally met was striking.

Not long before, walking near the Presnensky Ponds, full of my Bouchot terrorism, I had explained to a companion of my age the justice of the execution of Louis XVI.

'Quite so,' observed the youthful Prince O., 'but you know he was God's anointed!'

I looked at him with compassion, ceased to care for him and never asked to go and see him again.

There were no such barriers with Nick: his heart beat as mine did. He, too, had cast off from the grim conservative shore, and we had but to shove off together, and almost from the first day we resolved to work in the interests of the Tsarevich Constantine!

Before that day we had few long conversations. Karl Ivanovich pestered us like an autumn fly and spoilt every conversation with his presence; he interfered in everything without understanding, made remarks, straightened Nick's shirt collar, was in a hurry to get home: in fact, was detestable. After a month we could not pass two days without seeing each other or writing a letter; with all the impulsiveness of my nature I attached myself more and more to Nick, while he had a quiet, deep love for me.

From the very beginning our friendship was to take a serious tone. I do not remember that mischievous pranks were our foremost interest, particularly when we were alone. Of course we did not sit still: our age came into its own, and we laughed and played the fool, teased Sonnenberg and played with bows and arrows in our courtyard; but at the bottom of it all there was something very different from idle companionship. Besides our being of the same age, besides our 'chemical affinity,' we were united by the faith that bound us. Nothing in the world so purifies and ennobles early youth, nothing keeps it so safe as a passionate interest in the whole of humanity. We respected our future in ourselves, we looked at each other as 'chosen vessels,' predestined.

Nick and I often walked out into the country. We had our favourite places, the Sparrow Hills, the fields beyond the Dragomilovsky Gate. He would come with Sonnenberg to fetch me at six or seven in the morning, and if I were asleep would throw

---

[1] Ryleyev, Kondrati Fëdorovich (1795–1826), one of the leaders of the Decembrists: he was hanged for his part in the conspiracy. (R.)

sand and little pebbles at my window. I would wake up smiling and hasten out to him.

These walks had been instituted by the indefatigable Karl Ivanovich.

In the old-fashioned patriarchal education of Ogarëv, Sonnenberg plays the part of Biron.[2] When he made his appearance the influence of the old male nurse who had looked after the boy was put aside; the discontented oligarchy of the hall were forced against the grain to silence, knowing that there was no overcoming the damned German who fed at the master's table. Sonnenberg made violent changes in the old order of things. The old man who had been nurse positively grew tearful when he learnt that the wretched German had taken the young master *himself* to buy ready-made boots at a shop! Sonnenberg's revolution, like Peter I's, was distinguished by a military character even in the most peaceful matters. It does not follow from that that Karl Ivanovich's thin little shoulders had ever been adorned with epaulettes; but nature has so made the German that if he does not reach the slovenliness and *sans-gêne* of a philologist or a theologian, he is inevitably of a military mind even though he be a civilian. By virtue of this peculiarity Karl Ivanovich liked tight-fitting clothes, buttoned up and cut with a waist; by virtue of it he was a strict observer of his own rules, and, if he proposed to get up at six o'clock in the morning, he would get Nick up at one minute to six, and in no case later than one minute past, and would go out into the open air with him.

The Sparrow Hills, at the foot of which Karl Ivanovich had been so nearly drowned, soon became our 'sacred hills.'

One day after dinner my father proposed to drive out into the country. Ogarëv was with us and my father invited him and Sonnenberg to go too. These expeditions were not a joking matter. Before reaching the town gate we had to drive for an hour or more in a four-seated carriage 'built by Joachim,' which had not prevented it from becoming disgracefully shabby in its fifteen years of service, peaceful as they had been, and from being, as it always had been, heavier than a siege gun. The four horses of different sizes and colours which had grown fat and lazy in idleness were covered with sweat and foam within a quarter of an hour; the coachman Avdey was forbidden to let this happen, and so had no choice but to drive at a walk. The windows were usually up, however hot it might be; and with all

---

[2] Biron, favourite of the Empress Anna Ivanovna, was practically ruler of Russia during her reign and designated as successor by her. (*Tr.*)

this we had the indifferently oppressive supervision of my father and the restlessly fussy and irritating supervision of Karl Ivanovich. But we gladly put up with everything for the sake of being together.

At Luzhniki we crossed the river Moskva in a boat at the very spot where the Cossack had pulled Karl Ivanovich out of the water. My father walked, bent and morose as always; beside him Karl Ivanovich tripped along, entertaining him with gossip and scandal. We went on in front of them, and getting far ahead ran up to the Sparrow Hills at the spot where the first stone of Vitberg's temple was laid.

Flushed and breathless, we stood there mopping our faces. The sun was setting, the cupolas glittered, beneath the hill the city extended farther than the eye could reach; a fresh breeze blew on our faces, we stood leaning against each other and, suddenly embracing, vowed in sight of all Moscow to sacrifice our lives to the struggle we had chosen.

This scene may strike others as very affected and theatrical, and yet twenty-six years afterwards I am moved to tears as I recall it; there was a sacred sincerity in it, and our whole life has proved this. But apparently a like destiny defeats all vows made on that spot; Alexander was sincere, too, when he laid the first stone of that temple,[3] which, as Joseph II[4] said (although then mistakenly) at the laying of the first stone in some town in Novorossiya, was destined to be the last.

We did not know all the strength of the foe with whom we were entering into battle, but we took up the fight. That strength broke much in us, but it was not that strength that shattered us, and we did not surrender to it in spite of all its blows. The wounds received from it were honourable. Jacob's strained thigh was the sign that he had wrestled in the night with God.

From that day the Sparrow Hills became a place of worship for us and once or twice a year we went there, and always by ourselves. There, five years later, Ogarëv asked me timidly and shyly whether I believed in his poetic talent, and wrote to me afterwards (1833) from his country house: 'I have come away and feel sad, as sad as I have never been before. And it's all the Sparrow Hills. For a long time I hid my enthusiasm in myself;

---

[3] See 'Alexander Lavrentevich Vitberg,' pp. 199–209. (R.) Alexander I laid the foundation stone on 12th October, 1817. (A.S.)

[4] Joseph II of Austria paid a famous visit to Catherine II of Russia in 1780. (Tr.)

shyness or something else, I don't myself know what, prevented me from uttering it; but on the Sparrow Hills that enthusiasm was not burdened with solitude: you shared it with me and those moments have been unforgettable; like memories of past happiness they have followed me on my way, while round me I saw nothing but forest; it was all so blue, dark blue, and in my soul was darkness, darkness.

'Write then,' he concluded, 'how in this place' (that is, on the Sparrow Hills) 'the story of our lives, yours and mine, began to unfold.'[5]

Five more years passed. I was far from the Sparrow Hills, but near me their Prometheus, A. L. Vitberg, stood, austere and gloomy. In 1842, returning finally to Moscow, I again visited the Sparrow Hills, and once more we stood on the site of the foundation stone and gazed at the same view, two together, but the other was not Nick.

Since 1827 we had not been parted. In every memory of that time, general and particular, he with his boyish features and his love for me was everywhere in the foreground. Early could be seen in him that sign of grace which is vouchsafed to few, whether for woe or for bliss I know not, but certainly in order not to be one of the crowd. A large portrait of Ogarëv as he was at that time (1827–8), painted in oils, remained for long afterwards in his father's house. In later days I often stood before it and gazed at him. He is shown with an open shirt collar; the painter has wonderfully caught the luxuriant chestnut hair, the undefined, youthful beauty of his irregular features and his rather swarthy colouring; there was a pensiveness in the portrait that gave promise of powerful thought; an unaccountable melancholy and extreme gentleness shone out from his big grey eyes that suggested the future stature of a mighty spirit; such indeed he grew to be. This portrait, presented to me, was taken by a woman who was a stranger; perhaps these lines will meet her eyes and she will send it to me.

I do not know why the memories of first love are given such precedence over the memories of youthful friendship. The fragrance of first love lies in the fact that it forgets the difference of the sexes, that it is passionate friendship. On the other hand, friendship between the young has all the ardour of love and all its character, the same delicate fear of touching on its feelings

---

[5] The Sparrow Hills are now the Lenin Hills and the site of some high-rise paleostalinolithic buildings belonging to Moscow University, which, in name at least, was Herzen's and Ogarëv's alma mater. (*D.M.*)

with a word, the same mistrust of self and absolute devotion, the same agony at separation, and the same jealous desire for exclusive affection.

I had long loved Nick and loved him passionately, but had not been able to resolve to call him my friend, and when he was spending the summer at Kuntsevo I wrote to him at the end of a letter: 'Whether your friend or not, I do not yet know.' He first used the second person singular in writing to me and used to call me his Agathon after Karamzin,[6] while I called him my Raphael after Schiller.

You will smile, perhaps, but let it be a mild, good-natured smile, such as one smiles when one thinks of the time when one was fifteen. Or would it not be better to muse over the question, 'Was I like that when I was blossoming out?'[7] and to bless your fate if you have had youth (merely being young is not enough for this), and to bless it doubly if you had a friend then.

The language of that period seems affected and bookish to us now; we have become unaccustomed to its vague enthusiasm, its confused fervour that passes suddenly into languid tenderness or childish laughter. It would be as absurd in a man of thirty as the celebrated *Bettina will schlafen,*[8] but in its proper time this language of youth, this *jargon de la puberté,* this change of the psychological voice is very sincere; even the shade of bookishness is natural to the age of theoretical knowledge and practical ignorance.

Schiller remained our favourite.[9] The characters of his dramas were living persons for us; we analysed them, loved and hated them, not as poetic creations but as living men. Moreover we saw ourselves in them. I wrote to Nick, somewhat troubled by his being too fond of Fiesco, that behind every Fiesco stands his Verrina. My ideal was Karl Moor, but soon I was false to him and went over to the Marquis of Posa. I imagined in a hundred variations how I would speak to Nicholas, and how afterwards

---

[6] Karamzin, Nikolay Mikhaylovich (1766–1826), author of a great *History of the Russian State,* and also of novels in the sentimental romantic style of his period. (*Tr.*)

[7] From A. S. Pushkin: *Onegin's Travels.* (*A.S.*)

[8] See the *Tagebuch* of Bettina von Arnim for the account of her famous first interview with Goethe. (*Tr.*)

[9] Schiller's poetry has not lost its influence on me. A few months ago I read *Wallenstein,* that titanic work, aloud to my son. The man who has lost his taste for Schiller has grown old or pedantic, has grown hard or forgotten himself. What is one to say of these precocious *altkluge Burschen* who know his defects so well at seventeen?

he would send me to the mines or the scaffold. It is a strange
thing that almost all our day-dreams ended in Siberia or the
scaffold and hardly ever in triumph; can this be the way the
Russian imagination turns, or is it the effect of Petersburg with
its five gallows and its penal servitude reflected on the young
generation?

And so, Ogarëv, hand in hand we moved forward into life!
Fearlessly and proudly we advanced, generously we responded to
every challenge and single-heartedly we surrendered to every
inclination. The path we chose was no easy one; we have never
left it for one moment: wounded and broken we have gone forward and no one has outdistanced us. I have reached . . . not
the goal but the spot where the road goes downhill, and involuntarily I seek thy hand that we may go down together, that I may
press it and say, smiling mournfully, 'So this is all!'

Meanwhile in the dull leisure to which events have condemned me, finding in myself neither strength nor freshness for
new labours, I am writing down *our* memories. Much of that
which united us so closely has settled in these pages. I present
them to thee. For thee they have a double meaning, the meaning
of tombstones on which we meet familiar names.

. . . And is it not strange to think that had Sonnenberg
known how to swim, or had he been drowned then in the
Moskva, had he been pulled out not by a Cossack of the Urals
but by a soldier of the Apsheronsky infantry, I should not have
met Nick or should have met him later, differently, not in that
room in our old house, where, smoking cigars on the sly, we
entered so deeply into each other's lives and drew strength from
each other.

My Father

THE INSUFFERABLE DREARINESS of our house grew greater every
year. If my time at the university had not been approaching, if it
had not been for my new friendship, my political inclinations
and the liveliness of my disposition, I should have run away or
perished.

My father was hardly ever in a good humour; he was perpetually dissatisfied with everything. A man of great intelligence and great powers of observation, he had seen, heard, and remembered an immense amount; an accomplished man of the world, he could be extremely amiable and interesting, but he did not care to be so and sank more and more into wayward unsociability.

It is hard to say exactly what it was that put so much bitterness and spleen into his blood. Periods of passion, of great unhappiness, of mistakes and losses were completely absent from his life. I could never fully understand what was the origin of the spiteful mockery and irritability that filled his soul, the mistrustful unsociability and the vexation that consumed him. Did he bear with him to the grave some memory which he confided to no one, or was this simply the result of the combination of two elements so absolutely opposed to each other as the eighteenth century and Russian life, with the intervention of a third, terribly conducive to the development of capricious humour: the idleness of the serf-owning landed gentleman?

Last century produced in the West, particularly in France, a wonderful lode of men endowed with all the weak points of the Regency and all the strong points of Rome and Sparta. These men, Faublas[1] and Regulus together, opened wide the doors of the Revolution and were the first to rush in, crowding each other in their haste to reach the 'window' of the guillotine. Our age no longer produces these single-minded, violent natures; the eighteenth century, on the contrary, called them forth everywhere, even where they were not needed, even where they could not develop except into something grotesque. In Russia men exposed to the influence of this mighty Western wind became eccentric, but not historical figures. Foreigners at home, foreigners abroad, idle spectators, spoilt for Russia by Western prejudices and for the West by Russian habits, they were a sort of intellectual superfluity and were lost in artificial life, in sensual pleasure and in unbearable egoism.

To this circle belonged the Tatar Prince, N. B. Yusupov, a Russian grandee and a European *grand seigneur*, a foremost figure in Moscow, conspicuous for his intelligence and his wealth. About him gathered a perfect galaxy of grey-headed gallants and *esprits forts*. They were all quite cultured, well-educated people; having no work in life they flung themselves

---

[1] The hero of *La Vie du Chevalier de Faublas* (1787), by Louvet de Couvray, is the type of the effeminate rake and fashionable exquisite of the period. (*Tr.*)

upon pleasure, pampered themselves, loved themselves, good-naturedly forgave themselves all transgressions, exalted their gastronomy to the level of a Platonic passion and reduced love for women to a sort of voracious gourmandise.

The old sceptic and epicurean Yusupov, a friend of Voltaire and Beaumarchais, of Diderot and Casti,[2] really was gifted with artistic taste. To convince oneself of this, it is enough to make one visit to Arkhangelskoye and look at his galleries, that is, if they have not yet been sold bit by bit by his heir. He was magnificently fading out of life at eighty, surrounded by marble, painted and *living* beauty. In his house near Moscow Pushkin conversed with him, and dedicated to him a wonderful epistle, and Gonzaga[3] painted, to whom Yusupov dedicated his theatre.

By his education, by his service in the Guards, by position and connections, my father belonged to this circle, but neither his character nor his health permitted him to lead a frivolous life to the age of seventy: and he went to the opposite extreme. He tried to organise for himself a life of solitude, and there he found waiting for him a deadly dullness, the more because he tried to arrange it entirely *for himself*. His strength of will changed into obstinate caprice, and his unemployed energies spoilt his character, and made it disagreeable.

When he was being educated, European civilisation was still so new in Russia that to be educated meant being so much the less Russian. To the end of his days he wrote more fluently and correctly in French than in Russian. He had literally not read one single book in Russian, not even the Bible, though, indeed, he had not read the Bible in other languages either; he knew the subject-matter of the Holy Scriptures generally from hearsay and from extracts, and had no curiosity to look further into it. He had, it is true, a respect for Derzhavin[4] and Krylov:[5]

---

[2] Casti (1721–1803), an Italian poet, 'attached by habit and taste to the polished and frivolous society of the *ancien régime*, his sympathies were nevertheless liberal,' satirised Catherine II, and when exiled on that account from Vienna, had the spirit to resign his Austrian pension. The *Talking Animals*, a satire on the predominance of the foreigner in political life, is his best work. The influence of his poems on Byron is apparent in *Don Juan*. (*Tr.*)

[3] Gonzaga was a Venetian painter who came to Petersburg in 1792 to paint scenery for the Court Theatre. He planned the celebrated park at Pavlovsk. (*Tr.*)

[4] Derzhavin, Gavril Romanovich (1743–1816), was poet-laureate to Catherine II, and wrote numerous patriotic and a few other odes. (*Tr.*)

[5] Krylov, Ivan Andreyevich (1768–1844), was a very popular writer of fables in verse. (*Tr.*)

Derzhavin because he had written an ode on the death of his uncle, Prince Meshchersky, and Krylov because he had been a second with him at N. N. Bakhmetev's duel. My father did once pick up Karamzin's *History of the Russian State,* having heard that the Emperor Alexander had read it, but he laid it aside, saying contemptuously: 'It is nothing but Izyaslaviches and Olgoviches: to whom can it be of interest?'

For people he had an open, undisguised contempt—for everyone. Never under any circumstances did he count upon anybody, and I do not remember that he ever applied to any one with any considerable request. He himself did nothing for any one. In his relations with outsiders he demanded one thing only, the observance of the proprieties; *les apparences, les convenances* made up the whole of his moral religion. He was ready to forgive much, or rather to overlook it, but breaches of good form and good manners put him beside himself, and in such cases he was without any tolerance, without the slightest indulgence or compassion. I was rebellious so long against this injustice that at last I understood it. He was convinced beforehand that every man is capable of any evil act; and that, if he does not commit it, it is either that he has no need to, or that the opportunity does not present itself; in the disregard of formalities he saw a personal affront, a disrespect to himself; or a 'plebeian education,' which in his opinion excluded a man from all human society.

'The soul of man,' he used to say, 'is darkness, and who knows what is in any man's soul? I have too much business of my own to be interested in other people's, much less to judge and criticise their intentions; but I cannot be in the same room with an ill-bred man: he offends me, *il me froisse;* of course he may be the best-hearted man in the world and for that he will have a place in paradise, but I don't want him. What is most important in life is *esprit de conduite,* it is more important than the most superior intellect or any kind of learning. To know how to be at ease everywhere, to put yourself forward nowhere; the utmost courtesy with all and no familiarity with any one.'

My father disliked every sort of *abandon,* every sort of frankness; all this he called familiarity, just as he called every feeling sentimentality. He persistently posed as a man superior to all such petty trifles; for the sake of what, with what object? What was the higher interest to which the heart was sacrificed?—I do not know. And for whom did this haughty old man, who despised men so genuinely and knew them so well, play his part of impartial judge?—for a woman whose will he had broken although she sometimes contradicted him; for an invalid who lay

always at the mercy of the surgeon's knife; for a boy whose high
spirits he had developed into disobedience; for a dozen lackeys
whom he did not reckon as human beings!

And how much energy, how much patience were spent on it,
how much perseverance; and with what marvellous sureness the
part was played through to the end in spite of age and illness.
Truly the soul of man is darkness.

Later on when I was arrested, and afterwards when I was sent
into exile, I saw that the old man's heart was more open to love
and even to tenderness than I had thought. I never thanked him
for it, not knowing how he would take my gratitude.

Of course he was not happy: always on his guard, always
dissatisfied, he saw with a pang the hostile feelings he roused in
all his household; he saw the smile vanish from the face and the
words checked at his entrance; he spoke of it with mockery, with
vexation, but made not a single concession and went his way
with extreme persistence. Mockery, irony and cold, caustic,
utter contempt—these were the tools he wielded like an artist,
employing them equally against us and against the servants.
In early youth one can bear many things better than jeers.
Until I went to prison I was actually estranged from my father
and joined with the maids and men-servants in waging a little
war against him.

Add to everything else the fact that he had persuaded himself
that he was dangerously ill, and was continually undergoing
treatment; besides our own household doctor he was visited by
two or three others and had three or four consultations a year at
least. Visitors, seeing his continually unfriendly face and hearing nothing but complaints of his health, which was far from
being so bad as he thought, became fewer. He was angry at this
but never reproached a single person nor invited one. A terrible
dullness reigned in the house, particularly on the endless winter
evenings—two lamps lit a whole suite of rooms; wearing high
cloth or lamb's-wool boots, a velvet cap and a long, white lamb-
skin coat, bowed, with his hands clasped behind his back, the old
man walked up and down, followed by two or three brown dogs,
and never uttering a word.

A cautiousness, directed towards objects of no value, grew
with his melancholy. He managed the estate badly for himself
and badly for his peasants. The head-man and his *missi dominici*
robbed their master and the peasants; yet everything that could
be seen was subjected to double supervision: candles were saved
and the thin *vin de Graves* was replaced by sour Crimean wine
at the very time when a whole forest was cut down in one

village, and in another he was sold his own oats. He had his privileged thieves; the peasant whom he made collector of *obrok* payments in Moscow and whom he sent every summer to inspect the head-man, the kitchen-garden, the forest, and the field work, in ten years bought a house in Moscow. From a child I hated this 'minister without portfolio'; on one occasion he beat an old peasant in the courtyard in my presence. I was so furious that I clutched him by the beard and almost fainted. From that time until he died in 1845 I could not look at him calmly. I several times asked my father where did Shkun get the money to buy a house.

'That's what sobriety does,' the old man answered; 'he never takes a drop of liquor.'

◈   ◈   ◈

To give a full idea of our manner of life I will describe a whole day from the morning; it was just the monotony that was one of the most deadly things: our life went like an English clock regulated to go slowly—quietly, evenly, loudly recording each second.

At nine o'clock in the morning the valet who sat in the room next to the bedroom informed Vera Artamonovna, my ex-nurse, that the master was getting up. She went to prepare the coffee which he always drank alone in his study. Everything in the house assumed a different look: the servants began sweeping the rooms, or at any rate made a show of doing something. The hall, empty until then, filled up, and even the big Newfoundland dog Macbeth sat before the stove and watched the fire without blinking.

Over his coffee the old man read the *Moscow News* and the *Journal de St Pétersbourg*. I may mention that orders had been given for the *Moscow News* to be warmed, so his hands might not be chilled by the dampness of the paper, and that he read the political news in the French text, finding the Russian obscure. At one time he used to take in a Hamburg newspaper but could not reconcile himself to the fact that Germans printed in the German letters, and each time pointed out to me the difference between the French print and the German, saying that these freakish Gothic letters with their little tails weakened the eyesight. Later on he subscribed to the *Journal de Francfort*, but in the end he confined himself to the newspapers of his own country.

When he had finished reading he would observe that Karl

Ivanovich Sonnenberg was already in the room. When Nick was fifteen Karl Ivanovich had tried setting up a shop but, having neither goods nor customers, after wasting on this profitable undertaking the money he had somehow scraped up, he retired from it with the honourable title of 'merchant of Reval.' He was by then well over forty, and at that agreeable age he led the life of a bird of the air or a boy of fourteen, that is, did not know where he would sleep next day nor on what he would dine. He took advantage of my father's being somewhat well-disposed towards him; we shall now see what this meant.

In 1830 my father bought near our house another—bigger, better, and with a garden. The house had belonged to Countess Rostopchin, wife of the celebrated Governor of Moscow. We moved into it; after that he bought a third house which was quite unnecessary, but was next to it. Both these houses stood empty; they were not let for fear of fire (the houses were insured) and disturbance from tenants. Moreover they were not kept in repair, so they were on the sure road to ruin. In one of them the homeless Karl Ivanovich was permitted to live on condition that he did not open the gates after ten o'clock (not a difficult condition, since the gates were never closed), and that he bought his own firewood and did not get it from our store supplies (he did indeed buy it—from our coachman), and that he served my father in the capacity of an agent for private errands, that is, he came in the morning to inquire whether there were any orders, appeared for dinner and came in the evening, if there was no one else there, to entertain him with stories and the news.

Simple as Karl Ivanovich's duties might appear to be, my father knew how to inject so much bitterness into them that my poor merchant of Reval, accustomed to all the calamities which can fall upon the head of a man with no money, with no brains, who is small in stature, pock-marked and a German, could not endure it perpetually. At intervals of two years or eighteen months, Karl Ivanovich, deeply offended, would declare that 'this is absolutely intolerable,' would pack up, buy or exchange various articles of questionable soundness and dubious quality, and set off for the Caucasus. Ill-luck usually pursued him with ferocity. On one occasion his wretched nag—he was driving his own horse to Tiflis and the Kale Redoubt—fell down not far from the land of the Don Cossacks; on another, half his load was stolen from him; on another his two-wheeled gig upset and his French perfumes were spilt over the broken wheel, unappreciated by any one, at the foot of Elbrus; then he would lose something, and when he had nothing left to lose he lost his passport. Ten months later, as a rule, Karl Ivanovich, a little older, a little more battered, a little poorer, with still fewer teeth and less hair, would quite meekly present himself before my father with a store of Persian flea and bed-bug powder, of faded silks and rusty Circassian daggers, and would settle once more in the empty house on the conditions of running errands and using his own firewood to heat his stove.

Observing Karl Ivanovich, my father would at once commence some slight military operations against him. Karl Ivanovich would inquire after his health, the old man would thank him with a bow and then after a moment's thought would inquire, for instance;

'Where do you buy your pomade?'

I must mention here that Karl Ivanovich, the ugliest of mortals, was a fearful dangler after women, considered himself a Lovelace, dressed with pretensions to smartness and wore a curled golden wig. All this, of course, had long ago been weighed and assessed by my father.

'At Bouïs's on the Kuznetsky Most,' Karl Ivanovich would answer abruptly, somewhat piqued, and he would cross one leg over the other like a man ready to stand up for himself.

'What's the scent called?'

'*Nachtviolen*,' answered Karl Ivanovich.

'He cheats you: *la violette* is a delicate scent, *c'est un parfum*; but that's something strong, repellent—they embalm bodies with something of that sort! My nerves have grown so weak it's made me feel positively sick; tell them to give me the eau-de-Cologne.'

Karl Ivanovich would himself dash for the flask.

'Oh no, you must call someone, or you will come still closer. I shall be ill; I shall faint.'

Karl Ivanovich, who was reckoning on the effect of his pomade in the maids' room, would be deeply chagrined.

After sprinkling the room with eau-de-Cologne my father would invent some errands: to buy some French snuff and English magnesia, and to look at a carriage advertised for sale in the papers (he never bought anything). Karl Ivanovich, pleasantly bowing himself out and sincerely glad to get away, would be gone till dinner.

After Karl Ivanovich the cook appeared; whatever he had bought or whatever he had written down, my father thought extremely expensive.

'Ough, ough, how expensive! Why, is it because no supplies have come in?'

'Just so, sir,' answered the cook, 'the roads are very bad.'

'Oh very well, till they are mended you and I will buy less.'

After this he would sit down to his writing-table and write reports and orders to the villages, cast up his accounts, between whiles scolding me, receiving the doctor and, chiefly, quarrelling with his valet. The latter was the greatest sufferer in the whole house. A little, sanguine man, hasty and hot-tempered, he seemed to have been expressly created to irritate my father and provoke his sermons. The scenes that were repeated between them every day might have filled a farce, but it was all perfectly serious. My father knew very well that the man was indispensable to him and often put up with his rude answers, but never ceased trying to train him, in spite of his unsuccessful efforts for thirty-five years. The valet on his side would not have put up with such a life if he had not had his own distractions: more often than not he was somewhat tipsy by dinner-time. My father noticed this, but confined himself to roundabout allusions, advising him, for instance, to munch a little black bread and salt that he might not smell of vodka. Nikita Andreyevich had a habit, when he had had too much to drink, of bowing and scraping in a peculiar way as he handed the dishes. As soon as my father noticed this, he would invent some errand for him— would send him, for instance, to ask the barber Anton if he had changed his address, adding to me in French,

'I know he has not moved, but the fellow is not sober, he will drop the soup-tureen and smash it, drench the cloth and give me a turn. Let him go out for an airing. *Le grand air* will help.'

To such stratagems the valet usually made some reply, but if he could find nothing to say he would go out, muttering between his teeth. Then his master would call him and in the same calm voice ask him what he had said.

'I didn't address a single word to you.'

'To whom were you speaking, then? Except you and me there is no one in this room or the next.'

'To myself.'

'That's very dangerous; that's the way madness begins.'

The valet would depart in a rage and go to his room next to my father's bedroom; there he used to read the *Moscow News* and plait hair for wigs for sale. Probably to relieve his anger he would take snuff furiously; whether his snuff was particularly strong or the nerves of his nose were weak I cannot say, but this was almost always followed by his sneezing violently five or six times.

The master would ring. The valet would fling down his handful of hair and go in.

'Was that you sneezing?'

'Yes, sir.'

'Bless you.' And he would give a sign with his hand for the valet to withdraw.

On the last day of carnival, all the servants, according to ancient custom, would come in the evening to ask their master's forgiveness: on these solemn occasions my father used to go into the great hall, accompanied by his valet. Then he would pretend not to recognise some of them.

'Who is that venerable old man standing there in the corner?' he would ask the valet.

'Danilo, the coachman,' the valet would answer abruptly, knowing that all this was only a dramatic performance.

'Good gracious! how he has changed. I really believe that it is entirely from drink that men get old so quickly; what does he do?'

'He hauls the firewood in for the stoves.'

The old man assumed an expression of insufferable pain.

'How is it that in thirty years you have not learned how to speak? . . . Hauls: what's that—hauling firewood?—firewood is carried, not hauled. Well, Danilo, thank God, the Lord has thought me worthy to see you once more. I forgive you all your sins for this year, the oats which you waste so immoderately, and for not cleaning the horses, and do you forgive me. Go on hauling firewood while you have the strength, but now Lent is coming, so take less drink; it is bad for us at our age, and besides it is a sin.'

In this style he conducted the whole inspection.

We used to dine between three and four o'clock. The dinner lasted a long time and was very boring. Spiridon was an excellent cook, but my father's economy on the one hand, and his own on the other, rendered the dinner somewhat meagre, in spite of the fact that there were a great many dishes. Beside my father stood a red clay bowl into which he himself put various bits of food for the dogs; moreover, he used to feed them from his own fork, which gave fearful offence to the servants and consequently to me. Why? It is hard to say. . . .

Visitors on the whole seldom called upon us and dined more rarely still. I remember out of all those who visited us one man whose arrival to dinner would sometimes smooth the wrinkles out of my father's face, N. N. Bakhmetev. He was the brother of the lame general of that name and was himself a general also, though long on the retired list. My father and he had been friends as long before as the time when both had been officers in

the Izmaylovsky regiment. They had indulged themselves together in the days of Catherine, and in the reign of Paul had
both been court-martialled, Bakhmetev for having fought a duel
with someone and my father for having been his second; then
one of them had gone away to foreign lands as a tourist, and the
other to Ufa as Governor. There was no likeness between them.
Bakhmetev, a stout, healthy and handsome old man, liked a meal
and getting a little drunk after it; was fond of lively conversation and many other things. He used to boast that he had eaten
as many as a hundred sour-dough pies at a time; and when he
was about sixty he could, with complete impunity, make away
with up to a dozen buckwheat pancakes drowned in a pool of
butter. These experiments I have witnessed more than once.

Bakhmetev had some shade of influence over my father, or at
any rate did keep him in check. When Bakhmetev noticed that
my father's ill-humour was beyond bounds, he would put on his
hat and say with a military scrape:

'Good-bye—you are ill and stupid to-day; I meant to stay to
dinner, but I cannot endure sour faces at table! *Gehorsamer
Diener!*'

And my father by way of explanation would say to me: 'The
impresario! What a lively fellow N. N. still is! Thank God, he's
a healthy man and cannot understand a suffering Job like me;
there are twenty degrees of frost, but he dashes here all the way
from Pokrovka in his sledge as though it were nothing . . .
while I thank the Creator every morning that I have woken up
alive, that I am still breathing. Oh . . . oh . . . ough . . . ! it's
a true proverb; the well-fed don't understand the hungry!'

This was the utmost indulgence that could be expected from
him.

From time to time there were family dinners at which the
Senator, the Golokhvastovs and others were present, and these
dinners were not given casually, nor for the sake of any pleasure
to be derived from them, but were due to profound considerations of economy and policy. Thus on the 20th February, the
Senator's name-day, there was a dinner at our house, and on the
24th June, my father's name-day, the dinner was at the Senator's, an arrangement which, besides setting a moral example of
brotherly love, saved each of them from giving a much bigger
dinner at home.

Then there were various *habitués;* Sonnenberg would appear
ex officio, and having just before dinner swallowed a glass of
vodka and had a bite of Reval anchovy at home he would refuse
a minute glass of some specially infused vodka; sometimes my

last French tutor would come, a miserly old fellow with saucy phiz, fond of talking scandal. Monsieur Thirié so often made mistakes, pouring wine into his tumbler instead of beer and drinking it off apologetically, that at last my father would say to him,

'The *vin de Graves* stands on your right side, so you won't make a mistake again,' and Thirié, stuffing a huge pinch of snuff into his broad nose that turned up on one side, would spill snuff on his plate.

❖   ❖   ❖

But the real *souffre-douleurs* at dinner were various old women, the needy, nomadic hangers-on of Princess M. A. Khovansky, my father's sister. For the sake of a change, and also partly to find out how everything was going on in our house, whether there had been any quarrels in the family, whether the cook had not had a fight with his wife, and whether the master had not found out that Palashka or Ulyasha was with child, they would sometimes come on holidays to spend a whole day. It must be noted that these widows had forty or fifty years before, when they were still unmarried, been dependents in the household of my father's aunt, old Princess Meshchersky, and afterwards in that of her daughter, and had known my father since those days; that in this interval between their unsettled youth and the nomadic life of their old age they had spent some twenty years quarrelling with their husbands, restraining them from drunkenness, looking after them when they were paralysed, and taking them to the churchyard. Some had been trailing from one place to another in Bessarabia with a garrison officer and an armful of children; others had spent years with a criminal charge hanging over their husbands; and all these experiences of life had left upon them the marks of government offices and provincial towns, a dread of the powers of this world, a spirit of abasement and a sort of dull-witted bigotry.

Amazing scenes took place with them.

'Why is this, Anna Yakimovna; are you ill that you don't eat anything?' my father would ask.

Shrinking together, the widow of some inspector in Kremenchug, a wretched old woman with a worn, faded face, who always smelt strongly of sticking plaster, would answer with cringing eyes and deprecating fingers:

'Forgive me, Ivan Alexeyevich, sir, I am really ashamed, but there, it is my old-fashioned ways, sir. Ha, ha, ha, it's the fast before the Assumption now.'

'Oh, how tiresome! You are always so pious! It's not what goes into the mouth, dear lady, that defiles, but what comes out of it; whether you eat one thing or another, it all goes the same way; now what comes out of the mouth, you must watch over . . . your judgments of your neighbours. Come, you had better dine at home on such days, or we shall have a Turk coming next asking for pilau; I don't keep a restaurant *à la carte.'*

The frightened old woman, who had intended as well to ask for some dish made of flour or cereals, would fall upon the *kvas* and salad, making a show of eating a terrific meal.

But it is noteworthy that she, or any of the others, had only to begin eating meat during a fast for my father, though he never touched Lenten food himself, to say, shaking his head sadly:

'I should not have thought it was worth-while for you, Anna Yakimovna, to forsake the customs of your forefathers for the last few years of your life. I sin and eat meat, as comports with my many infirmities; but you, as you're allowed, thank God, have kept the fasts all your life and suddenly . . . what an example for *them.'*

He motioned towards the servants. And the poor old woman had to betake herself to *kvas* and salad again.

These scenes made me very indignant; sometimes I was so bold as to intervene and remind him of the contrary opinion he had expressed. Then my father would rise from his seat, take off his velvet cap by the tassel and, holding it in the air, thank me for the lesson and beg pardon for his forgetfulness; then he would say to the old lady:

'It's a terrible age! It's no wonder you eat meat during a fast, when children teach their parents! What are we coming to? It's dreadful to think of it! Luckily you and I won't see it.'

After dinner my father lay down to rest for an hour and a half. The servants at once dispersed to beer-shops and eating-houses. At seven o'clock tea was served; then sometimes someone would arrive, the Senator more often than any one; it was a time of leisure for all of us. The Senator usually brought various items of news and told them eagerly. My father affected complete inattention as he listened to him: he assumed a serious face, when his brother had expected him to be dying of laughter, and would cross-question him, as though he had not heard the point, when the Senator had been telling some astonishing story.

The Senator came in for it in a very different way when he

contradicted or differed from his younger brother (which rarely happened, however), and sometimes, indeed, when he did not contradict at all, if my father was particularly ill-humoured. In these tragi-comic scenes, what was funniest was the Senator's natural vehemence and my father's factitious *sang froid*.

'Well, you are ill to-day,' the Senator would say impatiently, and he would seize his hat and rush off.

Once in his vexation he could not open the door and pushed at it with all his might, saying, 'What a confounded door!' My father went up, coolly opened the door inwards, and in a perfectly composed voice observed:

'This door does its duty: it opens this way, and you try to open it that way, and lose your temper.'

It may not be out of place to mention that the Senator was two years older than my father and addressed him in the second person singular, while the latter as the younger brother used the plural form, 'you.'

When the Senator had gone, my father would retire to his bedroom, would each time inquire whether the gates were closed, would receive an answer in the affirmative, would express doubts on the subject but do nothing to make sure. Then began a lengthy routine of washings, fomentations, and medicines; his valet made ready on a little table by the bed a perfect arsenal of different objects—phials, nightlights, pill-boxes. The old man as a rule read for an hour Bourrienne's *Mémorial de Saint Hélène*[6] and other memoirs; then came the night.

Such was our household when I left it in 1834: so I found it in 1840, and so it continued until his death in 1846.

At thirty, when I returned from exile, I realised that my father had been right in many things, that he had unhappily an offensively good understanding of men. But was it my fault that he preached the truth itself in a way so provoking to a youthful heart? His mind, chilled by a long life in a circle of depraved men, put him on his guard against everyone, and his callous heart did not crave for reconciliation; so he remained on hostile terms with everyone on earth.

I found him in 1839, and still more so in 1842, weak and really ill. The Senator was dead, the desolation about him was greater than ever and he even had a different valet; but he himself was

---

[6] This book is not by Bourrienne but by E. de Las Cases (Paris, 1823–4). (*A.S.*)

just the same: only his physical powers were changed; there was the same spiteful intelligence, the same tenacious memory, he still persecuted everyone over trifles, and Sonnenberg, still unchanged, had his nomad's camp in the old house as before, and ran errands.

Only then did I appreciate all the cheerlessness of his life; I looked with an aching heart at the melancholy significance of this lonely, abandoned existence, dying out in the arid, harsh, stony wilderness which he had created about himself, but which he had not the will to change; he knew this; he saw death approaching and, overcoming weakness and infirmity, he jealously and obstinately controlled himself. I was dreadfully sorry for the old man, but there was nothing to be done: he was unapproachable.

Sometimes I passed softly by his study where, sitting in a hard, uncomfortable, deep armchair, surrounded by his dogs, he was playing all alone with my three-year-old son. It seemed as though the clenched hands and numbed nerves of the old man relaxed at the sight of the child, and he found rest from the incessant agitation, conflict, and vexation in which he had kept himself, as his dying hand touched the cradle.

The University

Oh, years of boundless ecstasies,
Of visions bright and free!
Where now your mirth untouched by spite,
Your hopeful toil and noisy glee?

N. P. Ogarëv, *Humorous Verse*

In spite of the lame general's sinister predictions my father nevertheless put my name down with Prince N. B. Yusupov for employment in the Kremlin Department. I signed a paper and there the matter ended; I heard nothing more of the service, except that about three years later Yusupov sent the Palace architect, who always shouted as though he were standing on the scaffolding of the fifth storey and there giving orders to workmen in the basement, to announce that I had received the first officer's grade. All these miracles, I may remark in passing, were unnecessary, for I rose at one jump, with the grades I received in the service, by passing the examination for my degree—it was not worth-while giving oneself much trouble for the sake of two or three years' seniority. And meanwhile this supposed post in the service almost prevented me from entering the university. The Council, seeing that I was reckoned as in the office of the Kremlin Department, refused me the right to take the examination.

For those in the government service there were special after-dinner courses of study, extremely limited in scope and qualifying one for entrance into the so-called 'committee examinations.' All the wealthy idlers, the young noblemen's sons who had learnt nothing, all those who did not want to serve in the army and were in a hurry to get the rank of assessor took the 'committee examinations'; they were by way of being gold mines presented to the old professors, who coached them *privatissime* for twenty roubles a lesson.

To begin my life with such a disaster of the Caudine Forks of learning was far from suiting my ideas. I told my father resolutely that if he could not find some other means I should resign from the service.

My father was angry, said that with my caprices I was preventing him from organising a career for me, and abused the teachers who had stuffed me with this nonsense; but, seeing that all this had very little effect upon me, he made up his mind to go to Yusupov.

Yusupov settled the matter in a trice, partly like a lord and partly like a Tatar. He called his secretary and told him to write me a leave of absence for three years. The secretary hesitated and hesitated, and at last, with some apprehension, submitted that leave of absence for longer than four months could not be given without the sanction of His Majesty.

'What nonsense, my man,' the prince said to him. 'Where is the difficulty? Well, if leave of absence is impossible, write that I commission him to attend the university course, to perfect himself in the sciences.'

His secretary wrote this and next day I was sitting in the amphitheatre of the Physico-Mathematical auditorium.

The University of Moscow and the Lycée of Tsarkoye Selo play a significant part in the history of Russian education and in the life of the last two generations.

Moscow University grew in importance together with the city itself after 1812. Degraded by the Emperor Peter from being the capital of the Tsars, Moscow was promoted by the Emperor Napoleon (partly intentionally, but twice as much unintentionally) to being the capital of the Russian people. The people realised their ties of blood with Moscow from the pain they felt at the news of its occupation by the enemy. From that time a new epoch began for the city. Its university became more and more the centre of Russian culture. All the conditions necessary for its development were combined—historical importance, geographical position, and the absence of the Tsar.

The intensified mental activity of Petersburg after the death of Paul came to a gloomy close on the Fourteenth of December (1825). Nicholas appeared with his five gibbets, with penal servitude, with the white strap and the light blue uniform of Benckendorf.[1]

Everything ran backwards: the blood rushed to the heart, the activity that was outwardly concealed boiled inwardly in secret. Moscow University remained firm and was the foremost to stand out in sharp relief from the general fog. The Tsar began to hate it from the time of the Polezhayev affair.[2] He sent A. Pisarev, the major-general of the *Evenings at Kaluga*,[3] as Director, commanded the students to be dressed in uniform, ordered them to wear a sword, then forbade them to wear a sword, condemned Polezhayev to be a common soldier for his verses and Kostenetsky and his comrades for their prose, destroyed the Kritskys[4] for a bust, sentenced us to exile for Saint-Simonism, then made Prince Sergey Mikhaylovich Golitsyn Director, and took no further notice of that 'hot-bed of depravity,' piously advising young men who had finished their studies at the lyceum or at the School of Jurisprudence not to enter it.

Golitsyn was an astonishing person: it was long before he could accustom himself to the irregularity of there being no lecture when a professor was ill; he thought the next on the list ought to take his place, so that Father Ternovsky sometimes had to lecture in the clinic on women's diseases and Richter, the gynæcologist, to discourse on the Immaculate Conception.

---

[1] The uniform of the gendarmes of the Third Division, the political police, of which Benckendorf was head, was light blue with a white strap. (*Tr.*)

[2] See pp. 117–19 for a full account of this. (*D.M.*)

[3] A collection of the works of various authors published in two parts by A. A. Pisarev in 1825.

[4] It was a young man called Zubov who was put in a madhouse for hacking a bust of the Tsar. The Kritsky brothers were punished for addressing insulting words to his portraits. (*A.S.*)

But in spite of that the university that had fallen into disgrace grew in influence; the youthful strength of Russia streamed to it from all sides, from all classes of society, as into a common reservoir; in its halls they were purified from the prejudices they had picked up at the domestic hearth, reached a common level, became like brothers and dispersed again to all parts of Russia and among all classes of its people.

Until 1848 the organisation of our universities was purely democratic. Their doors were open to everyone who could pass the examination, who was neither a serf, a peasant, nor a man excluded from his commune. Nicholas spoilt all this; he restricted the admission of students, increased the fees of those who paid their own expenses, and permitted none to be relieved of payment but poor *noblemen*. All these belonged to the series of senseless measures which will disappear with the last breath of that drag on the Russian wheel, together with the law about passports, about religious intolerance and so on.

Young men of all sorts and conditions coming from above and from below, from the south and from the north, were quickly fused into a compact mass of comrades. Social distinctions had not among us the offensive influence which we find in English schools and barracks; I am not speaking of the English universities: they exist exclusively for the aristocracy and for the rich. A student who thought fit to boast among us of his blue blood or his wealth would have been excluded from 'fire and water' and made the butt of his comrades.

The external distinctions—and they did not go very deep—that divided the students arose from other causes. Thus, for instance, the medical section which was on the other side of the garden was not so closely united with us as the other faculties; moreover, the majority of the medical students consisted of seminarists and Germans. The Germans kept a little apart and were deeply imbued with the Western bourgeois spirit. All the education of the luckless seminarists, all their ideas, were utterly different from ours; we spoke different languages. Brought up under the oppression of monastic despotism, stuffed with rhetoric and theology, they envied us our ease of manner; we were vexed by their Christian meekness.[5]

I entered the Faculty of Physics and Mathematics in spite of

---

[5] Immense progress has been made in this respect. All that I have heard of late of the theological academies, and even of the seminaries, confirms it. I need hardly say that it is not the ecclesiastical authorities but the spirit of the pupils that is responsible for this improvement.

the fact that I had never had a marked ability nor much liking for mathematics. Nick and I had been taught mathematics together by a teacher whom we loved for his anecdotes and stories; interesting as he was, he can hardly have developed any particular passion for his subject. His knowledge of mathematics extended only to conic sections, that is, exactly as far as was necessary for preparing high-school boys for the university; a real philosopher, he never had the curiosity to glance at the 'university' branches of mathematics. What was particularly remarkable, too, was that he never read more than one book, and that book, Francoeur's *Course*, he read constantly for ten years; but, being abstemious by temperament and having no love for luxury, he never went beyond a certain page.

I chose the Faculty of Physics and Mathematics because the natural sciences were taught in that Faculty, and just at that time I developed a great passion for natural science.

A rather strange meeting had led me to these studies.

After the famous division of the family property in 1822, which I have described, my father's older brother, Alexander, went to live in Petersburg. For a long time nothing was heard of him; then suddenly a rumour spread that he was getting married. He was at that time over sixty, and everyone knew that besides a grown-up son he had other children. He did in fact marry the mother of his eldest son; the 'young woman,' was over fifty. With this marriage he legitimised, as they said in the old days, his son. Why not all the children? It would be hard to say why, if we had not known his main purpose in doing what he did; his one desire was to deprive his brothers of the inheritance, and this he completely attained by legitimising the son. In the famous inundation of Petersburg in 1824 the old man was drenched with water in his carriage. He caught cold, took to his bed, and at the beginning of 1825 he died.

Of the son there were strange rumours. It was said that he was unsociable, refused to make acquaintances, sat alone for ever absorbed in chemistry, spent his life at his microscope, read even at dinner and hated feminine society. Of him it had been said in *Woe from Wit*,[6]

---

[6] Griboyedov's famous comedy, which appeared and had a large circulation in manuscript copies in 1824, its performance and publication being prevented by the censorship. When performed later it was in a very mutilated form. It was a lively satire on Moscow society and full of references to well-known persons, such as Izmaylov and Tolstoy 'the

He is a chemist, he is a botanist,
Our nephew, Prince Fëdor,
He flies from women and even from me.

His uncles, who transferred to him the rancour they had felt for his father, never spoke of him except as 'the Chemist,' using this word as a term of disparagement, and assuming that chemistry was a subject that could by no means be studied by a gentleman.

Before his death the father used to persecute his son dreadfully, not merely affronting him with the spectacle of his greyheaded father's cynical debauchery, but actually being jealous of him as a possible rival in his seraglio. The Chemist on one occasion tried to escape from this ignoble existence by means of laudanum. He happened to be rescued by a comrade, with whom he used to work at chemistry. His father was thoroughly frightened, and before his death had begun to treat his son better.

After his father's death the Chemist released the luckless odalisques, halved the heavy *obrok* laid by his father on the peasants, forgave all arrears and presented them gratis with the army receipts for the full quota of recruits, which the old man had used to sell when he sent his house-serfs for soldiers.

A year and a half later he came to Moscow. I wanted to see him, for I liked him for the way he treated his peasants and because of the undeserved ill-will his uncles bore him.

One morning a small man in gold spectacles, with a big nose, who had lost half his hair, and whose fingers were burnt by chemical reagents, called upon my father. My father met him coldly, sarcastically; his nephew responded in the same coin and gave him quite as good as he got: after taking each other's measure they began speaking of extraneous matters with external indifference, and parted politely but with concealed dislike. My father saw that here was a fighter who would not give in to him.

They did not become more intimate later. The Chemist very rarely visited his uncles; the last time he saw my father was after the Senator's death, when he came to ask him for a loan of thirty thousand roubles for the purchase of some land. My father would not lend it. The Chemist was moved to anger and, rub-

---

American.' Griboyedov was imprisoned in 1825 in connection with the Fourteenth of December. (*Tr.*)

   This passage, not entirely accurately quoted, is from Act III, scene 2. (*A.S.*)

bing his nose, observed with a smile, 'There is no risk whatever in it; my estate is entailed; I am borrowing money for its improvement. I have no children and we are each other's heirs.' The old man of seventy-five never forgave his nephew for this sally.

I took to visiting the Chemist from time to time. He lived in a way that was very much his own. In his big house on the Tverskoy Boulevard he used one tiny room for himself and one as a laboratory. His old mother occupied another little room on the other side of the corridor; the rest of the house was neglected and remained exactly as it had been when his father left it to go to Petersburg. The blackened candelabra, the unusual furniture, all sorts of rarities, a clock said to have been bought by Peter I in Amsterdam, an arm-chair said to have come from the house of Stanislas Leszczynski,[7] frames without pictures in them, pictures turned to the wall, were all left anyhow, filling up three big, unheated and unlighted rooms. Servants were usually playing the *torban* and smoking in the hall, where in old days they had scarcely dared to breathe or say their prayers. A man-servant would light a candle and escort one through this arsenal, observing every time that I had better not take my cloak off for it was very cold in the big rooms. Thick layers of dust covered the horned trophies and various curios, the reflections of which moved together with the candle in the elaborate mirrors; straw left from packing lay undisturbed here and there together with scraps of paper and bits of string.

Through a row of these rooms one reached at last a door hung with a rug, which led to the terribly overheated study. In this the Chemist, in a soiled dressing-gown lined with squirrel fur, was invariably sitting, surrounded by piles of books, and rows of phials, retorts, crucibles, and other apparatus. In that study where Chevalier's microscope now reigned supreme and there was always a smell of chlorine, and where a few years before terrible piteous deeds had been perpetrated—in that study I was born. My father, on his return from foreign parts, before his quarrel with his brother, stayed for some months in his house, and in the same house my wife was born in 1817. The Chemist sold the house two years later, and it chanced that I was in the house again at evening parties of Sverbeyev's,[8] arguing there

---

[7] Stanislas Leszczynski, King of Poland from 1702 to 1709. His daughter Maria was married to Louis XV of France. (*Tr.*)

[8] Sverbeyev, Dmitry Nikolayevich (1799–1876). Representatives of the 'Slavophils' and 'Westerners' used to meet in his house in Moscow. (*A.S.*)

about Pan-Slavism and getting angry with Khomyakov, who never lost his temper about anything. The rooms had been altered, but the front entrance, the vestibule, the stairs, the hall were all left as before, and so was the little study.

The Chemist's housekeeping was even less complicated, especially when his mother had gone away for the summer to their estate near Moscow and with her the cook. His valet used to appear at four o'clock with a coffee-pot, pour into it a little strong broth and, taking advantage of the chemical furnace, would set it there to warm, along with various poisons. Then he would bring bread and half a hazel-hen from an eating-house, and that made up the whole dinner. When it was over the valet would wash the coffee-pot and it would return to its natural duties. In the evening the valet would appear again, take from the sofa a heap of books, and a tiger-skin that had come down to the Chemist from his father, spread a sheet and bring pillows and a blanket, and the study was as easily transformed into a bedroom as it had been into a kitchen and a dining-room.

From the very beginning of our acquaintance the Chemist saw that I was interested in earnest, and began to try to persuade me to give up the 'empty' study of literature and the 'dangerous and quite useless pursuit of politics,' and take to natural science. He gave me Cuvier's speech on geological revolutions and Candolle's *Plant Morphology*. Seeing that these were not thrown away upon me he offered me the use of his excellent collections, apparatus, herbariums, and even his guidance. He was very interesting on his own ground, extremely learned, witty and even amiable; but for this one had to go no further than the apes; from the rocks to the orang-utan everything interested him, but he did not care to be drawn beyond them, particularly into philosophy, which he regarded as twaddle. He was neither a conservative nor a reactionary: he simply did not believe in people, that is, he believed that egoism is the sole source of all actions, and thought that it was restrained merely by the senselessness of some and the ignorance of others.

I was revolted by his materialism. The superficial Voltairianism of our fathers, which they were half afraid of, was not in the least like the Chemist's materialism. His outlook was calm, consistent, complete. He reminded me of the celebrated answer made by Lalande[9] to Napoleon. 'Kant accepts the hypothesis of

---

[9] Lalande, Joseph-Jérôme de (1732–1807), a French astronomer. (*Tr.*) This remark is usually attributed to Pierre Simon, Marquis de Laplace (1749–1827). (*R.*)

God,' Bonaparte said to him. 'Sire,' replied the astronomer, 'in my studies I have never had occasion to make use of that hypothesis.'

The Chemist's atheism went far beyond the sphere of theology. He considered Geoffroy Saint-Hilaire[10] a mystic and Oken[11] simply deranged. He closed the works of the natural philosophers with the same contempt with which my father had put aside Karamzin's *History*. 'They themselves invented first causes and spiritual forces, and then are surprised that they can neither find them nor understand them,' he said. This was a second edition of my father, in a different age and differently educated.

His views became still more comfortless on all the problems of life. He thought that there was as little responsibility for good and evil in man as in the beasts; that it was all a matter of organisation, circumstances, and condition of the nervous system in general, of which he said *more was expected than it was capable of giving*. He did not like family life, spoke with horror of marriage, and naïvely acknowledged that in the thirty years of his life he had never loved one woman. However, there remained one current of warmth in this frigid man and it could be seen in his attitude to his old mother; they had suffered a great deal together at the hands of his father, and their troubles had welded them firmly together; he touchingly surrounded her solitary and infirm old age, so far as he could, with tranquillity and attention.

He never advocated his theories, except those that concerned chemistry; they came out casually, evoked by me. He even showed reluctance in answering my romantic and philosophic objections; his answers were brief, and he made them with a smile and with the considerateness with which a big, old mastiff plays with a puppy, allowing him to tousle him and only gently pushing him away with his paw. But it was just that which provoked me most, and I would return to the charge without weariness—never gaining an inch of ground, however. Later on, twelve years afterwards, that is, I frequently recalled the Chemist's, just as I recalled my father's, observations. Of course, he had been right in three-quarters of everything that I had objected to;

---

[10] Geoffroy Saint-Hilaire (1772–1844), French naturalist and author of many books on zoology and biology, in which, in opposition to Cuvier, he advanced the theory of the variation of species under the influence of environment. (*Tr.*)

[11] Oken, Lorenz (1779–1851), a German naturalist, who aimed at deducing a system of natural philosophy from *a priori* propositions, and incidentally threw off some valuable and suggestive ideas. (*Tr.*)

but I had been right too, you know. There are truths (we have spoken of this already) which like political rights are not given to those under a certain age.

The Chemist's influence made me choose the Faculty of Physics and Mathematics; perhaps I should have done still better to enter the Medical Faculty, but there was no great harm in my first acquiring some degree of knowledge of the differential and integral calculus, and then completely forgetting it.

Without the natural sciences there is no salvation for modern man. Without that wholesome food, without that strict training of the mind by facts, without that closeness to the life surrounding us, without humility before its independence, the monastic cell remains hidden somewhere in the soul, and in it the drop of mysticism which might have flooded the whole understanding with its dark waters.

Before I completed my studies the Chemist had gone away to Petersburg, and I did not see him again until I came back from Vyatka. Some months after my marriage I went half secretly for a few days to the estate near Moscow where my father was then living. The object of this journey was to effect a final reconciliation with him, for he was still angry with me for my marriage.

On the way I halted at Perkhushkovo where we had so many times broken our journey in old days. The Chemist was expecting me there and had actually got a dinner and two bottles of champagne ready for me. In those four or five years he had not changed at all except for being a little older. Before dinner he asked me quite seriously:

'Tell me, please, frankly, how do you find married life: is it a good thing? or not very?'

I laughed.

'How venturesome of you,' he went on. 'I wonder at you; in a normal condition a man can never determine on such a terrible step. Two or three very good matches have been proposed to me, but when I imagine a woman taking up her abode in my room, setting everything in order according to her ideas, perhaps forbidding me to smoke my tobacco (he used to smoke rootlets from Nezhin),[12] making a fuss and an upset, I am so frightened that I prefer to die in solitude.'

'Shall I stay the night with you or go on to Pokrovskoye?' I asked him after dinner.

'I have no lack of room here,' he answered, 'but for you I think

---

[12] *Makhorka*, a strong, cheap tobacco produced, among other places, at Nezhin in the Ukraine. (*R.*)

it would be better to go on; you will reach your father at ten o'clock. You know, of course, that he is still angry with you; well—in the evening before going to bed old people's nerves are usually relaxed and drowsy—he will probably receive you much better to-day than he would to-morrow; in the morning you would find him quite ready for battle.'

'Ha, ha, ha! I recognise my teacher in physiology and materialism,' said I, laughing heartily. 'How your remark recalls those blissful days when I used to go to you like Goethe's Wagner to weary you with my idealism and listen with some indignation to your chilling opinions.'

'Since then,' he answered, laughing too, 'you have lived enough to know that all human affairs depend simply on the nerves and the chemical composition.'

Later on we had a difference: probably we were both wrong. . . . Nevertheless in 1846 he wrote me a letter. I was then beginning to be the fashion after the publication of the first part of *Who Is At Fault?* The Chemist wrote to me that he saw with grief that I was wasting my talent on idle pursuits.

'I became reconciled to you for the sake of your *Letters on the Study of Nature*. In them I understood German philosophy (so far as it is possible for the mind of man to do so)—why then instead of going on with serious work are you writing fairy-tales?' I sent him a few friendly lines in reply, and with that our intercourse ended.

If the Chemist's own eyes ever rest upon these lines, I would beg him to read them just after going to bed at night when his nerves are relaxed, and then I am sure he will forgive me this affectionate gossip, the more so since I retain a very genuine, kind memory of him.

And so at last the seclusion of the parental home was over. I was *au large*. Instead of solitude in our little room, instead of quiet, half-concealed meetings with Ogarëv alone, I was surrounded by a noisy family, seven hundred in number. I was more at home in it in a fortnight than I had been in my father's house from the day of my birth.

But the paternal home pursued me even at the university, in the shape of a footman whom my father ordered to accompany me, particularly when I went on foot. For a whole year I tried to get rid of my escort and only with difficulty succeeded in doing so officially. I say 'officially,' because my valet Pëtr Fëdorovich, upon whom the duty was laid, very quickly grasped, first, that I disliked being accompanied, and, secondly, that it was a great deal more pleasant for him in various places of entertainment than in the hall of the Faculty of Physics and Mathematics, where the only pleasures open to him were conversation with the two porters and the three of them treating each other and themselves to snuff.

What was the object of sending an escort to walk after me? Could Pëtr, who from his youth had been given to getting drunk for several days at a time, have prevented me from doing anything? I imagine that my father did not even suppose so, but his own peace of mind took steps, which were ineffective but were still steps, like people who do not believe but take the sacrament. It was part of the old-fashioned education of landowners. Up to seven years old, orders had been given that I should be led by the hand on the staircase, which was rather steep; up to eleven I was washed in my bath by Vera Artamonovna; therefore, very consistently, a servant was sent to walk behind me when I was a student; and until I was twenty-one, I was not allowed to be out after half-past ten. In practice I found myself at liberty, standing on my own feet, when I was in exile; had I not been exiled, probably the same régime would have continued up to twenty-five or even thirty-five.

Like the majority of lively boys brought up in solitude, I flung myself on everyone's neck with such sincerity and impulsiveness, built myself up with such senseless imprudence, and was so candidly fond of everyone, that I could not fail to call forth a warm response from my hearers, who consisted of lads of about my own age. (I was then in my seventeenth year.)

The sage rules—to be courteous to all, intimate with no one and to trust no one—did as much to promote this readiness to make friends as the ever-present thought with which we entered the university, the thought that here our dreams would be accomplished, that here we should sow the seeds and lay the foundation of a league. We were persuaded that out of this lecture-room would come the company which would follow in the footsteps of Pestel and Ryleyev, and that we should be in it.

They were a splendid set of young men in our year. It was just at that time that theoretical tendencies were becoming more and more marked among us. The scholastic method of learning and aristocratic indolence were alike disappearing, and had not yet been replaced by that German utilitarianism which enriches men's minds with science, as the fields with manure, for the sake of an increased crop. A tolerably large group of students no longer regarded science as a necessary but wearisome short-cut by which they would come to be collegiate assessors. The problems that were arising amongst us had no reference whatever to the Table of Ranks.

On the other hand the interest in science had not yet had time to degenerate into doctrinairianism; science did not draw us away from the life and suffering around us. Our sympathy with it raised the *social* morality of the students to an unusual extent. We said openly in the lecture-room everything that came into our heads; manuscript copies of *prohibited* poems passed from hand to hand, prohibited books were read with commentaries, but for all that I do not remember a single case of tale-bearing from the lecture-room or of betrayal. There were timid young men who turned away and held aloof, but they too were silent.[13]

One silly boy, questioned by his mother on the Malov affair,[14] under threat of the birch, did tell her something. The fond mother—an aristocrat and a princess—flew to the rector and passed on her son's information as proof of his penitence. We heard of this and tormented him so that he did not stay till the end of the course.

This affair, for which I too was imprisoned, deserves to be described.

Malov was a stupid, coarse, and uncultured professor in the Political Faculty. The students despised him and laughed at him.

'How many professors have you in your faculty?' the Director one day asked a student in the Politics lecture-room.

'Nine, not counting Malov,' answered the student.[15]

Well, this professor, who had to be left out of the reckoning in order that nine should remain, began to be more and more insolent in his treatment of the students; the latter made up their minds to drive him out of the lecture-room. After deliberating together they sent two delegates to our faculty to invite me to come with an auxiliary force. I at once proclaimed a declaration of war on Malov, and several students went with me; when we went into the Politics lecture-room Malov was present and saw us.

On the faces of all the students was written the same fear: that on that day he might say nothing rude to them. This fear soon

---

[13] At that time there were none of the inspectors and sub-inspectors who played the part of my Pëtr Fëdorovich in the lecture-rooms.

[14] The Malov affair happened on 16th March, 1831. (*A.S.*)

[15] A pun on the name—the phrase meaning also 'Nine all but a little.' (*Tr.*)

passed. The overflowing lecture-room was restless and a vague subdued hum rose from it. Malov made some observation; there began a scraping of feet.

'You express your thoughts like horses, with your feet,' observed Malov, probably imagining that horses think at a gallop or a trot; and a storm arose, whistling, hisses, shouts; 'Out with him, *pereat!*' Malov, white as a sheet, made a desperate effort to control the uproar but could not; the students jumped on to the benches. Malov quietly left the dais and, cowering down, tried to slip through to the door; his audience followed, saw him through the university court into the street and flung his galoshes after him. The last circumstance was important, for in the street the case at once assumed a very different character; but where in the world are there lads of seventeen or eighteen who would consider that?

The University Council was alarmed and persuaded the Director to present the affair as disposed of, and for that purpose to put the culprits, or somebody anyhow, in prison. This was prudent; it might otherwise easily have happened that the Tsar would have sent an aide-de-camp who, with a view to gaining a cross, would have turned the affair into a conspiracy, a rising, a rebellion, and would have proposed sending everyone to penal servitude, which the Tsar would graciously have commuted to service as common soldiers. Seeing that vice was punished and virtue triumphant, the Tsar confined himself to giving His Majesty's sanction to the confirmation of the wishes of the students, and dismissed the professor. We had driven Malov out as far as the university gates and he turned him out of them. It was *vae victis* with Nicholas, but this time we had no cause to reproach him.

And so the affair went merrily on; after dinner next day the watchman from the head office shuffled up to me, a grey-headed old man, who conscientiously assumed that the students' tips (given *na vodku*) were for vodka and therefore kept himself continually in a condition approximating more to drunkenness than sobriety. In the cuff of his greatcoat he brought a note from the rector; I was ordered to present myself before him at seven o'clock that evening. When he had gone a pale and frightened student appeared, a baron from the Baltic provinces, who had received a similar invitation and was one of the luckless victims led on by me. He began showering reproaches upon me and then asked advice as to what he was to say.

'Lie desperately, deny everything, except that there was an uproar and that you were in the lecture-room.'

'But the rector will ask why I was in the Politics lecture-room and not in ours.'

'What of it? Why, don't you know that Rodion Heyman did not come to give his lecture, so you, not wishing to waste your time, went to hear another.'

'He won't believe it.'

'Well, that's his affair.'

As we were going into the university courtyard I looked at my baron: his plump little cheeks were very pale and altogether he was in a bad way.

'Listen,' I said, 'you may be sure that the rector will begin with me and not with you, so you say exactly the same with variations. You did not do anything in particular, as a matter of fact. Don't forget one thing: for making an uproar and for telling lies ever so many of you will be put in prison, but if you blab, and implicate anyone in front of me, I'll tell the others and we'll poison your existence for you.'

The baron promised and kept his word honourably.

The rector at that time was Dvigubsky, one of the relics and patterns of the professors before the flood, or to be more accurate, before the fire, that is, before 1812. They are extinct now; with the directorship of Prince Obolensky the patriarchal period of Moscow University comes to an end. In those days the government did not trouble itself about the university; the professors lectured or did not lecture, the students attended or did not attend; besides, if they did attend, it was not in uniform jackets *ad instar* of light-cavalry officers, but in all sorts of outrageous and eccentric garments, in tiny little forage-caps that would scarcely stay on their virginal locks. The professors consisted of two camps or strata who quietly hated each other. One group was composed exclusively of Germans, the other of non-Germans. The Germans, among whom were good-natured and learned men, were distinguished by their ignorance of the Russian language and their disinclination to learn it, their indifference to the students, their spirit of Western favouritism and uninspired routine, their immoderate smoking of cigars and the immense quantity of decorations which they never took off. The non-Germans for their part knew not a single (living) language except Russian, were servile in their patriotism, as uncouth as seminarists, were sat upon, and instead of an immoderate consumption of cigars indulged in an immoderate consumption of liquor. The Germans for the most part hailed from Göttingen and the non-Germans were sons of priests.

Dvigubsky was one of the non-Germans: his appearance was so edifying that a student from a seminary, who came in for a list of classes, went up to kiss his hand and ask for his blessing, and always called him 'Father Rector.' At the same time he was awfully like an owl with an Anna ribbon round its neck, in which form another student, who had received a more worldly education, drew his portrait. When he came into our lecture-room either with the dean, Chumakov, or with Kotelnitsky, who had charge of a cupboard inscribed *Materia Medica*, kept for some unknown reason in the Mathematical lecture-room—or with Reiss, who had been bespoken from Germany because his uncle was a very good chemist, and who, when he read French, used to call a lamp-wick a *bêton de coton*, and poison, *poisson*, and pronounced the word for 'lightning' so unfortunately that many people supposed he was swearing—we looked at them with round eyes as at a collection of fossils.

But Dvigubsky was not at all a good-natured professor; he received us extremely curtly and was rude. I reeled off a fearful rigmarole and was disrespectful; the baron served the same story warmed up. The rector, irritated, told us to present ourselves next morning before the Council; and there for half an hour they questioned, condemned and sentenced us and sent the sentence to Prince Golitsyn for confirmation.

I had scarcely had time to give an imitation of the trial and the sentence of the University Senate to the students five or six times in the lecture-room when all at once, at the beginning of a lecture, the inspector, who was a major in the Russian army and a French dancing-master, made his appearance with a non-commissioned officer, bringing an order to take me and conduct me to the university prison. Some of the students came to see me on my way, and in the courtyard, too, there was a crowd of young men, so evidently I was not the first taken; as we passed they all waved their caps and their hands; the university soldiers tried to move them back but the students would not go.

In the dirty cellar which served as a prison I found two of the arrested men, Arapetov and Orlov; Prince Andrey Obolensky and Rosenheim had been put in another room; in all, there were six of us punished for the Malov affair. Orders were given that we should be kept on bread and water; the rector sent some sort of soup, which we refused, and it was well we did so. As soon as it got dark and the university grew empty, our comrades brought us cheese, game, cigars, wine, and liqueurs. The soldier in charge was angry and started grumbling, but accepted twenty kopecks and carried in the provisions. After midnight he went further and let several visitors come in to us; so we spent our time feasting by night and going to bed by day.

On one occasion it happened that the assistant-director, Panin, the brother of the Minister of Justice, faithful to his Horse-Guard habits, took it into his head to go the round of the State prison in the university cellar by night. We had only just lit a candle and put it under a chair so that the light could not be seen from outside, and were beginning on our nocturnal lunch-eon, when we heard a knock at the outer door; not the sort of knock that meekly begs a soldier to open, which is more afraid of being heard than of not being heard; no, this was a peremptory knock, a knock of authority. The soldier was petrified; we hid the bottles and our visitors in a little cupboard, blew out the candle and threw ourselves on our pallets. Panin came in.

'*I believe* you are smoking?' he said, so lost in thick clouds of smoke that we could hardly distinguish him from the inspector who was carrying a lantern. 'Where do they get a light? Do you give it to them?'

The soldier swore that he did not. We answered that we had tinder with us. The inspector undertook to remove it and to take away the cigars, and Panin withdrew without noticing that the number of caps in the room was double the number of heads.

On Saturday evening the inspector made his appearance and announced that I and one other of us might go home, but that the rest would remain until Monday. This proposal seemed to me insulting and I asked the inspector whether I might remain; he drew back a step, looked at me with that menacingly graceful air with which tsars and heroes in a ballet depict anger in a dance, and saying, 'Stay by all means,' went away. I got into more trouble at home for this last escapade than for the whole business.

And so the first nights I slept away from home were spent in prison. Not long afterwards it was my lot to have experience of a different prison, and there I stayed not eight days[16] but nine months, after which I went not home but into exile. All that comes later, however.

From that time forward I enjoyed the greatest popularity in the lecture-room. From the first I had been accepted as a good comrade. After the Malov affair I became, like Gogol's famous lady, a comrade 'agreeable in all respects.'

---

[16] In a written deposition given to the Commission of Inquiry in 1834, Herzen testified that he had been under arrest for seventy-two hours in 1831 in connection with the Malov case. (*A.S.*)

Did we learn anything with all this going on? Could we study? I suppose we did. The teaching was more meagre and its scope narrower than in the 'forties. It is not the function of a university, however, to give a complete training in any branch of knowledge; its business is to put a man in a position to continue to study on his own account; its work is to provoke inquiry, to teach men to ask questions. And this was certainly done by such professors as M. G. Pavlov, and on the other hand by such as Kachenovsky. But contact with other young men in the lecture-rooms and the exchange of ideas and of what they had been reading did more to develop the students than lectures and professors. . . . Moscow University did its work; the professors whose lectures contributed to the development of Lermontov, Belinsky,[17] Turgenev, Kavelin,[18] and Pirogov[19] may play their game of boston in tranquillity and still more tranquilly lie under the earth.

And what originals, what prodigies, there were among them—from Fëdor Ivanovich Chumakov, who adjusted formulas to those in Poinsot's course with the perfect liberty of a privileged landowner, adding letters and taking them away, taking squares for roots and x for the known quantity, to Gavriil Myagkov, who lectured on military tactics, the *toughest* science in the world. From perpetually dealing with heroic subjects Myagkov's very appearance had acquired a military mien; buttoned up to the throat and wearing a cravat that was quite unbending, he delivered his lectures as though giving words of command.

'Gentlemen!' he would shout; 'Into the field!—*Artillery!*'

This did not mean that cannon were advancing into the field of battle, but simply that such was the heading in the margin. What a pity Nicholas avoided visiting the university! If he had seen Myagkov, he would certainly have made him Director.

And Fëdor Fëdorovich Reiss, who in his chemistry lectures

---

[17] Belinsky, Vissarion Grigorevich (1810–48), was the greatest of Russian critics. See below. "Return to Moscow and Intellectual Debate," pp. 229–53. (*D.M.*)
[18] Kavelin, Konstantin Dmitriyevich (1818–85), a writer of brilliant articles on political and economic questions. A friend of Turgenev. (*Tr.*)
[19] Pirogov, Nikolay Ivanovich (1810–81), the great surgeon and medical authority, was the first in Russia to investigate disease by experiments on animals, and to use anaesthetics for operations. He took an active part in education and the reforms of the early years of Alexander II's reign, and published many treatises on medical subjects. To his genius and influence as Professor of Medicine in Petersburg University is largely due the very high standard of medical training in Russia. (*Tr.*)

never went beyond the second person of the chemical divinity,
i.e. hydrogen! Reiss, who had actually been made Professor of
Chemistry because not he, but his uncle, had at one time studied
that science! Towards the end of the reign of Catherine, the old
uncle had been invited to Russia; he did not want to come, so
sent his nephew instead. . . .

Among the exceptional incidents of my course, which lasted four
years (for the university was closed for a whole academic year
during the cholera), were the cholera itself, the arrival of
Humboldt and the visit of Uvarov.

Humboldt, on his return from the Urals, was greeted in
Moscow at a solemn session of the Society of Natural Scientists
at the university, the members of which were various senators
and governors—people, on the whole, who took no interest in the
sciences, natural or unnatural. The fame of Humboldt, a privy
councillor of His Prussian Majesty, on whom the Tsar had
graciously bestowed the Anna, and to whom he had also commanded that the insignia and diploma should be presented free
of charge, had reached even them. They were determined to keep
up their dignity before a man who had been on Chimborazo and
had lived at Sans-Souci.

To this day we look upon Europeans and upon Europe in the
same way as provincials look upon those who live in the capital,
with deference and a feeling of our own inferiority, knuckling
under and imitating them, taking everything in which we are
different for a defect, blushing for our peculiarities and concealing them. The fact is that we were intimidated, and had not
recovered from the jeers of Peter I, from Biron's insults, from the
arrogance of Germans in the services and of French instructors.
They talk in Western Europe of our duplicity and wily cunning;
they mistake the desire to show off and swagger a bit for the
desire to deceive. Among us the same man is ready to be naïvely
liberal with a Liberal or to pretend to agree with a Legitimist,
and this with no ulterior motive, simply from politeness and a
desire to please; the bump *de l'approbativité* is strongly developed on our skulls.

'Prince Dmitry Golitsyn,' observed Lord Durham, 'is a true
Whig, a Whig in soul!'

Prince D. V. Golitsyn was a respectable Russian gentleman,
but why he was a Whig and in what way he was a Whig I do
not understand. You may be certain that in his old age the
prince wanted to please Durham and so played the Whig.

The reception of Humboldt in Moscow and in the university

was no jesting matter. The Governor-General, various military
and civic chiefs, and the members of the Senate, all turned up
with ribbons across their shoulders, in full uniform, and the
professors wore swords like warriors and carried three-cornered
hats under their arms. Humboldt, suspecting nothing, came in a
dark-blue dress-coat with gold buttons, and, of course, was overwhelmed with confusion. From the vestibule to the great hall of
the Society of Natural Scientists ambushes were prepared for
him on all sides: here stood the rector, there a dean, here a
budding professor, there a veteran whose career was over and
who for that reason spoke very slowly; everyone welcomed him
in Latin, in German, in French, and all this took place in those
awful stone tubes, called corridors, in which one cannot stop for
a minute without being laid up with a cold for a month. Humboldt, hat in hand, listened to everything and replied to everything—I feel certain that all the savages among whom he had
been, red-skinned and copper-coloured, caused him less trouble
than his Moscow reception.

As soon as he reached the hall and sat down, he had to get up
again. The Director, Pisarev, thought it necessary, in brief but
vigorous language, to issue an *order of the day* in Russian concerning the services of his Excellency, the celebrated traveller;
after which Sergey Glinka,[20] 'the officer,' with an 1812 voice,
deep and hoarse, recited his poem which began:

> *Humboldt—Prométhée de nos jours!*

While Humboldt wanted to talk about his observation on the
magnetic needle and to compare his meteorological records on
the Urals with those of Moscow, the rector came up to show him
instead something plaited of the imperial hair of Peter I . . .
and Ehrenberg and Rose had difficulty in finding a chance to tell
him something about their discoveries.[21]

---

[20] S. N. Glinka, author of patriotic verses of no merit. Referred to as
'the officer' by Pushkin in a poem. (*Tr.*)
[21] How diversely Humboldt's travels were understood in Russia may be
gathered from the account of a Ural Cossack who served in the office
of the Governor of Perm; he liked to describe how he had escorted the
mad Prussian prince, Gumplot. What did he do? 'Well, the silliest things,
collecting grasses, looking at the sand; in the saltings he says to me,
through the interpreter, "Get into the water and fetch what's at the
bottom;" well, I got just what is usually at the bottom, and he asks, "Is
the water very cold at the bottom?" No, my lad, I thought, you won't
catch me. So I drew myself up at attention, and answered, "When it's
our duty, your Highness, it's of no consequence: we are glad to do our

Things are not much better among us in the non-official world: ten years later Liszt was received in Moscow society in much the same way. Enough silly things were done in his honour in Germany, but here his reception was of quite a different quality. In Germany it was all old-maidish exaltation, sentimentality, all *Blumenstreuen,* while with us it was all servility, homage paid to power, rigid standing at attention; with us it was all 'I have the honour to present myself to your Excellency.' And here, unfortunately, there was also Liszt's fame as a celebrated Lovelace to add to it all. The ladies flocked round him, as peasant-boys on country roads flock round a traveller while his horses are being harnessed, inquisitively examining himself, his carriage, his cap. . . . No one listened to anybody but Liszt, no one spoke to anybody else, nor answered anybody else. I remember that at one evening party Khomyakov, blushing for the honourable company, said to me,

'Please let us argue about something, that Liszt may see that there are people in the room not exclusively occupied with him.'

For the consolation of our ladies I can only say one thing, that in just the same way Englishwomen dashed about, crowded round, pestered and obstructed other celebrities such as Kossuth and afterwards Garibaldi and others. But alas for those who want to learn good manners from Englishwomen and their husbands!

Our second 'famous' traveller was also in a certain sense 'the Prometheus of our day,' only he stole the light not from Jupiter but from men. This Prometheus, sung not by Glinka but by Pushkin himself in his 'Epistle to Lucullus,' was the Assistant Minister of Public Instruction, S. S. (not yet Count) Uvarov. He amazed us by the multitude of languages and the heterogeneous hotch-potch which he knew; a veritable shopman behind the counter of enlightenment, he preserved in his memory samples of all the sciences, the concluding summaries, or, better, the rudiments. In the reign of Alexander, he wrote Liberal brochures in French; later on he corresponded on Greek subjects with Goethe in German. When he became Minister he discoursed on Slavonic poetry of the fourth century, upon which Kachenovsky observed to him that in those days our forefathers had enough to do to fight the bears, let alone singing ballads about the gods of Samothrace and the mercy of tyrants. He used to carry in his pocket, by way of a testimonial, a letter from

best." ' ('We are glad, etc.,' was the formula which soldiers were expected to shout when addressed on parade by a senior officer.) (*R.*)

Goethe, in which the latter paid him an extremely odd compliment, saying: 'There is no need for you to apologise for your style—you have succeeded in what I never could succeed in doing—forgetting German grammar.'

◈   ◈   ◈

In August 1830 we went to Vasilevskoye, stopped, as we usually did, at the Radcliffian castle of Perkhushkovo and, after feeding ourselves and our horses, were preparing to continue our journey. Bakay, with a towel round his waist like a belt, had already shouted: 'Off!' when a man galloped up on horseback, signalling to us to stop, and one of the Senator's postillions, covered with dust and sweat, leapt off his horse and handed my father an envelope. In the envelope was the news of the Revolution of July! There were two pages of the *Journal des Débats* which he had brought with the letter; I read them over a hundred times and got to know them by heart, and for the first time I found the country dull.

It was a glorious time; events came quickly. Scarcely had the meagre figure of Charles X had time to disappear into the mists of Holyrood, when Belgium flared up, the throne of the Citizen King tottered, and a hot, revolutionary breeze began to blow in debates and literature. Novels, plays, poems, all once more became propaganda and conflict.

At that time we knew nothing of the artificial stage-setting of the revolution in France, and we took it all for honest cash.

Anyone who cares to see how strongly the news of the July Revolution affected the younger generation should read Heine's description of how he heard in Heligoland 'that the great pagan Pan was dead.' There was no sham ardour there: Heine at thirty was as enthusiastic, as childishly excited, as we were at eighteen.

We followed step by step every word, every event, the bold questions and abrupt answers, the doings of General Lafayette, and of General Lamarque; we not only knew every detail concerning them but loved all the leading men (the Radicals, of course) and kept their portraits.

In the midst of this ferment all at once, like a bomb exploding close by, the news of the rising in Warsaw stunned us. This was not far away: this was at home, and we looked at each other with tears in our eyes, repeating our favourite line:

Nein! es sind keine leere Träume! [22]

---

[22] From J. W. van Goethe's *Hoffnung*. (For *keine* read *nicht*.) (*A.S.*)

We rejoiced at every defeat of Dibich; refused to believe in the failures of the Poles, and I at once added to my ikonostasis the portrait of Thaddeus Kościuszko.

It was just then that I saw Nicholas for the second time and his face was still more strongly engraved on my memory. The nobility and gentry were giving a ball in his honour. I was in the gallery of the Assembly Hall and could stare at him to my heart's content. He had not yet begun to wear a moustache. His face was still young, but I was struck by the change in it since the time of the coronation. He stood morosely by a column, staring coldly and grimly before him, without looking at anyone. He had grown thinner. In those features, in those pewtery eyes one distinctly could read the fate of Poland, and indeed of Russia as well. He was shaken, *frightened;* he doubted[23] the security of his throne and was ready to avenge himself for what he had suffered, for his fear and his doubts.

With the subjection of Poland all the restrained malignancy of the man was let loose. Soon we felt it, too.

The network of espionage cast about the university from the beginning of the reign began to be drawn tighter. In 1832 a Pole who was a student in our faculty disappeared. Sent to the university as a government scholar, not at his own initiative, he had been put in our course; I made friends with him; he was discreet and melancholy in his behaviour; we never heard a bitter word from him, but we never heard a word of weakness either. One

---

[23] Here is what Denis Davydov* tells in his memoirs: 'The Tsar said one day to A. P. Yermolov: "I was once in a very terrible situation during the Polish War. My wife was expecting her confinement; rebellion had broken out in Novgorod; I had only two squadrons of the Horse Guards left me; the news from the army was only reaching me through Königsberg. I was forced to surround myself with soldiers discharged from hospital." '

The memoirs of this partisan leave no room for doubt that Nicholas, like Arakcheyev, like all cold-hearted, cruel and vindictive people was a *coward.* Here is what General Chechensky told Davydov: 'You know that I can appreciate manliness and so you will believe my words. I was near the Tsar on the 14th December, and I watched him all the time. I can assure you on my honour that the Tsar, who was very *pale* all the time, *had his heart in his boots.*'

And Davydov himself tells us: 'During the riot in the Haymarket the Tsar only visited the capital on the second day, when order was restored. The Tsar was at Peterhof, and himself once observed casually, "Volkon-

* Davydov (see Tolstoy's *War and Peace*) and Yermolov were both leaders of the partisan or guerilla warfare against the French in 1812. (*Tr.*)

morning he was missing from the lectures; next day he was missing still. We began to make inquiries; the government scholars told us in secret that he had been fetched away at night, that he had been summoned before the authorities, and then people had come for his papers and belongings and had ordered them not to speak of it. There the matter ended: *we never heard anything of the fate of this unfortunate young man.*

A few months passed when suddenly there was a rumour in the lecture-room that several students had been seized in the night; among them were Kostenetsky, Kohlreif, Antonovich and others; we knew them well: they were all excellent fellows. Kohlreif, the son of a Protestant pastor, was an extremely gifted musician. A *court-martial* was appointed to try them; this meant in plain language that they were doomed to perish. We were all in a fever of suspense to know what would happen to them,[24] but from the first they too vanished without trace. The storm that was crushing the sprouts was close at hand. We no longer had a foreboding of its approach: we heard it, we saw it, and we huddled closer and closer together.

The danger strung up our exasperated nerves even tighter, made our hearts beat faster and made us love each other with greater fervour. There were five of us at first[25] and now we met Vadim Passek.

In Vadim there was a great deal that was new to us. With slight variations we had all developed in similar ways: that is, we knew nothing but Moscow and our country estates, we had all learned out of the same books, had lessons from the same

---

sky and I were standing all day on a mound in the garden, listening for the sound of cannon-shot from the direction of Petersburg." Instead of anxiously listening in the garden, and continually sending couriers to Petersburg,' Davydov adds, 'he ought to have hastened there himself; anyone of the slightest manliness would have done so. On the following day (when everything was quiet) the Tsar drove in his carriage into the crowd which filled the square, and shouted to it, "On your knees!" and the crowd hurriedly obeyed the order. The Tsar, seeing several people dressed in civilian clothes (among those following the carriage), imagined that they were suspicious characters, and ordered the poor wretches to be taken to the lock-up and, turning to the people, began shouting: "They are all vile Poles; they have egged you on." Such an ill-timed sally completely ruined the effect, in my opinion.'

A strange sort of bird was this Nicholas!

24 They were made to serve in the army as privates. (*A.S.*)

25 Herzen, Ogarëv, N. I. Sazonov, N. M. Satin, A. N. Savich. (*A.S.*)

tutors, and been educated at home or at a boarding-school preparatory for the university. Vadim had been born in Siberia during his father's exile, in the midst of want and privations. His father had been himself his teacher. He had grown up in a large family of brothers and sisters, under a crushing weight of poverty but in complete freedom. Siberia sets its own imprint on a man, which is quite unlike our provincial stamp; it is far from being so vulgar and petty; it displays more healthiness and better tempering. Vadim was a savage in comparison with us. His daring was of another kind, unlike ours, more that of the *bogatyr*,[26] and sometimes arrogant; the aristocracy of misfortune had developed in him a peculiar self-esteem; but he knew how to love others, too, and gave himself to them without stint. He was bold, even reckless to excess—a man born in Siberia, and in an exiled family too, has an advantage over us in not being afraid of Siberia.

Vadim from family tradition hated the autocracy with his whole soul, and he took us to his heart as soon as we met. We made friends very quickly—though, indeed, at that time, there was neither ceremony nor reasonable precaution, nothing like it, to be seen in our circle.

'Would you like to make the acquaintance of Ketscher, of whom you have heard so much?' Vadim said to me.

'I certainly should.'

'Come to-morrow evening, then, at seven o'clock; don't be late: he'll be at my place.'

I went—Vadim was not at home. A tall man with an expressive face and a good-naturedly menacing look behind his spectacles was waiting for him. I took up a book: he took up a book.

'But perhaps you,' he said as he opened it, 'perhaps you are Herzen?'

'Yes; and you're Ketscher?'

A conversation began and grew more and more lively. . . .

'Allow me,' Ketscher interrupted me roughly. 'Allow me: do me the kindness to use "thou" to me.'

'Let us use "thou." '

And from that minute (which may have been at the end of 1831) we were inseparable friends; from that minute the anger and kindness, the laugh and the shout of Ketscher have resounded at all the stages, in all the adventures of our life.

---

[26] Legendary hero. (*R.*)

Our meeting with Vadim introduced a new element into our Cossack brotherhood.

◈   ◈   ◈

A year passed, the trial of my arrested comrades was over. They were found guilty (just as we were later on, and later still the Petrashevsky group)[27] *of a design* to form a secret society, and of criminal conversations; for this they were sent as common soldiers to Orenburg. Nicholas made an exception of one of them, Sungurov. He had completed his studies, and was in the service, married and had children. He was condemned to be deprived of his rights of status and to be exiled to Siberia.

'What could a handful of young students do? They destroyed themselves for nothing!' All that is very sensible, and people who argue in that way ought to be gratified at the *good sense* of the younger generation of Russians that followed us. After our affair, which followed that of Sungurov, *fifteen years* passed in tranquillity before the Petrashevsky affair, and it was those fifteen years from which Russia is only just beginning to recover and by which two generations were broken, the elder smothered in violence, and the younger poisoned from childhood, whose sickly representatives we are seeing to-day.

After the Decembrists all attempts to form societies were, in effect, unsuccessful; the scantiness of our forces and the vagueness of our aims pointed to the necessity for another kind of work—for preliminary work upon ourselves. All that is true.

But what would young men be made of who could wait for theoretical solutions while calmly looking on at what was being done round them, at the hundreds of Poles clanking their fetters on the Vladimir Road, at serfdom, at the soldiers flogged in the Khodynsky field by some General Lashkevich, at fellow-students who disappeared and were never heard of again? For the moral purification of the generation, as a pledge of the future, they were bound to be so indignant as to be senseless in their attempts and disdainful of danger. The savage punishments inflicted on boys of sixteen or seventeen served as a stern lesson and a kind of hardening process; the paw of the beast hung over every one of us, proceeding from a breast without a heart, and dispelled for good all rosy hopes of indulgence for youth. It was dangerous to

---

[27] The members of the Petrashevsky group, of whom Dostoevsky was one, were condemned to death, and led out to the scaffold. At the last moment their sentence was commuted to penal servitude in Siberia. (*Tr.*)

play at Liberalism, and no one could dream of playing at conspiracy. For one badly concealed tear over Poland, for one boldly uttered word, there were years of exile, of the white strap,[28] and sometimes even the fortress; that was why it was important that those words were uttered and those tears were shed. Young people sometimes perished but they perished without checking the mental activity that was trying to solve the sphinx riddle of Russian life; indeed, they even justified its hopes.

Our turn came now. Our names were already on the lists of the secret police.[29] The first play of the light-blue cat with the mouse began as follows.

When the young men who had been condemned were being sent off to Orenburg on foot under escort without sufficient warm clothing, Ogarëv in our circle, I. Kireyevsky in his, got up subscriptions. All the condemned men were without money. Kireyevsky brought the money collected to the commander, Staal, a good-natured old man of whom I shall have more to say later. Staal promised to remit the money and asked Kireyevsky,

'But what are these papers?'

'The names of those who subscribed,' answered Kireyevsky, 'and the amounts.'

'You do believe that I shall remit the money?' asked the old man.

'There's no doubt of that.'

'And I imagine that those who have given it to you trust you. And so what is the use *of our keeping their names?*' With these words Staal threw the list into the fire, and of course it was an excellent thing to do.

Ogarëv himself took the money to the barracks, and this went off without a hitch; but the young men took it into their heads to send their thanks from Orenburg to their comrades, and, as a government official was going to Moscow, they seized the opportunity and asked him to take a letter, which they were afraid to trust to the post. The official did not fail to take advantage of this rare chance to prove all the ardour of his loyal sentiments, and presented the letter to the general of gendarmes in Moscow.

---

[28] *I.e.*, of supervision by the political police, whose light blue uniform was worn with a white strap. (*Tr.*)

[29] Ogarëv and Satin had been under secret police surveillance since the summer of 1833, in connection with the Sungurov affair. In December 1833, the police observed Ogarëv and Sokolovsky singing the '*Marseillaise*' at the entrance to the Maly Theatre. Oblensky had been under surveillance by the police since 1832. (*A.S.*)

The general of gendarmes at this time was Lesovsky, who was appointed to the post when A. A. Volkov went out of his mind, imagining that the Poles wanted to offer him the crown of Poland (an ironical trick of destiny to send a general of gendarmes mad over the crown of the Jagellons![30]). Lesovsky, himself a Pole, was not a bad man, and was no fool: having wasted his property over cards and a French actress, he philosophically preferred the place of general of gendarmes in Moscow to a place in the debtors' prison of the same city.

Lesovsky summoned Ogarëv, Ketscher, Satin, Vadim, I. Obolensky and the others, and charged them with being in communication with political criminals. On Ogarëv's observing that he had not written to any one, and that if any one had written to him he could not be responsible for it, and that, moreover, no letter had reached him, Lesovsky answered:

'You got up a subscription for them, *that's still worse*. For the first time the Sovereign is *so merciful* as to *pardon* you; only I warn you, gentlemen, a strict supervision will be kept over you: be careful.'

Lesovsky looked round at them all with a significant glance and, his eyes resting upon Ketscher, who was taller and a little older than the rest and who raised his eyebrows so fiercely, he added:

'You, my good sir, ought to be ashamed, in your station in life.'

It might have been supposed that Ketscher was vice-chancellor of the Russian Heraldry Office, while as a matter of fact he was only a humble district doctor.

I was not sent for: probably my name was not in the letter.

This threat was like a promotion, a consecration, a winning of our spurs. Lesovsky's advice threw oil on the fire, and as though to make their future task easier for the police we put on velvet *bérets à la* Karl Sand[31] and tied identical tricolour scarves round our necks.

❖   ❖   ❖

---

[30] The dynasty of kings of Poland from 1386 to 1572. (*Tr.*)
[31] Karl Sand, a student of Jena University, who in 1819 assassinated the German dramatist Kotzbue, because he ridiculed the *Burschenschaft* movement. (*Tr.*)

After the University

BEFORE THE STORM BROKE over our heads my time at the university was coming to an end. The ordinary anxieties, the nights without sleep spent in useless mnemonic tortures, the superficial study in a hurry and the thought of the examination overcoming all interest in science—all that was as it always is. I wrote a dissertation on *astronomy* for the gold medal, and got the silver one. I am certain that I am incapable of understanding now what I wrote then, and that it was worth its weight—in silver.

It has sometimes happened to me to dream that I am a student going in for an examination—I think with horror how much I have forgotten and feel that I shall be plucked—and I have woken up rejoicing from the bottom of my heart that the sea and passports, and years and visas cut me off from the university, that no one is going to torture me, and no one will dare to give me a horrid 'one.'[1] And, indeed, the professors would be surprised that I should have gone so far back in so few years. Indeed, this did once happen to me.[2]

After the final examination the professors shut themselves up to reckon the marks, while we, excited by hopes and doubts, hung about the corridors and entrance in little groups. Sometimes someone would come out of the council-room. We rushed to learn our fate, but for a long time there was still nothing settled. At last Heyman came out.

------

[1] Marks in Russian educational establishments range from one to five. (*R.*)

[2] In 1844 I met Perevoshchikov at Shchepkin's and sat beside him at dinner. Towards the end he could not resist saying: 'It is a pity, a very great pity, that circumstances prevented you from taking up work. You had excellent abilities.'

'But you know it's not for everyone to climb up to heaven behind you. We are busy here on earth at work of some sort.'

'Upon my word, to be sure that may be work of a sort. Hegelian philosophy perhaps. I have read your articles, and there is no understanding them; bird's language, that's queer sort of work. No, indeed!'

For a long while I was amused at this verdict, that is, for a long while I could not understand that our language really was poor; if it was a bird's it must have been the bird that was Minerva's favourite.

'I congratulate you,' he said to me, 'you are a graduate.'

'Who else, who else?'

'So-and-so, and So-and-so.'

I felt at once sad and gay; as I went out at the university gates I thought that I was not going out at them again as I had yesterday and every day; I was becoming estranged from the university, from that parental home where I had spent four years, so youthfully and so well; on the other hand I was comforted by the feeling of being accepted as completely grown-up, and, why not admit it? by the title of graduate I had gained all at once.[3]

Alma Mater! I am so greatly indebted to the university, and lived its life and with it so long after I had finished my studies, that I cannot think of it without love and respect. It will not charge me with ingratitude, though at least as regards the university gratitude is easy; it is inseparable from the love and bright memories of youth . . . and I send it my blessing from this far-off foreign land!

The year we spent after taking our degrees made a triumphant end to our early youth. It was one prolonged feast of friendship, exchange of ideas, inspiration, carousing. . . .

The little group of university friends who had survived the course did not part, but went on living in their common sympathies and fancies, and no one thought of his material situation or of arranging his future. I should not think well of this in men of mature age, but I prize it in the young. Youth, if only it has not been desiccated by the moral corruption of *petit bourgeois* ideas, is everywhere impractical, and is especially bound to be so in a young country which is full of strivings and has attained so little. Moreover, to be impractical is far from implying anything false: everything turned towards the future is bound to have a share of idealism. If it were not for the impractical characters, all the practical people would remain at the same dull stage of perpetual repetition.

---

[3] Among the papers sent me from Moscow I found a note in which I informed my *cousin* who was then in the country with the princess that I had taken my degree. 'The examination is over, and I am a graduate! You cannot imagine the sweet feeling of freedom after four years of work. Did you think of me on Thursday? It was a stifling day, and the torture lasted from nine in the morning till nine in the evening.' (26th June, 1833.) I fancy I added two hours for effect or to round off the sentence. But for all my satisfaction my vanity was stung by another student's (Alexander Drashusov) winning the gold medal. In a second letter of the 6th July, I find: 'To-day was the prizegiving, but I was not there. I did not care to be the *second* to receive a medal.'

Some enthusiasm preserves a man from *real* spills far more than any moral admonitions. I remember youthful orgies, moments of revelry that sometimes went beyond bounds, but I do not remember one really immoral affair in our circle, nothing of which a man would have to feel *seriously* ashamed, which he would try to forget and conceal. Everything was done openly, and what is bad is rarely done openly. Half, more than half, of the heart was turned away from idle sensuality and morbid egoism, which concentrate on impure thoughts and accentuate vices.

I consider it a great misfortune for a nation when their young generation has no youth; we have already observed that for this being young is not enough by itself. The most grotesque period of German student life is a hundred times better than the *petit bourgeois* maturity of young men in France and England. To my mind the *elderly* Americans of fifteen are simply repulsive.

In France there was at one time a brilliant aristocratic youth, and later on a revolutionary youth. All the Saint-Justs[4] and Hoches,[5] Marceaux[5] and Desmoulins,[6] the heroic children who grew up on the gloomy poetry of Jean-Jacques, were real youths. The Revolution was the work of young men: neither Danton nor Robespierre nor Louis XIV himself outlived his thirty-fifth year. With Napoleon the young men were turned into orderlies; with the Restoration, 'the revival of old age'—youth was utterly incompatible—everything became mature, businesslike, that is, *petit bourgeois*.

The last youth of France were the Saint-Simonists and the Fourierists. The few exceptions cannot alter the prosaically dull character of French youth. Escousse and Lebras[7] shot themselves because they were young in a society of old men. Others

---

[4] Louis de Saint-Just (1767–94) was a member of the Convention and the Committee of Public Safety, a follower of Robespierre and beheaded with him at the age of twenty-seven. (*Tr.*)

[5] Lazare Hoche (1768–97) and François-Séverin Marceau (1769–96), were generals of the French Revolutionary Army. Both were engaged in the pacification of La Vendée. Both perished before reaching the age of thirty. (*Tr.*)

[6] Camille Desmoulins (1760–94) was one of the early leaders of the French Revolution, and headed the attack on the Bastille; he was afterwards accused of being a Moderate and beheaded together with Danton at the age of thirty-four. (*Tr.*)

[7] Victor Escousse (b. 1813) and Auguste Lebras (b. 1816) were poets who wrote in collaboration a successful play, *Farruck le Maure*, followed by an unsuccessful one called *Raymond*. On the failure of the latter they committed suicide in 1832. Béranger wrote a poem on them. (*Tr.*)

struggled like fish thrown out of the water on to the muddy bank, till some were caught on the barricades and others on the hooks of the Jesuits.

But, since youth asserts its rights, the greater number of young Frenchmen work off their youth in a Bohemian period; that is, if they have no money, they live in little cafés with little *grisettes* in the Quartier Latin, and in grand cafés with grand *lorettes,* if they have money. Instead of a Schiller period, they have a Paul de Kock period; in this strength, energy, everything young is rapidly and rather wretchedly wasted and the man is ready—for a *commis* in a commercial house. The Bohemian period leaves at the bottom of the soul one passion only—the thirst for money, and the whole future is sacrificed to it—there are no other interests; these practical people laugh at theoretical questions and despise women (the result of numerous conquests over those whose trade it is *to be conquered*). As a rule the Bohemian period is passed under the guidance of some worn-out sinner, a faded celebrity, *d'un vieux prostitué,* living at someone else's expense, an actor who has lost his voice, or a painter whose hands tremble, and he is the model who is imitated in accent, in dress, and above all in a haughty view of human affairs and a profound understanding of good fare.

In England the Bohemian period is replaced by a paroxysm of pleasing originalities and amiable eccentricities. For instance, senseless tricks, absurd squandering of money, ponderous practical jokes, heavy, but carefully concealed vice, profitless trips to Calabria or Quito, to the north and to the south—with horses, dogs, races, and stuffy dinners by the way, and then a wife and an incredible number of fat, rosy babies; business transactions, *The Times,* Parliament, and the old port which weighs them to the earth.

We played pranks, too, and we caroused, but the fundamental tone was not the same, the diapason was too elevated. Mischief and dissipation never became our goal. Our goal was faith in our vocation; supposing that we were mistaken, still, believing it as a fact, we respected in ourselves and in each other the instruments of the common cause.

And in what did our feasts and orgies consist? Suddenly it would occur to us that in another two days it would be the sixth of December, St. Nicholas's day. The supply of Nikolays was terrific, Nikolay Ogarëv, Nikolay Satin, Nikolay Ketscher, Nikolay Sazonov. . . .

'Gentlemen, who is going to celebrate the name-day?'

'I! I! . . .'

'I shall the next day then.'

'That's all nonsense, what's the good of the next day? We will keep it in common—club together! And what a feast it will be!'

'Yes! yes! At whose rooms are we to meet?'

'Satin is ill, so obviously it must be at his.'

And so plans and calculations are made, and it is incredibly absorbing for the future guests and hosts. One Nikolay drives off to the Yar to order supper, another to Materne's for cheese and salami. Wine, of course, is bought in the Petrovka from Depré's, on whose price-list Ogarëv wrote the epigram:

> *De près ou de loin,*
> *Mais je fournis toujours.*

Our inexperienced taste went no further than champagne, and was so young that we sometimes even exchanged *Rivesaltes mousseux* for champagne. I once saw the name on a wine-list in Paris, remembered 1833 and ordered a bottle, but, alas, even my memories did not help me to drink more than one glass.

Before the festive day the wines would be tried, and so it would be necessary to send a messenger for more, for clearly the samples were liked.

For the celebration of the *four name-days* I wrote out a complete programme, which was deemed worthy of the special attention of the inquisitor Golitsyn, who asked me at the enquiry whether the programme had been carried out exactly.

'*À la lettre,*' I replied. He shrugged his shoulders as though he had spent his whole life in the Smolny Convent or keeping Good Friday.

After supper as a rule a *vital* question arose; a question that aroused controversy, i.e. how to prepare the punch. Other things were usually eaten and drunk *in good faith, like the voting in Parliament, without dispute,* but in this everyone must have a hand and, moreover, it was after supper.

'Light it—don't light it yet—light it how?—put it out with champagne or Sauternes?—put the fruit and pineapple in while it is burning or afterwards?'

'Obviously when it is burning, and then the whole aroma will go into the punch.'

'But, I say, pineapples float, the edges will be scorched, simply a calamity.'

'That's all nonsense,' Ketscher would shout louder than all, 'but what's not nonsense is that you must put out the candles.'

The candles were put out; all the faces looked blue, and the features seemed to quiver with the movement of the flame. And meantime the temperature in the little room was becoming tropical from the hot rum. Everyone was thirsty and the punch was not ready. But Joseph, the Frenchman sent from the Yar, was ready; he had prepared something, the antithesis of punch, an iced beverage of various wines *à la base de cognac*. A genuine son of the '*grand peuple*,' he explained to us, as he put in the French wine, that it was so good because it had twice passed the Equator. '*Oui oui, messieurs; deux fois l'équateur, messieurs!*'

When the beverage, remarkable for its arctic iciness, had been finished and in fact there was no need of more drink, Ketscher shouted, stirring the fiery lake in the soup-tureen and making the last lumps of sugar melt with a hiss and a wail,

'It's time to put it out! time to put it out!'

The flame blushes from the champagne, and runs along the surface of the punch, with a kind of anguish and foreboding.

Then comes a voice of despair:

'But I say, old man, you're mad: don't you see the wax is melting right into the punch?'

'Well, you try holding the bottle yourself in such heat so that the wax does not melt.'

'Well, something ought to be have been wrapped round it first,' the distressed voice continues.

'Cups, cups, have you enough? How many are there of us? Nine, ten, fourteen, yes, yes!'

'Where's one to find fourteen cups?'

'Well any one who hasn't got a cup must use a glass.'

'The glasses will crack.'

'Never, never; you've only to put a spoon in them.'

Candles are brought, the last flicker of flame runs across the middle, makes a pirouette and vanishes.

'The punch is a success!'

'It is a great success!' is said on all sides.

Next day my head aches—I feel sick. That's evidently from the punch, too mixed! And on the spot I make a sincere resolution never to drink punch for the future; it is a poison.

Pëtr Fëdorovich comes in.

'You came home in somebody else's hat, sir: our hat is a better one.'

'The devil take it entirely.'

'Should I run to Nikolay Mikhaylovich's Kuzma?'

'Why, do you imagine someone went home without a hat?'

'It won't hurt to go just in case.'

At this point I guess that the hat is only a pretext, and that Kuzma has invited Pëtr Fëdorovich to the field of battle.

'You go and see Kuzma; only first ask the cook to let me have some sour cabbage.'

'So, Lexandr Ivanych, the gentlemen kept their name-days in fine style?'

'Yes, indeed: there hasn't been such a supper in our time.'

'So we shan't be going to the university to-day?'

My conscience pricks me and I make no answer.

'Your papa was asking me, "How is it," says he, "he is not up yet?" I was pretty smart. I said, "His honour's head aches; he complained of it from early morning, so I did not even pull up the blinds." "Well," said he, "you did right there." '

'But do let me go to sleep, for Christ's sake. You wanted to go and see Kuzma, so go.'

'This minute, this minute, sir; first I'll run for the cabbage.'

A heavy sleep closes my eyes again; two or three hours later I wake up much refreshed. What can they be doing there? Ketscher and Ogarëv stayed the night. It's annoying that punch has such an effect on the head, for it must be owned it's very nice. It is a mistake to drink punch by the glass; henceforth and for ever I will certainly drink no more than a small cupful.

❖　❖　❖

So ends the first part of our youth; the second begins with prison. But before we enter upon it I must say something of the tendencies, of the ideas, with which it found us.

The period that followed the suppression of the Polish insurrection educated us rapidly. We were not tormented only by the fact that Nicholas had grown to his full stature and was firmly established in severity; we began with inward horror to perceive that in Europe, too, and especially in France, to which we looked for our political watchword and battle-cry, things were not going well; we began to look upon our theories with suspicion.

The childish liberalism of 1826, which gradually passed into the French political view preached by the Lafayettes and Benjamin Constant and sung by Béranger, lost its magic power over us after the ruin of Poland.

Then some of the young people, and Vadim among them, threw themselves into a profound, earnest study of Russian history.

Others took to the study of German philosophy.

Ogarëv and I belonged to neither of these sets. We had grown too closely attached to other ideas to part with them readily. Our faith in revolution of the festive Béranger stamp was shaken, but we looked for something else which we could find neither in the *Chronicle* of Nestor[8] nor in the transcendental idealism of Schelling.

In the midst of this ferment, in the midst of surmises, of confused efforts to understand the doubts which frightened us, the pamphlets of Saint-Simon and his followers, their tracts and their trial came into our hands. They impressed us.

Critics, superficial and not superficial, have laughed enough at Father Enfantin[9] and his apostles; the time has now come for some recognition of these forerunners of socialism.

These enthusiastic youths with their terry waistcoats and their budding beards made a triumphant and poetic appearance in the midst of the *petit bourgeois* world. They heralded a new faith; they had something to say; they had something in the name of which to summon the old order of things before their court of judgment, fain to judge them by the Code Napoléon[10] and the religion of Orléans.[11]

On the one hand came the *emancipation of woman*, the call to her to join in common labour, the giving of her destiny into her own hands, alliance with her as with an equal.

On the other hand the justification, the *redemption of the flesh, réhabilitation de la chair!*

Grand words, involving a whole world of new relations between human beings; a world of health, a world of spirit, a

---

[8] This is the earliest record of Russian history. It begins with the Deluge and continues in leisurely fashion up to the year 1110. Nestor, of whom nothing is really known, is assumed to have been a monk of the twelfth century. (*Tr.*)

[9] B. P. Enfantin (1796–1864), a French engineer, was one of the founders of Saint-Simonism. (*Tr.*)

[10] The Saint-Simonists were tried in 1832, under Article 291 of the Criminal Code, brought into effect in 1811, for an offence against public morals. Herzen is thinking of the philistinism and hypocrisy of this bourgeois Criminal Code, and also of the Civil Code of 1804, which was re-named in 1807 the 'Code Napoléon.'

[11] Herzen's irony. The period of the July (Orléans) Monarchy was marked by the extreme moral dissoluteness of the governing financial aristocracy. Moreover the July authorities accused the Saint-Simonists, who were preaching a 'new religion' and the equality of the sexes, of immorality and of advocating the 'community of women.'

world of beauty, the world of natural morality, and therefore of moral purity. Many scoffed at the emancipated woman and at the recognition of the rights of the flesh, giving to those words a filthy and vulgar meaning; our monastically depraved imagination fears the flesh, fears woman. Sensible people grasped that the purifying *baptism of the flesh* is the death-knell of Christianity; the religion of life had come to replace the religion of death, the religion of beauty to replace the religion of flagellation and mortification by prayer and fasting. The crucified body had risen again in its turn and was no longer ashamed of itself; man attained a harmonious unity and divined that he was a whole being and not made up like a pendulum of two different metals restraining each other, that the enemy that had been welded to him had disappeared.

What courage was needed in France to proclaim in the hearing of all those words of deliverance from the spirituality which is so strong in the notions of the French and so completely absent from their conduct!

The old world, ridiculed by Voltaire, undermined by the Revolution, but strengthened, patched up and made secure by the *petit bourgeois* for their own personal convenience, had never experienced this before. It wanted to judge the apostates on the basis of its secret conspiracy of hypocrisy, but these young men unmasked it. They were accused of being backsliders from Christianity, and they pointed above their judge's head to the holy picture that had been veiled after the Revolution of 1830. They were charged with justifying sensuality, and they asked their judge, was his life chaste?

The new world was pushing at the door, and our hearts and souls opened wide to meet it. Saint-Simonism lay at the foundation of our convictions and remained so in its essentials unalterably.

Impressionable, genuinely youthful, we were easily caught up in its mighty current and passed early over that boundary at which whole crowds of people remain standing with their arms folded, go back or look to the side for a ford—to cross the ocean!

But not everyone ventured with us. Socialism and realism remain to this day the touchstones flung on the paths of revolution and science. Groups of swimmers, tossed up against these rocks by the current of events or by process of reasoning, immediately divide and make two everlasting parties which, in various disguises, cut across the whole of history, across all upheavals, across innumerable political parties and even circles of no more than a dozen youths. One stands for logic, the other for history; one for dialectics, the other for embryogeny. One is more *correct*, the other more *practical*.

There can be no talk of choice; it is harder to bridle thought than any passion, it leads one on involuntarily; anyone who can check it by emotion, by a dream, by fear of consequences, will check it, but not all can. If thought gets the upper hand in any one, he does not inquire about its applicability, or whether it will make things easier or harder; he seeks the truth, and inexorably, impartially sets out his principles, as the Saint-Simonists did at one time, as Proudhon does to this day.

Our circle drew in still closer. Even then, in 1833, the Liberals looked at us askance, as having strayed from the true path. Just before we went to prison Saint-Simonism set up a barrier between N. A. Polevoy and me. Polevoy was a man of an unusually ingenious and active mind, which readily assimilated every kind of nutriment; he was born to be a journalist, a chronicler of successes, of discoveries, of political and learned controversies. I made his acquaintance at the end of my time at the university—and was sometimes in his house and at his brother Ksenofont's. This was the time when his reputation was at its highest, the period just before the prohibition of the *Telegraph*.

This man who lived in the most recent discovery, in the question of the hour, in the latest novelty in theories and in events, and who changed like a chameleon, could not, for all the liveliness of his mind, understand Saint-Simonism. For us Saint-Simonism was a revelation, for him it was insanity, a vain Utopia, hindering social development. To all my rhetoric, my expositions and arguments, Polevoy was deaf; he lost his temper and grew splenetic. Opposition from a student was particularly annoying to him, for he greatly prized his influence on the young, and saw in this dispute that it was slipping away from him.

On one occasion, affronted by the absurdity of his objections, I observed that he was just as old-fashioned a Conservative as those against whom he had been fighting all his life. Polevoy was deeply offended by my words and, shaking his head, said to me:

'The time will come when you will be rewarded for a whole life-time of toil and effort by some young man's saying with a smile, "Be off, you are behind the times." '

I felt sorry for him and ashamed of having hurt his feelings, but at the same time I felt that his sentence could be heard in his melancholy words. They were no longer those of a mighty champion, but of a superannuated gladiator who has served his time. I realised then that he would not advance, and would be incapable of standing still at the same point with a mind so active and on such unstable footing.

You know what happened to him afterwards: he set to work upon his *Parasha, the Siberian*.[12]

What luck a timely death is for a man who can neither leave the stage at the right moment nor move forward. I have thought that looking at Polevoy, looking at Pius IX, and at many others!

Appendix:
A. Polezhayev

To COMPLETE the gloomy record of that period, I ought to add a few details about A. Polezhayev.

As a student, Polezhayev was renowned for his excellent verses. Amongst other things he wrote a humorous parody of *Onegin* called *Sashka* in which, regardless of proprieties, he tilted at many things in a jesting tone, in very pleasant verses.

In the autumn of 1826 Nicholas, after hanging Pestel, Muravëv, and their friends, celebrated his coronation in Moscow. For other sovereigns these ceremonies are occasions for amnesties and pardons: Nicholas, after celebrating his apotheosis, proceeded again to 'strike down the foes of the father-land,' like Robespierre after his *Fête-Dieu*.

The secret police brought him Polezhayev's poem.

And so at three o'clock one night the Rector woke Polezhayev, told him to put on his uniform and go to the office. There the Director was awaiting him. After looking to see that all the necessary buttons were on his uniform and no unnecessary ones, he invited Polezhayev without any explanation to get into his carriage and drove off with him.

He conducted him to the Minister of Public Instruction. The latter put Polezhayev into his carriage and he too drove him off—but this time straight to the Tsar.

---

[12] A translation of *La Jeune Sibérienne* (1825) by Xavier de Maistre, who had known Parasha in St. Petersburg. (*R.* from private information.)

Prince Lieven[1] left Polezhayev in the great room—where several courtiers and higher officials were already waiting although it was only between five and six in the morning—and went into the inner apartments. The courtiers imagined that the young man had distinguished himself in some way and at once entered into conversation with him. A senator suggested that he might give lessons to his son.

Polezhayev was summoned to the study. The Tsar was standing leaning on his desk and talking to Lieven. He flung an angry, searching glance at the newcomer; there was a manuscript-book in his hand.

'Did you write these verses?' he inquired.

'Yes,' answered Polezhayev.

'Here, prince,' the Tsar continued, 'I will give you a specimen of university education. I will show you what young men learn there. Read the manuscript aloud,' he added, addressing Polezhayev again.

The agitation of Polezhayev was so great that he could not read. Nicholas's eyes were fixed immovably upon him. I know them and know nothing so terrifying, so hopeless, as those greyish, colourless, cold, pewtery eyes.

'I cannot,' said Polezhayev.

'Read!' shouted the imperial sergeant-major.

That shout restored Polezhayev's faculties; he opened the book. Never, he told us, had he seen *Sashka* so carefully copied and on such splendid paper.

At first it was hard for him to read; then as he got more and more into the spirit of the thing, he read the poem to the end in a loud and lively voice. At particularly cutting passages the Tsar made a sign with his hand to the Minister and the latter covered his eyes with horror.

'What do you say to that?' Nicholas inquired at the end of the reading. 'I shall put a stop to this corruption; these are the *last traces, the last remnants*; I shall root them out. What has his conduct been?'

The Minister, of course, knew nothing of his conduct, but some human feeling must have stirred in him, for he said:

'His conduct has been excellent, your Majesty.'

'That testimonial has saved you, but you must be punished, as an example to others. Would you like to go into the army?'

---

[1] The Minister of Public Instruction at this time was not K. A. Lieven but A. S. Shishkov. (*A.S.*)

Polezhayev was silent.

'I give you a means of purging yourself by service in the army. Well?'

'I must obey,' answered Polezhayev.

The Tsar went up to him, laid his hand on his shoulder, and saying to him,

'Your fate is in your own hands; if I forget you you may *write* to me,' *kissed him on the forehead*.

I made Polezhayev repeat the story of the kiss a dozen times, it seemed to me so incredible. He swore that it was true.

From the Tsar he was led off to Dibich, who lived on the spot in the palace. Dibich was asleep; he was awakened, came out yawning, and, after reading the paper, asked the aide-de-camp:

'Is this he?'

'Yes, your Excellency.'

'Well! it's a capital thing; you will serve in the army. I have always been in the army, and you see what I've risen to, and maybe you'll be a field-marshal.'

This misplaced, feeble, German joke was Dibich's equivalent of a kiss. Polezhayev was led off to the camp and enlisted.

Three years passed. Polezhayev remembered the Tsar's words and wrote him a letter. No answer came. A few months later he wrote a second; again there was no answer. Convinced that his letters did not reach the Tsar, he ran away, and ran away in order to present his petition in person. He behaved carelessly, saw his old friends in Moscow and was entertained by them; of course, that could not be kept secret. In Tver he was seized and sent back to his regiment as a deserter, on foot and in chains. The court-martial condemned him to run the gauntlet; the sentence was despatched to the Tsar for confirmation.

Polezhayev wanted to kill himself before the punishment. After searching in vain in his prison for a sharp instrument, he confided in an old soldier who liked him. The soldier understood him and respected his wishes. When the old man learned that the answer had come, he brought him a bayonet and, as he gave him it, said through his tears:

'I have sharpened it myself.'

The Tsar ordered Polezhayev not to be punished.

Then it was that he wrote his fine poem beginning:

I perished lonely,
No help was nigh.

My evil genius
Passed mocking by.[2]

Polezhayev was sent to the Caucasus. There for distinguished service he was promoted to be a non-commissioned officer. Years and years passed; his inescapable, dreary situation broke him down; become a police poet and sing the glories of Nicholas he could not, and that was the only way of getting rid of the knapsack.

There was, however, another means of escape, and he preferred it; he drank to win forgetfulness. There is a frightening poem of his, 'To John Barleycorn.'

He succeeded in getting transferred to a regiment of the Carabineers stationed in Moscow. This was a considerable alleviation of his lot, but a malignant consumption was already eating away his chest. It was at this period that I made his acquaintance, about 1833. He languished for another four years and died in a military hospital.

When one of his friends appeared to ask for the body for burial, no one knew where it was; a military hospital traffics in corpses—sells them to the university and to the Medical Academy, boils them down to skeletons, and so on. At last he found poor Polezhayev's body in a cellar; it was lying under a heap of others and the rats had gnawed off one foot.

After his death his poems were published, and his portrait in a private's uniform was to have been included in the edition. The censor thought this unseemly, and the poor martyr was portrayed with the epaulettes of an officer—he had been promoted in the hospital.

---

[2] Translated by Juliet Soskice.

PRISON

AND

EXILE

(1834-1838)

Ogarëv's Arrest

❖   ❖   ❖

'Taken? What do you mean?' I asked, jumping out of bed and feeling my head to make sure that I was awake.

'The *politsmeyster* came in the night with the district policeman and Cossacks, about two hours after you left, seized all the papers and took Nikolay Platonovich away.'

It was Ogarëv's valet speaking. I could not imagine what pretext the police had invented: of late everything had been quiet. Ogarëv had arrived only a day or two before . . . and why had they taken him and not me?

It was impossible to fold my arms and do nothing; I dressed and went out of the house with no definite purpose. This was the first misfortune that had befallen me. I felt dreadful: I was tortured by my impotence.

As I wandered about the streets I thought, at last, of one friend whose social position made it possible for him to find out what was the matter and, perhaps, to help. He lived terribly far away, in a summer villa beyond the Vorontsov Field; I got into the first cab I came across and galloped off to him. It was before seven in the morning.

I had made the acquaintance of ——[1] about eighteen months before; in his way he was a lion in Moscow. He had been educated in Paris, was wealthy, intelligent, cultured, witty, free-thinking, had been in the Peter-Paul fortress over the affair of the Fourteenth of December and was among those set free; he had had no experience of exile, but the glory of the affair clung to him. He was in the government service and had great influence with the Governor-General, Prince Golitsyn, who was fond of men of a liberal way of thinking, particularly if they expressed their views fluently in French. The prince was not strong in Russian.

V—— was ten years older than we were, and surprised us by his practical remarks, his knowledge of political affairs, his French eloquence and the ardour of his Liberalism. He knew so much and in such detail, talked so pleasantly and so easily; his opinions were so firmly traced; he had answers, good advice,

---

[1] V. P. Zubkov. (*A.S.*)

solutions for everything. He read everything, new novels, treatises, magazines, and poetry, was moreover a devoted student of zoology, wrote out schemes of reform for Prince Golitsyn and drew up plans for children's books.

His Liberalism was of the purest, trebly-distilled essence, of the left wing.

His study was hung with portraits of all the revolutionary celebrities. A whole library of prohibited books was to be found under this revolutionary ikonostasis. A skeleton, a few stuffed birds, some dried amphibians and entrails preserved in spirit, gave a serious tone of study and reflection to the too inflammatory character of the room.

We used to regard with envy his experience and knowledge of men; his delicate, ironical manner of arguing had a great influence on us. We looked upon him as a capable revolutionary, as a statesman *in spe*.

I did not find V—— at home: he had gone to town overnight for an interview with Prince Golitsyn. His valet told me he would certainly be home within an hour and a half. I waited.

V——'s summer villa was a splendid one. The study in which I sat waiting was a lofty, spacious room on the ground floor, and an immense door led to the verandah and into the garden. It was a hot day; the fragrance of trees and flowers came in from the garden and children were playing in front of the house with ringing laughter. Wealth, abundance, space, sunshine and shadow, flowers and greenery . . . while in prison it is cramped, stifling, dark. I do not know how long I had been sitting there absorbed in bitter thoughts, when suddenly the valet called me from the verandah with a peculiar animation.

'What is it?' I inquired.

'Oh, please, come here and look.'

I went out to the verandah, not to wound him by a refusal, and stood petrified. A whole semi-circle of houses were blazing, as though they had caught fire at the same moment. The fire was spreading with incredible rapidity.

I remained on the verandah; the valet gazed with a sort of nervous pleasure at the fire, saying:

'It's going splendidly. Look, that house on the right will catch fire! It will certainly catch!'

A fire has something revolutionary about it; it laughs at property and levels ranks. The valet understood that instinctively.

Half an hour later half the horizon was covered with smoke,

red below and greyish-black above. That day Lefortovo was burned down. This was the beginning of a series of cases of incendiarism, which went on for five months; we shall speak of them again.

At last V—— arrived. He was in high spirits, pleasant and cordial; he told me about the fire by which he had driven and about the general belief that it was a case of arson, and added, half in jest:

'It's Pugachëvshchina. You look: you and I won't escape; they'll stick us on a stake.'

'Before they put us on a stake,' I answered, 'I am afraid they will put us on a chain. Do you know that last night the police arrested Ogarëv?'

'The police—what are you saying?'

'That's what I have come to you about. Something must be done; go to Prince Golitsyn, find out what it's about and ask permission for me to see him.'

Receiving no answer, I glanced at V——, but where he had been it seemed as though an elder brother of his were sitting with a yellowish face and sunken features; he was groaning and greatly alarmed.

'What's the matter?'

'There, I told you; I always said what it would lead to. . . . Yes, yes, we ought to have expected it. There it is. I am not to blame in thought or in act but very likely they will put me in prison too, and that is no joking matter; I know what a fortress is like.'

'Will you go to the prince?'

'Goodness gracious me, whatever for? I advise you as a friend, don't even speak of Ogarëv; keep as quiet as you can, or it will be the worse for you. You don't know how dangerous these things are; my sincere advice is, keep out of it; do your utmost and you won't help Ogarëv, but you will ruin yourself. That's what autocracy means—no rights, no defence; are the lawyers and judges any use?'

On this occasion I was not disposed to listen to his bold opinions and cutting criticisms. I took my hat and went away.

At home I found everything in a turmoil. Already my father was angry with me on account of Ogarëv's arrest. Already the Senator was on the spot, rummaging among my books, taking away what he thought dangerous, and in a very bad humour.

On the table I found a note from M. F. Orlov inviting me to dinner. Could he not do something for us? I was beginning to be discouraged by experience: still, there was no harm in trying and the worst I could get was a refusal.

Mikhail Fëdorovich Orlov was one of the founders of the celebrated League of Welfare,[2] and that he had not found himself in Siberia was not his own fault, but was due to his brother, who enjoyed the special friendship of Nicholas and had been the first to gallop with his Horse Guards to the defence of the Winter Palace on December the Fourteenth. Orlov was sent to his estate in the country, and a few years later was allowed to live in Moscow. During his solitary life in the country he studied political economy and chemistry. The first time I met him he talked of his new system of nomenclature on chemistry. All energetic people who begin studying a science late in life show an inclination to move the furniture about and rearrange it to suit themselves. His nomenclature was more complicated than the generally accepted French system. I wanted to attract his attention, and by way of *captatio benevolentiae* began to try to prove to him that his system was good, but the old one was better.

Orlov contested the point and then agreed.

My effort to please succeeded: from that time we were on intimate terms. He saw in me a rising possibility; I saw in him a veteran of our views, a friend of our heroes, a noble figure in our life.

Poor Orlov was like a lion in a cage. Everywhere he knocked himself against the bars; he had neither space to move nor work to do and was consumed by a thirst for activity.

After the fall of France I more than once met people of the same sort, people who were disintegrated by the craving for public activity and incapable of finding their true selves within the four walls of their study or in home life. They do not know how to be alone; in solitude they are attacked by the spleen, they

---

[2] The League of Public Welfare was formed in the reign of Alexander I to support philanthropic undertakings and education, to improve the administration of justice, and to promote the economic welfare of the country. The best men in Russia belonged to it. At first approved by Alexander, it was afterwards repressed, and it split into the 'Union of the North,' which aimed at establishing constitutional government, and the 'Union of the South' led by Pestel, which aimed at republicanism. The two Unions combined in the attempt of December the Fourteenth, 1825. (*Tr.*)

become capricious, quarrel with their last friends, see intrigues against them on all hands, and themselves intrigue to reveal all these non-existent plots.

A stage and spectators are as necessary to them as the air they breathe; in the public view they really are heroes and will endure the unendurable. They have to be surrounded by noise, clamour and clash, they want to make speeches, to hear their enemies' replies, they crave the stimulus of struggle, the fever of danger, and without these tonics they are miserable, they pine, let themselves go and grow heavy, have an urge to break out, and make mistakes. Ledru-Rollin is one such, who, by the way, has a look of Orlov, particularly since he has grown moustaches.

Orlov was very handsome; his tall figure, fine carriage, handsome, manly features and completely bare skull, altogether gave an irresistible attractiveness to his appearance. The upper half of his body was a match to that of A. P. Yermolov, whose frowning, quadrangular brow, thick thatch of grey hair, and eyes piercing the distance gave him that beauty of the warrior chieftain, grown old in battles, which won Maria Kochubey's heart in *Mazeppa*.

Orlov was so bored that he did not know what to begin upon. He tried founding a glass factory, in which mediæval stained glass was made, costing him more than he sold it for; and began writing a book 'On Credit'—no, that was not the way his heart yearned to go, and yet it was the only way open to him. The lion was condemned to wander idly between the Arbat and Basmannaya Street, not even daring to let his tongue run freely.

It was a mortal pity to see Orlov endeavouring to become a learned man, a theorist. His intelligence was clear and brilliant, but not at all speculative, and he got confused among newly invented systems for long-familiar subjects—like his chemical nomenclature. He was a complete failure in everything abstract, but went in for metaphysics with intense obstinacy.

Careless and incontinent of speech, he was continually making mistakes; carried away by his first impression, which was always chivalrously lofty, he would suddenly remember his position and turn back half way. He was an even greater failure in these diplomatic countermarches than in metaphysics and nomenclature; and, having got his legs tangled in the traces once, he would do it two or three times more in trying to get clear. He was blamed for this; people are so superficial and inattentive that they look more to words than to actions, and attach more weight to separate mistakes than to the combination of the whole character. What is the use of blaming, from the rigorous viewpoint of a Regulus, a man? One must blame the sorry environment in which any noble feeling must be communicated, like contraband, under ground and behind locked doors; and, if one says a word aloud, one is wondering all day how soon the police will come. . . .

There was a large party at the dinner. I happened to sit beside General Rayevsky, the brother of Orlov's wife. He too had been in disgrace since the Fourteenth of December; the son of the celebrated N. N. Rayevsky, he had as a boy of fourteen been with his brother at Borodino by his father's side; later on he died of wounds in the Caucasus. I told him about Ogarëv, and asked him whether Orlov could do anything and whether he would care to.

A cloud came over Rayevsky's face: it was not the look of tearful self-preservation which I had seen in the morning, but a mixture of bitter memories and repulsion.

'There is no question here of caring or not caring,' he answered, 'only I doubt whether Orlov can do much; after dinner go to the study and I will bring him to you. So then,' he added after a pause, 'your turn has come, too; everyone will be dragged down into that slough.'

After questioning me, Orlov wrote a letter to Prince Golitsyn asking for an interview.

'The prince,' he told me, 'is a very decent man; if he doesn't do anything, he will at least tell us the truth.'

Next day I went for an answer. Prince Golitsyn said that Ogarëv had been arrested by order of the Tsar, that a committee of inquiry had been appointed, and that the material occasion had been some supper on the 24th June at which seditious songs had been sung. I could make nothing of it. That day was my father's name-day; I had spent the whole day at home and Ogarëv had been with us.

It was with a heavy heart that I left Orlov; he, too, was troubled; when I gave him my hand he stood up, embraced me, pressed me warmly to his broad chest and kissed me.

It was as though he felt that we were parting for long years.

I only saw him once afterwards, eight years later. His light was flickering out. The look of illness on his face, the melancholy and a sort of new angularity in it struck me; he was gloomy, was conscious that he was breaking up, knew things were all going wrong—and saw no way out. Two months later he died—the blood congealed in his veins.

. . . There is a wonderful monument[3] at Lucerne; carved by Thorwaldsen in the living rock. A dying lion is lying in a hollow: he is wounded to death; the blood is streaming from a wound in which the fragment of an arrow is sticking; he has laid his gallant head upon his paw, he is moaning, there is a look in his eyes of unbearable pain; all round it is empty, with a pond below, all this shut in by mountains, trees, and greenery; people pass by without seeing that here a royal beast is dying.

Once after sitting some time on a seat facing the stone agony, I was suddenly reminded of my last visit to Orlov. . . .

Driving home from Orlov's, I passed the house of the *ober-politsmeyster*,[4] and the idea occurred to me of asking him openly for permission to see Ogarëv.

I had never in my life been in the house of a police official. I was kept waiting a long time; at last the *oberpolitsmeyster* came in.

My request surprised him.

'What grounds have you for asking this permission?'

'Ogarëv is my kinsman.'

'Your kinsman?' he asked, looking straight into my face.

I did not answer, but I, too, looked straight into his Excellency's face.

'I cannot give you permission,' he said; 'your kinsman is *au secret*. Very sorry!'

Uncertainty and inactivity were killing me. Hardly any of my friends were in town; I could find out absolutely nothing. It seemed as though the police had forgotten or overlooked me. It was very, very dreary. But just when the whole sky was overcast with grey storm-clouds and the long night of exile and prison was approaching, a ray of light shone down on me.

A few words of deep sympathy, uttered by a girl of seventeen whom I had looked upon as a child, brought me to life again.

For the first time in my story a woman's figure[5] appears . . . and properly one single woman's figure appears throughout my life.

The passing fancies of youth and spring that had troubled my soul paled and vanished before it, like pictures in the mist; and no fresh ones came.

---

[3] The monument was raised in 1821 to the memory of the Swiss Guards who fell in the defence of the Tuileries in 1792. (*A.S.*)

[4] *Oberpolits(ey)meyster* (*Oberpolizeimeister*), the senior police-officer in Petersburg or Moscow. (*R.*)

[5] Natalya Alexandrovna Zakharin, Herzen's first cousin and wife. (*R.*)

We met in a graveyard. She stood leaning against a tombstone and spoke of Ogarëv, and my grief was put away.

'Till to-morrow,' she said and gave me her hand, smiling through her tears.

'Till to-morrow,' I answered . . . and stood a long time looking after her disappearing figure.

That was the nineteenth of July 1834.

My Arrest

'TILL TO-MORROW,' I repeated, as I fell asleep. . . . I felt uncommonly light-hearted and happy.

Between one and two in the morning[1] my father's valet woke me; he was not dressed and was frightened.

'An officer is asking for you.'

'What officer?'

'I don't know.'

'Well, I do,' I told him and threw on my dressing-gown.

In the doorway of the great hall a figure was standing wrapped in a military greatcoat; by the window I saw a white plume, and there were other persons behind—I made out the cap of a Cossack.

It was the *politsmeyster*, Miller.

He told me that by an order of the military Governor-General, which he held in his hand, he must look through my papers. Candles were brought. The *politsmeyster* took my keys; the district police superintendent and his lieutenant began rummaging among my books and my linen. The *politsmeyster* busied himself among my papers; everything seemed suspicious to him; he laid everything on one side and suddenly turned to me and said:

'I must ask you to dress meanwhile; you'll come along with me.'

'Where to?' I asked.

'To the Prechistensky police station,' answered the *politsmeyster* in a soothing voice.

'And then?'

---

[1] Of 21st July, 1834. (*A.S.*)

'There is nothing more in the Governor-General's order.'

I began to dress.

Meanwhile the frightened servants had woken my mother. She rushed out of her bedroom and was coming to my room, but was stopped by a Cossack at the doors between the drawing-room and the *salon*. She uttered a shriek: I shuddered and ran to her. The *politsmeyster* left the papers and came with me to the *salon*. He apologised to my mother, let her pass, swore at the Cossack, who was not to blame, and went back to the papers.

Then my father came up. He was pale but tried to maintain his studied indifference. The scene was becoming painful. My mother sat in the corner, weeping. My old father spoke of indifferent matters with the *politsmeyster*, but his voice shook. I was afraid that I could not stand this for long and did not want to afford the local police superintendent the satisfaction of seeing me in tears.

I pulled the *politsmeyster* by the sleeve,

'Let us go!'

'Let us go,' he said gladly.

My father went out of the room and returned a minute later. He brought a little ikon and put it round my neck, saying that his father had given it to him with his blessing on his deathbed. I was touched: this *religious* gift showed me the degree of fear and shock in the old man's heart. I knelt down while he was putting it on; he helped me up, embraced me and blessed me.

The ikon was a picture in enamel of the head of John the Baptist on a charger. What this was—example, advice, or prophecy?—I do not know, but the significance of the ikon struck me.

My mother was almost unconscious.

All the servants accompanied me down the staircase weeping and rushing to kiss my cheek or my hands. I felt as though I were present at my own funeral. The *politsmeyster* scowled and hurried me on.

When we went out at the gate he collected his detachment; he had with him four Cossacks, two police superintendents and two ordinary policemen.

'Allow me to go home,' a man with a beard who was sitting in front of the gate asked the *politsmeyster*.

'You can go,' said Miller.

'What man is that?' I asked, getting into the drozhki.

'The impartial witness; you know that without an impartial witness the police cannot enter a house.'

'Then why did you leave him outside the gate?'

'It's a mere form! It's simply keeping the man out of bed for nothing,' observed Miller.

We drove off accompanied by two Cossacks on horseback.

There was no special room for me in the police station. The *politsmeyster* directed that I should be put in the office until morning. He took me there himself; he flung himself in an easy-chair and, yawning wearily, muttered:

'It's a damnable service. I've been on the jump since three o'clock in the afternoon, and here I've been bothered with you till morning. I bet it's past three already and to-morrow I must go with the report at nine.

'Good-bye,' he added a minute later, and went out.

A non-commissioned officer locked me in, observing that if I needed anything I could knock at the door.

I opened the window. The day was already beginning and the morning wind was rising; I asked the non-commissioned officer for water and drank off a whole jugful. There was no thinking of sleep. Besides, there was nowhere to lie down; apart from the dirty leather chairs and one easy-chair, there was nothing in the office but a big table heaped up with papers and in the corner a little table with still more heaped up on it. A poor nightlight did not light the room, but made a flickering patch of light on the ceiling that grew paler and paler with the dawn.

I sat down in the place of the police superintendent and took up the first paper that was lying on the table, a document relating to the funeral of a serf of Prince Gagarin's and a medical certificate that he had died according to all the rules of science. I picked up another—it was a set of police regulations. I ran through it and found a paragraph which stated that 'Every arrested man has the right within three days after his arrest to know the reason for it or to be released.' I noted this paragraph for my own benefit.

An hour later I saw through the window our major domo bringing me a pillow, bedclothes, and a greatcoat. He asked the non-commissioned officer something, probably permission to come in to me; he was a grey-headed old man, to two or three of whose children I had stood godfather as a small boy. The non-commissioned officer gave him a rough and abrupt refusal; one of our coachmen was standing near; I shouted to them from the window. The non-commissioned officer fussed about and told them to take themselves off. The old man bowed to the waist to me and shed tears; the coachman, as he whipped up the horse, took off his hat and wiped his eyes, the drozhki rattled away and my tears fell in streams. My heart was brimming over; these were the first and last tears I shed while I was in prison.

Towards morning the office began to fill up; the clerk arrived still drunk from the day before, a consumptive-looking individual with red hair, a look of brutal vice on his pimply face. He wore a very dirty, badly-cut, shiny, brick-red dress-coat. After him another extremely free-and-easy individual arrived, in a non-commissioned officer's greatcoat. He at once addressed me with the question:

'Were you taken at the theatre, sir, or what?'

'I was arrested at home.'

'Did Fëdor Ivanovich himself arrest you?'

'Who's Fëdor Ivanovich?'

'Colonel Miller.'

'Yes.'

'I understand, sir.' He winked to the red-haired man who showed no interest whatever. He did not continue the conversation—he saw that I had been taken neither for disorderly conduct nor drunkenness, and so lost all interest in me; or perhaps was afraid to enter into conversation with a *dangerous* prisoner.

Not long afterwards various sleepy-looking police officials made their appearance and then came petitioners and litigants.

The keeper of a brothel brought a complaint against the owner of a beer-shop, that he had publicly abused her in his shop in such language as, being a woman, she could not bring herself to utter before the police. The shopkeeper swore that he had never used such language. The madam swore that he had uttered the words more than once and very loudly, and added that he had raised his hand against her and that, if she had not ducked, he would have laid her whole face open. The shopkeeper declared that, in the first place, she had not paid what she owed him, and, in the second, had insulted him in his own shop and, what was more, threatened that he should be thrashed within an inch of his life by her followers.

The brothel-keeper, a tall, untidy woman with puffy eyes, screamed in a loud, piercing voice and was extremely garrulous. The man made more use of mimicry and gesture than of words.

The police Solomon, instead of judging between them, cursed them both like a trooper.

'The dogs are too well fed, that's why they run mad,' he said; 'they should sit quiet at home, the beasts, seeing we say nothing

and leave them in peace. What an opinion they have of themselves! They quarrel and run at once to trouble the police. And
you're a fine lady! as though it were the first time—what's one
to call you if not a bad word, with the trade you follow?'

The shopkeeper shook his head and shrugged his shoulders to
express his profound gratification. The police officer at once
pounced upon him and said:

'What do you go barking from behind your counter for, you
dog? Do you want to go to the lock-up? You're a foul-tongued
brute! Raise your paw any more—do you want a taste of the
birch, eh?'

For me this scene had all the charm of novelty and it remained imprinted on my memory for ever; it was the first case
of patriarchal Russian justice I had seen.

The brothel-keeper and the police officer continued shouting
until the police superintendent came in. Without inquiring why
these people were there or what they wanted, he shouted in a still
more savage voice:

'Get out, be off! This isn't a public bath or a pot-house!'

Having driven 'the scum' out he turned to the police officer:

'You ought to be ashamed to allow such a disturbance! How
many times I have told you? Respect for the place is being lost.
After this every sort of riff-raff will turn it into a perfect Sodom.
You are too easy-going with these scoundrels. What man is this?'
he asked about me.

'A prisoner brought in by Fëdor Ivanovich, sir. Here is the
document.'

The superintendent ran through the document, looked at me,
met with disapproval the direct and unflinching gaze which I
fixed upon him, prepared at the first word to give as good as I
got, and said 'Excuse me.'

The affair of the brothel-keeper and the beer-shop man began
again. She insisted on making a deposition on oath. A priest
arrived. I believe they both made sworn statements; I did not see
the end of it. I was taken away to the *oberpolitsmeyster*'s. I do
not know why; no one said a word to me; then I was brought
back again to the police station, where a room had been prepared
for me under the watch tower. The non-commissioned officer
observed that if I wanted anything to eat I must send out to buy
it, that my government ration had not been allotted yet and that
it would not be for another two days or so; moreover, that it
consisted of three or four kopecks of silver and that the *better-
class* prisoners did not claim it.

There was a dirty sofa standing by the wall; it was past

midday: I felt fearfully tired, flung myself on the sofa and slept like the dead. When I woke up, all was quiet and serene in my heart. I had been worn out recently by uncertainty about Oga-rëv; now my turn too had come. The danger was no longer far off, but was all about me; the storm-cloud was overhead. This first persecution was to be our consecration.

Imprisonment

A MAN soon becomes used to prison, if only he has some inner resources. One quickly becomes used to the peace and complete freedom in one's cage—no anxieties, no distractions.

At first, I was not allowed any books; the superintendent assured me that it was forbidden to get books from home. I asked him to buy me some. 'Something instructive, a grammar now, I might get, perhaps, but for anything else you must ask the general.' The suggestion that I should while away the time by reading a grammar was immensely funny, nevertheless I seized it with both hands, and asked the superintendent to buy me an Italian grammar and lexicon. I had two red twenty-five rouble notes with me, and I gave him one; he at once sent an officer for the books and gave him a letter to the *oberpolitsmeyster* in which, on the strength of the paragraph I had read, I asked him to let me know the reason for my arrest or to release me.

The local superintendent, in whose presence I wrote the letter, tried to persuade me not to send it.

'It's a mistake, sir, upon my soul, it's a mistake to trouble the general; he'll say "they are restless people," it will do you harm and be no use whatever.'

In the evening the policeman appeared and told me that the *oberpolitsmeyster* had bidden him tell me verbally that I should know the reason for my arrest in due time. Then he pulled out of his pocket a greasy Italian grammar, and added, smiling, 'It luckily happened that there was a vocabulary in it so there was no need to buy a lexicon.' Not a word was said about the change. I should have liked to write to the *oberpolitsmeyster* again, but the role of a miniature Hampden at the Prechistensky police station struck me as too funny.

Ten days after my arrest a little swarthy, pock-marked policeman appeared some time after nine in the evening with an order for me to dress and set off to the commission of inquiry.

While I was dressing the following ludicrously vexatious incident occurred. My dinner was being sent me from home. A servant gave it to the non-commissioned officer on duty below and he sent it up to me by a soldier. It was permitted to let in for me from home half a bottle to a whole bottle of wine a day. N. Sazonov took advantage of this permission to send me a bottle of excellent Johannisberg. The soldier and I ingeniously uncorked the bottle with two nails; one could smell the *bouquet* some distance away. I looked forward to enjoying it for the next three or four days.

One must be in prison to know how much childishness remains in a man and what comfort can be found in trifles, from a bottle of wine to a trick at the expense of one's guard.

The pock-marked policeman sniffed out my bottle and turning to me asked permission to taste a little. I was vexed; however, I said that I should be delighted. I had no wine-glass. The monster took a tumbler, filled it incredibly full and drank it down without taking breath; this way of pouring down spirits and wine only exists among Russians and Poles; in the whole of Europe I have seen no other people empty a tumbler at a gulp, or who could toss off a wine-glassful. To make the loss of the wine still more bitter, the pock-marked policeman wiped his lips with a snuffy blue handkerchief, adding 'First-class Madeira.' I looked at him with hatred and spitefully rejoiced that he had not been vaccinated and nature had not spared him the smallpox.

This connoisseur of wines conducted me to the *oberpolits-meyster*'s house in Tverskoy Boulevard, showed me into a side-room and left me there alone. Half an hour later a stout man with a lazy, good-natured air came into the room from the inner apartments; he threw a portfolio of papers on to a chair and sent the gendarme standing at the door away on some errand.

'I suppose,' he said to me, 'you are concerned with the case of Ogarëv and the other young men who have lately been arrested?'

I said I was.

'I happened to hear about it,' he went on; 'it's an odd business: I don't understand it at all.'

'I've been a fortnight in prison in connection with the affair and I don't understand it at all, and, what's more, I simply know nothing about it.'

'A good thing, too,' he said, looking intently at me; 'and mind you don't know anything about it. You must forgive me if I give you a bit of advice; you're young, your blood is still hot, you long to speak out: that's the trouble. Don't forget that you know nothing about it: that's the only way to safety.'

I looked at him in surprise: his face expressed nothing evil; he guessed what I felt and said with a smile,

'I was a Moscow student myself twelve years ago.'

A clerk of some sort came in; the stout man addressed him and, after giving him his orders, went out with a friendly nod to me, putting his finger on his lips. I never met the gentleman afterwards and I do not know who he was, but I found out the genuineness of his advice.

Then a *politsmeyster* came in, not Miller, but another, called Tsynsky, and summoned me to the commission. In a large, rather handsome room five men were sitting at a table, all in military uniform, with the exception of one decrepit old man. They were smoking cigars and gaily talking together, lolling in easy chairs, with their uniforms unbuttoned. The *oberpolitsmeyster* presided.

When I went in, he turned to a figure sitting meekly in a corner, and said,

'If you please, Father.'

Only then I noticed that there was sitting in a corner an old priest with a grey beard and a reddish-blue face. The priest was half-asleep and yawning with his hand over his mouth; his mind was far away and he was longing to get home. In a drawling, somewhat chanting voice he began *admonishing* me, talking of the sin of concealing the truth before the persons appointed by the Tsar, and of the uselessness of such dissimulation considering the all-hearing ear of God; he did not even forget to refer to the eternal texts, that 'there is no power but of God' and 'to Cæsar the things that are Cæsar's.' In conclusion he said that I must put my lips to the Gospel and the *honourable* Cross in confirmation of the oath (which, however, I had not given, and he did not require) sincerely and candidly to reveal the whole truth.

When he had finished he began hurriedly wrapping up the Gospel and the Cross. Tsynsky, barely rising from his seat, told him that he could go. After this he turned to me and translated the spiritual speech into secular language:

'I will add only one thing to the priest's words—it is impossible for you to deny the charge, even if you wanted to.'

He pointed to the heaps of papers, letters, and portraits which were intentionally scattered about the table.

'Only a frank admission can mitigate your lot; to be at liberty, or Bobruysk, or in the Caucasus, depends on yourself.'

The questions were put to me in writing: the naïveté of some of them was striking: 'Do you not know of the existence of some secret society? Do you not belong to any society, literary *or other?* Who are its members? Where do they meet?'

To all this it was extremely easy to answer by the single word: 'No.'

'I see you know nothing,' said Tsynsky after looking through the answers. 'I have warned you, you are making your position more complicated.'

With that the first examination ended. . . .

A week or two later the pock-marked policeman came and took me to Tsynsky again. In the lobby several men in fetters were sitting or lying down, surrounded by soldiers with rifles; in the ante-room also there were several men of different classes, not chained but strictly guarded. The policemen told me that they were all incendiaries. Tsynsky was out at the fire and we had to await his return. We had arrived between nine and ten in the evening; no one had asked for me by one o'clock in the morning, and I was still sitting very quietly in the ante-room with the incendiaries. First one and then another of them was sent for, the police ran backwards and forwards, chains clanked, and the soldiers were so bored that they rattled their rifles and did arms-drill. About one o'clock Tsynsky arrived, sooty and grimy, and hurried straight through to his study without stopping. Half an hour passed and my policeman was sent for; he came back looking pale and out of countenance, with his face twitching convulsively. Tsynsky poked his head out of the door after him and said:

'The whole commission has been waiting for you all the evening, Monsieur Herzen; this *blockhead* brought you here when you were wanted at Prince Golitsyn's. I am very sorry you have had to wait here so long, but it is not my fault. What is one to do with such subordinates? I believe he has been fifty years in the service and he is still an idiot. Come, be off home now,' he added, changing to a much ruder tone as he addressed the policeman.

The little man repeated all the way:

'O Lord, what a calamity! a man has no thought, no notion what will happen to him. He will be the death of me now. He wouldn't care a bit if you had not been expected there, but since you were of course it is a disgrace to him. O Lord, how unlucky!'

I forgave him my wine, particularly when he told me that he had not been nearly so frightened when he had been almost drowned near Lisbon as he was now. This last circumstance was so unexpected that I was overcome with senseless laughter.

'Good lord, how very strange! However did you get to Lisbon?'

The old man had been a ship's officer for twenty-five years or so. One cannot but agree with the minister who assured Captain Kopeykin[1] that: 'It has never happened yet among us in Russia that a man who has deserved well of his country should be left a reward of some sort.' Fate had saved him at Lisbon only to be abused by Tsynsky like a boy, after forty years' service.

He was scarcely to blame, either.

The commission of inquiry formed by the Governor-General did not please the Tsar; he appointed a new one presided over by Prince Sergey Mikhaylovich Golitsyn. The members of this commission were Staal, the Commandant of Moscow, the other Prince Golitsyn, Shubinsky, a colonel of gendarmes, and Oransky, an ex-auditor.

In the instructions from the *oberpolitsmeyster* nothing was said about the commission's having been changed; it was very natural that the policeman from Lisbon took me to Tsynsky. . . .

There was great alarm at the police station, too; there had been three fires in one evening—and the commission had sent twice to inquire what had become of me, and whether I had not escaped. Anything that Tsynsky had left unsaid in his abuse the police station superintendent made up now to the man from Lisbon; which, indeed, was only to be expected, since the superintendent was himself partly to blame, not having inquired where I was to be sent. In a corner of the office someone was lying on some chairs, groaning; I looked: it was a young man of handsome appearance, neatly dressed, who was spitting blood and sighing. The police doctor advised his being taken to the hospital as early as possible in the morning.

When the non-commissioned officer took me to my room, I extracted from him the story of the wounded man. He was an ex-officer of the Guards, who had an intrigue with some maid-servant and had been with her when a wing of the house caught fire. This was the time of the greatest fright over arson; indeed, not a day passed without my hearing the bell ring the alarm three or four times; from my window I saw the glare of two or three fires every night. The police and the residents sought for the incendiaries with great persistence. To avoid compromising the girl the officer climbed over the fence as soon as the alarm

---

[1] See Gogol's *Dead Souls*. (*Tr.*)

was sounded, and hid in the stable of the next house, waiting for an opportunity to get away. A little girl who was in the yard saw him and told the first policeman who galloped up that the incendiary had hidden in the stable; they rushed in with a crowd of people and dragged the officer out in triumph. He was so thoroughly knocked about that he died next morning.

The people who had been captured began to be sorted out; about half were released, the others detained on suspicion. The *politsmeyster*, Bryanchaninov, used to come over every morning and cross-examine them for three or four hours. Sometimes the victims were thrashed or beaten; then their wailing, screams, entreaties and howls, and the moaning of women reached me, together with the harsh voice of the *politsmeyster* and the monotonous reading of the clerk. It was awful, intolerable. At night I dreamed of those sounds and woke in a frenzy at the thought that the victims were lying on straw only a few paces from me, in chains, with lacerated wounds on their backs, and in all probability quite innocent.

To know what the Russian prisons, the Russian lawcourts and the Russian police are like, one must be a peasant, a house-serf, an artisan or a town workman. Political prisoners, who for the most part belong to the upper class, are kept in close custody and punished savagely, but their fate bears no comparison with the fate of the poor. With them the police do not stand on ceremony. To whom can the peasant or the workman go afterwards to complain? Where can he find justice?

So terrible is the confusion, the brutality, the arbitrariness and the corruption of Russian justice and of the Russian police that a man of the humbler class who falls into the hands of the law is more afraid of the process of law itself than of any legal punishment. He looks forward with impatience to the time when he will be sent to Siberia; his martyrdom ends with the beginning of his punishment. And now let us remember that three-quarters of the people taken up by the police on suspicion are released by the courts, and that they have passed through the same tortures as the guilty.

Peter III abolished torture and the Secret Chamber.

Catherine II abolished torture.

Alexander I abolished it *again*.

Answers given 'under intimidation' are not recognised by law. The official who tortures an accused man renders himself liable to trial and severe punishment.

And yet all over Russia, from the Bering Straits to Taurogen, men are tortured; where it is dangerous to torture by flogging, they are tortured by insufferable heat, thirst, and salted food. In Moscow the police put an accused prisoner with bare feet on a metal floor at a temperature of ten degrees of frost; he sickened, and died in a hospital which was under the supervision of Prince Meshchersky, who told the story with indignation. The government knows all this, the governors conceal it, the Senate connives at it, the ministers say nothing; the Tsar, and the synod, the landowners and the police all agree with Selifan:[2] 'Why not thrash a peasant? A peasant sometimes needs a thrashing!'

The committee appointed to investigate the cases of incendiarism was investigating, that is, thrashing, for six months in a row, and had thrashed out nothing in the end. The Tsar was annoyed and ordered that the thing was to be finished in three days. The thing was finished in three days. Culprits were found and condemned to punishment by the knout, by branding, and by exile to penal servitude. The porters from all the houses were assembled to watch the terrible punishment of 'the incendiaries.' By then it was winter and at that time I was being held at the Krutitsky Barracks. The captain of gendarmes, a good-natured old man who had been present at the punishment, told me the details, which I pass on. The first man condemned to the knout told the crowd in a loud voice that he swore he was innocent, that he did not know himself what the pain had forced him to answer; then taking off his shirt he turned his back to the crowd and said: 'Look, good Christians!'

A groan of horror ran through the crowd: his back was a dark-blue striped wound, and on that wound he was to be beaten with the knout. The murmurs and gloomy aspect of the assembled people made the police hurry. The executioners dealt the legal number of blows, while others did the branding and others riveted fetters, and the business seemed to be finished. But this scene had impressed the inhabitants; in every circle in Moscow people were talking about it. The Governor-General reported upon it to the Tsar. The Tsar ordered a *new* trial to be held, and the case of the incendiary who had protested before his punishment to be particularly inquired into.

Several months afterwards, I read in the papers that the Tsar, wishing to compensate two men who had been punished by the knout, though innocent, ordered them to be given two hundred roubles a lash, and to be provided with a special passport testify-

---

[2] A character in Gogol's *Dead Souls*. (*Tr.*)

ing to their innocence in spite of the branding. These two were the incendiary who had spoken to the crowd and one of his companions.

The affair of the fires in Moscow in 1834, cases similar to which occurred ten years later in various provinces, remains a mystery. That the fires were caused by arson there is no doubt; fire, 'the red cock,' is in general a very national means of revenge among us. One is continually hearing of the burning by peasants of their owners' houses, barns, and granaries. but what was the cause of the incendiarism in Moscow in 1834 no one knows, and least of all the members of the commission of inquiry.

Before 22nd August, Coronation Day, some practical jokers dropped letters in various places in which they informed the inhabitants that they need not bother about illuminations, that the place would be lit up.

The cowardly Moscow authorities were in a great fluster. The police station was filled with soldiers from early morning and a squadron of Uhlans were stationed in the yard. In the evening patrols on horseback and on foot were incessantly moving about the streets. Artillery was kept in readiness in the drill-shed. *Politsmeysters* galloped up and down with Cossacks and gendarmes. Prince Golitsyn himself rode about the town with his aides-de-camp. This military look of modest Moscow was odd, and affected the nerves. Till late at night I lay by the window under my watch-tower and looked into the yard. . . . The Uhlans who had been hurried to the place were sitting in groups, near their horses, and others were mounting. Officers were walking about, looking disdainfully at the police; aides-de-camp with yellow collars arrived continually, looking anxious and, after doing nothing, rode away again.

There were no fires.

After this the Tsar himself came to Moscow. He was displeased with the inquiry into our case which was only beginning, was displeased that we were left in the hands of the ordinary police, was displeased that the incendiaries had not been found—in a word, he was displeased with everything and everyone.

We soon felt His Majesty's proximity.

Krutitsky Barracks

THREE DAYS after the Tsar's arrival, late in the evening—all these things are done in darkness to avoid disturbing the public—a police officer came to me with orders to collect my belongings and go with him.

'Where to?' I asked.

'You will see,' was the policeman's witty and polite reply. After this, of course, I did not continue the conversation, but collected my things and set off.

We drove on and on for an hour and a half, and at length we passed the Simonov Monastery and stopped at a heavy stone gate, before which two gendarmes with carbines were pacing up and down. This was the Krutitsky Monastery, converted into a barracks for gendarmes.

I was led into a small office. The clerks, the adjutants, the officers were all in light blue. The officer on duty, in a helmet and full uniform, asked me to wait a little and even suggested that I should light the pipe I held in my hand. After this he proceeded to write a receipt of having received a prisoner; giving it to the policeman he went away and returned with another officer.

'Your room is ready,' said the latter, 'let us go.'

A gendarme held a candle for us, and we went down some stairs and took a few steps across the courtyard and passed through a small door into a long corridor lit by a single lantern; on both sides were little doors, one of which the officer on duty opened; it led into a tiny guardroom beyond which was a small, damp, cold room that smelt like a cellar. The officer with an aiguillette who had conducted me then turned to me, saying in French that he was '*désolé d'être dans la nécessité*' of searching my pockets, but military service, duty, obedience. . . . After this eloquent introduction, he very simply turned to the gendarme and indicated me with his eyes. The gendarme at once thrust an incredibly large and hairy hand into my pocket. I observed to the courteous officer that this was quite unnecessary, and that I would myself, if he liked, turn my pockets inside out without such violent measures; moreover, what could I have after six weeks' imprisonment?

'We know,' said the polite officer with an aiguillette, with a smile of inimitable self-complacency, 'how things are done at police stations.'

The officer on duty also smiled sarcastically. However, they told the gendarme he need only look. I pulled out everything I had.

'Pour your tobacco out on the table,' said the officer who was *désolé*.

In my tobacco pouch I had a penknife and a pencil wrapped up in paper; from the very beginning I had been thinking about them and, as I talked to the officer, I played with the tobacco pouch, until I got the penkife into my hand. I held it through the material of the pouch, and boldly shook the tobacco out on the table. The gendarme poured it in again. The penknife and pencil were saved; so there was a lesson for the gendarme with the aiguillette for his proud disdain of the ordinary police.

This incident put me in the best of humours and I began gaily scrutinising my new domain.

Some of the monks' cells, built three hundred years before and sunk into the earth, had been turned into secular cells for political prisoners.

In my room there was a bedstead without a mattress, and a little table, with a jug of water on it, and a chair beside it. A thin tallow candle was burning in a big copper candlestick. The damp and cold pierced to one's bones; the officer ordered the stove to be lit, and then they all went away. A soldier promised to bring some hay; meanwhile, putting my greatcoat under my head, I lay down on the bare bedstead and lit my pipe.

A minute later I noticed that the ceiling was covered with 'Prussian' beetles. They had seen no candle for a long time and were running from all directions to where the light fell, bustling about, jostling each other, falling on to the table, and then racing headlong, backwards and forwards, along the edge of it.

I disliked black beetles, as I did every sort of uninvited guest; my neighbours seemed to me horribly nasty, but there was nothing to be done: I could not begin by complaining about the black beetles and my nerves had to submit. Two or three days later, however, all the 'Prussians' had moved beyond the partition to the soldier's room, where it was warmer; only occasionally a stray beetle would sometimes run in, prick up his whiskers and scurry back to get warm.

Though I continually asked the gendarme, he still kept the stove closed. I began to feel unwell and giddy; I tried to get up and knock for the soldier; I did actually get up, but with this all that I remember comes to an end. . . .

When I came to myself I was lying on the floor with a splitting head ache. A tall grey-haired gendarme was standing with his arms folded, staring at me blankly, as in the well known bronze statuettes a dog stares at a tortoise.

'You have been finely suffocated, your honour,' he said, seeing that I had recovered consciousness. 'I've brought you horseradish with salt and kvas; I have already made you sniff it, now you must drink it up.'

I drank it, he lifted me up and laid me on the bed. I felt very ill; there were double windows and no pane in them that opened; the soldier went to the office to ask permission for me to go into the yard; the officer on duty told him to say that neither the colonel nor the adjutant was there, and that he could not take the responsibility. I had to remain in the room full of charcoal fumes.

I got used even to the Krutitsky Barracks, conjugating the Italian verbs and reading some wretched little books. At first my confinement was rather strict: at nine o'clock in the evening, at the last note of the bugle, a soldier came into my room, put out the candle and locked the door. From nine o'clock in the evening until eight next morning I had to remain in darkness. I have never been a great sleeper, and in prison, where I had no exercise, four hours' sleep was quite enough for me; and not to have a candle was a real punishment. Moreover, every quarter of an hour from each end of the corridor the sentries uttered a loud, prolonged shout, to show that they were awake.

A few weeks later Colonel Semënov (brother of the celebrated actress, afterwards Princess Gagarin) allowed them to leave me a candle, forbade anything to be hung over the window, which was below the level of the courtyard, so that the sentry could see everything that was being done in the cell, and gave orders that the sentries should not shout in the corridor.

Then the commandant gave us permission to have ink and to walk in the courtyard. Paper was given in a fixed amount on condition that none of the leaves should be torn. I was allowed once in twenty-four hours to walk, accompanied by a soldier and the officer on duty, in the yard, which was enclosed by a fence and surrounded by a cordon of sentries.

Life passed quietly and monotonously; the military punctuality gave it a mechanical regularity like the cæsura in verse. In the morning, with the assistance of the gendarme, I prepared coffee on the stove; about ten o'clock the officer on duty appeared in gauntlets with enormous cuffs, in a helmet and a greatcoat, clanking his sabre and bringing in with him several cubic feet of frost. At one the gendarme brought a dirty napkin and a bowl of soup, which he always held by the edge, so that his two thumbs were perceptibly cleaner than his fingers. We were tolerably well fed, but it must not be forgotten that we were charged two paper roubles a day for our keep, which in the course of nine months' imprisonment ran up to a considerable sum for persons of no means. The father of one prisoner said quite simply that he had no money; he received the cool reply that it would be stopped out of his salary. If he had not been receiving a salary, it is extremely probable that he would have been put in prison.

I ought to add that a rouble and a half was sent to Colonel Semënov at the barracks for our board from the commandant's office. There was almost a row about this; but the adjutants, who got the benefit of it, presented the gendarmes' division with boxes for first performances and benefit nights, and with that the matter ended.

After sunset there followed a complete stillness, which was not disturbed at all by the footsteps of the soldier crunching over the snow just outside the window, nor by the far-away calls of the sentries. As a rule I read until one o'clock and then put out my candle. Sleep carried me into freedom; sometimes it seemed as though I woke up feeling—ough, what horrible dreams I have had—prison and gendarmes—and I would rejoice that it was all a dream; and then there would suddenly be the clank of a sabre in the corridor, or the officer on duty would open the door, accompanied by a soldier with a lantern, or the sentry would shout in a voice that did not sound human, 'Who goes there?' or a bugle under my very window would rend the morning air with its shrill reveille. . . .

In moments of dullness, when I was disinclined to read, I would talk with the gendarmes who guarded me, particularly with the old fellow who had looked after me when I was overcome by the charcoal fumes. The colonel used, as a sign of favour, to free his old soldiers from regular discipline, and detach them for the easy duty of guarding a prisoner; a corporal, who was a spy and a rogue, was set over them. Five or six gendarmes made up the whole staff.

The old man, of whom I am speaking, was a simple, good-hearted creature, devotedly grateful for any kind action, of which he had probably not had many in his life. He had been in the campaign of 1812 and his chest was covered with medals; he had served his full time and remained in the army of his own free will, not knowing where to go.

'Twice,' he told me, 'I wrote to my home in Mogilëv province, but I got no answer, so it seems as though there were none of my people left: and so it would be painful to go home; one would stay there a bit and then wander off like a lost soul, following one's nose to beg one's bread.'

How barbarously and mercilessly the army is organised in Russia with its monstrous term of service![1] A man's personality is everywhere sacrificed without the slightest mercy and with no reward.

Old Filimonov had pretensions to a knowledge of German which he had studied in winter quarters after the taking of Paris. He very felicitously adapted German words to the Russian spirit, calling a horse, *fert*, eggs, *yery*, fish, *pish*, oats, *ober*, pancakes, *pankukhi*.

There was a naïveté about his stories which made me sad and thoughtful. In Moldavia during the Turkish campaign of 1805 he had been in the company of a captain, the most good-natured man in the world, who looked after every soldier as though he were his own son and was always foremost in action.

'A Moldavian girl captivated him and then we saw our captain was worried, for, do you know, he noticed that the girl was making up to another officer. So one day he called me and a comrade—a splendid soldier, he had both his legs blown off afterwards at Maly-Yaroslavets—and began telling us how the Moldavian girl had wronged him and asked would we care to help him and give her a lesson. "To be sure, sir," we said, "we are always glad to do our best for your honour." He thanked us and pointed out the house in which the officer lived, and he says, "You wait on the bridge at night; she will certainly go to him. You seize her without any noise and drop her in the river." "We can do that, your honour," we tell him, and my comrade and I got a sack ready. We were sitting there, when towards midnight there's the Moldavian girl running up. "Why, are you in a hurry, madam?" we say, and we give her one on the head. She never uttered a squeal, poor dear, and we popped her into the sack and over into the river; and next day our captain goes to

---

[1] Service in the Russian army at this time, for those who were not officers, was for twenty-five years, and soldiers with bad records might be made to serve for life. Conscription was not general, and exemption could be bought. Under Alexander II, in 1874, the term was reduced to seven years; conscription became general and exemption could not be purchased. All recruits had to start in the ranks. (*R.*)

the other officer and says: "Don't you be angry with your Moldavian girl: we detained her a little, and now she is in the river, and I am ready to take a turn with you," he says, "with the sabre or with pistols, which you like." So they hacked at each other. The officer gave our captain a great stab in the chest, and the poor, dear man wasted away and a few months later gave up his soul to God.'

'And the Moldavian girl was drowned, then?' I asked.

'Yes, sir, she was drowned,' answered the soldier.

I looked with surprise at the childish unconcern with which the old gendarme told me this story. And he, as though guessing what I felt, or thinking about it for the first time, added, to soothe me and conciliate his conscience:

'A heathen woman, sir, as good as not christened, that sort of people.'

On every Imperial holiday the gendarmes are given a glass of vodka. The sergeant allowed Filimonov to refuse his share for five or six times and to receive them all at once. Filimonov scored on a wooden tally-stick how many glasses he had missed, and on the most important holidays he would go for them. He would pour this vodka into a bowl, crumble bread into it and eat it with a spoon. After this dish he would light a big pipe with a tiny mouthpiece, filled with tobacco of incredible strength which he used to cut up himself, and therefore rather wittily called 'sans-cracher.' As he smoked he would fold himself up on a little window-seat, bent double—there were no chairs in the soldiers' rooms—and sing his song:

> The maids came out into the meadow,
> Where was an anthill and a flower.

As he got more drunk the words would become more inarticulate until he fell asleep. Imagine the health of a man who had been twice wounded and at over sixty could still survive such carousals!

Before I leave these Flemish barrack scenes à la Wouverman and à la Callot, and this prison gossip, which is like the reminiscences of all prisoners, I shall say a few more words about the officers.

The greater number among them were quite decent men, by no means spies, but men who had come by chance into the gendarmes' division. Young gentlemen with little or no education and no fortune, who did not know where to lay their heads, they were gendarmes because they had found no other job. They performed their duties with military exactitude, but I never observed a shadow of zeal in any of them, except the adjutant, but that, of course, is why he was the adjutant.

When the officers had got to know me, they did all such little things as they could to alleviate my lot, and it would be a sin to complain of them.

One young officer told me that in 1831 he had been sent to find and arrest a Polish landowner, who was in hiding somewhere in the neighbourhood of his estate. He was charged with having relations with emissaries.[2] From evidence that the officer collected he found out where the landowner must be hidden, went there with his company, put a cordon round the house and entered it with two gendarmes. The house was empty—they walked through the rooms, peeping into everything and found no one anywhere, but yet a few trifles showed clearly that there had recently been people in the house. Leaving the gendarmes below, the young man went a second time up to the attic; looking round attentively he saw a little door which led to a closet or some small room; the door was fastened on the inside; he pushed it with his foot, it opened, and a tall, handsome woman stood before it. She pointed in silence to a man who held in his arms a girl of about twelve, who was almost unconscious. This was the Pole and his wife and child. The officer was embarrassed. The tall woman noticed this and asked him:

'And will you have the cruelty to destroy them?'

The officer apologised, saying the usual commonplaces about the inviolability of his military oath, and his duty, and, at last, in despair, seeing that his words had no effect, ended with the question:

'What am I to do?'

The woman looked proudly at him and said, pointing to the door:

'Go down and say there is no one here.'

'Upon my word, I don't know how it happened,' said the officer, 'or what was the matter with me, but I went down from the attic and told the corporal to collect the men. A couple of hours later we were diligently looking for him on another estate, while he was making his way over the frontier. Well—woman! I admit it!'

Nothing in the world can be more narrow-minded and more inhuman than wholesale condemnation of whole classes of

---

[2] Of the Polish government formed at the time of the rising of 1830–1. (*A.S.*)

people by a label, by a moral card-index, by the leading characteristics of their trade. Names are dreadful things. Jean-Paul Richter says with extraordinary certainty: 'If a child tells a lie, frighten him with his bad conduct, tell him he has told a lie, but don't tell him he is a *liar*. You destroy his moral confidence in himself by defining him as a liar. "That is a murderer," we are told, and at once we fancy a hidden dagger, a brutal expression, black designs, as though murder were a permanent employment, the trade of the man who has happened once in his life to kill someone. One cannot be a spy or trade in the vice of others and remain an honest man, but one may be an officer in the gendarmes without losing all human dignity; just as one may very often find womanliness, a tender heart and even nobility of character in the unhappy victims of "public incontinence." '

I have an aversion for people who cannot, or will not, or do not take the trouble to go beyond the name, to step over the barrier of crime, over a confused, false position, but either modestly turn aside, or harshly thrust it all away from them. This is usually done by dry, abstract natures, egoistic and revolting in their purity, or base, vulgar natures who have not yet managed, or have not needed, to exhibit themselves in practice. In sympathy they are at home in the dirty depths into which others have sunk.

Investigation and Sentence

BUT WITH ALL THIS what of our *case*, what of the investigation and the trial?

They were no more successful in the new commission than in the old. The police had been on our track for a long time, but in their zeal and impatience could not wait to find a sensible occasion, and did something silly. They had sent a retired officer called Skaryatka to lead us on and expose us; he made acquaintance with almost all of our circle, but we very soon guessed what he was and held aloof from him. Other young men, for the most part students, had not been so cautious, but these others had no serious connection with us.

One student, on completing his studies, had given a lunch-party to his friends on 24th June, 1834. Not one of us was at the festivity: indeed none of us had been invited. The young men drank too much, played the fool, danced the mazurka, and among other things sang Sokolovsky's[1] well-known song on the accession of Nicholas:

> *The Emperor of Russia*
> *Has gone to realms above,*
> *The operating surgeon*
> *Slit his belly open.*
>
> *The Government is weeping*
> *And all the people weep;*
> *There's coming to rule over us*
> *Constantine the freak.*
>
> *But to the King of Heaven,*
> *Almighty God above,*
> *Our Tsar of blessed memory*
> *Has handed a petition.*
>
> *When He read the paper,*
> *Moved to pity, God*
> *Gave us Nicholas instead,*
> *The blackguard, the . . . [2]*

In the evening Skaryatka *suddenly* remembered that it was his name-day, told a tale of how he had made a profit on the sale of a horse, and invited the students to his quarters, promising them a dozen of champagne. They all went; the champagne appeared, and the host, staggering, proposed that they should once more sing Sokolovsky's song. In the middle of the singing the door opened and Tsynsky with the police walked in. All this was crude, stupid, clumsy, and at the same time unsuccessful.

The police wanted to catch *us;* they were looking for external evidence to involve in the case some five or six men whom they had already marked, and only succeeded in catching twenty innocent persons.

It is not easy, however, to disconcert the Russian police. Within a fortnight they arrested us as *implicated* in the supper case. In Sokolovsky's possession they found letters from Satin, in

---

[1] It is probable that A. I. Polezhayev was the author of this song. (*A.S.*)
[2] The epithet in the last line is left to the imagination in Russian also. (*Tr.*) The word is probably *svoloch* ('off-scourings,' 'scum'; the Russian word is most opprobrious). (*R.*)

Satin's possession letters from Ogarëv, and in Ogarëv's possession my letters. Nevertheless, nothing was discovered. The first investigation failed. For the greater success of the second commission, the Tsar sent from Petersburg the choicest of the inquisitors, A. F. Golitsyn.

This breed of person is rare in Russia. It is represented among us by Mordvinov, the famous head of the Third Division, Pelikan, the rector of Vilna, and a few accommodating Baltic Germans and Poles[3] who have ratted.

But unluckily for the inquisition Staal, the Commandant of Moscow, was appointed the first member. Staal, a straightforward military man, a gallant old general, went into the case and found that it consisted of two circumstances that had no connection with each other: the affair of the supper party, which ought to have been punished by law, and the arrest, God knew why, of persons whose only guilt, so far as could be seen, lay in certain half-expressed opinions, for which it would be both difficult and absurd to try them.

Staal's opinion did not please Golitsyn junior. The dispute between them became caustic; the old warrior flared up, struck the floor with his sabre and said:

'Instead of ruining people, you had better draw up a report on the advisability of closing all the schools and universities; that would warn other unfortunates; however, you can do what you like, but you must do it without me. I shan't set foot in the commission again.'

With these words the old gentleman hastened out of the room. The Tsar was informed of this the same day.

In the morning when the commandant appeared with his report, the Tsar asked him why he would not attend the commission; Staal told him why.

'What nonsense!' replied the Tsar, 'to quarrel with Golitsyn, for shame! I trust you will attend the commission as before.'

'Sire,' answered Staal, 'spare my grey hairs. I have lived to reach them without the slightest stain on my honour. My zeal is known to Your Majesty, my blood, the remnant of my days are yours, but this is a question of my honour—my conscience revolts against what is being done in the commission.'

The Tsar frowned. Staal bowed himself out, and from that time was not once present in the commission.

---

[3] Among those who have distinguished themselves in this line of late years is the famous Liprandi, who drew up a scheme for founding an Academy of Espionage (1858).

This anecdote, the truth of which is not open to the slightest doubt, throws great light on the character of Nicholas. How was it that it did not enter his head that if a man whom he could not but respect, a brave warrior, an old man full of merit, so obstinately besought him to spare his honour, the business could not be quite clean? He should have done no less than require Golitsyn to present himself and insist on Staal's explaining the matter before him. He did not do this, but gave orders that we should be confined more strictly.

When Staal had gone there were only enemies of the accused in the committee, presided over by a simple-hearted old man, Prince S. M. Golitsyn, who after nine months knew as little about the case as he had nine months before it began. He preserved a dignified silence, very rarely put in a word, and at the end of an examination invariably asked:

'May we let him go?'

'We may,' Golitsyn junior would answer, and the senior would say with dignity to the prisoner,

'You may go.'

My first examination lasted four hours.

The questions were of two kinds. The object of the first was to discover a manner of thinking 'not akin to the spirit of the government, revolutionary opinions, imbued with the pernicious doctrines of Saint-Simon,' as Golitsyn junior and the auditor Oransky expressed it.

These questions were easy, but they were hardly questions. In the papers and letters that had been seized the opinions were fairly simply expressed; the questions could properly only relate to the material fact of whether a man had or had not written the words in question. The committee thought it necessary to add to every written phrase, 'How do you explain the following passage in your letter?'

Of course it was useless to explain; I wrote evasive and empty phrases in reply. In one letter the auditor discovered the phrase: 'All constitutional charters lead to nothing: they are contracts between a master and his slaves; the task is not to make things better for the slaves, but that there should be no slaves.' When I had to explain this phrase I observed that I saw no obligation to defend constitutional government, and that, if I had defended it, it would have been charged against me.

'A constitutional form of government may be attacked from two sides,' Golitsyn junior observed in his nervous, hissing voice; 'you do not attack it from the monarchical point of view, or you would not talk about slaves.'

'In that I err in company with the Empress Catherine II, who ordered that her subjects should not be called *slaves*.'

Golitsyn, breathless with anger at this ironical reply, said:

'You seem to imagine that we are assembled here to conduct scholastic arguments, that you are defending a thesis in the university.'

'With what object, then, do you ask for explanations?'

'You appear not to understand what is wanted of you.'

'I do not understand.'

'What obstinacy there is in *all of them*,' Golitsyn senior, the president, added, shrugging his shoulders and glancing at Shubinsky, the colonel of gendarmes. I smiled.

'Just like Ogarëv,' the good-hearted president wound up.

A pause followed. The commission was assembled in Golitsyn senior's library, and I turned to the bookshelves and began examining the books. Among others there was an edition in many volumes of the memoirs of the Duc de Saint-Simon.

'Here,' I said, turning to the president, 'is it not unjust? I am being tried on account of Saint-Simonism, while you, prince, have twenty volumes of his works.'

As the good old man had never read anything in his life, he could not think what to answer. But Golitsyn junior looked at me with the eyes of a viper and asked:

'Don't you see that those are the memoirs of the Duc de Saint-Simon at the time of Louis XIV?'

The president with a smile gave me a nod that signified, 'Well, my boy, a bit flashy, that remark of yours, wasn't it?' and said,

'You may go.'

While I was in the doorway the president asked:

'Is he the one who wrote about Peter I, that thing you were showing me?'

'Yes,' answered Shubinsky.

I stopped.

'*Il a des moyens*,' observed the president.

'So much the worse. Poison in clever hands is all the more dangerous,' added the inquisitor; 'a very pernicious and quite incorrigible young man.'

My sentence lay in those words.

A propos Saint-Simon. When the *politsmeyster* seized Ogarëv's books and papers, he laid aside a volume of Thiers' *History of the French Revolution*, then found a second volume . . . a third . . . an eighth. At last he could bear it no longer, and said:

'Good Lord! what a number of revolutionary books . . . and here is another,' he added, giving the policeman Cuvier's *Discours sur les révolutions du globe terrestre.*

The second kind of question was more confusing. In them various police traps and inquisitional tricks were made use of to confuse, entangle, and involve one in contradictions. Hints of information given by others and different moral torments were employed. It is not worth-while to tell them: it is enough to say that all their devices could not produce a single adequate confrontation among the four of us.[4]

After I had received my last question, I was sitting alone in the little room in which we wrote. All at once the door opened and Golitsyn junior walked in with a gloomy and anxious face.

'I have come,' he said, 'to have a few words with you before your evidence is completed. My late father's long connection with yours makes me take a special interest in you. You are young and may still make a career; to do so you must clear yourself of this affair . . . and fortunately it depends on yourself. Your father has taken your arrest deeply to heart and is living now in the hope that you will be released: Prince Sergey Mikhaylovich and I have just been speaking about it and we are genuinely ready to do all we can; give us the means of assisting you.'

I saw the drift of his words; the blood rushed to my head; I gnawed my pen with vexation.

He went on:

'You are going straight under the white strap, or to the fortress; on the way you will kill your father; he will not survive the day when he sees you in the grey overcoat of a soldier.'

I tried to say something but he interrupted me:

'I know what you want to say. Have a little patience! That you had designs against the government is evident. To merit the mercy of the Monarch you must give proofs of your penitence. You are obstinate, you give evasive answers and from a false sense of honour you spare men of whom we know more than you do and *who have not been so discreet as you,*[5] you will not help them, and they will drag you down with them to ruin. Write a letter to the commission, simply, frankly; say that you feel your guilt, that you were led away by your youth, name the unfortu-

---

[4] A. I. Herzen, N. P. Ogarëv, N. M. Satin and I. A. Obolensky. (*A.S.*)
[5] I need not say that this was a barefaced lie, a shameful police trap.

nate, misguided men who have led you astray. . . . Are you willing at this easy price to redeem your future and your father's life?'

'I know nothing and have not a word to add to my evidence,' I replied.

Golitsyn got up and said coldly:

'Ah, so you won't: it is not our fault!'

With that the examination ended.

In the January or February of 1835 I was before the commission for the last time. I was summoned to read through my answers, to add to them if I wished, and to sign them. Only Shubinsky was present. When I had finished reading them over I said to him:

'I should like to know what charge can be made against a man upon these questions and upon these answers? What article of the Code are you applying to me?'

'*The Code of laws is drawn up for crimes of a different kind,*' observed the light-blue colonel.

'That's a different point. After reading over all these literary exercises, I cannot believe that that makes up the whole business for which I have been in prison over six months.'

'But do you really imagine,' replied Shubinsky, 'that we believed you, that you have not formed a secret society?'

'Where is the society?'

'It is your luck that no traces have been found, that you have not succeeded in achieving anything. We stopped you in time, that is, to speak plainly, we have saved you.'

It was the story of the locksmith's wife and her husband in Gogol's *Inspector General* over again.

When I had signed, Shubinsky rang the bell and told them to summon the priest. The priest came up and wrote below my signature that all the evidence had been given by me voluntarily and without any compulsion. I need hardly say that he had not been present at the examination, and that he had not even the decency to ask me how it had been. (It was my impartial witness outside the gate again!)

At the end of the investigation, prison conditions were somewhat relaxed. Members of our families could obtain permits for interviews. So passed another two months.

In the middle of March our sentence was confirmed. No one knew what it was: some said we were being sent to the Caucasus, others that we should be taken to Bobruysk, others again hoped that we should all be released (this was the sentence which was proposed by Staal and sent separately by him to the

Tsar; he advised that our imprisonment should be taken as equivalent to punishment).

At last, on 31st March, we were all assembled at Prince Golitsyn's to hear our sentence. This was a gala day for us. We were seeing each other for the first time since our arrest.

Noisily, gaily embracing and shaking hands, we stood surrounded by a cordon of gendarme and garrison officers. This meeting cheered us all up; there was no end to the questions and the anecdotes.

Sokolovsky was present, pale and somewhat thinner, but as brilliantly amusing as ever.

The author of *The Creation of the World* and of *Khever* and other rather good poems, had much poetic talent by nature, but was not wildly original enough to dispense with development, nor sufficiently well-educated to develop. A charming rake, a poet in life, he was not in the least a political man. He was amusing, likeable, a merry companion in merry moments, a *bon vivant*, fond of having a good time—as we all were—perhaps rather more so.

Having dropped accidentally from a carousel into prison, Sokolovsky behaved extremely well; he grew up in confinement. The auditor of the commission, a pedant, a pietist, a detective, who had grown thin and grey-headed in envy, covetousness and slander, not daring from devotion to the throne and to religion to understand the last two verses of his poem in their grammatical sense, asked Sokolovsky,

'To whom do those insolent words at the end of the song refer?'

'Rest assured,' said Sokolovsky, 'not to the Tsar, and I would particularly draw your attention to that *extenuating* circumstance.'

The auditor shrugged his shoulders, lifted up his eyes unto the hills and after gazing a long time at Sokolovsky in silence took a pinch of snuff.

Sokolovsky was arrested in Petersburg and sent to Moscow without being told where he was being taken. Our police often perpetrate similar jests, and to no purpose at all. It is the form their poetical fancy takes. There is no occupation in the world so prosaic, so revolting that it has not its artistic yearnings for superfluous sumptuousness and decoration. Sokolovsky was taken straight to prison and put into a dark closet. Why was he put in prison while we were kept in various barracks?

He had two or three shirts with him and nothing else at all. In England every convict on being brought into prison is at once put into a bath, but with us they take every precaution against cleanliness.

If Dr Haas had not sent Sokolovsky a bundle of his own linen he would have been crusted with dirt.

Dr Haas was a very original eccentric. The memory of this 'crazy, deranged' man ought not to be choked among the weeds of the official necrologies describing the virtues of persons of the first two grades, which are not discovered until their bodies have rotted away.

A thin little, waxen-looking old man, in a black swallow-tail coat, breeches, black silk stockings and buckled shoes, he looked as though he had just come out of some drama of the eighteenth century. In this *grand gala* fit for funerals and weddings, and in the agreeable climate of fifty-nine degrees north latitude, Haas used every week to drive to the stage-post on the Sparrow Hills when a batch of convicts were being sent off. In the capacity of prison doctor he had access to them; he used to go to inspect them and always brought with him a basket full of all manner of things, victuals and dainties of all sorts—walnuts, cakes, oranges and apples for the women. This aroused the wrath and indignation of the *philanthropic* ladies who were afraid of giving pleasure by their philanthropy, and afraid of being more charitable than was necessary to save the convicts from dying of hunger and the ringing frost.

But Haas was not easy to move, and after listening mildly to reproaches for his 'foolish spoiling of the female convicts,' would rub his hands and say:

'Be so kind to see, gracious madam: a bit of bread, a copper everyone gives them; but a sweet or an orange for long they will not see; this no one gives them, that I can from your words deduce; I do them this pleasure for that it will not a long time be repeated.'

Haas lived in the hospital. A sick man came before dinner to consult him. Haas examined him and went into his study to write some prescription. On his return he found neither the patient nor the silver forks and spoons which had been lying on the table. Haas called the porter and asked him if any one had come in besides the sick man. The porter grasped the situation, rushed out and returned a minute later with the spoons and the patient, whom he had stopped with the help of another hospital porter. The rascal fell at the doctor's feet and besought him for mercy. Haas was overcome with embarrassment.

'Go for the police,' he said to one of the porters, and to the other, 'and you send a clerk here at once.'

The porters, pleased at the discovery, at the victory and at their share in the business altogether, ran off, and Haas, taking advantage of their absence, said to the thief,

"You are a false man, you have deceived and tried to rob me. God will judge you . . . and now run quickly out of the back gate before the porters come back . . . but stop: perhaps you haven't a farthing: here is half a rouble, but try to reform your soul; from God you will not escape as from a watchman.'

At this even the members of his own household protested. But the incorrigible doctor maintained his point:

'Theft is a great vice; but I know the police, I know how they torment them—they will question him, they will flog him; to give up one's neighbour to the lash is a far worse crime; besides, how can one tell: perhaps what I have done may touch his heart!'

His domestics shook their heads and said, '*Er hat einen Raptus*'; the benevolent ladies said, '*C'est un brave homme, mais ce n'est pas tout à fait en règle, cela,*' and tapped their foreheads. But Haas rubbed his hands and went his own way.

. . . Sokolovsky had hardly finished his anecdotes, when several others at once began to tell theirs; it was as though we had all returned from a long journey—there was no end to the questions, jokes, and witticisms.

Physically, Satin had suffered more than the rest; he was thin and had lost part of his hair. He had been at his mother's in the country in the Tambov province when he heard that we had been arrested, and at once set off for Moscow, for fear that his mother should be alarmed by a visit of the gendarmes; but he caught cold on the way and reached home in a high fever. The police found him in bed, and it was impossible to move him to the police station. He was placed under arrest at home, a soldier from the police station was put on guard inside the bedroom and the local police superintendent was set to act as a male nurse by the patient's bedside, so that on coming to himself after his delirium he met the *attentive* gaze of the one, or the wizened phiz of the other.

At the beginning of the winter he was moved to the Lefortovsky Hospital; it appeared there was not a single empty *private* room for a prisoner, but such trifles were not deemed worth considering; a corner partitioned off, *with no stove*, was found, the sick man was put in this southern verandah and a sentry posted to watch him. What the temperature in this stone closet was like in winter may be judged from the fact that the sentry was so benumbed with cold at night that he would go into the corridor to warm himself at the stove, begging Satin not to tell the duty officer of it.

The hospital authorities themselves saw that such tropical quarters were impossible in a latitude so near the pole, and moved Satin to a room near the one in which frost-bitten patients were rubbed.

Before we had time to describe and listen to half our adventures, the adjutants began suddenly bustling about, the gendarme officers drew themselves up, and the policemen set themselves to rights: the door opened solemnly and little Prince Sergey Mikhaylovich Golitsyn walked in *en grande tenue* with a ribbon across his shoulder; Tsynsky was in court uniform, and even the auditor, Oransky, had put on some sort of pale-green civil-military uniform for the joyful occasion. The commandant, of course, had not come.

Meanwhile the noise and laughter had risen to such a pitch that the auditor came menacingly into the room and observed that loud conversation and, above all, laughter, showed a subversive disrespect to the will of His Majesty, which we were to hear.

The doors were opened. Officers divided us into three groups: in the first was Sokolovsky, the painter Utkin, and an officer called Ibayev; we were in the second; in the third, the *tutti frutti*.

The sentence regarding the first category was read separately. It was terrible; condemned for *lèse-majesté* they were sent to the Schlüsselburg for an indefinite period. All three listened to this savage sentence like heroes.

When Oransky, drawling to give himself importance, read, with pauses, that for '*lèse-majesté* and insulting the Most August Family, *et cetera*,' Sokolovsky observed:

'Well, I never insulted the family.'

Among his papers besides that poem were found some resolutions written in jest as though by the Grand Duke Mikhail Pavlovich, with intentional mistakes in spelling, and those orthographical errors helped to convict him.

Tsynsky, to show that he could be free and easy and affable, said to Sokolovsky after the sentence:

'I say, you've been in Schlüsselburg before?'

'Last year,' Sokolovsky answered promptly, 'as though I felt in my heart what was coming, I drank a bottle of Madeira there.'

Two years later Utkin died in the fortress. Sokolovsky, half dead, was released and sent to the Caucasus; he died at Pyatigorsk. Some remnant of shame and conscience led the government after the death of two to transfer the third to Perm. Ibayev's death was *sui generis:* he had become a mystic.

Utkin, 'a free artist confined in prison,' as he described himself in his signature to questionnaires, was a man of forty; he had never taken part in any kind of politics, but, being of a generous and impulsive temperament, he gave free rein to his tongue in the commission and was abrupt and rude to the members of it. For this he was *done to death* in a damp cell, in which the water trickled down the walls.

Ibayev's greater guilt lay in his epaulettes. Had he not been an officer, he would never have been so punished. The man had happened to be present at *some* supper party, had probably drunk and sung like all the rest, but certainly neither more nor louder than the others.

Our turn came. Oransky wiped his spectacles, cleared his throat, and began reverently announcing His Majesty's will. In this it was represented that the Tsar, after examining the report of the commission and taking into special consideration the youth of the criminals, *commanded that we should not be brought to trial*, but that we should be notified that by law we ought, as men convicted of *lèse-majesté* by singing seditious songs, to lose our lives or, in virtue of other laws, to be transported to penal servitude for life. Instead of this, the Tsar in his infinite mercy forgave the greater number of the guilty, leaving them in their present abode under the supervision of the police. The more guilty he commanded to be put under reformatory treatment, which consisted in being sent to civilian duty for an indefinite period in remote provinces, to live under the superintendence of the local authorities.

It appeared that there were six of the 'more guilty': Ogarëv, Satin, Lakhtin, Obolensky, Sorokin, and I. I was to be sent to Perm. Among those condemned was Lakhtin, who had not been arrested at all. When he was summoned to the commission to hear the sentence, he supposed that it was as a warning, to be punished by hearing how others were punished. The story was that someone of Prince Golitsyn's circle, being angry with Lakhtin's wife, had obliged him with this agreeable surprise. A man of delicate health, he died three years later in exile.

When Oransky had finished reading, Colonel Shubinsky made a speech. In choice language and in the style of Lomonosov he informed us that it was due to the good offices of the noble gentleman who had presided at the committee that the Tsar had been so merciful.

Shubinsky waited for all of us to thank Prince Golitsyn, but this did not come off.

Some of those who were pardoned nodded, stealing a stealthy glance at us as they did so.

We stood with folded arms, making not the slightest sign that our hearts were touched by the Imperial and princely mercy.

Then Shubinsky thought of another dodge and, addressing Ogarëv, said:

'You are going to Penza; do you imagine that that is by chance? Your father is lying paralysed at Penza and the prince besought the Tsar to designate that town for you, that your being near might to some extent alleviate for him the blow of your exile. Do you not think you have reason to thank the prince?'

There was no help for it: Ogarëv made a slight bow. This was what they were trying to get.

The good-natured old man was pleased at this, and next, I do not know why, he summoned me. I stepped forward with the devout intention of not thanking him, whatever he or Shubinsky might say; besides, I was being sent farther away than any and to the nastiest town.

'You are going to Perm,' said Prince Golitsyn.

I said nothing. He was disconcerted and, for the sake of saying something, he added,

'I have an estate there.'

'Would you care to send some commission through me to your steward?' I asked with a smile.

'I do not give commissions to people like you—*Carbonari*,' added the resourceful old man.

'Then what do you wish of me?'

'Nothing.'

'I thought you called me.'

'You may go,' Shubinsky interposed.

'Allow me,' I replied, 'since I am here, to remind you that you told me, Colonel, last time I was before the commission, that no one accused me of being connected with the supper-party affair. Yet in the sentence it is stated that I was one of those guilty in connection with that affair. There is some mistake here.'

'Do you wish to object to His Majesty's decision?' observed

Shubinsky. 'You had better take care that Perm is not changed to something worse. I shall order your words to be taken down.'

'I meant to ask you to do so. In the sentence the words occur "on the report of the commission": I am protesting against your report and not against the will of His Majesty. I appeal to the prince: there was no question in my case of a supper party or of songs, was there?'

'As though you did not know,' said Shubinsky, beginning to turn pale with wrath, 'that you are ten times more guilty than those who were at the supper party. He, now'—he pointed to one of those who had been pardoned—'in a state of intoxication sang some filthy song, but afterwards he begged forgiveness on his knees with tears. But you are still far from any penitence.'

The gentleman at whom the colonel pointed said nothing, but hung his head and flushed crimson. . . . It was a good lesson: so he should, after behaving so vilely! . . .

'Excuse me, it is not the point whether my guilt is great or not,' I went on; 'but, if I am a murderer, I don't want to be considered a thief. I don't want it to be said of me, even in justification, that I did something in a "state of intoxication," as you expressed yourself just now.'

'If I had a son, my own son, who showed such stubbornness, I would myself beg the Tsar to send him to Siberia.'

At this point the *oberpolitsmeyster* interposed some incoherent nonsense. It is a pity that Golitsyn junior was not present, for it would have been an opportunity for his eloquence.

It all ended, of course, in nothing.

Lakhtin went up to Prince Golitsyn and asked that his departure might be deferred.

'My wife is with child,' he said.

'I am not responsible for that,' answered Golitsyn.

A wild beast, a mad dog when it bites, looks in earnest and puts its tail between its legs, but this crazy grandee, aristocrat, though he had the reputation of a good-natured man, was not ashamed to make this vulgar joke.

We stayed for a quarter of an hour more in the room, and, in spite of the zealous exhortations of the gendarme and police officers, embraced one another warmly and took a long farewell. Except Obolensky I saw none of them again until I came back from Vyatka.

Departure was before us.

Prison had been a continuation of our past; but our departure into the wilds was a complete break with it.

Our youthful existence in our circle of friends was over.

Our exile would probably last several years. Where and how should we meet, and should we ever meet? . . .

I regretted my old life, and I had to leave it so abruptly . . . without saying good-bye. I had no hope of seeing Ogarëv. Two of my friends had succeeded in seeing me during the last few days, but that was not enough for me.

If I could but once again see my youthful comforter and press her hand, as I had pressed it in the graveyard. . . . I longed both to take leave of my past and to greet my future in her person. . . .

We did see each other for a few minutes on the 9th of April, 1835, on the day before I was sent off into exile.

For years I kept that day sacred in my memory; it was one of the happiest moments in my life.

Why must the thought of that day and of all the bright days of my past bring back so much that is frightening? . . . The grave, the wreath of dark-red roses, two children holding my hand—torches, the crowd of exiles, the moon, the warm sea under the mountainside, the words that I did not understand and that wrung my heart. . . .

All is over![6]

Perm

❖   ❖   ❖

In Perm I was taken straight to the governor. He was holding a great reception; his daughter was being married that day to an officer. He insisted on my going in, and I had to present myself to the whole society of Perm in a dirty travelling coat, covered with mud and dust. The governor, after talking all sorts of non-sense, forbade me to make acquaintance with the Polish exiles and ordered me to come to him in a few days, saying that then he would find me work in the office.

This governor was a Little Russian; he did not oppress the exiles, and altogether was a harmless person. He was improving

---

[6] Herzen is recalling the burial of his wife in 1852. (*A.S.*)

his fortune somehow on the sly, like a mole working unseen underground; he was adding grain to grain and laying by a little something for a rainy day.

From some inexplicable idea of security and good order, he used to command all the exiles who lived in Perm to appear before him at ten o'clock in the morning on Saturdays. He would come out with his pipe and a list, verify whether we were all present, and, if anyone was not, send a policeman to find out the reason; then, after saying scarcely anything to anyone, he would dismiss us. In this way in his reception-room I became acquainted with all the Polish exiles, whose acquaintance he had warned me I must not make.

The day after my arrival the gendarme went away, and for the first time since my arrest I found myself at liberty.

At liberty . . . in a little town on the Siberian border, with no experience, with no conception of the environment in which I had to live.

From the nursery I had passed into the lecture-room, from the lecture-room to a circle of friends—it had all been theories, dreams, my own people, no active relationships. Then prison to let it all settle. Practical contact with life was beginning here near the Ural Mountains.

It manifested itself at once; the day after my arrival I went with a porter from the governor's office to look for a lodging and he took me to a big house of one storey. However much I explained that I was looking for a very small house or, still better, part of a house, he obstinately insisted on my going in.

The landlady made me sit down on her sofa and, learning that I came from Moscow, asked if I had seen Mr Kabrit in Moscow. I told her that I had never even heard the name.

'How is that?' observed the old woman; 'I mean Kabrit,' and she mentioned his Christian name and his father's name. 'Upon my word, sir, why, he was our Whist-Governor!'

'But I have been nine months in prison; perhaps that is why I have not heard of him,' I said, smiling.

'Maybe that is it. So you will take the house, my good sir?'

'It is too big, much too big; I told the man so.'

'You can't have too much of a good thing,' she said.

'That is so, but you will want more rent for so much of a good thing.'

'Ah, my good sir, but who has talked to you about my price? I have not said a word about it yet.'

'But I know that such a house cannot be let cheaply.'

'How much will you give?'

To get rid of her, I said that I would not give more than three hundred and fifty paper roubles.

'Well, I would be thankful for that. Bid the man bring your bits of trunks, my dear, and take a glass of Teneriffe.'

Her price seemed to me fabulously low. I took the house, and, just as I was on the point of going, she stopped me:

'I forgot to ask you: are you going to keep your own cow?'

'Good Heavens, no!' I answered, almost appalled by her question.

'Well, then, I will let you have cream.'

I went away thinking with horror where I was and what I was that I could be considered capable of keeping my own cow. But before I had time to look round, the governor informed me that I was being transferred to Vyatka because another exile who had been allotted to Vyatka had asked to be transferred to Perm, where he had relations. The governor wanted me to leave the next day. This was impossible: thinking to remain some time in Perm, I had bought all sorts of things, and I had to sell them even at half-price. After various evasive answers, the governor gave me permission to remain forty-eight hours, exacting a promise that I would not seek an opportunity of seeing the other exiles.

❖   ❖   ❖

On the day after we left Perm there was a heavy, unceasing downpour of rain ever since dawn, such as is common in forest districts, which lasted all day; about two o'clock we reached a very poor Votyak village. There was no house at the posting-station. Votyaks[1] (who could not read or write) performed the duties of overseers, looked through the permit for horses, saw whether there were two seals or one, shouted 'Ayda, ayda!' and harnessed the horses twice as quickly, I need hardly say, as it would have been done had there been a superintendent. I wanted to get dry and warm and to have something to eat. Before we reached the village the Perm gendarme had agreed to my suggestion that we should rest for a couple of hours. When I went into the stifling hut, without a chimney, and found that it was absolutely impossible to get anything, that there was not

---

[1] The Votyaks are a Mongolian tribe, found in Siberia and Eastern Russia; the geographical 'Vyatka' is a cognate noun. The people are known nowadays as Udmurty. (*Tr.*)

even a pot-house for five versts, I regretted our decision and was on the point of asking for horses.

While I was thinking whether to go on or not to go on, a soldier came in and reported that an escorting officer had sent to invite me to a cup of tea.

'With the greatest pleasure. Where is your officer?'

'In the hut near by, your honour,' and the soldier made the familiar left-about-turn.

I followed him.

A short, elderly officer with a face that bore traces of many anxieties, petty necessities, and fear of his superiors, met me with all the genial hospitality of deadly boredom. He was one of those unintelligent, good-natured 'old' soldiers who pull at the collar for twenty-five years in the service, and plod along without promotion and without reasoning about it, as old horses work, who probably suppose that it is their duty to put on their harness at dawn and haul something.

'Whom are you taking, and where to?'

'Oh, don't ask; it'd even break your heart. Well, I suppose my superiors know all about it; it is our duty to carry out orders and we are not responsible, but, looking at it as a man, it is an ugly business.'

'Why, what is it?'

'You see, they have collected a crowd of cursed little Jew boys of eight or nine years old. Whether they are taking them for the navy or what, I can't say. *At first the orders were to drive them to Perm; then there was a change and we are driving them to Kazan.* I took them over a hundred versts farther back. The officer who handed them over said, "It's dreadful, and that's all about it; a third were left on the way" (and the officer pointed to the earth). Not half will reach their destination,' he said.

'Have there been epidemics, or what?' I asked, deeply moved.

'No, not epidemics, but they just die off like flies. A Jew boy, you know, is such a frail, weakly creature, like a skinned cat; he is not used to tramping in the mud for ten hours a day and eating biscuit—then again, being among strangers, no father nor mother nor petting; well, they cough and cough until they cough themselves into their graves. And I ask you, what use is it to them? What can they do with little boys?'

I made no answer.

'When do you set off?' I asked.

'Well, we ought to have gone long ago, but it has been raining so heavily. . . . Hey, you there, soldier! tell them to get the small fry together.'

They brought the children and formed them into regular ranks: it was one of the most awful sights I have ever seen, those poor, poor children! Boys of twelve or thirteen might somehow have survived it, but little fellows of eight and ten. . . . Not even a brush full of black paint could put such horror on canvas.

Pale, exhausted, with frightened faces, they stood in thick, clumsy, soldiers' overcoats, with stand-up collars, fixing helpless, pitiful eyes on the garrison soldiers who were roughly getting them into ranks. The white lips, the blue rings under their eyes bore witness to fever or chill. And these sick children, without care or kindness, exposed to the icy wind that blows unobstructed from the Arctic Ocean, were going to their graves.

And note that they were being taken by a kind-hearted officer who was obviously sorry for the children. What if they had been taken by a military political economist?

What monstrous crimes are obscurely buried in the archives of the wicked, immoral reign of Nicholas! We are used to them, they were committed every day, committed as though nothing was wrong, unnoticed, lost in the terrible distance, noiselessly sunk in the silent sloughs of officialdom or kept back by the censorship of the police.

Have we not seen with our own eyes seven hungry peasants from Pskov, who were being forcibly removed to the province of Tobolsk, wandering, without food or lodging for the night, about Tverskoy Square in Moscow until Prince D. V. Golitsyn ordered them to be looked after at his own expense?

Vyatka

THE GOVERNOR of Vyatka did not receive me, but sent word that I was to present myself next morning at ten o'clock.

I found in the room next morning the district police-captain, the *politsmeyster*, and two officials: they were all standing talking in whispers and looking uneasily at the door. The door opened and there walked in a short, broad-shouldered old man with a head set on his shoulders like a bull-dog's, and with big jaws, which completed his resemblance to that animal and moreover wore a carnivorous-looking smile; the elderly and at the same time priapic expression of his face, the quick little grey eyes, and the sparse, stiff hair made an incredibly disgusting impression.

To begin with he gave the district police-captain a good dressing-down for the state of the road on which he had driven the day before. The district police-captain stood with his head somewhat bowed in token of respect and submission, and replied to everything as servants used to do in the old days,

'I hear, Your Excellency.'

When he had done with the district police-captain, he turned to me. He looked at me insolently and asked:

'Did you finish your studies at Moscow University?'

'I took my degree.'

'And then served?'

'In the Kremlin Department.'

'Ha, ha, ha! a fine sort of service! Of course, you had plenty of time there for supper parties and singing songs. Alenitsyn!' he shouted.

A scrofulous young man walked in.

'Listen, my boy: here is a graduate of Moscow University. I expect he knows everything except his duties in the service; it is His Majesty's pleasure that he should learn them with us. Take him into your office and send me special reports on him. To-morrow you will come to the office at nine o'clock, and now you may go. But stay, I forgot to ask how you write.'

I did not at once understand.

'Come, your handwriting.'

'I have nothing with me.'

'Bring paper and pen,' and Alenitsyn handed me a pen.

'What am I to write?'

'What you like,' observed the secretary. 'Write, "On inquiry it appears—" '

'Well, you won't be corresponding with the Tsar,' the governor remarked, laughing ironically.

Before I left Perm I had heard a great deal about Tyufyayev, but he far surpassed all my expectations.

What does not Russian life produce!

Tyufyayev was born at Tobolsk. His father had nearly been exiled, and belonged to the poorest class of townsfolk. At thirteen young Tyufyayev joined a troupe of travelling acrobats who wandered from fair to fair, dancing on the tight-rope, turning somersaults and cart-wheels, and so on. With these he travelled from Tobolsk to the Polish provinces, entertaining good Christian people. There, I do not know why, he was arrested, and since he had no passport he was treated as a vagrant, and sent on foot with a party of prisoners back to Tobolsk. His mother was by then a widow and was living in great poverty. The son rebuilt the stove with his own hands when it was broken: he had to find some trade; the boy had learned to read and write, and he was engaged as a copying clerk in the local court. Being naturally of a free-and-easy character and having developed his abilities by a many-sided education in the troupe of acrobats and the parties of convicts with whom he had passed from one end of Russia to the other, he had made himself an enterprising, practical man.

At the beginning of the reign of Alexander some sort of inspector came to Tobolsk. He needed capable clerks, and someone recommended Tyufyayev. The inspector was so well satisfied with him that he suggested that he should go with him to Petersburg. Then Tyufyayev, whose ambition, in his own words, had never risen above the post of secretary in a district court, formed a higher opinion of himself, and with an iron will resolved to make a career.

And he did make it. Ten years later we find him the indefatigable secretary of Kankrin,[1] who was at that time a general in the commissariat. A year later still he was superintending a department in Arakcheyev's secretariat which administered the whole of Russia. He was with Arakcheyev in Paris at the time when it was occupied by the allied troops.

Tyufyayev spent the whole time sitting in the secretariat of the expeditionary army and literally did not see one street in Paris. He sat day and night collating and copying papers with his worthy colleague, Kleinmikhel.

Arakcheyev's secretariat was like those copper mines into which men are sent to work only for a few months, because if they stay longer they die. Even Tyufyayev was tired at last in that factory of orders and decrees, of regulations and institutions, and began asking for a quieter post. Arakcheyev could not fail to like a man like Tyufyayev, a man free from higher pretensions, from all interests and opinions, formally honest, devoured by ambition, and regarding obedience as the foremost human virtue. Arakcheyev rewarded Tyufyayev with the post of deputy governor. A few years later he made him governor of the Perm Province. The province, through which Tyufyayev had walked once on a rope and once tied to a rope, lay at his feet.

---

[1] Tyufyayev was not Kankrin's secretary. (A.S.)

A governor's power generally increases in direct ratio to his distance from Petersburg, but it increases in geometrical progression in the provinces where there are no gentlefolk, as in Perm, Vyatka, and Siberia. Such a remote region was just what Tyufyayev needed.

He was an Oriental satrap, only an active, restless one, meddling in everything and for ever busy. Tyufyayev would have been a ferocious *Commissaire* of the Convention in 1794, a Carrier.[2]

Dissolute in his life, coarse by nature, intolerant of the slightest objection, his influence was extremely pernicious. He did not take bribes, though he did make his fortune, as it appeared after his death. He was strict with his subordinates, he punished without mercy those who were detected in wrongdoing, yet his officials stole more than ever. He carried the abuse of influence to an incredible point; for instance, when he sent an official on an inquiry he would (that is, if he was interested in the case) tell him that probably this or that would be discovered; and woe to the official if he discovered something else.

Perm was still full of the fame of Tyufyayev; there was a party of his adherents there, hostile to the new governor, who, of course, had surrounded himself with his own *coterie*.

On the other hand, there were people who hated him. One of them, a rather singular product of the warping influence of Russian life, particularly warned me what Tyufyayev was like. I am speaking of a doctor in one of the factories. This doctor, whose name was Chebotarëv, an intelligent, very nervous man, had made an unfortunate marriage soon after he completed his studies; then he was sent off to Yekaterinburg and without any experience stuck into the slough of provincial life. Though placed in a fairly independent position in these surroundings, none the less he was debased by them; all his activity took the form of a sarcastic persecution of the officials. He laughed at them to their faces, he said the most insulting things to them with leers and grimaces. Since no one was spared, no one particularly resented the doctor's spiteful tongue. He made a social position for himself by his attacks and forced a flabby set of people to put up with the lash with which he chastised them without resting.

---

[2] Jean-Baptiste Carrier (1756–94), was responsible for the *noyades* and massacre of hundreds of people at Nantes, while suppressing the counter-revolutionary rising of La Vendée. (*Tr.*)

I was warned that he was a good doctor, but crazy and extremely impertinent.

His gossip and jokes were neither coarse nor pointless; quite the contrary, they were full of humour and concentrated bile; they were his poetry, his revenge, his outcry of exasperation and, to some extent, perhaps, of despair as well. He had studied the circle of officials like an artist, and as a doctor he knew all their petty, concealed passions and, encouraged by their cowardice and lack of resource, took any liberty with them he liked.

At every word he would add, 'It won't make a ha'p'orth of difference to you.'

Once in joke I remarked upon his repeating this.

'Why are you surprised?' the doctor replied. 'The object of everything that is said is to convince. I hasten to add the strongest argument that exists. Convince a man that to kill his own father won't cost him a halfpenny, and he will kill him.'

Chebotarëv never refused to lend small sums of a hundred or two hundred paper roubles. When any one asked him for a loan, he would take out his note-book and inquire the exact date when the borrower would return the money.

'Now,' he would say, 'allow me to make a bet of a silver rouble that you won't repay it then.'

'Upon my soul,' the other would object, 'what do you take me for?'

'It makes not a ha'p'orth of difference to you what I take you for,' the doctor would answer, 'but the fact is I have been keeping a record for six years, and not one person has paid me up to time yet, and hardly any one has repaid me later either.'

The day fixed would pass and the doctor would very gravely ask for the silver rouble he had won.

A tax-farmer at Perm was selling a travelling coach. The doctor presented himself before him and made, without stopping, the following speech:

'You have a coach to sell, I need it; you are a wealthy man, you are a millionaire, everyone respects you for it and I have therefore come to pay you my respects also; as you are a wealthy man, it makes not a ha'p'orth of difference to you whether you sell the coach or not, while I need it very much and have very little money. You want to squeeze me, to take advantage of my necessity and ask fifteen hundred for the coach. I offer you seven hundred roubles. I shall be coming every day to bargain with you and in a week you will let me have it for seven-fifty or eight hundred; wouldn't it be better to begin with that? I am ready to give it.'

'Much better,' answered the astonished tax-farmer, and he let him have the coach.

Chebotarëv's anecdotes and mischievous tricks were endless. I will add two more.[3]

'Do you believe in magnetism?' a rather intelligent and cultured lady asked him in my presence.

'What do you mean by magnetism?'

The lady talked some vague nonsense in reply.

'It makes not a ha'p'orth of difference to you whether I believe in magnetism or not, but if you like I will tell you what I have seen in that way.'

'Please do.'

'Only listen attentively.'

After this he described in a very lively, witty and interesting way the experiments of a Kharkov doctor, an acquaintance of his.

In the middle of the conversation, a servant brought in some lunch on a tray.

As he was going out the lady said to him,

'You have forgotten to bring the mustard.'

Chebotarëv stopped.

'Go on, go on,' said the lady, a little scared already, 'I am listening.'

'Has he brought the salt?'

'So you are angry already,' said the lady, turning red.

'Not in the least, I assure you; I know that you were listening attentively. But I also know that, however intelligent a woman is and whatever is being talked about, she can never rise above the kitchen—so how could I dare to be angry with you personally?'

At Countess Polier's factory, where he also practised, he took a liking to a stout lad, and invited him to enter his service. The boy was willing, but the foreman said that he could not let him go without permission from the countess. Chebotarëv wrote to the lady. She told the foreman to let the lad have his passport on condition that the doctor paid five years' *obrok* in advance. The doctor promptly wrote to the countess that he agreed to her terms, but asked her as a preliminary to decide one point that troubled him: from whom could he recover the money if Encke's Comet should intersect the earth's orbit and knock it out of its course—which might occur a year and a half before the term fixed.

---

[3] These two anecdotes were not in the first edition. I recollected them when I was revising the sheets.

On the day of my departure for Vyatka the doctor appeared early in the morning and began with the following foolishness:

'Like Horace, once you sang, and to this day you are always being translated.'[4]

Then he took out his notecase and asked if I did not need some money for the journey. I thanked him and refused.

'Why won't you take any? It won't make a ha'p'orth of difference to you.'

'I have money.'

'That's bad,' he said; 'the end of the world must be at hand.' He opened his note-book and wrote down: 'After fifteen years of practice I have for the first time met a man who won't borrow, even though he is going away.'

Having finished playing the fool, he sat down on my bed and said gravely:

'You are going to a frightful man. Be on your guard against him and keep as far away from him as you can. If he likes you it will be a poor recommendation; if he dislikes you, he will finish you off by slander, chicanery, and I don't know what, but he will finish you, and it won't make a ha'p'orth of difference to him.'

With this he told me an incident the truth of which I had an opportunity of verifying afterwards from documents in the secretariat of the Minister of Home Affairs.

Tyufyayev carried on an open intrigue with the sister of a poor government clerk. The brother was made a laughing-stock and he tried to break the liaison, threatened to report it to the authorities, tried to write to Petersburg—in fact, he fretted and made such a to-do that on one occasion the police seized him and brought him before the provincial authorities to be certified as a lunatic.

The provincial authorities, the president of the court, and the inspector of the medical board, an old German who was very much liked by the working people and whom I knew personally, all found that Petrovsky, as the man was called, was mad.

Our doctor knew Petrovsky, who was a patient of his. He was asked too, as a matter of form. He told the inspector that Petrovsky was not mad at all, and that he proposed that they should make a fresh inquiry into the case, otherwise he would

---

[4] Pun on the Russian word for 'translate,' which also means 'transfer from one place to another.' (*Tr.*)

take the matter further. The local authorities were not at all opposed to this, but unluckily Petrovsky died in the madhouse without waiting for the day fixed for the second inquiry, although he was a robust young fellow.

The report of the case reached Petersburg. Petrovsky's sister was arrested (why not Tyufyayev?) and a secret investigation began. Tyufyayev dictated the answers; he surpassed himself on this occasion. To hush it up at once and to ward off the danger of a second involuntary journey to Siberia, Tyufyayev instructed the girl to say that her brother had been on bad terms with her ever since, carried away by youth and inexperience, she had been deprived of her innocence by the Emperor Alexander on his visit to Perm, for which she had received five thousand roubles through General Solomka.

Alexander's habits were such that there was nothing improbable in the story. To find out whether it was true was not easy, and in any case would have created a great deal of scandal. To Count Benckendorf's inquiry General Solomka answered that so much money passed through his hands that he could not remember the five thousand.

'*La regina ne aveva molto!*' says the *improvisatore* in Pushkin's *Egyptian Nights*. . . .

So this estimable pupil of Arakcheyev's and worthy comrade of Kleinmikhel's, the acrobat, vagrant, copying clerk, secretary, and governor, this tender heart, and disinterested man who locked up the sane in a madhouse and did them to death there, the man who slandered the Emperor Alexander to divert the attention of the Emperor Nicholas, was now undertaking to train me in the service.

I was almost completely dependent upon him. He had only to write some nonsense to the minister and I should have been sent off to some place in Irkutsk. And no need to write: indeed he had the right to transfer me to any outlandish town, Kay or Tsarevo-Sanchursk, without any communications, without any resources. Tyufyayev despatched a young Pole to Glazov because the ladies preferred dancing the mazurka with him to dancing it with His Excellency.

◈   ◈   ◈

The government office was incomparably worse than prison. Not that the actual work was great, but the stifling atmosphere, as of the Dogs' Grotto,[5] of those musty surroundings, and the fearful, stupid waste of time made the office intolerable. Alenitsyn did not worry me: he was, indeed, more polite than I expected; he had been at the Kazan High School and consequently had a respect for a graduate of Moscow University.

There were some twenty clerks in the office. For the most part they were persons of no education and no moral conceptions; sons of clerks and secretaries, accustomed from their cradle to regard the service as a source of profit, and the peasants as soil that yielded revenue, they sold certificates, took twenty kopecks and quarter-roubles, cheated for a glass of wine, demeaned themselves and did all sorts of shabby things. My valet gave up going to the 'billiard room,' saying that the officials cheated there worse than anybody, and one could not teach them a lesson because they were 'officers.'

So with these people, whom my servant did not thrash only on account of their rank, I had to sit every day from nine in the morning until two, and from five to eight in the evening.

Besides Alenitsyn, who was the head of the office, there was a head-clerk of the table at which I was put, who also was not an ill-natured creature, though drunken and illiterate. At the same table sat four clerks. I had to talk to and become acquainted with these, and, indeed, with all the others, too. Apart from the fact that these people would have paid me out sooner or later for being 'proud' if I had not, it is simply impossible to spend several hours of every day with the same people without making their acquaintance. Moreover it must not be forgotten that provincials make up to anyone from outside and particularly to anyone who comes from the capital, especially if there is some interesting story connected with him.

After spending the whole day in this galley, I would sometimes come home with all my faculties in a state of stupefaction and fling myself on the sofa, worn out, humiliated, and incapable of any work or occupation. I heartily regretted my Krutitsky cell with its charcoal fumes and black beetles, with a gendarme on guard and a lock on the door. There I had freedom, I did what I liked and no one interfered with me; instead of these vulgar remarks, dirty people, mean ideas and coarse feelings, there had been the stillness of death and undisturbed leisure. And when I remembered that after dinner I had to go again, and again to-

---

[5] At Terme d'Agnano, west of Naples, there is a grotto, filled at the bottom with carbon dioxide, where dogs suffocated. F. L. Lucas: *The Search for Good Sense* (Collins, 1958), p. 244. (*R.*)

morrow, I was at times overcome by fury and despair and tried
to find comfort in drinking wine and vodka.

And then, what is more, one of my fellow-clerks would look in
'on his way' and relieve his boredom by staying on talking until
it was time to go back to the office.

Within a few months, however, the office became somewhat
more bearable.

Prolonged, regular persecution is not in the Russian character
unless a personal or mercenary element comes in; and this is not
at all because the government does not want to stifle and crush a
man, but is due to the Russian carelessness, to our *laissez-aller*.
Russians in authority are as a rule ill-bred, audacious, and insolent; it is easy to provoke them to rudeness, but persistent
knocking about is not in their line: they have not enough
patience for it, perhaps because it brings them no profit.

In the first heat, in order to display, on the one hand their
zeal, and on the other their power, they do all sorts of stupid and
unnecessary things; then little by little they leave a man in
peace.

So it was with the office. The Ministry of Home Affairs had at
that time a craze for statistics: it had given orders for committees to be formed everywhere, and had issued programmes which
could hardly have been carried out even in Belgium or Switzerland; at the same time there were to be all sorts of elaborate
tables with maxima and minima, with averages and various
deductions from the totals for periods of ten years (made up on
evidence which had not been collected for *a year before!*), with
moral remarks and meteorological observations. Not a farthing
was assigned for the expenses of the committees and the collection of evidence; all this was to be done from love of statistics
through the rural police and put into proper shape in the governor's office. The clerks, overwhelmed with work, and the rural
police, who hate all peaceful and theoretical tasks, looked upon a
statistics committee as a useless luxury, as a caprice of the
ministry; however, the reports had to be sent in with tabulated
results and deductions.

This business seemed immensely difficult to the whole office; it
was simply impossible; but no one troubled about that: all they
worried about was that there should be no occasion for reprimands. I promised Alenitsyn to prepare a preface and introduction, and to draw up summaries of the tables with eloquent
remarks introducing foreign words, quotations, and striking
deductions, if he would allow me to undertake this very hard

work not at the office but at home. After parleying with Tyufyayev, Alenitsyn agreed.

The introduction to the record of the work of the committee, in
which I discussed their hopes and their plans, for in reality
nothing had been done at all, touched Alenitsyn to the depths
of his soul. Tyufyayev himself thought it was written in masterly
style. With that my labours in the statistical line ended, but
they put the committee under my supervision. They no longer
forced upon me the unpleasant task of copying papers, and the
drunken head-clerk who had been my chief became almost my
subordinate. Alenitsyn only required, from some consideration of
propriety, that I should go to the office for a short time every
day.

To show the complete impossibility of real statistics, I will
quote the facts sent in from the unimportant town of Kay. There,
among various absurdities, were for instance the entries:
Drowned—2. Causes of drowning not known—2, and in the
column of totals was set out the figure 4. Under the heading of
extraordinary incidents was reckoned the following tragic anecdote: So-and-so, townsman, having deranged his intelligence by
ardent beverages, hanged himself. Under the heading of the
morality of the town's inhabitants was the entry: 'There have
been no Jews in the town of Kay.' To the inquiry whether sums
had been allotted for the building of a church, a stock exchange,
or an almshouse, the answer ran thus: 'For the building of a
stock exchange was assigned—nothing.'

The statistics that rescued me from work at the office had the
unfortunate consequence of bringing me into personal relations
with Tyufyayev.

There was a time when I hated that man; that time is long
past and the man himself is past. He died on his Kazan estates
about 1845. Now I think of him without anger, as of a peculiar
beast met in the wilds of a forest which ought to have been
studied, but with which one could not be angry for being a
beast. At the time I could not help coming into conflict with
him; that was inevitable for any decent man. Chance helped
me or he would have done me great injury; to owe him a grudge
for the harm he did not do me would be absurd and paltry.

Tyufyayev lived alone. His wife was separated from him. The
governor's favourite, the wife of a cook who for no fault but
being married to her had been sent away to the country, was,
with an awkwardness which almost seemed intentional, kept out
of sight in the back rooms of his house. She did not make her
appearance officially, but officials who were particularly afraid of

inquiries formed a sort of court about the cook's wife, 'who was in favour.' Their wives and daughters paid her stealthy visits in the evening and did not boast of doing so. This lady was possessed of the same sort of tact as distinguished one of her brilliant predecessors—Potëmkin; knowing the old man's disposition and afraid of being replaced, she herself sought out for him rivals who were no danger to her. The grateful old man repeated this indulgent love with his devotion and they got on well together.

All the morning Tyufyayev worked and was in the office of the secretariat. The poetry of life only began at three o'clock. Dinner was for him no jesting matter. He liked a good dinner and he liked to eat it in company. Preparations were always made in his kitchen for twelve at table; if the guests were fewer than half that number he was mortified; if there were no more than two visitors he was wretched; if there was no one at all, he would go off on the verge of despair to dine in his Dulcinea's apartments. To procure people in order to feed them till they felt sick was no difficult task, but his official position and the terror he inspired in his subordinates did not permit them to enjoy his hospitality freely, nor him to turn his house into a tavern. He had to confine himself to councillors, presidents (but with half of these he was on bad terms, that is, he would not condescend to them), travellers (who were rare), rich merchants, tax-farmers, and the few visitors to the town and 'oddities.' Of course I was an oddity of the first magnitude at Vyatka.

Persons exiled 'for their opinions' to remote towns are somewhat feared, but are never confounded with ordinary mortals. 'Dangerous people' have for provincials the same attraction that notorious Lovelaces have for women and courtesans for men. Dangerous people are far more shunned by Petersburg officials and Moscow big pots than by provincials, and especially by Siberians.

Those who were exiled in connection with the Fourteenth of December were looked upon with immense respect. Officials paid their first visit on New Year's Day to the widow of Yushnevsky. Senator Tolstoy, when taking a census of Siberia, was guided by evidence received from the exiled Decembrists in checking the facts furnished by the officials.

Münnich[6] from his tower in Pelym superintended the affairs

---

6 Münnich (also spelt Minikh), Burchardt Christoph (Khristophor Antonovich), 1683–1767, was a minister and general prominent under Peter the Great and Anna. On the latter's death he brought about the downfall

of the Tobolsk Province. Governors used to go to consult him about matters of importance.

The working people are still less hostile to exiles: on the whole they are on the side of those who are punished. The word 'convict' disappears near the Siberian frontier and is replaced by the word 'unfortunate.' In the eyes of the Russian people a legal sentence is no disgrace to a man. The peasants of the Perm Province, living along the main road to Tobolsk, often put out kvas, milk, and bread in a little window in case an 'unfortunate' should be secretly slipping through that way from Siberia.

By the way, speaking of exiles, Polish exiles begin to be met beyond Nizhny Novgorod and their number increases rapidly after Kazan. In Perm there were forty, in Vyatka not fewer; there were several besides in every district town.

They lived quite apart from the Russians and avoided all contact with the inhabitants. There was great unanimity among them, and the rich shared with the poor like brothers.

On the part of the inhabitants I never saw signs of either hatred or special good-will towards them. They looked upon them as outsiders—the more so, as scarcely a single Pole knew Russian.

One tough old Sarmatian, who had been an officer in the Uhlans in Poniatowski's time and had taken part in Napoleon's campaigns, received permission in 1837 to return to his Lithuanian domains. On the eve of his departure he invited me and several Poles to dinner. After dinner my cavalry officer came up to me, goblet in hand, embraced me, and with a warrior's simplicity whispered in my ear, 'Oh, why are you a Russian!' I did not answer a word, but this observation sank deeply into my heart. I realised that *this* generation could never set Poland free.

From the time of Konarski[7] the Poles have come to look quite differently upon the Russians.

As a rule Polish exiles are not oppressed, but the material situation is awful for those who have no private means. The

---

of Biron, was exiled by Elizabeth, and finally brought back from Siberia by Catherine. (*Tr.*)

[7] Simon Konarski, a Polish revolutionary, also active in the 'Young Europe' (afterwards 'Young Italy') movement, lived in disguise and with a false passport in Poland, founding a printing press and carrying on active propaganda till he was caught and shot at Vilna in 1839. His admirers cut the post to which he was tied into bits which they preserved, like the relics of a saint. (*Tr.*) An attempt to liberate Konarski from the prison at Vilna was made by a secret organisation of Russian officers headed by Kuzmin-Karayev. (*A.S.*)

government gives those who have nothing *fifteen paper roubles a
month;* with that they must pay for lodging, food, clothes, and
fuel. In fairly big towns, in Kazan and Tobolsk, it was possible
to earn something by giving lessons or concerts, playing at balls,
executing portraits and teaching dancing. In Perm and Vyatka
they had no such resources. And in spite of that they would ask
for nothing from Russians.

Tyufyayev's invitations to his greasy Siberian dinners were a
real imposition on me. His dining-room was just like the office,
but in another form, less dirty but more vulgar, because it had
the appearance of free will and not of compulsion.

Tyufyayev knew his guests through and through, despised
them, showed them his claws at times, and altogether treated
them as a master treats his dogs: at one time with excessive
familiarity, at another with a rudeness which was beyond all
bounds—and yet he invited them to his dinners and they appeared before him in trembling and in joy, demeaning themselves, talking scandal, eavesdropping, trying to please, smiling,
bowing.

I blushed for them and felt ashamed.

Our friendship did not last long. Tyufyayev soon guessed that
I was not fit for 'high' Vyatka society.

A few months later he was dissatisfied with me, and a few
months later still he hated me, and I not only went no more to
his dinners but even gave up going to him at all. The Heir's
passage through Vyatka saved me from his persecution, as we
shall see later on.

I must observe that I had done absolutely nothing to deserve
first his attention and invitations, and afterwards his anger and
disfavour. He could not endure to see in me a man who behaved
independently, though not in the least insolently; I was always
en règle with him, and he demanded obsequiousness.

He loved his power jealously. He had earned it the hard way,
and he exacted not only obedience but an *appearance* of absolute
submission. In this, unhappily, he was typically native.

A landowner says to his servant, 'Hold your tongue; I won't
put up with your answering me back!'

The head of a department, turning pale with anger, observes
to a clerk who has made some objection, 'You forget yourself; do
you know *to whom* you are speaking?'

The Tsar sends men to Siberia 'for opinions,' does them to
death in dungeons for *a poem*—and all these three are readier to
forgive stealing and bribe-taking, murder and robbery, than the

impudence of human dignity and the insolence of a plain-spoken word.

Tyufyayev was a true servant of the Tsar. He was highly thought of, but not highly enough. Byzantine servility was exceptionally well combined in him with official discipline. Obliteration of self, renunciation of will and thought before authority went inseparably with harsh oppression of subordinates. He might have been a civilian Kleinmikhel; his 'zeal' might in the same way have overcome everything,[8] and he might in the same way have plastered the walls with the dead human bodies, have used living men's lungs to dry the damp walls of his palace, and have flogged the young men of the engineering corps even more severely for not being informers.

Tyufyayev had an intense, secret hatred for everything aristocratic; he had kept this from his bitter experiences. The hard labour of Arakcheyev's secretariat had been his first refuge, his first deliverance. Till then his superiors had never offered him a chair, but had employed him on menial errands. When he served in the commissariat, the officers had persecuted him, as is the custom in the army, and one colonel had horsewhipped him in the street at Vilna. . . . All this had entered into the copying clerk's soul and rankled there; now he was governor and it was his turn to oppress, to keep men standing, to call people 'thou,' to raise his voice more than was necessary, and sometimes to bring gentlemen of ancient lineage to trial.

From Perm Tyufyayev had been transferred to Tver. The gentry of the province, for all their submissiveness and servility, could not put up with him. They petitioned the minister, Bludov, to remove him. Bludov appointed him to Vyatka.

There he was quite at home again. Officials and contractors, factory-owners and government clerks—a free hand, and that was all he wanted. Everyone trembled before him, everyone stood up when he came in, everyone offered him drink and gave him dinners, everyone waited on his slightest wish; at weddings and name-day parties, the first toast was 'To the health of His Excellency!'

---

[8] The motto of the coat of arms granted by Nicholas I to Count Kleinmikhel was 'Zeal overcomes all.' (*A.S.*)

Misgovernment in Siberia

ONE OF THE most melancholy results of the Petrine revolution was the development of the official class. An artificial, hungry, and uncultivated class, capable of doing nothing but 'serving,' knowing nothing but official forms, it constitutes a kind of civilian clergy, celebrating divine service in the courts and the police forces, and sucking the blood of the people with thousands of greedy, unclean mouths.

Gogol lifted one corner of the curtain and showed us Russian officialdom in all its ugliness: but Gogol cannot help conciliating one with his laughter; his enormous comic talent gets the upper hand of his indignation. Moreover, in the fetters of the Russian censorship he could scarcely touch upon the melancholy side of that foul underworld, in which the destinies of the miserable Russian people are forged.

There, somewhere in grimy offices which we make haste to pass through, shabby men write and write on grey paper, and copy on to stamped paper—and persons, families, whole villages are outraged, terrified, ruined. A father is sent into exile, a mother to prison, a son for a soldier—and all this breaks like a thunderclap upon them, unexpected, for the most part undeserved. And for the sake of what? For the sake of money. A contribution . . . or an inquiry will be held into the dead body of some drunkard, burnt up by spirits and frozen to death. And the head-man collects and the village elder collects, the peasants bring their last kopeck. The police-commissary must live; the police-captain must live and keep his wife, too; the councillor must live and educate his children, for the councillor is an exemplary father.

Officialdom reigns supreme in the north-eastern provinces of Russia and in Siberia. There it has flourished unhindered, without looking back . . . it is a fearful long way, and everyone shares in the profits, stealing becomes *res publica*. Even the Imperial power, which strikes like grape-shot, cannot breach these boggy trenches that are dug in mud, that suck you down and are hidden under the snow. All the measures of government are enfeebled, all its intentions are distorted; it is deceived, fooled, betrayed, sold, and all under cover of loyal servility and with the observance of all the official forms.

Speransky[1] tried to improve the lot of the Siberian people. He introduced everywhere the collegiate principle, as though it made any difference whether the officials stole individually or in gangs. He discharged the old rogues by hundreds and engaged new ones by hundreds. At first he inspired such terror in the rural police that they actually *bribed the peasants* not to lodge petitions against them. Three years later the officials were making their fortunes by the new forms as well as they had done by the old.

Another eccentric was General Velyaminov. For two years he struggled at Tobolsk trying to check abuses, but, seeing his lack of success, threw it all up and quite gave up attending to business.

Others, more judicious, did not make the attempt, but got rich themselves and let others get rich.

'I shall eradicate bribe-taking,' said Senyavin, the Governor of Moscow, to a grey-haired peasant who had lodged a complaint against some obvious injustice. The old man smiled.

'What are you laughing at?' asked Senyavin.

'Why, you must forgive me, sir,' answered the peasant; 'it put me in mind of one fine young fellow who boasted he would lift the Tsar-pushka,[2] and he really did try, but he did not lift it for all that.'

Senyavin, who told the story himself, belonged to that class of unpractical men in the Russian service who imagine that rhetorical sallies on the subject of honesty, and the despotic persecution of two or three rogues who happen to be there, can remedy so universal a disease as Russian bribe-taking, which grows freely under the shadow of the censorship.

There are only two remedies for it: publicity, and an entirely different organisation of the whole machinery, the re-introduction of the popular principle of the arbitration courts, verbal proceedings, sworn witnesses, and all that the Petersburg administration detests.

---

[1] Speransky, Mikhail Mikhaylovich (1772–1839), a leading statesman of the early period of the reign of Alexander I, banished in 1812 on a trumped-up charge of treason, recalled by Nicholas. He was responsible for the codification of Russian laws. (*Tr.*)

[2] A cannon, cast in the seventeenth century, which weighs forty tons. It is in the Kremlin at Moscow and is said to be the biggest in the world. It has never been fired. (*R.*)

Pestel, the Governor-General of Western Siberia, father of the celebrated Pestel put to death by Nicholas, was a real Roman proconsul and one of the most violent. He carried on an open system of plunder in the whole region which was cut off from Russia by his spies. Not a single letter crossed the border without the seal being broken, and woe to the man who should dare to write anything about his government. He kept merchants of the first guild for a year at a time in prison in chains; he tortured them. He sent officials to the borders of Eastern Siberia and left them there for two or three years.

For a long time the people bore it; at last a working man of Tobolsk made up his mind to bring the condition of affairs to the knowledge of the Tsar. Afraid of the ordinary routes, he went to Kyakhta and from there made his way with a caravan of tea across the Siberian frontier. He found an opportunity at Tsarskoye Selo of giving Alexander his petition, beseeching him to read it. Alexander was amazed by the terrible things he read in it. He sent for the man, and after a long talk with him was convinced of the melancholy truth of his report. Mortified and somewhat embarrassed, he said to him:

'You go home now, my friend; the thing shall be inquired into.'

'Your Majesty,' answered the man, 'I shall not go home now. Better command me to be put in prison. My conversation with Your Majesty will not remain a secret and I shall be killed.'

Alexander shuddered and said, turning to Miloradovich, who was at that time Governor-General in Petersburg:

'You will answer to me for him.'

'In that case,' observed Miloradovich, 'allow me to take him into my own house.'

And the man actually remained there until the case was ended.

Pestel almost always lived in Petersburg. You may remember that the proconsuls as a rule lived in Rome. By means of his presence and connections, and still more by the division of the spoils, he anticipated all sorts of unpleasant rumours and scandals.[3] The Imperial Council took advantage of Alexander's

---

[3] This gave Count Rostopchin occasion for a biting jest at Pestel's expense. They were both dining with the Tsar. The Tsar, who was standing at the window, asked: 'What's that on the church, the black thing on the cross?' 'I can't make out,' observed Count Rostopchin. 'You must ask Ivan Borisovich, he has wonderful eyes, for he can see from here what is being done in Siberia.'

temporary absence at Verona or Aachen[4] to come to the intelligent and just decision that since the matter in a denunciation related to Siberia the case should be passed to Pestel to deal with, seeing that he was on the spot. Miloradovich, Mordvinov, and two others were opposed to this decision, and the case was brought before the Senate.

The Senate, with that outrageous injustice with which it constantly judges cases relating to higher officials, exculpated Pestel but exiled Treskin, the civilian governor of Tobolsk, deprived him of his rank and privileges as a member of the gentry and relegated him to somewhere or other. Pestel was only dismissed from the service.

Pestel was succeeded at Tobolsk by Kaptsevich, a man of the school of Arakcheyev. Thin, bilious, a tyrant by nature and a tyrant because he had spent his whole life in the army, a man of restless activity, he brought outward discipline and order into everything, fixed maximum prices for goods, but left everyday affairs in the hands of robbers. In 1824 the Tsar wished to visit Tobolsk. Through the Perm Province runs an excellent, broad high-road, which has been in use for ages and is probably good owing to the nature of the soil. Kaptsevich made a similar road to Tobolsk in a few months. In the spring, in the time of alternate thaw and frost, he forced thousands of workmen to make the road by levies from villages near and far; sickness broke out and half the workmen died, but 'zeal can overcome anything'— the road was made.

Eastern Siberia is still more negligently governed. It is so far away the news hardly reaches Petersburg. At Irkutsk, Bronevsky, the Governor-General, was fond of firing off cannon in the town when 'he was merry.' And another high official when he was drunk used to say mass in his house in full vestments and in the presence of the bishop. At least the noisiness of the one and the devoutness of the other were not so pernicious as Pestel's blockade and Kaptsevich's indefatigable activity.

It is a pity that Siberia is so rottenly governed. The choice of its governors-general has been particularly unfortunate. I do not know what Muravëv is like; he is well known for his intelligence and his abilities; the others were good for nothing. Siberia

---

[4] Congresses of the Holy Alliance were held in Aachen in 1818 and Verona in 1822. (*A.S.*)

has a great future: it is looked upon merely as a cellar, in which there are great stores of gold, fur, and other goods, but which is cold, buried in snow, poor in the means of life, without roads or population. This is not true.

The dead hand of the Russian government, which does everything by violence, everything with the stick, cannot give the vital impetus that would carry Siberia forward with American rapidity. We shall see what will happen when the mouths of the Amur are opened for navigation and America meets Siberia near China.

I said long ago that the *Pacific Ocean is the Mediterranean of the future.*[5] In that future the part played by Siberia, the land that lies between the ocean, Southern Asia, and Russia, will be extremely important. Of course Siberia is bound to extend to the Chinese frontier. Why freeze and shiver in Berëzov and Yakutsk when there are Krasnoyarsk, Minusinsk, and other such places?

Even the Russian immigrants into Siberia have elements in their nature that suggest a different development. Generally speaking, the Siberian race is healthy, well-grown, intelligent, and extremely steady. The Siberian children of settlers know nothing of the landowners' power. There is no upper class in Siberia and at the same time there is no aristocracy in the towns; the officials and the officers, who are the representatives of authority, are more like a hostile garrison stationed there by a victorious enemy than an aristocracy. The immense distances save the peasants from frequent contact with them; money saves the merchants, who in Siberia despise the officials and, though outwardly giving way to them, take them for what they are— their clerks employed in civil affairs.

The habit of using firearms, indispensable for a Siberian, is universal. The dangers and emergencies of his daily life have made the Siberian peasant more war-like, more resourceful, readier to offer resistance than the Great Russian. The remoteness of churches leaves his mind freer from fanaticism than in Russia; he is phlegmatic about religion and most often a schismatic. There are remote hamlets which the priest visits only three or four times a year and administers baptism wholesale, buries, marries, and hears confessions for the whole time since he was there last.

---

[5] I have seen with great pleasure that the New York papers have several times repeated this.

◇   ◇   ◇

Before the end of my time at Vyatka the Department of Crown Property was stealing so impudently that a commission of inquiry was appointed over it, which sent inspectors about the provinces. With that began the introduction of the new administration of Crown peasants.

Governor Kornilov was to appoint two officials from his staff for this inspection. I was one of those appointed. What things it was my lot to read!—sad, funny and nasty. The very headings of the cases struck me with amazement.

'Relating to the disappearance of the house of the Parish Council, *no one knows where to,* and to the gnawing of the plan of it by mice.'

'Relating to the loss of twenty-two government quit-rent articles,' *i.e.,* of fifteen versts of land.

'Relating to the registration of the peasant boy Vasily among the female sex.'

This last was so good that I at once read the case from cover to cover.

The father of this supposed Vasily wrote in his petition to the governor that fifteen years earlier he had a daughter born, whom he had wanted to call Vasilisa, but that the priest, being 'in liquor,' christened the girl Vasily and so entered it in the register. The circumstance apparently troubled the peasant very little; but when he realised that it would soon come to his family to furnish a recruit and pay the poll tax, he reported on the matter to the mayor and the rural police superintendent. The case seemed very odd to the police. They began by refusing the peasant's request, saying that he had let pass the ten-year limitation. The peasant went to the governor; the latter arranged a solemn examination of the boy of the female sex by a doctor and a midwife. . . . At this point a correspondence suddenly sprang up with the Consistory, and a priest, the successor of the one who, when 'in liquor,' had chastely failed to make fleshly distinctions, appeared on the scene, and the case went on for years and the girl was nearly left under the suspicion of being a man.

Do not imagine that this is an absurd figment made up by me for a joke; not at all: it is quite in harmony with the spirit of Russian autocracy.

In the reign of Paul a colonel in the Guards in his monthly report entered as dead an officer who was dying in the hospital.

Paul struck him off the list as dead. Unluckily the officer did not die, but recovered. The colonel persuaded him to withdraw to his country estate for a year or two, hoping to find an opportunity to rectify the error. The officer agreed, but unfortunately for the colonel the heirs who had read of the kinsman's death in the Orders refused on any consideration to acknowledge that he was alive and, inconsolable at their loss, demanded possession of the property. When the living corpse saw that he was likely to die a second time, not merely on paper but from hunger, he went to Petersburg and sent in a petition to Paul. The Tsar wrote with his own hand on the petition: 'Forasmuch as His Majesty's decree has been promulgated concerning this gentleman, the petition is to be refused.'

This is even better than my Vasilisa-Vasily. Of what consequence was the crude fact of life beside the decree of His Majesty? Paul was the poet and dialectician of autocracy!

Foul and muddy as this morass of officialdom is, I must add a few words more about it. To bring it into the light of day is the least poor tribute one can pay to those who have suffered and perished, unknown and uncomforted.

The government readily gives the higher officials uncultivated lands by way of reward. There is no great harm in that, though it would be more sensible to keep these reserves to provide for the increase of population. The regulations that govern the fixing of the boundaries of these lands are fairly detailed; forests containing building timber, the banks of navigable rivers, indeed both the banks of any river, must not be given away, nor under any circumstances may lands be so assigned that have been cultivated by peasants, even though the peasants have no right to the land except that of long usage. . . .[6]

All these restrictions of course are only on paper. In reality the assignment of land to private owners is a fearful source of plunder to the Treasury and of oppression to the peasants.

Great noblemen in receipt of lands usually either sell their rights to merchants, or try through the provincial authorities to gain some special privilege contrary to the regulations. Even

---

[6] In the province of Vyatka the peasants are particularly fond of moving to new settlements. Very often three or four *clearings* are suddenly discovered in the forest. The immense lands and forests (now half cut down) tempt the peasants to take this *res nullius* which is left unused. The Ministry of Finance has several times been obliged to confirm these squatters in possession of the land.

Count Orlov himself was *by chance* assigned a main road and lands on which flocks and herds are pastured in the province of Saratov.

It is therefore no wonder that one fine morning the peasants of Darovsky *volost*[7] in Kotelnichesky district had their land cut away right up to their woodyards and houses and given as private property to merchants who had bought them from some kinsman of Count Kankrin. The merchants fixed a rent for the land. This led to a lawsuit. The Court of Justice, bribed by the merchants and afraid of Kankrin's kinsman, confused the issues of the case. But the peasants were determined to persist with it. They chose two hard-headed peasants from amongst themselves and sent them to Petersburg. The case was brought before the Senate. The land-surveying department perceived that the peasants were in the right, but did not know what to do, so they asked Kankrin. He simply admitted that the land had been irregularly cut away, but considered that it would be difficult to restore it, because it *might* have changed hands since then, and its present owners *might* have made various improvements. His Excellency proposed, therefore, that advantage should be taken of the vast amount of Crown property available, and that the peasants should be assigned a full equivalent in another place. Everybody liked this except the peasants. In the first place, it is no light matter to bring fresh land under cultivation, and, in the second, the fresh land turned out to be swampy and unsuitable. Since the peasants of Darovsky *volost* were more interested in growing corn than in shooting snipe, they sent another petition.

Then the Court of Justice and the Ministry of Finance made a new case out of the old one and, finding a law in which it was said that, if the land that was assigned turned out to be unsuitable, it was not to be cancelled, but another half of the amount was to be added to it, they ordered the Darovsky peasants to be given another half swamp in addition to the swamp they already had.

The peasants once more petitioned the Senate, but, before their case came up for investigation, the land-surveying department sent them plans of their new land, bound and coloured, as is usual, with the points of the compass in the form of a star and appropriate explanations for the lozenge marked R.R.Z., and the lozenge marked Z.Z.R., and, what was most important, a demand for so much rent per acre. The peasants, seeing that far from

---

[7] An administrative district which included several villages. (*R.*)

giving them land they were trying to squeeze money out of them for the bog, refused point-blank to pay.

The police-captain reported it to Tyufyayev, who sent a punitive expedition under the command of the Vyatka *politsmeyster*. This man arrived, seized a few persons, flogged them, restored order in the *volost*, took the money, handed over the *guilty parties* to the Criminal Court, and was hoarse for a week afterwards from shouting. Several men were punished with the lash and sent into exile.

Two years later, when the Heir to the Throne passed through the *volost*, the peasants handed him a petition; he ordered the case to be investigated. It was upon this occasion that I had to draw up a report on it. Whether any sense came of this re-investigation I do not know. I have heard that the exiles returned, but whether the land was returned I have not heard.

In conclusion, I must mention the celebrated story of the potato revolt[8] and how Nicholas tried to bring the blessings of Petersburg civilisation to the nomad gypsies.

Like the peasantry of all Europe at one time, the Russian peasants were not very keen on planting potatoes, as though an instinct told the people that this was a trashy kind of food which would give them neither health nor strength. However, on the estates of decent landowners and in many Crown villages 'earth apples' had been planted long before the potato terror. But anything that is done of itself is distasteful to the Russian government. Everything must be done under threat of the stick and the drill-sergeant, and by numbers.

The peasants of the Kazan and of part of the Vyatka Province planted potatoes in their fields. When the potatoes were harvested, the idea occurred to the Ministry to set up a central potato-pit in each *volost*. Potato-pits were ratified, potato-pits were prescribed, potato-pits were dug; and at the beginning of winter the peasants, much against their will, took the potatoes to the central pits. But when in the following spring the authorities tried to make them plant *frozen* potatoes, they refused. There cannot, indeed, be a more flagrant insult to labour than a command to do something obviously absurd. This refusal was represented as a revolt. The Minister Kiselëv sent an official from Petersburg; he, being an intelligent and practical man,

[8] Herzen appears to be speaking of the 'potato revolt' of 1842; there had been an earlier one, less wide-spread, in 1834. (*A.S.*)

exacted a rouble apiece from the peasants of the first *volost* and allowed them not to plant the frozen potatoes.

He repeated this proceeding in the second *volost* and the third; but in the fourth the head-man told him point-blank that he would neither plant the potatoes nor pay him anything. 'You have let off these and those,' he told the official. 'It's clear you must let us off too.'

The official would have concluded the business with threats and thrashings, but the peasants snatched up stakes and drove the police away; the military governor sent Cossacks. The neighbouring *volosts* came in on their own people's side.

It is enough to say that it came to using grape-shot and bullets. The peasants left their homes and dispersed into the woods; the Cossacks drove them out of the thickets like wild beasts; then they were caught, put into irons, and sent to be court-martialled at Kosmodemyansk.

By an odd chance the old major in charge there was an honest, simple man; he good-naturedly said that the official sent from Petersburg was solely to blame. Everyone pounced upon him, his voice was stifled, he was suppressed; he was intimidated and even put to shame for 'trying to ruin an innocent man.'

And the inquiry followed the usual Russian routine: the peasants were flogged during the examination, flogged as a punishment, flogged as an example, flogged to extort money, and a whole crowd of them sent to Siberia.

It is worth noting that Kiselëv passed through Kosmodemyansk during the inquiry. He might, it may be thought, have looked in at the court-martial or have sent for the major.

He did not do so!

The famous Turgot, seeing the dislike of the peasants for the potato, distributed seed-potatoes among contractors, purveyors, and other persons under government control, strictly forbidding them to give them to the peasants. At the same time he gave them secret orders not to prevent the peasants from stealing them. In a few years a part of France was under potatoes.

Tout bien pris, is not that better than grape-shot, Pavel Dmitriyevich?[9]

In 1836 a party of gypsies came to Vyatka and settled in a field. These gypsies had wandered as far as Tobolsk and Irbit and, accompanied by their eternal trained bear and entirely un-

---

[9] P. D. Kiselëv. (*A.S.*)

trained children, had led their free, wandering existence from time immemorial, engaged in horse-doctoring, fortune-telling, and petty pilfering. They peacefully sang songs and robbed hen-roosts, but all at once the governor received instructions from His Majesty that if gypsies were found *without passports* (not a single gypsy had ever had a passport, and that Nicholas and his men knew perfectly well) they were to be given a fixed time within which they were to inscribe themselves as citizens of the village or town where the decree found them.

At the expiration of the time limit, it was ordained that those fit for military service should be taken for soldiers and the *rest* sent into exile, all but the children of the male sex.

This senseless decree, which recalled biblical accounts of the massacre and punishment of whole races and him that pisseth against the wall, disconcerted even Tyufyayev. He communicated the absurd *ukaz* to the gypsies and wrote to Petersburg that it was impossible to carry it out. To get themselves inscribed as citizens they would need both money for the officials and the consent of the town or village, which would also have been unwilling to accept the gypsies for nothing. It was necessary, too, to assume that the gypsies should themselves have been desirous of settling just there. Taking all this into consideration, Tyufyayev—and one must give him credit for it—asked the Ministry to grant postponements and exemptions.

The Minister answered by instructions that at the expiration of the time-limit this Nebuchadnezzar-like decree should be carried out. Most unwillingly Tyufyayev sent a squad of soldiers with orders to surround the gypsy camp; as soon as this was done, the police arrived with a garrison battalion, and what happened, I am told, was beyond all imagination. Women with streaming hair ran about in a frenzy, screaming and weeping, and falling at the feet of the police; grey-headed old mothers clung to their sons. But order triumphed and the lame *polits-meyster* took the boys and took the recruits—while the rest were sent by stages somewhere into exile.

But when the children had been taken away, the question arose what was to be done with them and at whose expense they were to be kept.

There had formerly been foundling hospitals connected with the Charitable Board, which cost the government nothing. But the Prussian chastity of Nicholas abolished them as detrimental to morals. Tyufyayev advanced money of his own and asked the Minister for instructions. Ministers never stick at anything. They ordered that the boys, until further instructions, were to be put into the care of the old men and women maintained in the almshouses.

Think of lodging little children with moribund old men and women, making them breathe the atmosphere of death—and charging old people who need peace and quiet with looking after children for nothing.

What imagination!

While I am on the subject I must describe what happened some eighteen months later to the head-man of my father's village in the province of Vladimir. He was a peasant of intelligence and experience who carried on the trade of a carrier, had several teams of three horses each, and had been for twenty years the head-man of a little village that paid *obrok* to my father.

Some time during the year I spent in Vladimir the neighbouring peasants asked him to hand over a recruit for them. Bringing the future defender of his country on a rope, he arrived in the town with great self-confidence as a man proficient in his business.

'This,' said he, combing with his fingers the fair, grizzled beard that framed his face, 'is all the work of men's hands, sir. The year before last we pitched on our lad, such a wretched, puny fellow he was—the peasants were fearfully afraid he wouldn't do. So I says, "And roughly how much, good Christians, will you go to? A wheel will not turn without being greased." We talked it over and the *mir*[10] decided to give twenty-five gold pieces. I went to the town and after talking in the government office I went straight to the president—he was a sensible man, sir, and had known me for ages. He told them to call me into his study and he had something the matter with his leg, so he was lying on a sofa. I put it all before him and he answered me with a laugh, "All right, all right; you tell me how many *of them* you have brought—you are a skinflint, I know you." I put ten gold pieces on the table and made him a low bow—he took the money in his hand and kept playing with it. "But I say," he said, "I am not the only one you will have to pay; what more have you brought?" I reported that I'd got together another ten. "Well," he said, "you can reckon yourself what you must do with it. Two to the doctor, two to the army receiver, then the clerk . . . and any treating won't come to

---

[10] Village council. (*R.*)

more than three—so you had better leave the rest with me and I will try to arrange the affair." '

'Well, did you give it to him?'

'To be sure I did—and they shaved the boy's head[11] all right.'

Trained in such a way of rounding off accounts, and accustomed to reckonings of this sort, and also, perhaps, to the five gold pieces about the fate of which he had been silent, the head-man was confident of success. But there may be many mishaps between the bribe and the hand that takes it. Count Essen, one of the Imperial adjutants, was sent to Vladimir for a levy of recruits. The head-man approached him with his gold pieces. Unfortunately the Count had, like the heroine of Pushkin's *Nulin*, been reared 'not in the traditions of his fathers,' but in the school of the Baltic aristocracy, which instils a German devotion to the Russian Tsar. Essen lost his temper, shouted at him and, what was worse than anything, rang the bell; the clerk ran in and gendarmes made their appearance. The head-man, who had never suspected the existence of men in uniform who would not take bribes, lost his head so completely that he did not deny the charge, did not vow and swear that he had never offered money, did not protest, might God strike him blind and might another drop never pass his lips, if he had thought of such a thing! He let himself be caught like a sheep and led off to the police station, probably regretting that he had offered the general too little and so offended him.

But Essen, not satisfied with the purity of his own conscience, nor the terror of the luckless peasant, and probably wishing to eradicate bribery *in Russland*, to punish vice and set a salutary example, wrote to the police, wrote to the governor, wrote to the recruiting office about the head-man's wicked attempt. The peasant was put in prison and committed for trial. Thanks to the stupid and grotesque law which metes out the same punishment to the honest man who gives a bribe to an official and to the official himself who accepts the bribe, things looked black and the head-man had to be saved at all costs.

I rushed to the governor; he refused to intervene in the matter; the president and councillors of the Criminal Court shook their heads, terrified at the interference of the Imperial adjutant. The adjutant himself, relenting, was the first to declare that he 'wished the man no harm, that he only wanted to give him a lesson, that he ought *to be tried and then let off*.' When I

---

[11] Took him as a recruit. (*R.*)

told this to the *politsmeyster,* he observed: 'The fact is, none of these gentry know how things are done; he should have simply sent him to me. I would have given the fool a good drubbing—to teach him to look before he leaps—and would have sent him home. Everyone would have been satisfied, but now how are things to be patched up with the Criminal Court?'

These two comments express the Imperial Russian conception of law so neatly and strikingly that I cannot forget them.

Between these pillars of Hercules of the national jurisprudence, the head-man had fallen into the deepest slough, that is, into the Criminal Court. A few months later the verdict was prepared that the head-man after being punished with the lash should be exiled to Siberia. His son and all his family came to me, imploring me to save their father, the head of the family. I myself felt fearfully sorry for the peasant, ruined though perfectly innocent. I went again to the president and the councillors, and pointed out to them once more that they were doing themselves harm by punishing the elder so severely; that they knew very well themselves that no business was ever done without bribes; that, in fact, they would have nothing to eat if they did not, like true Christians, consider that every gift is perfect and every gift is good. Entreating, bowing, and sending the head-man's son to bow still lower, I succeeded in gaining half my object. The elder was condemned to a few strokes of the lash within the prison walls, was allowed to remain in his place of residence, but was forbidden to act as intermediary for the other peasants.

I sighed with relief when I saw the governor and the prosecutor had agreed to this, and went to the police to ask for some mitigation of the severity of the flogging; the police, partly because they were flattered at my coming myself to ask them a favour, partly through compassion for a man who was suffering for something that concerned them all so intimately, and knowing, moreover, that the man was well off, promised me to make it a pure formality.

One morning a few days later the head-man appeared, thinner and greyer than before. I saw that for all his delight he was sad about something and weighed down by some thought that oppressed him.

'What are you worrying about?' I asked him.

'Well, I wish they'd settle it once for all.'

'I don't understand.'

'I mean, when are they going to punish me?'

'Why, haven't they punished you?'

'No.'

'Then how is it they have let you go? You are going home, aren't you?'

'Home, yes; but you see I keep thinking about the punishment. The secretary did read it out.'

I could really make nothing of it, and at last asked him whether they had given him any sort of paper. He gave it me. The whole verdict was written in it, and at the end it was stated that, punishment with the lash having been inflicted within the prison walls in accordance with the sentence of the Criminal Court, 'he was to be given a certificate to that effect and set free.'

I burst out laughing.

'Well, you have been punished already, then!'

'No, sir, I haven't.'

'Well, if you are dissatisfied, go back and ask them to punish you; perhaps the police will put themselves in your place, and see your point.'

Seeing that I was laughing, the old man smiled too, shaking his head dubiously and adding: 'Go on with you! What strange doings!'

'How irregular!' many people will say; but they must remember that it is only through such irregularity that life in Russia is possible.

Appendix: Alexander Lavrentevich Vitberg

AMONG THE GROTESQUE and greasy, petty and loathsome people and scenes, files and titles, in this setting of official routine and red-tape, I recall the noble and melancholy features of an artist, who was crushed by the government with cold and callous cruelty.

The leaden hand of the Tsar not merely smothered a work of genius in its cradle, not merely destroyed the very creation of the artist, entangling him in judicial snares and the wiles of a police inquiry, but tried to snatch from him his honourable name altogether with his last crust of bread, and brand him as a taker of bribes and a pilferer of government funds.

After ruining and disgracing A. L. Vitberg, Nicholas exiled him to Vyatka. It was there that we met.

For two years and a half I lived with the great artist and saw the strong man, who had fallen a victim to the autocracy of red-tape officialdom and barrack-discipline, which blockishly measures everything in the world by the standard of the recruiting officer and the copying clerk's ruler, breaking down under the weight of persecution and misery.

It cannot be said that he succumbed easily; he struggled desperately for full ten years. He came into exile still hoping to confound his enemies and vindicate himself; he came, in a word, still ready for conflict, bringing plans and projects. But he soon discerned that all was over.

Perhaps he could have dealt even with this discovery, but he had at his side a wife and children and ahead of him years of exile, poverty, and privation; and Vitberg was turning grey, growing old, growing old not by the day but by the hour. When I left him in Vyatka at the end of two years he was ten years older.

Here is the story of this long martyrdom.

The Emperor Alexander did not believe it was *his* victory over Napoleon: he was oppressed by the fame of it and genuinely gave the glory to God. Always disposed to mysticism and melancholy, in which many people saw the fretting of conscience, he gave way to it particularly after the series of victories over Napoleon.

When 'the last soldiers of the enemy had crossed the frontier,' Alexander issued a proclamation in which he vowed to raise in Moscow a huge temple to the Saviour.

Plans were invited from all sides, and a great competition was instituted.

Vitberg was at that time a young artist who had just completed his studies and won a gold medal for painting. A Swede by origin, he was born in Russia and at first was educated in the Engineers' Cadet Corps. The artist was enthusiastic, eccentric, and given to mysticism: he read the proclamation, read the appeal for plans, and flung aside all other pursuits. For days and nights he wandered about the streets of Petersburg, tormented by a persistent idea; it was stronger than he was: he locked himself up in his room, took a pencil and set to work.

To no one in the world did he confide his design. After some months of work he went to Moscow to study the city and the surrounding country and set to work once more, shutting himself up for months together and keeping his design a secret.

The date of the competition arrived. The plans were numerous: there were designs from Italy and from Germany and our Academicians sent in theirs. And the unknown young man sent in his among the rest. Weeks passed before the Emperor examined the plans. These were the forty days in the wilderness, days of temptation, doubt, and agonising suspense.

Vitberg's colossal design, filled with religious poetry, impressed Alexander. He came to a stop before it, and it was the first of which he inquired the authorship. They broke open the sealed envelope and found the unknown name of an Academy pupil.

Alexander desired to see Vitberg. He had a long talk with the artist. His bold and fervent language, his genuine inspiration and the mystical tinge of his convictions impressed the Emperor. 'You speak in stones,' he observed, examining Vitberg's design again.

That very day his design was accepted and Vitberg was chosen to be the architect and the director of the building committee. Alexander did not know that with the laurel wreath he was putting a crown of thorns on the artist's head.

There is no art more akin to mysticism than architecture; abstract, geometrical, mutely musical, passionless, it lives in symbol, in emblem, in suggestion. Simple lines, their harmonious combination, rhythm, numerical relationships, make up something mysterious and at the same time incomplete. The building, the temple, is not its own object, as is a statue or a picture, a poem, or a symphony; a building requires an inmate; it is a place mapped and cleared for habitation, an environment, the cuirass of the tortoise, the shell of the mollusc; and the whole point of it is that the receptacle should correspond with its spirit, its object, its inmate, as the cuirass does with the tortoise. The walls of the temple, its vaults and columns, its portal and façade, its foundation and its cupola must bear the imprint of the divinity that dwells within it, just as the convolutions of the brain are imprinted on the bone of the skull.

The Egyptian temples were their holy books. The obelisks were sermons on the high-road.

Solomon's temple was the Bible turned into architecture; just as St Peter's in Rome is the architectural symbol of the escape from Catholicism, of the beginning of the lay world, of the beginning of the secularisation of mankind.

The very building of temples was so invariably accompanied by mystic rites, symbolical utterances, mysterious consecrations that the mediaeval builders looked upon themselves as something apart, a kind of priesthood, the heirs of the builders of Solomon's temple, and made up secret guilds of stonemasons, which afterwards passed into Freemasonry.

From the time of the Renaissance architecture loses its properly mystical character. The Christian faith is struggling with philosophic doubt, the Gothic arch with the Greek pediment, spiritual holiness with wordly beauty. What gives St Peter's its lofty significance is that in its colossal dimension Christianity struggles towards life, the church becomes pagan and on the walls of the Sistine Chapel Michelangelo paints Jesus Christ as a broad-shouldered athlete, a Hercules in the flower of his age and strength.

After St Peter's basilica, church architecture deteriorated completely and was reduced at last to simple repetition, on a larger or smaller scale, of the ancient Greek peripteries or of St Peter's.

One Parthenon is called St Madeleine's church in Paris; the other, the Stock Exchange in New York.

Without faith and without special circumstances, it was hard to create anything living: there is an air of artificiality, of hypocrisy, of anachronism, about all new churches, such as the five-domed cruet-stands with onions instead of corks in the Indo-Byzantine manner, which Nicholas builds, with Ton for architect, or the angular, Gothic churches, so offensive to the artistic eye, with which the English decorate their towns.

But the circumstances under which Vitberg created his design, his personality, and the state of mind of the Emperor were all exceptional.

The war of 1812 had caused a violent upheaval in men's minds in Russia; it was long after the deliverance of Moscow before the ferment of thought and nervous irritation could subside. Events outside Russia, the taking of Paris, the story of the Hundred Days, the suspense, the rumours, Waterloo, Napoleon sailing over the ocean, the mourning for fallen kinsmen, apprehension for the living, the returning troops, the soldiers going home, all had a violent effect on even the coarsest natures. Imagine a youthful artist, a mystic, gifted with creative power and at the same time a fanatic, under the influence of all that was happening, under the influence of the Tsar's challenge and his own genius.

Near Moscow, between the Mozhaysk and Kaluga roads, there is a slight eminence which dominates the whole city. These are the Sparrow Hills of which I have spoken in the first reminiscences of my youth. The city lies stretched at their foot, and one of the most picturesque views of Moscow is from the top of them.

Here Ivan the Terrible, at that time a young profligate, stood weeping and watching his capital burn; here the priest Sylvester appeared before him and with stern words transformed that monster of genius for twenty years.

Napoleon with his army skirted this hill, here his strength was broken, it was at the foot of the Sparrow Hills that his retreat began.

Could a better spot be found for a temple to commemorate the year 1812 than the furthest point which the enemy reached?

But this was not enough: the hill itself was to be turned into the lower part of the temple; the open ground down to the river was to be encircled by a colonnade, and on this base, built on three sides by nature itself, a second and a third temple were to be raised, making up a marvellous whole.

Vitberg's temple, like the chief dogma of Christianity, was threefold and indivisible.

The lowest temple, carved out of the hill, had the form of a parallelogram, a coffin, a body: its exterior formed a heavy portal supported by almost Egyptian columns, and it merged into the hill, into rough, unhewn nature. This temple was lit up by lamps in tall Etruscan candelabra, and the daylight filtered sparsely into it from the second temple, passing through a transparent picture of the Nativity. In this crypt all the heroes who had fallen in 1812 were to be laid to rest. An eternal requiem was to be said for those slain on the field of battle; the names of all of them, from generals to private soldiers, were to be carved upon the walls.

Upon this tomb, upon this graveyard, the second temple—the temple of outstretched hands, of life, of suffering, of labour—was laid out in the form of a Greek cross with its four equal arms. The colonnade leading to it was decorated with statues from figures of the Old Testament. At the entrance stood the prophets: they stood outside the temple pointing the way which they were not destined to tread. The whole story of the Gospels and of the Acts of the Apostles was depicted within this temple.

Above it, crowning it and completing it, was a third temple in the form of a dome. This temple, brightly lit, was the temple of the spirit of untroubled peace, of eternity, expressed in its circular plan. Here there were neither pictures nor sculpture, only on the outside it was encircled by a ring of archangels and was covered by a colossal cupola.

I am now giving from memory Vitberg's main idea. He had it worked out to the minutest detail and everywhere perfectly in harmony with Christian theology and architectural beauty.

The amazing man spent his whole life over his design. During the ten years that he was on his trial he was occupied with nothing else and, though harassed by poverty and privation in exile, he devoted several hours every day to his temple. He lived in it, he did not believe that it would never be built; memories, consolations, glory, all were in the artist's portfolio.

Perhaps one day some other artist, after the martyr's death, will shake the dust off those sheets and with reverence publish that architectural martyrology, in which was spent and wasted a life full of strength—for a moment illuminated by radiant light, then smudged and crushed among a drill-sergeant Tsar, serf-senators, and pettifogging ministers.

The design was a work of genius, frightening, almost mad; that was why Alexander chose it, that is why it ought to have been carried out. It was said that the hill could not have borne the weight of the temple. I find that incredible, especially if we remember all the new resources of American and English engineers, the tunnels which a train takes eight minutes to pass through, the chain-bridges, and so on.

Miloradovich[1] advised Vitberg to make the thick columns of the lower temple of single blocks of granite. On this someone observed that it would be very expensive to bring the granite blocks from Finland.

'That is just why we ought to order them,' answered Miloradovich; 'if there were a granite-quarry on the River Moskva there would be nothing wonderful in putting them up.'

Miloradovich was a warrior poet and he understood poetry in general. Grand things are done by grand means.

Only nature does great things for nothing.

Even those who never had any doubt of Vitberg's honesty blame him most for having undertaken the duty of directing operations, though he was an inexperienced young artist who knew nothing of official business. He ought to have confined himself to the part of architect. That is true.

But it is easy to make such criticisms sitting at home in one's study. He undertook it just because he was young, inexperienced, and an artist; he undertook it because, when his design had been accepted, everything seemed easy to him; he undertook it because the Tsar himself had proposed it to him, encouraged him, supported him. Is there any man whose head would not have been turned? . . . Are there any so prudent, so sober, so re-

---

[1] See p. 10, fn. 10. (*D.M.*)

strained? Well, if there are, they do not design colossal temples nor do they make 'stones speak'!

It need hardly be said that Vitberg was surrounded by a crowd of rogues, men who look on Russia as a field for speculation, on the service as a profitable line of business, on a public post as a lucky chance to make a fortune. It was easy to understand that they would dig a pit under Vitberg's feet. But that, after falling into it, he should be unable to get out again, was due also to the envy of some and the wounded vanity of others.

Vitberg's colleagues on the committee were the metropolitan Filaret, the Governor-General of Moscow,[2] and Senator Kushnikov; they were all offended in advance by being associated with a young puppy, especially as he gave his opinion boldly and objected when he did not agree.

They helped to get him into trouble, they helped to slander him and with cold-blooded indifference completed his ruin afterwards.

They were helped in this first by the fall of the mystically-minded minister Prince A. N. Golitsyn, and afterwards by the death of Alexander.

With the fall of Golitsyn came the collapse of Freemasonry, of the Bible Societies, of Lutheran pietism, which in the persons of Magnitsky[3] at Kazan and of Runich[4] in Petersburg ran to grotesque extremes, to savage persecutions, to convulsive dances, to states of hysteria and God knows what strange doings.

Savage, coarse, ignorant orthodoxy had the upper hand. It was preached by Foty[5] the archimandrite of Novgorod, who lived on intimate terms (not physically, of course) with Countess Orlov. The daughter of the well known Alexey Grigorevich Orlov who smothered Peter III, she hoped to win redemption for her father's soul by devoting herself to frenzied fanaticism, by giving up to Foty and his monastery the greater part of her enormous estates, which had been forcibly seized from the monasteries by Catherine.

But the one thing in which the Petersburg government is

---

[2] Prince D. V. Golitsyn. *(A.S.)*

[3] Magnitsky, Mikhail Leontevich (1778–1855), reactionary official and mystic; Warden of Kazan educational district and University, 1820–6. *(A.S.)*

[4] Runich, Dmitry Pavlovich (1778–1860), reactionary official and mystic; Warden of Petersburg education district, 1821–6. *(A.S.)*

[5] Foty (1792–1838), archimandrite of the Yurevsky monastery at Novgorod. He took part in palace intrigues under Alexander I, and influenced his reactionary policy. *(A.S.)*

persistent, the one thing in which it does not change, however its principles and religion may change, is its unjust oppression and persecution. The fury of the Runiches and the Magnitskys was turned against the Runiches and the Magnitskys. The Bible Society, only yesterday patronised and approved—the prop of morality and religion—was to-day closed and sealed, and its members put almost on the level of counterfeit coiners; the *Messenger of Zion*, only yesterday recommended to all fathers of families, was more severely prohibited than Voltaire and Diderot, and its editor, Labzin, was exiled to Vologda.

Prince A. N. Golitsyn's downfall involved Vitberg; everyone fell upon him, the committee complained of him, the metropolitan was offended and the Governor-General was dissatisfied. His answers were 'insolent' ('insolence' is one of the principal charges in the indictment of him); his subordinates were *thieves* —as though there was any one in the government service who was not a thief. Though indeed it is likely that there was more thieving among Vitberg's subordinates than among others; he had had no practice in superintending houses of correction and highly placed thieves.

Alexander commanded Arakcheyev to investigate the case. He was sorry for Vitberg; he let him know through one of his intimates that he believed in his rectitude.

But Alexander died and Arakcheyev fell. Under Nicholas Vitberg's case at once took a turn for the worse. It dragged on for *ten* years, with incredible absurdities. On the points on which he was found guilty by the Criminal Court he was acquitted by the Senate. On those on which he was acquitted by the Court he was found guilty by the Senate. The committee of ministers found him guilty on all the charges. The Tsar, taking advantage of the 'best privilege of monarchs, to show mercy and mitigate punishment,' added exile to Vyatka to his sentence.

And so Vitberg was sent into exile, dismissed from the service 'for abuse of the confidence of the Emperor Alexander and causing loss to the treasury.' He was fined, I believe, a million roubles, all his property was seized and sold at public auction, and a rumour was circulated that he had transferred countless millions to America.

I lived in the same house with Vitberg for two years and remained on intimate terms with him up to the time I left Vyatka. He had not saved the barest crust of bread; his family lived in the most frightful poverty.

❖   ❖   ❖

Two years after Vitberg's exile the merchants of Vyatka formed a project to build a new church.

Nicholas, being desirous of killing all spirit of independence, of individuality, of imagination, and of freedom, everywhere and in everything, published a whole volume of frontages for churches sanctioned by His Majesty. If anyone wanted to build a church he was absolutely obliged to select one of the government plans. He is said to have forbidden the writing of Russian operas, considering that even those written by the adjutant Lvov, in the Third Division of his own Chancellery, were good for nothing. But that was not enough: he ought to have published a collection of musical airs sanctioned by His Majesty!

The Vyatka merchants after turning over the 'approved' plans had the audacity to differ from the Tsar's taste. Nicholas marvelled at the design they sent in; he sanctioned it and sent instructions to the provincial authorities to see that the architect's ideas were faithfully carried out.

'Who made this design?' he asked the secretary.

'Vitberg, your Majesty.'

'What, the same Vitberg?'

'The same, your Majesty.'

And behold, like a bolt from the blue, comes permission for Vitberg to return to Moscow or Petersburg. The man had asked leave to clear his character and it had been refused; he made a successful design, and the Tsar bade him return—as though anyone had ever doubted his artistic ability. . . .

In Petersburg, almost perishing of want, he made one last effort to defend his honour. It was utterly unsuccessful. Vitberg asked the assistance of A. N. Golitsyn, but the latter thought it impossible to raise the case again, and advised Vitberg to write a plaintive letter to the Heir with a request for financial assistance. He undertook to do his best for him with the assistance of Zhukovsky,[6] and promised to get him a thousand silver roubles.

Vitberg refused.

I was in Petersburg for the last time at the beginning of the

---

[6] Zhukovsky, Vasily Andreyevich, (1783–1852), the well known poet, was tutor to the Tsarevich, afterwards Alexander II. He was a man of fine and generous character. His original work is not of the first order, but as a translator from the European and classical languages he was of invaluable service in the development of Russian culture. (*Tr.*)

winter of 1846 and there saw Vitberg. He was completely crushed. Even his old wrath against his enemies which I had liked so much had begun to die down; he had no more hope, he did nothing to escape from his situation, blank despair was bringing him to his end, all the components of this existence had broken down and he was waiting for death.

If this was what Nicholas Pavlovich wanted he may be satisfied.

Whether the sufferer is still living I do not know, but I doubt it.

'If it were not for my family, my children,' he said at parting, 'I should tear myself away from Russia and go begging alms about the world. With the Vladimir Cross on my neck I would calmly hold out to passers-by the hand pressed by the Emperor Alexander and tell them of my design and the fate of an artist in Russia!'

'They shall hear in Europe of your fate, poor martyr,' I thought; 'I will answer for that.'

The society of Vitberg was a great solace to me in Vyatka. A grave serenity and a solemnity in his manner lent him something of a priestly air. He was a man of very pure morals and in general more disposed to asceticism than indulgence; but his severity did not detract from the wealth and luxuriance of his artistic nature. He could give to his mysticism so plastic a form and so exquisite a colouring that criticism died away on one's lips; one was sorry to analyse, to dissect the glittering images and misty pictures of his imagination.

Vitberg's mysticism was partly due to his Scandinavian blood; it was the same coldly-thought-out visionariness that we see in Swedenborg, and which in its turn is like the fiery reflection of sunbeams in the icy mountains and snows of Norway.

Vitberg's influence made me waver, but my realistic temperament nevertheless gained the upper hand. I was not destined to rise into the third heaven: I was born a quite earthly creature. No tables turn at the touch of my hands nor do rings swing at my glance. The daylight of thought is more akin to me than the moonlight of phantasy.

But I was more disposed to mysticism at the period when I was living with Vitberg than at any other time.

Separation, exile, the religious exaltation of the letters I was receiving, the love which was filling my heart more and more intensely, and at the same time the oppressive feeling of remorse, all reinforced Vitberg's influence.

And for two years afterwards I was under the influence of

ideas of a mystical socialist tinge, drawn from the Gospel and from Jean-Jacques, after the style of French thinkers like Pierre Leroux.[7]

Ogarëv plunged into the sea of mysticism even before I did. In 1833 he was beginning to write the words for Gebel's[8] oratorio, *The Lost Paradise*. 'In the idea of a "Lost Paradise," ' Ogarëv wrote to me, 'there is the whole history of humanity'; so at that time, he too mistook the paradise of the ideal that we are seeking for a paradise we have lost.

In 1838 I wrote historical scenes in the religious socialist spirit, and at the time took them for dramas. In some I pictured the conflict of the pagan world with Christianity. In these Paul entering Rome raised a dead youth to a new life. In others I described the conflict of the official Church with the Quakers and the departure of William Penn to America, to the New World.[9]

The mysticism of the Gospel was soon replaced in me by the mysticism of science; fortunately I rid myself of the second also.

❖   ❖   ❖

---

[7] Leroux, Pierre (1797–1871), a follower of Saint-Simon, of the first half of the nineteenth century. (*Tr.*)

[8] Gebel, Franz (1787–1843), a well known musical composer of the period. (*Tr.*)

[9] I thought fit, I don't understand why, to write these scenes *in verse*. Probably I thought that anybody could write unrhymed five-foot iambics, since even Pogodin* wrote them. In 1838 or 1840, I gave both the manuscripts to Belinsky to read and calmly awaited his praises. But the next day Belinsky sent them back to me with a note in which he said: "Do please have them copied to run on without being divided into lines, then I will read them with pleasure, but as it is I am bothered all the time by the idea that they are in verse.'

Belinsky killed both my dramatic efforts. It is always pleasant to pay one's debts. In 1841 Belinsky published a long dialogue upon literature in the *Notes of the Fatherland*. 'How do you like my last article?' he asked me, as we were dining together *en petit comité* at Dusseau's. 'Very much,' I answered. 'All that you say is excellent, but tell me, please, how could you go on struggling for two hours talking to that man without seeing at the first word that he was a fool?' 'That's perfectly true,' said Belinsky, dying with laughter. 'Well, my boy, that's killing! Why, he is a perfect fool!'

* Pogodin, Mikhail Petrovich (1800–5), chiefly known as a historian of a peculiar Slavophil tinge, was co-editor with Shevyrëv of the *Moskvityanin*, a reactionary journal, and wrote historical novels of little merit. (*Tr.*)

The Tsarevich's Visit

THE HEIR will visit Vyatka! The Heir is travelling about Russia to show himself and look at the country! This news interested everyone, but the governor, of course, more than any. He was harassed and did a number of incredibly stupid things: ordered the peasants along the high-road to be dressed in their holiday caftans, ordered the fences in the towns to be painted and the sidewalks to be repaired. At Orlov a poor widow who owned a small house told the mayor that she had no money to repair the sidewalk and he reported this to the governor. The latter ordered the floors in the house to be taken up (the sidewalks there are made of wood), and that, should they not be sufficient, the repairs should be made at the government expense and the money recovered from her afterwards, even if it were necessary to sell her house at public auction. Things did not go so far as a sale, but the widow's floors were broken up.

Fifty versts from Vyatka is the place at which the wonder-working ikon of St Nicholas of Khlynov appeared to the people of Novgorod. When emigrants from Novgorod settled at Khlynov (now Vyatka) they brought the ikon, but it disappeared and turned up again on the Great River fifty versts from Vyatka. They fetched it back again, and at the same time took a vow that if the ikon would stay they would carry it every year in a solemn procession to the Great River. This was the chief summer holiday in the Vyatka province; I believe it is on the 23rd of May. For twenty-four hours the ikon travels down the river on a magnificent raft with the bishop and all the clergy in full vestments accompanying it. Hundreds of all sorts of boats, rafts, and dug-out canoes filled with peasants, money and women, Votyaks, and artisans follow the sailing image in a motley throng, and foremost of all is the governor's decked boat covered with red cloth. This barbaric spectacle is very fine. Tens of thousands of people from districts near and far wait for the image on the banks of the Great River. They all camp in noisy crowds about a small village, and, what is strangest of all, crowds of unbaptised Votyaks, Cheremises, and even Tatars come to pray to the image; indeed, the festival has a thoroughly pagan appearance. Outside the monastery-wall Votyaks and Russians bring sheep and calves to be sacrificed; they are killed on the spot, a monk reads a service over them, and blesses and consecrates the meat, which is sold at a special window within the precincts. The meat is distributed in pieces to the people; in the old days it used to be given for nothing: now the monks charge a few kopecks for every piece; so that a peasant who had presented a whole calf has to pay something for a piece of his own consumption. In the monastery-yard sit whole crowds of beggars, the halt, the blind, the deformed of all sorts, who sing 'Lazar' in chorus.[1] Lads—priests' sons or boys from the town—sit on the tombstones near the church with inkpots[2] and cry: 'Who wants lists written? Who wants lists?' Peasant girls and women surround them, mentioning names, and the lads, deftly scratching with their pens, repeat: 'Marya, Marya, Akulina, Sepanida, Father Ioann, Matrëna. . . . Well, Auntie, you have got a lot; you've shelled out two kopecks, we can't take less than five; such a family—Ioann, Vasilisa, Iona, Marya, Yezpraxia, Baby Katerina. . . .'

In the church there is much jostling and strange preferences are shown; one peasant woman will hand her neighbour a candle with exact instructions to put it up 'for our guest,' another gives one for 'our host.' The Vyatka monks and deacons are continually drunk during the whole time of this procession. They stop at the bigger villages on the way, and the peasants treat them to enough to kill them.

So this popular holiday, to which the peasants had been accustomed for ages, the governor proposed to move to an earlier date, wishing to entertain the Tsarevich who was to arrive on the 19th of May; he thought there would be no harm in St Nicholas, the *guest*, going on his visit to his *host* three days earlier. Of course the consent of the bishop was necessary; fortunately he was an amenable person, and found nothing to protest at in the governor's intention of celebrating the 23rd of May on the 19th.

The governor sent a list of his ingenious plans for the reception of the Tsarevich to the Tsar—as though to say, 'See how we fête your son.' On reading this document the Tsar flew into a rage, and said to the Minister of Home Affairs: 'The governor and the bishop are fools; leave the holiday as it was.' The Minister gave the governor a good scolding, the Synod did the

---

[1] A plaintive, wheedling song sung by beggars. (*R.*)
[2] The lists of names were sent up to the priest, who said a prayer for the owner of each name. (*R.*)

same to the bishop, and St Nicholas the guest kept to his old habits.

Among the various instructions from Petersburg, orders came that in every provincial town an exhibition should be held of the various natural products and handicrafts of the district, and that the things exhibited should be arranged according to the three natural kingdoms. This division into animal, vegetable and mineral greatly worried the officials, and even Tyufyayev to some extent. In order not to make a mistake he made up his mind in spite of his ill will to summon me to give advice.

'Now, for instance, honey,' he said, 'where would you put honey? or a gilt frame—how are you to decide where it is to go?'

Seeing from my answers that I had wonderfully precise information concerning the three natural kingdoms, he offered me the task of arranging the exhibition.

While I was busy arranging wooden vessels and Votyak dresses, honey and iron sieves, and Tyufyayev went on taking the most ferocious measures for the entertainment of his Imperial Highness at Vyatka, the Highness in question was graciously pleased to arrive at Orlov, and the news of the arrest of the mayor of Orlov burst like a clap of thunder on the town. Tyufyayev turned yellow, and there was an uncertainty apparent in his gait.

Five days before the Tsarevich arrived at Orlov, the mayor had written to Tyufyayev that the widow whose floor had been broken up to make the sidewalk was making a fuss, and that So-and-so, a wealthy merchant and a prominent person in the town, was boasting that he would tell the Tsarevich everything. Tyufyayev disposed of the man very cleverly; he told the mayor to have doubts of his sanity (the precedent of Petrovsky pleased him[3]), and to send him to Vyatka to be examined by the doctors; while the affair was going on the Tsarevich would have left the province of Vyatka, and that would be the end of it. The mayor did as he was bid; the merchant was in the hospital at Vyatka.

At last the Tsarevich arrived.[4] He gave Tyufyayev a frigid bow, did not invite him to visit him, but at once sent Dr Enokhin to examine the arrested merchant. He knew all about it. The Orlov widow had given him her petition; the other merchants and townsmen had told him all that was going on. Tyufyayev's face was more awry than ever. Things looked black

3 See pp. 176–7. (D.M.)
4 18th May, 1837. (A.S.)

for him. The mayor said straight out that he had had written instructions for everything from the governor.

Dr Enokhin declared that the merchant was perfectly sane. Tyufyayev was lost.

Between seven and eight in the evening the Tsarevich visited the exhibition with his suite. Tyufyayev conducted him, explaining things incoherently, getting into a muddle and speaking of a 'Tsar Tokhtamysh.'5 Zhukovsky and Arsenev, seeing that things were not going well, asked me to show them the exhibition. I took them round.

The Tsarevich's expression had none of that narrow severity, that cold, merciless cruelty which was characteristic of his father; his features were more suggestive of good nature and listlessness. He was about twenty, but was already beginning to grow stout.

The few words he said to me were friendly and very different from the hoarse, abrupt tones of his Uncle Constantine and without his father's custom of making his hearer almost faint with terror.

When he had gone away Zhukovsky and Arsenev began asking me how I had come to Vyatka. They were surprised to hear a Vyatka official speak like a gentleman. They at once offered to speak of my situation to the Tsarevich, and did in fact do all that they could for me. The Tsarevich approached the Tsar for permission for me to travel to Petersburg. The Tsar replied that that would be unfair to the other exiles, but, in consideration of the Tsarevich's representations, he ordered me to be transferred to Vladimir which was geographically an improvement, being seven hundred versts nearer home. But of that later.

In the evening there was a ball at the Assembly Rooms. The musicians who had been sent for expressly from one of the factories had arrived dead drunk; the governor had arranged that they should be locked up for twenty-four hours before the ball, escorted straight from the police-station to their seats in the orchestra, which none of them should be allowed to leave till the ball was over.

The ball was a stupid, awkward, extremely poor and extremely gaudy affair, as balls always are in little towns on exceptional occasions. Police officers fussed about, government

---

5 The Tatar khan of the Golden Horde, who in 1382 sacked the Kremlin at Moscow and massacred 24,000 people. (*R.*)

officials in uniform huddled against the wall, ladies flocked round the Tsarevich as savages do round travellers. . . . *A propos* the ladies, in one little town a *goûter* was arranged after the exhibition. The Tsarevich took nothing but one peach, the stone of which he threw on the window-sill. Suddenly a tall figure saturated with spirits stepped out from the crowd of officials; it was the district assessor, notoriously a dissolute character, who with measured steps approached the window, picked up the stone and put it in his pocket.

After the ball or the *goûter*, he approached one of the ladies of most consequence and offered her the stone gnawed by royalty; the lady was in raptures. Then he approached a second, then a third: all were in ecstasies.

The assessor had bought five peaches, cut out the stones, and made six ladies happy. Which had the real one? Each was suspicious of the genuineness of her own stone. . . .

After the departure of the Tsarevich, Tyufyayev with a heavy heart prepared to exchange his *pashalik* for the chair of a senator; but worse than that happened.

Three weeks later the post brought from Petersburg papers addressed to 'the administrator of the province.' Everything was turned upside down in the secretariat; the registrar ran in to say that they had received an *ukaz;* the officer manager rushed to Tyufyayev; Tyufyayev gave out that he was ill and did not go to the office.

Within an hour we learned that he had been dismissed *sans phrase*.

The whole town was delighted at the fall of the governor; there was something stifling, unclean, about his rule, a fetid odour of red tape, but for all that it was nasty to watch the rejoicings of the officials.

Yes, every ass gave a parting kick to this wounded boar. The meanness of men was just as apparent as at the fall of Napoleon, though the catastrophe was on a different scale. Of late I had been on terms of open hostility with him, and he would have certainly sent me off to some obscure little town such as Kay, if he had not been sent away himself. I had held aloof from him, and I had no reason to change my behaviour to him. But the others, who only the day before had been cap in hand to him, who had grudged him his carriage, eagerly anticipating his wishes, fawning on his dog and offering snuff to his valet, now barely greeted him and made an outcry all over the town against the irregularities, the guilt of which *they* shared with him. This is nothing new; it has been repeated so continually in every age and in every place that we must accept this meanness as a common trait of humanity and at any rate feel no surprise at it.

The new governor, Kornilov, arrived. He was a man of quite a different type: a tall, stout, lymphatic man of about fifty with a pleasantly smiling face and a cultured manner. He expressed himself with unusual ordinary grammatical correctness, and at great length, with a precision and clarity calculated by their very excess to obscure the simplest subject. He had been at the Lyceum of Tsarskoye Selo, had been a schoolfellow of Pushkin's, had served in the Guards, bought the new French books, liked talking of important subjects, and gave me Tocqueville's book on democracy in America on the day after his arrival.

The change was very striking. The same rooms, the same furniture, but instead of a Tatar *baskak* (tax-collector), with the exterior of a Tungus and the habits of a Siberian—a doctrinaire, something of a pedant, but at the same time quite a decent man. The new governor was intelligent, but his intelligence seemed somehow to shed light without giving warmth, like a bright, winter day which is pleasant though one does not look for fruits from it. Moreover, he was a terrible formalist—not in a pettifogging way, but . . . how shall I express it? . . . it was formalism of the second degree, but just as tiresome as any other.

Since the new governor was really married, the house lost its ultra-bachelor and polygamous character. Of course this brought all the councillors back to their lawful spouses; bald old men no longer boasted of their conquests among the fair, but, on the contrary, alluded tenderly to their faded, stiff, angularly bony, or monstrously fat wives.

Kornilov had some years before coming to Vyatka been promoted to be civil governor somewhere, straight from being a colonel in the Semënovsky or Izmaylovsky regiment. He went to his province knowing nothing of his duties. To begin with, like all novices, he set to work to read everything. One day a document came to him from another province which he could make nothing of, though he read it two or three times.

He called the secretary and gave it to him to read. The secretary could not explain the business clearly either.

'What will you do with that document,' Kornilov asked him, 'if I pass it on to the office?'

'I shall hand it in to the third table, it's their job.'

'Then the head-clerk of the third table knows what to do?'

'To be sure he does, Your Excellency, he has been in charge of that table for seven years.'

'Send him to me.'

The head-clerk came in. Kornilov handed him the paper and asked what was to be done. The head-clerk glanced through the file and informed him that they ought to make an inquiry in the palace of justice and send an order to the police-captain.

'But order what?'

The head-clerk was nonplussed, and at last admitted that it was difficult to express it in words, but that it was easy to write it.

'Here is a chair: please write the answer.'

The head-clerk took up the pen and without hesitation briskly scribbled off two documents.

The governor took them, read them once, read them twice, but could make nothing of them.

'I saw,' he told me, smiling, 'that it really was an answer to the document, and I thanked God and signed it. Nothing more was heard of the business—the answer was completely satisfactory.'

The news of my transfer to Vladimir came just before Christmas; I was soon ready and set off.

My parting with Vyatka society was very warm. In that remote town I had made two or three genuine friends among the young merchants.

Everyone vied in showing sympathy and kindness to the exile. Several sledges accompanied me as far as the first posting-station, and in spite of all my efforts to defend myself my sledge was filled up with a perfect load of provisions and wine. Next day I reached Yaransk.

From Yaransk the road goes through endless pine forests. It was moonlight and very frosty at night. The little sledge flew along the narrow road. I have never seen such forests since; they go on like that unbroken as far as Arkhangel, and sometimes reindeer come through them to the province of Vyatka. The forest is for the most part composed of large trees; the pines, extraordinarily straight, ran past the sledge like soldiers, tall and covered with snow from under which their black needles stuck out like bristles; one would drop asleep and wake up again and still the regiments of pines would be marching rapidly by, sometimes shaking off the snow. The horses are changed at little clearings; there is a tiny house lost among the trees, the horses are tied up to a trunk, the sledge-bells begin tinkling, and two or three Cheremis boys in embroidered shirts run out, looking sleepy. The Votyak driver swears at his companion in a husky alto, shouts 'Ayda,' begins singing a song on two notes . . . and again pines and snow, snow and pines.

Just as I drove out of Vyatka Province it was my lot to take my last farewell of the official world, and it showed itself in all its glory *pour la clôture*.

We stopped at a posting-station, and the driver had begun unharnessing the horses, when a tall peasant appeared in the porch and asked:

'Who is travelling through?'

'What's that to do with you?'

'Why, the police-captain told me to inquire, and I am the messenger of the rural court.'

'Well then, go into the station hut; my travelling permit is there.'

The peasant went away and came back a minute later, saying to the driver,

'He is not to have horses.'

That was too much. I jumped out of the sledge and went into the hut. A half-tipsy police-captain was sitting on a bench, dictating to a half-tipsy clerk. A man with fetters on his hands and feet was sitting or rather lying on another bench in the corner. Several bottles, glasses, tobacco ash, and bundles of papers were scattered about.

'Where is the police-captain?' I asked in a loud voice as I went in.

'The police-captain's here,' answered the half-tipsy man whom I recognised as Lazarev, a man I had seen in Vyatka. As he spoke he fixed a rude and impudent stare upon me—and suddenly rushed at me with open arms.

I must explain that after Tyufyayev's dismissal the officials, seeing that I was on quite good terms with the new governor, had begun to be rather afraid of me.

I stopped him with my hand and asked him very gravely,

'How could you give orders that I shouldn't have horses? What nonsense is this, stopping travellers on the high-road?'

'Why, I was joking; upon my soul, aren't you ashamed to be angry? Here, horses, order the horses! Why are you standing there, you rascal?' he shouted to the messenger. 'Do me the favour of having a cup of tea with rum.'

'Thank you very much.'

'But haven't we any champagne? . . .' He hurried to the bottles; they were all empty.

'What are you doing here?'

'An inquiry, sir. This fine fellow here has killed his father and sister with an axe, in a quarrel, through jealousy.'

The police-captain was disconcerted. I glanced at the Cheremis; he was a young fellow of twenty, with nothing savage about his face, which was typically Oriental, with shining, narrow eyes and black hair.

It was all so nasty that I went out into the yard again. The police-captain ran out after me with a glass in one hand and a bottle of rum in the other, and pressed me to have a drink.

To get rid of him I drank some; he caught hold of my hand and said:

'I am sorry, there, I am sorry! there it is, but I hope you won't speak of this to His Excellency; don't ruin an honourable man!'.

With that the police-captain *seized my hand and kissed it*, repeating a dozen times over:

'For God's sake don't ruin an honourable man.'

I pulled away my hand in disgust and said to him:

'Oh get away; as though I were likely to tell him.'

'But how can I be of service to you?'

'See they make haste and harness the horses.'

'Look alive,' he shouted, 'Ayda, ayda!' and he himself began dragging at some ropes and straps of the harness.

This incident is vividly imprinted on my memory. In 1846, when I was in Petersburg for the last time, I had to go to the secretariat of the Minister of Home Affairs to try to get a passport. While I was talking to the head-clerk of the table, a gentleman passed . . . shaking hands familiarly with the magnates of the secretariat and bowing condescendingly to the head-clerks of the tables. 'Bah, devil take it,' I thought, 'can that be he!'

'Who is that?' I asked.

'Lazarev, a clerk of special commissions and of great influence with the Minister.'

'Was he once a police-captain in the Vyatka Province?'

'Yes.'

'Well, I congratulate you, gentlemen: nine years ago he kissed my hand.'

Petrovsky was a master hand at choosing men!

The Beginning of
My Life at Vladimir

WHEN I WENT OUT to get into my sledge at Kosmodemyansk it was harnessed in the Russian style, with three horses abreast: one between the shafts and two flanking it. The shaft horse, with its yoke, rang the bells gaily.

In Perm and Vyatka the horses are put in tandem, one before the other or two side by side and the third in front.

So my heart throbbed with delight when I saw the familiar troika.

'Come now, show us your mettle,' I said to the young lad who sat smartly in the driver's seat in a sheepskin coat, the bare side turned outwards, and stiff gauntlets which barely allowed his fingers to close enough to take fifteen kopecks from my hand.

'We'll do our best, sir, we'll do our best. Hey, darlings! Now, sir,' he said, turning suddenly to me, 'you just hold on; there is a hill yonder, so I'll let them go.'

It was a steep descent to the Volga; in the winter the way lay across the ice.

He certainly did let the horses go. The sledge did not so much run as bound from right to left, from left to right, as the horses whirled it down-hill; the driver was tremendously pleased, and indeed, sinful man that I am, so was I—it is the Russian temperament.

So my post-horses brought me into 1838—into the best, the brightest year of my life. I shall describe how we saw the New Year in.

Eighty versts from Nizhny Novgorod we, that is Matvey, my valet, and I, went into the station-superintendent's to warm ourselves. There was a very sharp frost, and it was windy too. The superintendent, a thin, sickly, pitiful-looking man, inscribed my travelling permit, dictating every letter to himself and yet making mistakes. I took off my fur-lined coat and walked up and down the room in my huge fur boots, Matvey was warming himself at the red-hot stove, the superintendent muttered, and a wooden clock ticked on a faint, cracked note.

'I say,' Matvey said to me, 'it will soon be twelve o'clock; it's the New Year, you know. I'll bring in something,' he added, looking at me half-inquiringly, 'from the stores they put in our sledge at Vyatka.' And without waiting for an answer he ran to fetch bottles and a bag with some food.

Matvey, of whom I shall have more to say later, was more than a servant: he was a friend, a younger brother to me. A man of Moscow, apprenticed to Sonnenberg, whose acquaintance we shall also make, to learn the art of bookbinding, in which Sonnenberg, however, was not very proficient, he passed into my hands.

I knew that if I refused it would disappoint Matvey, and besides I had nothing against celebrating the day at the posting-station. . . . The New Year is a station of a sort.

Matvey brought ham and champagne.

The champagne turned out to be frozen solid; the ham could have been chopped with an axe, and was all glistening with ice; but *à la guerre comme à la guerre*.

'May the New Year bring new happiness.' Yes indeed, new happiness. Was I not on the way back? Every hour was bringing me nearer to Moscow—my heart was full of hopes.

The frozen champagne did not exactly please the superintendent. I added half a glass of rum to his wine. This new 'half-and-half'[1] was very successful.

The driver, whom I had also invited to join us, was still more extreme in his views; he sprinkled pepper into his glass of foaming wine, stirred it with a spoon, drank it off at one gulp, uttered a painful sigh and almost with a moan added: 'It did scorch fine!'

The superintendent himself tucked me into the sledge, and was so zealous in his attentions that he dropped the lighted candle into the hay and could not find it afterwards. He was in great spirits and kept repeating:

'You've given me a New Year's Eve, too!'

The scorched driver started the horses off. . . .

At eight o'clock on the following evening I reached Vladimir and put up at the hotel, which is extremely faithfully described in V. A. Sollogub's *Tarantas* with its fowls in rice, its dough-like *pâtisserie*, and vinegar by way of Bordeaux.

'A man was asking for you this morning, he's probably waiting at the beer-shop,' the waiter told me after reading my name

---

[1] In English in the text. (*R.*)

on my travel permit. He wore the rakish parting and dashing lovelocks, which in old days were only affected by Russian waiters, but now are also worn by Louis Napoleon.

I could not conceive who this could be.

'But here he is, sir,' added the waiter, moving aside. What I saw first, however, was not a man but a tray of terrific size, on which were piles of all sorts of good things, a cake and cracknels, oranges and apples, eggs, almonds, raisins . . . and behind the tray appeared the grey head and blue eyes of the village headman, from my father's Vladimir estate.

'Gvrilo Semënych,' I cried, and rushed to embrace him. This was the first of our own people, the first figure out of my former life, whom I met after imprisonment and exile. I could not take my eyes off the intelligent old man, and felt as though I would never say all I had to say to him. He was the living proof of my nearness to Moscow, to my home, to my friends; only three days before he had seen them all, he brought me greetings from them all. . . . So it was not so far away!

The governor, who was a clever Greek called Kuruta, had a thorough knowledge of human nature, and had long become indifferent to good and evil. He grasped my situation at once and did not make the slightest attempt to be a nuisance to me. Official forms were not even referred to; he commissioned me and a master at the high-school to edit the *Vladimir Provincial News*—that was my only duty.

The work was familiar to me; in Vyatka I had put the unofficial part of the *Provincial News* on its feet, and had published in it an article which almost got my successor into trouble. Describing the festival on the Great River, I said that the mutton sacrificed to St Nicholas of Khlynov used in old days to be distributed to the poor, but now was sold. The bishop was incensed and the governor had difficulty in persuading him to let the matter drop.

These provincial newspapers were introduced in 1837. The very original idea of training the inhabitants of the land of silence and dumbness to express themselves in print occurred to Bludov, the Minister of Home Affairs. This man, famous for being chosen to continue Karamzin's *History*, though he never actually added a line to it, and for being the author of the report of the committee of investigation into the affair of the 14th of December, which it would have been better not to write at all, belonged to the group of doctrinaire statesmen who appeared on the scene at the end of the reign of Alexander. They were intel-

ligent, cultured, honourable old 'Arzamas geese'[2] who had risen
and grown old in the service. They could write Russian, were
patriots, and were so zealously engaged in the history of their
native land that they had no time to give serious attention to its
present condition. They all cherished the never-to-be-forgotten
memory of N. M. Karamzin, loved Zhukovsky, knew Krylov by
heart, and used to go to Moscow to converse with I. I. Dmitriyev
in his house in Sadovaya Street, where I too visited him as a
student, armed with romantic prejudices, a personal acquaintance with N. Polevoy, and a concealed disapproval of the fact
that Dmitriyev, who was a poet, should be Minister of Justice.
Great things were hoped of them, and like most doctrinaires of
all countries they did nothing. Perhaps they might have succeeded in leaving more permanent traces under Alexander, but
Alexander died and they were left with nothing but their *desire*
to do something worth doing.

At Monaco there is an inscription on the tombstone of one of
the hereditary princes: 'Here lies the body of Florestan So-and-
so—he *desired* to do good to his subjects.'[3] Our doctrinaires also
desired to do good, not to their own subjects but to the subjects of
Nicholas Pavlovich, but they reckoned without their host. I do
not know who hindered that Florestan, but these were hindered
by our Florestan. They were drawn into complicity in all the
measures detrimental to Russia and had to restrict themselves to
useless innovations, mere alternations of name and form. Every
head of a department among us thinks it his highest duty to
produce at intervals a project, an innovation, usually for the
worse but sometimes simply neutral. They thought it necessary
for instance to call the secretary in the governor's office by a
name of purely Russian origin,[4] while they left the secretary of
the provincial office untranslated into Russian.[5] I remember that
the Minister of Justice brought forward a plan for essential
changes in the uniforms of civil servants. This scheme opened in
a majestic and solemn style: 'Taking into special consideration
the lack of unity, of standard, in the make and pattern of certain
uniforms in the civil department and adopting as a fundamental
principle,' and so on.

---

[2] The reference is to the 'Arzamas,' a literary club of which Karamzin,
Batyushkov, Uvarov, this Bludov and some others were members. The
town Arzamas is noted for its geese. (*Tr.*)

[3] *Il a voulu le bien de ses sujets.*

[4] '*Pravitel' del*' (lit. 'manager of affairs'). (*R.*)

[5] '*Sekretar.*' (*R.*)

Possessed by the same mania for reform the Minister for Home Affairs replaced the rural assessors by police inspectors. The assessors lived in the towns and used to visit the villages. The police inspectors sometimes met together in the town but lived permanently in the country. In this way all the peasants were put under the supervision of the police and this was done with full knowledge of the predatory, carnivorous, corrupt character of our police officials. Bludov introduced the policeman into the secrets of the peasants' industry and wealth, into their family life, into the affairs of the *mir*, and in this way laid his hand on the last refuge of peasant life. Fortunately our villages are very many and there are only two police inspectors in a district.

Almost at the same time the same Bludov had the notion of establishing provincial newspapers. In Russia, although the government has no regard for popular education, it has great literary pretensions, and while in England, for instance, there are no official organs, every one of our departments has its own magazine, and so have the universities and the academy. We have journals relating to mining, to dry-salting, French and German ones, naval and military ones. All these are published at the government expense; contracts for literary articles are made in the ministries exactly as contracts are for fuel and candles, but without competition; there are plenty of statistics, invented figures and fantastic inferences from them. After monopolising everything else, the government has now taken the monopoly of talk and, imposing silence on everyone else, has begun chattering unceasingly. Continuing this system, Bludov commanded every provincial government to publish its own newspaper, which was to have an unofficial part for articles on historical, literary, and other subjects.

No sooner said than done, and the officials in fifty provinces were tearing their hair over this unofficial part. Priests with a seminary education, doctors of medicine, high-school teachers, all who could be suspected of a tinge of culture and ability to spell correctly were requisitioned. After much reflection and reading over of the *Library of Good Reading* and the *Notes of the Fatherland*, with tremors and false starts they at last wrote the articles.

The desire to see one's name in print is one of the strongest artificial passions in a man who has been corrupted by this bookish age. Nevertheless it needs a special occasion to induce people to expose their efforts to public criticism. People who would never have dared to dream of their essays being printed in the *Moscow News* or in a Petersburg magazine, began to publish them at home. And, meanwhile, the fatal habit of having a newspaper, the habit of publicity, took root. And, indeed, it may not be amiss to have an instrument ready. The printing press, too, is an unruly member![6]

---

[6] At this point Herzen begins the story of his wife, Natalie—his first cousin and, like him, the illegitimate child of a wealthy aristocrat: her solitary and unhappy childhood, their courtship and early married life. It takes up the last hundred pages of the first volume. They are omitted here—as are the last one hundred and seventy pages of the second volume, about their tragic later married life ("A Family Drama")—for reasons of theme and space as explained in the Preface. (*D.M.*)

❖   ❖   ❖

MOSCOW, PETERSBURG AND NOVGOROD

(1840-1847)

Return to Moscow and Intellectual Debate

AT THE BEGINNING of 1840 we left Vladimir and the poor, narrow River Klyazma. With anxiety and a heavy heart I left the little town where we were married. I foresaw that the same simple, profound intimate life would be no more, and that we should have to furl many of our sails.

Our long, solitary walks outside the town where, lost among the meadows, we felt so keenly the spring in nature and the spring in our hearts, would never come again. . . .

The winter evenings when, sitting side by side, we closed the book and listened to the crunch of sledge-runners and the jingle of bells, that reminded us of the 3rd of March, 1838, and our journey of the 9th of May[1] would never come again. . . .

They would never come again!

In how many keys and for how many ages men have known and repeated that 'The May of life blossoms once and never again,'[2] and yet the June of mature age with its hard, harvest-time work, with its stony roads, catches a man unawares. Youth, all unheeding, floats along in a sort of algebra of ideas, emotions and yearnings, is little interested in the particular, little touched by it; and then comes love, the unknown quantity found; all is concentrated on one person, through whom everything passes, in whom the universal becomes dear, in whom the elegant becomes beautiful; then, too, the young are untouched by the external, they are *given* to each other, and about them let no grass grow!

But it does grow, together with the nettles and the thistles, and sooner or later they begin to sting or hook on to you.

We knew that we could not take Vladimir with us, but still we thought that our May was not yet over. I even fancied that in going back to Moscow I was going back once more to my student days. All the surroundings helped to maintain the illusion. The same house, the same furniture—here was the room where Ogarëv and I, shut in together, used to conspire two paces away from the Senator and my father, and here was my father him-

---

[1] The dates of H.'s meeting in Moscow with his cousin Natalie, during H.'s secret visit, and of their arrival and marriage in Vladimir. (*A.S.*)

[2] From Schiller's poem 'Resignation.' (*A.S.*)

self, grown older and more bent, but just as ready to scold me for coming home late. 'Who is lecturing tomorrow? When is the rehearsal? I am going from the university to Ogarëv's. . . .' It was 1833 over again!

Ogarëv was actually there.

He had received permission to go to Moscow a few months before me. Again his house became a centre where old and new friends met. And although the old unity was no more, he was surrounded by all the nice people.

Ogarëv, as I have had occasion to observe already, was endowed with a peculiar magnetism, a feminine quality of attraction. For no apparent reason others are drawn to such people and cling to them; they warm, unite, and soothe them, they are like an open table at which everyone sits down, renews his powers, rests, grows calmer and more stout-hearted, and goes away a friend.

His acquaintances swallowed up a great deal of his time; he suffered from this at times, but he kept his door open, and met everyone with his gentle smile. Many people thought it a great weakness. Yes, time was lost and wasted, but love was gained, not only of intimate friends, but of outsiders, of the weak: and that is worth as much as reading and other interests.

I have never been able to understand clearly how it is that people like Ogarëv can be accused of idleness. The standards of the factory and the workhouse hardly apply here. I remember that in our student days Vadim and I were once sitting over a glass of Rhine wine when he became more and more gloomy, and suddenly with tears in his eyes, repeated the words of Don Carlos[3] (who quoted them from Julius Caesar): 'Twenty-three and nothing done for immortality!' This so mortified him that he brought his open hand down with all his might on the green wine-glass and cut it badly. All that is so, but neither Caesar nor Don Carlos and Posa, nor Vadim and I explained why we must do something *for immortality*. There is work and it has to be done, and is it to be done for the sake of the work, or for the sake of being remembered by mankind?

All that is somewhat obscure: and what is work?

Work, *business*.[4]. . . Officials recognise as such only civil and criminal affairs; the merchant regards as work nothing but commerce; military men call it their work to strut about like

---

[3] In Schiller's play of that name, Act II, scene 2. (*A.S.*)

[4] English in the original. (*Tr.*)

cranes and to be armed from head to foot in time of peace. To my thinking, to serve as the link, as the centre of a whole circle of people, is a very great work, especially in a society both disunited and fettered. No one has reproached me for idleness, and many people have liked some of the things I have done; but do they know how much of all that I have done has been the reflection of our talks, our arguments, the nights we spent idly strolling about the streets and fields, or still more idly sitting over a glass of wine?

❖   ❖   ❖

The circle of young people that formed itself round Ogarëv was not our old circle. Only two of his old friends, besides ourselves, were in it. Tone, interests, pursuits, all had changed. Stankevich's friends took the lead in it; Bakunin and Belinsky stood at their head, each with a volume of Hegel's philosophy in his hand, and each filled with the youthful intolerance inseparable from vital, passionate convictions.

Stankevich, also one of the *idle* people who accomplish *nothing*, was the first disciple of Hegel in the circle of young people in Moscow. He had made a profound study of German philosophy, which appealed to his aesthetic sense: endowed with exceptional abilities, he drew a large circle of friends into his favourite pursuit. This circle was extremely remarkable: from it came a regular legion of *savants*, writers and professors, among whom were Belinsky, Bakunin and Granovsky.

Before our exile there had been no great sympathy between our circle and Stankevich's. They disliked our almost exclusively political tendency, while we disliked their almost exclusively speculative interests. They considered us to be *Frondeurs* and French, we thought them sentimentalists and German. The first man who was acknowledged both by us and by them, who held out the hand of friendship to both and by his warm love for both and his conciliating character removed the last traces of mutual misunderstanding, was Granovsky; but when I arrived in Moscow he was still in Berlin, and poor Stankevich at the age of twenty-seven was dying on the shore of the Lago di Como.

Sickly in constitution and gentle in character, a poet and a dreamer, Stankevich was naturally bound to prefer contemplation and abstract thought to living and purely practical questions; his artistic idealism suited him; it was 'the crown of victory' set on the pale, youthful brow that bore the imprint of death. The others had too much physical vigour and too little poetical feeling to remain long absorbed in speculative thought without passing on into life. An exclusively speculative tendency is utterly opposed to the Russian temperament, and we shall soon see how the *Russian spirit* transformed Hegel's teaching and how the vitality of our nature asserted itself in spite of all those who took the tonsure of philosophical monasticism. But at the beginning of 1840 the young people surrounding Ogarëv had as yet no thought of rebelling against the letter on behalf of the spirit, against the abstract on behalf of life.

My new acquaintances received me as people do receive exiles and old champions, people who come out of prison or return from captivity or banishment, that is, with respectful indulgence, with a readiness to receive us into their alliance, though at the same time refusing to yield a single point and hinting at the fact that they are 'to-day' and we are already 'yesterday,' and exacting an unconditional acceptance of Hegel's *Phenomenology* and *Logic*, and their interpretation of them, too.

They discussed these subjects incessantly; there was not a paragraph in the three parts of the *Logic*, in the two of the *Aesthetic*, the *Encyclopaedia*, and so on, which had not been the subject of desperate disputes for several nights together. People who loved each other avoided each other for weeks at a time because they disagreed about the definition of 'all-embracing spirit,' or had taken as a personal insult an opinion on 'the absolute personality and its existence in itself.' Every insignificant pamphlet published in Berlin or other provincial or district towns of German philosophy was ordered and read to tatters and smudges, and the leaves fell out in a few days, if only there was a mention of Hegel in it. Just as Francoeur in Paris wept with emotion when he heard that in Russia he was taken for a great mathematician and that all the younger generation made use of the same letters as he did when they solved equations of various powers, tears might have been shed by all those forgotten Werders, Marheinekes, Michelets, Ottos, Watkes, Schallers, Rosenkranzes, and even Arnold Ruge himself,[5] whom Heine so wonderfully well dubbed 'the gate-keeper of Hegelian philos-

---

[5] Arnold Ruge (1802–80) began his political career with six years' imprisonment in connection with the *Burschenschaft* movement, founded the *Deutsche Jahrbücher*, the journal of the Young Hegelian School, and some ten years later *Die Reform*, a more definitely political paper. From 1849 he lived in England, advocated a universal democratic state, and wrote many books, of which his autobiography is now of most interest. (*Tr.*)

ophy,' if they had known what bloodshed, what declarations they were exciting in Moscow between the Maroseyka and the Mokhovaya,[6] how they were being read, and how they were being *bought*.

The young philosophers adopted a conventional language; they did not translate philosophical terms into Russian, but transferred them whole, even, to make things easier, leaving all the Latin words *in crudo*, giving them orthodox terminations and the seven Russian cases.

I have the right to say this because, carried away by the current of the time, I wrote myself exactly in the same way, and was actually surprised when Perevoshchikov, the well known astronomer, described this language as the 'twittering of birds.' No one in those days would have hesitated to write a phrase like this: 'The concretion of abstract ideas in the sphere of plastics presents that phase of the self-seeking spirit in which, defining itself for itself, it passes from the potentiality of natural immanence into the harmonious sphere of pictorial consciousness in beauty.' It is remarkable that here Russian words, as in the celebrated dinner of the generals of which Yermolov spoke, sound even more foreign than Latin ones.

German learning—and it is its chief defect—has become accustomed to an artificial, heavy, scholastic language of its own, just because it has lived in academies, that is, in the monasteries of idealism. It is the language of the priests of learning, a language for the *faithful*, and none of the catechumens understood it. A key was needed for it, as for a letter in cypher. The key is now no mystery; when they understood it, people were surprised that very sensible and very simple things were said in this strange jargon. Feuerbach was the first to begin using a more human language.

The mechanical copying of the German ecclesiastico-scientific jargon was the more unpardonable since the leading characteristic of our language is the extraordinary ease with which everything is expressed in it—abstract ideas, the lyrical emotions of the heart, 'life's mouse-like flitting,'[7] the cry of indignation, sparkling mischief, and shaking passion.

---

[6] V. P. Botkin lived in the Maroseyka, and Granovsky, Belinsky and Bakunin stayed with him there at various times. Moscow University is in the Mokhovaya. (*A.S.*)

[7] From A. S. Pushkin: *Verses Written during a Night of Sleeplessness*. (*A.S.*)

Another mistake, far graver, went hand in hand with this distortion of language. Our young philosophers distorted not merely their phrases but their understanding; their attitude to life, to reality, became schoolboyish and literary; it was that learned conception of simple things at which Goethe mocks with such genius in the conversation of Mephistopheles with the student. Everything that in reality was direct, every simple feeling, was exalted into abstract categories and came back from them without a drop of living blood, a pale, algebraic shadow. In all this there was a naïveté of a sort, because it was all perfectly sincere. The man who went for a walk in Sokolniky went in order to give himself up to the pantheistic feeling of his unity with the cosmos; and if on the way he happened upon a drunken soldier, or a peasant woman who got into conversation with him, the philosopher did not simply talk to them, but defined the essential substance of the people in its immediate and fortuitous manifestation. The very tear that started to the eye was strictly referred to its proper classification, to *Gemüth* or 'the tragic in the heart.'

It was the same thing in art. A knowledge of Goethe, especially of the second part of *Faust* (either because it is inferior to the first or because it is more difficult), was as obligatory as the wearing of clothes. The philosophy of music had a place in the foreground. Of course, no one ever spoke of Rossini; to Mozart they were indulgent, though they did think him childish and poor. To make up for this they carried out philosophical investigations into every chord of Beethoven and greatly respected Schubert, not so much, I think, for his superb melodies as for the fact that he chose philosophical themes for them, such as 'The Omnipotence of God' and 'Atlas.' French literature—everything French in fact, and, incidentally, everything political also—shared the interdict laid on Italian music.

From this it is easy to see on what field we were bound to meet and do battle. So long as we were arguing that Goethe was objective but that his objectivity was subjective, while Schiller as a poet was subjective but that his subjectivity was objective, and *vice versa*, everything went peaceably. Questions that aroused more passion were not slow to make their appearance.

While Hegel was Professor in Berlin, partly from old age, but twice as much from satisfaction with his position and the respect he enjoyed, he purposely screwed his philosophy up above the earthly level and kept himself in an ambience where all contemporary interests and passions became somewhat indistinguishable, like buildings and villages seen from an air-balloon; he did not like to be entangled in these accursed practical questions with which it is difficult to deal and which must receive a positive answer. How clamant this violent and insincere dualism was, in a doctrine which set out from the elimination of dualism, can be understood readily. The real Hegel was the modest Professor at Jena, the friend of Hoelderlin, who hid his *Phenomenology* under his coat when Napoleon entered the town; then his philosophy did not lead to Indian quietism, nor to the justification of the existing forms of society, nor to Prussian Christianity; then he had not given his lectures on the Philosophy of Religion, but had written things of genius such as the article on the executioner and the death penalty, printed in Rosenkranz's biography.

Hegel confined himself to the sphere of abstractions in order to avoid the necessity of touching upon empirical deductions and practical applications; the one domain which he, very adroitly, selected for the practical application of his theories was the calm, untroubled ocean of aesthetics. He rarely ventured into the light of day, and then only for a minute, wrapped up like an invalid; and even then he left behind in the dialectic maze just those questions that were most interesting to the modern man. The extremely feeble intellects (Gans is the only exception), who surrounded him, accepted the letter for the thing itself and were pleased by the empty play of dialectics. Probably at times the old man felt sad and ashamed at the sight of the limited outlook of his excessively complacent pupils. If the dialectic method is not the development of the reality itself, the educating of it to think, so to speak, it becomes a purely external means of making a farrago of things run the gauntlet of a system of categories, an exercise in logical gymnastics, as it was with the Greek Sophists and the mediaeval schoolmen after Abelard.

The philosophical phrase which did the greatest harm, and in virtue of which the German conservatives strove to reconcile philosophy with the political régime of Germany—'all that is real is rational'—was the principle of sufficient reason and of the correspondence of logic and facts expressed in other words. Hegel's phrase, wrongly understood, became in philosophy what the words of the Christian Girondist Paul once were: 'There is no power but from God.' But if all powers are from God, and if the existing social order is justified by reason, the struggle against it, if only it exists, is also justified. These two sentences accepted in their formal meaning are pure tautology; but, tautology or not, Hegel's phrase led straight to the recognition of the sovereign authorities, led to a man's sitting with folded arms, and that was just what the Berlin Buddhists wanted. However contrary such a view may be to the Russian spirit, our Moscow Hegelians were genuinely misled and accepted it.

Belinsky, the most active, impulsive, and dialectically passionate, fighting nature, was at that time preaching an Indian stillness of contemplation and theoretical study instead of conflict. He believed in that view and did not flinch before any of its consequences, nor was he held back by considerations of moral propriety nor the opinion of others, which has such terrors for the weak and those who lack independence. He was free from timidity for he was strong and sincere; his conscience was clear.

'Do you know that from your point of view,' I said to him, thinking to impress him with my revolutionary ultimatum, 'you can prove that the monstrous tyranny under which we live is rational and ought to exist?'

'There is no doubt about it,' answered Belinsky, and proceeded to recite to me Pushkin's 'Anniversary of Borodino.'

That was more than I could stand and a desperate battle raged between us. Our falling out reacted upon the others, and the circle fell apart into two camps. Bakunin wanted to reconcile, to explain, to *exorcise*, but there was no real peace. Belinsky, irritated and dissatisfied, went off to Petersburg, and from there fired off his last furious salvo at us in an article which he likewise called 'The Anniversary of Borodino.'

Then I broke off all relations with him. Bakunin, though he argued hotly, began to reconsider things; his sound revolutionary judgment pushed him in another direction. Belinsky reproached him for weakness, for concessions, and went to such exaggerated extremes that he scared his own friends and admirers. The chorus were on Belinsky's side, and looked down upon us, haughtily shrugging their shoulders and considering us to be behind the times.

In the midst of this intestine strife I saw the necessity *ex ipso fonte bibere* and began studying Hegel in earnest. I even think that a man who has not *lived through* Hegel's *Phenomenology* and Proudhon's *Contradictions of Political Economy*, who has not passed through that furnace and been tempered by it, is not complete, not modern.

When I had grown used to Hegel's language and mastered his method, I began to perceive that he was much nearer to our viewpoint than to that of his followers; he was so in his early works, he was so everywhere where his genius had taken the bit between its teeth and had dashed forward oblivious of the Brandenburg Gate. The philosophy of Hegel is the algebra of revolution; it emancipates a man in an unusual way and leaves not one stone upon another of the Christian world, of the world of tradition that has outlived itself. But, perhaps with intention, it is badly formulated.

Just as in mathematics—only there with more justification—men do not go back to the definition of space, movement, force, but continue the dialectical development of their laws and qualities; so also in the formal understanding of philosophy, after once becoming accustomed to the first principles, men go on merely drawing deductions. Anyone new to the subject, who has not stupefied himself by the method's being turned into a habit, grasps at just these traditions, these dogmas which have been accepted as thoughts. To people who have long been studying the subject, and are consequently not free from predilections, it seems astonishing that others should not understand things that are 'perfectly clear.'

How can anyone fail to understand such a simple idea as, for instance, 'that the soul is immortal and that what perishes is only the personality,' a thought so successfully developed in his book by the Berlin Michelet; or the still simpler truth that the absolute spirit is a personality, conscious of itself through the world, and at the same time having its own self-consciousness?

All these things seemed so easy to our friends, they smiled so condescendingly at 'French' objections, that for some time I was stifled by them and worked and worked to reach a precise understanding of their philosophic jargon.

Fortunately scholasticism is as little natural to me as mysticism, and I stretched its bow until the string snapped and the blindfold dropped from my eyes.

❖   ❖   ❖

Two or three months later, Ogarëv passed through Novgorod. He brought me Feuerbach's *Wesen des Christenthums;* after reading the first pages I leapt up with joy. Down with the trapping of masquerade; away with the stammering allegory! We are free men and not the slaves of Xanthos;[8] there is no need for us to wrap the truth in myth.

In the heat of my philosophic ardour I began my series of

---

[8] Aesop is said to have been the slave of Xanthos, a philosopher of Samos. (*R.*)

articles on 'Dilettantism in Science,' in which, among other things, I paid the doctor out.

Now let us go back to Belinsky.

A few months after his departure to Petersburg in 1840 we arrived there too. I did not go to see him. Ogarëv took my quarrel with Belinsky very much to heart; he knew that Belinsky's absurd opinion was a passing malady, and indeed I knew it too, but Ogarëv was kinder. At last by his letters he almost forced a meeting on us. Our interview was at first cold, unpleasant and strained, but neither Belinsky nor I was very diplomatic and in the course of trivial conversation I mentioned the article on 'The Anniversary of Borodino.' Belinsky jumped up from his seat and, flushing crimson, said with great simplicity,

'Well, thank God, we've come to it at last. Otherwise I am so stupid I should not have known how to begin. . . . You've won; three or four months in Petersburg have done more to convince me than all the arguments. Let us forget this nonsense. It is enough to tell you that the other day I was dining at a friend's and there was an officer of the Engineers there; my friend asked him if he would like to make my acquaintance. "Is that the author of the article on 'The Anniversary of Borodino' "? the officer asked him in his ear. "Yes." "No, thank you very much," he answered dryly. I heard it all and could not restrain myself. I pressed the officer's hand warmly and said to him: "You're an honourable man, I respect you. . . ." What more would you have?'

From that moment up to Belinsky's death we went hand in hand.

Belinsky, as was to be expected, fell upon his former opinion with all the stinging vehemence of his language and all his furious energy. The position of many of his friends was not very much to be envied. *Plus royalistes que le roi*, with the courage of misfortune they tried to defend their theories, while not averse to an honourable truce. All those with sense and vitality went over to Belinsky's side; only the obstinate formalists and pedants held aloof. Some of them reached such a point of German suicide through dead, scholastic learning that they lost all living interest and were themselves lost without a trace. Others became orthodox Slavophils. Strange as the combination of Hegel and Stefan Yavorsky[9] may appear, it is more possible than might be

---

[9] Stefan Yavorsky was a famous monk and theologian of the eighteenth century. (*Tr.*)

supposed; Byzantine theology is just such a superficial casuistry and play with logical formulas as Hegel's dialectics, formally accepted. Some of the articles in the *Moskvityanin* are a triumphant demonstration of the extremes to which, with talent, the sodomitical union of philosophy and religion can go.

Belinsky by no means abandoned Hegel's philosophy when he renounced his one-sided interpretation of it. Quite the contrary, it is from this point that there begins his living, apt, original combination of philosophical with revolutionary ideas. I regard Belinsky as one of the most remarkable figures of the period of Nicholas. After the liberalism which had somehow survived 1825[10] in Polevoy, after the gloomy article of Chaadayev,[11] Belinsky appears on the scene with his caustic scepticism, won by suffering, and his passionate interest in every question. In a series of critical articles he touches in season and out of season upon everything, true everywhere to his hatred of authority and often rising to poetic inspiration. The book he was reviewing usually served him as a starting-point, but he abandoned it half-way and plunged into some other question. The line 'That's what kindred are' in *Onegin* is enough for him to summon family life before the judgment seat and to pick blood relationships to pieces down to the last thread. What fidelity there is to his principles, what dauntless consistency, what adroitness in navigating between the shoals of the censorship, what boldness in his attacks on the literary aristocracy, on the writers of the first three grades, on the secretaries of state of literature who were always ready to defeat an opponent by foul means if not by fair, if not by criticism then by delation? Belinsky scourged them mercilessly, tearing to pieces the petty vanity of the conceited, limited writers of eclogues, lovers of culture, benevolence and tenderness; he turned into derision their dear, their heartfelt notions, the poetical dreams flowering under their grey locks, their naïveté, hidden under an Anna ribbon.

How they hated him for it!

The Slavophils on their side began their official existence with the war upon Belinsky; he drove them by his taunts to the *murmolka* and the *zipum*.[12] It is worth remembering that Belinsky had formerly written in *Notes of the Fatherland*, while

---

[10] The accession of Nicholas I and execution of the Decembrists. (*D.M.*)
[11] His first 'Philosophical Letter,' published in the *Telescope* in 1836. (*A.S.*)
[12] *Murmolka*, a peasant cap, and *zipum*, a long homespun peasant coat. (*Tr.*)

Kireyevsky began publishing his excellent journal under the title of *The European;* no better proof than these titles could be found to show that at first the difference was only between shades of opinion and not between parties.

Belinsky's articles were awaited with feverish expectation by the young people in Moscow and Petersburg from the 25th of every month. Half a dozen times the students would call in at the coffee-houses to ask whether *Notes of the Fatherland* had been received; the heavy volume was snatched from hand to hand. 'Is there an article by Belinsky?' 'Yes,' and it was devoured with feverish interest, with argument . . . and three or four cherished convictions and reputations were no more.

Sokobelev, the governor of the Peter-Paul fortress, might well say in jest to Belinsky when he met him on the Nevsky Prospect: 'When are you coming to us? I have a nice warm little cell all ready that I am keeping for you.'

I have spoken in another book of Belinsky's development and of his literary activity; here I will only say a few words about the man himself.

Belinsky was very shy and quite lost his head in an unfamiliar or very numerous company; he knew this and did the most absurd things in his desire to conceal it. Ketscher tried to persuade him to go to visit a lady; the nearer they came to her house the gloomier Belinsky became; he kept asking whether they could not go another day, and talked of having a head-ache. Ketscher, who knew him, would accept no evasions. When they arrived Belinsky set off running as soon as he got out of the sledge, but Ketscher caught him by the overcoat and led him to be introduced to the lady.

He sometimes put in an appearance at Prince Odoyevsky's literary-diplomatic evenings. At these there were crowds of people who had nothing in common except a certain fear of and aversion from each other: clerks from the embassies and Sakharov the archaeologist, painters and A. Meyendorf, several councillors of state of the cultured sort, Ioakinth Bichurin[13] from Pekin, people who were half gendarmes and half literary men, others who were wholly gendarmes and not at all literary men. The hostess concealed her affliction at her husband's vulgar tastes, and gave way to them much as Louis-Philippe at the beginning

---

[13] Ioakinth Bichurin (1777–1853), a monk and at one time an archimandrite, head of the Orthodox Mission to Pekin, and later a translator from the Chinese in the Ministry of Foreign Affairs. (*Tr.*)

of his reign indulged his electors by inviting to the balls at the Tuileries whole *rez-de-chaussée* of suspender-craftsmen, chandlers, shoe-makers, and other worthy citizens.

Belinsky was utterly lost at these evenings, between a Saxon ambassador who did not understand a word of Russian and an official of the Third Division who understood even words that were not uttered. He was usually ailing for two or three days afterwards and cursed the man who had persuaded him to go.

One Saturday, since it was New Year's Eve, Odoyevsky took it into his head to mix a punch *en petit comité* when the principal guests had dispersed. Belinsky would certainly have gone away, but he was prevented by a barricade of furniture; he was somehow stuck in a corner and a little table was set before him with wine and glasses on it; Zhukovsky in the white trousers of his uniform, with gold lace on them, sat down obliquely opposite him. Belinsky stood it for a long time but, seeing no chance of his lot improving, he began moving the table a little; the table yielded at first, but then lurched over and crashed to the floor, while the bottle of Bordeaux very deliberately began to empty itself over Zhukovsky. He jumped up, and the red wine trickled down his trousers; there was an uproar: one servant rushed up with a napkin to daub the wine on to the other parts of the trousers, and another picked up the broken wine-glasses . . . while this hubbub was going on Belinsky disappeared and, near to death as he was, ran home on foot.

Dear Belinsky! for what a long time he was angry and upset at such incidents, with what horror he used to recall them, walking up and down the room and shaking his head without the trace of a smile!

But in that shy man, that frail body, there dwelt a mighty spirit, the spirit of a gladiator! Yes, he was a powerful fighter! he could not preach or lecture; what he needed was a quarrel. If he met with no objection, if he was not stirred to irritation, he did not speak well, but when he felt stung, when his cherished convictions were called in question, when the muscles of his cheeks began to quiver and his voice to burst out, then he was worth seeing; he pounced upon his opponent like a panther, he tore him to pieces, made him a ridiculous, a piteous object, and incidentally developed his own thought, with unusual power and poetry. The dispute would often end in blood, which flowed from the sick man's throat; pale, gasping, with his eyes fixed on the man with whom he was speaking, he would lift his handkerchief to his mouth with shaking hand and stop, deeply mortified, crushed by his physical weakness. How I loved and how I pitied him at those moments!

Persecuted financially by the sharks of literature, morally persecuted by the censorship, surrounded in Petersburg by people for whom he had little sympathy, and consumed by a disease to which the Baltic climate was fatal, he became more and more irritable. He shunned outsiders, was *farouche*, and sometimes spent weeks together in melancholy inactivity. Then the publishers sent note after note demanding copy, and the enslaved writer, grinding his teeth, took up his pen and wrote the venomous articles quivering with indignation, the indictments which so impressed their readers.

Often, utterly exhausted, he would come to us to rest, and lie on the floor with our two-year-old child; he would play with him for hours together. While we were only the three of us things went swimmingly, but if there came a ring at the bell, a spasmodic grimace passed over his face and he would look about him uneasily, trying to find his hat; then, with the weakness of a Slav, he would often remain. Here one word, a remark that was not to his liking, would lead to the most extraordinary scenes and arguments. . . .

Once he went in Holy Week to dine with a literary man, and Lenten dishes were served.

'Is it long,' he asked, 'since you became so devout?'

'We eat Lenten fare,' answered the literary gentleman, 'simply and solely for the sake of the servants.'

'*For the sake of the servants*,' said Belinsky, and he turned pale. 'For the sake of the servants,' he repeated, and flung down his dinner napkin. 'Where are your servants? I'll tell them that they are deceived. Any open vice is better and more humane than this contempt for the weak and uneducated, this hypocrisy in support of ignorance. And do you imagine that you are free people? You are on the same level as all the tsars and priests and slave-owners. Good-bye. I don't eat Lenten fare for the edification of others; I have no servants!'

Among the Russians who might be classified as inveterate Germans, there was one, a *magister* of our university, who had lately arrived from Berlin; he was a good-natured man in dark-blue spectacles, stiff and decorous; he had come to a standstill for ever after upsetting and enfeebling his faculties with philosophy and philology. A doctrinaire and something of a pedant, he was fond of holding forth in edifying style. On one occasion, at a literary evening in the house of the novelist who kept the fasts for the sake of his servants, the *magister* was preaching some sort of *honnête et modéré* twaddle. Belinsky was lying on a sofa in the corner and as I passed him he took me by the tail of my coat and said:

'Do you hear the rubbish that monster is talking? My tongue has long been itching, but my chest hurts a bit and there are a lot of people. Be a father to me, make a fool of him somehow, squash him, crush him with ridicule, you can do it better—come, cheer me up.'

I laughed and told Belinsky that he was setting me on like a bull-dog at a rat. I scarcely knew the gentleman and had hardly heard what he said.

Towards the end of the evening, the *magister* in the blue spectacles, after abusing Koltsov for having abandoned the national costume, suddenly began talking of Chaadayev's famous 'Letter,' and concluded his commonplace remarks, uttered in that didactic tone which of itself provokes derision, with the following words: 'Be that as it may, I consider his action contemptible and revolting: I have no respect for such a man.'

There was in the room only one man closely associated with Chaadayev, and that was I. I shall have a great deal to say about Chaadayev later on; I always liked and respected him and was liked by him; I thought it was unseemly to let pass this savage remark. I asked him dryly whether he supposed that Chaadayev had had ulterior aims in writing his letter, or had been insincere.

'Certainly not,' answered the *magister*.

An unpleasant conversation followed; I demonstrated to him that the epithets 'revolting and contemptible' were themselves revolting and contemptible when applied to a man who had boldly expressed his opinion and had suffered for it. He expatiated to me on the oneness of the people, the unity of the fatherland, the crime of destroying that unity, and of sacred things that must not be touched.

Suddenly Belinsky mowed down the speech I was making: he leapt up from his sofa, came up to me as white as a sheet, slapped me on the shoulder and said:

'Here you have them, they have spoken out—the inquisitors, the censors—keeping thought in leading-strings . . .' and so he went on and on.

He spoke with formidable inspiration, seasoning serious words with deadly sarcasms:

'We are strangely sensitive: men are flogged and we don't resent it, sent to Siberia and we don't resent it; but here Chaadayev, you see, has rubbed the people's honour the wrong way: he mustn't dare to talk; to speak is insolence—a flunkey must never speak! Why is it that in more civilised countries, where one would expect susceptibilities, too, to be more developed than in Kostroma and Kaluga, words are not resented?'

'In civilised countries,' replied the *magister*, with inimitable self-complacency, 'there are prisons in which they confine the senseless creatures who insult what the whole people respect . . . and a good thing too.'

Belinsky seemed to tower: he was terrifying, great at that moment. Folding his arms over his sick chest and looking straight at the *magister*, he answered in a hollow voice:

'And in still more civilised countries there is a guillotine to deal with those who think that a good thing.'

Having said this, he sank exhausted in an easy-chair and spoke no more. At the word 'guillotine' our host turned pale, the guests were disquieted and a pause followed. The *magister* had been annihilated, but it is just at such moments that human vanity takes the bit between its teeth. I. Turgenev advises a man, when he has gone such lengths in argument that he begins to feel frightened himself, to move his tongue ten times round the inside of his mouth before uttering a word.

The *magister*, unaware of this homely advice, went on babbling feeble trivialities, addressing himself rather to the rest of the company than to Belinsky.

'In spite of your intolerance,' he said at last, 'I am certain that you will agree with one . . .'

'No,' answered Belinsky; 'whatever you said I shouldn't agree with anything!'

Everyone laughed and went in to supper. The *magister* picked up his hat and went away.

Suffering and privation soon completely undermined Belinsky's sickly constitution. His face, particularly the muscles about his lips, and the mournfully fixed look in his eyes, testified equally to the intense workings of his spirit and the rapid dissolution of his body.

I saw him for the last time in Paris in the autumn of 1847; he was in a very bad way and afraid of speaking aloud; it was only at moments that his former energy revived and its ebbing fires glowed brightly. It was at such a moment that he wrote his letter[14] to Gogol.

---

[14] The reference is to the open letter in which Belinsky expressed his passionate indignation at the *Correspondence with Friends*, by Gogol. (*Tr.*)

The news of the revolution of February found him still alive; he died taking its glow for the flush of the rising dawn!

So this chapter ended in 1854; since that time much has changed. I have been brought much *closer* to that time, closer because of my increasing remoteness from people here, and through the arrival of Ogarëv[15] and by two books: Annenkov's *Biography of Stankevich* and the first parts of Belinsky's complete works. From the windows suddenly thrown open the fresh air of the fields, the young breath of spring was wafted into the hospital wards. . . .

Stankevich's correspondence was unnoticed when it came out. It appeared at the wrong moment. At the end of 1857 Russia had not yet come to herself after the funeral of Nicholas; she was expectant and hopeful; that is the worst mood for reminiscences . . . but the book is not lost. It will remain in the paupers' burial-ground one of the rare memorials of its times from which any man who can read may learn what in those days was buried without a word. The pestilential streak, running from 1825 to 1855, will soon be completely cordoned off; men's traces, swept away by the police, will have vanished, and future generations will often come to a standstill in bewilderment before a waste land rammed smooth, seeking the lost channels of thought which actually were never interrupted. The current was apparently checked: Nicholas tied up the main artery—but the blood flowed along side-channels. It is just these capillaries which have left their trace in the works of Belinsky and the correspondence of Stankevich.

Thirty years ago the Russia of the future existed exclusively among a few boys, hardly more than children, so insignificant and unnoticed that there was room for them between the soles of the great boots of the autocracy and the ground—and in them was the heritage of the 14th of December, the heritage of a purely national Russia, as well as of the learning of all humanity. This new life sprouted like the grass that tries to grow on the lip of a still smouldering crater.

In the very jaw of the monster these children stand out unlike other children; they grow, develop, and begin to live an utterly different life. Weak, insignificant, unsupported—nay, on the contrary, persecuted by all, they may easily perish, leaving not the smallest trace, but they survive, or, if they die half-way, not

[15] Ogarëv, having left Russia for ever, came to H. in London on 9th April, 1856. (*A.S.*)

everything dies with them. They are the rudimentary germs, the embryos of history, barely perceptible, barely existing, like all embryos in general.

Little by little groups of them are formed. What is more nearly akin to them gathers round their centre-points; then the groups repel one another. This dismemberment gives them width and many-sidedness for their development; after developing to the end, that is to the extreme, the branches unite again by whatever names they may be called—Stankevich's circle, the Slavophils, or our little *coterie*.

The leading characteristic of them all is a profound feeling of alienation from official Russia, from their environment, and at the same time an impulse to get out of it—and in some a vehement desire to get rid of it.

The objection that these circles, unnoticed both from above and from below, form an exceptional, an extraneous, an unconnected phenomenon, that the education of the majority of these young people was exotic, strange, and that they sooner express a translation into Russian of French and German ideas than anything of their own, seems to us quite groundless.

Possibly at the end of the last century and the beginning of this there was in the aristocracy a fringe of Russian foreigners who had sundered all ties with the national life; but they had neither living interests, nor *coteries* based on convictions, nor a literature of their own. They were sterile and became extinct. Victims of Peter's break with the people, they remained eccentric and whimsical, they were not merely superfluous but undeserving of pity. The war of 1812 set a term to them—the older generation were living out their time, and none of the younger developed in that direction. To include among them men of the stamp of P. Ya. Chaadayev would be a most fearful mistake.

Protest, rejection, hatred of one's country if you will, has a completely different significance from indifferent aloofness. Byron, lashing at English life, fleeing from England as if from the plague, remained a typical Englishman. Heine, trying, from anger at the abominable political condition of Germany, to turn Frenchman, remained a genuine German. The highest protest against Judaism—Christianity—is filled with the spirit of Judaism. The rupture of the states of North America with England could lead to war and hatred, but it could not make the North Americans un-English.

As a rule it is with great difficulty that men abandon their physiological memories and the mould in which they are cast by heredity; to do so a man must be either peculiarly unpassioned and featureless or absorbed in abstract pursuits. The impersonality of mathematics and the unhuman objectivity of nature do not call forth those sides of the soul and do not awaken them; but as soon as we touch upon questions of life, of art, of morals, in which a man is not only an observer and investigator but at the same time himself a participant, then we find a physiological limit—which it is very hard to cross with one's old blood and brains unless one can erase from them all traces of the songs of the cradle, of the fields and the hills of home, of the customs and whole setting of the past.

The poet or the artist in his truest work always belongs to the people. Whatever he does, whatever aim and thought he may have in his work, he expresses, whether he will or not, some elements of the popular character and expresses them more profoundly and more clearly than the very history of the people. Even when renouncing everything national, the artist does not lose the chief features from which it can be recognised to what people he belongs. Both in the Greek *Iphigenia* and in the Oriental *Divan* Goethe was a German. Poets really are, as the Romans called them, prophets; only they utter not what is not and what will be by chance, but what is unrecognised, what exists in the dim consciousness of the masses, what is already slumbering in it.

Everything that has existed from time immemorial in the soul of the Anglo-Saxon people is held together, as if by a ring, by personality alone; and every fibre, every hint, every attempt, which has slowly come down from generation to generation, unconscious of itself, has taken on form and language.

Probably no one supposes that the England of the time of Elizabeth—particularly the majority of the people—had a precise understanding of Shakespeare; they have no precise understanding of him even now—but then they have no precise understanding of themselves either. But when an Englishman goes to the theatre he understands Shakespeare instinctively, through sympathy, of that I have no doubt. At the moment when he is listening to the play, something becomes clearer and more familiar to him. One would have thought that a people so capable of rapid comprehension as the French might have understood Shakespeare too. The character of Hamlet, for instance, is so universally human, especially in the stage of doubts and irresolution, in the consciousness of some black deeds being perpetrated round about them, some betrayal of the great in favour of the mean and trivial, that it is hard to imagine that he should not be understood; but in spite of every trial and effort, Hamlet remains alien to the Frenchman.

If the aristocrats of the last century, who systematically despised everything Russian, remained in reality incredibly more Russian than the house-serfs remained peasants, it is even more impossible that the younger generation could have lost their Russian character because they studied science and philosophy from French and German books. A section of the Slavs at Moscow, with Hegel in their hands, attained the heights of ultra-Slavism.

The very appearance of the circles of which I am speaking was a natural response to a profound, inward need in the Russian life of that time.

We have spoken many times of the stagnation that followed the crisis of 1825. The moral level of society sank, development was interrupted, everything progressive and energetic was struck out of life. Those who remained—frightened, weak and bewildered—were petty and insignificant; the trash of the generation of Alexander occupied the foremost place; little by little they changed into cringing officials, lost the savage poetry of junketing and lordliness together with any shadow of independent dignity; they served tenaciously, they served until they reached high positions, but they never became great personages. Their day was over.

Below this great world of society, the great world of the people maintained an indifferent silence; nothing was changed for them: their plight was bad, but no worse than before, the new blows fell not on their bruised backs. Their time had not yet come. Between this roof and this foundation the first to raise their heads were children, perhaps because they did not suspect how dangerous it was; but, let that be as it might, with these children Russia, stunned and stupefied, began to come to herself.

What halted them was the complete contradiction of the *words* they were taught with the *facts* of life around them. Their teachers, their books, their university spoke one language and that language was intelligible to heart and mind. Their father and mother, their relations, and their whole environment spoke another with which neither mind nor heart was in agreement—but with which the dominant authorities and financial interests were in accord. This contradiction between education and custom nowhere reached such dimensions as among the nobility and gentry of Russia. The shaggy German student with his round cap covering a seventh part of his head, with his world-shaking pranks, is far nearer to the German *Spiessbürger* than is supposed, and the French *collégien*, lank from vanity and emulation, is already *en herbe l'homme raisonnable qui exploite sa position.*

The number of educated people amongst us has always been extremely small; but those who were educated have always received an education, not perhaps very comprehensive, but fairly general and humane: it made men of all with whom it succeeded. But a man was just what was not wanted either for the hierarchical pyramid or for the successful maintenance of the landowning régime. The young man had either to dehumanise himself again—and the greater number did so—or to stop short and ask himself: 'But is it absolutely essential to go into the service? Is it really a good thing to be a landowner?' After that there followed for some, the weaker and more impatient, the idle existence of a cornet on the retired list, the sloth of the country, the dressing-gown, eccentricities, cards, wine; for others a time of ordeal and inner travail. They could not live in complete moral disharmony, nor could they be satisfied with a negative attitude of withdrawal; the stimulated mind required an outlet. The various solutions of these questions, all equally harassing for the younger generation, determined their distribution into various circles.

Thus our *coterie*, for instance, was formed, and at the university it met Sungurov's, already in existence. His, like ours, was concerned rather with politics than with learning. Stankevich's circle, which came into being at the same time, was equally near both and equally remote from both. He went by another path: his interests were purely theoretical.

Between 1830 and 1840 our convictions were too youthful, too ardent and passionate, not to be exclusive. We could feel a cold respect for Stankevich's circle, but we could not be intimate with its members. They traced philosophical systems, were absorbed in self-analysis, and found peace in a luxurious pantheism from which Christianity was not excluded. We were dreaming how to get up a new league in Russia on the pattern of the Decembrists and looked upon learning itself as a means to our end. The government did its best to strengthen us in our revolutionary tendencies.

In 1833 all Sungurov's circle was sent into exile and—vanished.

In 1835 we were exiled. Five years later we came back,

tempered by our experience. The dreams of youth had become the irreversible determination of maturity. This was the most brilliant period of Stankevich's circle. Stankevich himself I did not find in Moscow—he was in Germany; but it was just at that moment that Belinsky's articles were beginning to attract the attention of everyone.

On our return we measured our strength with them. The battle was an unequal one; basis, weapons, and language—all were different. After fruitless skirmishes we saw that it was our turn now to undertake serious study and we too set to work upon Hegel and the German philosophy. When we had sufficiently assimilated that, it became evident that there was no ground for dispute between us and Stankevich's circle.

The latter was inevitably bound to break up. It had done its work, and had done it most brilliantly; its influence on the whole of literature and academic teaching was immense—it is enough to mention the names of Belinsky and Granovsky; Koltsov was formed in it, Botkin, Katkov, and others belonged to it. But it could not remain a closed circle without passing into German doctrinairism—men who are alive and are Russian are not capable of that.

Close to Stankevich's circle, as well as ours, there was another, formed during our exile and in the same relationship to them as we were; its members were afterwards called Slavophils. The Slavs approached from the opposite direction the vital questions which occupied us, and were far more deeply immersed in living work and real conflict than Stankevich's circle.

It was natural that Stankevich's society should split up between them and us. The Aksakovs and Samarin joined the Slavophils, that is, Khomyakov and the Kireyevskys. Belinsky and Bakunin joined us. The closest friend of Stankevich, the most nearly akin to him in his whole nature, Granovsky, was one of us from the day he came back from Germany.

If Stankevich had lived, his circle would still have broken up. He would himself have gone over to Khomyakov or to us.

By 1842 the sifting in accordance with natural affinity had long been complete, and our camp stood in battle array face to face with the Slavophils. Of that conflict we shall speak in another place.[16]

In conclusion I shall add a few words about the elements of which Stankevich's circle was composed; this will throw a light of its own on the strange underground currents which were

---

[16] See "Our 'Opponents,' " pp. 287–305. (*D.M.*)

silently undermining the compact crust of the Russo-German régime.

Stankevich was the son of a wealthy landowner of the province of Voronezh, and was at first brought up in all the ease and freedom of a landowner's life in the country; then he was sent to the school at Ostrogozhsk (and that was something quite out of the way). For fine natures a wealthy and even aristocratic education is very good. A sufficiency gives unfettered freedom and space for growth and development of every sort; it does not constrict the young mind with premature anxiety and apprehension of the future, and it provides complete freedom to pursue the subjects to which it is drawn.

Stankevich's development was broad and harmonious; his artistic, musical, and at the same time reflective and contemplative nature showed itself from the very beginning of his university career. His special faculty, not only for deeply and warmly understanding, but also for reconciling, or as the Germans say 'removing' contradictions, was based on his artistic temperament. The need for harmony, proportion and enjoyment makes such people indulgent as to the means; to avoid seeing the well, they cover it over with canvas. The canvas will not stand a push, but the eye is not bothered by a yawning gulf. In this way the Germans attained to pantheistic quietism and rested upon it; but such a gifted Russian as Stankevich could not remain 'at peace' for long.

This is evident from the first question which involuntarily troubled him immediately after he left the university.

His pressing business was finished, he was left to himself, he was no longer led by others, *but he did not know what he should do*. There was nothing to go on with, there was no one and nothing around him that appealed to a lively man. A youth, when his mind had cleared and he had had time to look about him after school, found himself in the Russia of those days in the position of a traveller waking up in the steppe; one might go where one would—there were traces, there were bones of those who had perished, there were wild beasts and the empty desert on all sides with its dumb threat of danger, in which it is easy to perish and impossible to struggle. The one thing which could be pursued honourably and heartily was study.

And so Stankevich persevered in the pursuit of learning. He imagined that it was his vocation to be an historian, and began studying Herodotus; it could be foreseen that nothing would come of that pursuit.

He would have liked to be in Petersburg, where there was such ebullition of activity *of a sort* and to which he was attracted by the theatre and by nearness to Europe; he would have liked to be an honorary superintendent of the school at Ostrogozhsk. He determined to be of use in that 'modest career'—which was to be even less successful than Herodotus. He was in reality drawn to Moscow, to Germany, to his own university circle, to his own interests. He could not exist without intimate friends (another proof that there were at hand no interests very near to his heart). The need for sympathy was so strong in Stankevich that he sometimes invented intellectual sympathy and talents, and saw and admired in people qualities in which they were completely lacking.[17]

But—and in this lay his personal power—he did not often need to have recourse to such fictions; at every step he met wonderful people—he had the faculty of meeting them—and everyone to whom he opened his heart remained his passionate friend for life; and to every such friend Stankevich's influence was either an immense benefit or an alleviation of his burden.

In Voronezh Stankevich used sometimes to go to the one local library for books. There he used to meet a poor young man of humble station, modest and melancholy. It turned out that he was the son of a cattle-dealer who had business with Stankevich's father over supplies. Stankevich befriended the young man; the cattle-dealer's son was a great reader and fond of talking of books. Stankevich got to know him well. Shyly and timidly the youth confessed that he had himself tried his hand at writing verses and, blushing, ventured to show them. Stankevich was amazed at the immense talent not conscious nor confident of itself. From that minute he did not let him go until all Russia was reading Koltsov's songs with enthusiasm. It is quite likely that the poor cattle-dealer, oppressed by his relations, unwarmed by sympathy or recognition, might have wasted his songs on the empty steppes beyond the Volga over which he drove his herds, and Russia would never have heard those wonderful, truly native songs, if Stankevich had not crossed his path.

When Bakunin finished his studies at the school of artillery, he received a commission as an officer in the Guards. It is said that his father was angry with him and himself asked that he should be transferred into the army of the line. Cast away in some

---

[17] Klyushnikov vividly expressed this in the following image: 'Stankevich is a silver rouble that envies the size of a copper piece.'—Annenkov, *Biography of Stankevich*, p. 133.

God-forsaken village in White Russia with his guns, he grew
farouche and unsociable, left off performing his duties, and
would lie for whole days together on his bed wrapped in a
sheepskin coat. His commanding officer was sorry for him; he
had, however, no alternative but to remind him that he must
either carry out his duties or go on the retired list. Bakunin had
not suspected that he had a right to take the latter course and at
once asked to be relieved of his commission. On receiving his
discharge he came to Moscow, and from that date (about 1836)
for him life began in earnest. He had studied nothing before, had
read nothing, and hardly knew any German. With great dialectical abilities, with a gift for obstinate, persistent thinking, he
had strayed without map or compass into a world of fantastic
projects and efforts at self-education. Stankevich perceived his
talents and set him down to philosophy. Bakunin learnt German from Kant and Fichte and then set to work upon Hegel,
whose method and logic he mastered to perfection—and to
whom did he not preach it afterwards? To us and to Belinsky, to
ladies and to Proudhon.

But Belinsky drew as much from the same source; Stankevich's views on art, on poetry and its relation to life, grew in
Belinsky's articles into that powerful modern critical method,
that new outlook upon the world and upon life which impressed
all thinking Russia and made all the pedants and doctrinaires
recoil from Belinsky with horror. It was Stankevich's lot to
initiate Belinsky into the mysteries; but the passionate, merciless, fiercely intolerant talent that carried Belinsky beyond all
bounds wounded the aesthetically harmonious temperament of
Stankevich.

❖　　❖　　❖

Petersburg and
the Second Banishment

Though we were so comfortable in Moscow, we had to move to
Petersburg. My father insisted upon it. Count Strogonov, the
Minister for Home Affairs, commanded me to enter his secre-
tariat, and we set off there at the end of the summer of 1840.

◇   ◇   ◇

I was not long in the service. I got out of my duties in every possible way, and so I have not a great deal to tell about the service. The secretariat of the Ministry of Home Affairs had the same relationship to the secretariat of the Governor of Vyatka as boots that have been cleaned have to those who have not; the leather is the same, the sole is the same, but the one sort show mud, and the others polish. I did not see clerks drunk in Petersburg. I did not see twenty kopecks taken for looking up a reference, but yet I somehow fancied that under those close-fitting dress-coats and carefully combed heads there dwelt such vile, black, petty, envious, cowardly little souls that the head-clerk of my table at Vyatka seemed to me more of a man than any of them. As I looked at my new colleagues I recalled how, on one occasion, after having a drop too much at supper at the district surveyor's, he played a dance tune on the guitar, and at last could not resist leaping up with his instrument and beginning to join in the dance; but these Petersburg men are never carried away by anything: their blood never boils, and wine does not turn their heads. In some dancing class, in company with young German ladies, they can walk through a French quadrille, pose as disillusioned, repeat lines from Timofeyev[1] or Kukolnik[2] . . . they were diplomats, aristocrats, and Manfreds. It is only a pity that Dashkov, the Minister, could not train these Childe Harolds not to stand at attention and bow even at the theatre, at church, and everywhere.

The Petersburghers laugh at the costumes seen in Moscow; they are outraged by the caps and Hungarian jackets, the long hair and civilian moustaches. Moscow certainly is an unmilitary city, rather dishevelled and unaccustomed to discipline, but whether that is a good quality or a defect is a matter of opinion. The harmony of uniformity; the absence of variety, of what is personal, whimsical, and wayward; the obligatory wearing of uniform, and outward good form—all develop to the highest degree in the most inhuman condition in which men live—in

---

[1] Timofeyev, Alexey Vasilevich (1812–83), a sixth-rate writer of forgotten poems. (*Tr.*)
[2] Kukolnik, Nestor Vasilevich (1809–68), was a schoolfellow of Gogol's, and a very popular writer of stories and dramas in the most extreme romantic style—fearfully bombastic and unreal, and hyper-patriotic. (*Tr.*)

barracks. Uniforms and uniformity are passionately loved by despotism. Nowhere are fashions so respectfully observed as in Petersburg, and that shows the immaturity of our civilisation; our clothes are alien. In Europe people dress, but we dress up, and so are frightened if a sleeve is too full, or a collar too narrow. In Paris all that people are afraid of is being dressed without taste; in London all that they are afraid of is catching cold; in Italy everyone dresses as he likes. If one were to show him the battalions of exactly similar, tightly buttoned frock-coats of the fops on the Nevsky Prospect, an Englishman would take them for a squad of 'policemen.'

I had to do violence to my feelings every time I went to the Ministry. The chief of the secretariat, K. K. von Paul, a *Herrn-huter*,[3] and a virtuous and lymphatic native of the island of Dagö, induced a kind of pious boredom into all his surroundings. The heads of the sections ran anxiously about with portfolios and were dissatisfied with the head-clerks of the tables; the latter wrote and wrote and certainly were overwhelmed with work, and had the prospect before them of dying at those tables, or, at any rate, if not particularly fortunate, of sitting there for twenty years. In the Registry there was a clerk who for thirty-three years had been keeping a record of the papers that went out, and sealing the parcels.

My 'literary exercises' gained me some exemption here too; after experience of my incapacity for anything else the head of the section entrusted me with the composition of a general report on the Ministry from the various provincial secretariats. The foresight of the authorities had found it necessary to pro-pound certain findings in advance, not leaving them to the mercy of facts and figures. Thus, for instance, in the draft of the proposed report appeared the statement: 'From the examination of the number and nature of crimes' (neither their number nor their nature was yet known) 'Your Majesty may be graciously pleased to perceive the progress of national morality, and the increased zeal of the officials for its improvement.'

Fate and Count Benckendorf saved me from taking part in this spurious report. It happened in this way.

At nine o'clock one morning, early in December, Matvey told me that the superintendent of the local police station wished to

---

[3] The Moravian Brethren, called *Herrnhuter* from the little town of Herrnhut in Saxony, where they settled in 1722, are a Protestant sect who abjure military service, the taking of oaths, and all distinctions of rank. (*Tr.*)

see me. I could not guess what had brought him to me, and bade
Matvey show him in. The superintendent showed me a scrap of
paper on which was written that he *invited* me to be at the
Third Division of His Majesty's Own Chancellery at ten o'clock
that morning.

'Very well,' I answered. 'That is by Tsepnoy Bridge, isn't
it?'

'Don't trouble yourself,' he answered. 'I have a sledge downstairs. I will go with you.'

It is a bad business, I thought, with a pang at my heart.

I went into the bedroom. My wife was sitting with the baby,
who had only just begun to recover after a lòng illness.

'What does he want?' she asked.

'I don't know, some nonsense. I shall have to go with him.
. . . Don't worry.'

My wife looked at me and said nothing; she only turned pale
as though a cloud had passed over her face, and handed me the
child to say good-bye to it.

I felt at that moment how much heavier every blow is for a
man with a wife and children; the blow does not strike him
alone, he suffers for all, and involuntarily blames himself for
their sufferings.

The feeling can be restrained, stifled, concealed, but one must
recognise what it costs. I went out of the house in black misery.
Very different was my mood when I had set off six years before
with Miller, the *politsmeyster*, to the Prechistensky police
station.

We drove over the Tsepnoy Bridge and through the Summer
Garden and turned towards what had been Kochubey's house; in
the lodge there the secular inquisition founded by Nicholas was
installed: people who went in at its back gates, before which we
stopped, did not always come out of them again, or if they did, it
was perhaps to disappear in Siberia or perish in the Alexeyevsky
fortress. We crossed all sorts of courtyards and little squares, and
came at last to the office. In spite of the presence of the com-
missar, the gendarme did not admit us, but summoned an official
who, after reading the summons, left the policeman in the corridor and asked me to follow him. He took me to the Director's
room. At a big table near which stood several arm-chairs a thin,
grey-headed old man, with a sinister face, was sitting quite
alone. To maintain his importance he went on reading a paper to
the end, and then got up and came towards me. He had a star on
his breast, from which I concluded that he was some sort of
commanding officer in the army of spies.

'Have you seen General Dubelt?'[4]

'No.'

He paused. Then, frowning and knitting his brows, without looking me in the face, he asked me in a sort of threadbare voice (the voice reminded me horribly of the nervous, sibilant notes of Golitsyn junior at the Moscow commission of inquiry):

'I think you have not very long had permission to visit Petersburg or Moscow?'

'I received it last year.'

The old man shook his head. 'And you have made a bad use of the Tsar's graciousness. I believe you'll have to go back again to Vyatka.'

I gazed at him in amazement.

'Yes,' he went on, 'you've chosen a fine way to show your gratitude to the government that permitted you to return.'

'I don't understand in the least,' I said, lost in surmises.

'You don't understand? That's just what is bad, too! What connections! What pursuits! Instead of showing your zeal from the first, effacing the stains left from your youthful errors, using your abilities to good effect—no! not at all: it's nothing but politics and tattling, and all to the detriment of the government. This is what your talk has brought you to! How is it that experience has taught you nothing? How do you know that among those who talk to you there isn't each time some scoundrel[5] who asks nothing better than to come *here* a minute later to give information?'

'If you can explain to me what all this means, you will greatly oblige me. I am racking my brains and cannot understand what your words are leading up to, or what they are hinting at.'

'What are they leading to? Hm. . . . Come, did you hear that a sentry at the Blue Bridge killed and robbed a man at night?'

'Yes, I did,' I answered with great simplicity.

'And perhaps you repeated it?'

'I believe I did repeat it.'

'With comments, I dare say?'

'Very likely.'

---

[4] Dubelt, Leonty Vasilevich (1792–1862), Chief of Staff of the Corps of Gendarmes (from 1835) and Director of the Third Division (1839–56). (*A.S.*)

[5] I declare, on my word of honour, that the word 'scoundrel' was used by this worthy old gentleman.

'With what sort of comments? There it is: a propensity to censure the government. I tell you frankly, the one thing that does you credit is your sincere avowal: it will certainly be taken into consideration by the Count.'

'Upon my word,' I said, 'what is there to avow? All the town was talking of the story; it was talked of in the secretariat of the Ministry of Home Affairs and in the shops. What's surprising in my having spoken about the incident?'

'The diffusion of false and mischievous rumours is a crime that the laws do not tolerate.'

'You seem to be charging me with having invented the affair.'

'In the note of information to the Tsar it is merely stated that you assisted in the propagation of this mischievous rumour, upon which followed the decision of His Majesty concerning your return to Vyatka.'

'You are simply trying to frighten me,' I answered. 'How is it possible, for such a trivial business, to send a man with a family a thousand miles away, and, what's more, to condemn and sentence him without even inquiring whether it is true or not?'

'You have admitted it yourself.'

'But how was it the report was submitted and the matter settled before you spoke to me?'

'Read for yourself.'

The old man went over to a table, fumbled among a small heap of papers, composedly pulled one out and handed it to me. I read it and could not believe my eyes: such complete absence of justice, such insolent, shameless disregard of the law was amazing, even in Russia.

I did not speak. I fancied that the old gentleman himself felt that it was a very absurd and extremely silly business, so that he did not think it necessary to defend it further, but after a brief silence asked:

'I believe you said you were married?'

'I am married.'

'It is a pity that we did not know that before. However, if anything can be done the Count will do it. I shall tell him of our conversation. *In any case* you will be banished from Petersburg.'

He looked at me. I did not speak, but felt that my face was burning. Everything I could not utter, everything held back within me, could be seen in my face.

The old gentleman dropped his eyes, considered for a moment, and suddenly, in an apathetic voice, with an affectation of urbane delicacy, said to me:

'I shall not venture to detain you further. I sincerely wish you—however, you will hear later.'

I rushed home. My heart boiled with a consuming fury—that feeling of impotence; of having no rights, the condition of a caged beast, jeered at by a sneering street-boy, who knows that all the tiger's strength is not enough to break the bars.

I found my wife in a fever; she had been taken ill that day and, having another fright in the evening, was prematurely confined a few days later.[6] The baby only lived a day, and after three or four years she had hardly recovered her strength.

They say that that tender paterfamilias, Nicholas Pavlovich, wept when his daughter died. . . .

And passionately fond they are of raising a turmoil, galloping hell for leather, kicking up a dust, and doing everything at headlong speed, as though the town were on fire, the throne were tottering, or the dynasty in danger—and all this without the slightest necessity! It is the romanticism of the gendarmes, the dramatic exercises of the detectives, the lavish setting for the display of loyal zeal . . . the *oprichniki*,[7] the whippers-in, the hounds!

On the evening of the day on which I had been to the Third Division we were sitting sorrowfully at a small table—the baby was playing with his toys on it, and we were saying little; suddenly someone pulled the bell so violently that we could not help starting. Matvey rushed to open the door, and a second later an officer of gendarmes darted into the room, clashing his sabre and jingling his spurs, and began in choice language apologising to my wife. He could not have imagined, he had had no suspicion, no idea that there was a lady and children in the case. It was extremely unpleasant. . . .

Gendarmes are the very flower of courtesy; if it were not for their duty, for the sacred obligations of the service, they would never make secret reports, or even fight with post-boys and drivers at departures. I know this from the Krutitsky Barracks where the *désolé* officer was so deeply distressed at the necessity of searching my pockets.

Paul Louis Courier[8] observed in his day that executioners and

---

[6] H. was summoned to the Third Division on 7 December 1840: the child (Ivan) was born two months later, in February 1841. (*A.S.*)

[7] The lifeguards of Ivan IV. ('Ivan the Terrible.') (*R.*)

[8] Paul Louis Courier (1772–1825), a learned and brilliant writer of political pamphlets and letters, who discovered a complete manuscript of

prosecutors are the most courteous of men. 'My dear executioner,' writes the prosecutor, 'if it is not disturbing you too much, you will do me the greatest service if you will kindly take the trouble to chop off So-and-so's head to-morrow morning.' And the executioner hastens to answer that 'he esteems himself fortunate indeed that he can by so trifling a service do something agreeable for the prosecutor and remains, always his devoted and obedient servant, the executioner'; and the other man, the third, remains devoted without his head.

'General Dubelt asks you to see him.'

'When?'

'Upon my word! now, at once, this minute.'

'Matvey, give me my overcoat.'

I pressed my wife's hand—her face was flushed, her hand was burning. Why this hurry at ten o'clock in the evening? Had a plot been discovered? Had someone run away? Was the precious life of Nicholas Pavlovich in danger? I really had been unfair to that sentry, I thought. It was not surprising that with a government like this one of its agents should murder two or three passers-by; were the sentries of the Second and Third grades any better than their comrade on the Blue Bridge? And what about the head sentry of all?

Dubelt had sent for me in order to *tell me* that Count Benckendorf required my presence at eight o'clock the next morning to inform me of the decision of His Majesty!

Dubelt was an unusual person; he was probably more intelligent than the whole of the Third Division—indeed, than all three divisions of His Majesty's Own Chancellery. His sunken face, shaded by long, fair moustaches, his fatigued expression, particularly the furrows in his cheeks and forehead, clearly witnessed that his breast had been the battlefield of many passions before the pale-blue uniform had conquered, or rather concealed, everything that was in it. His features had something wolfish and even foxy about them, that is, they expressed the subtle intelligence of beasts of prey; there was at once evasiveness and arrogance in them. He was always courteous.

When I went into his study he was sitting in a uniform coat without epaulettes, and smoking a pipe as he wrote. He rose at once, asked me to sit down facing him and began with the following surprising sentence:

Longus's *Daphnis and Chloe*, of which he published a French translation. (*Tr.*)

'Count Alexander Khristoforovich has given me the opportunity of making your acquaintance. I believe you saw Sakhtynsky this morning?'

'Yes, I did.'

'I am very sorry that the reason I have had to ask you to see me is not an entirely pleasant one for you. Your imprudence has once more brought His Majesty's anger upon you.'

'I will say to you, General, what I said to Count Sakhtynsky: I cannot imagine that I shall be exiled simply for having repeated a street rumour, which you, of course, heard before me, and possibly spoke of just as I did.'

'Yes, I heard the rumour, and I spoke of it, and so far we are even; but this is where the difference begins: in repeating the absurd story I swore that there was nothing in it, while you made the rumour a ground for accusing the whole police force. It is all this unfortunate passion *de dénigrer le gouvernement*—a passion that has developed in all of you gentlemen from the pernicious example of the West. It is not with us as in France, where the government is at daggers drawn with the parties, where it is dragged in the mud. Our government is paternal: everything is done as privately as possible. . . . We do our very utmost that everything shall go as quietly and smoothly as possible, and here men, who in spite of painful experience persist in a fruitless opposition, alarm public opinion by stating verbally and in writing that the soldiers of the police murder men in the streets. Isn't that true? You have written about it, haven't you?'

'I attach so little importance to the matter that I don't think it at all necessary to conceal that I have written about it, and I will add to whom—to my father.'

'Of course it is not an important matter, but see what it has brought you to. His Majesty at once remembered your name, and that you had been at Vyatka, and commanded that you should be sent back there, and so the Count has commissioned me to inform you that you are to go to him to-morrow at eight o'clock and he will announce to you the will of His Majesty.'

'And so it is left that I am to go to Vyatka with a sick wife and a sick child on account of something that you say is not important?'

'Why, are you in the service?' Dubelt asked me, looking intently at the buttons of my half-dress uniform coat.

'In the office of the Minister of Home Affairs.'

'Have you been there long?'

'Six months.'

'And all the time in Petersburg?'

'All the time.'

'I had no idea of it.'

'You see,' I said, smiling, 'how discreetly I have behaved.'

Sakhtynsky did not know that I was married, Dubelt did not know that I was in the service, but both knew what I said in my own room, what I thought and what I wrote to my father. . . . The trouble was that I was just beginning to be friendly with Petersburg literary men, and to publish articles and, worse still, had been transferred by Count Strogonov from Vladimir to Petersburg, the secret police having no hand in it, and when I arrived in Petersburg I had not reported either to Dubelt or to the Third Division, which kindly persons had hinted that I should do.

'To be sure,' Dubelt interrupted me, 'all the information that has been collected about you is entirely to your credit. Only yesterday I was speaking to Zhukovsky and should be thankful to hear my sons spoken of as he spoke of you.'

'And yet I am to go to Vyatka?'

'You see it is your *misfortune* that the report had been handed in already, and that many circumstances had not been taken into consideration. Go you must: there's no altering that, but I imagine that another town might be substituted for Vyatka. I will talk it over with the Count: he is going to the Palace again to-day. We will try and do all that can be done to make things easier; the Count is a man of angelic kindness.'

I got up and Dubelt escorted me to the door of his study. At that point I could not restrain myself: I stopped and said to him:

'I have one small favour to ask of you, General. If you want me, please do not send constables or gendarmes. They are noisy and alarming, especially in the evening. Why should my sick wife be more severely punished than any one on account of the sentry business?'

'Oh! good heavens, how unpleasant that is,' replied Dubelt, 'how clumsy they all are! You may rest assured that I will not send a policeman again. And so till to-morrow; don't forget, eight o'clock at the Count's; we shall meet there.'

It was exactly as though we were agreeing to go to Smurov's to eat oysters together.

At eight o'clock next morning I was in Benckendorf's reception room. I found five or six petitioners waiting there; they stood gloomy and anxious by the wall, started at every sound, squeezed themselves together even more closely, and bowed to every adjutant that passed. Among their number was a woman in deep mourning, with tear-stained eyes. She sat with a paper rolled up in her hand, and the roll trembled like an aspen leaf. Three paces from her stood a tall, rather bent old man of seventy or so, bald and sallow, in a dark-green army great-coat, with a row of medals and crosses on his breast. From time to time he sighed, shook his head and whispered something under his breath.

Some sort of 'friend of the family,' a flunkey, or a clerk on duty, sat in the window, lolling at his ease. He got up when I went in, and looking intently at his face I recognised him; that loathsome figure had been pointed out to me at the theatre as one of the chief street spies, and his name, I remember, was Fabre. He asked me:

'Have you come with a petition to the Count?'

'I have come at his request.'

'Your surname?'

I mentioned it.

'Ah,' he said, changing his tone as though he had met an old acquaintance, 'won't you be pleased to sit down? The Count will be here in a quarter of an hour.'

It was horribly still and *unheimlich* in the room; the daylight hardly penetrated through the fog and frozen window-panes, and no one said a word. The adjutants ran quickly to and fro, and the gendarme standing at the door sometimes jingled his accoutrements as he shifted from foot to foot. Two more petitioners came in. A clerk on duty ran to ask each what he had come about. One of the adjutants went up to him and began telling him something in a half-whisper, assuming a desperately roguish air as he did so. No doubt it was something nasty, for they frequently interrupted their talk with noiseless, flunkeyish laughter, during which the worthy clerk, affecting to be quite helpless and ready to burst, repeated: 'Do stop, for God's sake stop, I can't bear it.'

Five minutes later Dubelt appeared, with his uniform unbuttoned as though he were off duty, cast a glance at the petitioners, at which they all bowed, and seeing me in the distance said: *'Bonjour, Monsieur Herzen. Votre affaire va parfaitement bien* . . . very well indeed.'

They would let me stay, perhaps! I was on the point of asking, but before I had time to utter a word Dubelt had disappeared. Next there walked into the room a general, scrubbed and decorated, tightly laced and stiffly erect, in white breeches and a scarf: I have never seen a finer general. If ever there is an exhibition of generals in London, like the Baby Exhibition at Cincinnati at this moment, I advise sending this very one from Petersburg. The general went up to the door from which Benckendorf was to enter and froze in stiff immobility; with great curiosity I scrutinised this sergeant's ideal. He must have flogged soldiers in his day for the way they paraded. Where do these people come from? He was born for military rules and regulations and files on parade. He was attended by the most elegant cornet in the world, probably his adjutant, with incredibly long legs, fair-haired, with a tiny face like a squirrel's, and that good-natured expression which often persists in mamma's darlings who have never studied anything, or at any rate have never succeeded in learning anything. This honeysuckle in uniform stood at a respectful distance from the model general.

Dubelt darted in again, this time assuming an air of dignity, and with his buttons done up. He at once addressed the general, and asked him what he could do for him. The general, with the correctness with which orderlies speak when reporting to their superior officers, announced:

'Yesterday I received through Prince Alexander Ivanovich His Majesty's command to join the active army in the Caucasus, and esteemed it my duty to report to His Excellency before leaving.'

Dubelt listened with religious attention to this speech, and with a slight bow as a sign of respect went out and returned a minute later.

'The Count,' he said to the general, 'sincerely regrets that he has not time to receive Your Excellency. He thanks you and has commissioned me to wish you a good journey.' Upon this Dubelt flung wide his arms, embraced the general, and twice touched his cheeks with his moustaches.

The general retreated at a solemn march, the youth with a squirrel's face and the legs of a crane set off after him. This scene compensated me for much of the bitterness of that day. The general's standing at attention, the farewell by proxy, and finally the sly face of *Reineke Fuchs* as he kissed the brainless countenance of His Excellency—all this was so ludicrous that I could only just contain myself. I fancied that Dubelt noticed this and began to respect me from that time.

At last the doors were flung open *à deux battants* and Benckendorf came in. There was nothing unpleasant in the exterior of the chief of the gendarmes; his appearance was rather typical of the Baltic barons and of the German aristocracy generally. His face looked creased and tired, he had the deceptively good-natured expression which is often found in evasive and apathetic people.

Possibly Benckendorf did not do all the harm he might have done, being the head of that terrible police, being outside the law and above the law, and having a right to meddle in everything. I am ready to believe it, especially when I recall the vapid expression of his face. But he did no good either; he had not enough will-power, energy, or heart for that. To shrink from saying a word in defence of the oppressed is as bad as any crime in the service of a man as cold and merciless as Nicholas.

How many innocent victims passed through Benckendorf's hands, how many perished through his lack of attention, through his absent-mindedness, or because he was engaged in gallantry—and how many dark images and painful memories may have haunted his mind and tormented him on the steamer on which, having prematurely collapsed and grown decrepit, he sailed off to seek, in betrayal of his own religion, the intercession of the Catholic Church with its all-forgiving indulgences. . . .

'It has come to the knowledge of His Imperial Majesty,' he said to me, 'that you take part in the diffusion of rumours injurious to the government. His Majesty, seeing how little you have reformed, deigned to order that you should be sent back to Vyatka; but I, at the request of General Dubelt, and relying upon information collected about you, have reported to His Majesty about the illness of your wife, and His Majesty has been pleased to alter his decision. His Majesty forbids you to visit Petersburg and Moscow, and you will be under police supervision again, but it is left to the Ministry of Home Affairs to appoint the place of your residence.'

'Allow me to tell you frankly that even at this moment I cannot believe that there has been no other reason for exiling me. In 1835 I was exiled on account of a supper-party at which I was not present! Now I am being punished for a rumour about which the whole town was talking. It is a strange fate!'

Benckendorf shrugged his shoulders and, turning out the palms of his hands like a man who has exhausted all the resources of argument, interrupted me.

'I make known to you the Imperial will, and you answer me with criticisms. What good will come of all that you say to me, or that I say to you? It is a waste of words. Nothing can be changed now. What will happen later partly depends on you, and, since you have referred to your first trouble, I particularly recommend you not to let there be a third. You will certainly not get off *so easily* a third time.'

Benckendorf gave me a benevolent smile and turned to the petitioners. He said very little to them; he took their petition, glanced at it, and then handed it to Dubelt, interrupting the petitioners' observations with the same graciously condescending smile. For months together these people had been pondering and preparing themselves for this interview, upon which their honour, their fortune, their family depended; what labour, what effort had been employed before they were received; how many times they had knocked at the closed door and been turned away by a gendarme or porter. And how great, how poignant must the necessities have been that brought them to the head of the secret police; no doubt all legal channels had been exhausted first. And this man gets rid of them with commonplaces, and in all probability some Head of a Table proposed *some* decision, in order to pass the case on to *some* other secretariat. And what was he so absorbed in? Where was he in a hurry to go to?

When Benckendorf went up to the old man with the medals, the latter fell on his knees and said:

'Your Excellency, put yourself in my place.'

'How abominable!' cried the Count; 'you are disgracing your medals,' and full of noble indignation he passed by without taking his petition. The old man slowly got up, his glassy eyes were full of horror and craziness, his lower lip quivered and he babbled something.

How inhuman these people are when the whim takes them to be human!

Dubelt went up to the old man and said: 'Whatever did you do that for? Come, give me your petition. I'll look through it.'

Benckendorf had gone to see the Tsar.

'What am I to do?' I asked Dubelt.

'Settle on any town you choose with the Minister of Home Affairs; we shall not interfere. We will send the whole case on there to-morrow. I congratulate you on its having been so satisfactorily settled.'

'I am very much obliged to you!'

From Benckendorf I went to the Ministry. Our Director, as I have mentioned, belonged to that class of Germans who have something of the lemur about them, lanky, sluggish, and dilatory. Their brains work slowly, they do not catch the point at once and they labour a long time if they are to reach any sort of conclusion. My account unfortunately arrived before the communication from the Third Division; he had not expected it at all, and so was completely bewildered, uttered incoherent phrases, noticed this himself, and in order to recover himself said to me: '*Erlauben Sie mir deutsch zu sprechen.*' Possibly his remarks came out more correct grammatically in German, but they did not become any clearer or more definite in meaning. I distinctly perceived two feelings struggling in him: he grasped all the injustice of the affair, but considered himself bound as Director to justify the action of the government; at the same time, he did not want to show himself a barbarian before me, nor could he forget the hostility which invariably reigned between the Ministry and the secret police. So the task of expressing all this jumble was in itself not easy. He ended by admitting that he could say nothing until he had seen the Minister, and by going off to see him.

Count Strogonov sent for me, inquired into the matter, listened attentively to the whole thing, and said to me in conclusion:

'It's a police trick, pure and simple—well, all right: I'll pay them out for it.'

I imagined, I confess, that he was going straight off to the Tsar to explain the business to him; but ministers do not go so far as that.

'I have received His Majesty's command concerning you,' he went on: 'here it is. You see that it is left to me to select the place of your exile and to employ you in the service. Where would you like to go?'

'To Tver or Novgorod,' I answered.

'To be sure. . . . Well, since the choice of a place is left to me, and it probably does not matter to you to which of those towns I appoint you, I shall give you the first councillor's vacancy in the provincial government. That is the highest position that you can receive with your seniority, so get yourself a uniform made with an embroidered collar,' he added jocosely.

So that was how I recouped myself, though not in my own suit.

A week later Strogonov recommended me to the Senate for an appointment as councillor at Novgorod.

It really is very funny to think how many secretaries, assessors, and district and provincial officials had been long soliciting, passionately and persistently soliciting, to get that post; bribes had been given, the most sacred promises had been received, and here, all at once, a Minister, to carry out His Majesty's will and at the same time to have his revenge on the secret police, *punished* me with this promotion and, by way of gilding the pill, flung this post, the object of ardent desires and ambitious dreams, at the feet of a man who accepted it with the firm intention of throwing it up at the first opportunity.

❖   ❖   ❖

Meanwhile the months passed, the winter was over, and no one reminded me about going away. I was forgotten and I gave up being *sur le qui-vive*, particularly after the following meeting. Bolgovsky, the military governor of Vologda, was at that time in Petersburg; being a very intimate friend of my father, he was rather fond of me and I was sometimes at his house. He had taken part in the killing of Paul, as a young officer in the Semënovsky Regiment, and was afterwards mixed up in the obscure and unexplained Speransky[9] affair in 1812. He was at that time a colonel in the army at the front. He was suddenly arrested, brought to Petersburg, and then sent to Siberia. Before he had time to reach his place of exile Alexander pardoned him, and he returned to his regiment.[10]

One day in the spring I went to see him; a general was sitting in a big easy-chair with his back towards the door so that I could not see his face, but only one silver epaulette.

'Let me introduce you,' said Bolgovsky, and then I recognised Dubelt.

'I have long enjoyed the pleasure of Leonty Vasilyevich's attention,' I said, smiling.

'Are you going to Novgorod soon?' he asked me.

'I supposed I ought to ask you about that.'

'Oh! not at all! I had no idea of reminding you. I simply asked the question. We have handed you over to Count Strogonov, and we are not trying to hurry you, as you see. Besides, with such a legitimate reason as your wife's illness. . . .'

He really was the politest of men!

At last, at the beginning of June, I received the Senate's *ukaz*, confirming my appointment as councillor in the Novgorod Provincial Government. Count Strogonov thought it was time for me to set off, and about the 1st of July I arrived in Novgorod, the 'City in the keeping of God and of Saint Sophia,' and settled on the bank of the Volkhov, opposite the very barrow from which

---

[9] Mikhail Mikhaylovich Speransky (1772–1839), a liberal and an able and trusted minister of Alexander I, was suddenly dismissed and on 17 March 1812, was relegated to Nizhny Novgorod. (*R.*)

[10] The biographical details of Bolgovsky, given by H., are not accurate. (*A.S.*)

the Voltairians of the twelfth century threw the wonder-working statue of Perun[11] into the river.

Councillor at Novgorod

BEFORE I WENT AWAY Count Strogonov told me that the military governor of Novgorod, Elpidifor Antiokhovich Zurov, was in Petersburg; he said that he had spoken to him about my appointment, and advised me to call upon him. I found him a rather simple and good-natured general, short, middle-aged and with a very military exterior. We talked for half an hour, he graciously escorted me to the door and there we parted.

When I arrived in Novgorod I went to see him, and the change of *décor* was amazing. In Petersburg the governor had been a visitor, here he was at home; he actually seemed to me to be taller in Novgorod. Without any provocation on my part, he thought it necessary to inform me that he did not permit councillors to voice their opinions, or put them in writing; that it delayed business, and that, if anything were not right, they could talk it over, but that if it came to giving opinions, one or another would have to take his discharge. I observed with a smile that it was hard to frighten me with a threat of discharge, since the sole object of my service was to get my discharge from it; and I added that while bitter necessity forced me to serve in Novgorod I should probably have no occasion for giving my opinion.

This conversation was quite enough for both of us. As I went away I made up my mind to avoid coming into close contact with him. So far as I could observe, the impression I made on the governor was much the same as that which he made upon me, that is, we could not bear each other, so far as this was possible on so brief and superficial an acquaintance.

When I looked a little into the work of the provincial government I saw that my position was not only very disagreeable but also extraordinarily dangerous. Every councillor was responsible for his own department and shared the responsibility for all the rest. To read the papers concerning all the departments was

[11] Perun was the god of sky and of thunder, the chief god of the ancient Slavs. (*Tr.*)

absolutely impossible, so one had to sign them on trust. The governor, in accordance with his theory that a councillor should never give counsel, put his signature, contrary to the law and good sense, next after that of the councillor whose department the file concerned. For me personally this was excellent; in his signature I found something of a safeguard, since he shared the responsibility, and also because he often, with a peculiar expression, talked of his lofty honesty and Robespierre-like incorruptibility. As for the signatures of the other councillors, they were very little comfort to me. They were case-hardened old clerks who by dozens of years of service had worked their way up to being councillors, and lived only by the service, that is, only by bribes. There was nothing to blame them for in this; a councillor, I think, received one thousand two hundred paper roubles a year: a man with a family could not possibly live on that. When they understood that I was not going to share with them in dividing the common spoil, nor to plunder on my own account, they began to look upon me as an uninvited guest and a dangerous witness. They did not become very intimate with me, especially when they had discovered that there was very slight friendship between the governor and myself. They stood by one another and watched over one another's interests, but they did not care about me.

Moreover, my worthy colleagues were not afraid of big monetary penalties or of deficiencies in their accounts, because they had nothing. They could risk it, and the more readily the more important the affair was; whether the deficit was of five hundred roubles or of five hundred thousand, it was all the same to them. In case of a deficit a fraction of their salary went to the reimbursement of the Treasury, and this might last for two or three hundred years, if the official lasted so long. Usually either the official died or the Tsar did, and then in his rejoicing the heir forgave the debts. Such manifestoes are also published during the life-time of the same Tsar, by reason of a royal birth or coming of age, and odds and ends like that; the officials counted on them. In my case, on the contrary, the part of the family estate and the capital which my father had assigned to me would have been seized.

If I could have relied on my own head-clerks, things would have been easier. I did a great deal to gain their attachment, treated them politely and helped them with money, but my efforts only resulted in their ceasing to obey me. They feared only those councillors who treated them as though they were schoolboys; and they took to coming to the office half-drunk.

They were very poor men with no education and no expectations. All the imaginative side of their lives was confined to little pot-houses and strong drink, so I had to be on my guard in my own department, too.

At first the governor gave me Department Four, in which all business dealing with contracts and money matters was dealt with. I asked him to exchange me; he would not, saying that he had no right to make an exchange without the consent of the other councillor. In the governor's presence I asked the councillor in charge of Department Two: he consented and we exchanged. My new department was less attractive; its work was concerned with passports, circulars of all sorts, cases of the abuse of power by landowners, schismatics, counterfeiters and people under the supervision of the police.

Anything sillier and more absurd cannot be imagined; I am certain that three-quarters of the people who read this will not believe it,[1] and yet it is the downright truth that I, as a councillor in the provincial government, head of the Second Department, counter-signed every three months the *politsmeyster*'s report on *myself*, as a man under police supervision. The *politsmeyster* from politeness made no entry in the column for 'behaviour,' and in the column for 'occupation' wrote: 'Engaged in the government service.' Such are the Hercules' pillars of insanity that can be reached when there are two or three police forces antagonistic to one another, official forms instead of laws, and a sergeant-major's conception of discipline in place of a governing intelligence.

This absurdity reminds me of an incident that occurred at Tobolsk some years ago. The civil governor was on bad terms with the vice-governor. The quarrel was carried on on paper, and they wrote each other all sorts of biting and sarcastic things in official form. The vice-governor was a ponderous pedant, a formalist, a good-natured specimen of the divinity student; he composed his *caustic* answers himself with immense labour and, of course, made this quarrel his aim in life. It happened that the governor went to Petersburg for a time. The vice-governor took over his duties and, as governor, received an insolent document from himself, sent the day before. Without hesitation he ordered the secretary to answer it, signed the answer and, receiving it as

---

[1] This is so true that a German who has abused me a dozen times in the *Morning Advertiser* [of November 29 and December 6, 1855] adduced as proof that I had never been exiled the fact that I had the post of councillor in a provincial government.

vice-governor, set to work again to rack his brains and scribble an insulting letter to himself. He regarded this as a proof of the highest probity.

For six months I pulled in harness in the provincial government. It was disagreeable and extremely tedious. Every morning at eleven o'clock I put on my uniform, buckled on my civilian sword, and went to the office. At twelve o'clock the military governor arrived; taking no notice of the councillors, he walked straight to a corner and stood his sword there. Then, after looking out of the window and straightening his hair, he went towards his arm-chair and bowed to those present. As soon as the sergeant, with fierce, grey moustaches that stood up at right angles to his lips, had solemnly opened the door and the clank of the sword had become audible in the office, the councillors got up and remained standing with backs bent until the governor bowed to them. One of my first acts of protest was to take no part in this collective rising and reverential expectation, but to sit quietly and to bow only when he bowed to us.

There were no great discussions or heated arguments; it rarely happened that a councillor asked the governor's opinion in advance, still more rarely that the governor put some business question to the councillors. Before everyone lay a heap of papers and everyone signed his name: it was a signature factory.

Remembering Talleyrand's celebrated injunction, I did not try to make any particular show of zeal and attended to business only so far as was necessary to escape reprimand or avoid getting into trouble. But there were two kinds of work in my department towards which I considered I had no right to take so superficial an attitude: these were matters relating to schismatics and to the abuse of power by the landowners.

Schismatics are not consistently persecuted in Russia, but something suddenly comes over the Synod or the Ministry of Home Affairs, and they make a raid on some hermitage, or some community, plunder it, and then subside again. The schismatics usually have intelligent agents in Petersburg who warn them from there of coming danger; the others at once collect money, hide their books and their ikons, stand the Orthodox priest a drink, stand a drink to the Orthodox police-captain and buy themselves off; and with that the matter ends for ten years or so.

In Novgorod Province there were in the reign of Catherine a great many Dukhobors.[2] Their leader, the old head of the post-

---

[2] I am not certain whether these were Dukhobors.

ing drivers, in Zaitsevo, I think it was, enjoyed enormous respect. When Paul was on his way to Moscow to be crowned he ordered the old man to be summoned, probably with the object of converting him. The Dukhobors, like the Quakers, do not take off their caps, and the grey-headed old man went up to the Emperor of Gatchina[3] with his head covered. This was more than the Tsar could bear. A petty, touchy readiness to take offence is a particularly striking characteristic of Paul, and of all his sons except Alexander; having savage power in their hands, they have not even the wild beast's consciousness of strength which keeps the big dog from attacking the little one.

'Before whom are you standing in your cap?' shouted Paul, breathing hard, with all the marks of frenzied rage: 'do you know me?'

'I do,' answered the schismatic calmly; 'you are Pavel Petrovich.'

'Put him in chains! to penal servitude with him! to the mines!' Paul continued.

The old man was seized and the Tsar ordered the village to be set fire to on four sides and the inhabitants to be sent to live in Siberia. At the next stopping-place one of the Tsar's intimates threw himself at his feet and said that he had ventured to delay the carrying out of His Majesty's will, and was waiting for him to repeat it. Paul, now somewhat sobered, perceived that setting fire to villages and sending men to the mines without a trial was a strange way of recommending himself to the people. He commanded the Synod to investigate the peasants' case and ordered the old man to be incarcerated for life in the Spaso-Yefimyevsky Monastery; he thought that the Orthodox monks would torment him worse than penal servitude; but he forgot that our monks are not merely good Orthodox Christians but also men who are very fond of money and vodka; and the schismatics drink no vodka and are not sparing of their money.

The old man acquired among the Dukhobors the reputation of a saint. They came from the ends of Russia to do homage to him, and paid with gold for admission to see him. The old man sat in his cell, dressed all in white, and his friends draped the walls and the ceiling with linen. After his death they obtained permission to bury his body with his kindred and solemnly carried him upon their shoulders from Vladimir to the province of Novgorod. Only the Dukhobors know where he is buried. They are per-

---

[3] So the "mad tsar," Paul, was called, from one of his suburban palaces. See p. 46, fn. 16. (*D.M.*)

suaded that he had the gift of working miracles in his life-time
and that his body is incorruptible.

I heard all this partly from the governor of Vladimir, I. E.
Kuruta, partly from the post-drivers at Novgorod, and partly
from a church-attendant in the Spaso-Yefimyevsky Monastery.
Now there are no more political prisoners in this monastery,
although the prison is full of various priests and ecclesiastics,
disobedient sons of whom their parents have complained, and so
on. The archimandrite, a tall, broad-shouldered man in a fur
cap, showed us the prison-yard. When he went in, a non-commissioned officer with a rifle went up to him and reported: 'I have
the honour to report to your Reverence that all is well in the
prison and that there are so many prisoners.' The archimandrite
in answer gave him his blessing—what a mix-up!

The business about the schismatics was of such a kind that it
was much best not to stir them up again. I looked through the
documents referring to them and left them in peace. On the
contrary the cases of the abuse of landowners' power needed a
thorough overhauling. I did all I could, and scored several victories in those sticky lists; I delivered one young girl from persecution and put her under the guardianship of a naval officer.
This I believe was the only service I did in my official career.

A certain lady was keeping a servant-girl in her house without
any documentary evidence of ownership; the girl petitioned that
her rights to freedom should be inquired into. My predecessor
had very sagaciously thought fit to leave her, until her case
should be decided, in complete bondage with the lady who
claimed her. I had to sign the documents; I approached the
governor and observed that the girl would not be in a very
enviable situation in her lady's house after lodging this petition
against her.

'What's to be done with her?'

'Keep her in the police station.'

'At whose expense?'

'At the expense of the lady, if the case is decided against
her.'

'And if it is not?'

Luckily at that moment the provincial prosecutor came in. A
prosecutor from his social position, from his official relationships,
from the very buttons on his uniform, is bound to be an enemy
of the governor, or at least to thwart him in everything. I purposely continued the conversation in his presence. The governor
began to get angry and said that the whole question was not

worth wasting a couple of words on. The prosecutor was quite indifferent to what would happen, and what became of the girl, but he immediately took my side and advanced a dozen different points from the code of laws in support of it. The governor, who in reality cared even less, said to me, smiling ironically:

'It's much the same whether she goes to her mistress or to prison.'

'Of course it's better for her to go to prison,' I observed.

'It will be more consistent with the intention expressed in the code,' observed the prosecutor.

'Let it be as you like,' the governor said, laughing more than ever. 'You've done your *protégée* a service: when she has been in prison for a few months she will thank you for it.'

I did not continue the argument; my object was to rescue the girl from domestic persecution; I remember that a couple of months later she was released and received her complete freedom.

Among the unsettled cases in my department there was a complicated correspondence which had lasted for several years, concerning acts of violence by a retired officer called Strugov-shchikov and all sorts of wrongs committed on his estate. The affair began with a petition by his mother, and after that the peasants complained. He had come to some arrangement with his mother, and had himself accused the peasants of intending to kill him, without, however, adducing any serious testimony. Meanwhile it was obvious from the evidence of his mother and his house-serfs that the man was guilty of all sorts of frantic actions. The business had been sleeping the sleep of the just for more than a year; it is always possible to drag a case out with inquiries and unnecessary correspondence and then, reckoning it to be settled, to file it in the archives. A recommendation had to be made to the Senate that he should be put under wardship, but for this purpose a declaration from the Marshal of Nobility was necessary. The Marshal of Nobility usually declines, not wishing to lose a vote. It rested entirely with me to get the case moving, but a *coup de grâce* from the marshal was essential.

The marshal of the Novgorod Province, a nobleman who had served in the militia in 1812 and had a Vladimir medal, tried to show me, when we met, that he was a well-read man, by talking in the bookish language of the period before Karamzin; once, pointing to a monument which the nobility of Novgorod had raised *to itself* in recognition of its patriotism in 1812, he alluded with some feeling to the difficult, so to speak, and sacred, but none the less flattering, duties of a marshal.

All this was to my advantage.

The marshal came to the office about certifying the insanity of some ecclesiastic; when all the presidents of all the courts had exhausted their whole store of foolish questions, from which the lunatic might well have concluded that they too were not quite in their right minds, and he had finally been elevated to the post of madman, I drew the marshal aside and told him about the case. The marshal shrugged his shoulders, assuming an air of horror and indignation, and ended by referring to the officer as an arrant scoundrel 'who cast a shadow over the well born community of the nobility and gentry of Novgorod.'

'Probably,' I said, 'you would give us the same answer in writing, if we asked you?'

The marshal, caught unawares, promised to answer according to his conscience, adding that 'honour and truthfulness were the invariable attributes of the nobility of Russia.'

Though I had some doubt of the invariability of those attributes, I did set the business in motion, and the marshal kept his word. The case was brought before the Senate, and I remember very well the sweet moment when the *ukaz* of the Senate was passed to my department, appointing trusteeship over the officer's estate and putting him under the supervision of the police. The officer had been convinced that the case was closed, and after the *ukaz* he appeared at Novgorod like one thunderstruck. He was at once told how it had happened; the infuriated officer was prepared to fall upon me from behind a corner, to engage ruffians and have me ambushed, but, being unaccustomed to campaigns on land, he quietly disappeared from sight in some district capital.

Unfortunately the 'attributes' of brutality, debauchery, and violence with house-serfs and peasants are more 'invariable' than those of 'honour and truthfulness' among our nobility. Of course there is a small group of cultured landowners who do not knock their servants about from morning to night, do not thrash them every day; but even among them there are 'Penochkins'[4]; the rest have not yet advanced beyond the stage of Saltychikha[5] and the American planters.

Rummaging about in the files, I found the correspondence of

---

[4] The landowner in 'The Agent,' one of Turgenev's *Sportsman's Sketches*. (*Tr.*)

[5] Saltychikha was a lady notorious in the reign of Catherine for her cruelty to her serfs. She was eventually brought to justice. (*Tr.*)

the provincial government of Pskov concerning a certain Madame Yaryzhkin, a landed lady. She had flogged two of her maids to death, was tried on account of a third, and was almost completely acquitted by the Criminal Court, who based their verdict among other things on the fact that the third maid did not die. This woman invented the most amazing punishments, hitting with a flat iron, with gnarled sticks or with a beetle.

I do not know what the girl in question had done, but her mistress surpassed herself. She made the girl kneel in filth, or on boards into which nails had been driven; in this position she beat her about the back and the head with a beetle and, when she had exhausted herself, called the coachman to take her place; luckily he was not in the servants' quarters, and she went out to find him, while the girl, half frantic with pain and covered with blood, rushed out into the street with nothing on but her smock and ran to the police station. The police-inspector took her evidence and the case went its regular course. The police busied themselves and the Criminal Court busied itself over it for a year; at last the court, obviously bribed, very sagaciously decided to summon the lady's husband and suggest to him that he should restrain his wife from such punishments, and they obliged her, while leaving her under suspicion of having brought about the death of two servants, to sign an undertaking not to inflict punishments in future. On this understanding the unfortunate girl, who had been kept somewhere else while the case was going on, was handed over to her mistress again.

The girl, terrified by what lay before her, began writing one petition after another; the matter reached the ears of the Tsar; he ordered it to be investigated, and sent an official from Petersburg. Probably Madame Yaryzhkin's means were not equal to bribing the Petersburg, the ministerial and the political police investigators, and the case took a different turn. The lady was relegated to Siberia and her husband was put under ward. All the members of the Criminal Court were tried; how their case ended I do not know.

In another place[6] I have told the story of the man flogged to death by Prince Trubetskoy and of the *Kammerherr* Bazilevsky who was thrashed by his own servants. I will add one more story of a lady.

The maid of the wife of a colonel of gendarmes at Penza was carrying a tea-pot full of boiling water. Her mistress's child ran

---

[6] *Property in Serfs.*

against the servant, who spilt the boiling water, and the child
was scalded. The mistress, to exact her vengeance in the same
coin, ordered the servant's child to be brought and scalded its
hand from the samovar. . . .

Panchulidzev, the governor, hearing of this monstrous proceeding, expressed his heartfelt regret that his relations with the
colonel of gendarmes were somewhat fragile, and that consequently he felt it improper to start proceedings which might be
thought to be instigated by personal motives!

And then sensitive hearts wonder at peasants murdering landowners with their whole families, or at the soldiers of the
military settlements at Staraya Russa[7] massacring all the Russian Germans and all the German Russians.

In halls and maids' rooms, in villages and the torture-
chambers of the police, are buried whole martyrologies of frightful villainies; the memory of them works in the soul and in
course of generations matures into bloody, merciless vengeance
which it is easy to prevent, but will hardly be possible to stop
once it has begun.

Staraya Russa, the military settlements! Frightful words! Can
it be that history (bribed beforehand by Arakcheyev's *pourboire*[8])
will never pull away the shroud under which the government
has concealed the series of crimes coldly and systematically
perpetrated at the introduction of the military settlements?
There have been plenty of horrors everywhere, but here there
was added the peculiar imprint of Petersburg and Gatchina, of
German and Tatar. The beating with sticks and flogging with
rods of the insubordinate went on for months together . . . the

---

[7] In July 1831. (*A.S.*) The military settlements were entirely the idea
of Alexander I. They were foreshadowed in a manifesto of 1814. [For
the term of military service in Russia during his reign see p. 149, fn. 1.
(*D.M.*)] He wished the soldiers, in peace time, to live with their families on the land and work it. The project started when one battalion of
Grenadier Guards was settled in the Novgorod Province in 1815, but
nothing was made public then about the settlements. 'It was a healthy,
practical idea . . .' says E. M. Almedingen in *The Emperor Alexander I*
(The Bodley Head, 1964, p. 176), 'a mixture of humaneness and economic foresight. . . . A poisonous plant grew out of that good seed.' (*R.*)
[8] Arakcheyev left, I believe, a hundred thousand roubles in a bank to be
paid a hundred years later, together with the accumulated interest, to
the man who should write the best history of the reign of Alexander I.
[It was 50,000 roubles that Arakcheyev deposited in a bank for this
purpose in 1833. (*A.S.*)]

blood was never dry on the floors of the village offices . . . every crime that may be committed by the people against their executioners on that small tract of land is justified beforehand.

The Mongolian side of the Moscow period which distorted the Slav character of the Russians, the flat-of-the-sword inhumanity which distorted the period of Peter were embodied in the full splendour of their hideousness in Count Arakcheyev. Arakcheyev was undoubtedly one of the most loathsome figures that rose after Peter I to the heights of the Russian government. That 'sneaking thrall of the crowned soldier,' as Pushkin said of him, was the model of an ideal corporal as he floated in the dreams of the father of Frederick the Second; he was made up of inhuman devotion, mechanical correctness, the exactitude of a chronometer, routine and activity, a complete lack of feeling, just as much intelligence as was necessary to carry out orders, and just enough ambition, spleen and envy to prefer power to money. Such men are a real treasure to Tsars. Only the petty resentment of Nicholas can explain the fact that he made no use of Arakcheyev, but confined himself to his underlings.

Paul had discovered Arakcheyev through sympathy. So long as Alexander's sense of shame lasted he kept him at some distance; but, carried away by the family passion for discipline and drill, he entrusted to him the secretariat of the army. Of the victories of this general of artillery we have heard little[9]; he rather performed civilian duties in the military service: his battles were fought on the soldiers' backs; his enemies were brought to him in chains: they had been conquered beforehand. In the latter years of Alexander I, Arakcheyev governed all Russia. He meddled in everything, he had a right to everything, *carte blanche*, in fact. As Alexander grew feebler and sank into gloomy melancholy, he wavered a little between Prince A. N. Golitsyn and Arakcheyev and in the end naturally inclined towards the latter.

At the time of Alexander's Taganrog visit the house-serfs on

---

[9] Arakcheyev was a pitiful coward, as Count Toll tells us in his *Memoirs,* and the Secretary of State Marchenko in a little story of the Fourteenth of December published in *The Pole Star.* [V. R. Marchenko's account appeared not in *Polyarnaya Zveda* but in the *Istorichesky sbornik volnoy russkoy tipografii v Londone* (London, 1859), pp. 70–1. (*A.S.*)] I have heard that he was in hiding during the Staraya Russa rising, and was in deadly terror of Reikhel, the general of Engineers.

Arakcheyev's estate in Gruzino killed the Count's sweetheart; this murder gave rise to the investigation of which to this day, seventeen years later, that is, the officials and inhabitants of Novgorod speak with horror.

The sweetheart of Arakcheyev, an old man of sixty, was one of his serf-girls; she persecuted the servants, fought with them and told tales, and the Count thrashed them according to the information she laid. When their patience was completely exhausted, the cook killed her. The crime was committed so adroitly that there was no clue to the culprit.

But a culprit was needed for the vengeance of the doting old man; he threw aside the affairs of the whole Empire and galloped to Gruzino. In the midst of tortures and blood, in the midst of groans and dying shrieks, Arakcheyev, with the blood-stained kerchief round his neck which had been taken from his concubine's body, wrote touching letters to Alexander, and Alexander replied: 'Come and find rest from your unhappiness on the bosom of your friend.'

The baronet Wylie[10] must have been right when he declared that the Emperor had water on the brain before his death.

But the culprits were not discovered. The Russian is wonderfully good at holding his tongue.

Then, utterly infuriated, Arakcheyev appeared at Novgorod, where a crowd of martyrs was brought. With his face yellow and livid, with mad eyes, and still with the blood-stained kerchief round his neck, he began a new investigation, and here the affair assumes monstrous dimensions. Some eighty persons were seized once more. In the town people were arrested on the strength of one word, on the slightest suspicion, for a distant acquaintanceship with some lackey of Arakcheyev's, for an incautious word. People passing through the town were seized and flung into prison. Merchants and clerks were kept waiting for weeks in the police station to be questioned. . . . The inhabitants hid in their houses and were afraid to go about the streets; the affair itself no one dared to refer to.

---

[10] Sir James Wylie (1768–1854), a Scot who entered the Russian service. He was surgeon-in-ordinary to Paul I whose body he embalmed, certifying that he had died of apoplexy; and physician-in-ordinary to Alexander I, whom he accompanied on his campaigns. He was knighted by the Prince Regent in 1814, when Alexander visited England, and made a baronet later in the same year at the Tsar's special request. He continued to enjoy the Imperial confidence under Nicholas I. (*R.*)

Kleinmikhel, who served under Arakcheyev, took part in this investigation. . . .

The governor transformed his house into a torture chamber; people were tortured near his study from morning till night. The police-captain of Staraya Russa, a man accustomed to horrors, broke down at last and, when he was ordered to question under the rods a young woman who was several months gone with child, he was not equal to the task. He went in to the governor (it took place in the time of old Popov, who told me about it) and told him that the woman could not be flogged, and it was clean against the law; the governor leapt up from his seat and, mad with fury, rushed at the police-captain *brandishing his fist:* 'I order you to be arrested at once: I will have you tried: you are a *traitor.*' The police-captain was arrested and resigned his commission; I am truly sorry I do not know his surname,[11] but may his previous sins be forgiven him for the sake of that minute—I say it in all seriousness—of heroism; in dealing with these ruffians it was no trifling matter to show human feeling.

The woman was tortured; she knew nothing about the crime . . . but she died.[12]

And Alexander 'of blessed memory' died too. Not knowing what was coming, these monsters made one last effort, and succeeded in tracing the culprit; he was condemned to the knout, of course. In the midst of this triumph for the investigators came an order from Nicholas that they should be tried and that the whole case should be stopped.

It was commanded that the governor[13] should be tried by the Senate . . . even by them he could not be acquitted. Nicholas issued a gracious manifesto after his coronation. The friends of Pestel and Muravëv did not come under it, but this scoundrel did. Two or three years later, the same man was tried at Tambov

---

[11] The chief of the Novgorod rural police at this time was V. Lyalin who, on the advice of A. F. Musin-Pushkin, president of the Criminal Court, decided not to subject the thirty-year-old peasant woman, Darya Konstantinov, who was pregnant, to the ninety-five blows of the knout to which she had been sentenced. Both officials were relieved of their duties and arrested, and were suspected of interceding for the 'criminal woman' of malice prepense. (*A.S.*)

[12] Darya Konstantinov, who was punished together with five other 'ringleaders,' survived the torment and was to be sent to hard labour; three of those condemned died of their floggings. (*A.S.*)

[13] I am extremely sorry that I have forgotten the Christian name of this worthy head of a province. I remember his surname was Zherebtsov.

for the abuse of power on his own property. Yes, he came under Nicholas's manifesto: he was beneath it.

At the beginning of 1842 I was hopelessly weary of provincial government and was trying to invent an excuse to get out of it. While I was hesitating between one means and another, a quite extraneous incident decided in my favour.

One cold winter's morning as I reached the office I found a peasant woman of about thirty standing in the front hall; seeing me in uniform she fell on her knees before me and bursting into tears besought my protection. Her master, Musin-Pushkin, was sending her with her husband to a settlement, while their son, a boy of ten, was to remain behind; she begged to be allowed to take the child with her. While she was telling me this the military governor came in; I motioned her towards him and passed on her petition. The governor explained to her that children of ten or over are kept by the landowners. The mother, not understanding the stupid law, went on entreating him. He was bored; the woman, sobbing, clutched at his legs, and he pushed her away roughly, saying: 'What a fool you are; don't I tell you in plain Russian that I can do nothing? Why do you keep on so?' After this he went with a firm, resolute step to the corner, where he put his sword.

And I went too . . . I had had enough. . . . Did not that woman take me for one of *them?* It was high time to put an end to the farce.

'Are you unwell?' asked a councillor called Khlopin, who had been transferred from Siberia for some shortcomings or other.

'I am ill,' I answered, and I got up, took my leave and went away. The same day I sent in a declaration that I was ill, and from that day never set foot in the office of the provincial government. Then I asked for my discharge on the ground 'of illness.' The Senate gave me my discharge accompanying it with promotion to the grade of Aulic Councillor; but Benckendorf at the same time informed the governor that I was forbidden to visit Petersburg or Moscow and was commanded to live at Novgorod.

When Ogarëv returned from his first tour abroad, he did his utmost in Petersburg to procure permission for us to move to Moscow. I had little faith in the success of such a patron and was fearfully bored in the wretched little town with the great historical name. Meanwhile Ogarëv managed our business for us. On the 1st of July, 1842, the Empress, taking advantage of some family festivity, asked the Tsar to allow me to live in Moscow in consideration of my wife's illness and her desire to move there. The Tsar agreed and three days later my wife received from Benckendorf a letter in which he informed her that I was permitted to accompany her to Moscow in consequence of the Tsaritsa's intercession. He concluded the letter with the agreeable notification that I should remain under police supervision there also.

I felt no regret at leaving Novgorod and made haste to get away as soon as possible. Before I left it, however, there occurred almost the only pleasant event in my sojourn there.

I had no money! I did not want to wait for a remittance from Moscow and so I commissioned Matvey to try to borrow fifteen hundred paper roubles for me. An hour later Matvey appeared with an innkeeper called Gibin, whom I knew, and at whose hotel I had stayed for a week. Gibin, a stout merchant with a good-natured expression, bowed and handed me a packet of notes.

'How much interest do you want?' I asked him.

'Well, you see,' answered Gibin, 'I don't do this sort of business and I don't lend money at interest, but since I heard from Matvey Savelyevich that you need money for a month or two, and we very much approve of you, and thank God have the money to spare, I've brought it along.'

I thanked him and asked him which he would like, a simple receipt for the money or a promissory note; but to this, too, Gibin answered: 'Extra work; I trust your word more than a piece of stamped paper.'

'Upon my word, but I may die you know.'

'Well then, in my sorrow at your decease I shouldn't worry much about the loss of the money.'

I was touched and pressed his hand warmly instead of giving him a receipt. Gibin embraced me in the Russian fashion and said: 'We know it all, of course; we know you were not serving of your own will and didn't behave yourself like the other officials, the Lord forgive them, but stood up for the likes of us and the ignorant people, so I am glad a chance has come to do you a good turn too.'

As we were driving out of the town late in the evening our driver pulled up the horses at the inn and Gibin gave me a pie the size of a cart-wheel as provision for the journey. . . .

That was my 'medal for good service.'

❖   ❖   ❖

Our Friends

WITH OUR VISIT to Pokrovskoye and the quiet summer [1843] we spent there begins the gracious, grown-up, active part of our Moscow life, which lasted till my father's death and perhaps until we went abroad.

Our nerves, overstrained in Petersburg and Novgorod, had relaxed, our inner storms had subsided. The agonising analysis of ourselves and of each other, the useless reopening with our words of recent wounds, the incessant return to the same painful subjects were over; and our shaken faith in our own infallibility gave a truer and more earnest quality to our lives. My article 'On a Drama' was the last word of the sickness we had passed through.

Externally the only restriction we suffered from was police supervision; I cannot say it was very tiresome, but the unpleasant feeling of a cane of Damocles, wielded by the local police-constable, was very disagreeable.

Our new friends received us warmly, much better than two years before. Foremost among them stood Granovsky: to him belongs the chief place in those five years. Ogarëv was abroad almost all the time. Granovsky filled his place for us, and we are indebted to him for the happiest moments of that time. There was a wonderful power of love in his nature. With many I was more in agreement in opinion, but to him I was nearer—somewhere deep down in the soul.

Granovsky and all of us were very busy, all hard at work, one lecturing at the university, another contributing to reviews and magazines, another studying Russian history; the first beginnings of all that was done afterwards date from this time.

By now we were far from being children; in 1842 I was thirty; we knew only too well where our work was leading us, but we went on. We went along our chosen path, not rashly but deliberately, with the calm, even step to which experience and family life had trained us. This did not mean that we had grown old: no, we were still young, and that is how it was that some speaking in the university lecture-room, others publishing articles or editing a newspaper were every day in danger of being arrested, dismissed, exiled.

Such a circle of talented, cultured, versatile and pure-hearted people I have met nowhere since, neither in the highest ranks of the political nor on the summits of the literary and artistic worlds. Yet I have travelled a great deal, I have lived everywhere and with all sorts of people. I have been thrust by revolution into the extremes of progress, beyond which there is nothing, and conscientiously I am bound to say the same thing.

The finished, self-contained personality of the Western European, which surprises us at first by his specialisation, surprises us later by his one-sidedness. He is always satisfied with himself, and his *suffisance* offends us. He never forgets his personal views, his position is generally cramped and his morals only appropriate to paltry surroundings.

I do not think that men were always like this here; the Western European is not in a normal condition, *he is moulting*. Unsuccessful revolutions have been absorbed and none of them has transformed him, but each has left its trace and confused his ideas, while the natural surge of historical process has splashed up into the foreground the slimy stratum of the *petit bourgeois*, under which the fossilised aristocratic class is buried and the rising masses submerged. *Petite bourgeoisie* is incompatible with the Russian character—and thank God for it!

Whether it is due to our carelessness, or our lack of moral stability and of defined activity, or our youth in the matter of education, or the aristocratic way in which we are brought up, yet we are in our living on the one hand more artists, and on the other far simpler than Western Europeans; we have not their specialised knowledge, but to make up for that we are more versatile than they. Well developed personalities are not common amongst us, but their development is richer, wider in its scope, free from hedges and barriers. It is quite different in Western Europe.

When you are talking to the most likeable people here[1] you immediately reach contradictions where you and they have nothing in common, and it is impossible to convince. In this stubborn obstinacy and unintentional incomprehension you seem to be knocking your head against the frontier of a world that is completed.

Our theoretical differences, on the contrary, brought more living interest into our lives, and a need for active exchange of opinions kept our minds more vigorous and helped us to progress; we grew in this friction against each other, and in reality

---

[1] Written in England. (*Tr.*)

were the stronger thanks to that 'composite' workmen's association which Proudhon has so superbly described in the field of
mechanical labour.

I love to dwell on that time of work in unison, of a full exalted
pulse, of harmonious order and virile struggle, on those years in
which we were young for the last time! . . .

Our little circle assembled frequently, at the house sometimes
of one, sometimes of another, and oftenest of all at mine. Together with chatter, jest, supper and wine, there was the most
active, the most rapid exchange of ideas, news and knowledge;
everyone handed on what he had read and learned. Opinion was
disseminated through arguments and what had been worked out
by each became the property of all. There was nothing of significance in any sphere of knowledge, in any literature or in any
art, which did not come under the notice of some one of us, and
was not at once communicated to all.

It was just this quality of our gatherings that dull pedants and
tedious scholars failed to understand. They saw the meat and the
bottles, but they saw nothing else. Feasting goes with fullness of
life; ascetic people are usually dry and egoistical. We were not
monks: we lived on all sides and, sitting round the table, learnt
rather more and did no less than those fasting toilers who grub
in the backyards of science.

I will not have anything said against you, my friends, nor
against that bright, splendid time; I think of it with more than
love: almost with envy. We were not like the emaciated monks
of Zurbaran; we did not weep over the sins of this world—we
only sympathised with its sufferings, and were ready with a
smile for anything, and not depressed by a foretaste of our sacrifices to come. Ascetics who are for ever morose have always
excited my suspicion; if they are not pretending, either their
mind or their stomach is out of order.

❖   ❖   ❖

Our 'Opponents'

> *Yes, we were their opponents, but very strange ones. We had the same love, but not the same way of loving—and like Janus or the two-headed eagle we looked in different directions, though the heart that beat within us was but one.*
>
> The Bell, p. 90 (*On the death of K. S. Aksakov*)

SIDE BY SIDE with our circle were our opponents, *nos amis les ennemis,* or more correctly, *nos ennemis les amis*—the Moscow Slavophils.

The conflict between us ended long ago and we have held out our hands to each other; but in the early 'forties we could not but be antagonistic—without being so we could not have been true to our principles. We might have been able not to quarrel with them over their childish homage to the childhood of our history; but accepting their Orthodoxy as meant in earnest, seeing their ecclesiastical intolerance on both sides—in relation to learning and in relation to sectarianism—we were bound to take up a hostile attitude to them. We saw in their doctrines fresh oil for anointing the Tsar, new chains laid upon thought, new subordination of conscience to the servile Byzantine Church.

The Slavophils are to blame for our having so long failed to understand either the Russian people or its history; their ikon-painter's ideals and incense smoke hindered us from seeing the realities of the people's existence and the foundations of village life.

The Orthodoxy of the Slavophils, their historical patriotism and over-sensitive, exaggerated feeling of nationality were called forth by the extremes on the other side. The importance of their outlook, what was true and essential in it, lay not in Orthodoxy, and not in exclusive nationalism, but in those elements of Russian life which they unearthed from under the manure of an artificial civilisation.

The idea of nationality is in itself a conservative idea—the demarcation of one's rights, the opposition of self to another; it includes both the Judaic conception of superiority of race, and the aristocratic claim to purity of blood and to the right of primo-

geniture. Nationalism as a standard, as a war-cry, is only surrounded with the halo of revolution when a people is fighting
for its independence, when it is trying to throw off a foreign
yoke. That is why national feeling with all its exaggerations is
full of poetry in Italy and in Poland, while in Germany it is
vulgar.

For us to display our nationalism would be even more absurd
than it is for the Germans; even those who abuse us do not doubt
it; they hate us from fear, but they do not refuse to recognise us,
as Metternich did Italy. We have had to set up our nationalism
against the Germanised government and our own renegades.
This domestic struggle could not be raised to the epic level. The
appearance of the Slavophils as a school, and as a special doctrine, was quite in place; but if the Slavophils had had no other
standard than the banner of the Church, no other ideal than the
Domostroy[1] and the very Russian but extremely tedious life
before Peter I, they would have passed away as an eccentric
party of changelings and cranks belonging to another age. The
strength and the future of the Slavophils did not lie in that.
Their treasure may have been hidden in the liturgical objects of
their Church, with their old-fashioned workmanship; but its
value was to be found neither in vessels nor in forms. They did
not distinguish them in the beginning.

To their own historical traditions were added the traditions of
all the Slav peoples. Our Slavophils sympathised with the Western Panslavists for identity of cause and policy, forgetting that
exclusive nationalism there was at the same time the cry of a
people oppressed by a foreign yoke. Western Panslavism on its
first appearance was taken by the Austrian government itself for
a conservative movement. It developed at the melancholy epoch
of the Congress of Vienna. It was a time of restorations and
resurrections of all sorts, a period of every possible Lazarus,
fresh or stinking. Alongside Teutschthum,[2] which looked for the
renaissance of the *happy days* of Barbarossa and the Hohen-
staufens, Czech Panslavism made its appearance. The governments were pleased with this movement and at first encouraged the development of international hatreds; the masses once

---

[1] The *Domostroy* was a sixteenth-century book of moral precepts and
practical advice written by the priest Sylvester, the adviser of Ivan the
Terrible. (*Tr.*)
[2] Deutschthum was the nationalist movement in Germany. It was considered more patriotic to spell it Teutschthum. (*Tr.*)

more clung round the idea of racial kinship, the bond of which was drawn tighter, and were again turned aside from the general demands for the improvement of their lot. Frontiers became more impassable, ties and sympathies between peoples were broken. It need hardly be said that only among apathetic and feeble peoples was nationalism allowed to awaken, and only so long as it confined itself to archaeological and linguistic disputes. In Milan and in Poland where nationalism was by no means confined to grammar, it was held in with spiked gloves.

Czech Panslavism provoked Slavonic sympathies in Russia.

Slavanism, or Russianism, not as a theory, not as a doctrine, but as a wounded national feeling, as an obscure memory and a true instinct, as antagonism to an exclusively foreign influence, had existed ever since Peter I cut off the first Russian beard.

There has never been any interval in the resistance to the Petersburg culture terrorism; it reappears in the form of the mutinous Streltsy, executed, quartered, hanged on the crenellations of the Kremlin and there shot by Menshikov and other buffoons of the Tsar; in the form of the Tsarevich Alexey poisoned in the dungeons of the Petersburg fortress; as the party of the Dolgorukys in the reign of Peter II; as the hatred for the Germans at the time of Biron; as Pugachëv in the time of Catherine II; as Catherine herself, the Orthodox German in the reign of the Prussian Holsteiner, Peter III; as Elizabeth who ascended the throne through the support of the Slavophils of those days (the people in Moscow expected all the Germans to be massacred at her coronation).

All the schismatics are Slavophils.

All the clergy, both white and black, are Slavophils of another sort.

The soldiers who demanded the removal of Barclay de Tolly[3] on account of his German name were the precursors of Khomyakov and his friends.

The war of 1812 greatly developed the feeling of national consciousness and love for the Fatherland. But there was nothing of the Old Believers' Slavonic spirit in the patriotism of 1812 which we see in Karamzin and Pushkin, and in the Emperor Alexander himself. Practically it was the expression of that instinct of strength which all powerful nations feel when they are provoked by others; afterwards it was the triumphant feeling

---

[3] Barclay de Tolly was one of the ablest of the Russian generals of 1812. He was, as a matter of fact, of Scottish, not of German, descent. (*Tr.*)

of victory, the proud sense of successful resistance. But it was weak on the theoretical side; in order to love Russian history the patriots adapted it to European manners; in general they translated Greek and Roman patriotism from French into Russian and did not go beyond the line '*Pour un coeur bien né que la patrie est chère!*'[4] Shishkov[5] was raving even then, it is true, about the restoration of archaic forms of language, but his influence was limited. As for the real speech of the people, the only person who showed a knowledge of it was the Frenchified Count Rostopchin in his proclamations and manifestoes.[6]

As the war was forgotten this patriotism subsided and finally degenerated on the one hand into the mean cynical flattery of the *Northern Bee*, on the other into the vulgar patriotism of Zagoskin, which called Shuya Manchester, and Shebuyev[7] Raphael, and boasted of bayonets and the distance from the ice of Torneo to the mountains of the Crimea.

In the reign of Nicholas patriotism became something associated with the knout, with the police, especially in Petersburg, where this savage movement ended, conformably to the cosmopolitan spirit of the town, in the *invention* of a national hymn after Sebastian Bach[8] and in Prokopy Lyapunov[9]—after Schiller![10]

---

[4] Misquoted from Voltaire's *Tancred* (Act III, scene 1). (*A.S.*)

[5] Shishkov, Alexander Semënovich (1754–1841), began his career as a naval officer and attained the rank of vice-admiral but, disapproving of the reforms of the early years of Alexander's reign, left the navy. From 1812 be became prominent as a writer and president of the Academy, and from 1824 to 1828 was Minister of Public Instruction. Intensely conservative and patriotic, he bitterly opposed every new movement in literature and politics. (*Tr.*) He was a leader of the 'Slavonic' party. (*R.*)

[6] Herzen is referring ironically to the pseudo-homespun language of the patriotic proclamations issued in 1812 by F. V. Rostopchin, Commander-in-Chief and Military Governor of Moscow. (*A.S.*)

[7] Shebuyev, Vasily Kuz'mich (1776–1855), was a well known painter of historical pictures in the pseudo-classical style. (*Tr.*)

[8] At first the national hymn was very naïvely sung to the tune of 'God Save the King,' and indeed it was scarcely ever sung. It was among the innovations of Nicholas. From the time of the Polish War the national hymn composed by Colonel Lvov of the *Corps of Gendarmes* was, by Imperial command, sung at all the royal festivities and at large concerts.

The Emperor Alexander was too well educated to like crude flattery; he listened with disgust in Paris to the Academicians' despicable speeches grovelling at the feet of the Conqueror. On one occasion meeting Chateaubriand in his front hall he showed him the latest number of the *Journal des Débats*, and added: 'I assure you I have never seen such dull abjectness in any Russian paper.' But in the time of Nicholas there

To cut himself off from Europe, from enlightenment, from the revolution of which he had been frightened since the Fourteenth of December, 1825, Nicholas on his side raised the banner of Orthodoxy, autocracy, and nationalism, embellished after the fashion of the Prussian standard and supported by anything that came to hand—the barbaric novels of Zagoskin, barbaric ikon-painting, barbaric architecture, Uvarov,[11] the persecution of the Uniats[12] and 'The Hand of the Most High Saved the Father-land.'[13]

The encounter of the Moscow Slavophils with the Petersburg Slavophilism of Nicholas was a great misfortune for the former. Nicholas was simply flying to nationalism and Orthodoxy from revolutionary ideas. The Slavophils had nothing in common with him but words. Their extremes and absurdities were at all events disinterestedly absurd, and had no connection with the Third Division or with ecclesiastical jurisdiction; which of

---

were literary men who justified his monarchical confidence, and beat into a cocked hat all the journalists of 1814 and even some of the prefects of 1852. Bulgarin wrote in the *Northern Bee* that among the other advantages of the railway between Moscow and Petersburg, he could not think without emotion that the same man would be able to hear a service for the health of His Imperial Majesty in the morning in the Kazan Cathedral, and in the evening in the Kremlin! One would have thought it difficult to excel this awful absurdity, but there was found a literary man in Moscow who surpassed Bulgarin in elegance. On one of Nicholas's visits to Moscow a learned professor [M. P. Pogodin (*A.S.*)] wrote an article in which, speaking of the mass of people crowding before the palace, he added that the Tsar had but to express the faintest desire—and those thousands who had come to gaze at him would gladly fling themselves into the River Moskva. The sentence was erased by Count S. G. Strogonov, who told me this nice anecdote.

[9] Lyapunov, a national hero who fought the Poles in the 'Time of Troubles.' Several plays were written about him—one by Stepan Alexandrovich Gedeonov (1816–78), on which Turgenev wrote a criticism.

[10] I was at the first performance of *Lyapunov* in Moscow and saw the hero tuck up his sleeves and say something like, 'I shall amuse myself with the shedding of Polish blood.' A hollow groan of repulsion broke from the whole body of the theatre; even the gendarmes, policemen, and people in the stalls, so undistinguished that even the numbers on their seats seemed to have been worn away, could not find the strength to applaud.

[11] Uvarov, Sergey Semënovich (1786–1855), president of the Academy of Sciences, 1818–55; Minister for Public Enlightenment, 1833–49. (*R.*)

[12] The Uniats are members of the Greek Church who accept the supremacy of the Pope. (*Tr.*)

[13] 'The Hand of the Most High Saved the Fatherland' is the title of a play by N. V. Kukolnik, 1809–68. (*Tr.*)

course did not in any way prevent their absurdities from being extraordinarily absurd.

For instance there was staying in Moscow, on his way through, at the end of the 'thirties the Panslavist Gay who afterwards played an obscure part as a Croatian agitator and was at the same time closely connected with the Ban of Croatia, Jellachich.[14] Moscow people as a rule trust all foreigners: Gay was more than a foreigner, more than one of themselves; he was both at once; so he had no difficulty in touching the hearts of our Slavophils with the fate of their suffering Orthodox brothers in Dalmatia and Croatia; a huge subscription was raised in a few days, and more than this, Gay was given a dinner in the name of all Serbian and Ruthenian sympathies. At the dinner one of the mildest of the Slavophils, both in voice and interests, a man of the *reddest* Orthodoxy, probably vexed by the toasts to the Montenegrin prelate and to various great Bosnians, Czechs and Slovaks, improvised some verses in which the following not quite Christian expression occurred:

> *I shall slake my thirst with the blood*
> *of Magyar and German.*

All who were not deranged heard this phrase with repulsion. Fortunately the witty statistician Androsov rescued the blood-thirsty singer; he jumped up from his chair, clutched a dessert knife, and said: 'Excuse me, gentlemen: I'm going to leave you for a minute: it occurs to me that my landlord Dietz, an old piano-tuner, is a German. I'll just run and cut his throat and be back directly.'

A roar of laughter drowned the indignation.

It was while we were in exile and when I was living in Petersburg and Novgorod that the Moscow Slavophils formed themselves into a party that was so bloodthirsty in its *toasts*.

Their passionate and generally polemical character developed specially in consequence of the appearance of Belinsky's critical articles; and even before that they had had to close their ranks and take a definite stand on the appearance of Chaadayev's *Letter* and the commotion it caused.

The *Letter* was in a sense the last word, the limit. It was a

---

[14] Baron Joseph Jellachich, an Austrian general, who was also a poet and politician. In 1848 he was appointed Ban of Croatia, and took part in suppressing the revolt of the Hungarians. (*Tr.*)

shot that rang out in the dark night; whether it was something foundering that proclaimed its own wreck, whether it was a signal, a cry for help, whether it was news of the dawn or news that there would not be one—it was all the same: one had to wake up.

What, one may wonder, is the significance of two or three pages published in a monthly review? And yet such is the might of speech, such is the power of the spoken word in a land of silence, unaccustomed to free speech, that Chaadayev's *Letter* shook all thinking Russia. And well it might. There had not been one literary work since *Woe from Wit* which made so powerful an impression. Between that play and the *Letter* there had been ten years of silence, the Fourteenth of December, the gallows, penal servitude, Nicholas. The Petrine period was broken off at both ends. The empty place left by the powerful men who had been exiled to Siberia had not been filled. Thought languished: men's minds were working, but nothing was yet attained. To speak was dangerous, and indeed there was nothing to say; suddenly a mournful figure quietly rose and asked for a hearing in order calmly to utter his *lasciate ogni speranza*.

In the summer of 1836 I was sitting quietly at my writing-table in Vyatka when the postman brought me the latest number of the *Telescope*. One must have lived in exile and in the wilds to appreciate a new book. I abandoned everything, of course, and set to work to cut the *Telescope*. I saw 'Philosophical Letters,' written to a lady, unsigned. In a footnote it was stated that these letters had been written by a Russian in French, that is, that it was a translation. This put me against them rather than for them, and I proceeded to read the 'criticism' and the 'miscellany.'

At last the turn came for the *Letter;* from the second or third page I was struck by the mournfully earnest tone. Every word breathed of prolonged suffering, which by now was calmer, but was still bitter. It was written as only men write who have been thinking for many years, who have thought much and learned much from life and not from theory. . . . I read further: the letter grew and developed, it turned into a dark denunciation of Russia, the protest of one who, in return for all he has endured, longs to utter some part of what is accumulated in his heart.

Twice I stopped to take breath and collect my thoughts and feelings, and then again I read on and on. And this was published in Russian by an unknown author. . . . I was afraid I had gone out of my mind. Afterwards I read the *Letter* aloud to

Vitberg, then to Skvortsov, a young teacher in the Vyatka High School; then I read it again to myself.

It is most likely that exactly the same thing was happening in various provincial and district capitals, in Moscow and Petersburg and in country gentlemen's houses. I learned the author's name a few months later.

Long cut off from the people, part of Russia had been suffering in silence under the most incapable and prosaic yoke, which gave them nothing in return. Everyone felt the oppression of it, everyone had something weighing on his heart, and yet all were silent; at last a man had come who in his own way told them what it was. He spoke only of pain; there was no ray of light in his words, nor indeed in his view. Chaadayev's *Letter* was a merciless cry of pain and reproach against Petrine Russia, which deserved the indictment; had it shown pity or mercy to the author or any one else?

Of course such an utterance was bound to provoke opposition, or Chaadayev would have been perfectly right in saying that Russia's past was empty, its present insufferable, and that there was no future for it at all; that it was 'a *lacuna* of the intellect, a stern lesson given to the nations of the plight to which a people can be brought by alienation and slavery.' This was both penitence and accusation; to know beforehand the means of reconciliation is not the business of penitence, nor the business of protest—or consciousness of guilt becomes a jest, and expiation insincere.

But it did not pass unnoticed; for a minute everyone, even the drowsy and the stunned, recoiled in alarm at this ominous voice. All were astounded and most were offended, but a dozen men loudly and warmly applauded its author. Talk in the drawing-rooms anticipated government measures—provoked them. The Russian patriot of German origin Vigel (well known and not for the right side of him, from Pushkin's epigram) set them going.[15]

The review was at once prohibited; Boldyrev, the censor, an old man, and the Rector of Moscow University, was dismissed; Nadyezhdin the publisher was sent to Ust-Sysolsk; Nicholas ordered Chaadayev himself to be declared insane, and to be obliged to sign an undertaking to write nothing. Every Saturday he was visited by the doctor and the *politsmeyster*; they

---

[15] Herzen was misled by false rumours. The decision to close down the *Telescope* was taken before Vigel's delation. Pushkin's epigram begins 'Cursed town of Kishiner.' (*A.S.*)

interviewed him and made a report, that is, gave out over their signature fifty-two false statements by the command of His Majesty—an intelligent and moral proceeding. It was they of course who were punished. Chaadayev looked with profound contempt on these tricks of the truly insane arbitrariness of power. Neither the doctor nor the *politsmeyster* ever hinted at what they had come for.

I had seen Chaadayev once before my exile. It was on the very day of Ogarëv's arrest. I have mentioned already that on that day there was a dinner party at M. F. Orlov's. All the guests were assembled when a man, bowing coldly, walked into the room. His unusual appearance, handsome, with a striking air of independence, was bound to attract everyone's attention. Orlov took me by the hand and introduced me: it was Chaadayev. I remember little of that first meeting; I had no thoughts to spare for him; he was as always cold, grave, clever, and malicious. After dinner Madame Rayevsky, Orlov's mother-in-law, said to me:

'How is it you are so sad? Oh you young people! I don't know what has come over you in these days.'

'Then you do think,' said Chaadayev, 'that there still are young people in these days?'

That is all that has remained in my memory.

On my return to Moscow I made friends with him and from the time until I went away we were on the best of terms.

Chaadayev's melancholy and peculiar figure stood out sharply like a mournful reproach against the faded and dreary background of Moscow 'high life.'[16] I liked looking at him among the tawdry aristocracy, feather-brained Senators, grey-headed scapegraces, and venerable nonentities. However dense the crowd, the eye found him at once. The years did not mar his graceful figure; he was very scrupulous in his dress, his pale, delicate face was completely motionless when he was silent, as though made of wax or of marble—'a forehead like a bare skull,'[17] —his grey-blue eyes were melancholy and at the same time there was something kindly in them, though his thin lips smiled ironically. For ten years he stood with folded arms, by a column, by a tree on the boulevard, in drawing-rooms and theatres, at the club and, an embodied veto, a living protest, gazed at the vortex of faces senselessly whirling round him. He became whimsical and

---

[16] In English. (*R.*)
[17] From Pushkin's *Polkovodets*. (*A.S.*)

eccentric, held himself aloof from society, yet could not leave it altogether, then uttered his message, which he had quietly concealed, just as in his features he concealed passion under a skin of ice. Then he was silent again, again showed himself whimsical, dissatisfied, irritated; again he was an oppressive influence in Moscow society, and again he could not leave it. Old and young alike were awkward and ill at ease with him; they were abashed, God knows why, by his immobile face, his direct gaze, his mournful mockery, his malignant condescension. What made them receive him, invite him . . . still more, visit him? It is a very difficult question.

Chaadayev was not wealthy, particularly in his later years; he was not eminent—a retired captain of cavalry with the iron Kulm cross[18] on his breast. It is true, as Pushkin writes, that he would

> *In Rome have been a Brutus,*
> *In Athens Pericles,*
> *But here, under the yoke of Tsars,*
> *Was only Captain of Hussars.*[19]

Acquaintance with him could only compromise a man in the eyes of the ruling police. To what did he owe his influence? Why did the 'swells' of the English Club, and the patricians of Tverskoy Boulevard flock on Mondays to his modest little study in Old Basmannaya Street? Why did fashionable ladies gaze at the cell of the morose thinker? Why did generals who knew nothing about civilian affairs feel obliged to call upon the old man, to pretend awkwardly to be people of culture, and brag afterwards, garbling some phrase of Chaadayev's uttered at their expense? Why did I meet at Chaadayev's the savage Tolstoy 'the American,' and the savage Adjutant-General Shipov who destroyed culture in Poland?

Chaadayev not only made no compromise with them, but worried them and made them feel very clearly the difference between himself and them.[20] Of course these people went to see

---

18 It was not this decoration that Chaadayev received after the battle of Kulm, but the order of St Anna, fourth class. (*A.S.*)

19 A misquotation from Pushkin's lines 'To a Portrait of Chaadayev.' (*A.S.*)

20 Chaadayev was often at the English Club. On one occasion Menshikov, Minister of Naval Affairs, went up to him with the words: 'How is it, Pëtr Yakovlevich, you don't recognise your old acquaintances?' 'Oh, it is you,' answered Chaadayev. 'I really had not recognised you. But how is

him and invited him to their gatherings from vanity, but that is
not what matters; what is important is the involuntary recognition that thought had become a power, that it had its honoured
place in spite of His Majesty's command. In so far as the authority of the 'insane' Captain Chaadayev was recognized, the 'insane' power of Nicholas Pavlovich was diminished.

Chaadayev had his eccentricities, his weaknesses: he was
embittered and spoilt. I know no society less indulgent, or more
exclusive than that of Moscow; it is just that which gives it a
provincial flavour and reminds one that its culture is of recent
growth. How could a solitary man of fifty who had been deprived of almost all his friends, who had lost his property, who
lived a great deal in thought, and had suffered many mortifica-
tions, fail to have his whims and habits?

Chaadayev had been Vasilchikov's adjutant at the time of the
celebrated Semënovsky affair.[21] The Tsar was at the time, if I
remember right, at Verona or Aachen for a congress. Vasilchikov
sent Chaadayev to him with a report and he was somehow or
other an hour or two behind time, and arrived later than a
courier sent by the Austrian ambassador Lebzeltern. The Tsar,
annoyed at the news, and at that time completely influenced
towards reaction by Metternich, who was delighted at the news
of the Semënovsky affair, received Chaadayev very harshly,
reprimanded him, lost his temper and then, recovering himself,
directed that he should be offered the post of an Imperial
adjutant; Chaadayev declined the honour and asked only one
favour—his discharge. Of course this was not liked, but he received his discharge.

Chaadayev was in no haste to return to Russia; on relinquish-
ing his gold-laced uniform he devoted himself to study. Alexander died—the Fourteenth of December came—Chaadayev's

---

it you are wearing a black collar? I fancy that you used to wear a red
one.' 'Why, don't you know I am Minister of Naval Affairs?' 'You! why,
I imagine you have never steered a boat.' 'You don't need much wit to
bake a pot, you know,' answered Menshikov, a little bit displeased. 'Oh,
well, if it is on that principle. . . .' answered Chaadayev.

A Senator was complaining vehemently of being very busy. 'With
what?' asked Chaadayev. 'Upon my soul, the mere reading of papers
and files!' and the Senator made a gesture indicating a pile a yard
from the floor. 'But you don't read them?' 'Oh yes, sometimes I do, quite
a lot; and besides, it is often necessary to give my opinion on them.'
'Well, I don't see any necessity for that,' answered Chaadayev.

[21] A reference to the mutiny of the Semënovsky Regiment of Guards
in 1820. I. V. Vasilchikov at that time commanded the Corps of Guards.
(*A.S.*)

absence saved him from almost certain persecution[22]—about 1830 he returned.

In Germany Chaadayev made friends with Schelling; the acquaintance probably did a great deal to turn him towards mysticism. In his case it developed into revolutionary Catholicism to which he remained faithful all his life. In his *Letter* he attributes half the calamities of Russia to the Greek Church, to its severance from the all-embracing unity of the West.

❖   ❖   ❖

On a Russian, such Catholicism was bound to have an even stronger effect. It formally contained all that was lacking in Russian life which was left to itself and oppressed only by the material power, and was seeking a way out by its own instinct alone. The strict ritual and proud independence of the Western Church, its consummate limitedness, its practical applications, its irreversible assurance and supposed removal of all contradictions by its higher unity, by its eternal *fata Morgana*, and its *urbi et orbi*, by its contempt for the temporal power, must easily have dominated an ardent mind which began its education in earnest only after reaching maturity.

When Chaadayev returned to Russia he found there a different society and a different tone. Young as I was, I remember how conspicuously aristocratic society deteriorated and became nastier and more servile after the accession of Nicholas. The dash of the officers of the Guards, the aristocratic independence of the reign of Alexander, had all vanished from 1826 onwards.

There were germs of a new life springing up, young creatures, not yet fully conscious of themselves, still wearing an open collar *à l'enfant*, or studying at boarding schools or in lycées. There were young literary men beginning to try their strength and their pen, but all that was still hidden, and did not exist in the world in which Chaadayev lived.

His friends were in penal servitude; at first he was left quite alone in Moscow, then he was joined by Pushkin, and there were two of them and later on Orlov made three. After the death of both these friends Chaadayev often used to point out two small patches on the wall above the sofa-back where they used to lean their heads!

---

[22] We now know for certain from Yakushkin's *Diary* that Chaadayev was a member of the Decembrist society.

It is infinitely sad to set side by side Pushkin's two epistles to Chaadayev, separated not only by their life but by a whole epoch, the life of a whole generation, racing hopefully forward and rudely flung back again. Pushkin as a youth writes to his friend:

> *Comrade, have faith. That dawn will break*
> *Of deep intoxicating joy;*
> *Russia will spring from out her sleep*
> *And on the fragments of a fallen tyranny*
> *Our names will be recorded,*[23]

but the dawn did not rise; instead Nicholas rose to the throne, and Pushkin writes:

> *Chaadayev, dost thou call to mind*
> *How in the past, by youthful ardour prompted,*
> *I dreamt to add that fatal name*
> *Unto the rest of those that lie in ruins?*
> *. . . But now within my heart by tempests chastened*
> *Silence and lassitude prevail, unchallenged,*
> *And with a glow of tender inspiration*
> *Upon the stone by friendship sanctified*
> *I write our names . . .*[24]

Nothing in the world was more opposed to the Slavophils than the hopeless pessimism which was Chaadayev's vengeance on Russian life, the deliberate curse wrung out of him by suffering, with which he summed up his melancholy existence and the existence of a whole period of Russian history. He was bound to awaken violent opposition in them; with bitterness and dismal malice he offended all that was dear to them, from Moscow downwards.

'In Moscow,' Chaadayev used to say, 'every foreigner is taken to look at the great cannon and the great bell—the cannon which cannot be fired and the bell which fell down before it was rung. It is an amazing town in which the objects of interest are distinguished by their absurdity; or perhaps that great bell without a tongue is a hieroglyph symbolic of this huge, dumb

---

[23] Translated by Juliet Soskice. (*R.*)
[24] Translated by Juliet Soskice. (*R.*) These and the preceding verses are quotations, not always exact, from two of A. S. Pushkin's poems *To Chaadayev* (1818 and 1824). H. attributes a wrong date to the second poem. (*A.S.*)

land, inhabited by a race calling themselves Slavs as though wondering at the possession of human speech.'[25]

Chaadayev and the Slavophils alike stood facing the unsolved Sphinx of Russian life, the Sphinx sleeping under the overcoat of the soldier and the watchful eye of the Tsar; they alike were asking: 'What will come of this? To live like this is impossible: the oppressiveness and absurdity of the present situation is obvious and unendurable—where is the way out?'

'There is none,' answered the man of the Petrine epoch of exclusively Western civilisation, who in Alexander's reign had believed in the European future of Russia. He sadly pointed to what the efforts of a whole age had led to. Culture had only given new methods of oppression, the church had become a mere shadow under which the police lay hidden; the people still tolerated and endured, the government still crushed and oppressed. 'The history of other nations is the story of their emancipation. Russian history is the development of serfdom and autocracy.' Peter's upheaval made us into the worst that men can be made into—*enlightened* slaves. We have suffered enough, in this oppressive, troubled moral condition, misunderstood by the people, struck down by the government—it is time to find rest, time to bring peace to one's soul, to find something to lean on . . . this almost meant 'time to die,' and Chaadayev thought to find in the Catholic Church the rest promised to all that labour and are heavy laden.

From the point of view of Western civilisation in the form in which it found expression at the time of restorations, from the point of view of Petrine Russia, this attitude was completely justified. The Slavophils solved the question in a different way.

Their solution implied a true consciousness of the *living soul* in the people; their instinct was more penetrating than their reasoning. They saw that the existing condition of Russia, however oppressive, was not a *fatal disease*. And while Chaadayev had a faint glimmer of the possibility of saving individuals, but not the people, the Slavophils had a clear perception of the ruin of individuals in the grip of that epoch, and faith in the salvation of the people.

'The way out is with us,' said the Slavophils, 'the way out lies in renouncing the Petersburg period, in going back to the people from whom we have been separated by foreign education and foreign government; let us return to the old ways!'

---

25 The name *Slav* is probably derived from *slovo*, word. (*Tr.*)

But history does not turn back; life is rich in materials, and never needs old clothes. All reinstatements, all restorations have always been masquerades. We have seen two; the Legitimists did not go back to the days of Louis XIV nor the Republicans to the 8th of Thermidor. What has once happened is stronger than anything written; no axe can hew it away.

More than this, we have nothing to go back to. The political life of Russia before Peter was ugly, poor and savage, yet it was to this that the Slavophils wanted to return, though they did not admit the fact; how else are we to explain all their antiquarian revivals, their worship of the manners and customs of old days, and their very attempts to return, not to the existing (and excellent) dress of the peasants but to the clumsy, antiquated costumes?

In all Russia no one wears the *murmolka* but the Slavophils. K. S. Aksakov wore a dress so national that people in the street took him for a Persian, as Chaadayev used to tell for a joke.

They took the return to the people in a very crude sense too, as the majority of Western democrats did also, accepting the people as something complete and finished. They supposed that sharing the prejudices of the people meant being at one with them, that it was a great act of humility to sacrifice their own reason instead of developing reason in the people. This led to an affectation of devoutness, the observance of rites which are touching when there is a naïve faith in them and offensive when there is visible premeditation. The best proof of the lack of reality in the Slavophils' return to the people lies in the fact that they did not arouse in them the slightest sympathy. Neither the Byzantine Church nor the Granovitaya Palata[26] will do anything more for the future development of the Slav world. To go back to the village, to the workmen's guild, to the meeting of the *mir*,[27] to the Cossack system is a different matter; but we must return to them not in order that they may be fixed fast in immovable Asiatic crystallisations, but to develop and set free the elements on which they were founded, to purify them from all that is extraneous and distorting, from the proud flesh with which they are overgrown—this, of course, is our vocation. But we must make no mistake; all this lies outside the purview of the State: the Moscow period will help here as little as the Petersburg—

---

[26] Granovitaya Palata, the hall in the Kremlin in which the Tsar and his councillors used to meet before the time of Peter the Great. (*Tr.*)
[27] Village council. (*R.*)

indeed at no time was it better. The Novgorod[28] bell which used to call the citizens to their ancient moot was merely melted into a cannon by Peter but had been taken down from the belfry by Ivan III; serfdom was only confirmed by the census under Peter but had been introduced by Boris Godunov; in the *Ulozheniye*[29] there is no longer any mention of sworn witnesses, and the knout, the rods and the lash made their appearance long before the day of *Spiessruten* and *Fuchteln*.

The mistake of the Slavophils lay in their thinking that Russia once had an individual culture, obscured by various events and finally by the Petersburg epoch. Russia never had this culture and never could have had it. That which is now reaching our consciousness, that of which we are beginning to have a presentiment, a glimmer in our thoughts, that which existed unconsciously in the peasants' hut and in the open country, is only now beginning to grow in the pastures of history, manured by the blood, the tears and the sweat of twenty generations.

The foundations of our life are not memories; they are the living elements, existing not in chronicles but in the actual present; but they have merely *survived* under the difficult historical process of building up a single state and under the oppression of the state they have only been preserved not developed. I even doubt whether the inner forces for their development would have been found without the Petrine epoch, without the period of European culture.

The immediate foundations of our way of life are insufficient. In India there has existed for ages and exists to this day a village commune very like our own and based on the partition of fields; yet the people of India have not gone very far with it.

Only the mighty thought of the West, with which all its long history is united, is able to fertilise the seeds slumbering in the patriarchal mode of the life of the Slavs. The workmen's guild and the village commune, the sharing of profits and the partition of fields, the meeting of the *mir* and the union of villages into self-governing *volosts*, are all the corner-stones on which the mansion of our future, freely communal existence will be built.

---

28 Novgorod, the most famous city in the earliest period of Russian history, was to some extent a republic under the rule of its princes from Rurik onwards. It was almost destroyed and was deprived of its liberties by Ivan III in 1471. (*Tr.*)
29 The *Ulozheniye* was the code of laws of Tsar Alexis Mikhaylovich (father of Peter the Great), issued in 1649. (*Tr.*)

But these corner-stones are only stones . . . and without the thought of the West our future cathedral would not rise above its foundations.

This is what happens with everything truly *social:* it involuntarily attracts into the reciprocal security of peoples. . . . Holding themselves aloof, isolating themselves, some remain at the barbaric stage of the commune, others get no further than the abstract idea of communism which, like the Christian soul, hovers over the decaying body.

The receptive character of the Slavs, their *femininity*, their lack of initiative, and their great capacity for assimilation and adaptation, made them pre-eminently a people that stands in need of other peoples; they are not fully self-sufficing. Left to themselves the Slavs readily 'lull themselves to sleep with their own songs' as a Byzantine chronicler observed, 'and doze.' Awakened by others they go to extreme consequences; there is no people which might more deeply and completely absorb the thought of other peoples while remaining true to itself. The persistent misunderstanding which exists to-day, as it has for a thousand years, between the Germanic and the Latin peoples does not exist between them and the Slavs. The need to surrender and to be carried away is innate in their sympathetic, readily assimilative, receptive nature.

To be formed into a princedom, Russia needed the Varangians;[30] to be formed into a kingdom, the Mongols.

Contact with Europe developed the kingdom of Muscovy into the colossal empire ruled from Petersburg.

'But for all their receptiveness, have not the Slavs shown everywhere a complete incapacity for developing a modern European political order without continually falling into the most hopeless despotism or helpless disorganisation?'

This incapacity and this incompleteness are great *talents* in our eyes.

All Europe has now reached the inevitability of despotism in order to uphold somehow the existing political order against the pressure of social ideas striving to instal a new structure, towards which Western Europe, though frightened and recalcitrant, is being carried with incredible force.

---

[30] The Varangians were Scandinavian and Norman tribes whose rulers were, according to tradition, summoned in 862 by the northern Slavs to rule over them. (*Tr.*)

There was a time when the half-free West looked proudly at a Russia crushed under the throne of the Tsars, and cultivated Russia gazed sighing at the good fortune of its elder brothers. That time has passed. The equality of slavery has been established.

We are present now at an amazing spectacle: even those lands in which free institutions have survived are offering themselves to despotism. Humanity has seen nothing like it since the days of Constantine, when free Romans sought to become slaves in order to escape civic burdens.

Despotism or socialism—there is no other choice.

Meanwhile Europe has shown a surprising incapacity for social revolution.

We believe that Russia is not so incapable of it, and in this we are at one with the Slavophils. On this our faith in its future is founded, the faith which I have been preaching since the end of 1848.

Europe has chosen despotism, has preferred imperialism. Despotism means a military camp, empires mean war, the emperor is the commander-in-chief. Everyone is under arms, there will be war, but where is the real enemy? At home—down below in the depths—and yonder beyond the Niemen.

The war now beginning[31] may have intervals of truce but will not end before the beginning of the general revolution which will shuffle all the cards and begin a new game. It is impossible that the two great historical powers, the two veteran champions of all West European history, representatives of two worlds, two traditions, two principles—of the State and of personal freedom—should not check, should not shatter the third which, dumb, nameless, and bannerless comes forward so inopportunely with the rope of slavery on its neck and rudely knocks at the doors of Europe and the doors of history, with an insolent claim to Byzantium, with one foot on Germany and the other on the Pacific Ocean.

Whether these three will try their strength and shatter each other in the trying; whether Russia will break up into pieces or Europe, enfeebled, sink into Byzantine dotage; whether they will give each other their hands, reanimated for a new lease of life and for an amicable step forward, or will slaughter each other endlessly—one thing we have discovered for certain and it will not be eradicated from the consciousness of the coming generations; this is: that the *free and rational development of*

---

31 Written at the time of the Crimean War.

Russian national life coincides with the aspirations of Western socialism.

❖   ❖   ❖

To Petersburg for a Passport

A few months before my father's death Count Orlov was appointed to succeed Benckendorf.[1] I then wrote to Olga Alexandrovna to ask whether she could manage to procure me a passport for abroad or permission on some pretext or other to go to Petersburg to get one for myself. My old friend answered that the latter was easier to arrange and a few days later I received from Orlov His Majesty's permission to go to Petersburg for a short time to arrange my affairs. My father's illness, his death, the actual arrangement of my affairs, and some months spent in the country, delayed me till winter. At the end of November I set off for Petersburg, having first sent a request for a passport to the Governor-General. I knew that he could not grant it because I was still under *strict* police supervision: all I wanted was that he should send on the request to Petersburg.

On the day of my departure I sent in the morning for a permit from the police, but instead of a permit there came a policeman to say that there were certain difficulties and that the local police-superintendent himself would come to me. He did come, and, asking me to see him alone, he mysteriously made known to me the news that five years before I had been forbidden to go to Petersburg, and, without His Majesty's orders he would not sign the permit.

'That won't stand in our way,' I said, laughing, and took the letter out of my pocket.

The police-superintendent was greatly astonished; he read it and asked permission to show it to the *oberpolitsmeyster*, and two hours later sent me my permit and the letter.

---

[1] This happened in September 1844; *i.e.*, nearly two years before the death of H.'s father. (*A.S.*)

I must mention that my police-superintendent carried on half the conversation in unusually polished French. How mischievous it is for a police-superintendent, or indeed any Russian policeman, to know French, he had learnt by very bitter experience.

Some years previously a French traveller, the Legitimist Chevalier Preaux, arrived in Moscow from the Caucasus. He had been in Persia and in Georgia, had seen a great deal, and was so incautious as to be severely critical of the military operations in the Causasus at that time, and especially of the administration. Afraid that Preaux would say the same thing in Petersburg, the Governor-General of the Caucasus prudently wrote to the Minister of War that Preaux was a very dangerous military agent of the French government. Preaux was living with an easy mind in Moscow and had been well received by Prince D. V. Golitsyn, when suddenly the latter got an order to send the Frenchman from Moscow across the frontier accompanied by a police-officer. To do anything so stupid and so rude is always more difficult to an acquaintance, and so after two days of hesitation Golitsyn invited Preaux to his house, and beginning with an eloquent introduction told him finally that reports of some sort, probably from the Caucasus, had reached the Tsar, who had ordered that he should leave Russia; that he would, however, even be given an escort. . . .

Preaux was incensed and observed to Golitsyn that, seeing that the government had the right to eject him he was prepared to go, but that he would not accept an escort, since he did not consider himself a criminal who needed to be escorted.

Next day when the *politsmeyster* came to Preaux, that latter met him with a pistol in his hand and told him point-blank that he would not permit a police-officer to enter his room or his carriage, and that he would put a bullet through his head if he attempted to use force.

Golitsyn was, on the whole, a very decent man, which made it the more difficult for him; he sent for Weyer, the French consul, to ask his advice what to do. Weyer found an expedient; he asked for a police-officer who spoke French well and promised to present him to Preaux as a traveller who was asking Preaux to let him have a place in his carriage in return for half the travelling expenses.

From the consul's first words Preaux guessed what was up.

'I don't deal in seats in my carriage,' he said to the consul.

'This man will be desperate.'

'Very well,' said Preaux, 'I'll take him for nothing, but he must undertake a few little services in return; he's not an ill-humoured fellow I suppose: if he is I shall leave him in the road.'

'The most obliging man in the world; he will be entirely at your disposal. I thank you on his behalf.' And the consul galloped off to Prince Golitsyn to announce his success.

In the evening Preaux and the *bona fide* traveller set off. Preaux did not speak all the way; at the first posting-station he went indoors and lay down on a sofa.

'Hi,' he shouted to his companion, 'come here and take off my boots.'

'Upon my word, why should I?'

'I tell you, take off my boots, or I shall leave you in the road; I am not keeping you, you know.'

The police-officer took off the boots.

'Knock the dirt off and polish them.'

'That's really too much!'

'Very well: stay here!'

The officer polished the boots.

At the next station there was the same story with his clothes, and so Preaux went on tormenting him till they reached the frontier. To console this martyr of the secret service, the Sovereign's special attention was drawn to him and eventually he was made a police-superintendent.

The second day after my arrival in Petersburg the house porter came to ask me from the local police: 'With what papers have you come to Petersburg?' The only paper I had, the decree concerning my retirement from the service, I had sent to the Governor-General with my request for a passport. I gave the house-porter my permit, but he came back to say that it was valid for leaving Moscow but not for entering Petersburg. A police-officer came too, with an invitation to the *oberpolitsmeyster*'s office. I went to Kokoshkin's office, which was lit by lamps although it was daytime, and after an hour he arrived. Kokoshkin more than other persons of the same selection was the picture of a servant of the Tsar with no ulterior designs, a man in favour, ready to do any dirty job, a favourite with no conscience and no bent for reflection. He served and made his pile as naturally as birds sing.

Perovsky told Nicholas that Kokoshkin was a great bribe-taker.

'Yes,' answered Nicholas, 'but I sleep peacefully at night knowing that he is *politsmeyster* in Petersburg.'

I looked at him while he was dealing with other people. . . . What a battered, senile, depraved face he had; he was wearing a curled wig which was glaringly incongruous with his sunken features and wrinkles.

After conversing with some German women in German and with a familiarity that showed they were old acquaintances, which was evident also from the way the women laughed and whispered, Kokoshkin came up to me, and looking down asked in a rather rude voice:

'Why, are not you forbidden by His Majesty to enter Petersburg?'

'Yes, but I have permission.'

'Where is it?'

'I have it here.'

'Show it. How's this? You are using the same permit twice.'

'Twice?'

'I remember that you came here before.'

'I didn't.'

'And what is your business here?'

'I have business with Count Orlov.'

'Have you been at the Count's, then?'

'No, but I have been at the Third Division.'

'Have you seen Dubelt?'

'Yes.'

'Well, I saw Orlov himself yesterday and he says that he has sent you no permit.'

'It's in your hands.'

'God knows when this was written, and the time has expired.'

'It would be an odd thing for me to do, wouldn't it? to come without permission and begin with a visit to General Dubelt.'

'If you don't want any trouble, be so good as to go back, and not later than the next twenty-four hours.'

'I was not proposing to remain here long, but I must wait for Count Orlov's answer.'

'I cannot give you leave to do so; besides, Count Orlov is much displeased at your coming without permission.'

'Kindly give me my permit and I will go to the Count at once.'

'It must remain with me.'

'But it is a letter to me, addressed to me personally, the only document on the strength of which I am here.'

'The document will remain with me as a proof that you have been in Petersburg. I earnestly advise you to go to-morrow in order that nothing worse may befall you.'

He nodded and went out. Much good it is talking to them!

Old General Tuchkov had a lawsuit with the Treasury. His village head-man undertook a contract, did some swindling and was caught with a deficit. The court ordered that the money should be paid by the landowner who had given the head-man the authorisation. But no authorisation in regard to this undertaking ever had been given and Tuchkov said so in his answer. The case was brought before the Senate, and the Senate again decided: 'Inasmuch as Lieutenant-General Tuchkov, retired, gave an authorisation . . . then . . .' To which Tuchkov again answered: 'But inasmuch as Lieutenant-General Tuchkov, retired, gave no authorisation . . . then . . .' A year passed, and the police made their pronouncement again, sternly repeating: 'Inasmuch as Lieutenant-General, etc.,' and once more the old gentleman wrote his answer. I do not know how this interesting case ended. I left Russia without waiting for the decision.

All this is not at all exceptional but quite the normal thing. Kokoshkin holds in his hands a document of the genuineness of which there is no doubt, on which there is a number and date so that it can be easily verified, in which it is written that I am permitted to visit Petersburg, and says: 'Since you have come without permission you must go back,' and puts the document in his pocket.

Chaadayev was right indeed when he said of these gentry: 'What rogues they all are!'

I went to the Third Division and told Dubelt what had happened. He burst out laughing. 'What a muddle they everlastingly make of everything! Kokoshkin reported to the Count you had come without permission and the Count said you were to be sent away, but I explained the position to him afterwards; you can stay as long as you like. I'll have the police written to at once. But now about your petition: the Count does not think it would be of any use to ask permission for you to go abroad. The Tsar has refused you twice, the last time when Count Strogonov interceded for you; if he refuses a third time, you won't get to *the waters* during this reign, for certain.'

'What am I to do?' I asked in horror, for the idea of travel and freedom had taken such deep root in my heart.

'Go to Moscow: the Count will write a private letter to the Governor-General telling him that you want to go abroad for the sake of your wife's health, assuring him that he knows nothing of you but what is good, and asking him whether he thinks it would be possible to relieve you from police supervision. He can make no answer but "yes" to such a question. We shall report to the Tsar the removal of police supervision, then you take out a passport for yourself like anybody else, and you can go to any *watering-place* you like, and good luck to you.'

All this seemed to me extraordinarily complicated, and indeed I fancied it was a device simply to get rid of me. They could not refuse me point-blank, for it would have brought down upon them the wrath of Olga Alexandrovna, whom I visited every day. When once I had left Petersburg I could not come back again; corresponding with these gentry is a difficult business. I communicated some of my doubts to Dubelt; he began frowning, that is, grinning more than ever with his lips and screwing up his eyes.

'General,' I said in conclusion, 'I do not know, but the fact is I do not even feel certain that Strogonov's representation reached the Tsar.'

Dubelt rang the bell and ordered the file about me to be brought. While waiting for it he said to me goodnaturedly: 'The Count and I are suggesting to you the course of proceeding by which we think you most likely to get your passport; if you have more certain means at your disposal, make use of them; you may be sure that we shall not hinder you.'

'Leonty Vasilevich is perfectly right,' observed a sepulchral voice. I turned round; beside me, looking older and more grey-headed than ever, stood Sakhtynsky, who had received me five years before at the same Third Division. 'I *advise* you to be guided by his opinion if you want to go.'

I thanked him.

'And here's the file,' said Dubelt, taking a thick writing-book from the hands of a clerk (what would I not have given to read the whole of it! In 1850 I saw my *dossier* in Carlier's office in Paris; it would have been interesting to compare them). After rummaging in it he handed it to me open; there was Benckendorf's report after Strogonov's letter petitioning for permission for me to go for six months to a watering-place in Germany. In the margin was written in big letters in pencil: 'Too soon.' The pencil marks were glazed over with varnish, and below was written in ink: ' "Too soon" written by the hand of his Imperial Majesty.—Count A. Benckendorf.'[2]

---

[2] Benckendorf's report to the Tsar of 7 April 1843, contained the solicitation of S. G. Strogonov, then Warden of Moscow University, that H. might be permitted, in consequence of his wife's illness, to go to Italy for some months. The report is endorsed in the hand of Nicholas I: '*peregovorim*'—'Let us talk it over', and there is a postscript by Bencken-

'Do you believe me now?' asked Dubelt.

'Yes, I do,' I answered, 'and I am so sure of your words that I shall go to Moscow to-morrow.'

'Well, you can stay and amuse yourself here a little; the police will not worry you now, and before you go away look in, and I'll tell them to show you the letter to Shcherbatov. Good-bye. *Bon voyage*, if we don't meet again.'

'A pleasant journey,' added Sakhtynsky.

We parted, as you see, on friendly terms.

On reaching home I found an invitation, from the superintendent of the Second Admiralty Police Station I believe it was. He asked me when I was going.

'To-morrow evening.'

'Upon my word, but I believe, I thought . . . the general said to-day. His Excellency will put it off, of course. But will you allow me to make certain of it?'

'Oh yes, oh yes; by the way, give me a permit.'

'I will write it in the police station and send it to you in two hours' time. By what convenience are you thinking of going?'

'The Serapinsky, if I can get a seat.'

'Very good, and if you do not succeed in getting a seat kindly let us know.'

'With pleasure.'

In the evening a policeman turned up again; the superintendent sent to tell me that he *could not* give me the permit, and that I must go at *eight o'clock* next morning to the *oberpolitsmeyster*'s.

What a plague and what a bore! I did not go at eight o'clock, but in the course of the morning I looked in at the office of the *oberpolitsmeyster*. The police station superintendent was there; he said to me:

'You cannot go away: there is a paper from the Third Division.'

'What has happened?'

'I don't know. The general gave orders you were not to be given a permit.'

'Does the director know?'

'Of course he knows,' and he pointed out to me a colonel in uniform and wearing a sword sitting at a big table in another room; I asked him what was the matter.

'To be sure,' he said, 'there was a paper, and here it is.' He

---

dorf: '*ne pozvolyayet*'—'He does not give leave'; the document was countersigned by Dubelt on 9 April 1843. (*A.S.*)

read it through and handed it to me. Dubelt wrote that I had a perfect right to come to Petersburg and could remain *as long as I liked*.

'And is that why you won't let me go? Excuse me, I can't help laughing; yesterday the *oberpolitsmeyster* was chasing me away against my will, to-day he is keeping me against my will, and all this on the ground that the document gives me leave to remain *as long as I like*.'

The absurdity was so evident that even the colonel-secretary laughed.

'But why should I throw money away, paying for a place in the *diligence* twice over? Please tell them to write me a permit.'

'I cannot, but I will go and inform the general.'

Kokoshkin ordered them to write me a permit, and as he walked through the office said to me reproachfully: 'It's beyond anything. First you want to stay, then you want to go; why, you have been told that you can stay.'

I made no answer.

When we had driven out of the city gates in the evening and I saw once more the endless plain stretching away towards the Four Hands,[3] I looked at the sky and vowed with all my heart never to return to that city of the despotism of blue, green, and variegated police, of official muddle, of flunkeyish insolence, of gendarme romance, in which the only civil man was Dubelt, and he chief of the Third Division.

Shcherbatov answered Orlov reluctantly. He had at that time a secretary who was not a colonel but a pietist, who because of my articles hated me as an 'atheist and Hegelian.' I went myself to deal with him. The pious secretary, in an oily voice and with Christian unction, told me that the Governor-General knew nothing about me, that he did not doubt my lofty moral qualities, but that he would have to make inquiries of the *oberpolitsmeyster*. He wanted to drag the business out; moreover, this gentleman did not take bribes. In the Russian service disinterested men are the most frightful of all; the only ones who do not take bribes in all simplicity are Germans; if a Russian does not take money he will take it out in something else, and from such villains God spare us. Fortunately *oberpolitsmeyster* Luzhin gave me a good character.

On returning home ten days later I bumped into a gendarme

---

[3] The name of the first stage-post on the way from Petersburg to Moscow. A sign-post stood at the cross-roads indicating the directions of Moscow, Tsarskoye Selo, Peterhof and Petersburg. (*A.S.*)

at my door. The appearance of a police-officer in Russia is as bad as a tile falling on one's head, and therefore it was not without a particularly unpleasant feeling that I waited to hear what he had to say to me; he handed me an envelope. Count Orlov informed me of his Imperial Majesty's command that I should be relieved from police supervision. Together with this I received the right to a foreign passport.

> *Rejoice with me, for I am free at last!*
> *Free to set forth to foreign lands at will!*
> *But is it not a dream, deceiving me?*
> *Not so! To-morrow come the post-horses,*
> *And then "von Ort zu Ort" I'll gallop on,*
> *Paying for passports what the price may be. . . .*
> *Well, I'll set forth! And then—what shall I find?*
> *I know not! I have faith! And yet—and yet—*
> *God knows alone what still may be my fate. . . .*
> *With fear and doubt I stand before the gate*
> *Of Europe. And my heart is full*
> *Of hope, of troubled, shadowy dreams. . . .*
> *I am in doubt, my friend, you see,*
> *I shake my head despondingly. . . .*

N. P. Ogarëv, *Humorous Verse*, Part II[4]

'Six or seven sledges accompanied us as far as Chërnaya Gryaz. There for the last time we clinked glasses and parted, sobbing.'

'It was evening, the covered sledge crunched through the snow . . . you looked sadly after us but did not guess that it meant a funeral and eternal separation. All were there, only one was missing, the nearest of the near: he alone was ill, and by his absence, as it were, washed his hands of my departure.

'It was the 21st of January, 1847 . . .'

The sergeant gave me back the passports; a little old soldier in a clumsy shako covered with oilskin, carrying a rifle of incredible size and weight, lifted the barrier; a Ural Cossack with narrow little eyes and broad cheekbones, holding the reins of his little, shaggy, dishevelled nag, which was covered all over with little icicles, rode up to wish me a happy journey; the pale, thin, dirty little Jewish driver with rags twisted four times round his neck clambered on the box.

'Good-bye! Good-bye!' said our old acquaintance, Karl Ivano-

---

4 Translated by Juliet Soskice. (*R.*)

vich, who was seeing us as far as Taurogen, and Tata's wet-nurse, a handsome peasant woman, dissolved in tears as she said farewell.

The little Jew whipped up his horses, the sledge moved off. I looked back, the barrier had been lowered, the wind swept the snow from Russia on to the road and blew to one side the tail and mane of the Cossack's horse.

The nurse in a sarafan and a warm jacket was still looking after us and weeping; Sonnenberg, that symbol of the parental home, that comic figure from the days of childhood, waved his silk handkerchief—all round us was the endless steppe of snow.

'Good-bye, Tatyana! Good-bye, Karl Ivanovich!'

Here was a milestone and on it, covered with snow, a thin, *single-headed* eagle with outspread wings . . . and that's a good thing: one head less.

❖   ❖   ❖

PARIS—
ITALY—
PARIS

(1847-1852)

When I began to publish yet another part of My Past and Thoughts, *I paused in hesitation before the discontinuity of the narratives, the pictures and of my, so to speak, interlinear comments on them. There is less external unity in them than in the earlier parts. I cannot weld them into one. In filling in the gaps it is very easy to give the whole thing a different background and a different lighting—the truth of* that time *would be lost.* My Past and Thoughts *is not an historical monograph, but the reflection of historical events on a man who has accidentally found himself in their path. That is why I have decided to leave my disconnected chapters as they were, stringing them together like the mosaic pictures in Italian bracelets—all of which refer to one subject but are only held together by the setting and the chain.*

My Letters from France and Italy *are essential for completing this part, especially in regard to the year 1848; I had meant to make extracts from them, but that would have involved so much reprinting that I could not make up my mind to it.*

Many things that have not appeared in The Pole Star *have been put into this edition, but I cannot give everything to my readers yet, for reasons both personal and public. The time is not far off when not only the pages and chapters here omitted, but the whole volume, which is the most dear to me, will be published.*

GENEVA, 29th July, 1866

The Journey

AT LAUTZAGEN the Prussian gendarmes invited me into the guard-room. An old sergeant took the passports, put on his spectacles, and with extraordinary precision began reading aloud all that was unnecessary:

Auf Befehl s.k. M. Nikolai des Ersten.. . . allen und jeden denen daran gelegen, etc. etc. . . . *Unterzeichner Peroffski, Minister des Innern, Kammerherr, Senator und Ritter des Ordens St. Wladimir . . . Inhaber eins goldenen Degens mit der Inschrift für Tapferkeit . . .*

This sergeant who was so fond of reading reminds me of another one. Between Terracino and Naples a Neapolitan carabineer came to the *diligence* four times, asking every time for our visas. I showed him the Neapolitan visa: this and the half *carlino* were not enough for him; he carried off the passports to the office, and returned twenty minutes later with the request that my companion and I should go to see the brigadier. The latter, a drunken old non-commissioned officer, asked me rather rudely:

'What is your surname and where do you come from?'

'Why, that is all in the passport.'

'I can't read it.'

We conjectured that reading was not the brigadier's strong point.

'By what law,' asked my companion, 'are we bound ro read you our passports aloud? We are bound to have them and to show them, but not to dictate them; I might dictate anything.'

'*Accidenti!*' muttered the old man, '*va ben, va ben!*' and he gave back our passports without writing anything.

The learned gendarme at Lautzagen was of a different type; after reading three times in the three passports all General Perovsky's decorations, including his clasp for an unblemished record, he asked me:

'But who are you, *Euer Hochwohlgeboren?*'

I stared, not understanding what he wanted of me.

'*Fräulein Maria E., Fräulein Maria K., Frau H.*[1]—they are women, there is not one man's passport here.'

I looked: there really were only the passes of my mother and

---

[1] Maria Kasparovna Ern (Reichel), Maria Fëdorovna Korsh and Luiza Ivanovna Haag, H.'s mother. (*R.*)

two ladies we knew who were travelling with us; a cold shudder ran down my back.

'They would not have let me through at Taurogen without passport.'

'*Bereits so*, but you can't go further.'

'What am I to do?'

'Perhaps you have forgotten it at the guard-room. I'll tell them to harness a sledge for you; you can go yourself, and your people can warm themselves here meanwhile. *Heh! Kerl! Lass er mal den Braunen anspannen.*'

I cannot remember this stupid incident without laughing, just because I was so utterly disconcerted by it. I was overwhelmed by losing that passport of which I had been dreaming for several years, which I had been trying to obtain for two years, and losing it the minute after crossing the frontier. I was certain I had put it in my pocket, so I must have dropped it—where could I look for it? It would be covered by snow. . . . I should have to ask for a new one, to write to Riga, perhaps to go myself: and then they would send in a report, would notice that I was going to the mineral waters in January. In short, I felt as though I were in Petersburg again; visions of Kokoshkin and Sakhtynsky, Dubelt and Nicholas, passed through my mind. Good-bye to my journey, good-bye to Paris, to freedom of the press, to concerts and theatres . . . . once more I should see the clerks in the ministry, police—and every other sort of watcher, town constables with the two bright buttons on their backs that they use for looking behind them . . . and first of all I should see again the little scowling soldier in a heavy shako with the mysterious number '4' inscribed on it, the frozen Cossack horse . . .

Meanwhile they put a big, melancholy, angular horse into a tiny sledge. I got in beside a driver in a military overcoat and high boots; he gave the traditional crack of the traditional whip—and suddenly the learned sergeant ran out into the porch wearing only his breeches, and shouted: '*Halt! Halt! Da ist der vermaledeite Pass,*' and he held it unfolded in his hands.

I was overtaken by hysterical laughter.

'What's this you're doing to me? Where did you find it?'

'Look,' he said, 'your Russian sergeant folded them one inside the other: who could tell it was there? I never thought of unfolding them.'

And yet he had read three times over: *Es ergehet deshalb an alle hohen Mächte und an alle und jede, welchen Standes und welcher Würde sie auch sein mögen.* . . .

'I reached Königsberg[2] tired out by the journey, by anxiety, by many things. After a good sleep in an abyss of feathers, I went out next day to look at the town. It was a warm winter's day: the hotel-keeper suggested that we should take a sledge. There were bells on the horses and ostrich feathers on their heads . . . and we were gay; a load was lifted from our hearts: the unpleasant sensation of fear, the gnawing feeling of suspicion, had flown away. Caricatures of Nicholas were exhibited in the window of a bookshop, and I rushed in at once to buy a whole stock of them. In the evening I went to a small, dirty, inferior theatre, but came back from it excited, not by the actors but by the audience, which consisted mostly of workmen and young people; in the intervals everyone talked freely and loudly, and all put on their hats (an extremely important thing, as important as the right to wear a beard, etc.). This ease and freedom, this element of greater serenity and liveliness impresses the Russian when he arrives abroad. The Petersburg government is still so coarse and unpolished, so absolutely nothing but despotism, that it positively likes to inspire fear; it wants everything to tremble before it—in short, it desires not only power but the theatrical display of it. To the Petersburg Tsars the ideal of public order is the ante-room and the barracks.'

. . . When we set off for Berlin I got into the carriage, and a gentleman muffled up in wraps took the seat beside me; it was evening and I could not examine him as we drove. Learning that I was a Russian he began to question me about the strictness of the police and about passports; and of course I told him all I knew. Then we passed on to Prussia; he spoke highly of the disinterestedness of the Prussian officials, the excellence of the administration, praised the King, and concluded with a violent attack on the Poles of Posen on the ground that they were not good Germans. This surprised me; I objected, and told him bluntly that I did not share his views at all, and then said no more.

Meanwhile it had got light; I noticed only then that my conversative neighbour spoke through his nose, not because he had a cold in it, but because he had not one, or at least had not the most conspicuous part. He probably noticed that this discovery did not afford me any particular satisfaction, and so thought it necessary to tell me, by way of apology, the story of how he had lost his nose and how it had been restored. The first

---

[2] From *Letters from France and Italy*, Letter I. (*A.S.*)

part was somewhat confused, but the second was very circum-stantial: Diffenbach himself had carved him a new nose out of his hand; his hand had been bound to his face for six weeks; *Majestät* had come to the hospital to look at it, and was gra-ciously pleased to wonder and approve.

> *Le roi de Prusse, en le voyant,*
> *A dit: c'est vraiment étonnant.*

Apparently Diffenbach had been busy at the time with some-thing else and had carved him a very ugly nose; but I soon discovered that his hand-made nose was the least of his defects.

Travelling from Königsberg to Berlin was the most difficult part of our journey. The belief has somehow gained ground among us that the Prussian posting service is well organised: that is all nonsense. Travelling by post-chaise is good only in France, Switzerland, and England. In England the post-chaises are so well built, the horses so elegant, and the drivers so skilful that one may travel for pleasure. The carriage moves at full speed over the very longest stages, whether the road runs uphill or downhill. Now, thanks to the railway, this question is becoming one of historical interest, but in those days we learned by experi-ence what German posting-chaises and their screws could be. They were worse than anything in the world except the German coachmen.

The way from Königsberg to Berlin is very long; we took seven places in the *diligence* and set off. At the first station the guard told us to take our luggage and get into another *diligence*, sensibly warning us that he would not be responsible for the safety of our things. I observed that I had inquired at Königs-berg and was told that we should keep the same seats: the guard pleaded the snow, and said that we must get into a *diligence* provided with runners; there was nothing to be said against that. We began to transfer ourselves with our belongings and our children in the middle of the night in the wet snow. At the next station there was the same business again, and the guard did not even trouble himself to explain the change of carriages. We did half the journey in this way; then he informed us quite simply that we 'should be given only five seats.'

'Five? Here are my tickets.'

'There are no more seats.'

I began to argue; a window in the posting-station was thrown open with a bang and a grey-headed man with moustaches asked rudely what the wrangling was about. The guard said that I demanded seven seats, and that he had only five; I added that I had tickets and a receipt for the fares for seven seats. Paying no attention to me, the head said to the guard in a strangled, insolent, Russo-German military voice:

'Well, if this gentleman does not want the five seats, throw his things out, let him wait till there are seven seats free.'

Whereupon the worthy station-master, whom the guard addressed as *Herr Major*, and whose name was Schwerin, shut the window with a slam. After considering the matter, being Russians, we decided to go on. Benvenuto Cellini in like circumstances would, being an Italian, have fired his pistol and killed the station-master.

My neighbour who had been repaired by Diffenbach was in the restaurant at the time; when he had clambered on to his seat and we had set off, I told him the story. He was in a very genial mood, having had a drop too much; he showed the greatest sympathy with us and asked me to give him a note on the subject when we got to Berlin.

'Are you an official in the posting service?' I asked.

'No,' he answered, still more through his nose; 'but that doesn't matter . . . you . . . see . . . I am in what is called the central police service.'

I found this revelation even more unpleasant than the hand-made nose.

The first person to whom I expressed my liberal opinions in Europe was a spy—but he was not the last.

Berlin, Cologne, Belgium—all flashed past before our eyes; we looked at everything half absent-mindedly, in passing; we were in haste to arrive, and at last we did arrive.

. . . I opened the heavy, old-fashioned window in the Hôtel du Rhin; before me stood a column:

> . . . *with a cast-iron doll,*
> *With scowling face and hat on head,*
> *And arms crossed tightly on his breast.*[3]

And so I was really in Paris, not in a dream but in reality: this was the Vendôme column and the Rue de la Paix.

In Paris—the word meant scarcely less to me than the word 'Moscow'! Of that minute I had been dreaming since my childhood. If I might only see the Hôtel de Ville, the Café Foy in the Palais Royal, where Camille Desmoulins picked a green leaf, stuck it on his hat for a cockade and shouted '*à la Bastille!*'

I could not stay indoors; I dressed and went out to stroll about

---

[3] From A. S. Pushkin's *Yevgeny Onegin*, VII, 19. (*A.S.*)

at random . . . to look up Bakunin, Sazonov: here was Rue St-Honoré, the Champs-Élysées—all those names to which I had felt akin for long years . . . and here was Bakunin himself. . . .

I met him at a street corner; he was walking with three friends and, just as in Moscow, discoursing to them, continually stopping and waving his cigarette. On this occasion the discourse remained unfinished; I interrupted it and took him with me to find Sazonov and surprise him with my arrival.

I was beside myself with happiness!

And on that happiness I shall stop.

I am not going to describe Paris once more. My first acquaintance with European life, the triumphant tour of an Italy that had just leapt up from sleep, the revolution at the foot of Vesuvius, the revolution before St Peter's, and finally the news—like a flash of lightning—of the 24th of February—all that I have described in my *Letters from France and Italy*. I could not now with the same vividness reproduce impressions half effaced and overlaid by others. They make an essential part of my *Notes* —for what are letters but notes of a brief period?

The Honeymoon of the Republic

'TOMORROW WE ARE GOING to Paris; I am leaving Rome full of animation and excitement. What will come of it all? Can it last? The sky is not free from clouds; at times there is a chilly blast from the sepulchral vaults bringing the smell of a corpse, the odour of the past; the historical *tramontana* is strong, but whatever happens I am grateful to Rome for the five months I have spent there. The feelings I have passed through remain in the soul, and the reaction will not extinguish quite everything.'

This is what I wrote at the end of April 1848, sitting at a window in the Via del Corso and looking out into the *People's* Square, in which I had seen and felt so much.

I left Italy in love with her and sorry for her: there I had met not only great events but also the first people I had found *sympathiques*—but still I went away. It would have seemed like a betrayal of all my convictions not to be in Paris when there

was a republic there. Doubts are apparent in the lines I have
quoted, but faith got the upper hand, and with inward pleasure I
looked at the consul's seal on my visa at Cività on which were
engraved the formidable words, 'République Française'—I did
not reflect that the very fact that a visa was needed showed that
France was not a republic.

We went by a mail steamer. There were a great many passengers on board, and as usual they were of all sorts: there were
passengers from Alexandria, Smyrna, and Malta. One of the
fearful winds common in spring blew up just after we passed
Leghorn: it drove the ship along with incredible swiftness and
with insufferable rolling; within two or three hours the deck
was covered with sea-sick ladies; by degrees the men too succumbed, except a grey-headed old Frenchman, an Englishman
from Canada in a fur-jacket and a fur-cap, and myself. The
cabins, too, were full of sufferers, and the stuffiness and heat in
them alone were enough to make one ill. At night we three sat
on deck amidships on our portmanteaus, covered with our overcoats and railway rugs, amid the howling of the wind and the
splashing of the waves, which at times broke over the fore-deck.
I knew the Englishman; the year before I had travelled in the
same steamer with him from Genoa to Cività Vecchia. It happened we were the only two at dinner; he did not say a word all
through the meal, but over the dessert, softened by the Marsala
and seeing that I on my side had no intention of entering upon a
conversation, he gave me a cigar and said that he had brought
his cigars himself from Havana. Then we talked: he had been in
South America and California, and told me that he had often
intended to visit Petersburg and Moscow, but should not go until
there were *regular* and direct communications between London
and Petersburg.[1]

'Are you going to Rome?' I asked, as we approached Cività.

'I don't know,' he answered.

I said no more, supposing that he considered my question
indiscreet, but he immediately added:

'That depends on whether I like the climate in Cività.'

'Then you are stopping here?'

'Yes; the steamer leaves to-morrow.'

At that time I knew very few Englishmen, and so I could
hardly conceal my laughter, and was quite unable to do so when
I met him next day, as I was strolling in front of the hotel, in

---

[1] There is this now.

the same fur-coat, carrying a portfolio, a field-glass, and a little dressing-case, followed by a servant laden with his portmanteau and various belongings.

'I am off to Naples,' he said as he came up to me.

'Why, don't you like the climate?'

'It's horrid.'

I forgot to mention that on our first journey together he occupied the berth which was directly over mine. On three occasions during the night he almost killed me, first with fright, and then with his feet; it was deadly hot in the cabin and he went several times to have a drink of brandy and water and each time, climbing down or climbing up, he trod on me and shouted loudly in alarm: 'Oh—beg pardon—*J'ai avais soif.*'

'*Pas de mal!*'

So on this journey we met like old friends; he highly praised my immunity from sea-sickness, and offered me his Havana cigars. As was perfectly natural the conversation soon turned on the revolution of February. The Englishman, of course, looked upon revolution in Europe as an interesting spectacle, as a source of curious, new observations and experiences, and he described the revolution in the Republic of New Colombia.[2]

The Frenchman took a different part in these matters . . . within five minutes an argument had sprung up between him and me: he answered evasively, intelligently and with the utmost courtesy, conceding nothing, however. I defended the republic and revolution. Without directly attacking it, the old gentleman championed the traditional forms of government as the only ones durable, popular and capable of satisfying the just claims of progress and the necessity for settled security.

'You cannot imagine,' I said to him jokingly, 'what a peculiar satisfaction you give me by what you leave out. I have been for fifteen years speaking about the monarchy just as you speak about the republic. Our rôles are changed; in defending the republic, I am the conservative, while you, defending the legitimist monarchy, are a *perturbateur de l'ordre politique.*'

The old gentleman and the Englishman burst out laughing. The Comte d'Argout,[3] a tall, gaunt gentleman, whose nose has

---

[2] That is the rising of Colombia against Spanish domination in 1810. (*A.S.*)

[3] Antoine Maurice, Comte d'Argout (1782–1858), had much to do in bringing about the fall of Charles X, and held several important ministerial appointments under Louis-Philippe. (*Tr.*)

been immortalised by *Charivari*[4] and Philipon came up to us. (*Charivari* used to declare that his daughter did not marry because she did not want to sign herself 'So-and-so, *née d'Argout.'*) He joined in the conversation, addressed the old gentleman with deference, but looked at me with a surprise not far removed from repulsion; I noticed this, and began to be at least four times *redder* in my remarks.

'It is a very remarkable thing,' the grey-headed old Frenchman said to me: 'you are not the first Russian I have met of the same way of thinking. You Russians are either the most absolute slaves of your Tsar, or—*passez-moi le mot*—anarchists. And it follows from that, that it will be a long time before you are free.'[5]

Our political conversation continued in that strain.

When we were approaching Marseilles and all the passengers were busy looking after their luggage, I went up to the old gentleman and, giving him my card, said that I was glad to think that our discussion on the rolling boat had left no unpleasant results. The old gentleman said good-bye to me very nicely, delivered himself of another epigram at the expense of the republicans whom I should see at last at closer quarters, and gave me his card. It was the Duc de Noailles, a kinsman of the Bourbons and one of the leading counsellors of Henri V.[6]

Though this incident is quite unimportant, I have told it for the benefit and education of our 'dukes' of the first three ranks. If some senator or privy councillor had been in Noailles's place he would simply have taken what I said for insolent breach of discipline and would have sent for the captain of the ship.

In the year 1850 a certain Russian minister[7] sat with his family in his carriage on the steamer to avoid all contact with passengers who were common mortals. Can one imagine anything more ridiculous than sitting in an unharnessed carriage

---

[4] *Le Charivari* was the French *Punch* (earlier in date, however, *Punch* being called 'The London Charivari' as a sub-title), founded in 1831 by Charles Philipon (1802–62), a caricaturist of great talent. (*Tr.*)

[5] I have heard this criticism a dozen times since.

[6] The Comte de Chambord, grandson of Charles X, was by the royalists called Henri V. (*Tr.*) In part of an early edition of *Letters from France and Italy* H. speaks of a 'courteous old gentleman,' who is called the Duc de Rohan. There was a D. de R. who participated (as H. writes there) in Napoleon's Russian campaign. It has been impossible to establish whether there was such a Duc de Noailles as he describes here. (*A.S.*)

[7] The celebrated Victor Panin.

. . . and on the sea, too, and for a man double the ordinary size into the bargain!

The arrogance of our great dignitaries is not due to aristocratic feeling—the grand gentleman is dying out; it is the feeling of liveried and powerful flunkeys in great houses, extremely abject in one direction and extremely insolent in the other. The aristocrat is a personality, while our faithful servants of the throne are entirely without personality; they are like Paul's medals, which bear the inscription:[8] 'Not unto us, not unto us, but unto thy name.' Their whole training leads up to this: the soldier imagines that the *only* reason why he must not be beaten with rods is that he wears the Anna ribbon; the station superintendent considers his position as an officer the barrier that protects his cheek from the traveller's hand; an insulted clerk points to his Stanislav or Vladimir ribbon—'not by us, not by us . . . but by our rank!'

On leaving the steamer at Marseilles, I met a great procession of the National Guard, which was carrying to the Hôtel de Ville the figure of Liberty, *i.e.* of a woman with huge curls and a Phrygian cap. With shouts of *'Vive la République!'* thousands of armed citizens were marching in it, among them workmen in blouses who had joined the National Guard after 24th of February. I need hardly say that I followed them. When the procession reached the Hôtel de Ville, the general, the mayor, and the *commissaire* of the Provisional Government, Démosthène Ollivier, came out into the portico. Démosthène, as might be expected from his name, prepared to make a speech. A big circle of people formed about him: the crowd, of course, moved forward, the National Guards pressed it back, the crowd would not yield; this offended the armed workmen: they lowered their rifles, turned round and began to squash with the butts the toes of the people who stood in front; the citizens of the 'one and indivisible Republic' stepped back. . . .

This proceeding surprised me the more because I was still completely under the influence of the manners of Italy, and especially of Rome, where the proud sense of personal dignity and the inviolability of the person is fully developed in every man—not merely in the *facchino* and the postman, but even in the beggar who holds out his hand for alms. In the Romagna such insolence would have been greeted with twenty *coltellate*.[9]

---

[8] This is the inscription not on 'Paul's medals' but on those issued by Alexander I as memorials of the Patriotic War of 1812. (*A.S.*)

[9] *I.e.*, stabs with a dagger. (*Tr.*)

The French drew back—perhaps they had corns?

This incident affected me unpleasantly. Moreover, when I reached the hotel I read in the newspapers what had happened at Rouen.[10] What could be the meaning of it? Surely the Duc de Noailles was not right?

But when a man wants to believe, his belief is not easily uprooted, and before I reached Avignon I had forgotten the rifle-butts at Marseilles and the bayonets at Rouen.

In the *diligence* with us there was a full-bodied, middle-aged abbé of stately deportment and pleasant appearance. For the sake of propriety he at first took to his breviary, but to avoid dropping asleep put it back soon afterwards in his pocket and began talking pleasantly and intelligently. With the classical correctness of the language of Port-Royal and the Sorbonne, and with many quotations and chaste witticisms.

Indeed, it is only the French who know how to talk. The Germans can make declarations of love, confide their secrets, preach sermons or swear. In England routs are so much liked just because they make conversation impossible . . . there is a crowd, no room to move, everyone is pushing and being pushed, no one knows anybody; while if people come together in a small party they immediately have wretchedly poor music, singing out of tune, or boring little games, or with extraordinary heaviness the hosts and guests try to keep the ball of conversation rolling, with sighs and pauses, reminding one of the luckless horses on the tow-path who almost at their last gasp drag a loaded barge against the current.

I wanted to tease the abbé about the republic, but I did not succeed. He was very glad that liberty had come without *excesses*, above all without bloodshed and fighting, and looked upon Lamartine as a great man, something in the style of Pericles.

'And of Sappho,' I added, without, however, entering upon an argument. I was grateful to him for not saying a word about religion. So talking we arrived at Avignon at eleven o'clock at night.

'Allow me,' I said to the abbé as I filled his glass at supper, 'to

---

[10] At the Rouen elections for the Constituent Assembly in April the Socialist candidates were heavily defeated; the workmen, suspecting some fraud, assembled, unarmed, before the Hôtel de Ville, to protest. They were attacked by soldiers and National Guards; eleven were killed and many wounded. (*Tr.*)

propose a rather unusual toast: "To the Republic, *et pour les hommes d'église qui sont républicains*." The abbé got up, and concluded some Ciceronian sentences with the words: "*À la République future en Russie*."

'*À la République universelle!*' shouted the guard of the *diligence* and three men who were sitting at the table. We clinked glasses.

A Catholic priest, two or three shopmen, the guard and some Russians—we might well drink to the universal republic!

But it really was very jolly.

'Where are you bound for?' I inquired of the abbé, as we took our seats in the *diligence* once more, and I asked his pastoral blessing on my smoking a cigar.

'For Paris,' he answered; 'I have been elected to the National Assembly. I shall be delighted to see you if you will call; this is my address.' He was the Abbé Sibour, *doyen* of something or other and brother of the Archbishop of Paris.

A fortnight later there came the fifteenth of May, that sinister *ritournelle* which was followed by the fearful days of June. That all belongs not to my biography but to the biography of mankind. . . .

I have written a great deal about those days.

I might end here like the old captain in the old song:—

> *Te souviens-tu?* . . . *mais ici je m'arrête,*
> *Ici finit tout noble souvenir.*

But with these accursed days the last part of my life begins.

Western European Arabesques, I

1. THE DREAM

Do YOU REMEMBER, friends, how lovely was that winter day, bright and sunny, when six or seven sledges accompanied us to Chërnaya Gryaz, when for the last time we clinked glasses and parted, sobbing?

. . . Evening was coming on, the sledge crunched over the

snow; you looked sadly after us and did not divine that it was a
funeral and a parting for ever. All were there but one, the
dearest of all; he alone was far away, and by his absence seemed
to wash his hands of my departure.[1]

That was the 19th January, 1847.

Seven years have passed since then, and what years! Among
them were 1848 and 1852.

All sorts of things happened in those years, and everything
was shattered—public and private: the European revolution and
my home, the freedom of the world and my personal happiness.

Of the old life not one stone was left upon another. *Then* my
powers had reached their fullest development; the previous years
had given me pledges for the future. I left you boldly, with
headlong self-reliance, with haughty confidence in life. I was in
haste to tear myself away from the little group of people who
were so thoroughly accustomed to each other and had come so
close, bound by a deep love and a common grief. I was beckoned
to by distance, space, open conflict, and free speech. I was seeking
an independent arena, I longed to try my powers in freedom. . . .

Now I no longer expect anything: after what I have seen and
experienced nothing will move me to any particular wonder or
to deep joy; joy and wonder are curbed by memories of the past
and fear of the future. Almost everything has become a matter of
indifference to me, and I desire as little to die to-morrow as to
live long; let the end come as casually and senselessly as the
beginning.

And yet I have found all that I sought, even recognition from
this old, complacent world—and along with this I experienced
the loss of all my beliefs, all that was precious to me meeting
with betrayal, treacherous blows from behind, and in general a
moral corruption of which you have no conception.

It is hard for me, very hard, to begin this part of my story; I
have avoided it while I wrote the preceding parts, but at last I
am face to face with it. But away with weakness: he who could
live through it must have the strength to remember.

From the middle of the year 1848 I have nothing to tell of but
agonising experiences, unavenged offences, undeserved blows.
My memory holds nothing but melancholy images, my own mistakes and other people's: mistakes of individuals, mistakes of

---

[1] *I.e.*, N. P. Ogarëv, then living on his Penza estate, Staroye Aksheno.
(*A.S.*)

whole peoples. Where there was a possibility of salvation, death crossed the path. . . .

. . . The last days of our life in Rome conclude the bright part of my memories, that begin with the awakening of thought in childhood and our youthful vow on the Sparrow Hills.

Alarmed by the Paris of 1847, I had opened my eyes to the truth for a moment, but was carried away again by the events that seethed about me. All Italy was 'awakening' before my eyes! I saw the King of Naples tamed and the Pope humbly asking the alms of the people's love—the whirlwind which set everything in movement carried me, too, off my feet; all Europe took up its bed and walked—in a fit of somnambulism which we took for awakening. When I came to myself, it had all vanished; *la Sonnambula*, frightened by the police, had fallen from the roof; friends were scattered or were furiously slaughtering one another. . . . And I found myself alone, utterly alone, among graves and cradles—their guardian, defender, avenger, and I could do nothing because I tried to do more than was usual.

And now I sit in London where chance has flung me—and I stay here because I do not know what to make of myself. An alien race swarms confusedly about me, wrapped in the heavy breath of ocean; a world dissolving into chaos, lost in a fog in which outlines are blurred, in which a lamp gives only murky glimmers of light.

. . . And that other land—washed by the dark-blue sea under the canopy of a dark-blue sky . . . it is the one shining region left until the far side of the grave.

O Rome, how I love to return to your deceptions, how eagerly I run over day by day the time when I was intoxicated with you!

. . . A dark night. The Corso is filled with people, and here and there are torches. It is a month since a republic was proclaimed in Paris. News has come from Milan—there they are fighting, the people demand war,[2] there is a rumour that Charles Albert is on the way with troops. The talk of the angry crowd is like the intermittent roar of a wave, which alternately comes noisily up the beach and then pauses to draw breath.

The crowds form into ranks. They go to the Piedmontese ambassador to find out whether war has been declared.

'Fall in, fall in with us,' shout dozens of voices.

---

[2] This refers to the successful rising in Milan on 18th March, 1848 against the Austrian dominion in Lombardy. Charles Albert, King of Piedmont, also declared war on Austria. (*A.S.*)

'We are foreigners.'

'All the better; *Santo Dio*, you are our guests.'

We joined the ranks.

'The front place for the guests, the front place for the ladies, *le donne forestiere!*'

And with passionate shouts of approval the crowd parted to make way. Ciceruacchio and with him a young Russian poet, a poet of popular songs, pushed their way forward with a flag, the tribune shook hands with the ladies and with them stood at the head of ten or twelve thousand people—and all moved forward in that majestic and harmonious order which is peculiar to the Roman people.

The leaders went into the Palazzo, and a few minutes later the drawing-room doors opened on the balcony. The ambassador came out to appease the people and to confirm the news of war; his words were received with frantic joy. Ciceruacchio was on the balcony in the glaring light of torches and candelabra, and beside him under the Italian flag stood four young women, all four Russians—was it not strange? I can see them now on that stone platform, and below them the swaying, innumerable multitude, mingling with shouts for war and curses for the Jesuits, loud cries of '*Evviva le donne forestiere!*'

In England they and we should have been greeted with hisses, abuse, and perhaps stones. In France we should have been taken for venal agents. But here the aristocratic proletariat, the descendants of Marius and the ancient tribunes, gave us a warm and genuine welcome. We were received by them into the European struggle . . . and with Italy alone the bond of love, or at least of warm memory, is still unbroken.

And was all that . . . intoxication, delirium? Perhaps—but I do not envy those who were not carried away by that exquisite dream. The sleep could not last long in any case: the inexorable Macbeth of real life had already raised his hand to murder sleep and . . .

My dream was past—it has no further change.

2. THE REALITY

ON THE EVENING of the 24th of June [1848] coming back from the Place Maubert, I went into a café on the Quai d'Orsay. A few minutes later I heard discordant shouting, which came nearer and nearer. I went to the window: a grotesque comic *banlieue* was coming in from the surrounding districts to the support of order; clumsy, rascally fellows, half peasants, half shopkeepers, somewhat drunk, in wretched uniforms and old-fashioned shakos, they moved rapidly but in disorder, with shouts of 'Vive Louis-Napoléon!'

That ominous shout I now heard for the first time. I could not restrain myself, and when they reached the café I shouted at the top of my voice: 'Vive la République!' Those who were near the windows shook their fists at me and an officer muttered some abuse, threatening me with his sword; and for a long time afterwards I could hear their shouts of greeting to the man who had come to destroy half the revolution, to kill half the republic, to inflict himself upon France, as a punishment for forgetting in her arrogance both other nations and her own proletariat.

At eight o'clock in the morning of the 25th or 26th of June Annenkov and I went out to the Champs-Elysées. The cannonade we had heard in the night was now silent; only from time to time there was the crackle of rifle-fire and the beating of drums. The streets were empty, but the National Guards stood on either side of them. On the Place de la Concorde there was a detachment of the *Garde mobile;* near them were standing several poor women with brooms and some ragpickers and *concierges* from the houses near by. All their faces were gloomy and shocked. A lad of seventeen was leaning on a rifle and telling them something; we went up to them. He and all his comrades, boys like himself, were half drunk, their faces blackened with gunpowder and their eyes bloodshot from sleepless nights and drink; many were dozing with their chins resting on the muzzles of their rifles.

'And what happened then can't be described.' He paused, and then went on: 'Yes, and they fought well, too, but we paid them out for our comrades! A lot of them really caught it! I stuck my bayonet right up to the hilt in five or six of them; they'll remember us,' he added, trying to assume the air of a hardened malefactor. The women were pale and silent; a man who looked like a *concierge* observed: 'Serve them right, the blackguards!' . . . but this savage comment evoked not the slightest response. They were all of too ignorant a class to sympathise with the massacre and with the unfortunate boy who had been made into a murderer.

Silent and sad, we went to the Madeleine. Here we were stopped by a cordon of the National Guard. At first, after searching our pockets, they asked where we were going, and let us through; but the next cordon, beyond the Madeleine, refused to let us through and sent us back; when we went back to the first cordon we were stopped once more.

'But you saw us pass here just now!'

'Don't let them pass,' shouted an officer.

'Are you making fools of us, or what?' I asked.

'It's no use talking,' a shopman in uniform answered rudely. 'Take them up—and to the police: I know one of them' (he pointed at me); 'I have seen him more than once at meetings. The other must be the same sort too; they are neither of them Frenchmen. I'll answer for everything—march.'

We were taken away by two soldiers with rifles in front, two behind, and one on each side. The first man we met was a *représentant du peuple* with a silly badge in his button-hole; it was Tocqueville, who had written about America. I addressed myself to him and told him what had happened: it was not a joking matter; they kept people in prison without any sort of trial, threw them into the cellars of the Tuileries, and shot them. Tocqueville did not even ask who we were; he very politely bowed himself off, delivering himself of the following banality: 'The legislative authority has no right to interfere with the executive.' How could he have helped being a minister under Napoleon III!

The 'executive authority' led us along the boulevard to the Chaussée d'Antin to the *commissaire de police.* By the way, it will do no harm to mention that neither when we were arrested, nor when we were searched, nor when we were on our way, did I see a single policeman; all was done by the *bourgeois*-warriors. The boulevard was completely empty, all the shops were closed and the inmates rushed to their doors and windows when they heard our footsteps, and kept asking who we were: '*Des émeutiers étrangers,*' answered our escort, and the worthy *bourgeois* looked at us and gnashed their teeth.

From the police station we were sent to the Hôtel des Capucines; the Ministry of Foreign Affairs had its quarters there, but at that time there was some temporary police committee there. We went with our escort into a large study. A bald old gentleman in spectacles, dressed entirely in black, was sitting alone at a table; he asked us over again all the questions that the *commissaire* had asked us.

'Where are your passports?'

'We never carry them with us when we are out for a walk.'

He took up a manuscript book, looked through it for a long time, apparently found nothing, and asked one of our escort:

'Why did you arrest them?'

'The officer gave the order; he says they are very suspicious characters.'

'Very well,' said the old gentleman; 'I will inquire into the case; you may go.'

When the escort had gone the old gentleman asked us to explain the cause of our arrest. I put the facts before him, adding that the officer might perhaps have seen me on the fifteenth of May at the Assembly; and then I told him of an incident of the previous day. I had been sitting in the Café Caumartin when suddenly there was a false alarm, a squadron of dragoons rode by at full gallop and the National Guard began to form ranks. Together with some five people who were in the café, I went up to a window; a National Guardsman standing below shouted rudely,

'Didn't you hear that windows were to be shut?'

His tone justified me in supposing that he was not addressing me, and I did not take the slightest notice of his words; besides, I was not alone, though I happened to be standing in front. Then the defender of order raised his rifle and, since this was taking place on the *rez-de-chaussée*, tried to thrust at me with his bayonet, but I saw his movement and stepped back and said to the others:

'Gentlemen, you are witnesses that I have done nothing to him—or is it the habit of the National Guard to bayonet foreigners?'

'*Mais c'est indigne, mais cela n'a pas de nom!*' my neighbours chimed in.

The frightened café-keeper rushed to shut the windows; a vile-looking sergeant appeared with an order to turn everyone out of the café—I fancied he was the same gentleman who had ordered us to be stopped. Moreover, the Café Caumartin was a couple of steps from the Madeleine.

'So that's how it is, gentlemen: you see what imprudence leads to. Why walk out at such a time?—minds are exasperated, blood is flowing. . . .'

At that moment a National Guardsman brought in a maid-servant, saying that an officer had caught her in the very act of trying to post a letter addressed to Berlin. The old gentleman took the envelope and told the soldier to go.

'You can go home,' he said to us; 'only, please do not go by the same streets as before, and especially not by the cordon which arrested you. But stay, I'll send someone to escort you! he'll take you to the Champs-Élysées—you can get through that way.'

'And you,' he said, addressing the servant, giving her back the letter which he had not touched, 'post it in another letter-box, further away.'

And so the police gave protection from the armed *bourgeois!*

On the night of the 26th–27th of June, so Pierre Leroux relates, he went to Sénart to beg him to do something for the prisoners who were being suffocated in the cellars of the Tuileries. Sénart, a man well known as a desperate conservative, said to Pierre Leroux:

'And who will answer for their lives on the way? The National Guard will kill them. If you had come an hour earlier you would have found two colonels here: I had the greatest difficulty in bringing them to reason, and ended by telling them if these horrors went on I should give up the president's chair in the Assembly and take my place behind the barricades.'

Two hours later, on our returning home, the *concierge* made his appearance accompanied by a stranger in a dress-coat and four men in workmen's blouses which badly disguised the moustaches of *municipales* and the deportment of gendarmes. The stranger unbuttoned his coat and waistcoat and, pointing with dignity to a tricoloured scarf, said that he was Barlet, the *commissaire* of police (the man who on the 2nd of December, in the National Assembly, took by the collar the man who in his time had taken Rome—General Oudinot), and that he had orders to search my quarters. I gave him my key, and he set to work exactly as *politsmeyster* Miller had in 1834.

My wife came in: the *commissaire,* like the officer of gendarmes who once came to us from Dubelt, began apologising. My wife looked at him calmly and directly and, when at the end of his speech he begged her indulgence, said:

'It would be cruelty on my part not to imagine myself in your place; you are sufficiently punished already by being obliged to do what you are doing.'

The *commissaire* blushed, but did not say a word. Rummaging among the papers and laying aside a whole heap of them, he suddenly went up to the fireplace, sniffed, touched the ashes and, turning to me with an important air, asked:

'What was your object in burning papers?'

'I haven't been burning papers.'

'Upon my word, the ash is still warm.'

'No, it is not warm.'

'*Monsieur, vous parlez à un magistrat!*'

'The ash is cold, all the same, though,' I said, flaring up and raising my voice.

'Why, am I lying?'

'What right have you to doubt my word? . . . here are some *honest workmen* with you, let them test it. Besides, even if I had burnt papers: in the first place, I have a right to burn them; and in the second, what are you going to do?'

'Have you no other papers?'

'No.'

'I have a few letters besides, and very interesting ones; come into my room,' said my wife.

'Oh, your letters . . .'

'Please don't stand on ceremony . . . why, you are only doing your duty; come along.'

The *commissaire* went in, glanced very slightly at the letters, which were for the most part from Italy, and was about to go. . . .

'But you haven't seen what is underneath here—a letter from the Conciergerie, from a prisoner, you see; don't you want to take it with you?'

'Really, Madame,' answered the policeman of the republic, 'you are so prejudiced; I don't want that letter at all.'

'What do you intend to do with the Russian papers?' I asked.

'They will be translated.'

'The point is, where you will take your translator from. If he is from the Russian Embassy, it will be as good as laying information; you will destroy five or six people. You will greatly oblige me if you will mention at the *procès-verbal* that I beg most urgently that a Polish *émigré* shall be chosen as a translator.'

'I believe that can be done.'

'I thank you; and I have another request: do you know Italian at all?'

'A little.'

'I will show you two letters; in them the word France is not mentioned. The man who wrote them is in the hands of the Sardinian police; you will see by the contents that it will go badly with him if they get hold of the letters.'

'*Mais, ah ça!*' observed the *commissaire*, his dignity as a man beginning to be aroused; 'you seem to imagine that we are connected with the police of all the *despotic* powers. We have nothing to do with other countries. We are unwillingly compelled to take measures at home when blood is flowing in the streets and when foreigners interfere in our affairs.'

'Very well: then you can leave the letters here.'

The *commissaire* had not lied; he really did know *a little*

Italian, and so, after turning the letters over, he put them in his pocket, promising to return them.

With that his visit ended. The letters from the Italian he gave back next day, but my papers vanished completely. A month passed; I wrote a letter to Cavaignac,[3] inquiring why the police did not return my papers nor say what they had found in them—a matter of very little consequence to them, perhaps, but of the greatest importance for my honour.

What gave rise to this last phrase was as follows. Several persons of my acquaintance had intervened on my behalf, considering the visit of the *commissaire* and the retention of my papers outrageous.

'We wanted to make certain,' Lamoricière[4] told them, 'whether he was not *an agent of the Russian government.*'

This was the first time I heard of this abominable suspicion; it was something quite new for me. My life had been as open, as public, as though it had been lived in a glass hive, and now all at once this filthy accusation, and from whom?—from a republican government!

A week later I was summoned to the prefecture. Barlet was with me. We were received in Ducoux's room by a young official very like some free and easy Petersburg head-clerk.

'General Cavaignac,' he told me, 'has charged the Prefect to return your papers without any examination. The information collected concerning you renders it quite superfluous; no suspicion rests upon you; here is your portfolio. Will you be good enough to sign this paper first?'

It was a receipt stating that *all* the papers had been returned to me complete.

I stopped and asked whether it would not be more in order for me to look the papers through.

'They have not been touched. Besides, here is the seal.'

'The seal has not been broken,' observed Barlet soothingly.

'My seal is not here. Indeed, it was not put on them.'

'It is my seal, but you know you had the key.'

Not wishing to reply with rudeness, I smiled. This enraged

---

[3] Cavaignac, Louis-Eugène (1802–57), the youngest of the three distinguished Frenchmen of that name, was Commander-in-Chief in 1848, and an unsuccessful candidate for the presidency of the republic when Louis-Napoleon (afterwards Napoleon III) was elected on 10th December, 1848. (*Tr.*)

[4] Lamoricière, Louis de (1806–65), a prominent politician and general, was exiled in December 1848, and afterwards took command of the Papal troops. (*Tr.*)

them both: the head-clerk became the head of a department; he
snatched up a penknife and, cutting the seal, said rudely
enough: 'Pray look, if you don't believe, but I have not so much
time to waste,' and walked out with a dignified bow. Their resentment convinced me that they really had not looked at the
papers, and so, after a cursory glance at them, I signed the receipt
and went home.

The Revolution
of 1848 in France

I LEFT PARIS in the autumn of 1847, without having formed any
ties there; I remained completely outside the literary and political circles. There were many reasons for that. No immediate
occasion of contact with them presented itself, and I did not care
to seek one. To visit them simply in order to look at celebrities, I
thought unseemly. Moreover, I particularly disliked the tone of
condescending superiority which Frenchmen assume with Russians: they approve of us, encourage us, commend our pronunciation and our wealth; we put up with it all, and behave as though
we were asking them a favour, or were even partly guilty,
delighted when, from politeness, they take us for Frenchmen.
The French overwhelm us with a flood of words, we cannot keep
pace with them; we think of an answer, but they do not care to
hear it; we are ashamed to show that we notice their blunders
and their ignorance—they take advantage of all that with hopeless complacency.

To get on to a different footing with them one would have to
impress them with one's consequence; to do this one must possess
various rights, which I had not at that time, and of which I took
advantage at once when they came to be at my disposal.

Moreover, it must be remembered that there are no people in
the world with whom it is easier to strike up a nodding acquaintance than the French—and no people with whom it is more
difficult to get on to really intimate terms. A Frenchman likes to
live in company, in order to display himself, to have an audience, and in that respect he is as much a contrast to the
Englishman as in everything else. An Englishman looks at

people because he is bored; he looks at men as though from a stall in a theatre; he makes use of people as an entertainment, or as a means of obtaining information. The Englishman is always asking questions, the Frenchman is always giving answers. The Englishman is always wondering, always thinking things over; the Frenchman knows everything for certain, he is finished and complete, he will go no further: he is fond of preaching, talking, holding forth—about what, to whom, he does not care. He feels no need for personal intimacy; the café satisfies him completely. Like Repetilov in *Woe from Wit*, he does not notice that Chatsky is gone and Skalozub is in his place, that Skalozub is gone and Zagoretsky is in his place—and goes on holding forth about the jury-room, about Byron (whom he calls 'Biron'), and other important matters.

Coming back from Italy not yet cooled from the February Revolution, I stumbled on the 15th of May, and then lived through the agony of the June days and the state of siege. It was then that I obtained a deeper insight into the *tigre-singe* of Voltaire—and I lost even the desire to become acquainted with the mighty ones of this republic.

On one occasion a possibility almost arose of common work which would have brought me into contact with many persons, but that did not come off either. Count Ksawery Branicki gave seventy thousand francs to found a magazine to deal principally with foreign politics and other nations, and especially with the Polish question. The usefulness and appropriateness of such a magazine were obvious. French papers deal little and badly with what is happening outside France; during the republic, they thought it sufficient to encourage all the heathen nations now and then with the phrase *solidarité des peuples,* and the promise that as soon as they had time to turn round at home they would build a world-wide republic based upon universal brotherhood. With the means at the disposal of the new magazine, which was to be called *La Tribune des Peuples,* it might have been made the international *Moniteur* of movement and progress. Its success was the more certain because there is no international periodical at all; there are sometimes excellent articles in *The Times* and the *Journal des Débats* on special subjects, but they are occasional and disconnected. The *Augsburg Gazette* would really be the most international organ if its *black-and-yellow* proclivities were not so glaringly conspicuous.

But it seems that all the good projects of the year 1848 were doomed to be born in their seventh month and to die before

cutting their first tooth. The magazine turned out poor and
feeble—and died at the slaughter of the innocent papers after
the 14th of June, 1849.

When everything was ready and standing by, a house was
taken and fitted up with big tables covered with cloth and little
sloping desks; a lean French *littérateur* was engaged to watch
over international mistakes in spelling; a committee to edit it
was set up of former Polish nuncios and senators, and Mickiewicz was appointed head to this with Chojecki as his assistant;—
all that was left to arrange was a triumphal opening ceremony,
and what date could be more suitable for that than the anniversary of February the 24th, and what form could it more decently
take than a supper?

The supper was to take place at Chojecki's. When I arrived I
found a good many guests already there, and among them
scarcely a single Frenchman; to make up for this other nationalities, from the Sicilians to the Croats, were well represented. I
was really interested in one person only—Adam Mickiewicz; I
had never seen him before. He was standing by the fireplace
with his elbow on the marble mantelpiece. Anyone who had seen
his portrait in the French edition of his works, taken, I believe,
from the medallion executed by David d'Angers, could have
recognised him at once in spite of the great change wrought by
the years. Many thoughts and sufferings had passed over his
face, which was rather Lithuanian than Polish. The whole
impression made by his figure, by his head, his luxuriant grey
hair and weary eyes, was suggestive of unhappiness endured, of
acquaintance with spiritual pain, and of the exaltation of sorrow—he was the moulded likeness of the fate of Poland. The
same impression was made on me later by the face of Worcell,
though the features of the latter, while even more expressive of
suffering, were more animated and gracious than those of
Mickiewicz. It seemed as though Mickiewicz were held back,
preoccupied, distracted by something: that 'something' was the
strange mysticism into which he retreated further and further.

I went up to him and he began questioning me about Russia:
his information was fragmentary; he knew little of the literary
movement after Pushkin, having stopped short at the time when
he left Russia.[1] In spite of his basic idea of a fraternal league of
all the Slavonic peoples—a conception he was one of the first to

---

[1] A. Mickiewicz had been in Russia in 1824 and 1825 to participate in
the work of the secret patriotic society of the Philarets. He met and made
friends with Pushkin, Ryleyev, Baryatynsky, Vyazemsky, Zhukovsky,
Krylov, Griboedov and others. (*A.S.*)

develop—he retained some hostility to Russia. And indeed it could hardly be otherwise after all the atrocities perpetrated by the Tsar and his satraps; besides, we were speaking at a time when the terrorism of Nicholas was at its very worst.

The first thing that surprised me disagreeably was the attitude to him of the Poles, his followers: they approached him as monks approach an abbot, with self-abasement and reverent awe; some of them kissed him on the shoulder. He must have been accustomed to these expressions of submissive affection, for he accepted them with great *laisser aller*. To be recognised by people of the same way of thinking, to have influence on them, to see their affection, is desired by everyone who is devoted, body and soul, to his convictions and lives by them; but external signs of sympathy and respect I should not like to accept—they destroy equality and consequently freedom. Moreover, in that respect we can never catch up with bishops, heads of departments, and colonels of regiments.

Chojecki told me that at the supper he was going to propose a toast 'to the memory of the 24th of February, 1848,' that Mickiewicz would respond with a speech in which he would expound his views and the spirit of the new magazine; he wished me as a Russian to reply to Mickiewicz. Not being accustomed to public speaking, especially without preparation, I declined his invitation, but promised to propose the health of Mickiewicz and to add a few words describing how I had first drunk his health in Moscow at a public dinner given to Granovsky in the year 1844. Khomyakov had raised his glass with the words, 'To the great Slavonic poet who is absent!' The name (which we dared not pronounce) was not needed; everyone raised his glass and, standing in silence, drank to the health of the exile. Chojecki was satisfied. Having thus arranged our *extempore* speeches, we sat down to the table. At the end of the supper, Chojecki proposed his toast. Mickiewicz got up and began speaking. His speech was elaborate and clever, and extremely adroit—that is to say Barbès[2] and Louis-Napoleon could both have applauded it sincerely; it made me wince. As he developed his thought I began to feel painfully distressed and, that not the slightest doubt might be left, waited for one word, one name: it was not slow to appear![3]

Mickiewicz worked up to the theme that democracy was now

[2] Barbès, Armand (1809–70), called the 'Bayard de la démocratie,' was a people's representative in 1848, imprisoned in 1849, and set free in 1854. (*Tr.*)

[3] *I.e.*, Louis-Napoleon. (*A.S.*)

preparing to enter a new, open camp, at the head of which stood France; that it would once more rush to the liberation of all oppressed peoples under the same eagles, under the same standards, at the sight of which all tsars and powers had turned pale; and that it would once more be led forward by a member of that dynasty which had been crowned by the people, and, as it seemed, ordained by Providence itself to guide revolution by the well-ordered path of authority and victory.[4]

When he had finished a general silence followed, except for two or three exclamations of approval from his adherents. Chojecki was very well aware of Mickiewicz's blunder and, wishing to efface the effect of the speech as quickly as possible, came up with a bottle, filled my glass and whispered to me:

'Well?'

'I am not going to say a word after that speech.'

'Please do say something.'

'Nothing will induce me.'

The silence continued; some people kept their eyes fixed on their plates, others scrutinised their glasses, others fell into private conversation with their neighbours. Mickiewicz changed colour; he wanted to say something more, but a loud '*Je demande la parole*' put an end to the painful situation. Everyone turned to the man who had risen to his feet. A rather short man of about seventy, grey-haired, with a fine vigorous exterior, stood with a glass in his trembling hand; anger and indignation were apparent in his large, black eyes and excited face. It was Ramón de la Sagra.[5]

'To the 24th of February,' he said: 'that was the toast proposed by our host. Yes, to the 24th of February, and to the downfall of every despotism whatever its name is, king or emperor, Bourbon or Bonaparte. I cannot share the views of our friend Mickiewicz

---

[4] In 1848 Adam Mickiewicz had shown himself to be a revolutionary and a democrat; but, like many other workers in the Polish national-liberation movement, he was imbued with Napoleonic illusions, which came out particularly clearly after 10 December 1849, when Napoleon I's nephew, Louis Bonaparte, was elected President of France. M. saw in him the continuation of the work of Napoleon I, which had been the work of the revolution. Although M. had become disappointed in Louis-Napoleon even in 1849, he could not even so fully overcome his illusions about Napoleon I. (*A.S.*)

[5] Ramón de la Sagra (1798–1871), a Spanish economist, took part in the revolutionary movement of 1848 in France, and wrote advocating the views of Proudhon. In 1854 he returned to Spain, and was several times elected a member of the Cortes. He was, of course, not seventy in 1848, as Herzen mistakenly assumes, but fifty. (*Tr.*)

—he can look at things like a poet, and from his own point of view he is right; but I don't want his words to pass without protest in such a gathering'; and so he went on and on, with all the fire of a Spaniard and the authority of an old man.

When he had finished, twenty glasses, mine among them, were held out to clink with his.

Mickiewicz tried to retrieve his position, and said a few words of explanation, but they were unsuccessful. De la Sagra did not give way. Everyone got up from the table and Mickiewicz went away.

There could scarcely have been a worse omen for the new journal; it succeeded in existing after a fashion till the 13th of June, and its disappearance was as little noticed as its existence. There could be no unity in the editing of it. Mickiewicz had rolled up half his imperial banner *usé par la gloire.* The others did not dare to unfurl theirs; hampered both by him and by the committee many of the contributors abandoned the journal at the end of the month; I never sent them a single line. If the police of Napoleon had been more intelligent the *Tribune des Peuples* would never have been prohibited for a few lines on the 13th of June. With Mickiewicz's name and devotion to Napoleon, with its revolutionary mysticism and its dream of a democracy in arms, with the Bonapartes at its head, the journal might have become a veritable treasure for the President, the clean organ of an unclean cause.

Catholicism, so alien to the Slavonic genius, has a destructive effect upon it. When the Bohemians no longer had the strength to resist Catholicism, they were crushed; in the Poles Catholicism has developed that mystical exaltation which supports them perpetually in their world of phantoms. If they are not under the direct influence of the Jesuits, then instead of liberty they either invent some idol for themselves, or come under the influence of some visionary. Messianism, that mania of Wronski's, that delirium of Towjanski's, had turned the brains of hundreds of Poles, Mickiewicz himself[6] among them. The worship of Napoleon

---

[6] Chagrin at the defeat of 1830–1 and the loss of hope in the liberation of Poland bred a mood of mysticism among the Polish emigrants and contributed to the rise of ideas of Messianism. Polish Messianism was the teaching of the peculiar rôle of 'martyred Poland' in the history of peoples, according to which the Polish-people-Messiah was redeeming and liberating all the other peoples by its sufferings and its struggle. The representative of this doctrine was Joseph Wronski, a mathematician and philosopher, the author of *Messianism.* From his idealistic system, which he called 'Messianistic,' Wronski with the aid of the 'universal

stands in the foreground of this insanity. Napoleon had done nothing for them; he had no love for Poland, but he liked the Poles who shed their blood for him with the titanic, poetic courage displayed in their famous cavalry attack of Sommo Sierra. In 1812 Napoleon said to Narbonne: 'I want a camp in Poland, not a forum. I will not permit either Warsaw or Moscow to open a club for demagogues'—and of this man the Poles made a military incarnation of God, setting him on a level with Vishnu and Christ.

Late one winter evening in 1848 I was walking with one of the Polish followers of Mickiewicz along the Place Vendôme. When we reached the column the Pole took off his cap. 'Is it possible? . . .' I thought, hardly daring to believe in such stupidity, and meekly asked what was his reason for taking off his cap. The Pole pointed to the bronze emperor. How can we expect men to refrain from domineering or oppressing others when it wins so much devotion!

Mickiewicz's private life was dark; there was something unfortunate about it, something gloomy, some 'visitation of God.' His wife was for a long time out of her mind. Towjanski recited incantations over her, and is said to have done her good; this made a great impression on Mickiewicz, but traces of her illness remained . . . things went badly with them. The last years of the great poet, who outlived himself, were spent in gloom. He died in Turkey while taking part in an absurd attempt to organise a Cossack legion, which the Turkish government would not permit to be called Polish. Before his death he wrote a Latin ode to the honour and glory of Louis-Napoleon.

After this unsuccessful attempt to take part in the magazine I withdrew even more into a small circle of friends, enlarged by the arrival of new *émigrés*. Formerly I had sometimes visited a

---

mathematical formula' originated by himself deduced the idea of the unity of the Slavonic peoples. The Messianic-mystic mood overcame Mickiewicz, too, and induced his spiritual crisis in the 1830s and the early 1840s, when he joined the mystic sect of the adventurer Andrei Towjanski who came to Paris from Lithuania in 1840 and gave out that he was a prophet. In one of his letters written in 1841 Chopin, speaking of Towjanski as a clever rogue who could dull people's wits, grieves that M. has not seen through Towjanski. M.'s religious and mystic tendencies left their stamp on his work in the 1830s and 1840s and affected his life and activity for the worse. Yet even in the years of his spiritual crisis his revolutionary inclination had the upper hand and grew steadily stronger. He found inspiration in the revolution of 1848 and was brought ideologically closer to it and to Polish revolutionary democracy. (*A.S.*)

club, and I had participated in three or four banquets, that is I
had eaten cold mutton and drunk sour wine, while I listened to
Pierre Leroux or Father Cabet and joined in the '*Marseillaise.*'
Now I was sick of that, too. With profound sorrow I watched and
recorded the success of the forces of dissolution and the decline of
the republic, of France, of Europe. From Russia came no gleam
of light in the distance, no good news, no friendly greeting:
people had given up writing to me; personal, intimate, family
relations were suspended. Russia lay speechless, as though dead,
covered with bruises, like an unfortunate peasant-woman at the
feet of her master, beaten by his heavy fists. She was then entering upon those fearful five years from which she is at last emerg-
ing now that Nicholas[7] is buried.

Those five years were for me, too, the worst time of my life; I
have not now such riches to lose or such beliefs to be destroyed. . . .

. . . The cholera raged in Paris; the heavy air, the sunless
heat produced a languor; the sight of the frightened, unhappy
population and the rows of hearses which started racing each
other as they drew near the cemeteries—all this corresponded
with what was happening.

The victims of the pestilence fell near by, at one's side. My
mother drove to St Cloud with a friend, a lady of five-and-
twenty. When they were coming back in the evening, the lady
felt rather unwell; my mother persuaded her to stay the night
with us. At seven o'clock the next morning they came to tell me
that she had cholera. I went in to see her, and was aghast. Not
one feature was unchanged; she was still handsome; but all
the muscles of her face were drawn and contracted and dark
shadows lay under her eyes. With great difficulty I succeeded in
finding Rayer[8] at the Institute, and brought him home with me.
After glancing at the sick woman, Rayer whispered to me:

'You can see for yourself what is to be done here.' He prescribed something and went away.

The sick woman called me and asked:

'What did the doctor say? He did tell you something, didn't
he?'

'To send for your medicine.'

She took my hand, and her hand amazed me even more than
her face: it had grown thin and angular as though she had been

---

[7] Written in 1856.
[8] Rayer, P. F. O., was a distinguished French physician and the author
of numerous medical works. (*Tr.*)

through a month of serious illness since she had fallen sick: she fixed upon me a look that was full of suffering and horror and said:

'Tell me, for God's sake, what he said . . . is it that I am dying? . . . You are not afraid of me, are you?' she added.

I felt fearfully sorry for her at that moment; that frightful consciousness not only of death, but of the infectiousness of the disease that was rapidly sapping her life, must have been intensely painful. Towards the morning she died.

Ivan Turgenev was about to leave Paris; the lease of his flat was up, and he came to me for a night. After dinner he complained of the suffocating heat; I told him that I had had a bath in the morning; in the evening he too went for a bath. When he came back he felt unwell, drank some soda-water with some wine and sugar in it, and went to bed. In the night he woke me.

'I am a lost man,' he said; 'it's cholera.'

He really was suffering from sickness and spasms; fortunately he escaped with ten days' illness.

After burying her friend my mother had moved to the Ville d'Avray. When Turgenev was taken ill I sent Natalie and the children there and remained alone with him; when he was a great deal better I moved there too.

On the morning of June the 12th Sazonov came to see me there. He was in the greatest exaltation: he talked of the popular outbreak that was impending, of the certainty of its being successful, of the glory awaiting those who took part in it, and urgently pressed me to join in reaping the laurels. I told him that he knew my opinion of the present state of affairs—that it seemed to me stupid, without believing in it, to co-operate with people with whom one had hardly anything in common.

To this the enthusiastic agitator remarked that of course it was quieter and safer to stay at home and write sceptical articles while others were in the market-place championing the liberty of the world, the solidarity of peoples, and much else that was good.

A very vile emotion, but one that has led and will lead many men into great errors, and even crimes, impelled me to say:

'But what makes you imagine I am not going?'

'I concluded that from your words.'

'No: I said it was stupid, but I didn't say that I never do anything stupid.'

'That is just what I wanted! That's what I like you for! Well, it's no use losing time; let us go to Paris. This evening the Germans and other refugees are meeting at nine o'clock; let us go to them first.'

'Where are they meeting?' I asked him in the train.

'In the Café Lamblin, in the Palais Royal.'

This was my first surprise.

'In the Café Lamblin?'

'That is where the "reds" usually meet.'

'That's just why I think that to-day they ought to have met somewhere else.'

'But they are all used to going there.'

'I suppose the beer is very good!'

In the café various *habitués* of the revolution were sitting with dignity at a dozen little tables, looking darkly and consequentially about them from under wide-brimmed felt hats and caps with tiny peaks. These were the perpetual suitors of the revolutionary Penelope, those inescapable actors who take part in every popular demonstration and form its *tableau*, its background, and who are as menacing from afar as the paper dragons with which the Chinese wished to intimidate the English.

In the troubled times of social storms and reconstructions in which states forsake their usual grooves for a long time, a new generation of people grows up who may be called the choristers of the revolution; grown on shifting, volcanic soil, nurtured in an atmosphere of alarm when work of every kind is suspended, they become inured from their earliest years to an environment of political ferment—they like the theatrical side of it, its brilliant, pompous *mis en scène*. Just as to Nicholas marching drill was the most important part of the soldier's business, to them all those banquets, demonstrations, protests, gatherings, toasts, banners, are the most important part of the revolution.

Among them there are good, valiant people, sincerely devoted and ready to face a bullet; but for the most part they are very limited and extraordinarily pedantic. Immobile conservatives in everything revolutionary, they stop short at some programme and do not advance.

Dealing all their lives with a small number of political ideas, they only know their rhetorical side, so to speak, their sacerdotal vestments, that is the commonplaces which successively cut the same figure, *à tour de rôle*, like the ducks in the well known children's toy—in newspaper articles, in speeches at banquets and in parliamentary devices.

In addition to naïve people and revolutionary doctrinaires, the unappreciated artists, unsuccessful literary men, students who did not complete their studies, briefless lawyers, actors without talent, persons of great vanity but small capability, with huge pretensions but no perseverance or power of work, all naturally drift into this *milieu*. The external authority which guides and pastures the human herd in a lump in ordinary times is weakened in times of revolution; left to themselves people do not know what to do. The younger generation is struck by the ease, the apparent ease, with which celebrities float to the top in times of revolution, and rushes into futile agitation; this inures the young people to violent excitements and destroys the habit of work. Life in the clubs and cafés is attractive, full of movement, flattering to vanity and free from restraint. One must not be left behind, there is no need to work: what is not done to-day may be done to-morrow, or may even not be done at all.

The choristers of the revolution, like the chorus in Greek tragedies, are further divided into two semi-choruses; the botanical classification may be applied to them: some of them may be called *cryptogamous* and the others *phanerogamous*. Some of them become eternal conspirators, and several times change their lodgings and the shape of their beards. They mysteriously invite one to extraordinarily important interviews, at night if possible, or in some inconvenient place. Meeting their friends in public, they do not like saluting them with a bow, but greet them with a significant glance. Many of them keep their address a secret, never tell one what day they are going away, never say where they are going, write in cypher or invisible ink news which is plainly printed in printer's ink in the newspapers.

I was told by a Frenchman that in the days of Louis-Philippe, E., who had been mixed up in some political business, was in hiding in Paris. With all its attractions such a life becomes *à la longue* wearisome and tedious. Delessert, a *bon vivant* and a rich man, was Police Prefect at that time; he served in the police not from necessity but for the love of it, and sometimes like a festive dinner. He and E. had many friends in common. One day 'between the pear and the cheese,' as the French say, one of them said to him:

'What a pity it is that you so persecute poor E.! We are deprived of a capital talker, and he is obliged to hide like a criminal.'

'Upon my soul,' said Delessert, 'his case is completely forgotten! Why is he in hiding?'

His friend smiled ironically.

'I shall try to convince him that he's behaving absurdly—and you, too.'

On reaching home he sent for one of his chief spies and asked him,

'Is E. in Paris?'

'Yes,' answered the spy.

'Is he in hiding?' asked Delessert.

'Yes,' answered the spy.

'Where?' asked Delessert.

The spy took out his notebook, looked in it, and read out E.'s address.

'Good; then go to him early to-morrow morning and tell him that he need not be anxious; we are not looking for him and he can live peacefully at his flat.'

The spy carried out his orders exactly, and two hours after his visit E. mysteriously informed his friends that he was leaving Paris and would be in hiding in a remote town, because the Prefect had discovered where he had been hiding!

Just as conspirators try to conceal their secret with a transparent veil of mystery and an eloquent silence, so do the phanerogamous try to display and blurt out all that is in their hearts.

They are the permanent tribunes of the clubs and cafés; they are perpetually dissatisfied with everything, and fuss about everything; they tell about everything—even things that have not happened, while things that have happened they square and cube, like mountains on a relief map. One's eye is so used to seeing them that one involuntarily looks for them at every street row, at every demonstration, at every banquet.

. . . The spectacle of the Café Lamblin was still new to me; at that time I was not familiar with the back premises of the revolution. It is true that I had been about in Rome and in the Cafe delle Belle Arti and in the square; I had been in the Circolo Romano and in the Circolo Popolare; but the movement in Rome had not then that character of political garishness which particularly developed after the failures of 1848. Ciceruacchio and his friends had a naïveté of their own, their southern gesticulations which strike one as commonplace and their Italian phrases which seem to us to be rant; but they were in a period of youthful enthusiasm, they had not yet come to themselves after three centuries of sleep. *Il popolano* Ciceruacchio was not in the least a political agitator by trade; he would have liked nothing better than to retire once more in peace to his little house in

Strada Ripetta and to carry on his trade in wood and timber within his family-circle like a *paterfamilias* and free *civis romanus*.

The men surrounding him were free from that brand of vulgar, babbling pseudo-revolutionism, of that *taré* character which is so dismally common in France.

I need hardly say that in speaking of the café agitators and revolutionary *lazzaroni* I was not thinking of those mighty workers for the emancipation of humanity, those martyrs for the love of their fellow-creatures and fiery evangelists of independence whose words could not be suppressed by prison, exile, proscription or poverty—of the drivers, the motive powers of events, by whose blood, tears and words a new historical order is established. I was talking about the incrusted border covered with barren weeds, for which agitation itself is goal and reward, who like the process of national revolution for its own sake, as Chichikov's Petrushka[9] liked the process of reading, or as Nicholas liked military drill.

There is nothing for reaction to rejoice at in this, for it is overgrown with worse burdocks and toadstools, not only on the borders but everywhere. In its ranks are whole multitudes of officials who tremble before their superiors, prying spies, volunteer assassins ready to fight on either side, officers of every repulsive species from the Prussian *junker* to the predatory French Algerian, from the guardsman to the *page de chambre*—and here we still have touched only on the secular side of the reaction, and have said nothing of the mendicant fraternity, the intriguing Jesuits, the priestly police, or the other members of the ranks of angels and archangels.

If there are among reactionaries any who resemble our dilettante revolutionaries, they are the courtiers employed for ceremonies, the men of exits and entrances, the people who are conspicuous at *levées*, christenings, royal weddings, coronations, and funerals, the people who exist for the uniform, for gold lace, who represent the rays and fragrance of power.

In the Café Lamblin, where the desperate *citoyens* were sitting over their *petits verres* and big glasses, I learned that they had no plan, that the movement had no real centre of momentum and no programme. Inspiration was to descend upon them as the Holy Ghost once descended upon the heads of the apostles. There was only one point on which all were agreed—*to come to the meeting-place unarmed*. After two hours of empty

---

[9] A character in Gogol's *Dead Souls*. (*Tr.*)

chatter we went off to the office of the *True Republic*, agreeing
to meet at eight o'clock next morning at the Boulevard Bonne
Nouvelle, facing the Château d'Eau.

The editor was not at home: he had gone to the 'Montagnards'[10] for instructions. About twenty people, for the most
part Poles and Germans, were in the big, grimy, poorly lit and
still more poorly furnished room which served the editorial
board as an assembly hall and a committee room. Sazonov took a
sheet of paper and began writing something; when he had
written it he read it out to us: it was a protest in the name of the
émigrés of all nationalities against the occupation of Rome, and
a declaration of their readiness to take part in the movement.
Those who wished to immortalise their names by associating
them with the glorious morrow he invited to sign it. Almost all
wished to immortalise their names, and signed. The editor came
in, tired and dejected, trying to suggest to everyone that he knew
a great deal but was bound to keep silent; I was convinced that
he knew nothing at all.

'*Citoyens,*' said Thorez, '*la Montagne est en permanence.*'

Well, who could doubt its success—*en permanence!* Sazonov
gave the editor the protest of the democracy of Europe. The
editor read it through and said:

'That's splendid, splendid! France thanks you, *citoyens;* but
why the signatures? There are so few that if we are unsuccessful
our enemies will vent all their anger upon you.'

Sazonov insisted that the signatures should remain; many
agreed with him.

'I won't take the responsibility for it,' the editor objected;
'excuse me, I know better than you the people we have to deal
with.'

With that he tore off the signatures and delivered the names
of a dozen candidates for immortality to a holocaust in the
candle, and the text he sent to the printer.

It was daybreak when we left the office; groups of ragged boys
and wretched, poorly dressed women were standing, sitting, and
lying on the pavement near the various newspaper offices, waiting for the piles of newspapers—some to fold them, and others to
run with them all over Paris. We walked out on to the boulevard: there was absolute stillness; now and then one came upon

---

[10] The Jacobins were called *Montagnards* in 1793 because they occupied
the highest seats in the Parliament. In 1848–9 the name was given to
the supporters of Ledru-Rollin in the Constituent Assembly. (*A.S.*)

a patrol of National Guards, and police-sergeants strolled about looking slyly at us.

'How free from care the city sleeps,' said my comrade, 'with no foreboding of the storm that will wake it up to-morrow!'

'Here are those who keep vigil for us all,' I said to him, pointing upwards—that is, to a lighted window of the *Maison d'Or.*

'And very appropriately, too. Let us go in and have some absinthe; my stomach is a bit upset.'

'And I feel empty; it wouldn't be amiss to have some supper too. How they eat in the Capitole I don't know, but in the Conciergerie the food is abominable.'

From the bones left after our meal of cold turkey no one could have guessed either that cholera was raging in Paris, or that in two hours' time we were going to change the destinies of Europe. We ate at the *Maison d'Or* as Napoleon slept before Austerlitz.

Between eight and nine o'clock, when we reached the Boulevard Bonne Nouvelle, numerous groups of people were already standing there, evidently impatient to know what they were to do; their faces showed perplexity, but at the same time something in the peculiar look of the groups manifested great exasperation. Had those people found real leaders the day would not have ended in a farce.

There was a minute when it seemed to me that something was really going to happen. A gentleman rode on horseback rather slowly down the boulevard. He was recognised as one of the ministers (Lacroix), who probably was having a ride so early not for the sake of fresh air alone. He was surrounded by a shouting crowd, who pulled him off his horse, tore his coat and then let him go—that is, another group rescued him and escorted him away. The crowd grew; by ten o'clock there may have been twenty-five thousand people. No one we spoke to, no one we questioned, knew anything. Chersosi, a *carbonaro* of old days assured us that the *banlieue* was coming to the Arc de Triomphe with a shout of '*Vive la République!*'

'Above all,' the elders of the democracy repeated again, 'be unarmed, or you will spoil the character of the affair—the sovereign people must show the National Assembly its will peacefully and solemnly in order to give the enemy no occasion for calumny.'

At last columns were formed; we foreigners made up an honorary phalanx immediately behind the leaders, among whom were E. Arago in the uniform of a colonel, Bastide, a former minister, and other celebrities of 1848. We moved down the boulevard, voicing various cries and singing the Marseillaise. One who has not heard the Marseillaise, sung by thousands of voices in that state of nervous excitement and irresolution which is inevitable before certain conflict, can hardly realise the overwhelming effect of the revolutionary hymn.

At that minute there was really something grand about the demonstration. As we slowly moved down the boulevards all the windows were thrown open; ladies and children crowded at them and came out on to the balconies; the gloomy, alarmed faces of their husbands, the fathers and proprietors, looked out from behind them, not observing that in the fourth storeys and attics other heads, those of poor seamstresses and working girls, were thrust out—they waved handkerchiefs, nodded and greeted us. From time to time, as we passed by the houses of well known people, various shouts were uttered.

In this way we reached the point where the Rue de la Paix joins the boulevards; it was closed by a squad of the Vincennes Chasseurs, and when our column came up to it the chasseurs suddenly moved apart like the scenery in a theatre, and Changarnier,[11] mounted upon a small horse, galloped up at the head of a squadron of dragoons. With no summons to the crowd to disperse, with no beat of drum or other formalities prescribed by law, he threw the foremost ranks into confusion, cut them off from the others and, deploying the dragoons in two directions ordered them to clear the street in quick time. The dragoons in a frenzy fell to riding down people, striking them with the flat of their swords and using the edge at the slightest resistance. I hardly had time to take in what was happening when I found myself nose to nose with a horse which was almost snorting in my face, and a dragoon swearing likewise in my face and threatening to give me one with the flat if I did not move aside. I retreated to the right, and in an instant was carried away by the crowd and squeezed against the railings of the Rue Basse des Remparts. Of our rank the only one left beside me was Müller-Strübing. Meanwhile the dragoons were pressing back the foremost ranks with their horses, and people who had no room to get away were thrust back upon us. Arago leaped down into the Rue Basse des Remparts, slipped and dislocated his leg; Strübing and I jumped down after him. We looked at each other in a frenzy of indignation; Strübing turned round and shouted loudly: '*Aux*

---

[11] Changarnier, Nicolas (1793–1877), a prominent politician and general, was exiled at the *coup d'état* of 1851, but lived to serve in the Franco-Prussian War of 1870. (*Tr.*)

armes! Aux armes!' A man in a workman's blouse caught him by the collar, shoved him out of the way and said:

'Have you gone mad? Look there!'

Thickly bristling bayonets were moving down the street—the Chaussée d'Antin it must have been.

'Get away before they hear you and cut off all escape. All is lost, all!' he added, clenching his fist; he hummed a tune as though there was nothing the matter, and walked rapidly away. We made our way to the Place de la Concorde. In the Champs-Elysées there was not a single squad from the *banlieue;* why, Chersosi must have known that there was not. It had been a diplomatic lie to save the situation, and it would perhaps have been the destruction of anyone who had believed it.

The shamelessness of attacking unarmed people aroused great resentment. If anything really had been prepared, had there been leaders, nothing would have been easier than for fighting to have begun in earnest. Instead of showing itself in its full strength the *Montagne,* on hearing how ludicrously the sovereign people had been dispersed by horses, hid itself behind a cloud. Ledru-Rollin carried on negotiations with Guinard.[12] Guinard, the artillery commander of the National Guard, wanted to join the movement, wanted to give men, agreed to give cannon, but would not on any consideration give ammunition—he seems to have wished to act by the moral influence of the guns; Forestier[13] was doing the same with his legion. Whether this helped them much we saw by the Versailles trial.[14] Everyone wanted to do something, but no one dared; the most foresight was shown by some young men who hoped for a new order—they bespoke themselves prefects' uniforms, which they declined to take after the failure of the movement, and the tailor was obliged to hang them up for sale.

When the hurriedly rigged-up government was installed at the *Arts et Métiers* the workmen, after walking about the streets with inquiring faces and finding neither advice nor leadership,

---

[12] Guinard, Auguste-Joseph (born 1799), had been one of the first to proclaim the republic in February 1848, and at the head of the 8th Legion had occupied the Hôtel de Ville. (*Tr.*)

[13] Forestier, Henri-Joseph (born 1787), was a painter of merit. He was colonel of the 8th Legion of the National Guard. (*Tr.*)

[14] After the crushing of the demonstration of 13 June 1849, in Paris, and of a series of manifestations in the provinces, the government of Odilon Barrot deprived thirty-three *Montagnards* of their status as deputies, declared them to be enemies of the state and delivered them over for trial. Those who had emigrated were tried *in absentia.* (*A.S.*)

went home, convinced once more of the bankruptcy of the *Montagnard* fathers of the country: perhaps they gulped down their tears like the man who said to us, 'All is lost!'—or perhaps laughed in their sleeves at the way the *Montagne* had been tousled.

But the dilatoriness of Ledru-Rollin, the pedantry of Guinard —these were the external causes of the failure, and were just as *à propos* as are decisive characters and fortunate circumstances when they are needed. The internal cause was the poverty of the republican idea in which the movement originated. Ideas that have outlived their day may hobble about the world for years— may even, like Christ, appear after death once or twice to their devotees; but it is hard for them ever again to lead and dominate life. Such ideas never gain complete possession of a man, or gain possession only of incomplete people. If the *Montagne* had been victorious on the 13th of June, what would it have done? There was nothing new they could call their own. It would have been a photograph in black and white of the grim, glowing Rembrandt or Salvator Rosa picture of 1793 without the Jacobins, without the war, without even the naïve guillotine. . . .

After the 13th of June [1849] and the attempted rising at Lyons, arrests began. The mayor came to us with the police at Ville d'Avray to look for Karl Blind[15] and Arnold Ruge; some of our acquaintances were seized. The Conciergerie was full to overflowing. In one small room there were as many as sixty men; in the middle stood a large slop-bucket, which was emptied once in the twenty-four hours—and all this in civilised Paris, with the cholera raging. Having not the least desire to spend some two months among those comforts, fed on rotten beans and putrid meat, I got a passport from a Moldo-Wallachian and went to Geneva.[16]

◈   ◈   ◈

---

[15] Blind, Karl (1826–1907), a writer and revolutionary, was for the part he took in the insurrections in South Germany sentenced to eight years' imprisonment, but was rescued by the mob. He settled in England, where he continued journalistic and propaganda work up to the time of his death. (*Tr.*)

[16] How well founded my apprehensions were was shown by a police search of my mother's house at Ville d'Avray two days after my de- parture. They seized all the papers, even the correspondence of her maid with my cook. I thought it inopportune to publish my account of the 13th of June at the time.

In Geneva with
the Exiles of 1848

THERE WAS A TIME when in a fit of irritation and bitter mirth I
intended to write a pamphlet in the style of Grandville's[1] illus-
trations: *Les réfugiés peints par eux-mêmes.* I am glad I did not
do it. Now I look at things more calmly and I am less moved to
laughter and indignation. Besides, exile is both lasting too long
and is weighing too heavily on people. . . .

Nevertheless I do say even now that exile, not undertaken
with any definite object, but forced upon men by the triumph of
the opposing party, checks development and draws men away
from the activities of life into the domain of phantasy. Leaving
their native land with concealed anger, with the continual
thought of going back to it once more on the morrow, men do not
move forwards but are continually thrown back upon the past;
hope prevents them from settling down to any permanent work;
irritation and trivial but exasperated disputes prevent their
escaping from the familiar circle of questions, thoughts and
memories which make up an oppressive, binding tradition. Men
in general, and especially men in an exceptional position, have
such a passion for formalism, for the guild spirit, for looking
their part, that they immediately fall into a professional groove
and acquire a doctrinaire stamp.

All *émigrés*, cut off from the living environment to which
they have belonged, shut their eyes to avoid seeing bitter truths,
and grow more and more acclimatised to a closed, fantastic circle
consisting of inert memories and hopes that can never be
realised.

If we add to this an aloofness from all who are not exiles and

---

[1] Grandville, Jean Ignace Isidore (1803–47), was one of the most celebrated book-illustrators of his time. Perhaps his most famous book is
Les animaux peints par eux-mêmes. He was deeply interested in animals,
insects, and fishes, and drew them wonderfully. He edited *La Caricature,*
in which all the most eminent people of his time in Paris are depicted
He died insane. (*Tr.*)

an element of exasperation, suspicion, exclusiveness and jealousy, this new, stiff-necked Israel becomes perfectly comprehensible.

The exiles of 1849 did not yet believe in the permanence of
their enemies' triumph; the intoxication of their recent successes
had not yet passed off, the applause and songs of the exultant
people were still ringing in their ears. They firmly believed that
their defeat was a momentary reverse, and did not move their
clothes from their trunks to a wardrobe. Meanwhile Paris was
under police supervision, Rome had fallen under the onslaught
of the French,[2] the brother of the Prussian King was brutally
triumphing in Baden,[3] and Paskevich in the Russian style had
outwitted Görgei[4] in Hungary by bribes and promises. Geneva
was full to overflowing with refugees; it became the Coblenz[5] of
the revolution of 1848. There were Italians from all parts;
Frenchmen escaping from the Bauchart[6] inquiry and from the
Versailles trial; Baden militiamen, who entered Geneva marching in regular formation with their officers and with Gustav
Struve; men who had taken part in the rising of Vienna;
Bohemians and Poles from Posen and Galicia. All these people
were crowded together between the Hôtel des Bergues and the
Café de la Poste. The more sensible of them began to guess that
this exile would not be over soon, talked of America, and went
away. With the majority it was just the opposite, especially with
the French who, true to their temperament, were in daily expectation of the death of Napoleon and the birth of a republic—

---

[2] French troops under General Oudinot entered Rome on 3rd July, 1849.
(*A.S.*)

[3] In 1848 there was an insurrection in Baden, headed by Struve and
Hecker, which aimed at establishing a republic. The troops sided with
the insurgents, the Grand Duke fled, and in May 1848 a Constituent
Assembly was called. After several battles the Grand Duke was reinstated
by Prussian aid in July of the same year. (*Tr.*)

[4] Görgei, Arthur (1818–1916), Commander-in-Chief of the Hungarian
forces in 1848, was victorious over the Austrians in the spring of that
year, but was defeated early in August by the Russian general, Paskevich, and on the 13th of that month surrendered the Hungarian army
unconditionally to Rüdiger, another Russian general. He was accused of
treachery. (*Tr.*)

[5] Coblenz was one of the chief centres to which the *émigrés* of the great
French Revolution flocked from 1790 onwards. (*Tr.*)

[6] The Commission of Inquiry was presided over by Odilon Barrot; the
report, drawn up by one Bauchart, is described as a '*monument impéris-
sable de mauvaise foi et de basse fureur.*' (*Tr.*)

some looking for a republic both democratic and socialistic,
others for one that should be democratic and not at all socialistic.

A few days after my arrival, as I was walking in Les Paquis, I
met an elderly gentleman who looked like a Russian village
priest, wearing a low, broad-brimmed hat and a *black* white
overcoat, and walking along with a sort of priestly unction;
beside him walked a man of terrific dimensions, who looked as
though he had been casually put together of huge chunks of
human flesh. F. Kapp,[7] the young writer, was with me.

'Don't you know them?' he asked me.

'No; but, if I'm not mistaken, it must be Noah or Lot out for a
walk with Adam, who has put on a badly cut overcoat instead of
his fig-leaves.'

'They are Struve and Heinzen,' he answered, laughing;
'would you like to make their acquaintance?'

'Very much.'

He introduced me.

The conversation was trivial. Struve was on his way home,
and invited us to come in; so we went with him. His small
lodging was crowded with people from Baden. A tall woman,
very good-looking from a distance, with a mass of luxuriant hair
flowing loose in an original fashion, was sitting in the midst of
them; this was his wife, the celebrated Amalie Struve.

Struve's face made a strange impression on me from the very
first; it expressed that moral rigidity which fanaticism gives to
bigots and schismatics. Looking at his strong, narrow forehead,
at the untroubled expression of his eyes, at his uncombed beard,
his slightly grizzled hair, and his whole figure, I could have
fancied that this was either a fanatical pastor of the army of
Gustavus Adolphus who had forgotten to die, or a Taborite[8]
preaching repentance and communion in both kinds. There was
a surly coarseness about the appearance of Heinzen,[9] that

---

[7] Kapp, Friedrich (1820–84), a German historian, after the revolution of
1848 went to New York, but returned to Berlin in 1870, and became a
Liberal member of the Reichstag. (*Tr.*)

[8] The more thoroughgoing of the followers of John Huss were called
Taborites, from their headquarters at Mt. Tabor in Bohemia. (*Tr.*)

[9] Heinzen, Karl Peter (1827–80), wrote for the *Leipzige Allgemeine
Zeitung* and the *Rheinische Zeitung*, and his articles led to the suppression of these two papers. He published an attack on the government, '*Die
preussische Bureaukratie*,' for which he was prosecuted. In 1848 he was
one of the leaders of the Baden revolution. Later on he escaped to
America, where he edited *The Pioneer*. (*Tr.*)

Sobakevich[10] of the German revolution; full-blooded and clumsy, he looked out angrily from under his brows, and was sparing of words. He wrote later on that it would be sufficient to *massacre two millions* of the inhabitants of the globe and the cause of revolution would go swimmingly. Anybody who had once seen him would not be surprised at his writing this.

I cannot refrain from relating an extremely funny incident which happened to me in connection with this cannibalistic project. There was, and indeed still is, living in Geneva a Dr R., one of the most good-natured men in the world and one of the most constant and Platonic lovers of the revolution, the friend of all the refugees; he doctored them gratis as well as giving them food and drink. However early one might arrive at the Café de la Poste, the Doctor would already be there and already reading his third or fourth newspaper; he would beckon one mysteriously and murmur in one's ear:

'I fancy it will be a hot day in Paris to-day.'

'Why so?'

'I can't tell you from whom I heard it, but only that it was a man closely connected with Ledru-Rollin; he was here on his way through. . . .'

'Why, you were expecting something yesterday and the day before yesterday too, weren't you, my dear Doctor?'

'Well, what of that? *Stadt Rom war nicht in einem Tage gebaut.*'

So it was to him as a friend of Heinzen's that I appealed in the very same café when the latter published his philanthropic programme.

'Why,' I said to him, 'does your friend write such pernicious nonsense? The reaction is making an outcry, and indeed it has every reason to: he's a regular Marat in a German setting! And how can one ask for two million heads?'

R. was confused, but did not like to give up his friend.

'Listen,' he said at last; 'you have lost sight of one fact, perhaps: Heinzen is speaking of the whole human race; in that number there would be at least *two hundred thousand Chinese.*'

'Oh, well, that's a different matter; why spare them?' I answered and for a long time afterwards I could never think of this mitigating consideration without bursting into insane laughter.

Two days after our meeting in Les Paquis, the *garçon* of the Hôtel des Bergues, where I was staying, ran up to my room and announced with an air of importance:

---

[10] A character in *Dead Souls* by N. V. Gogol. (*A.S.*)

'General Struve and his adjutants.'

I imagined either that someone had sent the *garçon* up as a joke, or that he had made some blunder; but the door opened and—

> *Mit bedächtigem Schritt*
> *Gustav Struve tritt . . .*[11]

and with him four gentlemen: two were in the military uniform worn in those days by German *Freischärler*,[12] and had in addition red armlets adorned with various emblems. Struve presented his suite to me, democratically referring to them as 'brothers in exile.' I learnt with pleasure that one of them, a young man of twenty, who looked like a *Bursch* who had recently emerged from being a '*Fuchs*,'[13] was already successfully occupying the post of Minister of Home Affairs *per interim*.

Struve at once began instructing me in his theory of the seven scourges, *der sieben Geisseln*—Popes, priests, kings, soldiers, bankers, etc.—and of the establishment of some new democratic, revolutionary religion. I remarked that, if it depended upon us whether to found a new religion or not, it would be better not to found one, but to leave it to the will of God, since from the very nature of the affair it was more His concern. We argued, Struve made some remark about the *Weltseele*; I observed that, in spite of Schelling's having so clearly defined the world-soul by calling it *das Schwebende*, I found great difficulty in grasping it. He jumped up from his chair and, coming as close to me as possible, with the words, 'Excuse me, allow me,' began playing on my head with his fingers, pressing it with them, as though my skull had been composed of the keyboard of a concertina. 'Yes, indeed,' he commented, addressing his four brothers in exile, '*Bürger Herzen hat kein, aber auch gar kein Organ der Venerazion!*' All were satisfied with the lack of the 'bump of reverence' in me, and so was I.

Hereupon he informed me that he was a great phrenologist, and had not only written a book on Gall's[14] system but had even

---

[11] A paraphrase of two lines from Schiller's *The Glove:*
  Und hinein mit bedächtigem Schritt
  Ein Löwe tritt. . . . (A.S.)
[12] Volunteers. *(R.)*
[13] Undergraduates in their first year were called 'foxes' in German universities. *(Tr.)*
[14] Gall, Franz Joseph (1758–1828), an Austrian doctor, the discoverer of phrenology. *(A.S.)*

selected his Amalie from it, after first feeling her skull. He
assured me that the bump of the passions was almost completely
absent in her, and that the back part of the skull where they are
located was almost flat. On these grounds, sufficient for a divorce,
he married her.

Struve was a very queer fish: he ate nothing but Lenten food,
with the addition of milk, drank no wine, and kept his Amalie
on a similar diet. He thought that this was not enough, and he
went every day to bathe with her in the Arve, the water of
which scarcely reaches a temperature of eight degrees in the
middle of summer, since it flows down from the mountains so
swiftly that it has not time to get warm.

Later on, it often happened that we talked of vegetarianism. I
raised the usual objections: the structure of the teeth, the great
loss of energy in the assimilation of vegetable fibre, and the
lower development of the brain in herbivorous animals. He
listened blandly without losing his temper, but stuck to his opinion. In conclusion, apparently wishing to impress me, he said:

'Do you know that a man always nourished on vegetable food
so purifies his body as to be quite free from smell after death?'

'That's very pleasant,' I replied; 'but what advantage will that
be to me? I won't be sniffing myself after death.'

Struve did not even smile, but said to me with serene conviction:

'You will speak very differently one day!'

'When my bump of reverence develops,' I added.

At the end of 1849 Struve sent me the calendar he had newly
devised for 'free' Germany. The days, the months, everything
had been translated into an ancient German jargon difficult to
understand; instead of saints' days, every day was dedicated to
the memory of two celebrities—Washington and Lafayette, for
instance; but to make up for this every tenth day was devoted to
the memory of the enemies of mankind—Nicholas and Metternich, for instance. The holidays were the days when remem-
brance fell upon particularly great men, such as Luther,
Columbus and so on. In this calendar Struve had gallantly
replaced the twenty-fifth of December, the birth of Christ, by the
festival of Amalie!

Meeting me in the street one day, he said among other things
that there ought to be published in Geneva a journal common to
all the exiles, in three languages, which would carry on the
struggle against the 'seven scourges' and maintain the 'sacred

fire' of the peoples that were now crushed by reaction. I answered that of course it would be a good thing.

The publishing of papers was at that time an epidemic disease: every two or three weeks new schemes were started, specimen copies appeared, prospectuses were sent about, then two or three numbers would come out—and it would all disappear without a trace. People who were incapable of anything none the less considered themselves competent to edit a paper, scraped together a hundred francs or so, and spent them on the first and last issue. Struve's intention, therefore, did not surprise me at all; but I was surprised, very much so, by his calling upon me at seven o'clock the next morning. I thought some misfortune had happened, but Struve, after calmly sitting down, brought a sheet of paper out of his pocket and said, as he prepared to read it: *'Bürger,* since you and I agreed yesterday on the need to publish a magazine, I have come to read you the prospectus of it.'

When he had read it he informed me that he was going to Mazzini and many others to invite them to meet at Heinzen's for a conference. I went to Heinzen's too: he was sitting fiercely at the table, holding a manuscript in one huge paw; the other he held out to me, muttering thickly, *'Bürger, Platz!'*

Some eight people, French and German, were present. Some representative of the people in the French legislative Assembly was making an estimate of the costs, and writing something in slanting lines. When Mazzini came in Struve proposed reading the prospectus that had been written by Heinzen. Heinzen cleared his throat and began reading it in German, although the only language common to us all was French.

Since they had not the faintest shadow of a new idea, the prospectus was only the thousandth variation of those democratic lucubrations which constitute the same sort of rhetorical exercise on revolutionary texts as church sermons are on those of the Bible. Indirectly anticipating a charge of socialism, Heinzen said that the democratic republic would of itself solve the economic question to the general satisfaction. The man who did not flinch from a demand for two million heads was afraid that his organ would be considered communistic.

I urged some objection to this when the reading was finished, but from his abrupt replies, from Struve's intervention and from the gestures of the French deputy I perceived that we had been invited to the council to accept Heinzen's and Struve's prospectus, not at all to discuss it; it was in complete agreement, by the way, with the theory of Elpidifor Antiokhovich Zurov, the military governor of Novgorod.

Mazzini listened with a melancholy air, but agreed, and was almost the first to subscribe for two or three shares. '*Si omnes consentiunt ego non dissentio,*' I thought *à la* Grimm in Schiller's *Robbers*, and I too subscribed.

But the subscribers appeared to be too few; however often the French deputy calculated and verified, the sum subscribed was insufficient.

'Gentlemen,' said Mazzini, 'I have found a means of overcoming this difficulty: publish the journal at first only in French and German; as for the Italian translation, I shall print any *remarkable* articles in my *Italia del Popolo*—that will save you one-third of the expenses.'

'To be sure! what could be better!'

Mazzini's proposition was accepted by everybody and he grew more cheerful. I was awfully amused, and very eager to show him that I had seen the trick he had played. I went up to him and watched for a moment when no one was near us; then I said:

'How capitally you got out of the journal!'

'Well,' he observed, 'an Italian part is really superfluous, you know.'

'So are the two others!' I added.

A smile glided over his face and vanished as quickly as though it had never been there.

This was the second time that I saw him. Mazzini, who knew of my stay in Rome, had wanted to make my acquaintance. One morning I went with L. Spini[15] to see him at Les Paquis.

When we went in Mazzini was sitting dejectedly at the table listening to what was being said by a rather tall, graceful, handsome young man with fair hair. This was Garibaldi's bold companion-in-arms, the defender of Vascello, the leader of the Roman legionaries, Giacomo Medici. Another young man with an expression of melancholy preoccupation sat plunged in thought, paying no attention to what was going forward—this was Mazzini's colleague in the triumvirate, Marco Aurelio Saffi.[16]

[15] Spini, Leopold, an *émigré* who had taken part in the Italian movement for national liberation. (*A.S.*)

[16] Saffi was instructor in Italian language and literature at Oxford University from 1853–60. (*A.S.*)

Mazzini got up and, looking me straight in the face with his piercing eyes, held out both hands in a friendly way. Even in Italy a head so severely classical, so elegant in its gravity, is rarely to be met with. At moments the expression of his face was harshly austere, but it quickly grew soft and serene. An active, concentrated intelligence sparkled in his melancholy eyes; there was an infinity of persistence and strength of will in them and in the lines on his brow. All his features showed traces of long years of anxiety, of sleepless nights, of storms endured, of powerful passions, or rather of one powerful passion, and also some element of fanaticism—perhaps of asceticism.

Mazzini is very simple and amiable in his manner, but the habit of ruling is apparent, especially in argument; he can scarcely conceal his annoyance at contradiction, and sometimes he does not conceal it. He knows his strength, and genuinely despises all the external signs of a dictatorial setting. His popularity was at that time immense. In his little room, with the everlasting cigar in his mouth, Mazzini at Geneva, like the Pope in the old days at Avignon, held in his hands the threads that like a spiritual telegraph system brought him into living communication with the whole peninsula. He knew every heartthrob of his party, felt the slightest tremor in it, promptly responded to everyone, and, with an indefatigability that was striking, gave general guidance to everything and everybody.

A fanatic and at the same time an organiser, he covered Italy with a network of secret societies connected together and devoted to one object. These societies branched off into arteries that defied detection, split up, grew smaller and smaller, and vanished in the Apennines and the Alps, in the regal *palazzi* of aristocrats and the dark alleys of Italian towns into which no police can penetrate. Village priests, *diligence* guards, the *principi* of Lombardy, smugglers, innkeepers, women, bandits, all were made use of, all were links in the chain that was in contact with him and was subject to him.

From the times of Menotti[17] and the brothers Bandiera,[18]

---

17 The 'Bolognese insurrection' began on 2nd February, 1831, at the house of Ciro Menotti at Modena. There thirty-one conspirators surprised by the ducal troops held the soldiers at bay for hours. (*Tr.*)
18 Attilio and Emilio Bandiera, two young Venetians, lieutenants in the Austrian navy, attempted an insurrection in 1843. On its failure they escaped to Corfu; but, misled by false information, landed in Calabria with twenty companions, and were caught and shot at Cosenza in July of the same year. Their letters to Mazzini in London had been opened by the English authorities, who then resealed them and sent the informa-

enthusiastic youths, vigorous men of the people, vigorous aristocrats, sometimes old men, have come forward in constant succession . . . and follow the lead of Mazzini, who had been
consecrated by the elder Buonarrotti, the comrade and friend of
Gracchus Babeuf,[19] and advance to the unequal combat, disdainful of chains and the block, and sometimes at the point of death
adding to the shout of '*Viva l'Italia!*' that of '*Evviva Mazzini!*'

There has never been such a revolutionary organisation anywhere, and it would hardly be possible anywhere but in Italy,
unless in Spain. Now it has lost its former unity and its former
strength; it is exhausted by the ten years of martyrdom, it is
dying from loss of blood and worn out with waiting; its ideas
have aged; and yet what outbursts, what heroic examples, there
are still:

    Pianori, Orsini, Pisacane!

I do not think that by the death of one man a country could be
raised from such decline as France has fallen into now.[20]

I do not seek to justify the plan on which Pisacane made his
landing;[21] it seemed to me as ill-timed as the two previous
attempts at Milan: but that is not the point. I only mean to
speak here of the way in which it was actually carried out.
These men overwhelm one with the grandeur of their tragic
poetry, of their frightening strength, and silence all blame and
criticism. I know no instance of greater heroism, among either
the Greeks or the Romans, among the martyrs of Christianity or
of the Reformation!

A handful of vigorous men sail to the luckless shore of Naples,
serving as a challenge, an example, a living witness that all is
not yet dead in the people. The handsome young leader is the
first to fall, with the flag in his hand—and after him the rest
fall, or worse still find themselves in the clutches of the Bourbon.

---

tion so gained to the Austrian government. Sir James Graham and Lord
Aberdeen were principally responsible. (*Tr.*)

[19] Babeuf, François Noël, nicknamed Gracchus (1760–97), conspired
against the *Directoire*, was condemned to death, but stabbed himself. He
advocated a form of communism called *babouvisme*. (*Tr.*)

[20] The reference is to Orsini's attempt to assassinate Napoleon III on
14th January, 1858. (*Tr.*)

[21] 'In 1857 Pisacane seized the steamer *Cagliari*, freed the political prisoners on the island of Ponza, and with a small force effected a landing
on the Neapolitan coast at Sapri, hoping to join others of the republican
party: Met by overwhelming numbers, he fell at the head of his men,
most of them falling with him.' (*Tr.*)

The death of Pisacane and the death of Orsini were two fearful thunderclaps in a sultry night. Latin Europe shuddered—the
wild boar,[22] terrified, retreated to Caserta and hid himself in his
lair.

Pale with horror, the man who was driving France in her
funeral hearse to the graveyard swayed on the box.

❖   ❖   ❖

The Italian refugees were not superior to the other refugees
either in talent or education. The greater number of them knew
nothing, indeed, but their own poets and their own history. But
they were free from the stereotyped, commonplace stamp of the
French rank and file democrats (who argue, declaim, exult and
feel exactly the same thing in herds, and express their feelings in
an identical manner), as well as from the unpolished, coarse, pot-
house, state-educated-seminarist character which distinguishes
the German emigrants. The French democrat who comes by the
dozen is a *bourgeois in spe;* the German revolutionary, like the
German *Bursch*, is just the philistine over again, but at a different stage of development. The Italians are more original, more
individual.

The French are turned out ready-made by thousands on the
same pattern. The present government did not originate this
curtailment of individuality, but it has grasped the secret of it.
Absolutely in the French spirit, it has organised public education—that is all education, for there is no home education in
France. In every town in the empire the same thing is being
taught on the same day, at the same hour, from the same books.
At all examinations the same questions are asked, the same
examples set; teachers who deviate from the text, or alter the
syllabus, are promptly removed. This soulless, stereotyped education has only put into a compulsory, inherited form what was
fermenting in men's minds before. It is the conventional democratic notion of equality applied to intellectual development.
There is nothing of the sort in Italy. The Italian, a federalist and
an artist by temperament, flies with horror from every sort of
barrack discipline, uniformity and geometrical regularity. The
Frenchman is innately a soldier; he loves discipline, the military
detachment, the uniform; he loves to inspire fear. The Italian, if

---

22 The 'wild boar' is, of course, Ferdinand II of Naples, nicknamed
Bomba because of the cruel bombardment of Naples and other cities
during the suppression of the insurrection. (*Tr.*)

it comes to that, is rather a bandit than a soldier, and by this I do not mean to say anything at all against him. He prefers at the risk of capital punishment to kill his enemy at his own desire rather than to kill by order; but it is without throwing any responsibility on others. He is fonder of living penuriously in the mountains, and concealing smugglers, than of discovering them, and serving honourably in the gendarmes.

The educated Italian, like us Russians, has been elaborated spontaneously, by life, by his passions and by the books that have fallen into his hands, and has found his way to understanding of one sort or another. This is why in him and in ourselves there are gaps, discords. He and we are in many respects inferior to the specialised finish of the French and the theoretical learning of the Germans; but to make up for this the colours are more brilliant both in us and in the Italians.

We even have the same defects as they. The Italian has the same tendency to laziness as we: he does not think of work as pleasure; he does not like the anxiety of it, the weariness, the lack of leisure. Industry in Italy is almost as backward as it is with us; the Italians, like us, have treasures lying under their feet and they do not dig them up. Manners in Italy have not been influenced by the modern *bourgeois* tendency to the same degree as in France and in England.

The history of the Italian *petite bourgeoisie* is quite unlike the development of the *bourgeoisie* in France and in England. The wealthy *bourgeois*, the descendants *del popolo grasso,* have more than once successfully rivalled the feudal aristocracy, have been rulers of cities, and therefore they have been not further from but nearer to the plebeians and *contadini* than the rapidly enriched vulgarians of other lands. The *bourgeoisie* in the French sense is properly represented in Italy by a special class which has been formed since the first revolution,[23] and which might be called, as in geology, the Piedmont stratum. It is distinguished in Italy as in the whole continent of Europe by being constantly liberal in *many* questions, and afraid in all of them of the people and of too indiscreet talk about labour and wages, and also by always giving way to the enemy above and never to its own followers below.

The Italian exiles were drawn from every possible stratum of society. There were all sorts to be found about Mazzini, from the old names that occur in the chronicles of Guicciardini and

---

[23] Presumably the French Revolution of 1789–94. (*A.S.*)

Muratori, to which the people's ear has been accustomed for centuries, such as the Litti and Borromei, del Verme, Belgiojoso, Nani, Visconti, to some half-savage runaway Romeo from the Abruzzi with his dark, olive-coloured face and indomitable daring! Here were clericals too, like Sirtori, the heroic priest who, at the first shot in Venice, tucked up his cassock, and all through the siege and defence of Marghera fought, rifle in hand, in the foremost ranks under a hail of bullets; and here were the brilliant staff of Neapolitan officers, such as Pisacane, Cosenz, and the brothers Mezzacapo. Here, too, were plebeians from Trastevere, case-hardened in loyalty and privations, rough, surly, dumb in distress, modest and invincible, like Pianori; and by their side Tuscans, effeminate even in pronunciation, but equally ready for the struggle. Lastly, there were Garibaldi, a figure taken straight out of Cornelius Nepos, with the simplicity of a child and the valour of a lion; and Felice Orsini, whose beautiful head has so lately rolled from the steps of the scaffold.

But on their names I must dwell awhile.

I myself made Garibaldi's acquaintance in 1854, when he sailed from South America as the captain of a ship and lay in the West India Dock; I went to see him accompanied by one of his comrades in the Roman war and by Orsini. Garibaldi, in a thick, light-coloured overcoat, with a bright scarf round his neck and a cap on his head, seemed to me more a genuine sailor than the glorious leader of the Roman militia, statuettes of whom in fantastic costume were being sold all over the world. The good-natured simplicity of his manner, the absence of all affectation, the cordiality with which he received one, all disposed one in his favour. His crew consisted almost entirely of Italians; he was their chief and their authority, and I am sure he was a strict one, but they all looked gaily and affectionately at him; they were proud of their captain. Garibaldi gave us lunch in his cabin, regaling us with specially prepared oysters from South America, dried fruits, port—when suddenly he leapt up, saying, 'Wait a bit! With you I shall drink a different wine,' and ran up on deck; then a sailor brought in a bottle; Garibaldi looked at it with a smile and filled our glasses. . . . One might have expected anything from a man who had come from across the ocean, but it was nothing more nor less than Bellet from his native town, Nice, which he had brought with him to London from America.

Meanwhile, in his simple and unceremonious talk one was conscious little by little of the presence of strength; *sans phrases*, without commonplaces the people's leader, who had amazed old

soldiers by his valour, was revealed, and it was easy to recognise
in the ship's captain the wounded lion who, snarling at every
step, retreated after the taking of Rome and, having lost his
followers, mustered again at San Marino, at Ravenna, in Lombardy, in the Tyrol, at Tessino, soldiers, peasants, bandits,
anyone of any sort to strike once more at the foe—and all this
beside the body of his wife,[24] who had succumbed to the hard-
ships and privations of the campaign.

In 1854 his opinions diverged widely from those of Mazzini,
although he was on good terms with him. He told him in my
presence that Piedmont ought not to be irritated, that the chief
aim now was to shake off the Austrian yoke, and he greatly
doubted whether Italy was as ready for union and a republic as
Mazzini thought. He was entirely opposed to all ventures and
experiments in insurrection.

When he was about to sail for coal to Newcastle upon Tyne
and was from there setting off to the Mediterranean, I told him
how immensely I liked his seafaring life, and that of all the
exiles he was the one who had chosen the better part.

'And who forbids them doing the same?' he replied with
warmth. 'This was my cherished dream; you may laugh at it if
you like, but I cherish it still. I am known in America: I could
have three or four such ships under my command. I could take
all the refugees on them: the sailors, the lieutenants, the workmen, the cooks, might all be exiles. What can they do now in
Europe? Grow used to slavery and be false to themselves, or go
begging in England. Settling in America is worse still—that's
the end, that's the land of "forgetting one's country": it is a new
fatherland, there are other interests, everything is different; men
who stay in America fall out of the ranks. What is better than
my idea? (his face beamed); 'what could be better than gathering together round a few masts and sailing over the ocean,
hardening ourselves in the rough life of sailors, in conflict with
the elements and with danger? A floating revolution, ready to
put in at any shore, independent and unassailable!'

At that moment he seemed to me a hero of antiquity, a figure
out of the *Aeneid* . . . who—had he lived in another age—
would have had his legend, his '*Arma virumque cano!*'

Orsini was a man of quite a different sort. He gave proof of his

---

[24] Anita Riveira de Silva, a beautiful creole, whom G. eloped with and
then married. She was his companion on his earliest campaigns and bore
him two sons and a daughter. She died in July 1849. (*R.*)

wild strength and terrific energy on the 14th of January, 1858,[25] in the Rue Lepelletier; they won him a great name in history, and brought his thirty-six-year-old head under the knife of the guillotine. I made his acquaintance at Nice in 1851; at times we were even very intimate, then we drifted apart, came together again, and in the end 'a grey cat ran between us' in 1856 and, though we were reconciled, we no longer felt the same towards each other.

Such personalities as Orsini developed only in Italy; but to make up for this they appear there at all times and in all ages: they are conspirators and artists, martyrs and adventurers, patriots, *condottieri*, Teverinos[26] and Rienzis,[27] anything you like, but not vulgar, petty, commonplace, *bourgeois*. Such personalities stand out vividly in the chronicles of every Italian city. They amaze us by their goodness, they amaze us by their wickedness; they impress us by the strength of their passions and by the strength of their will. The yeast of restlessness is fermenting in them from early years—they must have danger, they must have laurels, glory, praise; they are purely Southern natures, with hot blood in their veins, with passions almost beyond our understanding, ready for any privation, for any sacrifice, from a sort of thirst for enjoyment. Self-denial and devotion in them go hand in hand with revengefulness and intolerance; in much they are simple, and cunning in much. Reckless as to the means they use, they are reckless, too, of dangers; descendants of the Roman 'fathers of their country' and children in Christ of the Jesuit Fathers, reared on classical memories and the traditions of mediaeval turmoils, a mass of ancient virtues and catholic vices is fermenting in their souls. They set no value on their own lives nor on the life of their neighbour, either; their terrific persistence is on a level with Anglo-Saxon obstinacy. On the one hand there is a naïve love of the external, an *amour propre* bordering on vanity, on a voluptuous desire to drink their fill of power, applause and glory; on the other, all the Roman heroism in face of privation and death.

People with energy of this sort can only be halted by the guillotine; otherwise, scarcely do they escape from the gendarmes of Sardinia before they begin hatching plots in the very claws of the Austrian hawk; and the day after a miraculous

---

[25] The date of Orsini's attempt on the life of Napoleon III. (*A.S.*)

[26] The hero of George Sand's novel of the same name. (*A.S.*)

[27] Rienzi, Cola di (1313–54), seized power in Rome in 1347 and fought for the unification of Italy. He was unsuccessful and had to flee. (*A.S.*)

rescue from the dungeons of Mantua they begin, with their arms still bruised from the leap to freedom, to sketch a plan with *grenades;* then, face to face with danger, they hurl them under a carriage. In the hour of failure they grow to colossal dimensions, and by their death deal a blow more powerful than a bursting grenade. . . .

As a young man Orsini had fallen into the hands of the secret police of Pope Gregory XVI; he was condemned for taking part in the movement in Rome and sentenced to the galleys, and remained in prison till the amnesty of Pius IX. From this life with smugglers, with bravoes, with survivors of the Carbonari, he gained a temper of iron and an immense knowledge of the national spirit. From these men, who were in constant, daily conflict with the society which oppressed them, he learnt the art of self-control, the art of being silent not only before a judge but even with his friends.

Men like Orsini have a powerful influence on others: people are attracted by their reserved nature and at the same time are not at home with them; one looks at them with the nervous pleasure mingled with tremors with which one admires the graceful movements and velvety gambols of a panther. They are children, but wicked children. Not only is Dante's hell 'paved' with them, but all the later centuries nurtured on his menacing poetry and the malignant wisdom of Machiavelli are full of them. Mazzini, too, belongs to their family, as did Cosimo de' Medici, Orsini, and Giovanni Procida.[28] One cannot even exclude from them the great 'adventurer of the sea,' Columbus, nor the greatest 'bandit' of recent ages, Napoleon Bonaparte.

Orsini was strikingly handsome; his whole appearance, elegant and graceful, could not but attract attention; he was quiet, spoke little, gesticulated less than his fellow-countrymen, and never raised his voice. The long black beard, as he wore it in Italy, made him look like some young Etruscan priest. His whole head was unusually beautiful, only a little marred by the irregular line of the nose.[29] And with all this there was something in Orsini's features, in his eyes, in his frequent smile and his gentle voice, that discouraged intimacy. It was evident that he was

---

[28] Procida, G. (*c.* 1225; d. after 1299), fought for the liberation of Sicily from France. (*A.S.*)

[29] Napoleon, so the newspapers wrote, ordered Orsini's head to be steeped in nitric acid that it might be impossible to take a death mask from it. What progress in humanity and chemistry since the days when the head of John the Baptist was given on a golden dish to the daughter of Herod!

reining himself in, that he never fully let himself go and was wonderfully in command of himself; it was evident that not one word fell from those smiling lips without intention, that there were depths behind those inwardly shining eyes, that, where people like us would hesitate and shy away, he would smile and, without changing his expression or raising his voice, go forward remorseless and undoubting.

In the spring of 1852 Orsini was expecting very important news about his family affairs: he was tormented at not getting a letter; he told me so several times, and I knew in what anxiety he was living. At dinner-time one day, when two or three outsiders were present, the postman came into the entry: Orsini sent to ask whether there was a letter for him; it appeared that there was; he glanced at it, put it in his pocket, and went on with the conversation. An hour and a half later, when I was alone with him, Orsini said to me: 'Well, thank God, at last I have got an answer, and all is quite well.' I, knowing that he was expecting a letter, had not guessed that this was it, with so unconcerned an air had he opened it and then put it into his pocket. A man like that is a born conspirator; and indeed he was one, all his life.

And what was accomplished by him with his energy, by Garibaldi with his daring, by Pianori with his revolver, by Pisacane and the other martyrs whose blood is not yet dry? Italy will be delivered from the Austrians, if at all, by Piedmont; from the Bourbon of Naples by fat Murat, both under the patronage of Bonaparte. Oh, *divina commedia*—or simply *commedia!* in the sense in which Pope Chiaramonti[30] said it to Napoleon at Fontainebleau. . . .

One evening an argument sprang up between Mazzini and me about Leopardi.

There are poems of Leopardi with which I am passionately in sympathy. Much of his work, like Byron's, is spoilt by theorising, but sometimes a line of his, like one of Byron's, stabs, hurts, wrings the heart. There are such words, such lines, in Lermontov.

---

[30] Pope Pius VII signed the Concordat of 15th July, 1801 with Napoleon, was forced by the latter to come to Paris to consecrate him as Emperor in 1804, was later on kept prisoner at Fontainebleau, and only returned to Rome in 1814. (*Tr.*) In January 1813 Napoleon visited Pius VII at Fontainebleau and obtained his consent to a new Concordat, by which the Catholic Church became subject to the authority of the Emperor of the French, and the secular authority of the Pope in Rome was abolished. (*R.*)

Leopardi was the last book Natalie read, the last she looked at before her death. . . .

To men of action, to agitators who move the masses, this venomous irresoluteness, these shattering doubts are incomprehensible. They see in them nothing but profitless lamentation, nothing but feeble despondency. Mazzini could not sympathise with Leopardi, that I knew beforehand; but he attacked him with bitterness. I was greatly vexed; of course, he was angry with him for being of no use to him for propaganda. In the same way Frederick II might have been angry . . . I do not know . . . well, with Mozart, for instance, because he was of no use as a guardsman. This is the shocking restriction of the personality, the subjecting of men to categories and *cadres*—as though historical development were serf-labour to which the bailiffs drive weak and strong, willing and unwilling alike, without consulting their wishes.

Mazzini was angry. I said to him, half in jest and half in earnest:

'I believe you have your knife into poor Leopardi for not having taken part in the Roman revolution; but you know he has an excellent reason to urge in his defence—you keep forgetting it!'

'What reason?'

'Why, the fact that he died in 1837.'

When a man who has long been watching black curls and black eyes suddenly turns to a fair-haired woman with light eyebrows who is pale and nervous, his eyes always receive a shock and cannot at once get over it. The difference, of which he has not been thinking and which he has forgotten, forces itself upon him physically through no desire of his.

Exactly the same thing happens when one turns quickly from Italian *émigré* circles to German.

Undoubtedly the Germans are more developed on the theoretical side than any other people, but they have not gained much by it so far. From Catholic fanaticism they have passed to the Protestant pietism of transcendental philosophy and the romance of philology, and are now gradually making the transition to exact science; the German 'studies diligently at all his stages,' and his whole history is summed up in that, and he will get marks for it on the Day of Judgment. The common people of Germany, who have studied less, have suffered a great deal; they bought the right to Protestantism by the Thirty Years' War, the right to an independent existence—that is, to a colourless existence under the supervision of Russia—by the struggle with Napoleon. The liberation in 1814–15 was a complete victory of the reaction; and when, in place of Jérôme Bonaparte, *der Landesvater* appeared in a powdered wig and an old-fashioned uniform long laid by, and announced that next day was fixed, let us say, for the forty-fifth parade (the one before, the forty-fourth, had taken place before the revolution), then all the liberated people felt as though they had suddenly lost touch with the present and gone back to another age, and everyone felt his head to see whether he had not grown a pigtail with a ribbon on it. The people accepted this with simple-hearted stupidity, and sang Körner's songs. Science and learning advanced. Greek tragedies were performed in Berlin, there were dramatic festivals for Goethe—at Weimar.

The most radical men among the Germans remain philistines in their private life. Bold as they are in logic, they feel no obligation to be consistent in practice, and fall into glaring contradictions. The German mind, in matters revolutionary as well as in everything else, accepts the general idea in its absolute, of course—that is, inoperative—significance, and is satisfied with an ideal construction of it, imagining that a thing is done if it is conceived, and that the fact as easily follows the thought as the meaning of the fact is grasped by the consciousness.

The English and the French are full of prejudices, while a German is free from them; but both French and English are more consistent in their lives—the rule they follow is perhaps absurd, but it is what they have accepted. A German accepts nothing except reason and logic, but he is ruled in many things by *other considerations*—which means acting against one's conscience in return for bribes.

The Frenchman is not morally free: though rich in initiative in practical life, he is poor in abstract thought. He thinks in received conceptions, in accepted forms; he gives a fashionable cut to commonplace ideas, and is satisfied with them. It is hard for him to take in anything new, although he does rush at it. The Frenchman oppresses his family and believes it is his duty to do so, just as he believes in the 'Legion of Honour' and the judgments of the lawcourts. The German believes in nothing, but takes advantage of public prejudices where it suits him. He is accustomed to a petty prosperity, to *Wohlbehagen*, to peace and quiet and, as he goes from his study to the *Prunkzimmer* or his bedroom, sacrifices his freedom of thought to his dressing-gown, to his peace and quiet and to his kitchen. The German is a great sybarite, and this is not noticed in him, because his scanty comfort and petty mode of life are not conspicuous; but the Eskimo who is ready to sacrifice everything for fish-fat is as much an epicurean as Lucullus. Moreover the German, lymphatic by temperament, soon puts on weight and sends down a thousand roots into his familiar mode of life; anything that might disturb him in his habits terrifies his philistine temper.

All German revolutionaries are great cosmopolitans, *sie haben überwunden den Standpunkt der Nationalität*, and are filled with the most touchy, most obstinate patriotism. They are ready to accept a universal republic, to abolish the frontiers between states, but Trieste and Danzig must belong to Germany. The Vienna students did not disdain to set off for Lombardy and to put themselves under the command of Radetsky; they even, under the leadership of some professor, took a cannon, which they presented to Innsbruck.

With this arrogant, bellicose patriotism, Germany has, from the time of the first revolution and up to this day, looked with horror to the right and with horror to the left. On this side, France with standards unfurled is crossing the Rhine; on that side, Russia is crossing the Niemen, and the people numbering twenty-five millions finds itself utterly forlorn and deserted, curses in its fright, hates because it is frightened and to comfort itself proves theoretically, according to the sources, that the existence of France is no longer existence, and the existence of Russia is not yet existence.

The 'council of war' assembled in St Paul's Church at Frankfurt, and consisting of various worthy professors, physicians, theologians, pharmacists and philologists, *sehr ausgezeichneten in ihrem Fache*, applauded the Austrian soldiers in Lombardy and oppressed the Poles in Posen. The very question of Schleswig-Holstein (*stammverwandt!*) touched on the quick only from the point of view of '*Teutschthum.*' The first free word, uttered after centuries of silence by the representatives of liberated Germany, was against weak, oppressed nationalities. This incapacity for freedom, these clumsily displayed inclinations to retain what had been wrongfully acquired, provoke irony: one forgives insolent pretensions only in return for vigorous actions, and there were none of these.

The revolution of 1848 had everywhere the character of precipitateness and instability, but there was scarcely anything absurd about it in France or in Italy; in Germany, except in Vienna, it was full of a comicality incomparably more humorous than the comicality of Goethe's wretched comedy, *Der Bürgergeneral.*

There was not a town, not a spot in Germany where at the time of the rising there was not an attempt at a 'committee of public safety' with all its principal actors, with a frigid youth as Saint-Just, with sombre terrorists, and a military genius representing Carnot. I knew two or three Robespierres personally: they always wore clean shirts, washed their hands and cleaned their nails. To make up for these there were also dishevelled Collot d'Herbois; and if in the club there was a man fonder of beer than the rest and more openly given to dangling after *Stubenmädchen*—he was the Danton, *eine schwelgende Natur!*

French weaknesses and defects are partly dissipated by their owners' prompt, easy nature. In the German the same defects get a more solid, steady development, and hence are more conspicuous. One must see for oneself these German efforts to play *so einen burschikosen Kamin de Paris* in politics in order to appreciate them. They have always reminded me of the playfulness of a cow when that good, respectable animal, garnished with domestic benevolence, starts frisking and frolicking in the meadow, and with a perfectly serious mien kicks up her two hind legs or gallops sideways chasing her own tail.

After the Dresden affair,[31] I met in Geneva one of the agitators who had taken part in it, and at once began questioning him about Bakunin. He praised him highly, and began describing how he had himself commanded a barricade under his orders. Inflamed by his own narrative he went on:

'A revolution is a thunderstorm; in it one must listen neither to the dictates of the heart nor to considerations of ordinary justice. . . . One must oneself have taken part in such events in order fully to understand the *Montagne* of 1794. Imagine: we suddenly observe a vague movement in the royalist party, false reports are intentionally circulated, suspicious-looking men appear. I reflected and reflected, and at last resolved to terrorise my street. *"Männer!"* I said to my detachment, "under pain of court-martial which in a 'state of siege' like this, may at once deprive you of life in case of disobedience, I order you that everyone, without distinction of sex, age or calling, who attempts to cross the barricade, shall be seized and brought under close guard to me." This was kept up for more than twenty-four hours. If the *Bürger* who was brought to me was a good patriot, I let him

---

31 In May 1849 M. A. Bakunin led a rising in Dresden. He was arrested and sentenced to be hanged; but the sentence was commuted to imprisonment for life. (*A.S.*)

through; but if he was a suspicious character, then I gave a sign to the guard.'

'And,' I said with horror, 'and they?'

'And they took him off home,' the terrorist replied with pride and satisfaction.

◈   ◈   ◈

All these absurd failings, together with the peculiar *Plumpheit* of the Germans, jar upon the Southern nature of the Italians and rouse in them a zoological, racial hatred. The worst of it is that the good side of the Germans, that is, their philosophical culture, is either of no interest to the Italian or beyond his grasp; while the vulgar, ponderous side always strikes his eye. The Italian often leads the most frivolous and idle life, and that is why he can least put up with the bear-like joking and clumsy familiarity of the jovial German.

The Anglo-Germanic race is much coarser than the Franco-Roman. There is no help for that: it is its physical characteristic; it is absurd to be angry with it. The time has come to understand once for all that the different breeds of mankind, like different breeds of animals, have their different natures and are not to blame for this. No one is angry with the bull for not having the beauty of the horse or the swiftness of the stag; no one reproaches the horse because the meat of its fillet does not taste so good as that of the ox: all that we can require of them in the name of animal brotherhood is to graze peaceably in the same field without kicking or goring each other. In nature everything attains to whatever it is capable of attaining to, is formed as chance determines, and so takes its generic *pli:* training goes to a certain stage, corrects one thing and grafts on another; but to demand beefsteaks from horses, or an ambling pace from bulls, is nevertheless absurd.

To get a visible conception of the difference between the two opposite traditions of the European races, one has but to glance at the street-boys in Paris and in London; it is they that I take as an example because they are absolutely spontaneous in their rudeness.

Look how the Parisian *gamins* jeer at any English eccentric, and how the London street-boys mock at a Frenchman; in this little example the two opposite types of two European races are sharply defined. The Parisian *gamin* is insolent and persistent, he can be insufferable: but, in the first place, he is witty, his mischief is confined to jests, and he is as amusing as he is annoying; and, in the second, there are words at which he blushes and at once desists, there are words which he never uses; it is difficult to stop him by rudeness, and if the victim lifts his stick I do not answer for the consequences. It should be noted, too, that for French boys there must be something striking: a red waistcoat with dark-blue stripes, a brick-coloured coat, an unusual muffler, a flunkey carrying a parrot or a dog, things done only by Englishmen and, take note, only outside England. To be simply a foreigner is not enough to make them mock and run after you.

The wit of the London street-boy is simpler. It begins with guffawing at the sight of a foreigner,[32] if only he has a moustache, a beard, or a wide-brimmed hat; then they shout a score of times: 'French pig! French dog!' If the foreigner turns to them with some reply, the neighings and bleatings are doubled; if he walks away, the boys run after him—then all that is left is the *ultima ratio* of lifting a stick, and sometimes bringing it down on the first that comes to hand. After that the boys run away at break-neck speed, with showers of oaths and sometimes throwing mud or a stone from a distance.

In France a grown-up workman, shopman, or woman street-vendor never takes part with the *gamins* in the pranks they play upon foreigners; in London all the dirty women, all the grown-up shopmen grunt like pigs and abet the boys.

In France there is a shield which at once checks the most persistent boy—that is, poverty. In England, a country that knows no word more insulting than the word *beggar*, the foreigner is the more persecuted the poorer and more defenceless he is.

One Italian refugee, who had been an officer in the Austrian cavalry and had left his country after the war, completely destitute, went about when winter came, in his army officer's greatcoat. This excited such a sensation in the market through which he had to pass every day, that the shouts of 'Who's your tailor?' the laughter, and finally tugs at his collar, went so far that the Italian gave up wearing his greatcoat and, shivering to the marrow of his bones, went about in his jacket.

This coarseness in street mockery, this lack of delicacy and tact in the common people, helps to explain how it is that women are nowhere beaten so often and so badly as in En-

---

[32] All this has greatly changed since the Crimean War. (1866.)

gland,[33] and how it is that an English father is ready to cast dishonour on his own daughter and a husband on his wife by taking legal proceedings against them.

The rude manners of the English streets are a great offence at first to the French and the Italians. The German, on the contrary, receives them with laughter and answers with similar swear-words; an interchange of abuse is kept up, and he remains very well satisfied. They both take it as a kindness, a nice joke. 'Bloody dog!'[34] the proud Briton shouts at him, grunting like a pig. 'Beastly John Bull!' answers the German, and each goes on his way.

This behaviour is not confined to the streets: one has but to look at the polemics of Marx, Heinzen, Ruge, *et consorts*, which never ceased after 1849 and are still kept up on the other side of the ocean. We are accustomed to see such expressions in print, such accusations: nothing is spared, neither personal honour, family affairs nor confidential secrets.

Among the English, coarseness disappears as we rise higher in the scale of intelligence or aristocratic breeding; among the Germans it never disappears. The greatest poets of Germany (with the exception of Schiller) fall into the most uncouth vulgarity.

One of the reasons of the *mauvais ton* of Germans is that breeding in our sense of the word does not exist in Germany at all. Germans are taught, and taught a great deal, but they are not educated at all, even in the aristocracy, in which the manners of the barracks, of the *Junker*, are predominant. In their daily life they are completely lacking in the aesthetic sense. The French have lost it, just as they have lost the elegance of their language; the Frenchman of to-day rarely knows how to write a letter free from legal or commercial expressions—the counter and the barrack-room have deformed his manners.

◇   ◇   ◇

I stayed in Geneva 'til the middle of December. The persecution which the Russian government was secretly commencing against

---

[33] *The Times* reckoned two years ago that on an average in every police district in London (there are ten) there were two hundred cases of assaults on women and children *per annum*; and how many assaults never lead to proceedings?

[34] In English in the text. (*R.*)

me compelled me to go to Zürich to try to save my mother's property, into which the never-to-be-forgotten Emperor had stuck his Imperial claws.

This was a frightful period in my life. A lull between two thunderclaps, an oppressive, heavy lull, but there was nothing pleasant about it . . . there were threatening signs, but even then I still turned away from them. Life was uneven, inharmonious, but there were bright days in it; for those I am indebted to the grand, natural scenery of Switzerland.

Remoteness from men, and beautiful natural surroundings, have a wonderfully healing effect. From experience I wrote in *A Wreck:*

'When the soul bears within it a great grief, when a man has not mastered himself sufficiently to grow reconciled with the past, to grow calm enough for understanding, he needs distance and mountains, the sea and warm, mild air. He needs them that grief may not turn into obduracy and despair, that he may not grow hard. . . .'

I was longing for rest from many things even then. A year and a half spent in the centre of political upheavals and dissensions, in constant provocation, in the midst of bloody sights, fearful downfalls and petty treacheries, had left a sediment of much bitterness, anguish and weariness at the bottom of my soul. Irony began to take a different character. Granovsky wrote to me after reading *From the Other Shore,* which I wrote just at that time: 'Your book has reached us. I read it with joy and a feeling of pride . . . but for all that there is something of fatigue about it; you stand too much alone, and perhaps you will become a great writer, but what in Russia was lively and attractive to all in your talent seems to have disappeared on foreign soil. . . .' Then Sazonov who, just before I left Paris in 1849, read the beginning of my story, *Duty Before Everything,* written two years previously, said to me: 'You won't finish that story, and you will never write anything more like it. Your light laugh and good-natured jokes are gone for ever.'

But could a man live through the ordeal of 1848 and 1849 and remain the same? I was myself conscious of the change. Only at home, when no outsiders were present, we sometimes found moments as of old, not of 'light laughter' but of light sadness, which recalled the past and our friends, recent scenes of our life in Rome; beside the cots of our sleeping children or watching their play, the soul was attuned as formerly, as once upon a time—there came upon it a breath of freshness, of youthful

poetry, of gentle harmony; there was peace and content in the
heart, and under the influence of such an evening life was easier
for a day or two.

These minutes were not frequent; a painful, melancholy distraction prevented them. The number of visitors kept increasing
about us, and by the evening our little drawing-room in the
Champs-Élysées was full of strangers. For the most part, these
were newly arrived *émigrés*, good, unfortunate people, but I was
intimate with only one man. . . . And why was I intimate with
him? . . .[35]

I was glad to leave Paris, but in Geneva we found ourselves in
the same society, though the persons in it were different and it's
dimensions were narrower. In Switzerland at that time everything had been hurled into politics; everything—*tables d'hôte*
and coffee-houses, watchmakers and women—all were divided
into parties. An exclusive preoccupation with politics, particularly in the oppressive lull that always follows unsuccessful
revolutions, is extremely wearisome with its barren aridity and
monotonous censure of the past. It is like summer-time in big
cities where everything is dusty and hot, airless, where through
pale trees the glistening walls and the hot paving-stones reflect
the glaring sun. A living man craves for air which has not yet
been breathed a thousand times over, which does not smell of the
picked bones of life, or ring with discordant jangling, where
there is no greasy, putrid stench and incessant noise.

Sometimes we did tear ourselves away from Geneva, visit the
shores of Lake Léman and go to the foot of Mont Blanc; and the
sombre, frowning beauty of the mountain scenery with its intense shadows screened all the vanity of vanities, refreshing soul
and body with the cold breath of its eternal glaciers.

I do not know whether I should like to stay for ever in
Switzerland. To us dwellers in the valleys and meadows, the
mountains after a time get in the way; they are too huge and too
near, they press in upon us and confine us; but sometimes it is
good to stay for a while in their shadow. Moreover a pure, good-
hearted race lives in the mountains, a race of people poor but not
unhappy, with few wants, accustomed to a life of sturdy independence. The scum of civilisation, its verdigris, has not settled

---

[35] Georg Herwegh (1817–75), a German poet and radical who seduced
Herzen's wife: see "A Family Drama" at the end of Volume II of his
Memoirs (not included in this selection) and E. H. Carr's *The Romantic
Exiles* (Gollancz, 1933). (*D.M.*)

on these people; historical changes pass like clouds beneath their feet and scarcely affect them. The Roman world still endures in Graubünden: anywhere in Appenzell the time of the peasant wars has scarcely passed. Perhaps in the Pyrenees, in the Tyrol or other mountains such a healthy stock of population is to be found, but it has ceased to exist in Europe as a whole.

◇   ◇   ◇

Western European Arabesques, II

1. A LAMENT

AFTER THE JUNE DAYS I saw that the revolution was vanquished, but I still believed in the vanquished, in the fallen; I believed in the wonder-working power of the relics, in their moral strength. At Geneva I began to understand more and more clearly that the revolution not only had been vanquished, but had been bound to be vanquished.

My head was dizzy with my discoveries, an abyss was opening before my eyes and I felt that the ground was giving way under my feet.

It was not the reaction that vanquished the revolution. The reaction showed itself everywhere densely stupid, cowardly, in its dotage; everywhere it retreated ignominiously round the corner before the shock of the popular tide, furtively biding its time in Paris, and at Naples, Vienna and Berlin. The revolution fell, like Agrippina, under the blows of its own children, and, what was worse than anything, without their being conscious of it; there was more heroism, more youthful self-sacrifice, than good judgment; and the pure, noble victims fell, not knowing for what. The fate of the survivors was almost more grievous. Absorbed in wrangling among themselves, in personal disputes, in melancholy self-deception, and consumed by unbridled vanity, they kept dwelling on their unexpected days of triumph, and

---

* Herzen's title is *"Il Pianto,"* fr. Italian *piangere*, to weep. I have taken the liberty of translating it as "A Lament." (*D.M.*)

were unwilling to take off their faded laurels or wedding garments, though it was not the bride who had deceived them.

Misfortunes, idleness and need induced intolerance, obstinacy and exasperation. . . . The *émigrés* broke up into little groups, which rallied not to principles but to names and hatreds. The fact that their thoughts continually turned to the past, and that they lived in an exclusive, closed circle, began to find expression in speech and thought, in manners and in dress; a new class was formed, the class of refugees, and ossified alongside the others. And just as once Basil the Great wrote to Gregory Nazianzen that he 'wallowed in fasting and delighted in privations,' so now there appeared voluntary martyrs, sufferers by vocation, wretches by profession, among whom were some very conscientious people; and indeed Basil the Great was sincere when he wrote to his friend of orgies of mortification of the flesh and of the voluptuous ecstasy of persecution. With all this, consciousness did not move a step forward and thought slumbered. . . . If these people had been summoned by the sound of a new trumpet and a new tocsin they would, like the nine sleeping maidens, have gone on with the day on which they fell asleep.

My heart almost broke at these painful truths; I had to live through a difficult page of my education.

. . . I was sitting mournfully one day in my mother's dining-room at gloomy, disagreeable Zürich; this was at the end of December 1849. I was going next day to Paris. It was a cold, snowy day; two or three logs, smoking and crackling, were unwillingly burning on the hearth. Everyone was busy packing; I was sitting quite alone. My life at Geneva floated before my mind's eye; everything ahead looked dark; I was afraid of something, and it was so unbearable that if I could have, I would have fallen on my knees and wept and prayed; but I could not and instead of a prayer I wrote my *curse*—my *Epilogue to 1849*.

'Disillusionment, fatigue, *Blasiertheit!*' The democratic critics said of those lines I vomited up. Disillusionment, yes! Fatigue, yes!. . . Disillusionment is a vulgar, hackneyed word, a veil under which lie hidden the sloth of the heart, egoism posing as love, the noisy emptiness of vanity with pretensions to everything and strength for nothing. All these exalted, unrecognised characters, wizened with envy and wretched from pretentiousness, have long wearied us in life and in novels. All that is perfectly true; but is there not something real, peculiarly characteristic of our times, at the bottom of these frightful spiritual sufferings which degenerate into absurd parodies and vulgar masquerade?

The poet who found words and voice for this malady was too proud to pose and to suffer for the sake of applause; on the contrary, he often uttered his bitter thought with so much humour that his kind-hearted readers almost died of laughing. Byron's disillusionment was more than caprice, more than a personal mood; Byron was shattered because life deceived him. And life deceived him not because his demands were unreal, but because England and Byron were of two different ages, of two different educations, and met just at the epoch when the fog was dispersing.

This rupture existed in the past, too, but in our age it has come to consciousness; in our age the impossibility of the intervention of any beliefs is becoming more and more manifest. After the break-up of Rome came Christianity; after Christianity, the belief in civilisation, in humanity. Liberalism is the *final religion*, though its church is not of the other world but of this. Its theology is political theory; it stands upon the earth and has no mystical conciliations, for it must have conciliation in fact. Triumphant and then defeated liberalism has revealed the rift in all its nakedness; the painful consciousness of this is expressed in the irony of modern man, in the scepticism with which he sweeps away the fragments of his shattered idols.

Irony gives expression to the vexation aroused by the fact that logical truth is not the same as the truth of history, that as well as dialectical development it has its own development through chance and passion, that as well as reason it has its romance.

Disillusionment[1] in our sense of the word was not known before the Revolution; the eighteenth century was one of the most religious periods of history. I am no longer speaking of the great martyr Saint-Just or of the apostle Jean-Jacques; but was not Pope Voltaire, blessing Franklin's grandson in the name of God and Freedom, a fanatic of his religion of humanity?

Scepticism was proclaimed together with the republic of the 22nd of September, 1792.

The Jacobins and revolutionaries in general belonged to a minority, separated from the life of the people by their culture: they constituted a sort of secular clergy ready to shepherd their human flocks. They represented the *highest* thought of their

---

[1] On the whole 'our' scepticism was not known in the last century; England and Diderot alone are the exceptions. In England scepticism has been at home for long ages, and Byron follows naturally on Shakespeare, Hobbes, and Hume.

time, its *highest* but not its *general consciousness*, not the *thought of all*.

This new clergy had no means of coercion, either physical or fancied: from the moment that authority fell from their hands, they had only one weapon—conviction; but for conviction to be *right* is not enough; their whole mistake lay in supposing so; something more was necessary—*mental equality*.

So long as the desperate conflict lasted, to the strains of the hymn of the Huguenots and the hymn of the Marseillaise, so long as the faggots flamed and blood flowed, this inequality was not noticed; but at last the oppressive edifice of feudal monarchy crumbled, and slowly the walls were shattered, the locks struck off . . . one more blow struck, one more wall breached, the brave men advanced, gates are opened and the crowd rushes in . . . but it is not the crowd that was expected. Who are these men; to what age do they belong? They are not Spartans, not the great *populus Romanus*. An irresistible wave of filth flooded everything. The inner horror of the Jacobins was expressed in the Terror of 1793 and 1794: they saw their fearful mistake, and tried to correct it with the guillotine; but, however many heads they cut off, they still had to bow their own before the might of the rising stratum of society. Everything gave way before it; it overpowered the Revolution and the reaction, it submerged the old forms and filled them up with itself because it constituted the one effective majority of its day. Sieyès was more right than he thought when he said that the *petite bourgeoisie was everything*.

The *petits bourgeois* were not produced by the Revolution; they were ready with their traditions and their customs, which were alien, in a different mode, to the revolutionary idea. They had been held down by the aristocracy and kept in the background; set free, they walked over the corpses of their liberators and established their own régime. The minority were either crushed or dissolved in the *petite bourgeoisie*.

A few men of each generation remained, in spite of events, as the tenacious preservers of the idea; these Levites, or perhaps ascetics, are unjustly punished for their monopoly of an exclusive culture, for the mental superiority of the well-fed castes, the leisured castes that had time to work not only with their muscles.

We were angered, moved to fury, by the absurdity, by the injustice of this fact. As though someone (not ourselves) had promised that everything in the world should be just and elegant and should go like clockwork. We have marvelled enough at the abstract wisdom of nature and of historical development; it is time to perceive that in nature as in history there is a great deal that is fortuitous, stupid, unsuccessful and confused. Reason, fully developed thought, comes last. Everything begins with the dullness of the new-born child; potentiality and aspiration are innate in him, but before he reaches development and consciousness he is exposed to a series of external and internal influences, deflections and checks. One has water on the brain; another falls and flattens it; both remain idiots. A third does not fall nor die of scarlet fever—and becomes a poet, a military leader, a bandit or a judge. On the whole we know best, in nature, in history and in life, the advances and successes: we are only now beginning to feel that all the cards are not so well pre-arranged as we had thought, because we are ourselves a failure, a losing card.

It mortifies us to realise that the idea is impotent, that truth has no binding power over the world of actuality. A new sort of Manichaeism takes possession of us, and we are ready, *par dépit*, to believe in rational (that is, purposive) evil, as we believed in rational good—that is the last tribute we pay to idealism.

The anguish will pass with time; its tragic and passionate character will calm down: it scarcely exists in the New World of the United States. This young people, enterprising and more practical than intelligent, is so busy building its own dwelling-place that it knows nothing at all of our agonies. Moreover, there are not two cultures there. The persons who constitute the classes in the society of that country are constantly changing, they rise and fall with the bank balance of each. The sturdy breed of English colonists is multiplying fearfully; if it gets the upper hand people will not be more fortunate for it, but they will be better contented. This contentment will be duller, poorer, more arid than that which hovered in the ideals of romantic Europe; but with it there will be neither tsars nor centralisation, and perhaps there will be no hunger either. Anyone who can put off from himself the old Adam of Europe and be born again a new Jonathan had better take the first steamer to some place in Wisconsin or Kansas; there he will certainly be better off than in decaying Europe.

Those who *cannot* will stay to live out their lives, as patterns of the beautiful dream dreamt by humanity. They have lived too much by fantasy and ideals to fit into the age of American good sense.

There is no great misfortune in this: we are not many, and we shall soon be extinct.

But how is it men grow up so out of harmony with their environment? . . .

Imagine a hothouse-reared youth, the one, perhaps, who has described himself in Byron's *The Dream*; imagine him face to face with the most boring, with the most tedious society, face to face with the monstrous Minotaur of English life, clumsily welded together of two beasts—the one decrepit, the other knee-deep in a miry bog, weighed down like a Caryatid whose muscles, under a constant strain, cannot spare one drop of blood for the brain. If he could have adapted himself to this life he would, instead of dying in Greece at thirty, now have been Lord Palmerston or Lord John Russell. But since he could not it is no wonder that, with his own Childe Harold, he says to his ship:

> *Nor care what land thou bearest me to,*
> *But not again to mine.*

But what awaited him in the distance? Spain cut up by Napoleon, Greece sunk back into barbarism, the general resurrection after 1814 of all the stinking Lazaruses; there was no getting away from them at Ravenna or at Diodati. Byron could not be satisfied like a German with theories *sub specie aeternitatis,* nor like a Frenchman with political chatter; he was broken, but broken like a menacing Titan, flinging his scorn in men's faces and not troubling to gild the pill.

The rupture of which Byron, as a poet and a genius, was conscious forty years ago, now, after a succession of new experiences, after the filthy transition from 1830 to 1848, and the abominable one from 1848 to the present, shocks many of us. And we, like Byron, do not know what to do with ourselves, where to lay our heads.

The realist Goethe, like the romantic Schiller, knew nothing of this rending of the spirit. The one was too religious, the other too philosophical. Both could find peace in abstract spheres. When the 'spirit of negation' appears as such a jester as Mephistopheles, then the swift *disharmony* is not yet a fearful one; his mocking and for ever contradictory nature is still blended in the higher harmony, and in its own time will ring out with everything—*sie ist gerettet*. Lucifer in *Cain* is very different; he is the rueful angel of darkness and on his brow shines with dim lustre the star of bitter thought; he is full of an inner disintegration which can never be put together again. He does not make a jest of denial, he does not seek to amuse with the impudence of his unbelief, he does not allure by sensuality, he does not procure artless girls, wine or diamonds; but he quietly prompts to murder, draws towards himself, towards crime—by that incomprehensible power with which at certain moments a man is enticed by still, moonlit water, that promises nothing in its comfortless, cold, shimmering embraces, nothing but death.

Neither Cain nor Manfred, neither Don Juan nor Byron, makes any inference, draws any conclusion, any 'moral.' Perhaps from the point of view of dramatic art this is a defect, but it gives a stamp of sincerity and indicates the depth of the gulf. Byron's epilogue, his last word, if you like, is *The Darkness;* here is the finish of a life that began with *The Dream.* Complete the picture for yourselves.

Two enemies, hideously disfigured by hunger, are dead, they are devoured by some crab-like animals . . . their ship is rotting away—a tarred rope swings in the darkness of dim waters; there is fearful cold, the beasts are dying out, history has died already and space is being cleared for new life: our epoch will be reckoned as belonging to the fourth geological formation—that is, if the new world gets as far as being able to count up to four.

Our historical vocation, our work, consists in this: that by our disillusionment, by our sufferings, we reach resignation and humility in face of the truth, and spare following generations from these afflictions. By means of us humanity is regaining sobriety; we are its head-ache next morning, we are its birth-pangs; but we must not forget that the child or mother, or perhaps both, may die by the way, and then—well, then history, like the Mormon it is, will start a new pregnancy. . . . *È sempre bene,* gentlemen!

We know how Nature disposes of individuals: later, sooner, with no victims or on heaps of corpses, she cares not; she goes her way, or goes any way that chances. Tens of thousands of years she spends building a coral reef, every spring abandoning to death the ranks that have run ahead too far. The polyps die without suspecting that they have served the *progress* of the reef.

We, too, shall serve something. To enter into the future as an element in it does not yet mean that the future will fulfil our ideals. Rome did not carry out Plato's idea of a republic nor the Greek idea in general. The Middle Ages were not the development of Rome. Modern Western thought will pass into history and be incorporated in it, will have its influence and its place, just as our body will pass into the composition of grass, of sheep, of cutlets, and of men. We do not like that kind of immortality, but what is to be done about it?

Now I am accustomed to these thoughts; they no longer frighten me. But at the end of 1849 I was stunned by them; and in spite of the fact that every event, every meeting, every contact, every person vied with each other to tear away the last green leaves, I still frantically and obstinately sought a *way out*.

That is why I now prize so highly the courageous thought of Byron. He saw that there is *no way out*, and proudly said so.

I was unhappy and perplexed when these thoughts began to haunt me; I tried by every means to run away from them . . . like a lost traveller, like a beggar, I knocked at every door, stopped people I met and asked the way, but every meeting and every event led to the same result—to *meekness* before the *truth*, to self-sacrificing acceptance of it.

Three years ago I sat by Natalie's sick-bed and saw death drawing her pitilessly, step by step, to the grave; that life was my whole fortune. Darkness spread around me; I was a savage in my dull despair, but did not try to comfort myself with hopes, did not betray my grief for one moment by the stultifying thought of a meeting beyond the grave.

So it is less likely that I should be false to myself over the impersonal problems of life.

2. POSTSCRIPT

ON PETIT BOURGEOIS

I KNOW that my view of Europe will meet with a bad reception at home. We for our own comfort *want* a different Europe and believe in it as Christians believe in paradise. Destroying dreams is always a disagreeable business, but some inner force which I cannot overcome makes me come out with the truth even on occasions when it does me harm.

As a rule we know Europe from school, from literature—that is, we do not know it, but judge it *à livre ouvert*, from books and pictures, just as children judge the real world from their *Orbis pictus*, imagining that all the women in the Sandwich Islands hold their hands above their heads with a sort of tambourine, and that where-ever there is a naked negro there is sure to be standing five paces from him a lion with a tousled mane or a tiger with angry eyes.

Our *classic* ignorance of the Western European will be productive of a great deal of harm; racial hatreds and bloody collisions will still develop from it.

In the first place all we know is the top, *cultured* layer of Europe, which conceals the heavy substratum of popular life formed by the ages, and evolved by instinct and by laws that are little known in Europe itself. Western culture does not penetrate into those Cyclopean works by which history has become rooted to the ground and borders upon geology. The European states are welded together of two peoples whose special characteristics are sustained by utterly different up-bringings. There is here none of the Oriental oneness, in consequence of which the Turk who is a Grand Vizier and the Turk who hands him his pipe resemble each other. Masses of the country population have, since the religious wars and the peasant risings, taken no active part in events; they have been swayed by them to right and left like standing corn, never for a minute leaving the ground in which they are rooted.

Secondly, that stratum with which we are acquainted, with which we do enter into contact, we only know historically, not as it is to-day. After spending a year or two in Europe we see with surprise that the men of the West do not on the whole correspond with our conception of them, that they are *greatly inferior* to it.

Elements of truth enter into the ideal we have formed, but either these no longer exist or they have completely changed. The valour of chivalry, the elegance of aristocratic manners, the stern decorum of the Protestants, the proud independence of the English, the luxurious life of Italian artists, the sparkling wit of the Encyclopaedists and the gloomy energy of the Terrorists—all this has been melted down and transmuted into one integral combination of different predominant manners, *bourgeois* ones. They constitute a complete whole, that is, a finished, self-contained outlook upon life with its own traditions and rules, with its own good and evil, with its own ways and its own morality *of a lower order*.

As the knight was the prototype of the feudal world, so the merchant has become the prototype of the new world; feudal lords are replaced by employers. The merchant in himself is a colourless intermediate figure; he is the middle-man between the producer and the consumer; he is something of the nature of a means of communication, of transport. The knight was more himself, more of a person, and kept up his dignity as he understood it, whence he was in essence not dependent either on wealth or on position; his personality was what mattered. In the *petit bourgeois* the personality is concealed or does not stand out, because it is not what matters; what matters is the ware, the produce, the thing; what matters is *property*.

The knight was a fearful ignoramus, a bully, a swashbuckler, a bandit and a monk, a drunkard and a pietist, but he was open and genuine in everything: moreover he was always ready to lay down his life for what he thought right; he had his moral laws, his code of honour—very arbitrary, but one from which he did not depart without loss of his self-respect or the respect of his peers.

The merchant is a man of peace and not of war, stubbornly and persistently standing up for his rights, but weak in attack; calculating, parsimonious, he sees a deal in everything and, like the knight, enters into single combat with everyone he meets, but measures himself against him in *cunning*. His ancestors, mediaeval townsmen, were forced to be sly to save themselves from violence and pillage; they purchased peace and wealth by evasiveness, by secretiveness and pretence, keeping themselves close and holding themselves in check. His ancestors, cap in hand and bowing low, cheated the knight; shaking their heads and sighing, they talked to their neighbours of their poverty, while they secretly buried money in the ground. All this has naturally passed into the blood and brains of their descendants, and has become the physiological sign of a particular human species called the *middle estate*.

While it was in a condition of adversity and joined with the enlightened fringe of the aristocracy to defend its faith and win its rights, it was full of greatness and poetry. But this did not last long, and Sancho Panza, having taken possession of his palace and lolling at full liberty without ceremony, let himself go and lost his peasant humour and his common sense; the vulgar side of his nature got the upper hand.

Under the influence of the *petit bourgeois* everything was changed in Europe. Chivalrous honour was replaced by the honesty of the book-keeper, elegant manners by propriety, courtesy by affectation, pride by a readiness to take offence, parks by kitchen gardens, palaces by hotels open to *all* (that is all who have money).

The former, out-of-date but consistent conceptions of relationships between people were shaken, but no new consciousness of the *true* relationships between people was discovered. This chaotic liberty contributed greatly to the development of all the bad, shallow sides of *petite bourgeoisie* under the all-powerful influence of unbridled acquisition.

Analyse the moral principles current for the last half-century, and what a medley you will find! Roman conceptions of the state together with the Gothic division of powers, Protestantism and political economy, *salus populi* and *chacun pour soi*, Brutus and Thomas à Kempis, the Gospel and Bentham, book-keeping and Jean-Jacques Rousseau. With such a hotch-potch in the head and with a magnet in the breast for ever attracted towards gold, it was not hard to arrive at the absurdities reached by the foremost countries of Europe.

The whole of morality has been reduced to the duty of him who *has not*, to acquire by every possible means; and of him who *has*, to preserve and increase his property; the flag which is run up in the market-place to show that trading may begin has become the banner of a new society. The man has *de facto* become the appurtenance of property; life has been reduced to a perpetual struggle for money.

The political question since 1830 has been becoming exclusively the *petit bourgeois* question, and the age-long struggle is expressed in the passions and inclinations of the ruling class. Life is reduced to a gamble on the Stock Exchange; everything— the publication of newspapers, the elections, the legislative chambers—all have become money-changers' shops and markets. The English are so used to putting everything into shop nomenclature that they call their old Anglican Church the 'Old Shop.'[2]

All parties and shades of opinion in the *petit bourgeois* world have gradually divided into two chief camps: on one hand the *bourgeois* property-owners, obstinately refusing to abandon their monopolies; on the other the *bourgeois* who have nothing, who want to tear the wealth out of the others' hands but have not the power: that is on the one hand *miserliness*, on the other hand *envy*. Since there is no real moral principle in all this, the adherence of any individual to one or the other side is determined by external conditions of fortune and social position. One wave of the opposition after another achieves a victory: that is, property or position, and passes naturally from the side of envy to the side of miserliness. For this transition nothing can be more favourable than the fruitless swing backwards and for-

---

[2] In English in the text. Herzen has remembered a trifle incorrectly the phrase used by certain Anglicans to describe the Established Church: 'The Old Firm.' (*R.*)

wards of parliamentary debates—it gives movement and sets limits to it, provides an appearance of *doing something,* and an external show of public interest in order to attain its private ends.

Parliamentary government, not as it follows from the popular foundations of the Anglo-Saxon *Common Law* but as it has taken shape in the law of the State, is simply the wheel in a squirrel's cage—and the most colossal one in the world. Would it be possible to stand still on one spot more majestically—while simulating a triumphant march forward—than is performed by the two English Houses of Parliament?

But just that maintenance of appearance is the main point.

Upon everything belonging to contemporary Europe two traits, obviously derived from the shop, are deeply imprinted: on one hand hypocrisy and secretiveness; on the other ostentation and *étalage.* It is all window-dressing, buying at half-price, passing off rubbish for the real thing, show for reality, concealing some condition, taking advantage of a literal meaning, *seeming* instead of *being,* behaving *decorously* instead of behaving *well,* keeping up external *Respektabilität* instead of inner dignity.

In this world everything is so much a stage-set that even the coarsest ignorance has achieved an appearance of education. Which of us has not been left blushing for the ignorance of Western European society? (I am not speaking here of men of learning, but of the people who make up what is called society.) There can be no serious theoretical education; it requires too much time and is too distracting from *business.* Since nothing that lies outside trading operations and the 'exploitation' of their social position is essential in the *petit bourgeois* world, their education is bound to be limited. That is what accounts for the absurdity and slowness of mind which we see in the *petit bourgeois* whenever he has to step off the beaten track. Cunning and hypocrisy on the whole are by no means so clever and so far-sighted as is supposed; their endurance is poor, and they are soon out of their depth.

The English are aware of this and so do not leave the beaten track, and put up with the not merely burdensome but, what is worse, absurd inconveniences of their mediaevalism through fear of any change.

The French *petit bourgeois* have not been so careful, and for all their slyness and duplicity have fallen headlong into an empire.

Full of confidence in their victory they proclaimed universal suffrage as the basis of their new régime. This arithmetical banner suited their taste; the truth was determined by addition and subtraction, it could be verified by figures, and marked by pins.

And what did they put to the decision of the *votes of all* in the present state of society? The question of the existence of the republic. They wanted to kill it by means of the people, to make of it an empty word, because they did not like it. Is anyone who respects the truth going to ask the opinion of the first stray man he meets? What if Columbus or Copernicus had put America or the movement of the earth to the vote?

It was shrewdly conceived, but in the end the good souls miscalculated.

The gap between the *parterre* and the actors, covered at first by the faded carpet of Lamartine's eloquence, grew wider and wider; the blood of June washed the channel deeper; and then the question of the president was put to the irritated people. As answer to the question, Louis-Napoleon, rubbing his sleepy eyes, stepped out of the gap and took everything into his hands—that is the *petit bourgeois* too, who fancied, from memory of old days, that he would *reign* and they would *govern*.

What you see on the great stage of political events is repeated in microscopic form at every hearth. The corruption of *petite bourgeoisie* has crept into all the secret places of family and private life. Never was Catholicism, never were the ideas of chivalry, impressed on men so deeply, so multifariously, as the *bourgeois* ideas.

Noble rank had its obligations. Of course, since its rights were partly imaginary, its obligations were imaginary too, but they did provide a certain mutual guarantee between equals. Catholicism laid still more obligations. Feudal knights and believing Catholics often failed to carry out their obligations, but the consciousness that by so doing they were breaking the social alliance recognised by themselves prevented them from being lawless in their defections and from justifying their behaviour. They had their festival attire, their official stage-setting, which were not a lie but were rather their ideal.

We are not now concerned with the nature of that ideal. They were tried and their cause was lost long ago. We only want to point out that *petite bourgeoisie* on the contrary involves no obligations, not even the obligation to serve in the army, so long as there are volunteers; or rather, its only obligation is *per fas et nefas* to have property. Its gospel is brief: 'Heap up wealth, multiply thy riches 'til they are like the sands of the sea, use and misuse thy financial and moral capital, without ruining thyself, and in fullness and honour thou shalt attain length of years, marry thy children well, and leave a good memory behind thee.'

The rejection of the feudal and Catholic world was essential, and was the work not of the *petit bourgeois* but simply of free men, that is of men who had renounced all wholesale classifications. Among them were knights like Ulrich von Hutten, gentlemen like Voltaire, watchmakers' apprentices like Rousseau, army doctors like Schiller, and merchants' sons like Goethe. The *petit bourgeois* took advantage of their work and showed themselves emancipated, not only from monarchs and slavery but from all social obligations, except that of contributing to the hire of the government who guarded their security.

Of Protestantism they made *their own* religion, a religion that reconciles the conscience of the Christian with the practice of the usurer, a religion so *petit bourgeois* that the common people, who shed their blood for it, have abandoned it. In England the working class goes to church less than any.

Of the Revolution they wanted to make *their own* republic, but it slipped between their fingers, just as the civilisation of antiquity slipped away from the barbarians—that is, with no place in real life, but with hope for *instaurationem magnam*.

The Reformation and the Revolution were both so frightened by the emptiness of the world which they had come into that they sought salvation in two forms of monasticism: the cold, dreary bigotry of Puritanism and the dry, artificial, civic morality of republican formalism. Both the Quaker[3] and the Jacobin forms of intolerance were based on the fear that the ground was not firm under their feet; they saw that they needed to take strong measures, to persuade one group of men that this was the church, and the other that this was freedom.

Such is the general atmosphere of European life. It is most oppressive and intolerable where the modern Western system is most developed, where it is most true to its principles, where it is most wealthy and most *cultured*—that is, most industrial. And that is why it is not so unendurably stifling to live in Italy or Spain as it is in England or France. . . . And that is why poor, mountainous, rustic Switzerland is the only corner of Europe into which one can retreat in peace.

◈ ◈ ◈

---

[3] Here Herzen ignorantly uses the word 'Quaker' as equivalent to 'Nonconformist,' or perhaps, 'Puritan.' It is needless to point out that tolerance is one of the most prominent principles of the Society of Friends. (*Tr.*)

Money and the Police

IN THE DECEMBER of 1849 I learnt that the authorisation for the mortgage of my estate sent from Paris and witnessed at the Embassy had been destroyed, and that after that a distraint had been laid on my mother's fortune. There was no time to be lost and I at once left Geneva and went to my mother's.

It would be stupid and hypocritical to affect to despise property in our time of financial disorder. Money is independence, power, a weapon; and no one flings away a weapon in time of war, though it may have come from the enemy and even be rusty. The slavery of poverty is frightful; I have studied it in all its aspects, living for years with men who have escaped from political shipwrecks in the clothes they stood up in. I thought it right and necessary, therefore, to take every measure to extract what I could from the bear's paws of the Russian government.

Even so I was not far from losing everything. When I left Russia I had had no definite plan; I only wanted to stay abroad as long as possible. The revolution of 1848 arrived and drew me into its vortex before I had done anything to secure my property. Worthy persons have blamed me for throwing myself headlong into political movements and leaving the future of my family to the will of the gods. Perhaps it was not altogether prudent; but if, when I was living in Rome in 1848, I had sat at home considering ways and means of saving my property while an awakened Italy was seething before my windows, then I should probably not have remained in foreign countries, but have gone to Petersburg, entered the service once more, might have become a vice-governor, have sat at the head prosecutor's table, and should have addressed my secretary with insulting familiarity and my minister as 'Your Exalted Excellency.'

I had no such self-restraint and good sense, and I am infinitely thankful for it now. My heart and my memory would be the poorer if I had missed those shining moments of faith and enthusiasm! What would have compensated me for the loss of them? Indeed, why speak of me? What would have compensated her whose broken life was nothing afterwards but suffering that ended in the grave? How bitterly would my conscience have reproached me if, from over-prudence, I had robbed her of almost the last minutes of untroubled happiness! And after all I did do the important thing: I did save almost all our property except the Kostroma estate.

After the June days my situation became more dangerous. I made the acquaintance of Rothschild, and proposed that he should change for me two Moscow Savings Bank bonds. Business then was not flourishing, of course, and the exchange was very bad; his terms were not good, but I accepted them at once, and had the satisfaction of seeing a faint smile of compassion on Rothschild's lips—he took me for one of the innumerable *princes russes* who had run into debt in Paris, and so fell to calling me *Monsieur le Comte.*

On the first bonds the money was paid promptly; but on the later ones for a much larger sum, although payment was made, Rothschild's agent informed him that a distraint had been laid on my capital—luckily I had withdrawn it all.

In this way I found myself in Paris with a large sum of money in very troubled times, without experience or knowledge what to do with it. Yet everything was settled fairly well. As a rule, the less impetuosity, alarm and uneasiness there is in financial matters, the better they succeed. Grasping money-grubbers and financial cowards are as often ruined as spendthrifts.

By Rothschild's advice I bought myself some American shares, a few French ones and a small house in the Rue Amsterdam which was let to the Havre Hôtel.

One of my first revolutionary steps, which cut me off from Russia, plunged me into the respectable class of conservative idlers, brought me acquaintance with bankers and notaries, taught me to keep an eye on the Stock Exchange—in short, turned me into a Western European *rentier.* The rift between the modern man and the environment in which he lives brings a fearful confusion into private behaviour. We are in the very middle of two currents which are getting in each other's way; we are flung and shall continue to be flung first in one direction and then in the other, until one current or the other finally wins and the stream, still restless and turbulent but now flowing in one direction, makes things easier for the swimmer by carrying him along with it.

Happy the man who knows how to manoeuvre so that, adapting and balancing himself among the waves, he still swims on his own course!

On the purchase of the house I had the opportunity of looking more closely into the business and *bourgeois* world of France.

The bureaucratic pedantry over completing a purchase is not inferior to ours in Russia. The old notary read me several documents, the statute concerning the reading of the *main levée*, then the actual statute itself—all this making up a complete folio volume. In our final negotiation concerning the price and the legal expenses, the owner of the house said that he would make a concession and take upon himself the very considerable expenses of the legal conveyance, if I would immediately pay the whole sum to him personally. I did not understand him, since from the very first I had openly stated that I was buying it for ready money. The notary explained to me that the money must remain in his hands for at least three months, during which a notice of sale would be published and all creditors who had any claims on the house would be called upon to state their case. The house was mortgaged for seventy thousand, but there might be further mortgages in other hands. In three months' time, after inquiries had been made, the *purge hypothécaire* would be handed to the purchaser and the former owner would receive the purchase money.

The owner declared that he had no other debts. The notary confirmed this.

'Your honour and your hand on it,' I said to him: 'you have no other debts which would concern the house?'

'I willingly give you my word of honour.'

'In that case I agree, and shall come here to-morrow with Rothschild's cheque.'

When I went next day to Rothschild's his secretary flung up his hands in horror:

'They are cheating you! This is impossible: we will stop the sale if you like. It's something unheard of, to buy from a stranger on such terms.'

'Would you like me to send someone with you to look into the business?' Baron James himself suggested.

I did not care to play the part of an ignorant boy, so I said that I had given him my word, and took a cheque for the whole sum. When I reached the notary's I found there, besides the witnesses, the creditor who had come to receive his seventy thousand francs. The deed of purchase was read over, we signed it, the notary congratulated me on being a Parisian house-owner—all that was left was to hand over the cheque. . . .

'How vexing!' said the house-owner, taking it from my hands; 'I forgot to ask you to draw it in two cheques. How can I pay out the seventy thousand separately now?'

'Nothing is easier: go to Rothschild's, they'll give it you in two cheques; or, simpler still, go to the bank.'

'I'll go if you like,' said the creditor.

The house-owner frowned and answered that that was his business, and he would go.

The creditor frowned. The notary good-naturedly suggested that they should go together.

Hardly able to refrain from laughter I said to them:

'Here's your receipt; give me back the cheque, I will go and change it.'

'You will infinitely oblige us,' they said with a sigh of relief; and I went.

Four months later the *purge hypothécaire* was sent me, and I gained about ten thousand francs by my rash trustfulness.

After the 13th of June, 1849, Rébillaud, the Prefect of Police, laid information against me; it was probably in consequence of his report, that some unusual measures were taken by the Petersburg government against my estate. It was these, as I have said, that made me go with my mother to Paris.

We set off through Neuchâtel and Besançon. Our journey began with my forgetting my greatcoat in the posting-station yard at Berne; since I had on a warm overcoat and warm galoshes I did not go back for it. All went well till we reached the mountains, but in the mountains we were met by snow up to the knees, eight degrees of frost, and the cursed Swiss *bise*. The *diligence* could not go on and the passengers were transferred by twos and threes into small sledges. I do not remember that I have ever suffered so much from cold as I did on that night. My feet were simply in agony, and I dug them into the straw; then the driver gave me a collar of some sort, but that was not much help. At the third stage I bought a shawl from a peasant woman for fifteen francs, and wrapped myself in it; but by that time we were already on the descent, and with every mile it became warmer.

This road is magnificently fine on the French side; the vast amphitheatre of immense mountains, so varied in outline, accompanies one as far as Besançon itself; here and there on the crags the ruins of fortified feudal castles are visible. In this landscape there is something mighty and harsh, solid and grim; with his eyes upon it, there grew up and was formed a peasant boy, the descendant of old country stock, Pierre-Joseph Proudhon. And indeed one may say of him, though in a different sense, what was said by the poet of the Florentines:

E tiene ancor del monte e del macigno.[1]

---

[1] Dante, *Inferno*, XV, 63. (*A.S.*)

Rothschild agreed to take my mother's bond, but would not cash it in advance, referring to Gasser's letter. The Board of Trustees did in fact refuse payment. Then Rothschild instructed Gasser to request an interview with Nesselrode[2] and to inquire of him what was wrong. Nesselrode replied that, though there was no doubt about the bonds and Rothschild's claim was valid, the Tsar had ordered the money to be stopped, for secret, political reasons.

I remember the surprise in Rothschild's office on the reception of this reply. The eye involuntarily sought at the bottom of the document for the mark of Alaric or the seal of Genghis Khan. Rothschild had not expected such a trick even from so celebrated a master of despotic affairs as Nicholas.

'For me,' I said to him, 'it is hardly surprising that Nicholas should wish to purloin my mother's money in order to punish me, or hope to catch me with it as a bait; but I could not have imagined that your name would carry so little weight in Russia. The bonds are yours and not my mother's; when she signed them she transferred them to the bearer (*au porteur*), but ever since you endorsed them that *porteur*[3] has been you; and you have received the insolent answer: "The money is yours, but master orders me not to pay." '

My speech was successful. Rothschild grew angry, and walked about the room saying:

'No, I shan't allow myself to be trifled with; I shall bring an action against the bank; I shall demand a categorical reply from the Minister of Finance!'

'Well,' thought I, 'Vronchenko won't understand this at all. A "confidential" reply would still have been all right, but not a "categorical" one!'

'Here you have a sample of how familiarly and *sans gêne* the autocracy, upon which the reaction is building such hopes, disposes of property. The communism of the Cossack is almost more dangerous than that of Louis Blanc.'

'I shall think it over,' said Rothschild; 'we can't leave it like this.'

Three days or so after this conversation, I met Rothschild on the boulevard.

'By the way,' he said, stopping me, 'I was speaking of your

---

2 Nesselrode, Karl Vasilevich (1780–1862), Russian Minister for Foreign Affairs, 1816–56. (*A.S.*) Also inventor of Nesselrode pudding. (*D.M.*)
3 This endorsement is done for security in sending cheques, in order that a cheque may not be sent unendorsed, by means of which anybody would be able to receive the money.

business yesterday to Kiselëv.[4] You must excuse me, but I ought to tell you that he expressed a very unfavourable opinion of you, and does not seem willing to do anything for you.'

'Do you often see him?'

'Sometimes, at evening parties.'

'Be so good as to tell him that you have seen me to-day, and that I have the worst possible opinion of him, but that even so I don't think it would be at all just to rob his mother on that account.'

Rothschild laughed; I think that from that time he began to surmise that I was not a *prince russe,* and now he took to addressing me as Baron; he elevated me thus, I imagine, to make me worthy of conversing with him.

Next day he sent for me; I went at once. He handed me an unsigned letter to Gasser, and added:

'Here is the draft of our letter; sit down, read it carefully and tell me whether you are satisfied with it. If you want to add or change anything, we shall do it at once. Allow me to go on with my work.'

At first I looked about me. Every minute a small door opened and one Bourse agent after another came in, uttering a number in a loud voice; Rothschild, going on reading, muttered without raising his eyes: 'Yes—no—good—perhaps—enough—' and the number walked out. There were various gentlemen in the room, rank and file capitalists, members of the National Assembly, two or three exhausted tourists with youthful moustaches and elderly cheeks, those everlasting figures who drink—wine—at watering-places and are presented at courts, the feeble, lymphatic suckers that drain the sap from aristocratic families and shove their way from the gaming table to the Bourse. They were all talking together in undertones. The Jewish autocrat sat calmly at his table, looking through papers and writing something on them, probably millions, or at least hundreds of thousands.

'Well,' he said, turning to me, 'are you satisfied?'

'Perfectly,' I answered.

The letter was excellent, curt and emphatic as it should be when one power is addressing another. He wrote to Gasser telling him to request an immediate audience with Nesselrode and the Minister of Finance; he was to tell them that Rothschild was not interested to know to whom the bonds had belonged; that he has bought them and demands payment, or a clear legal declara-

---

[4] This was not P. D. Kiselëv, who was in Paris later, the well known Minister of Crown Property, a very decent man; but another one: N. D. Kiselëv, afterwards transferred to Rome.

tion why payment had been stopped; that in case of refusal he would submit the affair to the judgment of the legal authorities; and he advised careful reflection on the consequences of a refusal, which was particularly strange at a time when the Russian government was negotiating through him for the conclusion of a new loan. Rothschild wound up by saying that in case of further delays he would have to give the matter publicity through the press, in order to warn other capitalists. He recommended Gasser to show the letter to Nesselrode.

'I'm very glad . . . but . . .' he said, holding a pen in his hand and looking me straight in the face with a somewhat ingenuous air . . . 'but, my dear Baron, do you really think that I shall sign this letter which, *au bout du compte*, might put me on bad terms with Russia—and that for a commission of one half of one per cent?'

I was silent.

'In the first place,' he continued, 'Gasser will have disbursements—nothing is done for nothing in your country—and of course they must be at your expense; and in addition to that—how much do you propose?'

'I think,' I said, 'it is for you to propose and for me to agree.'

'Well, five: what do you say? That's not much.'

'Let me think about it. . . .'

I simply wanted to calculate.

'As long as you like. Besides,' he added with an expression of Mephistophelean irony, 'you can manage this business for nothing. Your mother's rights are incontestable. She is a subject of Württemberg: apply to Stuttgart—the Minister for Foreign Affairs is bound to support her and exert himself to procure payment. For my part, to tell you the truth, I shall be very glad to get this unpleasant affair off my shoulders.'

We were interrupted. I left the office impressed by all the old-fashioned simplicity in his look and his question. If he had asked for ten or fifteen per cent, I should have agreed then and there. His help was essential to me, and he knew this so well that he even put himself out for a Russified subject of Württemberg; but, allowing myself to be guided as of old by the Russian rules of political economy, which ordain that, for whatever distance an *izvozchik* asks for twenty kopecks, one should still try to get him to take fifteen, I told Schomburg, on no sufficient basis, that I proposed that a commission of one per cent might be added. Schomburg promised to tell him and asked me to come back in half an hour.

When half an hour later I was mounting the staircase of the

Winter Palace of Finance in the Rue Laffitte, the rival of Nicholas was coming down it.

'Schomburg has told me,' said His Majesty, smiling graciously, and majestically holding out his own august hand, 'that the letter has been signed and sent off. You will see how they will come round. I'll teach them to trifle with me.'

'Only not for half of one per cent,' I thought, and I felt inclined to drop on my knees and to offer an oath of allegiance together with my gratitude, but I confined myself to saying: 'If you feel perfectly certain of it, allow me to open an account, if only for half of the whole sum.'

'With pleasure,' answered His Majesty the Emperor, and went his way into the Rue Laffitte.

I made my obeisance to His Majesty and, since it was so close, went into the *Maison d'Or*.

Within a month or six weeks Nicholas Romanov, that Petersburg merchant of the first guild, who had been so stingy about paying up, now terrified of competition and of publication in the newspapers, did at the Imperial command of Rothschild pay over the illegally detained money, together with the interest and the interest on the interest, justifying himself by his ignorance of the laws, which in his social position he certainly could not be expected to know.

From that time forth I was on the best of terms with Rothschild. He liked in me the field of battle on which he had beaten Nicholas; I was for him something like Marengo or Austerlitz, and he several times recited the details of the action in my presence, smiling faintly, but magnanimously sparing his vanquished opponent.

While this action of mine was going on—and it occupied about six months—I was staying at the Hôtel Mirabeau, in the Rue de la Paix. One morning in April I was told that a gentleman was waiting for me in the hall and wished to see me without fail. I went in there. A cringing figure that looked like an old government clerk was standing in the hall.

'The *Commissaire* of Police of the *Tuileries arrondissement:* So-and-so.'

'Pleased to see you.'

'Allow me to read you a decree of the Ministry of Home Affairs, communicated to me by the Prefect of Police, and relating to you.'

'Pray do so; here is a chair.'

'We, the Prefect of Police—In accordance with paragraph

seven of the law of the 13th and 21st of November and 3rd of December of 1849, giving the Ministry of Home Affairs the power to expel (*expulser*) from France any foreigner whose presence in France may be subversive of order and dangerous to public tranquillity, and in view of the ministerial circular of the 3rd of January, 1850,

'Do command as follows:

'The here-mentioned' (*le N——é*, that is, *nommé*, but this does not mean 'aforesaid' because nothing has been said about me before; it is merely an illiterate attempt to designate a man as rudely as possible) 'Herzen, Alexandre, aged 40' (they added two years), 'a Russian subject, living in such a place, is to leave Paris at once after this intimation, and to quit the boundaries of France within the shortest possible time.

'It is forbidden for him to return in future on pain of the penalties laid down by the eighth paragraph of the same law (imprisonment from one to six months and a money fine).

'All necessary measures will be taken to secure the execution of these orders.

'Done (*Fait*) in Paris, April 16th, 1850.

'Prefect of Police,

'A. Carlier.

'Confirmed by the general secretary of the *Préfecture*.

'Clément Reyre.'

On the margin:

'Read and approved April 19th, 1850,

'Minister of Home Affairs,

'G. Baroche.

'In the year eighteen hundred and fifty, April the twenty-fourth.

'We, Emile Boullay, *Commissaire* of Police of the city of Paris and in particular of the *Tuileries arrondissement*, in execution of the orders of *M. le Préfet de Police* of April 23rd:

'Have notified the Sieur Alexandre Herzen, telling him in words as written herewith.' Here follows the whole text over again. It is just as children tell the story of the White Bull, prefacing it every time they tell it with the same phrase: 'Shall I tell you the tale of the White Bull?'

Then: 'We have invited *le dit Herzen* to present himself in the course of the next twenty-four hours at the Prefecture for the obtaining of a passport and the assignment of the frontier by which he will quit France.

'And that *le dit Sieur Herzen n'en prétende cause d'ignorance* (what jargon!) *nous lui avons laissé cette copie tant du dit arrêté en tête de cette présente de notre procès-verbal de notification.*'

Oh, my Vyatka colleagues in the secretariat of Tyufyayev; oh, Ardashov, who would write a dozen sheets at one sitting, Veprëv, Shtin, and my drunken head-clerk! Would not their hearts rejoice to know that in Paris, after Voltaire, Beaumarchais, George Sand and Hugo, documents are written like this?

And, indeed, not only they would be delighted, but also my father's village foreman, Vasily Yepifanov, who from profound considerations of politeness would write to his master: 'Your commandment by this present preceding post received, and by the same I have the honour to report . . .'

Ought there to be left one stone upon another of this stupid, vulgar temple *des us et coutumes,* only fitting for a blind, doting old goddess like Themis?

The reading of this document did not produce the result expected; a Parisian thinks that exile from Paris is as bad as the expulsion of Adam from Paradise, and without Eve into the bargain. To me, on the contrary, it was a matter of indifference, and I had already begun to be sick of Parisian life.

'When am I to present myself at the Prefecture?' I asked, assuming a polite air in spite of the wrath which was tearing me to pieces.

'I advise ten o'clock to-morrow morning.'

'With pleasure.'

'How early the spring is beginning this year!' observed the *commissaire* of the city of Paris, and in particular of the *Tuileries arrondissement.*

'Extraordinarily.'

'This is an old-fashioned hotel. Mirabeau used to dine here; that is why it bears his name. Have you really been well satisfied with it?'

'Very well satisfied. Only fancy what it must be to leave it so abruptly!'

'It's certainly unpleasant. . . . The hostess is an intelligent, beautiful woman—Mlle Cousin; she was a great friend of the celebrated Le Normand.'[5]

'Imagine that! What a pity I did not know it! Perhaps she has inherited her art of fortune-telling and might have predicted my *billet doux* from Carlier.'

'Ha, ha! . . . It is my duty, you know. Allow me to wish you good-day.'

'To be sure, anything may happen. I have the honour to wish you good-bye.'

---

[5] Mlle Le Normand (1772–1843), was a well known fortune-teller of the period. (*Tr.*)

Next day I presented myself in the Rue Jérusalem, more celebrated than Le Normand herself. First, I was received by some sort of a youthful spy, with a little beard, a little moustache, and all the manners of an abortive journalist and an unsuccessful democrat. His face and the look in his eyes bore the stamp of that refined corruption of soul, that envious hunger for enjoyment, power, and acquisition, which I have so well learned to read on Western European faces, and which is completely absent from those of the English. It cannot have been long since he had taken up his appointment; he still took pleasure in it, and therefore spoke somewhat condescendingly. He informed me that I must leave within three days, and except for particularly important reasons it was impossible to defer the date. His impudent face, his accent and his gestures were such that without entering into further discussion with him I bowed and then asked, first putting on my hat, when I could see the Prefect.

'The Prefect only receives persons who have asked him for an audience in writing.'

'Allow me to write to him at once.'

He rang the bell, and an old *huissier* with a chain on his breast walked in; saying to him with an air of importance, 'Pen and paper for this gentleman,' the youth nodded at me.

The *huissier* led me into another room. There I wrote to Carlier that I wished to see him in order to explain to him why I had to defer my departure.

On the evening of the same day I received from the Prefecture the laconic answer: '*M. le Préfet* is ready to receive So-and-So tomorrow at two o'clock.'

The same repulsive youth met me next day: he had his own room, from which I concluded that he was something in the nature of the head of a department. Having begun his career so early and with such success, he will go far, if God grants him a long life.

This time he led me into a big office. There a tall, stout, rosy-cheeked gentleman was sitting in a big easy-chair at a huge table. He was one of those persons who are always hot, with white flesh, fat but flabby, plump, carefully tended hands, a necktie reduced to a minimum, colourless eyes and the jovial expression which is usually found in men who are completely immersed in love for their own well-being, and who can have recourse, coldly and without great effort, to extraordinary infamies.

'You wished to see the Prefect,' he said to me; 'but he asks you to excuse him; he has been obliged to go out on very important business. If I can do anything in any way for your pleasure I ask nothing better. Here is an easy-chair: will you sit down?'

All this he brought out smoothly, very politely, screwing up his eyes a little and smiling with the little cushions of flesh which adorned his cheekbones. 'Well, this fellow has been in the service for a long time,' I thought.

'You surely know what I've come about.' He made that gentle movement of the head which everyone makes on beginning to swim, and did not answer.

'I have received an order to leave within three days. Since I know that your minister has the right of expulsion without giving a reason or holding an inquiry, I am not going to inquire why I am being expelled, nor to defend myself; but I have, besides my own house . . .'

'Where is your house?'

'Fourteen, Rue Amsterdam . . . very important business in Paris, and it is difficult for me to abandon it at once.'

'Allow me to ask, what is your business? Is it to do with the house or . . . ?'

'My business is with Rothschild. I have to receive four hundred thousand francs.'

'What?'

'A little over a hundred thousand silver roubles.'

'That's a considerable sum!'

'*C'est une somme ronde.*'

'How much time do you need for completing your business?' he asked, looking at me more blandly, as people look at pheasants stuffed with truffles in the shop-windows.

'From a month to six weeks.'

'That is a terribly long time.'

'My action is being settled in Russia. I should not wonder if it is thanks to that that I am leaving France.'

'How so?'

'A week ago Rothschild told me that Kiselëv spoke ill of me. Probably the Petersburg government wishes to hush up the business; I dare say the ambassador has asked for my expulsion as a favour.'

'*D'abord,*' observed the offended patriot of the Prefecture, assuming an air of dignity and profound conviction, 'France will not permit any other government to interfere in her domestic affairs. I am surprised that such an idea could enter your head. Besides, what can be more natural than that the government, which is doing its utmost to restore order to the suffering people, should exercise its right to remove from the country, in which there is so much inflammable material, foreigners who abuse the hospitality she grants them?'

I determined to get at him by money. This was as sure a method as the use of texts from the Gospel in discussion with a Catholic, and so I answered with a smile:

'For the hospitality of Paris I have paid a hundred thousand francs, and so I considered I had almost settled my account.'

This was even more successful than my *somme ronde*. He was embarrassed, and saying after a brief pause, 'What can we do? It is our duty,' he took my *dossier* from the table. This was the second volume of the novel, the first part of which I had once seen in the hands of Dubelt. Stroking the pages, as though they were good horses, with his plump hand:

'Now look,' he observed, 'your connections, your association with ill-disposed journals' (almost word for word what Sakhtynsky had said to me in 1840), 'and finally the considerable *subventions* which you have given to the most pernicious enterprises, have compelled us to resort to a very unpleasant but necessary step. That step can be no surprise to you. Even in your own country you brought political persecution upon yourself. Like causes lead to like results.'

'I am certain,' I said, 'that the Emperor Nicholas himself has no suspicion of this solidarity; you cannot really approve of his administration.'

'*Un bon citoyen* respects the laws of his country, whatever they may be. . . .'

'Probably on the celebrated principle that it is in any case better there should be bad weather than no weather at all.'

'But to prove to you that the Russian government has no hand in it, I promise to try to get the Prefect to grant a postponement for one month. You will surely not think it strange if we make inquiries of Rothschild concerning your business; it is not so much a question of doubting. . . .'

'Do by all means make inquiries. We are at war, and if it had been of any use for me to have resorted to stratagem in order to remain, do you suppose I should not have employed it?'

But this nice *alter ego* of the Prefect, this man of the world, would not be outdone.

'People who talk like you never say what is untrue,' he replied.

A month later my business was still not completed. We were visited by an old doctor, Palmier, whose agreeable duty it was to make a weekly examination of an interesting class of Parisian women at the Prefecture. Since he gave such a number of certificates of health to the fair sex, I thought he would not refuse to write me out a certificate of sickness. Palmier was acquainted, of course, with everyone in the Prefecture: he promised me to give X. personally the history of my indisposition. To my extreme surprise Palmier came back without a satisfactory answer. This trait is worth noting because there is in it a fraternal similarity between the Russian and French bureaucracies. X. had given no answer but had shuffled, being offended at my not having come in person to inform him that I was ill, in bed, and unable to get up. There was no help for it: I went next day to the Prefecture, glowing with health.

X. asked me most sympathetically about my illness. As I had not had the curiosity to read what the doctor had written, I had to invent an illness. Luckily I remembered Sazonov who, with his great corpulence and insatiable appetite, complained of aneurism. I told X. that I had heart disease and travelling might be very bad for me.

X. was sorry to hear it, and advised me to take care of myself; then he went into the next room, and returned a minute later, saying:

'You may stay for another month. The Prefect has charged me to tell you at the same time that he hopes and desires that your health may be restored during that period; if this should not be so, he would greatly regret it, for he cannot postpone your departure a third time.'

I understood this, and made ready to leave Paris about the 20th of June.

I came across the name of X. once more a year later. This patriot and *bon citoyen* had noiselessly withdrawn from France, forgetting to account for some thousands of francs belonging to people who were not well off, or even poor, who had taken tickets in a Californian lottery run under the patronage of the Prefecture! When the worthy citizen saw that for all his respect for the laws of his country he might find himself in the galleys for swindling, he decided that he preferred a steamer, and went to Genoa. He was a consistent person and although he had failed he did not lose his head. He took advantage of the notoriety he had acquired from the scandal of the Californian lottery and at once offered his services to a society of speculators that had been formed at that time at Turin for building railways; since he was such a trustworthy man the society hastened to accept his services.

The last two months I spent in Paris were insufferable. I was literally *gardé à vue;* my letters arrived shamelessly unsealed and a day late; wherever I went I was followed at a distance by a loathsome individual, who at the corners passed me on with a wink to another.

It must not be forgotten that this was the time of the most frenzied activity of the police. The stupid conservatives and revolutionaries of the Algiers-Lamartine persuasion helped the rogues and knaves surrounding Napoleon, and Napoleon himself, to prepare a network of espionage and surveillance, in order that, by spreading it over the whole of France, they might at any given minute reach out by telegraph from the Ministry of Home Affairs and the Élysée and catch all the active forces in the country and strangle them. Napoleon cleverly used the weapon entrusted to him against these men themselves. The 2nd of December meant the elevation of the police to the rank of a state authority.

There has never anywhere, even in Austria or in Russia, been such a political police as existed in France after the time of the Convention. There are many causes for this, apart from the peculiar *national* bent for a police. Except in England, where the police have nothing in common with Continental espionage, the police are everywhere surrounded by hostile elements and consequently thrown on their own resources. In France, on the contrary, the police is the most popular institution. Whatever government seizes power, its police is *ready;* part of the population will help it with a zest and a fanaticism which have to be restrained and not intensified, and will help it, too, with all the frightful means at the disposal of private persons which are impossible for the police. Where can a man hide from his shop-keeper, his concierge, his tailor, his washerwoman, his butcher, his sister's husband or his brother's wife, especially in Paris, where people do not live in separate houses as they do in London, but in something like coral reefs or hives with a common staircase, a common courtyard and a common concierge?

Condorcet escapes from the Jacobin police and successfully makes his way to a village near the frontier; tired and harassed, he goes into a little inn, sits down before the fire, warms his hands and asks for a piece of chicken. The good-natured old woman who keeps the inn, and who is a great patriot, reasons like this: 'He is covered with dust, so he must have come a *long way;* he asks for chicken, so he must have *money;* his hands are white, so he must be an *aristocrat.*' Putting the chicken into the stove she goes to another inn; there the patriots are in session: a *citoyen,* who is Mucius Scaevola; the liquor-seller and *citoyen,* who is Brutus, and Timoleon, the tailor. They ask for nothing better, and ten minutes later one of the wisest leaders of the

French Revolution is in prison and handed over to the police of Liberty, Equality and Fraternity!

Napoleon, who had the police talent developed to the highest degree, turned his generals into spies and informers. The hangman of Lyons, Fouché, founded a complete theory, system, science of espionage, through the prefects, unbeknown to the prefects, through wanton women and blameless shopkeepers, through servants and coach-men, through doctors and barbers. Napoleon fell, but his tool remained, and not only his tool but the man who wielded it. Fouché went over to the Bourbons; the strength of the espionage lost nothing; on the contrary, it was reinforced by monks and priests. Under Louis-Philippe, in whose reign bribery and easy profit became one of the moral forces of government, half the *petits bourgeois* became his spies, his police chorus, a result to which their service in the National Guard, in itself a police duty, specially contributed.

During the February Republic three or four branches of genuinely secret police forces were formed and several professedly secret ones. There was the police of Ledru-Rollin and the police of Caussidière, there was the police of Marrast and the police of the provisional government, there was the police of order and the police of disorder, the police of Louis-Napoleon and the police of the Duc d'Orléans. All were on the look-out, all were watching each other and informing on each other; if we assume that these secret reports were made from conviction, with the best of motives and gratis, yet they were still secret reports. . . . This pernicious custom, encountering on the one hand sorry failures, and on the other morbid, unbridled thirst for money or pleasure, corrupted a whole generation.

We must not forget, either, the moral indifference, the vacillation of opinion, which was left like sediment from intermittent revolutions and restorations. Men had grown used to regarding as heroism and virtue on one day what would on the next be a crime punished with penal servitude; the laurel wreath and the executioner's brand alternated several times on the same head. By the time they had become accustomed to this a nation of spies was ready.

All the latest discoveries of secret societies and conspiracies, all the denunciations of refugees have been made by false members of societies, bribed friends, men who had won confidence with the object of betrayal.

There were examples on all hands of cowards who, through fear of prison and exile, revealed secrets and destroyed their friends, as a faint-hearted comrade destroyed Konarski. But neither among us nor in Austria is there a legion of young men, cultured, speaking *our* language, making inspired speeches in clubs, writing revolutionary articles and serving as spies.

Moreover, the government of Napoleon is excellently placed for making use of informers of all parties. It represents the revolution and the reaction, war and peace, the year 1789 and Catholicism, the fall of the Bourbons and the four-and-a-half per cents. It is served both by Falloux the Jesuit, Billault the socialist, La Rochejaquelin the legitimist, and a mass of people to whom Louis-Philippe has been a benefactor. The corruption of all parties and shades of opinion naturally flows together and ferments in the Palace of the Tuileries.

◈   ◈   ◈

P.-J. Proudhon

AFTER THE FALL of the June barricades the printing-presses fell too. The frightened journalists were silent. Only old Lamennais rose up like the sombre shadow of a judge, cursed Cavaignac— the Duc of Alba of the June days—and his companions, and sombrely said to the people: 'And you be silent: you are too poor to have the right to speak!'

When the first fright at the state of siege had passed and the newspapers began coming to life again, they found themselves confronted, not with violence, but with a perfect arsenal of legal chicanery and judicial tricks. The old baiting, *par force,* of editors began, the process in which the ministers of Louis-Philippe distinguished themselves. The trick consisted in exhausting the guaranteed fund by a series of lawsuits that invariably ended in prison and a money fine. The fine is paid out of the fund; until this is made up again the paper cannot be published; as soon as it is made good, there is a new lawsuit. This game is always successful, for the legal authorities are always hand in glove with the government in all political prosecutions.

At first Ledru-Rollin, and afterwards Colonel Frappoli[1] as the representative of Mazzini's party, contributed large sums of

---

[1] Frappoli, Ludovico (1815–78), an Italian politician who took part in the revolutionary movement of 1848, was a partisan of Garibaldi's, and always on the extreme left in the Italian Parliament. He reintroduced Freemasonry into Italy. (*Tr.*)

money, but could not save *La Réforme*. All the more outspoken
organs of socialism and republicanism were destroyed by this
method. Among these, and at the very beginning, was Proudhon's *Le Représentant du Peuple*, and later on his *Le Peuple*.
Before one prosecution was over, another began.

One of the editors—it was Duchesne, I think—was brought
three times out of prison to the lawcourts on fresh charges; and
every time was sentenced once more to prison and a fine. When
on the last occasion before the ruin of the paper the verdict was
declared, he said to the prosecutor: *'L'addition, s'il vous plaît!'*
As a matter of fact, it added up to ten years in prison and a fine
of fifty thousand francs.

Proudhon was on trial when his newspaper was stopped after
the 13th of June. The National Guard burst into his printing-
office on that day, broke the printing-press and scattered the
type, as though to assert, in the name of the armed *bourgeois*,
that the period of the utmost violence and despotism of the police
was coming on in France.

The indomitable gladiator, the stubborn Besançon peasant,
would not lay down his arms, but at once contrived to publish a
new journal, *La Voix du Peuple*. It was necessary to find twenty-
four thousand francs for the guarantee fund. Emile Girardin
would have been ready to give it, but Proudhon did not want to
be dependent on him, and Sazonov suggested that I should contribute the money.

I was under a great obligation to Proudhon for my intellectual
development, and after a little consideration I consented, though
I knew that the fund would soon be gone.

The reading of Proudhon, like reading Hegel, gives one a special
method, sharpens one's weapon and furnishes not results but
means. Proudhon is pre-eminently the dialectician, the contro-
versialist of social questions. The French look in him for an
experimentalist and, finding neither an estimate for a Fourierist
phalanstery nor the ecclesiastical jurisdiction of Cabet's Icaria,
shrug their shoulders and lay the book aside.

It is Proudhon's own fault, of course, for having put as the
motto on his *Contradictions*: *'Destruo et aedificabo';* his strength
lay not in creation but in criticism of the existing state of things.
But this mistake has been made from time immemorial by all
who have broken down what was old. Man dislikes mere destruction: when he sets to work to break something down, he is
involuntarily haunted by some ideal of future construction,
though sometimes this is like the song of a mason as he pulls
down a wall.

In the greater number of sociological works the ideals advocated, which almost always either are unattainable at present or boil down to some one-sided solution, are of little consequence; what is of importance is what, in arriving at them, is seen as the question. Socialism touches not only on what was decided by the old empirico-religious way of living, but also on what has passed through the consciousness of partial science; not only on juridical conclusions founded on traditional legislation, but also the conclusions of political economy. It treats the rational way of living of the epoch of guarantees and of the bourgeois economic system as unmediated rudiments for itself to work upon, just as political economy is related to the theocratic-feudal state.

It is in this negation, this volatilisation of the old social tradition, that the fearful power of Proudhon lies; he is as much the poet of dialectics as Hegel is, with the difference that one stands on the tranquil summit of the philosophic movement, and the other thrusts into the hurly-burly of popular commotions and the hand-to-hand fighting of parties.

Proudhon is the first of a new series of French thinkers. His works constitute a revolution in the history not only of socialism but also of French logic. There is more power and fluency in his dialectical robustness than in the most talented of his fellow-countrymen. Intelligent and clear-thinking men like Pierre Leroux[2] and Considérant[3] do not grasp either his point of departure or his method. They are accustomed to play with ideas as with cards already arranged, to walk in a certain attire along the beaten track to familiar places. Proudhon often drives ahead bodily, not afraid of crushing something in his path, with no regret for running down anything he comes across, or for going too far. He has none of that sensitiveness, that rhetorical revolutionary chastity, which in the French takes the place of Protestant pietism . . . that is why he remains a solitary figure among his own people, rather alarming than convincing them with his power.

People say that Proudhon has a German mind. That is not true; on the contrary, his mind is absolutely French: he has that ancestral Gallo-Frankish genius which appears in Rabelais, in Montaigne, in Voltaire, and in Diderot . . . even in Pascal. It is only that he has assimilated Hegel's dialectical method, as he

---

[2] Leroux, Pierre (1797–1871), a prominent follower of Saint-Simon. (*Tr.*)

[3] Considérant, Victor (1808–93), a philosopher and political economist, an advocate of Fourierism. (*Tr.*)

has assimilated also all the methods of Catholic controversy. But neither Hegelian philosophy nor the Catholic theology furnished the content or the character of his writings; for him these are the weapons with which he tests his subject, and these weapons he has squared and adapted in his own way just as he has adapted the French language to his powerful and vigorous thought. Such men stand much too firmly on their own feet to resign themselves to anything or to allow themselves to be lassoed.

'I like your system very much,' an English tourist said to Proudhon.

'But I have no system,' Proudhon answered with annoyance, and he was right.

It is just this that puzzles his fellow-countrymen, who are accustomed to a moral at the end of the fable, to systematic formulae, to classification, to binding, abstract prescriptions.

Proudhon sits by a sick man's bedside and tells him that he is in a very bad way for this reason and for that. You do not help a dying man by constructing an ideal theory of how he might be well if he were not ill, or by suggesting remedies, excellent in themselves, which he cannot take or which are not to be had.

The external signs and manifestations of the financial world serve him, just as the teeth of the animals served Cuvier, as a ladder by which he descends into the mysteries of social life; by means of them he studies the forces that are dragging the sick body towards decomposition. If after every such observation he proclaims a new victory for death, is that his fault? There are no relations here whom one is afraid of alarming: we are ourselves dying this death. The crowd shouts indignantly: 'Remedies! Remedies! Or be quiet about the disease!' But why not speak of it? It is only under despotic governments that we are forbidden to speak of crops failing, of epidemic diseases and of the numbers slain in war. The remedy, obviously, is not easily to be found; they have made plenty of experiments in France since the days of the immoderate blood-letting of 1793; they have treated her with victories and violent exercise, making her march to Egypt and to Russia; they have tried parliamentarianism and *agiotage*, a little republic and a little Napoleon—and has anything done her any good? Proudhon himself once tried his own pathology and came to grief over the People's Bank—though in itself his idea was a good one. Unfortunately, he does not believe in magic charms, or else he would have added to everything: 'League of Nations! League of Nations! Universal Republic! Brotherhood of all the World! *Grande Armeé de la Démocratie!*' He does not use these phrases, he does not spare the Old Believers of the revolution, and for that reason the French look upon him as an egoist, as an individualist, almost as a renegade and a traitor.

I remember Proudhon's works, from his reflections *On Property* to his *Financial Guide;* many of his ideas have changed—a man could hardly live through a period like ours and whistle the same duet in A minor like Platon Mikhaylovich in *Woe from Wit.* What leaps to the eye in these changes is the inner unity that binds them all together, from the essay written as a school task at Besançon Academy to the *carmen horrendum* of Stock Exchange depravity,[4] which has recently been published; the same order of thought, developing, varying in aspect, reflecting events, runs through the *Contradictions of Political Economy,* through his *Confessions* and through his *Journal.*

Sluggishness of thought is an appurtenance of religion and doctrinairianism; they assume a wilful narrow-mindedness, a definitive circumscription, living apart or in a narrow circle of its own that rejects everything new that life offers . . . or at any rate not troubling itself about it. The real truth must lie under the influence of events, must reflect them, while remaining true to itself, or it would be not the *living truth,* but an eternal truth, at rest from the tempests of this world in the deadly stillness of sacred stagnation.[5] Where, and on what occasion, I have sometimes asked, was Proudhon false to the organic basis of his view of things? I have been answered each time that he was so in his political mistakes, his blunders in revolutionary diplomacy. For his political mistakes he was, of course, responsible as a journalist; but even here it was not before himself that he was guilty: on the contrary, some of his mistakes were due to his believing more in his principles than in the party to which he, against his own will, belonged and with which he had

---

[4] "Even in despair [because he couldn't support his family after he was released from prison in 1852] Proudhon had no difficulty in refusing . . . a subvention of 20,000 francs offered through the patronage of Prince Jerome Bonaparte. He preferred to earn his living by hack work and brought out an anonymous Manual for Speculators on the Exchange."—J. Hamden Jackson: *Marx, Proudhon and European Socialism* (Macmillan, n.d.). "In this year," adds Jackson, "Karl Marx, in London, had to borrow two pounds to pay for his daughter's coffin and pawned his overcoat to [finance] a pamphlet." The 1850s weren't kind to radicals. (*D.M.*)

[5] In Stuart Mill's new book *On Liberty,* he uses an excellent expression in regard to these truths settled once and for ever: 'the deep slumber of a decided opinion.'

nothing in common and was only associated by hatred for a common foe.

It was not in political activity that his strength lay; it was not there that he found the basis of the thought which he invested in the panoply of his dialectic. Quite the contrary: it is everywhere plainly to be seen that politics in the sense of the old liberalism and constitutional republicanism were, in his eyes, of secondary importance, as something passing, half elapsed. He was not indifferent to political questions and was ready to make compromises because he did not ascribe any special importance to the forms, which in his view were not essential. All who have abandoned the Christian point of view stand in a similar relationship to the religious question. I may recognise that the constitutional religion of Protestantism is somewhat more liberal than the autocracy of Catholicism, but I cannot take to heart the question of church or creed; in consequence of this I probably make mistakes and concessions which the most ordinary graduate in divinity or parish priest would avoid.

Doubtless there was no place for Proudhon in the National Assembly as it was constituted, and his individuality was lost in that den of the *petite bourgeoisie*. In the *Confessions of a Revolutionary* Proudhon tells us that he was completely at a loss in the Assembly. And indeed what could have been done there by a man who said to Marrast's constitution, that sour fruit of the seven months' work of seven hundred heads: 'I give my vote against your constitution, not only because it's bad, but because it's a constitution.'

The parliamentary rabble greeted one of his speeches:[6] 'The speech to the *Moniteur*, the speaker to the madhouse!' I do not think that in the memory of man there had been many of such parliamentary scenes from the days when the Archbishop of

---

[6] On 13 July 1848, the Constituent Assembly debated Proudhon's Utopian Bill which proposed the taxation of movable and real property by a single tax at the rate of one third of the revenue from it. This enraged the *bourgeois* majority in the Assembly and the *bourgeois* press. His speech was accompanied by obstruction from the deputies, cries that the speaker should be sent to a madhouse, etc. Marx observed that Proudhon's speech in defence of his project was 'an act of lofty manliness,' although it also displayed how little he understood all that had happened. The chief speaker who opposed Proudhon was Thiers. The Assembly rejected Proudhon's project (only two votes were cast for him, one of them his own) as an incitement to attack property and 'an abominable *attentat* on the principles of social morality.' (*A.S.*)

Alexandria brought with him to Ecumenical Councils lay
brothers armed with clubs in the name of the Virgin, till the
days of the Washington Senators who proved the benefits of
slavery to each other with the stick.[7]

But even there Proudhon succeeded in rising to his full height
and left in the midst of the wrangling a glowing footprint.

Thiers in rejecting Proudhon's financial scheme made an
insinuation about the moral depravity of the men who disseminated such doctrines. Proudhon mounted the tribune, and with
his stooping figure and his menacing air of a stocky dweller in
the fields said to the smiling old creature:

'Speak of finance, but do not speak of morality: I may take
that as personal, as I have already told you in committee. If you
persist, I—I shall not challenge you to a duel' (Thiers smiled);
'no, your death is not enough for me—that would prove nothing.
I challenge you to another sort of contest. Here from this tribune
I shall tell the whole story of my life, fact by fact, and anyone
may remind me if I forget or omit something; and then let my
opponent tell the story of his!'

The eyes of all were turned upon Thiers; he sat scowling, and
there was no trace of the smile, and no answer either.

The hostile Chamber fell silent and Proudhon, looking contemptuously at the champions of religion and the family, came
down from the platform. That was where his strength lay: in
these words of his is clearly heard the language of the new world
coming with its own standards and its own penalties.

After the Revolution of February Proudhon was foretelling
what France had come to; in a thousand different keys he repeated, 'Beware, do not trifle; "this is not Catiline at your gates,
but death."' The French shrugged their shoulders. The skull,
the scythe, the hour-glass—all the trappings of death—were not
to be seen. How could it be death?—it was 'a momentary eclipse,
the after-dinner nap of a great people!' Eventually many people
discerned that things were in a bad way. Proudhon was less
downcast than others, less frightened, because he had foreseen it;

---

[7] In the Senate debate on the Kansas-Nebraska Act (1856), Senator
Charles Sumner of Massachusetts, a leading opponent of slavery, denounced the Act as "a swindle" and its two main defenders, Senators
Douglas and Butler, as "myrmidons of slavery." Two days later a young
Congressman, one Preston Brooks of South Carolina, Butler's nephew,
achieved his Oswaldian footnote in history by invading the Senate
chamber, shouting that Sumner had libeled his uncle and his state and
then attacking him with a heavy cane. It took Sumner three years to
recover. (*D.M.*)

then he was accused of callousness and even of having invited disaster. They say the Chinese Emperor pulls the Court star-gazer's pigtail every year when the latter announces that the days are beginning to draw in.

The genius of Proudhon is actually antipathetic to the rhetori-cal French; his language is offensive to them. The Revolution developed its own special puritanism, narrow and intolerant, its own obligatory jargon; and patriots reject everything that is not written in the official form, just as the Russian judges do. Their criticism stops short at their symbolic books, such as the *Contrat Social* and *Declaration of the Rights of Man*. Being men of faith, they hate analysis and doubt; being men of conspiracy, they do everything in common and turn everything into a party ques-tion. An independent mind is hateful to them as a disturber of discipline and they dislike original ideas even in the past. Louis Blanc is almost vexed by the eccentric genius of Montaigne. It is upon this Gallic feeling, which seeks to subject individuality to the herd, that their partiality for *equalising*, for the uniformity of military formation, for centralisation—that is, for despotism— is based.

The blasphemy of the French and their sweeping judgments, are more due to naughtiness, love of mischief, the pleasure of teasing, than the need for analysis, than the scepticism that sucks the soul. The Frenchman has an endless number of little prejudices, minute religions, and these he will defend with the fire of a Don Quixote and the obduracy of a *raskolnik*.[8] That is why they cannot forgive Montaigne or Proudhon for their free-thinking and lack of reverence for generally accepted idols. Like the Petersburg censorship, they permit a jest at a titular coun-cillor, but you must not touch a privy councillor. In 1850 Girardin printed in the *Presse* a bold, new idea, that the bases of right are not eternal but vary with the development of history. What an uproar this article excited! The campaign of abuse, of cries of horror, of charges of immorality, promoted by the *Gazette de France* was kept up for months.

To assist in re-establishing such an organ as the *Peuple* was worth a sacrifice; I wrote to Sazonov and Chojecki that I was ready to supply the guarantee fund.

Until then I had seen very little of Proudhon; I had met him twice at the lodgings of Bakunin, with whom he was very inti-mate. Bakunin was living at that time with Adolf Reichel in an extremely modest lodging at the other side of the Seine in the

---

[8] Schismatic. (*R.*)

Rue de Bourgogne. Proudhon often went there to listen to
Reichel's Beethoven and Bakunin's Hegel: the philosophical
discussions lasted longer than the symphonies. They reminded
me of the famous all-night vigils of Bakunin with Khomyakov at
Chaadayev's and at Madame Yelagin's, also over Hegel. In 1847
Karl Vogt, who also lived in the Rue de Bourgogne, and often
visited Reichel and Bakunin, was bored one evening with listening to the endless discussions on phenomenology, and went home
to bed. Next morning he went round for Reichel, for they were
to go to the Jardin des Plantes together; he was surprised to hear
conversation in Bakunin's study at that early hour. He opened
the door—Proudhon and Bakunin were sitting in the same places
before the burnt-out embers in the fireplace, finishing in a brief
summing-up the argument begun overnight.

At first, afraid of the humble rôle of our fellow-countrymen,
and of being patronised by great men, I did not try to become
intimate even with Proudhon himself, and I believe I was not
altogether wrong. Proudhon's letter in answer to mine was
courteous, but cold and somewhat reserved.

I wanted to show him from the very first that he was not
dealing with a mad *prince russe* who was giving the money from
revolutionary dilettantism, and still more from ostentation, nor
with an orthodox admirer of French journalists, deeply grateful
for their accepting twenty-four thousand francs from him, nor,
finally, with a dull-witted *bailleur de fonds* who imagined that
providing the guarantee funds for such a paper as the *Voix du
Peuple* was a serious business investment. I wanted to show him
that I knew very well what I was doing, that I had my own
definite object, and so wanted to have a definite influence on the
paper. While I accepted unconditionally all that he wrote about
money, I demanded in the first place the right to insert articles,
my own and other people's; secondly, the right to superintend all
the foreign section, to recommend editors, correspondents, and so
on for it, and to require payment for these for articles published.
This last may seem strange, but I can confidently assert that the
National and the *Réforme* would have opened their eyes wide if
any foreigner had ventured to ask to be paid for an article. They
would take it for impudence or madness.

Proudhon agreed to my requirements, but still they made him
wince. This is what he wrote to me at Geneva on the 29th of
August, 1849: 'And so the thing is settled: under my general
direction you have a share in the editorship of the paper; your
articles must be accepted with *no restriction*, except that to
which the editors are bound by respect for their *own opinions*
and fear of legal responsibility. Agreed in ideas, we can only

differ in conclusions; as for commenting on events abroad, we leave them entirely to you. You and we are missionaries of one idea. You will see our line in general controversy, and you will have to support it: I am sure I shall never have to *correct your views;* I should regard that as the greatest calamity. I tell you frankly, the whole success of the paper depends on our agreement. The democratic and social question must be raised to the level of the undertaking of a European League. To suppose that we shall not agree means to suppose that we have not the essential conditions for publishing the paper, and that *we had better be silent.'*

To this severe missive I replied by the despatch of twenty-four thousand francs and a long letter, perfectly friendly, but firm. I told him how completely I agreed with him theoretically, adding that, like a true Scythian, I saw with joy that the old world was falling into ruins, and believed that it was our mission to announce to it its imminent demise. *'Your fellow-countrymen are far from sharing these ideas.* I know one liberal Frenchman—that is you. Your revolutionaries are conservatives. They are Christians without knowing it, and monarchists fighting for a republic. You alone have raised the question of negation and revolution to a scientific level, and you have been the first to tell France that there is no salvation for an edifice that is crumbling from within, and that there is nothing worth saving from it; that its very conceptions of freedom and revolution are saturated with conservatism and reaction. As a matter of fact the political republicans are but one of the variations on the same constitutional tune on which Guizot, Odilon Barrot and others are playing their own variations. This is the view that should be pursued in the analysis of the latest European events, in attacking reaction, Catholicism and monarchism, not in the ranks of our enemies—that is extremely easy—but in our own camp. We must reveal the mutual guarantees existing between the democrats and the authorities. If we are not afraid to touch the victors, let us not from false sentimentality be afraid to touch the vanquished also.

'I am thoroughly convinced that if the inquisition of the Republic does not kill our newspaper, it will be the best newspaper in Europe.'

Even now I am convinced of this. But how Proudhon and I could think that Napoleon's government, which never stood on ceremony, would put up with a paper like that, it is difficult to explain.

Proudhon was pleased with my letter, and wrote to me on the 15th of December from the Conciergerie prison:

'I am very glad to have been associated with you in the same or similar work. I, too, have written something in the nature of the philosophy[9] of revolution under the title of *The Confessions of a Revolutionary*. You will not perhaps find in it the *verve barbare* to which you have been trained by German philosophy. Do not forget that I am writing for the French who, for all their revolutionary fire, are, it must be admitted, far inferior to their rôle. However limited my view may be, it is a hundred thousand *toises* higher than the loftiest heights of our journalistic, academic and literary world. I have enough in me to be a giant among them for another ten years.

'I entirely share your opinion of the so-called Republicans; of course, they are only one species of the whole genus doctrinaire. As regards these questions there is no need for us to try to convince each other; you will find in me and my colleagues men who will go hand in hand with you. . . .

'I too think a peaceful methodical advance by imperceptible transitions, such as the political economists and philosophical historians want, is no longer possible for the revolution; we must make fearful leaps. But as journalists announcing the coming catastrophe, it is not for us to present it as something inevitable and just, or we shall be hated and kicked out; and we have got to live. . . .'

The paper was a wonderful success. Proudhon from his prison cell conducted his orchestra in masterly fashion. His articles were full of originality, fire and that exasperation which is fanned by imprisonment.

'What are you, *M. le Président?*' he writes in one article, speaking of Napoleon; 'tell us—man, woman, hermaphrodite, beast or fish?' And we still thought that such a paper might be kept going!

The subscribers were not numerous, but the street sales were large; thirty-five thousand to forty thousand copies a day were sold. The sale of particularly remarkable numbers, those, for instance, in which Proudhon's articles appeared, was even greater; fifty thousand to sixty thousand were printed, and often on the following day copies were being sold for a franc instead of a sou.[10]

But for all that, by the 1st of March, that is, six months later,

---

[9] I had then published *Vom andern Ufer* (*From the Other Shore*).

[10] My answer to the speech of Donoso Cortés of which fifty thousand copies were printed, was sold out; and when two or three days later I asked for a few copies for myself, they had to be searched for and bought in bookshops.

not only was there no cash in hand, but already part of the
guarantee fund had gone in payment of fines. Ruin was inevitable and Proudhon hastened it considerably. This was how it
happened. On one occasion at his rooms in Ste Pélagie, I found
d'Alton-Shée and two of the editors. D'Alton-Shée is that peer of
France who frightened all the peers by his answer from the
platform to the question,

'Why, are you not a Catholic?'

'No! and what's more, I am not a Christian at all, and I don't
know whether I am a deist.'

He was saying to Proudhon that the last numbers of the *Voix
du Peuple* were feeble: Proudhon was looking through them and
growing more and more morose; then, thoroughly incensed, he
turned to the editors:

'What is the meaning of this? You take advantage of my being
in prison, and go to sleep there in the office. No, gentlemen: if
you go on like this I shall refuse to have anything to do with the
paper, and shall publish the grounds for my refusal. I don't want
my name to be dragged in the mud; you need someone to stand
behind you and look over every line. The public takes it for my
newspaper: no, I must put a stop to this. To-morrow I shall send
an article to cancel the bad effects of your scribbling, and I shall
show how I understand what ought to be the spirit of our paper.'

Seeing his irritation, it might have been expected that the
article would not be of the most moderate, but he surpassed our
expectations: his *'Vive l'Empereur!'* was a dithyramb of irony—
frightful, virulent irony.

In addition to a new action against the paper the government
avenged itself on Proudhon in its own way. He was transferred
to a horrible room—that is, given a far worse one than before:
the window was half boarded up so that nothing could be seen
but the sky; no one was admitted to see him, and a special sentry
was stationed at the door. And these measures, unseemly for the
correction of a naughty boy of sixteen, were taken seven years
ago against one of the greatest thinkers of our age. Men have
grown no wiser since the days of Socrates, no wiser since the
days of Galileo; they have only become more petty. This disrespect for genius, however, is a new phenomenon that has reappeared during the last ten years. From the time of the
Renaissance talent has to some extent become a protection;
neither Spinoza nor Lessing was shut in a dark room or stood in
a corner. Such men are sometimes persecuted and killed, but
they are not humiliated in trivial ways; they are sent to the
scaffold, but not to the workhouse.

Bourgeois Imperial France is fond of equality.

Though persecuted, Proudhon still struggled in his chains; he still made an effort to bring out the *Voix du Peuple* in 1850; but this attempt was strangled at once. My guarantee money had been seized to the last farthing; the one man in France who still had something to say had no choice but to be silent.

I saw Proudhon in Ste Pélagie; for the last time.[11] I was being expelled from France, while he still had two years of prison. It was a mournful parting; there was no shadow of hope in the near future. Proudhon maintained a concentrated silence, whilst I was boiling with vexation; we both had many thoughts in our minds, but no desire to speak.

I have heard a great deal of his roughness, *rudesse*, and intolerance; I have had no experience of anything like it in my own case. What soft people call his harshness was the tense muscle of the fighter; his scowling brow showed only the powerful working of his mind: in his anger he reminded me of a wrathful Luther or of Cromwell ridiculing the Rump. He knew that I understood him and, knowing too how few did understand him, appreciated it. He knew that he was considered an undemonstrative man; and hearing from Michelet of the disaster that had overtaken my mother and Kolya, he wrote to me from Ste Pélagie, among other things: 'Is it possible that fate must attack us from that direction too? I cannot get over this terrible calamity. I love you, and carry your image deep here in this heart which so many think is of stone.'

Since then I have not seen him: in 1851 when, by the kindness of Léon Faucher, I visited Paris for a few days, he had been sent away to some central prison. A year later, when I was passing through Paris in secret, Proudhon was ill at Besançon.

Proudhon had his sensitive spot that had been bruised before, and there he was incorrigible; there the limit of his character was reached and, as is always the case, beyond it he was a conservative and a follower of tradition. I am speaking of his views of family life and of the significance of woman in general.

'How lucky is our friend N.!' Proudhon would say jestingly; 'his wife is not so stupid that she can't make a good *pot-au-feu* and not clever enough to discuss his articles. That's all that is necessary for domestic happiness.'

In this jest Proudhon laughingly expressed the essential basis of his view of woman. His conceptions of family relationships were coarse and reactionary, but they expressed not the *bourgeois* element of the townsman, but rather the stubborn feeling

---

[11] In the first three weeks of June 1850. (*A.S.*)

of the rustic *paterfamilias*, haughtily regarding woman as a subordinate worker and himself as the autocratic head of the family.

A year and a half after this was written, Proudhon published his great work on *Justice in the Church and in Revolution*.

This book, for which France, now become *farouche*, condemned him once more to three years' imprisonment,[12] I read through attentively, and I closed the third volume oppressed by gloomy thoughts.

A grievous . . . grievous time! . . . The atmosphere of decomposition stupefies the strongest. . . .

This 'brilliant fighter,' too, could not endure it, and was broken: in his last work I see the same might of controversy, the same flourish, but it brings him now to preconceived results; it is no longer free in the very fullest sense. Towards the end of the book I watched over Proudhon as Kent watched over King Lear, expecting him to recover his reason, but he raved more and more—there were the same fits of intolerance, of unbridled speech, as in Lear; and in the same way 'every inch' reveals talent, but . . . a talent that is 'touched' . . . and he runs with a corpse, only not a daughter's but a mother's, whom he takes to be living.[13]

Latin thought, religious in its very negation, superstitious in doubt, rejecting one set of authorities in the name of another, has rarely gone further, rarely plunged more deeply *in medias res* of reality, rarely freed itself from all fetters, with such dialectic boldness and certainty as in this book. In it not only the crude dualism of religion but the subtle dualism of philosophy is cast off; the mind is set free not only from heavenly phantoms but from those of the earth, it strides beyond the sentimental apotheosis of humanity and the fatalism of progress, and has none of the invariable litanies of brotherhood, democracy, and progress which are so pitifully wearisome in the midst of wrangling and violence. Proudhon sacrificed the idols and the language of revolution to the understanding of it, and transferred morality to its only real basis, the heart of man, recognising reason alone, and no other gods but it.

And after all that, the great iconoclast was frightened of human nature's being set free; for, having freed it abstractly, he fell back once more into metaphysics, endowed it with a *fictitious will*, could not manage it, and led it to be immolated to an

---

[12] In 1858. Proudhon did not serve this sentence, but emigrated to Belgium, where he lived till 1862. (*A.S.*)

[13] I have partly modified my opinion of this work of Proudhon (1866).

inhuman god, the cold god of *justice*, the god of equilibrium, of quiet and repose, the god of the Brahmins, who seek to lose all that is personal and to be dissolved, to come to rest in an infinite world of nothingness.

On the empty altar were set up scales. This would be a new Caudine Forks for humanity.

The 'justice' which is his goal is not even the artistic harmony of Plato's Republic, the elegant equilibrium of passion and sacrifice; the Gallic tribune takes nothing from 'anarchic and frivolous Greece'; he stoically tramples personal feelings under foot, and does not seek to conciliate them with the sacrifice of the family and the commune. His 'free personality' is a sentry and a workman with no fixed terms of service; he will serve and must stand on guard until he is relieved by death; he must kill in himself all personal passion, everything outside duty, because he is not himself: his meaning, his essence, lie outside himself; he is the instrument of justice; he is pre-destined, like the Virgin Mary, to bear the idea in suffering and to bring it into the world for the salvation of the state.

The family, the first cell of society, the first cradle of justice, is doomed to everlasting, inescapable toil; it must serve as the altar of purification from the personal; in it the passions must be stamped out. The austere Roman family in the workshop of to-day is Proudhon's ideal. Christianity has softened family life too much: it has preferred Mary to Martha, the dreamer to the housewife: it has forgiven the sinner and held out a hand to the penitent, because she loved much; but in Proudhon's family, just what is needed is to love little. And that is not all: Christianity puts the individual far higher than his family relationships. It has said to the son: 'Forsake father and mother and follow me'— to the son who in the name of Proudhon's *incarnation of justice* must be shackled once more in the stocks of absolute paternal authority, who in his father's lifetime can have no freedom, least of all in the choice of a wife. He is to be tempered in slavery, to become in his turn a tyrant over the children who are born without love, from duty, for the continuation of the family. In this family marriage will be indissoluble, but in return it will be as cold as ice. Marriage is properly a victory over love; the less love there is between the cook-wife and the workman-husband the better. And to think that I should meet these old, shabby bogeys from right wing Hegelianism in the writings of Proudhon!

Feeling is banished, everything is frozen, the colours have vanished, nothing is left but the dull, exhausting, inescapable toil of the proletariat of to-day, the toil from which at least the aristocratic family of ancient Rome, based on slavery, was free: the poetic beauty of the Church is no more, nor the delirium of faith, nor hopes of paradise; even verse by that time 'will no longer be written,' so Proudhon asserts, but in return work will 'be increased.' For individual freedom, for the right of initiative, for independence, one may well sacrifice the lullaby of religion; but to sacrifice everything for the incarnation of the idea of justice—what nonsense!

Man is doomed to toil: he must labour till his hand drops and the son takes from the cold fingers of his father the plane or the hammer and carries on the everlasting work. But what if among the sons there happens to be one with a little more sense, who lays down the chisel and asks:

'But what are we wearing ourselves out for?'

'For the triumph of justice,' Proudhon tells him.

And the new Cain answers:

'But who charged me with the triumph of justice?'

'Who?—why, is not your whole vocation, your whole life, the incarnation of justice?'

'Who set up that object?' Cain will answer. 'It is too stale; there is no God, but the Commandments remain. Justice is not my vocation; work is not a duty but a necessity; for me the family is not life-long fetters but the setting for my life, for my development. You want to keep me in slavery, but I rebel against you, against your yard-stick, just as you have been re-volting all your life against bayonets, capital, and Church, just as all the French revolutionaries rebelled against the feudal and Catholic tradition. Or do you think that after the taking of the Bastille, after the Terror, after war and famine, after *bourgeois* king and *bourgeois* republic, I shall believe you when you say that Romeo had no right to love Juliet because those old fools of Montagues and Capulets kept up an everlasting feud, and that, even at thirty or forty, I must not choose the companion of my life without my father's permission, that a woman who has been betrayed must be punished and disgraced? Why, what do you take me for with your justice?'

And in support of Cain, we would add, from our dialectical side, that Proudhon's whole conception of an *aim* is utterly inconsistent. This teleology is also theology; this is the February Republic, that is, the same as the July Monarchy, but without Louis-Philippe. What difference is there between predetermined expediency and providence?[14]

---

[14] Proudhon himself said: '*Rien ne ressemble plus à la préméditation que la logique des faits.*'

After emancipating human nature beyond the limit, Proudhon took fright when he looked at his contemporaries, and, in order that these convicts, these 'ticket-of-leave' men, might do no mischief, he tried to catch them in the trap of the Roman family.

The doors of the restored *atrium*, without its *Lares* and *Penates*, have been flung open; but through them no longer is Anarchy seen, or the annihilation of authority and the state, but a strict order of seniority, with centralisation, with interference in family affairs, with inheritance and deprivation of it as a punishment; and with these all the old Roman sins look out of every crevice with the dead eyes of statues.

The family of antiquity naturally implies the ancient conception of the fatherland with its jealous patriotism, that ferocious virtue which has shed ten times more blood than all the vices put together.

Man bound in serfdom to the family becomes once more the bondslave of the soil. His movements are circumscribed, he has put down roots into his land; only upon it he is what he is: 'the Frenchman living in Russia,' says Proudhon, 'is a Russian, and not a Frenchman.' No more colonies, no more factories abroad; let every man live at home. . . .

'Holland will not perish,' said William of Orange in the fearful hour; 'she will go aboard ships and sail off to Asia, and here we shall break down the dykes.' It is peoples like that who are free.

The English are like that: as soon as they begin to be oppressed, they sail over the ocean and there found a younger, freer England. And yet nobody, of course, could say of the English that they do not love their country, or that they are lacking in national feeling. Sailing out in all directions, England has peopled half the world; while France, lacking in sap, has lost one set of colonies and does not know what to do with the rest. She does not even need them; France is pleased with herself and clings more and more to her centre, and the centre to its master. What independence can there be in such a country?

On the other hand, how can one abandon France, *la belle France*? 'Is not she even now the freest country in the world, is not her language the best language, her literature the finest literature, is not her syllabic line more musical than the Greek hexameter?' Moreover her universal genius appropriates to herself the thought and the works of all ages and all countries: 'have not Shakespeare and Kant, Goethe and Hegel been made at home in France?' And what is more: Proudhon forgot that she refined them and dressed them, as landowners dress peasants when they take them into their household.

Proudhon concludes his book with a Catholic prayer adapted to socialism; all he had to do was to secularise a few Church phrases, and to put the Phrygian cap on them in the place of the cowl, for the prayer of the 'Byzantine' bishops to be at once the very thing for the bishop of socialism.

What chaos! Proudhon, emancipated from everything except reason, wished to remain not only a husband after the style of Bluebeard, but also a French nationalist—with his literary chauvinism and his unlimited paternal authority; and therefore after the strong, vigorous mind of a free man one seems to hear the voice of a savage greybeard, dictating his will and wishing now to preserve for his children the tottering edifice that he has been undermining all his life.

The Latin world does not like freedom, it only likes to sue for it; it sometimes finds the force for liberation, never for freedom. Is it not sad to see such men as Auguste Comte and Proudhon setting up with their last word, the one a sort of mandarin hierarchy, the other his domestic penal servitude and apotheosis of an inhuman *pereat mundus, fiat justitia!*

Appendix: Second Thoughts on the Woman Question

I

. . . ON ONE HAND we have Proudhon's family, submissively welded and tightly clinched together, indissoluble marriage, indivisible paternal authority—a family in which for the sake of the community the persons perish, *except one*, the ferocious marriage in which is accepted the unchangeability of feelings and the abracadabra of a vow; on the other hand we have the doctrines that are springing up in which marriage and the family are unbound from each other, the irresistible force of passion is recognised, the non-liability of the past and the independence of the individual.

On one hand we have woman almost stoned for infidelity; on the other jealousy itself put *hors la loi* as a morbid, monstrous feeling of egoism and proprietorship and the romantic subversion of natural, healthy ideas.

Where is the truth . . . where is the middle line? Twenty-three years ago I was already seeking a way out of this forest of contradictions.

We are bold in denial and always ready to fling any of our Peruns[1] into the river, but the Peruns of home and family life are somehow 'waterproof,'[2] they always bob up. Perhaps there is no sense left in them—but life is left; evidently the weapons used against them simply glided over their snaky scales, have felled them, stunned them . . . but have not killed them.

Jealousy . . . Fidelity . . . Infidelity . . . Purity. . . . Dark forces, menacing words, thanks to which rivers of tears have flowed, and rivers of blood—words that set us shuddering like the memory of the Inquisition, of torture, of the plague . . . and yet they are the words under the shadow of which, as under the sword of Damocles, the family has lived and is living.

There is no turning them out of doors by abuse or by denial. They remain round the corner, slumbering, ready on the slightest occasion to destroy everything near and far, to destroy us ourselves. . . .

Clearly we must abandon our honourable intention of utterly extinguishing these smouldering flames and modestly confine ourselves to humanely guiding and subduing the consuming fire. You can no more bridle passions with logic than you can justify them in the lawcourts. Passions are facts and not dogmas.

Jealousy, moreover, has always enjoyed special privileges. In itself a violent and *perfectly natural* passion, which hitherto, instead of being muzzled and kept under, has only been stimulated. The Christian doctrine which, through hatred of the body, sets everything fleshly on an extraordinary height, and the aristocratic worship of blood and purity of race, have developed to the point of absurdity the conception of a mortal affront, a blot that cannot be washed off. Jealousy has received the *jus gladii*, the right of judgment and revenge. It has become a duty of *honour*, almost a virtue. All this will not stand a moment's criticism—but yet there still remains at the bottom of the heart a very real, insurmountable feeling of pain, of unhappiness, called jealousy, a feeling as elementary as the feeling of love itself, resisting every effort to deny it, an 'irreducible' feeling.

. . . Here again are the everlasting limits, the Caudine Forks

---

[1] '. . . the Prince' (Vladimir) '. . . ordered that Perun should be bound to a horse's tail and dragged along Borichev to the river. . . . After they had thus dragged the idol along they cast it in to the Dnieper.' Samuel H. Cross: *The Russian Primary Chronicle* (Cambridge, Mass., 1930), p. 204. (*R.*)

[2] English in the original. (*R.*)

under which history drives us. On both sides there is truth, on both there is falsehood. A brusque *entweder–oder* will lead you nowhere. At the moment of the complete negation of one of the terms it comes back, just as after the last quarter of the moon the first appears on the other side.

Hegel removed these boundary-posts of human reason, by rising to the *absolute spirit;* in it they did not vanish but were *transmuted, fulfilled,* as German theological science expressed it: this is mysticism, philosophical theodicy, allegory and reality purposely mixed up. All religious reconciliations of the irreconcilable are won by means of *redemptions,* that is, by sacred transmutation, sacred deception, a solution which solves nothing but is taken on trust. What can be more antithetical than free-will and necessity? Yet by faith even they are easily reconciled. Man will accept without a murmur the justice of punishment for an action which was pre-ordained.

Proudhon himself, in a different range of questions, was far more humane than German philosophy. From economic contradictions he escapes by the recognition of both sides under the restraint of a higher principle. Property as a right and property as theft are set side by side in everlasting balance, everlastingly complementary, under the ever-growing *Weltherrschaft* of *justice.* It is clear that the argument and the contradictions are transferred to another sphere, and that it is the conception of justice we have to call to account rather than the right of property.

The simpler, the less mystical and the less one-sided, the more real and practically applicable the higher principle is, the more completely it brings the contradictory terms to their lowest denomination.

The absolute, 'all-embracing' spirit of Hegel is replaced in Proudhon by the menacing idea of justice.

But the problem of the passions is not likely to be solved by that either. Passion is intrinsically unjust; justice is abstracted from the personal, it is 'interpersonal'—passion is only individual.

The solution here lies not in the lawcourt but in the humane development of individual character, in its removal from emotional self-centredness into the light of day, in the development of common interests.

The radical elimination of jealousy implies eliminating love for the individual, replacing it by love for woman or for man, by love of the sex in general. But it is just the personal, the individual, that pleases; it is just that which gives colouring, tone, sensuality to the whole of our life. Our emotion is personal, our happiness and unhappiness are personal happiness and unhappiness.

Doctrinairianism with all its logic is of as little comfort in personal sorrow as the consolations of the Romans with their rhetoric. Neither the tears of loss nor the tears of jealousy can be wiped away, nor should they be, but it is right and possible that they should flow humanely . . . and that they should be equally free from monastic poison, the ferocity of the beast, and the wail of the wounded owner of property.[3]

II

To REDUCE the relationships of man and woman to a casual sexual encounter is just as impossible as to exalt and bolt them together in marriage which is indissoluble before the planks of the coffin. Both the one and the other may be met with at the extremes of sexual and marital relationships, as a special case, as an exception, but not as a general rule. The sexual relationship will be broken off or will continually tend towards a closer and firmer union, just as the indissoluble marriage will tend towards liberation from external bonds.

People have continually protested against both extremes. Indissoluble marriage has been accepted by them hypocritically, or

---

[3] As I was correcting the proofs of this I came upon a French newspaper with an extremely characteristic incident in it. Near Paris a student had a liaison with a girl, which was discovered. The girl's father went to the student and on his knees besought him, with tears, to rehabilitate his daughter's honour and marry her; the student refused with contumely. The kneeling father gave him a slap in the face, the student challenged him, they shot at each other; during the duel the old man had a stroke which crippled him. The student was disconcerted, and 'decided to marry,' and the girl was grieved, and also decided to marry. The newspaper adds that this happy *dénouement* will no doubt do much to promote the old father's recovery. Can this have happened outside a madhouse? Can China or India, at whose grotesqueries and follies we mock so much, furnish anything uglier or stupider than this story? I will not say more immoral. This Parisian romance is a hundredfold more wicked than all the roastings of widows or buryings of vestal virgins. In those cases there was religious faith, which removed all personal responsibility, but in this case there is nothing but conventional, visionary ideas of external honour, of external reputation. . . . Is it not clear from this story what the student was like? Why should the destiny of the girl be shackled to him *à perpétuité?* Why was she ruined to save her reputation? Oh, Bedlam! (1866.)

in the heat of the moment. Casual intimacy has never had complete recognition; it has always been concealed, just as marriage has been a subject of boasting. All attempts at the official regulation of brothels, although aiming at their restriction, are offensive to the moral sense of society, which in organisation sees acceptance. The scheme of a gentleman in Paris, in the days of the Directorate, for establishing privileged brothels with their own hierarchy and so on, was even in those days received with hisses and overwhelmed by a story of laughter and contempt.

The healthy, normal life of man avoids the monastery just as much as the cattle-yard; the sexlessness of the monk, which the Church esteems above marriage, as much as the childless gratification of the passions. . . .

Marriage is for Christianity a concession, an inconsistency, a weakness. Christianity regards marriage as society regards concubinage.

The monk and the Catholic priest are condemned to perpetual celibacy by way of reward for their foolish triumph over human nature.

Christian marriage on the whole is sombre and unjust; it establishes inequality, which the Gospel preaches against, and delivers the wife into slavery to the husband. The wife is sacrificed, love (hateful to the Church) is sacrificed; after the Church ceremony it becomes a superfluity, and is replaced by duty and obligation. Of the brightest and most joyous of feelings Christianity has made a pain, a weariness, and a sin. The human race had either to die out or be inconsistent. Outraged nature protested.

It protested not only by acts followed by repentance and the gnawing of conscience, but by sympathy, by rehabilitation. The protest began in the very heyday of Catholicism and chivalry.

The threatening husband, Raoul, the Bluebeard in armour with the sword, tyrannical, jealous, and merciless; the barefoot monk, sullen, senseless, superstitious, ready to avenge himself for his privations, for his unnecessary struggle; jailers, hangmen, spies, . . . and in some cellar or turret a sobbing woman, a page in chains, for whom no one will intercede. All is darkness, savagery, blood, bigotry, violence, and Latin prayers chanted through the nose.

But behind the monk, the confessor and the jailer who, with the threatening husband, the father and the brother stand guard over the marriage, the folk-legend is forming in the stillness, the ballad is heard and is carried from place to place, from castle to castle, by troubadour and minnesinger—it champions the unhappy woman. The court smites, the song emancipates. The Church hurls its anathema at love outside marriage, the ballad curses marriage without love. It defends the love-sick page, the fallen wife, the oppressed daughter, not by reasoning but with sympathy, with pity, with tears, lamentation. The song is for the people its secular prayer, its other escape from the cold and hunger of life, from suffocating misery and heavy toil.

On holidays the litanies to the Madonna were replaced by the mournful strains, *des complaintes*, which did not abandon an unfortunate woman to infamy, but wept for her, and set above all the Virgin of Sorrows, beseeching Her intercession and forgiveness.

From ballads and legends the protest grows into the novel and the drama. In the drama it becomes a force. In the theatre outraged love and the gloomy secrets of family injustice found their tribunal, their public hearing. Their case has shaken thousands of hearts, wringing tears and cries of indignation against the serfdom of marriage and the fetters of the family riveted on by force. The jury of the stalls and the boxes have over and over again pronounced the acquittal of individuals and the guilt of institutions.

Meanwhile, in the period of political reconstructions and secular tendencies in thought, one of the two strong props of marriage has begun to break down. As it becomes less and less of a sacrament—that is, loses its ultimate basis—it has leaned more and more on the police. Only by the mystic intervention of a higher power can Christian marriage be justified. Here there is a certain logic—senseless, but still logic. The police-officer, putting on his tricolour scarf and celebrating the wedding with the civil code in his hand, is a far more absurd figure than the priest in his vestments, surrounded by the fumes of incense, holy images and miracles. Even the First Consul, Napoleon, the most prosaic *bourgeois* in matters of love and family, perceived that marriage at the police station was a mighty poor affair, and tried to persuade Cambacérès[4] to add some obligatory phrase, some moral sentence, particularly one that would impress upon the bride her duty to be faithful to her husband (not a word about him) and to obey him.

As soon as marriage emerges from the sphere of mysticism, it

---

[4] Cambacérès, Jean-Jacques (1753–1824), one of the nearest advisers of Napoleon, and compiler of the *Code Civil*. He attempted to dissuade Napoleon from the invasion of Russia. (*Tr.*)

becomes *expédient,* an external course of action. It was introduced by the frightened 'Bluebeards' (shaven nowadays, and
changed into 'blue-chins') in judges' wigs, and academic tail-
coats, popular representatives and liberals, the priests of the civil
code. Civil marriage is simply a measure of state economy, freeing the state from responsibility for the children and attaching
people more closely to property. Marriage without the intervention of the Church became a contract for the bodily enslavement
of each to the other for life. The legislator has nothing to do
with faith, with mystic ravings, so long as the contract is
fulfilled, and if it is not he will find means of punishment and
enforcement. And why not punish it? In England, the traditional country of juridical development, a boy of sixteen, made
drunk by ales and gin and enrolled in a regiment by an old
recruiting sergeant with ribbons on his hat, is subjected to the
most fearful tortures. Why not punish a girl? Why not punish
with shame, ruin, and forcible restoration to her master the girl
who, with no clear understanding of what she is about, has
contracted to love for life, and has admitted an *extra,* forgetting
that the 'season-ticket' is not transferable. But these 'blue-chins'
too have been attacked by the *trouvères* and novelists. Against
the marriage of legal contract a psychiatrical, physiological
dogma has been set up, the dogma of *the absolute infallibility of
the passions and the incapacity of man to struggle against them.*

Those who were yesterday the slaves of marriage are now
becoming the slaves of love. There is no law for love, there is no
strength that can resist it.

After this, all rational control, all responsibility, every form of
self-restraint is effaced. That man is in subjection to irresistible
and ungovernable forces is a theory utterly opposed to that
freedom of reason and by reason, to that formation of the character of a free man which all social theories aim at attaining by
different paths.

Imaginary forces, if men take them for real, are just as powerful as real ones; and this is so because the substance generated
by a human being is the same whatever the force that acts upon
him. The man who is afraid of ghosts is afraid in exactly the
same way as the man who is afraid of mad dogs, and may as
easily die of fright. The difference is that in one case the man
can be shown that his fears are nonsensical, and in the other he
cannot.

I refuse to admit the sovereign position given to *love* in life; I
deny it autocratic power and protest against the pusillanimous
excuse of having been carried away by it.

Surely we have not freed ourselves from every restraint on earth, from God and the devil, from the Roman and the criminal law, and proclaimed reason as our sole guide and governor, in order to lie down humbly, like Hercules at the feet of Omphale, or to fall asleep in the lap of Delilah? Surely woman has not sought to be free from the yoke of the family, from perpetual tutelage and the tyranny of father, husband, or brother, has not striven for her right to independent work, to learning and the standing of a citizen, only to begin over again cooing like a turtle-dove all her life and pining for a dozen Leone Leonis[5] instead of one.

Yes, while considering this theme it is for woman that I am sorriest of all; she is irreparably gnawed and destroyed by the all-devouring Moloch of love. She has more faith in it and she suffers more from it. She is more concentrated on the sexual relationship alone, more driven to love. . . . She is both intellectually more unstable and intellectually less trained than we.

I am sorry for her.

III

HAS ANYONE made a serious and honest attempt to break down conventional prejudices in female education? They are broken down by experience, and so it is life and not convention that suffers.

People skirt the questions we are discussing, as old women and children go round a graveyard or places where some villainy has been committed. Some are afraid of impure spirits, others of the pure truth, and are left with an imagined derangement amid uninvestigated obscurity. There is as little serious consistency in our view of sexual relationships as in all practical spheres. We still dream of the possibility of combining Christian morality, which starts from the trampling underfoot of the flesh and leads towards the other world, with the realistic, earthly morality of this world. People are annoyed because the two moralities do not get on with each other and, to avoid spending time tormenting themselves over the solution of the problem, they pick out according to their tastes and retain what they like of the Church teaching, and reject what they do not care for, on the same

---

[5] Leone Leoni is the hero, or rather villain, whose name supplies the title of one of George Sand's earlier novels. (*Tr.*)

principle as those who do not keep fasts will zealously eat
pancakes and, while observing the gay religious customs, avoid
the dull ones. Yet I should have thought it was high time to
bring more harmony and manliness into conduct. Let him who
respects the law remain under the law and not break it, but let
him who does not accept it show himself openly and consciously
independent of it.

A sober view of human relationships is far harder for women
than for us; of that there is no doubt; they are more deceived by
education and know less of life, and so they more often stumble
and break their heads and hearts than free themselves. They are
always in revolt, and remain in slavery; they strive for revolution and more than anything they support the existing régime.

From childhood the girl is frightened by the sexual relationship as by some *fearful unclean secret* of which she is warned
and scared off as though it were a sin that had some magical
power; and afterwards this same monstrous thing, this same
magnum ignotum which leaves an ineffaceable stain, the remotest hint at which is shameful and sets her blushing, is made
the object of her life. As soon as a boy can walk, he is given a tin
sword to train him to murder, and an hussar's uniform and
epaulettes are predicted for him; the girl is lulled to sleep with
the hope of a rich and handsome bridegroom, and she dreams of
epaulettes not on her own shoulders but on the shoulders of her
future husband.

> *Dors, dors, mon enfant,*
> *Jusqu'à l'âge de quinze ans,*
> *À quinze ans faut te réveiller,*
> *À quinze ans faut te marier.*

One must marvel at any fine human nature that does not
succumb to such an upbringing: we ought to have expected that
all the little girls lulled to sleep like this would, from the age of
fifteen, set to work speedily to replace those who had been slain
by the boys trained from childhood to murderous weapons.

Christian teaching inspires terror of the 'flesh' before the
organism is conscious of its sex; it awakens a dangerous question
in the child, instils alarm into the adolescent soul, and when the
time to answer it is come—another doctrine exalts, as we have
said, for the girl her sexual assignment into a sought-for ideal:
the school-girl becomes the bride, and the same mystery, the
same sin, but purified, becomes the crown of her upbringing, the

desire of all her relations, the goal of all her efforts, almost a social duty. Arts and sciences, education, intelligence, beauty, wealth, grace, all these are directed to the same object, all are the roses strewn on the path to her *sanctioned* fall . . . to the very same sin, the thought of which was looked on as a crime but which has now changed its substance by a miracle like that by which a Pope, when anhungered on a journey, blessed *a meat dish into a Lenten one.*

In short, the whole training, negative and positive, of a woman remains a training for sexual relationships; round them revolves her whole subsequent life. From them she runs, towards them she runs, by them is disgraced, by them is made proud. . . . To-day she preserves the negative holiness of chastity, to-day she whispers, blushing, to her bosom friend of love; to-morrow, in the presence of the crowd, in glare and noise, to the light of chandeliers and to strains of music, she is flung into the arms of a man.

Bride, wife, mother, scarcely in old age, as a *grandmother,* is a woman set free from sexual life, and becomes an independent being, especially if the grandfather is dead. Woman, marked by love, does not soon escape from it. . . . Pregnancy, suckling, child-rearing are all the evolution of the same mystery, the same act of love; in woman it persists not in the memory only, but in blood and body, in her it ferments and ripens and tears itself away—without breaking its tie.

Christianity breathed with its feverish monastic asceticism, with its romantic ravings, upon this physiologically strong, deep relationship, and fanned it into a senseless and destructive flame—of jealousy, revenge, punishment, outrage.

For a woman to extricate herself from this chaos is an heroic feat: only rare and exceptional natures accomplish it; the other women are tortured, and if they do not go out of their minds it is only thanks to the frivolity with which we all live without over-subtlety in the face of menacing blows and collisions, thought-lessly passing from day to day, from fortuity to fortuity and from contradiction to contradiction.

What breadth, what beauty and power of human nature and development there must be in a woman to get over all the palisades, all the fences, within which she is held captive!

I have seen one such struggle and one such victory. . . .

❖   ❖   ❖

ENGLAND

(1852-1858)

The Fogs of London

WHEN AT DAYBREAK on the 25th of August, 1852, I passed along a wet plank on to the shore of England and looked at its dirty white promontories, I was very far from imagining that years would pass before I should leave those chalk cliffs.

Entirely under the influence of the ideas with which I had left Italy, stunned and sick, bewildered by a series of blows which had followed one on the other with such brutal rapidity, I could not look clearly at what I was doing. It seemed as though I had needed to be brought again and again into physical contact with familiar truths in order that I might renew my belief in what I had long known or ought to have known.

I had been false to my own logic and forgotten how different the man of to-day is in opinions and in actions, how noisily he begins and how modestly he carries out his programmes, how genial are his desires and how feeble his muscles.

Two months had been filled with unnecessary meetings, fruitless seeking, painful and quite useless conversations, and I was still expecting something . . . expecting something. But my real nature could not remain for long in that world of phantoms. I began little by little to grasp that the edifice I was raising had no solid ground beneath it, and that it would inevitably crumble into ruins.

I was humiliated, my pride was outraged and I was angry with myself. My conscience gnawed at me for the sacrilegious deterioration of my grief, for a year of vain anxiety; and I was aware of a fearful, inexpressible weariness. . . . How I needed then the breast of a friend who, without judging and condemning, would have received my confession and shared my unhappiness; but the desert about me extended more and more; there was no one near to me, not one human being . . . and perhaps that was even for the best.

I had not thought of staying longer than a month in London, but little by little I began to perceive that I had absolutely nowhere to go and no reason to go anywhere. Nowhere could I have found the same hermit-like seclusion as in London.

Having made up my mind to remain there, I began by taking a house in one of the remotest parts of the town, beyond Regent's Park, near Primrose Hill.

The little girls remained in Paris; only Sasha was with me. As the fashion is here, the house was divided into three storeys. The whole middle storey consisted of a huge, cold, uncomfortable 'drawing-room.' I turned it into a study. The owner of the house was a sculptor and had cluttered up the whole of this room with various statuettes and models; a bust of Lola Montes was always before my eyes, together with Victoria.

When on the second or third day after our crossing, having unpacked and settled in, I went into that room in the morning, sat down in a big arm-chair and spent a couple of hours in complete stillness, worried by no one, I felt myself somehow free for the first time after a long, long time. My heart was not the lighter for this freedom, but yet I looked out of the window with a greeting to the sombre trees in the park, which were hardly visible through the smoky fog, and thanked them for the peacefulness.

For whole mornings I used now to sit utterly alone, often doing nothing, not even reading; Sasha would sometimes run in, but he did not interfere with my solitude. Haug, who lived with me, never came in—without some pressing need—before dinner which was between six and seven. In this leisure I went, fact by fact, over the whole past, words and letters, other people and myself. I found mistakes to the right, mistakes to the left, vacillation, weakness, action hindered by irresolution and over-readiness to be influenced by others. And in the course of this analysis, by degrees, a revolution took place within me . . . there were bitter moments and more than once tears rolled down my cheeks; but there were other moments, not of gladness but of courage: I was conscious of power in myself. I no longer relied on anyone else, but my confidence in myself grew stronger; I grew more independent of everyone.

The emptiness about me strengthened me and gave me time to collect myself; I grew unaccustomed to others: that is, I did not seek real intimacy with them: I avoided no one, but people became indifferent to me. I saw that I had no ties that rested on earnest, profound feelings. I was a stranger among outsiders; I had more sympathy for some than for others, but was in no close intimacy with any. It had been so in the past, too, but I had not noticed it, being continually carried away by my own thoughts; now the masquerade was over, the dominoes had been removed, the garlands had fallen from the heads, the masks from the faces, and I saw features different from those that I had surmised. What was I to do? I could help showing that I liked many people less, that is, I knew them better, but I could not help feeling it; and, as I have said, these discoveries did not rob me of my courage, but rather strengthened it.

London life was very favourable for such a break. There is no town in the world which is more adapted for training one away from people and training one into solitude than London. The manner of life, the distances, the climate, the very multitude of the population in which personality vanishes, all this together with the absence of Continental diversions conduces to the same effect. One who knows how to live alone has nothing to fear from the tedium of London. The life here, like the air here, is bad for the weak, for the frail, for one who seeks a prop outside himself, for one who seeks welcome, sympathy, attention; the moral lungs here must be as strong as the physical lungs, whose task it is to separate oxygen from the smoky fog. The masses are saved by battling for their daily bread, the commercial classes by their absorption in heaping up wealth, and all by the bustle of business; but nervous and romantic temperaments—fond of living among people, fond of intellectual sloth and of idly luxuriating in emotion—are bored to death and fall into despair.

Wandering lonely about London, through its stony lanes and stifling passages, sometimes not seeing a step before me for the thick, opaline fog, and colliding with shadows running—I lived through a great deal.

In the evening, when my son had gone to bed, I usually went out for a walk; I scarcely ever went to see anyone; I read the newspapers and stared in taverns at the alien race, and lingered on the bridges across the Thames.

On one side the stalactites of the Houses of Parliament would loom through the darkness, ready to vanish again; on the other, the inverted bowl of St Paul's . . . and street-lamps . . . street-lamps . . . street-lamps without end in both directions. One city, full-fed, went to sleep: the other, hungry, was not yet awake—the streets were empty and nothing could be heard but the measured tread of the policeman with his lantern. I used to sit and look, and my soul would grow quieter and more peaceful. And so for all this I came to love this fearful ant-heap, where every night a hundred thousand men know not where they will lay their heads, and the police often find women and children dead of hunger beside hotels where one cannot dine for less than two pounds.

But this kind of transition, however quickly it approaches, is not achieved all at once, especially at forty. A long time passed while I was coming to terms with my new ideas. Though I had made up my mind to work, for a long time I did nothing, or did not do what I wanted to do.

The idea with which I had come to London, to seek the tribunal of my own people, was a sound and right one. I repeat this even now, with full, considered conviction. To whom, in fact, are we to appeal for judgment, for the re-establishment of the truth, for the unmasking of falsehood?

It is not for us to litigate in the court of our enemies, who judge by other principles, by laws which we do not recognise.

One can settle one's quarrels for oneself; no doubt one can. To take the law in one's own hands is to snatch back by force what has been taken by force, and so restore the balance; vengeance is just as sound and simple a human feeling as gratitude; but neither revenge nor taking the law into one's own hands explains anything. It may happen that a clear explanation is what matters most to a man. The re-establishment of the truth may be dearer to him than revenge. My own error lay not in the main proposition but in the underlying assumption; in order that there may be a tribunal of one's own people one must first of all have one's own people. Where were mine . . . ?

I had had my own people once in Russia. But I was so completely cut off in a foreign land; I had at all costs to get into communication with my own people; I wanted to tell them of the weight that lay on my heart. Letters were not allowed in, but books would get through of themselves; writing letters was impossible: I would print; and little by little I set to work upon *My Past and Thoughts*, and upon setting up a Russian printing-press.

The Emigrants in London

By the waters of Babylon we sat down and wept.

PSALMS 137:1

If any one had conceived the idea of writing from the outside the inner history of the political *émigrés* and exiles from the year 1848 in London, what a melancholy page he would have added to the records of contemporary man. What sufferings, what privations, what tears . . . and what triviality, what narrowness, what poverty of intellectual powers, of resources, of understanding, what obstinacy in wrangling, what pettiness of wounded vanity! . . .

On one hand those simple-hearted men, who by heart and instinct have understood the business of revolution and have made for its sake the greatest sacrifice a man can make, that of voluntary beggary, form the small group of the blessed. On the other hand there are men, actuated by secret, ill-concealed ambition, for whom the revolution meant office, *position sociale*, and who scuttled into exile when they failed to attain a position. Then there were all kinds of fanatics, monomaniacs with every sort of monomania, madmen with every variety of madness. It was due to this nervous, strained, irritable condition that table-turning numbered so many victims among the exiles. Almost every one was turning tables, from Victor Hugo and Ledru-Rollin to Quirico Filopanti[1] who went farther still and found out everything that a man was doing a thousand years ago.

And with all that not a step forward. They are like the court clock at Versailles, which pointed to one hour, the hour at which the King died. . . . And, like the clock, it has been forgotten to move them on from the time of the death of Louis XV. They point to one event, the extinction of some event. They talk about it, they think about it, they go back to it. Meeting the same men, the same groups, in five or six months, in two or three years, one becomes frightened: the same arguments are still going on, the same personalities and recriminations: only the furrows drawn by poverty and privation are deeper; jackets and overcoats are shabbier; there are more grey hairs, and they are all older together and bonier and more gloomy . . . and still the same things are being said over and over again.

The revolution with them has remained the philosophy of social order, as it was in the 'nineties, but they have not and cannot have the naïve passion for the struggle which in those days gave vivid colouring to the most meagre generalisations and body to the dry outlines of their political framework; generalisations and abstract concepts were a joyful novelty, a revelation in those days. At the end of the eighteenth century men for the first time—not in books but in actual fact—began to free themselves from the fatal, mysteriously oppressive world of theological tradition, and were trying to base on conscious understanding the whole political system which had grown up apart from will or consciousness. In the attempt at a rational state, as in the attempt to found a religion of reason, there was in 1793 a mighty, titanic poetry, which bore its fruits, but for all that, has withered and weakened in the last sixty years. Our

---

[1] The pseudonym of Giuseppe Barilli (1812–94), mathematician, philosopher and patriot. (*R.*)

heirs of the Titans do not notice this. They are like the monks of
Mount Athos, who busy themselves about their own affairs, deliver the same speeches which were delivered in the time of
Chrysostom and keep up a manner of life blocked long ago by
the Turkish sovereignty, which now is drawing towards an end
itself . . . and they go on meeting together on certain days to
commemorate certain events with the same ritual, the same
prayers.

Another brake that slows down the *émigrés* is their constant
defending of themselves against each other; this is fearfully
destructive of intellectual effort and every sort of conscientious
work. They have no objective purpose; all the parties are obstinately conservative, and a movement forward seems to them a
weakness, almost a desertion. You have stood under the banner?
Then stand under it, even though in time you have seen that its
colours are not quite what they seemed.

So the years pass: gradually everything about them changes.
Where there were snowdrifts, the grass is growing; where there
were bushes, there is a forest; where there was a forest are only
tree-stumps . . . they notice nothing. Some ways out have completely crumbled away and are blocked up: they go on knocking
at them; new chinks have opened and beams of light pierce
through them, but they look the other way.

The relationships formed between the different *émigrés* and
the English might furnish by themselves wonderful data for the
chemical affinity of various nationalities.

English life at first dazzles the Germans, overwhelms them,
then swallows them up, or rather breaks them down into inferior
Englishmen. As a rule, if a German undertakes any kind of
business, he at once shaves, turns his shirt collar up to his ears,
says *yes* instead of *ja* and *well* where there is no need to say
anything at all. In a couple of years, he writes his letters and his
notes in English, and lives entirely in an English circle. Germans never treat Englishmen as equals, but behave with them as
our workpeople behave with officials, and our officials behave
with noblemen of ancient standing.

When they enter English life, Germans do not really become
Englishmen, but affect to be English, and partly cease to be
Germans. The English are as whimsical in their relationships
with foreigners as they are in everything else; they rush at a
new arrival as they do at a comic actor or an acrobat and give
him no peace, but they hardly disguise their sense of their own
superiority and even a certain aversion they feel for him. If the
foreigner keeps to his own dress, his own way of doing his hair,

his own hat, the offended Englishman jeers at him, but by degrees grows used to recognising him as an independent person. If in his first alarm the foreigner begins to adapt his manners to the Englishman's, the latter does not respect him but treats him superciliously from the height of his British haughtiness. Here it is sometimes hard, even with great tact, to steer one's course so as not to err either on the minus or the plus side; it may well be imagined what the Germans do, who are devoid of all tact, are familiar and servile, too stiff and also too simple, sentimental without reason and rude without provocation.

But if the Germans look upon the English as upon a higher species of the same genus, and feel themselves to be inferior to them, it by no means follows that the attitude of the French, and especially of the French refugees, is any wiser. Just as the German respects everything in England without discrimination, the Frenchman protests against everything and loathes everything English. This peculiarity sometimes, I need hardly say, is pushed to the most comically grotesque extreme.

The Frenchman cannot forgive the English, in the first place, for not speaking French; in the second, for not understanding him when he calls Charing Cross Sharan-Kro, or Leicester Square Lessesstair-Skooar. Then his stomach cannot digest the English dinners consisting of two huge pieces of meat and fish, instead of five little helpings of various ragouts, *fritures*, *salmis* and so on. Then he can never resign himself to the 'slavery' of restaurants being closed on Sundays, and the people being *bored to the glory of God*, though the whole of France is bored to the glory of Bonaparte for seven days in the week. Then the whole *habitus*, all that is good and bad in the Englishman, is detestable to the Frenchman. The Englishman pays him back in the same coin, but looks with envy at the cut of his clothes and like a caricature attempts to imitate him.

All this is of significance for the study of comparative physiology, and I am not describing it in order to amuse. The German, as we have observed, recognises that he is, in a civilian capacity at any rate, an inferior specimen of the same breed to which the Englishman belongs, and subordinates himself to him. The Frenchman, belonging to a different breed, not so distinct that he may be indifferent, as the Turk is to the Chinese, hates the Englishman, especially because both nations are each blindly convinced of being the foremost people in the world. The German, too, is inwardly convinced of this, particularly *auf dem theoretischen Gabiete*, but is ashamed to own it.

The Frenchman is really the opposite of the Englishman in

every respect. The Englishman is a solitary creature, who likes to live alone in his own lair, obstinate and impatient of control; the Frenchman is a gregarious animal, impudent but easily shepherded. Hence two completely parallel lines of development with the Channel lying between them. The Frenchman is constantly anticipating things, meddling in everything, educating everybody, giving instructions about everything. The Englishman waits to see, does not meddle at all in other people's business and would be readier to be taught than to teach, but has not the time: he has to get to his shop.

The two corner-stones of the whole of English life, personal independence and family tradition, hardly exist for the Frenchman. The coarseness of English manners drives the Frenchman frantic, and it really is repugnant and poisons life in London, but behind it he fails to see the rude strength with which this people has stood up for its rights, the stubbornness of character which makes it impossible to turn an Englishman into the slave who delights in the gold lace on livery and is in raptures over his chains entwined with laurel, though by flattering his passions you may do almost anything else with him.

The world of self-government, decentralisation, expanding capriciously of its own initiative, seems to the Frenchman so savage, so incomprehensible that, however long he lives in England, he never understands its political and civic life, its rights and its judicial forms. He is lost in the incongruous multiplicity of precedents on which English law rests, as in a dark forest, and does not observe the immense and majestic oaks that compose it, nor see the charm, the poetry, and the significance of its very variety. His little Codex, with its sanded paths, its clipped shrubs and policemen-gardeners in every avenue, is a very different matter.

Shakespeare and Racine again.

If a Frenchman sees drunken men fighting in a tavern and a policeman looking at them with the serenity of an outsider and the curiosity of a man watching a cock-fight, he is furious with the policeman for not flying into a rage and carrying someone off *au violon*. He does not reflect that personal freedom is only possible when a policeman has no parental authority, when his intervention is reduced to passive readiness to come when he is summoned. The confidence that every poor fellow feels when he shuts the door of his cold, dark, damp little hovel transforms a man's attitude. Of course, behind these jealously guarded, strictly observed rights, the criminal sometimes hides—and so be it. It is far better that the clever thief should go unpunished than that every honest man should be trembling like a thief in his own room. Before I came to England every appearance of a policeman in the house in which I lived gave me an irresistibly nasty feeling, and morally I stood *en garde* against an enemy. In England the policeman at your door or within your doors only adds a feeling of security.

❖ ❖ ❖

As the successor of Maximilien Robespierre, Louis Blanc worshipped Rousseau, and was somewhat cold in his attitude to Voltaire. In his *History* he has separated all leading men into two flocks in biblical fashion—on the right hand, the sheep of brotherhood, on the left, the goats of greed and egoism. For the egoists such as Montaigne he had no mercy, and he caught it properly. Louis Blanc did not stick at anything in this classification, and meeting the speculator, Law, he boldly reckoned him among the brotherhood, which the reckless Scot had certainly never expected.

In 1856 Barbès arrived in London from The Hague. Louis Blanc brought him to see me. I looked with emotion at the sufferer who had spent almost his whole life in prison. I had seen him once before, and where? At the window of the Hôtel de Ville, on the 15th of May, 1848, a few minutes before the National Guard broke in and seized him.[2]

I invited them to dine with me next day; they came, and we sat on till late at night.

They sat on recalling the year 1848; when I had seen them into the street, and gone back alone into my room, I was overcome by an immense sadness. I sat down at my writing-table and was ready to weep.

I felt what a son must feel on returning to the parental home after a long absence: he sees how everything in it has grown dingy and warped; his father has grown old without being aware of it, but the son is very well aware of it, and he is cramped, he feels that the grave is not far off; he conceals this, but the meeting wearies him instead of cheering and rejoicing him.

---

[2] The pitch reached by the ferocity of the guardians of order on that day may be judged by the fact that the National Guard seized Louis Blanc on the boulevard, though he ought not to have been arrested at all, and the police at once ordered him to be released. On receiving this order the National Guard who held him seized him by the finger, thrust his nails into it and twisted the last joint backwards.

Barbès, Louis Blanc! Why, they were old friends, honoured friends of my effervescent youth. *L'Histoire de dix ans*, the trial of Barbès before the Chamber of Peers—all that had so long ago been absorbed into my brain and my heart, we were so closely related to all this—and here they were in person.

Their most malicious enemies have never dared suspect the incorruptible honesty of Louis Blanc, nor cast a slur on the chivalrous valour of Barbès. Everyone had seen, had known both men in every situation; they had no private life, they had no closed doors. One of them we had seen, a member of the government, the other half an hour from the guillotine. On the night before his execution Barbès did not sleep, but asked for paper and began to write: those lines[3] have been preserved and I have read them. There is French idealism in them, and religious dreams, but there is not a trace of weakness; his spirit was not troubled nor cast down; with serene consciousness he was preparing to lay his head on the block and was calmly writing when the gaoler's hand knocked loudly at the door. 'It was at dawn, I was expecting the executioners' (he told me this himself), 'but his sister came in instead and flung herself on his neck. Without his knowledge she had begged from Louis-Philippe a commutation of his sentence and had been galloping with post-horses all night to reach him in time.

Louis-Philippe's prisoner rose some years later to the pinnacle of civic glory; the chains were removed by the exultant populace, and he was led in triumph through Paris. But the upright heart of Barbès was not confused: he was the first to attack the Provisional Government for the killings at Rouen. The reaction grew up round him, the republic could only be saved by impudent audacity and, on the 15th of May, Barbès dared what neither Ledru-Rollin nor Louis Blanc did and what Caussidière was afraid to do. The *coup d'état* failed and Barbès, now a prisoner of the republic, was once more before the court. At Bourges, just as in the Chamber of Peers, he told the lawyers of the *petit bourgeois* world, as he had told the old sinner Pasquier: 'I do not recognise you as judges: you are my enemies and I am your prisoner of war; do with me what you will, but I do not recognise you as my judges.' And again the heavy door of life-long imprisonment closed behind him.

By chance, against his will, he came out of prison. Napoleon III thrust him out almost in mockery, after reading during the

---

[3] Probably the pamphlet of Barbès, *Deux jours de condamnation à mort*, written in prison at Nîmes in March 1847. (*A.S.*)

Crimean War the letter in which Barbès, in a fit of Gallic chauvinism, speaks of the military glory of France. Barbès tried retiring to Spain, but the scared, dull-witted government expelled him. He went to Holland and there found a tranquil, secluded refuge.

And now this hero and martyr, together with some of the chief leaders of the February Republic, together with the foremost statesman of socialism, had been recalling and criticising the past days of glory and misfortune!

And I was oppressed by a weight of distress; I saw with unhappy clarity that they, too, belonged to the history of *another decade*, which was finished to the last page, to the cover. Finished, not for them personally but for all the *émigrés* and for all the political parties of the day.

Living and noisy ten, even five years before, they had passed out of the channel and were being lost in the sand, imagining that they were still flowing to the ocean. They had no longer the words which, like the word 'republic,' roused whole nations, nor the songs like the Marseillaise which set every heart throbbing. Even their enemies were not of the same grandeur, not of the same standard: there were no more old feudal privileges of the Crown with which it would have been hard to do battle; there was no king's head which, rolling from the scaffold, would have carried away a whole ruling system with it. You may execute Napoleon III, but that will not bring you another 21st of January; pull the Mazas Prison to bits stone by stone, and that will not bring you the taking of the Bastille! In those days, amid those thunders and lightnings, a new discovery was made, the discovery of the State founded upon Reason, a new means of redemption from the gloomy slavery of mediaevalism. Since those days the redemption by revolution has been proved insolvent: the State has not been founded upon Reason. The political reformation has degenerated like the religious one into rhetorical babble, preserved by the weakness of some and the hypocrisy of others. The Marseillaise remains a sacred hymn, but it is a hymn of the past, like *Ein' feste Burg*; the strains of both songs evoke even now a row of majestic images, like the procession of shades in *Macbeth*, all kings, but all dead.

The last is hardly still visible from behind, and of the new there are only rumours. We are in an *interregnum*; till the heir arrives the police have seized everything in the name of outward order. There can be no mention here of rights; it is lynch law in history, a case of temporary necessities, of executive measures, police cordons, quarantine precautions. The new régime, combining all that is oppressive in monarchy and all that is ferocious in Jacobinism, is defended, not by ideas, not by prejudices, but by fears and uncertainties. While some were afraid others fixed bayonets and took up their positions. The first who breaks through their chain may perhaps even occupy the chief place, which is occupied by the police; only he will at once become a policeman himself.

This reminds me of how on the evening of the 24th of February Caussidière arrived at the Prefecture with a rifle in his hand, sat down in the chair just vacated by the escaping Delessert, called the secretary, told him that he had been appointed Prefect and ordered him to give him his papers. The secretary smiled as respectfully as he had to Delessert, as respectfully bowed and went to fetch the papers, and the papers went their regular course; nothing was changed, only Delessert's supper was eaten by Caussidière.

Many have found out the password to the Prefecture, but have never learned the watchword of history. These men, when the time came, behaved exactly like Alexander I. They wanted a blow to be struck at the old régime, but not a mortal blow; and there was no Bennigsen or Zubov[4] among them.

And that is why if they go down into the arena again they will be horrified by the ingratitude of men. And may they dwell on that thought: may they think it is only ingratitude! That is a gloomy thought, but easier to bear than many others.

But it would be still better if they did not go there at all; let them stay and tell us and our children of their great deeds. There is no need to resent this advice; what is living changes, and the unchanging becomes a monument. They have left their furrow, just as those who come after them will leave theirs, and these a fresh wave will over-take in its turn, and then everything: furrows, the living and the monuments, will be covered by the universal amnesty of everlasting oblivion!

Many people are angry with me for saying these things openly. 'In your words,' a very worthy man said to me, 'one hears an outside spectator speaking.'

But I did not come to Europe as an outsider, you know. An outsider is what I have become. I am very long-suffering, but at last I am worn out.

For five years I have not seen one bright face, I have not heard spontaneous laughter, I have not encountered an understanding

---

4 The assassins of Paul I. (*Tr.*)

look, I have been surrounded by *feldshers*[5] and *prosectors*.[6] The *feldshers* have been continually trying their remedies, while the others have been proving to them on the corpse that they have blundered—well, eventually, I have snatched up a scalpel too; perhaps, through being unused to it, I have cut too deeply.

I have spoken not as an outside spectator, not to find fault: I have spoken because my heart was full, because the lack of general understanding has put me out of patience. That I was sobered earlier than the rest has been of no alleviation to me. Even of *feldshers* only the worst smile with satisfaction as they look at the dying patient and say: 'Didn't I tell you he would turn up his toes by the evening? And he has.'

For what, then, have I held out?

In 1856 the best of all the German emigrants, Karl Schurz,[7] arrived in Europe from Wisconsin. On his return from Germany he told me that he had been struck by the moral desolation of the Continent. I translated to him aloud my *West European Sketches*, and he tried to defend himself from my conclusions, as though they had been ghosts in which a man is unwilling to believe, but of which he is afraid.

'A man who understands contemporary Europe as you do,' he said to me, 'ought to abandon it.'

'That is what you have done,' I observed.

'Why is it that you don't?'

'It is very simple. I can answer you as a certain honest German, before me, answered in a fit of proud independence: "I have a king of my own in Swabia." I have my own people in Russia!'

❖　　❖　　❖

---

[5] Male nurses or doctors' assistants. (*Tr.*)

[6] Dissecting demonstrators. (*Tr.*)

[7] Schurz, Karl (1829–1906), fought in the revolutionary movement of 1848. In 1852 he went to the United States, where he lectured, took part in politics and fought in the Civil War, as a major-general of volunteers. In 1869 he was elected to the Senate, and in 1877 appointed Secretary of the Interior. He edited a paper, and wrote lives of Henry Clay and of Lincoln. (*Tr.*)

John Stuart Mill
and His Book on Liberty

I HAVE HAD to smart a good deal for taking a gloomy view of
Europe, and for speaking my mind simply, without fears or
regrets. Since I published my 'Letters from the Avenue Marigny'
in the *Contemporary*[1] some of my friends and unfriends have
shown signs of impatience and indignation, and have objected
. . . and then, as though to spite them, with every development
things in Europe have become darker, more suffocating, and
neither Paradol's wise articles nor the worthless clerico-liberal
stuff of Montalembert, nor the superseding of a king of Prussia
by a Prussian prince, have been able to distract the eyes of
seekers after truth. People in Russia do not care to know this,
and naturally they are angry with the indiscreet discoverer.

We need Europe as an ideal, a reproach, a good example; if
she were not these things it would be necessary to invent her.
Did not the naïve free-thinkers of the eighteenth century, Voltaire and Robespierre among them, say that even if there were
no immortality of the soul it would be necessary to preach that
there was, in order to maintain people in fear and virtue? And
do we not see in history how the great have sometimes concealed
the serious illness or sudden death of a king, and have governed
in the name of a corpse or a madman, as happened not long ago
in Prussia?

A pious lie may be a good thing, but not everyone is capable
of it.

I was not cast down, however, by censure, but consoled myself
by thinking that here, too, the thoughts I uttered were no better
received, and still more by considering that they were objec-
tively true, that is independent of personal opinions and even of
good intentions in education, correction of morals and the like.
Everything true of itself sooner or later rises up and reveals
itself, *kommt an die Sonnen*, as Goethe says.

While I was being scolded by the heads of the literary depart-

---

[1] The Russian perodical *Sovremennik*, October and November 1847. (*R.*)

ments, time went on its way, and at last ten whole years had gone. Much of what in 1849 had been new had become a cliché in 1859; what then had seemed an extravagant paradox had been transformed into public opinion, and many eternal and unshakeable truths had gone out with that year's fashions in clothes.

Serious minds in Europe began to take a serious view. There are very few of them, and this only confirms my opinion of the West, but they will go far, and I well remember how Thomas Carlyle smiled over the remains of my faith in English ways. But now there appears a book that goes far beyond anything I have said. *Pereant qui ante nos nostra dixerunt*, and thanks be to those who after us confirm with their authority what we have said, and with their talent clearly and forcefully hand on what we have feebly expressed.

The book that I am speaking of was not written by Proudhon, nor even by Pierre Leroux nor by any other angry socialist exile: —not at all: it was written by one of the most celebrated political economists, recently a member of the India Board, to whom Lord Stanley three months ago offered a place in the government. This man enjoys enormous, well merited authority; in England the Tories read him with reluctance and the Whigs with anger; on the Continent he is read by the few people (specialists excepted) who read anything at all except newspapers and pamphlets.

The man is John Stuart Mill.

A month ago he published a strange book in defence of *liberty of thought, speech and the person*; I say 'strange' for is it not strange that, where Milton wrote two centuries ago of the same thing, it should be necessary for a voice once more to be raised 'On Liberty'? But men like Mill, you know, cannot write out of satisfaction: his whole book is imbued with a profound sadness, not fretful but virile, censorious, Tacitean. He has spoken up because evil has become worse. Milton defended freedom of speech against the attacks of authority, against violence, and all that was noble and vigorous was on his side. Mill's enemy is quite different: he is standing up for liberty not against an educated government but against *society*, against custom, against the deadening force of indifference, against petty intolerance, against 'mediocrity.'

This is not the indignant old courtier of Catherine's time who, passed over for promotion at Court, grumbles at the younger generation, runs down the Winter Palace and cries up the Hall of Facets. No: this man, full of energy, long versed in affairs of state and theories deeply thought out, accustomed to regard the world calmly, like an Englishman and a thinker—this man at least could bear it no longer and, exposing himself to the wrath of the registrars of civilisation who live on the Neva and the bookmen with a Western education by the Moscow River, cried: 'We are drowning!'

He was horrified by the constant deterioration of personalities, taste and style, by the inanity of men's interests and their absence of vigour; he looks closely, and sees clearly that everything is becoming shallow, commonplace, shoddy, trite, more 'respectable,' perhaps, but more banal. He sees in England (what Tocqueville observed in France) that standard, indistinguishable types are being evolved and, gravely shaking his head, he says to his contemporaries: 'Stop! Think again! Do you know where you are going? Look: *your soul is ebbing away.*'

But why does he try to wake the sleepers? What path, what way out has he devised for them? Like John the Baptist of old he threatens them with what is coming and summons them to repentance; people will hardly be got moving a second time with this renunciatory lever. Mill cries shame on his contemporaries as Tacitus cried shame on his: he will not halt them by this means any more than Tacitus did. A few sad reproaches will not stem *the ebbing of the soul,* nor perhaps will any dam in the world.

'Men of another stamp,' he says, 'made England what *it has been,* and only men of another stamp can prevent its *decline.*'

But this deterioration of individuality, this want of temper, are only pathological facts, and admitting them is a very important step towards the way out; but it is not the way out. Mill upbraids the sick man and points to his sound ancestors: an odd sort of treatment, and hardly a magnanimous one.

Come: are we now to begin to reproach the lizard with the antediluvian ichthyosaurus? Is it the fault of one that it is little and the other was big? Mill, frightened by the moral worthlessness, the spiritual mediocrity of his environment, cried out passionately and sorrowfully, like the champions in our old tales: 'Is there a man alive in the field?'

Wherefore did he summon him? To tell him that he was a degenerate descendant of mighty forebears, and consequently ought to try to make himself like them.

For what? —Silence.

Robert Owen, too, was calling upon people for seventy years running, and equally to no purpose; but he was summoning them *for something.* Whether this *something* was Utopia, phantasy or the truth is not our business now; what is important to us is that his summons had an object; but Mill, smothering his contemporaries in the grim, Rembrandtesque shadows of the time of Cromwell and the Puritans, wants shopkeepers who are everlastingly giving short weight and short measure to turn from some poetic necessity, by some spiritual gymnastics, into— heroes!

We could likewise call up the monumental, menacing figures of the French Convention and set them beside the past, future and present French spies and *espiciers,* and begin a speech like Hamlet's:

> *Look here, upon this picture, and on this . . .*
> *Hyperion's curls; the front of Jove himself;*
> *An eye like Mars . . .*
> > *Look you now, what follows:*
> *Here is your husband . . .*

This would be very just, and even more offensive; but would this make anyone leave his vulgar but comfortable life, and that in order to be majestically bored like Cromwell or stoically take his head to the block like Danton?

It was easy for them to act as they did because they were ruled by a passionate conviction—*une idée fixe.*

Catholicism was such an *idée fixe* at one time, then Protestantism, science in the age of the Renaissance, revolution in the eighteenth century.

Where is that sacred monomania, that *magnum ignotum,* that riddle of the Sphinx of our civilisation? Where is the mighty conception, the passionate belief, the burning hope, which could temper the body like steel and bring the soul to such a pitch of feverish obduracy as feels neither pain nor privation but walks with a firm step to the scaffold or the stake?

Look about you: what is capable of heartening individuals, uplifting peoples, shaking the masses? The religion of the Pope with his Immaculate Conception of the Mother of God, or the religion with no Pope and its abstention from beer on the Sabbath Day? The arithmetical pantheism of universal suffrage or the idolatrous worship of monarchy? Superstitious belief in a republic or in parliamentary reform? . . . No, no: all this pales, ages and is bundled away, as once the gods of Olympus were bundled away when they descended from heaven, dislodged by new rivals risen from Golgotha.

Unfortunately our blackened idols do not command these sources of inspiration, or at all events Mill does not point them out.

On the one hand, the English genius finds repellent an abstract generalisation, a bold, logical consistency; with his scepticism the Englishman feels that the extremes of logic, like the laws of pure mathematics, are not applicable without the introduction of the factor of the living environment. On the other hand, he has been accustomed physically and morally to do up all the buttons of his overcoat and turn up his collar, which protects him from damp winds and harsh intolerance. In that same book of Mill's we see an example of this. With two or three blows of unusual dexterity he overturned Christian morality, somewhat unsteady on its feet, without saying anything in his whole book about Christianity.

Instead of suggesting any way out Mill suddenly observes: 'In the development of peoples there is a limit, it seems, after which the people stands still, and *becomes a China.*'

When does this happen?

It happens, he replies, when individualities begin to be effaced, to disappear among the masses; when everything is subjected to received customs, when the conception of good and evil is confused with the conception of conformity or non-conformity with what is accepted. The oppression of custom halts development, which properly consists in aspiration towards *what is better*, away from what is customary. The whole of history is made up of this struggle and, if the greater part of humanity has no history, this is because its life is utterly subjected to custom.

Now let us see how our author regards the present state of the educated world. He says that, in spite of the intellectual excellence of our times, everything is moving towards *mediocrity*, that faces are being lost in the crowd. This 'conglomerated mediocrity' hates everything that is sharply defined, original, outstanding: it imposes a common level upon everyone. And, just as in an average section of people there is not much intelligence and not many desires, so the miscellaneous mediocrity, like a viscous bog, submerges, on the one hand, everything that desires to extricate itself and, on the other, forestalls the disorderliness of eccentric individuals by educating new generations in the same flaccid mediocrity. The moral basis of behaviour consists principally in living as other people do: 'Woe to the man, and especially to the woman, who thinks of doing *what nobody does;* but woe also to those who do not do *what every one does.*' For this sort of morality no intelligence nor any particular will-power is required: people occupy themselves with their own *affairs*, and now and again, by way of diversion, with some 'philanthropic hobby,' and they remain respectable but commonplace.

To this mean belong power and authority; the very government is powerful in proportion as it serves as the organ of the dominant mean and understands its instinct.

What sort of thing is this sovereign mean? 'In America all whites belong to it; in England the ruling stratum is composed of the *middle class*.'

Mill finds one difference between the lifeless inertia of Oriental peoples and the modern *petit bourgeois* state; and in this, I think, is the bitterest drop in the whole goblet of wormwood that he offers. Instead of a sluggish, Asiatic quiescence, modern Europeans, he says, live in vain unrest, in senseless changes: 'In getting rid of singularities we do not get rid of changes, so long as they are performed each time by *everyone*. We have cast away our fathers' individual, personal way of dressing, and are ready to change the cut of our clothes two or three times a year, but only so long as everybody changes it; and this is done not with an eye to beauty or convenience but for the sake of change itself!'

If individuals cannot get free of this clogging slough, this befouling bog, then 'Europe, despite its noble antecedents and its Christianity, *will become a China*.'

So we have come back and are facing the same question. On what principle are we to wake the sleeper? In the name of what shall the flabby personality, magnetised by trifles, be inspired, be made discontented with its present life of railways, telegraphs, newspapers and cheap goods?

Individuals do not step out of the ranks because there is not sufficient occasion. For whom, for what, or against whom are they to come forward? The absence of energetic men of action is not a cause but a consequence.

The point, the line, beyond which the struggle between the desire for *something better* and the conservation of *what is* finishes in favour of conservation, comes (it seems to us) when the dominant, active, *historic* part of a people approaches a form of life that suits it; this is a kind of repletion, saturation: everything reaches an equilibrium, settles down and eternally pursues one and the same course—until a cataclysm, renovation or destruction. *Semper idem* requires neither enormous efforts nor menacing warriors. Of whatever kind they may be, they will be superfluous: in the midst of peace there is no need of generals.

Not to go as far as China, look close at hand, at the country in the West which has become the most sedentary—the country where Europe's hair is beginning to turn grey—Holland. Where are her great statesmen, her great artists, her subtle theologians, her bold mariners? But what would be the purpose of them? Is she unhappy because she chafes and blusters no longer, because these men are no more? She will show you her smiling villages on the drained marshes, her laundered towns, her ironed gardens, her comfort, her liberty, and will say: 'My great men obtained for me this freedom, my mariners bequeathed me this wealth, my great artists embellished my walls and churches: it is well with me—what do you want me to do? Have a sharp struggle with the government? But is it oppressive? We have more liberty even now than there ever was in France.'

But what comes of a life like this?

What comes of it? Well, what *comes* of life at all? And then: are there no private romances in Holland? no clashes or scandals? Do people not fall in love in Holland, weep, laugh, sing songs, drink *Schiedam*, dance till morning in every village? What is more, it should not be forgotten that, on the one hand, they enjoy all the fruits of education, science and art, and, on the other, they have a mass of business: the great patience-game of trade, interminable household puzzles, the education of their children in the form and semblance of their own. The Dutchman has not the time to look round him, to enjoy some leisure, before he is carried off to 'God's acre' in an elegant, lacquered coffin, while his son is already harnessed to the trade-wheel, which must be turned incessantly or business will come to a stop.

Life may be lived like this for a thousand years if it is not interrupted by a second accession of the brother of a Bonaparte.

I beg leave to digress from the elder brothers to the younger.

We do not possess enough facts, but we may suppose that the races of animals, as they have established themselves, represent the ultimate result of the long, vacillating succession of different changes of species, of a series of consummations and attainments. This history was performed at leisure by the bones and muscles, the convolutions of the brain and the ripples of the nerves.

The antediluvian beasts represent a kind of heroic age in this *Book of Being:* they are the Titans or paladins; they diminish in size, adapt themselves to a new environment and, as soon as they attain to a type that is sufficiently skilful and stable, they begin to repeat themselves in conformity with their type, to such a degree that the dog of Ulysses in the *Odyssey* is as like all our dogs as two drops of water. And that is not all: has anyone said that political or social animals, not only living in a herd but possessing organisation of some sort, like ants and bees, established their ant-hills or nests out of hand? I do not think so at all. Millions of generations lay down and died before they built and stabilised their *Chinese* ant-hills.

I should like to explain from this that, if any people arrives at this condition, where its external social structure conforms to its requirements, then there is no internal need, before a change of requirements, for it to progress, make war, rebel or produce eccentric individuals.

An inactive absorption in the herd or the swarm is one of the prime conditions for the conservation of what has been achieved.

The world of which Mill speaks has not arrived at this state of complete repose. After all its revolutions and shocks it cannot precipitate its lees: there is a mass of muck at the top, and everything is turbid: there is not the cleanness of Chinese porcelain nor the whiteness of Dutch linen. There is much in it that is immature, misshapen, even sick, and in this connection there lies before it one more step forward on its own path. It must acquire not energetic personalities or eccentric passions, but the particular morality of its situation. For the Englishman to stop giving false weight, for the Frenchman to refuse to give assistance to every police-force, it is not only 'respectability' that is required, but a stable mode of living.

Then, in Mill's words, England can turn into a China (an improved one, of course), retaining all her trade and all her freedom and perfecting her legislation, that is, easing it in proportion to the growth of obligatory custom, which deadens the will better than any lawcourts or punishments; and France at the same time can launch herself into the beautiful, martial stream-bed of Persian life, which is enlarged with everything that an educated centralisation puts in the hands of authority, rewarding herself for the loss of all the rights of man with brilliant attacks on her neighbours and shackling other peoples to the fortunes of a centralised despotism . . . already the features of Zouaves belong more to Asia than to Europe.

Forestalling ejaculations and maledictions I hasten to say that I am not speaking here of my desires, or even of my opinions. My task is the purely logical one of trying to *eliminate the brackets* from the formula in which Mill's result is expressed; from his individual differentials to form the historical integral.

So the question cannot be whether it is polite to prophesy for England the fate of China (and it was not I who did this, but Mill himself), or in good taste to foretell that France will be a

Persia; although in all fairness I do not know, either, how it comes that China and Persia may be insulted with impunity. The really important question, that Mill does not touch upon, is this: do there exist the sources of a new vigour to renovate the old blood? Are there sprouts and sound shoots to grow up through the dwindling grass? And what this question adds up to is whether a people will let itself be used once and for all to manure the soil for a new China and a new Persia, condemned inescapably to unskilled labour, to ignorance and hunger, accepting in return that one in ten thousand, as in a lottery, for an example, encouragement and appeasement to the rest, shall grow rich and turn from eaten to eater?

This problem will be solved by events: it cannot be solved theoretically.

If the people is overcome, the new China and new Persia are inevitable.

But if the people overcomes, what is unavoidable is a *social revolution.*

Is this not indeed an *idea* that may be promoted to an *idée fixe,* in spite of the shoulder-shrugging of the aristocracy and the tooth-grinding of the *petite bourgeoisie?*

The people feels this: very much so. Gone is its earlier, childish belief in the legality—or at all events the justice—of what happens: there is fear in the face of violence, and inability to exalt private pain into a general rule; but blind faith there is not. In France the people menacingly declared its protest at the very time when the middle class, flushed with authority and power, was crowning itself king under the name of a republic, was lolling with Marrast in Louis XV's armchairs at Versailles and dictating laws. The people rose in despair, seeing that again it was being left outside the door and without a piece of bread; it rose like barbarians, with nothing decided, no plan, no leaders, no resources; but of vigorous personalities it had no lack and, what is more, it evoked from the other side such predatory, bloodthirsty kites as Cavaignac.

The people was utterly routed. The likelihood of a Persia *increased* and it has been increasing ever since.

How the English working man will put his social question we do not know, but his ox-like stubbornness is great. He has the numerical majority on his side, but not the power. Numbers prove nothing. Two or three Cossacks of the line with two or three garrison soldiers each of them take five hundred convicts from Moscow to Siberia.

If the people in England is routed, as it was in Germany at the time of the Peasants' Wars and in France during the July days, then the China foretold by John Stuart Mill is not far off. The transition to it will take place imperceptibly; not a single right, as we have said, will be lost, not one freedom will be diminished: all that will be diminished is *the ability to make use of these rights and this freedom.*

Timid and sensitive people say that this is impossible. I desire nothing better than to agree with them: but I see no reason to. The tragic inevitability consists in just this: the idea that might rescue the people and steer Europe towards new destinies is *unprofitable* for the ruling class; and for this class, if it were consistent and audacious, the only thing that is *profitable* is ruling—combined with an American system of slavery!

German Emigrants

THE GERMAN EMIGRANTS were distinguished from the others[1] by their ponderous, prosy and cantankerous nature. There were no enthusiasts among them, as there were among the Italians, no hotheads nor sharp tongues, as among the French.

The other emigrants had little to do with them; the difference of manners, of *habitus,* kept them at a certain distance: French arrogance has nothing in common with German boorishness. The absence of a commonly accepted notion of good manners, the heavy, scholastic doctrinairism, the excessive familiarity, the excessive naïveté of the Germans hampered their relationships with people who were not used to them. They did not make many advances themselves . . . considering, on the one hand, that they greatly excelled others in their scientific development and, on the other, feeling in the presence of others the awkwardness of a provincial in a *salon* at the capital and of a civil service clerk in a coterie of aristocrats.

Internally the German emigrants displayed the same friability as their country did. They had no common plan; their unity was supported by mutual hatred and malicious persecution of each

---

[1] After the rout of the rising in the Palatinate and Baden in 1848 there was a wave of emigration from Germany. The overwhelming majority travelled to Switzerland and thence to England and the U.S.A. In the autumn of 1850 London became their headquarters. (*A.S.*)

other. The better among the German exiles were conscious of this. Vigorous men, intelligent men, like Karl Schurz, August Willich and Oskar Reichenbach, had gone to America. Men of gentle disposition, like Freiligrath, were making use of business, of distant London, to hide behind. The rest, except for a few of the leaders, were tearing each other to pieces with indefatigable frenzy, unsparing of family secrets or the most criminal accusations.

Soon after my arrival in London I went to Brighton to see Arnold Ruge, who had been intimately acquainted with Moscow University circles in the 1840s; he had published the celebrated *Hallische Jahrbücher*, and we had drawn from them our philosophical radicalism. I had met him in 1849 in Paris, where the soil had not yet cooled and was still volcanic. There was no time then for the study of personalities. He had come as one of the agents of the insurrectionary government of Baden to invite Mieroslawski, who knew no German, to take command of the army of *Freischärler* and hold discussions with the government of France, which was not at all eager to recognise revolutionary Baden. Karl Blind was with him. After 13th June he and I had to flee from France. Blind was several hours late and was imprisoned in the Conciergerie. I did not see Ruge after that till the autumn of 1852.

I found him at Brighton, a grumbling old man, angry and spiteful. Abandoned by his former friends, forgotten in Germany, without influence on affairs and at variance with his fellow emigrants, Ruge was absorbed in slanderous gossip. In constant touch with him there were two or three most inept newspaper correspondents, penny-a-liners, those petty free-lances of publicity, who are never to be seen in time of battle and always afterwards, cockchafers of the political and literary worlds, who rootle about every evening, gloating and busy, in the discarded remnants of the day. Ruge composed newspaper paragraphs with these men, goaded them on, gave them copy and produced several periodicals in Germany and America.

I dined with him and spent the evening. He complained the whole time about the emigrants and ran them down.

'Have you heard,' he said, 'how things are going with our forty-five-year-old Werther and the baroness?[2] It's said that when he revealed his love for her he tried to captivate her with

---

[2] The reference is to August Willich and Baroness Brüning, a Russian by birth, who had helped to arrange Kinkel's escape from prison. (*A.S.*)

the chemical prospect of a child of genius, to be born of an aristocratic mother and a communist father. The baron, they say, who was no amateur of physiological experiments, chucked him out neck and crop. Is that true?'

'How can you believe such absurdities?'

'No, in point of fact I don't really believe it. I live this parochial life here and only hear from the Germans what is going on in London; all of them, and particularly the emigrants, tell God knows what lies; they're all quarrelling and slandering each other. I think that this Kinkel set that rumour going as a token of gratitude to the baroness, who got him out of prison. He would have run after her himself, you know, but he's not free to: his wife doesn't let him get into mischief. "You got me away from my first husband," she says, "and that's quite enough. . . ."'

There is a sample of philosophical conversation with Arnold Ruge!

He did once alter his tone and talk with friendly interest about Bakunin, but recollected himself half-way and added:

'However, he's begun to go to seed recently; he's been raving about revolutionary tsarism, panslavism or something.'

I left him with a heavy heart and a firm determination never to come back.

A year later he gave some lectures in London about the philosophical movement in Germany. The lectures were bad; the Berlin–English accent struck the ear unpleasantly, and besides he pronounced all the Greek and Latin names in the German way, so that the English could not make out who these Yofis and Yunos were. . . . A dozen people came to the second lecture, and to the third two—Worcell and I. As he walked through the empty hall past us Ruge shook me by the hand, and added:

'Poland and Russia have come, but Italy's not here; I shan't forgive Mazzini or Saffi this when there's a new people's rising.'

When he left, wrathful and menacing, I looked at Worcell's sardonic smile and said:

'Russia invites Poland to dine with her.'

'*C'en est fait d'Italie,*' Worcell observed, shaking his head, and we set off.

Kinkel was one of the most remarkable German emigrants in London. A man of irreproachable conduct, who had laboured in the sweat of his brow—a thing which, however strange this seems, was practically never met with among the emigrants—

Kinkel was Ruge's sworn enemy. Why? That is just as hard to explain as that Ruge, the advocate of atheism, was a friend of the neo-Catholic Ronge. Gottfried Kinkel was one of the heads of the forty times forty[3] German schisms in London.

When I looked at him I always marvelled that the majestic head of a Zeus had found itself on the shoulders of a German professor, and how a German professor had found himself first on the field of battle and then, wounded, in a Prussian prison; but perhaps the oddest thing of all is that all this *plus* London did not change him in the least, and he remained a German professor. A tall man, with grey hair and a grizzled beard, he had a look that of itself was stately and inspired respect; but he added to it as it were an official unction, *Salbung*, something judicial and episcopal, solemn, stiff, and modestly self-satisfied. This *nuance*, in different variations, is encountered in fashionable priests, ladies' physicians, and especially in mesmerisers, advocates who are the special guardians of morals and the headwaiters of aristocratic hotels in England. Kinkel had studied theology a good deal as a young man; when he got free of it he retained the priestly manner. There is nothing surprising in this: Lamennais himself, who cut so deeply at the roots of Catholicism, kept the appearance of an abbot until he was an old man. Kinkel's deliberate, fluent speech, correct and eschewing extremes, ran on as if part of an edifying discussion; he listened to the other side with studied indulgence and to himself with frank self-satisfaction.

He had been a professor at Somerset House[4] and at several institutes of higher education, and had lectured publicly on aesthetics in London and Manchester: this could not be forgiven him by the liberators, roaming hungrily and idly about London, of thirty-four German fatherlands. Kinkel was constantly abused in American newspapers, which became the main channel for German libels, and at the scantily attended meetings held every year in memory of Robert Blum, of the first *Schilderhebung* in Baden, the first Austrian *Schwertfahrt*, etc. He was abused by all his compatriots, who never gave any lessons and were constantly asking for loans, never gave back what they had borrowed and

---

[3] By tradition there were said to be forty times forty churches in Moscow. (*R.*)

[4] In 1771 the king granted the Royal Academy apartments in old Somerset House, and in 1780 in new Somerset House, where they remained till 1830 when they removed to the National Gallery. (*R.*)

were always ready, in case of refusal, to denounce a man as a spy
or a thief. Kinkel did not reply. . . . The scribblers barked; they
barked and, as Krylov puts it, began to lag behind; only now and
then a rough, hairy, uncombed mongrel darts out from the
bottom floor of German democracy into the *feuilleton* that is read
by nobody and bursts out into a vicious yapping to recall the
happy times of fraternal insurrections in the various Tübingens,
Darmstadts and Brunswick-Wolfenbüttels.

In Kinkel's house, at his lectures, in his conversation, it was
all good and sensible—but there was some kind of grease lacking
in the wheels, so that everything went round stiffly; his wife, a
well known pianist, played splendid pieces: and the boredom
was deadly. Only the children as they jumped about introduced a
brighter element; their little shining eyes and resounding voices
augured less virtue, perhaps, but . . . more grease in the
wheels.

'Ich bin *ein Mensch der Möglichkeit*,' Kinkel has said to me
more than once to describe his position among the extremist
parties; he thinks he is a possibility for a future minister in the
coming Germany; I do not think so, but Johanna, his wife, has
no doubt of it.

A propos, a word about their relationship. Kinkel always preserved his dignity and she always marvelled at him. Between
themselves they talk of the most everyday matters in the style of
edifying comedies (modish *haute comédie* in Germany!) and
moral novels.

'*Beste Johanna*,' says he sonorously and without haste, '*du bist,
mein Engel, so gut, schenke mir noch eine Tasse von den vortreff
lichen Thee, den du so gut machst, ein!*'

'*Es ist zu himmlisch, lieber Gottfried, dass er dir geschmeckt
hat. Tue, mein Bester, für mich einige Tropfen Schmand hinein!*'

And he lets some cream drip in, regarding her with tenderness, and she gazes at him with gratitude. Johanna persecuted
her husband fiercely with her perpetual, inexorable solicitude:
when there was a fog she handed him a revolver in some sort of
special belt; begged him to protect himself from the wind, from
evil people, from harmful food, and *in petto* from women's eyes,
which were more harmful than any winds and *pâté de foie
gras*. . . . In a word, she poisoned his life with her acute jealousy and implacable, ever-stimulated love. In return she supported him in his idea that he was a genius, at any rate not
inferior to Lessing, and that in him a new Stein was being
provided for Germany; Kinkel knew that this was true, and

mildly restrained Johanna in the presence of outsiders when her praises went rather too far.

'Johanna, have you heard about Heine?' Charlotte asked her once, running in much upset.

'No,' answers Johanna.

'He's dead . . . yesterday night. . . .'

'Really?'

'*Zu wahr.*'

'Oh, how glad I am. I was always afraid that he would write some caustic epigram against Gottfried: he had such a venomous tongue. You do amaze me,' she added, catching herself up; 'what a loss for Germany.'[5]

. . . . [6]

The source of these hatreds lies partly in a consciousness of the political second-ratedness of the German fatherland, and in their pretensions to play the chief part. Nationalistic fanfaronade is ludicrous even in the French, but at least the French can say that in a certain manner they have shed their blood for the sake of humanity. The pretension to some enormous national importance, going hand in hand with a doctrinaire cosmopolitanism, is the more ridiculous that it exhibits no other right to its claim than a disbelief in consideration for others, a desire *sich geltend zu machen.*

'Why do the Poles not like us?' a German seriously asked in a gathering of *Gelehrter.*

There happened to be a journalist there, an intelligent man, who had lived in England for a long time.

'Well, that's not so hard to understand,' he answered. 'You'd do better to ask who does like us, or why everyone hates us.'

'How do you mean, everyone hates us?' asked the astonished professor.

'All foreigners do, at any rate: Italians, Danes, Swedes, Russians, Slavs.'

'Excuse me, *Herr Doktor:* there are some exceptions,' returned the disquieted and embarrassed *Gelehrte.*

'Without the least doubt: and what are they? France and England.'

The man of learning began to blossom out:

---

[5] I am sorry, in my turn, that I wrote these lines. Soon after this the poor woman threw herself out of a third-storey window into a paved yard. Jealousy and a disease of the heart brought her to this fearful death.

[6] There is a hiatus here in the text. (*R.*)

'And do you know why? France is afraid of us and England despises us.'

The situation of the German is really a sad one, but his sadness is not interesting. They all know that they can settle with the internal and external enemy, but they do not know how to. How comes it, for instance, that peoples of the same stock as the Germans—England, Holland, Sweden—are free, and the Germans are not? Incapability also has its obligations, like nobility, and to modesty most of all. The Germans are conscious of this, and have recourse to desperate measures in order to get the upper hand: they point to England and the North American states[7] as representatives of Germanism in the sphere of political *Praxis*. Ruge, infuriated by Edward Bauer's inane pamphlet on Russia, entitled, I think, *Kirche und Staat*, and suspecting that it was I who had led Bauer into temptation, wrote to me (and later published the same thing in the *Jersey Almanac*) that Russia was only rough material, undisciplined and disorganised, whose strength, glory and beauty proceeded only from German genius having given her its own form and likeness.

Every Russian who appears on the scene encounters in the Germans that malevolent amazement that not so long ago was directed by those same Germans at our men of learning who wished to become professors at Russian universities and the Russian Academy. 'Colleagues' who had been imported into Russia thought this was insolence, ingratitude, usurpation of other people's posts.

Bakunin nearly lost his head, for the sake of the Germans, at the hands of a Saxon headsman, and Marx, who knew him very well, *denounced him as a Russian spy*. In his paper he told a complete story[8] of how George Sand had heard from Ledru-

---

[7] Ruge evinced similar ideas in a letter of his to H. seeking to prove the rights of the Germans to a dominion 'from Kamchatka to Ostend,' and reproaching H. for Russian 'nationalism.' He did not restrict himself to this: he plainly included both England and the U.S.A. in the 'German world.' (*A.S.*)

[8] Marx never denounced Bakunin as a Russian spy. This slander was spread by the Russian embassy in Paris before the revolution of 1848; it was taken up by certain circles of Polish emigrants, and was current, after the March revolution in Germany, at Breslau, where B. had gone at the end of April to be nearer the Russian frontier. A Paris journalistic agency passed on this rumour to newspapers, among them Marx's paper *Neue Rheinische Zeitung*. Everbeck, a German *émigré*, included it in his correspondence with his newspaper, citing the finding at George Sand's of compromising documents of a Russian revolutionary: the ac-

Rollin that, while he had been Minister of the Interior, he had seen a correspondence which compromised Bakunin. At that time Bakunin was in prison[9] awaiting sentence, and suspected nothing. The slander tended to thrust him towards the scaffold, and to sever the last contact of love between the martyr and the mass that sympathised in silence. Adolf Reichel, a friend of Bakunin, wrote to George Sand at Nohant and asked her what the truth was. She answered Reichel at once and sent a letter to the editor of Marx's paper expressing the greatest friendship for Bakunin; she added that *she had never talked* about Bakunin to Ledru-Rollin, in virtue of which she could not have repeated what the newspaper said. Marx exonerated himself cleverly and printed George Sand's letter with a note which said that the notice about Bakunin had been printed 'at a time when he was absent.'

The finale was a completely German one: it would have been impossible not only in France, where the *point d'honneur* is so scrupulous and where the editor would have buried all the dirtiness of the affair under a heap of phrases, words, circumlocutions

---

count appeared on 6th July, 1848. 'The *publication* of the accusation,' Marx wrote later, 'was in the interests of the cause and in the interests of Bakunin.'

Bakunin's protest and his request to George Sand to refute the rumour appeared in a Breslau newspaper; they were at once reprinted in Marx's paper of 16th July, 1848. On 3rd August Marx printed a complete rehabilitation of Bakunin by George Sand, and gave his reasons for publishing the slander, one of which was to give Bakunin an opportunity of vindicating himself. Bakunin was satisfied. He and Marx met in Berlin towards the end of 1848 and 'renewed their friendship.' (*A.S.*)

This gloss by the Academy of Sciences is more academic than scientific. An editor who prints a slanderous rumor about an opponent does afford the latter "an opportunity of vindicating himself," in a sense—a Pickwickian sense. But assuming Marx's chief concern was, as he states, to protect "the interests of Bakunin," one might expect a simpler, less ambiguous method to occur to that formidable brain, namely, to ask George Sand about it before he printed anything. One wonders whether Marx reprinted the Sand refutation of the *canard* (and after Reichel, not Marx, had asked her to set the matter straight) as the foreseen climax of a Bakunin vindication campaign? Or whether he was simply, and cruelly, caught with his polemical pants down? I'm also curious about the source of "renewed their close friendship"—perhaps some Comrade Smooth-It-Away in the Soviet Academy? That Marx and Bakunin, given their politics—and their temperaments—were ever close friends, however briefly, seems unlikely, nor does this friendship figure in any histories or biographies I have read. (*D.M.*)

[9] Bakunin was arrested for participating in the Dresden rising of May 1849—almost a year after the correspondence appeared in Marx's newspaper. (*A.S.*)

and moral aphorisms, and would have masked it with his despair *qu'on avait surpris sa religion;* but even an English editor, though incomparably less punctilious, would not have dared to shift the responsibility to his colleagues.[10]

A year after my arrival in London Marx's party returned again to their vile calumny of Bakunin, who was then entombed in the Alexeyevsky ravelin.

In England, this time-honoured country of the crazed, one of the most egregious positions is occupied by David Urquhart, a man of talent and energy, an ex-conservative radical, who is obsessed by two notions: first, that Turkey is a superlative country with a great future, in virtue of which he has furnished himself with Turkish cooking, a Turkish bath and Turkish sofas; secondly, that Russian diplomacy is the slyest and most astute in the whole of Europe, and that it bribes and bamboozles all the statesmen in every country in the world, principally in England. Urquhart worked for years to find a proof that Palmerston was in the pay of the cabinet in Petersburg. He published articles and pamphlets on this, introduced motions in Parliament and held forth at meetings. At first people were angered by him, replied to

---

[10] In spite of the fact that England takes fearful liberties. To give an idea of them I shall tell of something that happened to Louis Blanc. *The Times* published a report that Louis Blanc, when he was a member of the Provisional Government, had spent '1,500,000 francs of the government's money, to form for himself a party among the workers.' Blanc replied to the editor that he had been misinformed about him and that, however much he had wanted to, he would not have been able to steal or to spend 1½ million francs because, during all the time that he was at the head of the Luxemburg Commission, he had not had at his disposal more than 30,000 francs. *The Times* did not print his reply. Louis Blanc went to the editorial office himself and requested an interview with the editor-in-chief. He was told that there was *no such person* as an editor-in-chief; that *The Times* was published as it were by a committee. Blanc demanded an accountable committee-man: he was told that nobody was personally answerable for anything.

'Whom, then, should I see, from whom demand an account of why my letter about an affair which concerned my good name, was not published.'

'Here,' one of the officials on *The Times* told him, 'things are not done as they are in France; we have neither a *gérant responsable* nor a legal obligation to print replies.'

'There is absolutely no accountable editor?' Louis Blanc asked.

'No.'

'It's a very great pity,' remarked Louis Blanc, smiling angrily, 'that there is no editor-in-chief; otherwise I should certainly have boxed his ears. Good-bye, gentlemen.'

'Good day, Sir, good day. God bless you!' repeated *The Times*'s official, coolly and courteously opening the door.

him and abused him; then they became accustomed to him. Those he accused and those who listened to the accusations began to smile; they paid no attention . . . finally they burst out laughing.

Lecturing to a meeting in one of the big towns Urquhart was so carried away by his *idée fixe* that, representing Kossuth as a man not to be trusted, he added that even if Kossuth had not been bought by Russia he was under the influence of a man who clearly was working on behalf of Russia . . . *and that man was Mazzini!* Like Dante's Francesca, that day he read no more. At the name of Mazzini there rose such a gale of Homeric laughter that David himself remarked that he had not knocked over the Italian Goliath with his sling, but had dislocated his own arm.

A man who thought and openly said that from Guizot and Derby to Espartero, Cobden and Mazzini, they were all Russian agents, was a boon to the gang of unacknowledged German statesmen who surrounded an unrecognised genius of the first order—Marx. They made, of their unsuccessful patriotism and fearful pretensions, a kind of *Hochschule* of calumny and suspicion of anyone who came on to the stage with greater success than theirs. They were in need of an honourable name: Urquhart gave them one.

Urquhart had at that time great influence with *The Morning Advertiser*, one of those newspapers that are very peculiarly run. This paper is not to be seen in the clubs, at the big news agents or on the tables of respectable people, but it has a bigger circulation than the *Daily News*, and it is only recently that cheap sheets like the *Daily Telegraph* and *The Morning* and *Evening Star* have pushed *The Morning Advertiser* into the background. It is a purely English phenomenon: *The Morning Advertiser* is the public-house newspaper, and no tavern would be without it.

With Urquhart and the customers of public houses the Marxists and their friends[11] declared themselves in the pages of *The Morning Advertiser*. 'Where there is beer, there will be Germans.'

One fine morning[12] *The Morning Advertiser* suddenly raised

---

[11] In reality Marx not only did not keep up any close connection with *The Morning Advertiser* but even expressed himself very sharply more than once about the paper's politics and about the personal qualities of the editor and publishers. He considered it to be 'Pam's [*i.e.*, Palmerston's (*D.M.*)] barrel-organ.' (*A.S.*)

[12] 2nd August, 1853. (*A.S.*)

the question: 'Was Bakunin a Russian agent or not?' Of course, the answer was in the affirmative. This act was so outrageous that it perturbed even people who took no particular interest in Bakunin.

The affair could not possibly be left there. However annoying it was to have to sign a joint protestation[13] with Golovin (there will be a separate chapter on this subject),[14] there was no choice. I invited Worcell and Mazzini to associate themselves with our protest, and they agreed at once. One might have thought that, after the testimony of the President of the Polish democratic Central Government and of such a man as Mazzini, the whole thing was finished; but the Germans were not satisfied with this: they dragged on a most boring polemic with Golovin, who kept it up on his side to interest in himself the customers of London public-houses.

My protest, and the fact that I had written to Mazzini and Worcell, was bound to direct Marx's rage against me. This anyhow was the time when the Germans realised their mistake, and began to encompass me with a boorish hostility on a par with the boorish advances that they had formerly made to me. They no longer wrote me panegyrics, as at the time when *Vom andern Ufer* and *Letters from Italy* appeared, but spoke of me as 'the insolent barbarian who dares to look down his nose at Germany.'[15] One of the Marxist *Gesellen* wrote a complete book against me and sent it to Hofmann and Campe, who declined to publish it. Then he got it printed (I learnt this much later) in *The Leader,* of which I have spoken. I do not recollect his name.

The Marxists were soon joined by a knight with his visor

---

[13] The letter signed by Golovin, Herzen and Worcell, appeared in *The Morning Advertiser* of 29th August, 1853. See also the letter from Marx printed in *The Morning Advertiser* of 2nd September. (*A.S.*)

[14] Later Herzen devotes twenty pages to his depressing encounters with I. Golovin, which are omitted here. Judging from Herzen's account, concrete and documented as usual, I. Golovin was a paranoid adventurer and clearly a man to avoid. But, unlike Marx, Herzen was unable to be reclusive either by temperament or on principle. "I was visited for the first time by I. Golovin, who until then was known to me only from his mediocre writings and from his exceedingly bad reputation as an insolent and quarrelsome man," he writes as of 1848. But ten years later he was still entangled with the Golovin tar-baby. (*D.M.*)

[15] This was written by one Kolachek in an American periodical on the subject of the second French edition of *On the Development of Revolutionary Ideas in Russia.* The piquancy of it lies in the fact that *the whole text* of this book had been formerly published in German by . . . that same Kolachek!

lowered, Karl Blind, then a *famulus* of Marx, now his enemy. In his account in New York papers, mention was made of a dinner given to us by the American consul in London:[16] 'At this dinner there was a Russian, A. H. by name, who passes himself off as a socialist and republican. H. lives in close association with Mazzini, Kossuth and Saffi. . . . It is extremely careless of people who are at the head of movements to admit a Russian to their acquaintance. We hope that they will not have to repent of this when it is too late.'

Whether Blind himself, or one of his assistants, wrote this I do not know: I have not the text before me, but I will answer for the sense of it.

While I am on the subject I must observe that both on Blind's side and on Marx's, whom I did not know at all, all this hatred was purely Platonic—impersonal, so to speak: they were sacrificing me to their *Vaterland* out of patriotism. At the American dinner, by the way, they were infuriated by the absence of a German—so they took it out on the Russian.

This dinner, which made a great deal of noise on both sides of the Atlantic, came about in the following way. President Pierce was being sulky with the old European governments and playing all sorts of schoolboy pranks. This was possibly in order to gain greater popularity at home, and partly to divert the eyes of all the radical parties in Europe from the main jewel on which his whole policy turned—the imperceptible expansion and consolidation of slavery.

This was the time of the embassy of Soulé to Spain and of Robert Owen's son[17] to Naples, soon after Soulé's duel with Turgot and his insistent request to be allowed to travel, notwithstanding Napoleon's order, through France and Brussels, which the Emperor of the French could not make up his mind to refuse. 'We send ambassadors,' the Americans said, 'not to kings but to peoples.' Hence arose the idea of giving a diplomatic dinner to the enemies of all existing governments.

I had no notion of the dinner that was being arranged. I

---

16 On 21st February, 1854. (*A.S.*)

17 Pierre Soulé had emigrated in 1824 from France to the U.S.A. He went as ambassador to Spain in 1853; he fought a duel with the Marquis de Turgot, the French ambassador, in Madrid. Robert Dale Owen took an active part in American politics from the 1830s onwards, and from 1853-8 was United States ambassador at the Court of the Two Sicilies. (*A.S.*)

suddenly received an invitation from Saunders, the American consul; with the invitation was enclosed a little note from Mazzini: he asked me not to refuse, saying that the dinner was being given to annoy someone and to demonstrate sympathy with somebody else.

There were at the dinner Mazzini, Kossuth, Ledru-Rollin, Garibaldi, Orsini, Worcell, Pulszki and myself, one Englishman, Joshua Wolmsley, M.P., and Buchanan, the United States ambassador, and all the embassy officials.

It should be mentioned that one of the objects of the *red* dinner, given by the defender of *black* slavery, was that Kossuth and Ledru-Rollin should meet. The idea was not to reconcile them, for they had never quarrelled, but to introduce them to each other officially. The reasons why they had not made each other's acquaintance was as follows. Ledru-Rollin was already in London when Kossuth arrived from Turkey. The question arose, which should call first, Ledru-Rollin on Kossuth or Kossuth on Ledru-Rollin. The question greatly agitated their friends and supporters, their Court, the brigade of guards and the rabble that followed them. The *pro* and *contra* were considerable. One had been dictator of Hungary; the other had not been a dictator, but then he was a *Frenchman*. One was a guest of honour in England, a lion of the first magnitude, at the zenith of his glory which was about to decline; to the other England was like a home, and calls are paid by the newer arrivals. . . . In a word this problem, like the squaring of the circle or the *perpetuum mobile*, was found by both courts to be insoluble . . . therefore it was solved by a decision that neither should call on the other, and a meeting between them was left to the will of God and to chance. . . . For three or four years Ledru-Rollin and Kossuth, living in the same town, having friends and interests in common and a common cause, had to ignore each other, and chance there was none. Mazzini decided to give destiny a helping hand.

Before dinner, and after Buchanan had shaken hands with all of us, expressing to each one his great pleasure at making his acquaintance personally, Mazzini took Ledru-Rollin by the arm, and at the same time Buchanan carried out the same manoeuvre with Kossuth and, both gently leading forward the two men who were the occasion of the dinner, brought them almost into collision and named each to the other. The new acquaintances did not hang back, and showered each other with compliments— Oriental and florid from the great Magyar, full of power and the colour and eloquence of the Convention from the great Gaul.

All the time that this scene was being played I stood by the window with Orsini . . . as I looked at him I was fearfully glad to see a slight smile, more in his eyes than on his lips.

'Let me tell you,' I said, 'what nonsense has come into my head. In 1847 I saw in Paris, at the *Théâtre de l'Histoire*, a very stupid play about a war, in which the chief part was acted by smoke and shooting and the second by horses, cannon and drums. In one of the acts the commanders of both armies came from opposite sides of the stage to negotiate; they walked bravely towards each other and, as they came near, one took off his hat and said, "Suvorov—Masséna!" to which the other, also hatless, answered, "Masséna—Suvorov!" '

'I've hardly been able to keep from laughing myself,' said Orsini to me, with a completely grave face.

The sly old man Buchanan, who was then already dreaming, in spite of his seventy years, of the presidency, and therefore was constantly talking of the happiness of retirement, of the idyllic life and of his own infirmity, made up to us as he had made up to Orlov and Benckendorf at the Winter Palace when he was ambassador in the time of Nicholas. Kossuth and Mazzini he knew already; to the others he paid compliments specially selected for each, much more reminiscent of an experienced diplomatist than of the austere citizen of a democratic republic. To me he said nothing except that he had been in Russia for a long time, and had brought away the conviction that she had a great future. I made no reply to that, of course, but observed that I remembered him from the time of Nicholas's coronation. 'I was a boy, but you were so conspicuous in your simple, black frock-coat and round hat, in that crowd of embroidered, gilded, uni-formed notables.'

To Garibaldi he remarked: 'You have the same reputation in America as you have in Europe, only in America you have an-other title to fame as well: you're known there . . . you're known there as a distinguished sailor.'

At dessert, when Madame Saunders had gone and we had been offered cigars with another large quantity of wine, Buchanan, who was sitting opposite Ledru-Rollin, told him that he had 'a friend in New York who had said he was prepared to travel from America to France only to make Ledru-Rollin's acquaintance.'

Unfortunately Buchanan mumbled rather and Ledru-Rollin did not understand English well; so that a most amusing *quid pro quo* occurred—Ledru-Rollin thought that Buchanan was speaking of himself, and with a French *effusion de reconnais-sance* started to thank him, and held out his huge hand to him across the table. Buchanan accepted the thanks and the hand and, with the imperturbable coolness in difficult circumstances with which Englishmen and Americans go down with their ship or lose half their fortune, observed to him, 'I think this is a mistake; it was not I who thought so: it was one of my best friends in New York.'

The festal evening ended when, late at night, after Buchanan left, and when Kossuth did not think it possible to remain any longer, and went away with his Minister without Portfolio, the consul began begging us to go back into the dining-room, where he wished to make for us with his own hands an American punch of old Kentucky whisky. What was more, Saunders wanted to compensate himself there for the absence at dinner of vehement toasts to the future universal (white) republic, which the cautious Buchanan must have forbidden. At dinner we had drunk to the health of two or three of the guests and Saunders, without speeches.

While he was burning some alcohol and seeing to the flavour-ing, seasoning and spicing, he proposed a ceremonial singing of the Marseillaise in chorus. It proved that only Worcell knew the tune properly, but he had an *extinction* of the voice, and Mazzini knew it slightly—so the American Mrs Saunders had to be summoned, and she played the Marseillaise on the guitar.

Meanwhile her spouse, having finished his concoction, tried it, was pleased with it and poured us out big teacups. With no thought of danger I took a big mouthful, and for a minute I could not draw breath. When I had recovered, and saw that Ledru-Rollin was preparing to gulp it just as eagerly, I stopped him with the words:

'If life is dear to you, approach the Kentucky refreshment with more circumspection: I am a Russian, and even so I've scorched my palate, my throat and my whole alimentary canal: what will happen to you? Punch in Kentucky must be made from red pepper with an infusion of oil of vitriol.'

The American smiled ironically, rejoicing at the feebleness of Europeans. I, having followed from my youth in the footsteps of Mithridates, was the only one who held out my empty cup and asked for more. The chemical affinity with alcohol raised me terribly high in the consul's eyes.

'Yes, yes,' he said: 'it's only in America and Russia that people know how to drink.'

'Well,' I thought, 'there is an even more flattering affinity: it's only in America and Russia that they know how to flog serfs to death.'

With punch, then, of 70 degrees there came to an end this dinner, which did more harm to the blood of German *folliculaires* than it did to the stomachs of the diners.

The transatlantic dinner was followed by the venture of an International Committee—the last endeavour of the Chartists and exiles to declare, with united power, their mode of life and their alliance. The idea of this committee came from Ernest Jones. He wanted to revivify Chartism, which was decrepit, considering its age, by bringing together the English workers and French socialists. The public enactment of this *entente cordiale* was to be a political meeting in memory of 24th February, 1848.

The International Committee elected me a member, among a dozen others, and asked me to make a speech about Russia. I thanked them for their letter and declined to make a speech. The matter would have rested there if Marx and Golovin had not compelled me to spite them by appearing on the platform at St Martin's Hall.[18]

To begin with Jones received a letter from some German protesting against the choice of me. He wrote that I was a known panslavist, that I had written of the necessity for conquering Vienna, which I called the Slavonic capital, and that I preached the serfdom of Russia as an ideal for an agricultural population. In all this he relied on my letters to Linton (*La Russie et le vieux monde*). Jones threw the patriotic slander away and paid no attention.

But this letter was only a reconnaissance patrol. At the next meeting Marx declared that he considered my election inconsistent with the object of the committee and proposed that it should be quashed. Jones remarked that this was not as easy as he thought; that the committee, which had elected a person who had expressed no desire to be a member, and had communicated to him his official election, could not alter its decision at the wish of one member; let Marx make his accusations formally and submit them for the consideration of the committee.

To this Marx replied that he did not know me personally, that he had no private accusation to make against me, but for him it was sufficient that I was a Russian, and, moreover, *a Russian who supported Russia in everything he wrote*; in short, if the

---

[18] On 27th February, 1855. (*A.S.*) This was the meeting at which Marx declined to be present because Herzen would be there. (*R.*)

committee did not exclude me, he and all his people would be obliged to go.

Ernest Jones, the French, the Poles, the Italians, two or three Germans and the English voted for me. Marx was left with a tiny minority. He rose and, with his faithful followers, left the committee and did not return.

Beaten in the committee, the Marxists withdrew to their stronghold, *The Morning Advertiser*. Hurst and Blackett had published one volume of *My Past and Thoughts*, which included 'Prison and Exile.' In order to get a good sale for their wares they had not hesitated to put 'My Exile in Siberia' in the table of contents. *The Express* was the first to notice this piece of showing off. I wrote a letter to the publisher and another to *The Express*. Hurst and Blackett affirmed that the heading had been put in by them; that it was not in the original, but that Hofmann and Campe also had put 'in Siberia' in the German translation. All this was printed by *The Express*. It seemed that the affair was over; but *The Morning Advertiser* began to stick a pin into me two or three times a week. It said that I had used the word 'Siberia' to get the book a better sale; that I had protested five days after the appearance of the book: that is, giving time for the edition to sell. I replied; they printed a headline: 'The Case of Mr H.,' as reports of murders are usually printed, or of criminal cases. The *Advertiser*'s Germans doubted not only the 'Siberia' affixed by the publisher, but even my banishment itself. 'At Vyatka and Novgorod Mr H. was on *Imperial* service: where was he banished to, and when?'[19]

---

[19] The Marxists' accusation was both plausible and damaging. Siberian exile, such as Dostoevsky suffered in the same period (cf. *The House of the Dead*), was to Herzen's as Leavenworth is to parole. Herzen was not a convict like Dostoevsky—or Bakunin, Lenin or Trotsky later. He was a well-connected but imprudent aristocrat who was banished but not imprisoned; *i.e.*, was merely required to live in certain provincial towns (on the Western, civilized, non-Siberian side of the Urals) as a minor government official. So *My Exile in Siberia* was indeed a phoney title for his book, and his Marxist enemies made the most of it. Too much. Did they really believe their charge except as effective demagogy? (Marxists weren't over-delicate in such matters then, from my reading, nor are they now, from my experience.) Herzen's explanation—that his English publishers, without consulting him, put "Siberia" into the title for the usual publishers' reasons—seems to me convincing because: (a) unless he was a fool, he must have realized that (since he reveals at length just where and when he was exiled; see the chapters on Perm, Vyatka, Vladimir and Novgorod) the most cursory reader would detect the fakery

Eventually interest evaporated and *The Morning Advertiser* forgot me.[20]

◇   ◇   ◇

—and Herzen wasn't a fool; (b) he was jealous of his honor to the point of touchiness; (c) he tended to minimize his achievements like a gentleman rather than to inflate them like a careerist; and (d) even granting, for argument's sake, that he was a foolish scoundrel careerist —which is his Marxian enemies' polemical assumption—he was a rich man, the wealthiest revolutionary in London, including Engels, and really didn't need the extra royalties that "Siberia" hype might have brought him. As for the Marxists' accusation that Herzen was "On Imperial Service," this is the factual lie of demagogy: narrowly true and deeply false. When Tolstoy "served" his Tsar at Sevastopol as an artillery officer (the same Tsar Nicholas Herzen had "served," more critically and less bloodily, twenty years earlier) he was also "On Imperial Service." Considering the writings that came out of these "services," the formulation seems inadequate. (*D.M.*)

[20] In Volume XI (1957), pp. 678–80, of the Soviet Academy's edition of Herzen's works there is an account of the disparity in view and the hostility to each other of Herzen and Marx. They never met, although they were living in London in the 1850s and 1860s. (*R.*) See Appendix for a translation, made by Mr. Higgens at my request, of the Soviet Academy's history of, and political glosses on, the Marx-Herzen antagonism, which was mutual, intense and lifelong; also for some glosses of my own on their glosses. (*D.M.*)

Robert Owen [1]

Shut up the world at large, let Bedlam out
And you will be perhaps surprised to find
All things pursue exactly the same route,
As now with those of soi-disant sound mind;
This I could prove beyond a single doubt
Were there a jot of sense among mankind;
But till that point d'appui *is found, alas!*
Like Archimedes, I leave earth as 'twas.

BYRON, *Don Juan*, XIV, 84

I

SOON AFTER MY ARRIVAL in London in 1852 I received an invitation from a lady[2] to stay for a few days at her house in the country near Sevenoaks.[3] I had made her acquaintance through Mazzini at Nice in 1850. My life was still sunny when she came to see us, and so it was when she left. I wanted to see her again, so I went.

Our meeting was awkward. There had been too much darkness in my life since we had seen each other.[4] If a man does not boast of his misfortunes he feels ashamed of them, and this feeling of

---

[1] The significance of this chapter extends far beyond a mere characterization of Owen and memories of him. It contains sharp criticism of bourgeois society and is remarkable for expressing the tendencies towards historical optimism in Herzen's *Weltanschauung*, of his faith in the role of historical activity [by] progressive people and of the importance of progressive thought. (*A.S.*) I agree with the Soviet academicians about the chapter's importance though I see it as a noble statement of Herzen's political philosophy which, like Owen's, was idealistic, moralistic, anarchistic and humanistic—in short, all the Soviet Academy of Sciences despises and the opposite of what it means by "progressive." (*D.M.*)

[2] Matilda Biggs, the daughter of James Stansfeld, whose whole family was on friendly terms with the democratic *émigrés* in London, and in particular with Herzen. (*A.S.*)

[3] A home was found for Owen at Park Farm, Sevenoaks, where he lived from 1853 until his death. (*R.*)

[4] Herzen is referring to the 'Family Drama' and the death of Natalya, his wife. (*A.S.*)

shame comes to the surface at every meeting with former
acquaintances.

She had not had an easy time, either. She gave me her hand
and took me into a park. This was the first old English park that
I had seen, and one of the most magnificent. It had not been
touched by human hands since the days of Elizabeth; shady,
gloomy, it had grown without hindrance and spread more
thickly in its aristocratic, monastic remoteness from the world.
The ancient mansion of purely Elizabethan architecture was
empty. Although a solitary old lady lived in it there was nobody
to be seen; only a grey-haired porter, sitting at the gates, remarked with some pomposity to people going into the park that
they should not walk past the mansion at dinner-time. It was so
quiet in the park that the fallow deer trooped across the rides
and came calmly to a stop, raising their muzzles and sniffing the
air. Nowhere was there an extraneous sound, and the crows
cawed just as they had in our old garden at Vasilevskoye. Somewhere hereabouts I thought I might have lain down under a tree
and tried to imagine myself at thirteen. . . . We came from
Moscow only yesterday, and somewhere here, not far away, our
old gardener is making some peppermint water. We dwellers in
the oak-woods feel more kinship with forests and trees than with
seas and mountains.

We talked of Italy, of my journey to Mentone; we talked of
Medici, with whom she was slightly acquainted, and of Orsini,
and we did not speak of what at that time probably occupied the
minds of both of us more than anything else.

I saw the sincere sympathy in her eyes and silently thanked
her for it. What could I have said to her that was new?

Soon rain began to fall and, since it might rain harder and
might be lasting, we went back.

In the drawing-room there was a little, frail old gentleman,
with snow-white hair, with an unusually good-natured expression and a bright, clear, gentle eye—that blue, child-like eye
which remains with people until extreme old age, a reflection of
their great kindness.

My hostess's daughters ran to their white-haired grandfather:
it was obvious that they were friends.

I had stopped at the garden door.

'Here is something that could not have happened more appropriately,' said their mother, putting out her hand to the old
gentleman. 'To-day I have a treat for you. Let me introduce our
Russian friend. I think,' she added, turning to me, 'you will
enjoy meeting one of *your patriarchs*.'

'Robert Owen,' said the old gentleman, smiling good-naturedly. 'I'm very, very pleased.'

I took his hand with a feeling of filial respect; if I had been younger I might perhaps have knelt and asked the old man to lay his hands on me.

So this was how he came by his kind, bright eye; this was why the children loved him. . . . This was he, the one sober, courageous jury-man 'among the drunken ones' (as Aristotle once said of Anaxagoras), who dared to pronounce 'not guilty' over humanity, 'not guilty' over the criminal. This was the second eccentric who was grieved for the publican and pitied the fallen and who, without sinking, walked, if not over the sea, yet over the bog of vulgarity of English life—not only without sinking but even without getting dirty!

. . . Owen's manner was very simple; but with him, as with Garibaldi, there shone through his kindliness a strength and a consciousness of the possession of authority. In his affability there was a feeling of his own excellence; it was the result perhaps of continual dealings with wretched associates: on the whole, he bore more resemblance to a ruined aristocrat, to the younger son of a great family, than to a plebeian and a socialist.

At that time I spoke no English, and Owen knew no French and was noticeably deaf, so the lady's eldest daughter offered to act as our dragoman: Owen was accustomed to talking to foreigners like this.

'I am expecting great things from your country,' he said to me. 'With you the field is clearer and the priests are not so powerful, prejudices are not so deeply rooted . . . and such strength! If the Emperor were willing to go into, to understand, the new requirements of the harmonious world that is coming into being, how easy it would be for him to become one of the greatest of men.'

With a smile I asked my dragoman to tell Owen that I had very little hope that Nicholas would become a follower of his.

'But he came to see me at Lanark,[5] you know.'

---

[5] Nicholas visited Owen in 1815 at New Lanark, where the cotton-mill was that Owen had established. Owen tells in his autobiography how the Grand Duke Nicholas invited him to move to Russia and set up there, with support from the Tsar's government, industrial communities like New Lanark. Owen declined the invitation. (*A.S.*) According to Podmore (I, 173), Nicholas wished to take one of Owen's younger sons, David Dale Owen, to Russia and find him a place at his court; and, knowing that these islands were thought by some statesmen to be over-populated, he suggested that O. should come to Russia and bring two

'And I'm sure he understood nothing.'

'He was young then, and'—Owen laughed—'and was very sorry that my eldest son was so tall and was not going into the army. He did invite me to Russia, though.'

'Now he's old, but he understands just as little, and probably is even sorrier that not every tall man goes for a soldier. I've seen the letter you wrote to him and, I tell you frankly, I don't understand your purpose in writing it. You can't really have any hope?'

'While a man is alive one must not despair of him. There are so many kinds of happening that may lay open the soul. Well, and if my letter doesn't work and he throws it away, where's the harm? I shall have done what I could. It is not his fault that his upbringing and the environment in which he lives have made him incapable of understanding the truth. In such a case, one must not be angry but feel pity.'

So this old man extended his all-embracing forgiveness of sins not only to thieves and criminals but even to Nicholas. For a minute I felt ashamed.

Is not this why people have forgiven Owen nothing, not even his mental torpor before he died and his half-sick ravings about spirits?

When I met Owen he was eighty-one (he was born in 1771). For *sixty years* he had not left the arena.

Three years after Sevenoaks I saw Owen again for a moment. His body was worn out, his mind was dulled and sometimes rambled unchecked about the mystical spheres of spectres and shades. But the same energy was there, the same blue gaze of child-like goodness and the same hope for man. He harboured no grudge, he had forgotten old scores, he was the same young enthusiast, the founder of New Lanark, hard of hearing, grey, feeble, but still preaching the abolition of punishments and the harmonious life of communal labour. One could not see without deep veneration this old man walking slowly, with uncertain step, on to the platform, where *once* he had been greeted by the fervent applause of a brilliant audience, and where now his yellowed white locks evoked a whisper of indifference and an ironical laugh. The crazy old man, with the seal of death upon

---

million of the surplus people with him. Both offers were gratefully declined. (*R.*)

his face, stood without anger, asking meekly and with love for an hour of their time. He might surely have been given that hour in return for his sixty-five years of blameless service; but he was refused: he bored them, he kept repeating the same thing and, most important, he deeply offended the crowd. He wanted to take away from them the right to dangle from the gallows and to watch others dangling there; he wanted to take away from them the loathsome wheel that pushes them on from behind and to open the locked cage, that inhuman *mater dolorosa* of the soul, which the secular inquisition has substituted for the monkish chests filled with knives. For this sacrilege the crowd was ready to stone Owen to death, but the crowd, too, had become more *humane:* stones had gone out of fashion; they preferred mud, hisses and articles in the newspapers.

Another old man, just such a fanatic, was more fortunate than Owen when, with his feeble, hundred-year-old hands he blessed small and great on Patmos and only murmured, 'Children, love one another!' The simple and the poor did not laugh at him, did not say that his commandment was absurd: these plebeians did not know the golden mean of the vulgar world—a world more hypocritical than ignorant, more narrow-minded than stupid. Compelled to abandon his New Lanark, Owen crossed the ocean ten times, thinking that the seeds of his teaching would grow better in *new soil*, forgetting that this had been cleared by Quakers and Puritans, and probably not foreseeing that five years after his death[6] the republic of Jefferson, the first to proclaim the rights of man, would collapse over the right to flog Negroes. When he was unsuccessful there too, Owen appeared on the old soil again and went round battering at every door, at palaces and hovels, starting markets which would serve as a model of the Rochdale community[7] and of the co-operative associations, publishing books and magazines, writing epistles, holding meetings, making speeches, availing himself of every opportunity. Governments from all over the world were sending delegates to the 'World Exhibition.'[8] Owen was among them at once, asking them to take with them an olive branch and the news of a call to a life of reason and concord—but they did not

---

[6] Robert Owen died in 1858. (*A.S.*)
[7] The first consumers' co-operative society was founded at Rochdale in 1844 by workers in the textile industry. (*A.S.*)
[8] In London in 1851. (*A.S.*)

listen to him, for they were thinking of the jewelled crosses and snuff-boxes to come. Owen was not discouraged.

On a foggy October day in 1858 Lord Brougham, knowing very well that the leak in the ramshackle barn of society was always gaining but still hoping that it could be caulked so that it would last our time, sought advice about *oakum and pitch* at Liverpool at the second meeting of the Social Science Association.

Suddenly there was a stir, and Owen, ill and pale, was gently carried on a stretcher on to the platform. He had overtaxed his strength and had come from London on purpose to give again his good news of the possibility of a society fed and clothed, of a society without a hangman. Lord Brougham received the old gentleman with deference (they had been intimates at one time); Owen stood up quietly and in a faint voice began to speak of the different time that was approaching, of a new harmony[9]— his strength failed him and his speech stopped . . . Brougham finished his sentence for him and gave a sign: the old man's body was drooping and he was insensible; he was gently placed on a stretcher and carried in dead silence through the crowd, who this time were struck with a kind of reverence: it was as though they felt that this was the beginning of a funeral not entirely of the usual sort, that something great, something sacred, something outraged was being extinguished.

A few days went by; Owen recovered a little and one morning told his friend and assistant, Rigby, to pack, because he wanted to leave.

'To London again?' Rigby asked.

'No. Take me to the place where I was born. That is where I shall lay my bones.'

And Rigby took him to Newtown in Montgomeryshire, where eighty-eight years before this strange man had been born, an apostle among mill-owners. . . .

'His breathing stopped so gently,' writes his eldest son, who alone managed to get to Newtown before Owen's death, 'that I, who was holding his hand, hardly noticed it. There was not the slightest struggle, not one convulsive movement.'

In exactly the same way neither England nor the whole world noticed when this witness *à la décharge* in the criminal action against humanity ceased to breathe.

An English priest troubled his dust with a funeral service, in

---

[9] New Harmony was the name of a co-operative labouring community founded by Owen in Indiana, U.S.A., in 1824. It came to an end in 1829. (*R*.)

spite of the wishes of a small group of friends who had come to the burial; the friends dispersed, Thomas Allsop[10] protested boldly, nobly—and 'all was over.'

I wished to write a few words about him but, carried away by the general *Wirbelwind*, I did nothing; his tragic shade withdrew farther and farther and began to disappear behind the heads of others, behind painful events and the dust of every day. Suddenly, the other day, I remembered Owen and my intention of writing something about him.

Turning over the pages of the *Westminster Review*[11] I came across an article about him, and I read the whole of it with attention. The article was written not by an enemy of Owen's but by a reasonable, reliable man who could give merits their due and defects their desert; nevertheless, I put down the magazine with an odd feeling of pain, of outrage, of something stifling, with a feeling approaching hatred of what I had been subjected to.

Perhaps I was unwell, in a bad humour, did not understand? I took the periodical up again, read here and there—the effect was still the same.

'More than the last twenty years of Owen's life are without interest for the public.

Ein unnütz Leben ist ein früher Tod.[12]

'He summoned meetings, but hardly anyone came, because he went on repeating his old principles which everybody had long forgotten. Those who wanted to hear from him something *useful for themselves* had to hear again how the whole life of society was based on false foundations. To this dotage there was soon added a belief in the rapping of spirits . . . the old man harped on his talks with the Duke of Kent, with Byron, Shelley and so on. . . .

'There is not the least danger that Owen's teachings will be accepted in practice. They were such *feeble* chains as cannot *hold* a whole people. Long before his death his principles were *refuted*, forgotten, but he continued to imagine himself the benefactor of the human race, a sort of *atheistical Messiah*.

---

[10] He refused to be present at the religious ceremony. (*A.S.*)

[11] The *Westminster and Foreign Quarterly Review* published in its issue of October 1860 a long article, unsigned, about Owen. (*A.S.*)

[12] Goethe: *Iphigenie auf Tauris*, I, 2. (*A.S.*)

'His turning to the rappings of spirits is not in the least surprising. People *of no education* constantly pass with extraordinary ease from extreme scepticism to extreme superstition. They wish to determine every question by the light of nature alone. Study, reasoning and care in judgment are unknown to them. . . .'

'In the foregoing pages,' the author adds at the end of the article, 'we have dealt more with Owen's life than with his teachings; we desired to *express our sympathy* with the practical good which he brought about, and at the same time to announce our complete disagreement with his theories. The story of his life is more interesting than his writings. While the former may be useful and entertaining (*amusé*), the latter can only bewilder and bore the reader. But here, too, we feel that he *lived too long:* too long for himself; too long for his friends, and even longer for his biographers!'

The shade of the mild old man hovered before me: there were bitter tears in his eyes and, mournfully shaking his old, old head he seemed to try to say: 'Have I deserved this?' but he could not, and fell sobbing on his knees, and it was as though Lord Brougham hastened to screen him once more and made a sign to Rigby for him to be carried back as quickly as possible to the graveyard, before the frightened crowd had time to come to its senses and upbraid him with everything, everything that to him was dear and sacred, and even with having lived so long, with spoiling the lives of others, with unnecessarily taking up room by the fire. In fact, Owen, I think, was of the same age as Wellington, that sublime *incompetent* in time of peace.

'In spite of his mistakes, his pride, his fall, Owen *deserves our recognition.*'—What more could he expect?

Yet how is it that the curses of a Bishop of Oxford, Winchester or Chichester, damning Owen, are easier for us to bear than this requital of his services? It is because on that side there is passion, outraged faith, and on this, narrow dispassionateness—the dispassionateness not simply of a man but of the judge in the court of first instance. In the court of ecclesiastical jurisdiction it is all very easy to judge the behaviour of some ordinary libertine, but not of such a man as Mirabeau or Fox. With a folding foot-rule it is easy to measure cloth with great accuracy, but it is very inconvenient for estimating sidereal space.

It is possible that for correctness in judging affairs which are outside the competence of either a police court or arithmetical verification, *partiality* is more necessary than justice. Passion may not only blind, but may also penetrate more deeply into the

object, embrace it in its own fire and be blind to everything
else.

Give a pedantic schoolmaster, if only he is not endowed by
nature with aesthetic understanding—give him to analyse anything you like—*Faust, Hamlet*—and you will see how the 'fat'
prince of Denmark wastes away, crumpled up by a secondary-
school doctrinaire. With the cynicism of Noah's son he will display the nakedness and deficiencies of dramas which are the
delight of generation after generation.

There is in the world nothing great or poetical that could
endure the gaze—*not of stupidity, and not of wisdom*—either: I
mean the gaze of ordinary, vital intelligence. The French have
hit the mark so accurately with their proverb that no man is a
hero to his valet.

'If a beggar gets hold of a horse,' as people say and as the critic
of the *Westminster Review* repeats, 'he'll hop on to its back and
gallop off to the devil. . . . An "ex-linen-draper" ' (this expression is used several times)[13] 'who has suddenly become' (mark:
after twenty years of unremitting toil and colossal success) 'an
important personage, on a friendly footing with dukes and
ministers, must naturally become puffed up and make himself
*ridiculous, since he has not much moderation and not much
sense.*' The ex-linen-draper became so puffed up that his village
was too cramped for him and he wanted to reconstruct the
world; with these pretensions he ruined himself, failed in everything and covered himself with *ridicule*.

But this is not all. If Owen had preached only his economic
revolution, that folly would have been forgiven him, the first
time, in the *classic* land of madness. This is proved by the fact
that ministers and bishops, parliamentary committees and congresses of mill-owners sought his advice. The success of New
Lanark attracted everyone: not a single statesman, not a single
learned man left England without having travelled to see Owen;
even (as we have seen) Nicholas Pavlovich himself visited him,
and wanted to entice him to Russia and his son into the army.
Crowds of people filled the passages and vestibules of the halls
where Owen was speaking. But Owen, with his audacity, destroyed at one blow, in a quarter of an hour, this colossal popularity which was based on colossal incomprehension of what he

---

[13] Fourier began by being an assistant in a shop of his father's where
cloth was sold. Proudhon was the son of an illegitimate peasant. What
a base beginning for socialism! Is it from such demi-gods and semi-robbers
that dynasties draw their origins?

was saying; he saw this, and dotted the i, and the most dangerous i, too.

It happened on 21st August, 1817. The Protestant hypocrites,
the most troublesome and glutinously boring, had long been
plaguing him. Owen declined disputing with them, so far as he
was able, but they gave him no peace. A certain inquisitor and
owner of a paper-mill, Philips by name, went so far in his
ecclesiastical fury that, in a parliamentary committee, suddenly,
out of the blue, in the middle of an important discussion, he
started badgering Owen with a cross-examination on what he
believed and what he did not believe.

Instead of answering the paper-mill-owner with any such
subtleties as Faust uses with Gretchen, Owen, the ex-linen-
draper, preferred to reply from the height of a platform, before a
huge gathering of people, at a public meeting *in England, in
London, in the City, in the London Tavern!*[14] On this side of
Temple Bar, near the umbrella of the cathedral under which the
old City clings together, in the neighbourhood of Gog and
Magog, within sight of Whitehall and of the secular cathedral-
synagogue of the Bank, he announced clearly and unequivocally,
loudly and extraordinarily simply, that the chief obstacle to the
harmonious development of a new society was—*religion.* 'The
absurdities of fanaticism have made of man a feeble, crazy beast,
an insane bigot, a canting hypocrite. With the existing religious
concepts,' Owen concluded, 'not only will the communal villages
proposed by me not be built, but with them Paradise would not
long continue to be Paradise.'[15]

Owen was so convinced that this act of 'folly' was an act of
honour and apostleship, the inevitable consequence of his teaching, that he was compelled by probity and candour, by his whole
life, to promulgate his opinion *thirty years afterwards,* when he

---

14 Owen's speech of 21st August, 1817, to which Herzen refers, was
printed at the same time, with the title 'A New State of Society.' (*A.S.*)
15 Herzen's quotation of Owen's words is not exact. (*A.S.*) Frank Podmore in *Robert Owen* . . . (Hutchinson, 1906), I, 246–7, quotes this
passage of Owen's speech as follows: 'Then, my friends, I tell you, that
hitherto you have been prevented from even knowing what happiness
really is, solely in consequence of the errors—gross errors—that have
been combined with the fundamental notions of every religion that has
hitherto been taught to man. And, in consequence, they have made man
the most incompetent, the most miserable being in existence. By the
errors of these systems he has been made a weak, imbecile animal; a
furious bigot and fanatic; or a miserable hypocrite; and should these
qualities be carried, not only into the projected villages, but *into Paradise
itself, a Paradise would no longer be found!* . . .' (*R.*)

wrote: 'That was the greatest day in my life: I carried out my duty.'

An impenitent sinner was this Owen! And he was paid out for it!

'Owen,' says the *Westminster Review,* 'was not torn in pieces for this: the time of physical vengeance in matters of religion had gone by. But no one, even nowadays, *can offend our cherished prejudices with impunity!'*

English priests do not, in fact, use surgical methods any more, although they are not squeamish about other, more spiritual means. 'From that moment,' says the author of the article, 'Owen brought down upon himself the fearful hatred of the clergy, and after that meeting begins *the long list of failures which makes ridiculous the last forty years of his life.* He was not a martyr, but he was an outlaw.'

Enough, I think. I may put the *Westminster Review* aside. I am very grateful to it for such a vivid reminder not only of the saintly old man but also of the environment in which he lived. Let us turn to business, that is, to Owen himself and his teaching.

One thing I shall add as I bid farewell to the unwashed critic and to Owen's other biographer,[16] also unwashed, less severe but no less earnest—that, while I am not an entirely envious man, I envy them from the bottom of my heart. I would give much for their imperturbable consciousness of their own excellence, for their calm satisfaction with themselves and with their comprehension, for their sometimes pliant, always just and now and then slightly ironical condescension. What tranquillity must be conferred by this complete confidence in their knowledgeability, and in the fact that they are wiser and more practical than Owen was; that, if they had his energy and his money they would not behave so stupidly, but would be rich, like Rothschild, and ministers, like Palmerston!

II

ROBERT OWEN called one of the articles in which he set out his system, 'An attempt to change this *lunatic asylum* into a Rational World.'[17]

---

[16] Herzen is probably referring to William L. Sargant and his book, *Robert Owen and his Social Philosophy* (London, 1860). (*A.S.*)

[17] In English in the original. (*R.*) Owen's article 'The World a great lunatic asylum' was published in the first issue of *Robert Owen's Journal*

One of Owen's biographers, prompted by this, tells how a madman who was confined in a hospital said: 'The whole world thinks me insane, and I think the whole world is so; the pity is that the *majority* is on the side of the whole world.'

This expands Owen's title and throws a clear light on the whole business. I am sure that the biographer did not consider how accurate his comparison was nor how far it carried. He only wanted to hint that Owen was mad, and I shall not dispute that . . . but what his reason is *for supposing that that whole world of his is sane*, this I do not understand.

If Owen was mad it was by no means because the world thought him so and he paid it back in its own coin, but because, knowing well that he lived in a madhouse and was surrounded by the sick, he talked to them *for sixty years* as though they were well.

Here the *number* of the sick means nothing: sanity has its justification not in the majority of votes but in its own logical arbitrariness. If the whole of England is convinced that a certain medium can summon up the spirits of the dead, and one Faraday says that this is rubbish, then truth and sanity will be on his side and not on the side of the whole population of England. More: if even Faraday does not say this, then the truth about this subject will not exist at all as something recognised; but none the less the absurdity accepted unanimously by the whole people will still be an absurdity.

The majority of which the sick man complained was not frightening because it was wise or foolish, right or wrong, false or true, but because it was powerful and because it held the keys of Bedlam.

Power does not admit consciousness within its understanding as a necessary condition; on the contrary, it is the more irresistible the madder it is, the more to be feared the more it lacks consciousness. From an insane man it is possible to save oneself, from a pack of furious wolves it is harder, and before the irrational elements a man can only fold his arms and perish.

The act of Owen's that in 1817 struck England with horror would not in 1617 have astonished the country of Vanini and Giordano Bruno, would not have scandalised France or Germany in 1717; but England, after half a century, cannot remember him without exasperation. Perhaps somewhere in Spain the

(London, 2nd November, 1850), and ends almost literally as in Herzen's quotation: 'To change this lunatic asylum into a rational world, will be the work to be accomplished by this journal.' (*A.S.*)

monks might have incited the savage rabble against him, the *alguazils* of the Inquisition might have put him in prison or burnt him on a bonfire, but the humane part of society would have been on his side. . . .

Could Goethe and Fichte, Kant and Schiller, or Humboldt in our time and Lessing a hundred years ago, have concealed their way of thinking or have had the unscrupulousness to preach their philosophy, in books and in the academies, for six days a week, and on the seventh to listen pharisaically to the pastor, and bamboozle the mob, *la plèbe*, with their devout Christianity?

The same thing in France: Not Voltaire nor Rousseau nor Diderot, not all the Encyclopaedists, nor the school of Bichat and Cabanis, nor Laplace nor Comte, pretended to be ultramontanists or bowed in veneration before 'cherished prejudices,' and this did not lower or diminish their importance by one iota.

The Continent, politically enslaved, is morally freer than England; the mass of ideas and doubts in circulation is much more extensive. They have become habitual and society does not shake with either fear or indignation before a free man—

Wenn er die Kette bricht.[18]

On the Continent people are powerless before authority: they endure their chains, but do not respect them. The Englishman's liberty is more in his institutions than in himself or in his conscience. His freedom is in the 'common law,' in *habeas corpus*, not in his morals or his way of thinking. Before the prejudices of society the proud Brit inclines without a murmur, with an appearance of respect. It stands to reason, then, that wherever there are people there are lies and pretence, but openness is not considered a vice, the boldly uttered conviction of a thinker is not confused with the indecency of a lewd woman who boasts of her own fall; but hypocrisy is not exalted to the degree of a social and therewith obligatory virtue.[19]

---

[18] From Schiller's poem 'Die Worte des Glaubens.' (*A.S.*) The couplet runs: '*Vor dem Sklaven, wenn er die Kette bricht, Vor dem freien Menschen erzittert nicht.*' (*R.*)

[19] In the present year Temple, a justice of the peace, would not accept the evidence of a woman from Rochdale because she refused to take the oath in the form prescribed, saying that she did not believe in punishment in the world to come. Trelawney (the son of the celebrated friend

Of course, David Hume and Gibbon did not pretend to mystical beliefs. But the England that listened to Owen in 1817 was not the same in time or in profundity. The sense of understanding was no longer restricted to a choice circle of educated aristocrats and scholars. On the other hand, the country had spent fifteen years in a prison cell which Napoleon had locked upon it—in one way, it had moved out of the current of ideas, and in another, life had thrust forward a huge majority of that 'conglomerated mediocrity' of John Stuart Mill. In the new England a man like Byron or Shelley wanders as a foreigner; he begs the wind to carry him away, but not to his native shore; another man the judges, with the help of a family crazed with fanaticism, rob of his children because he does not believe in God.[20]

The intolerance, then, directed against Owen bestows no right to deduce the falsity or truth of his doctrine; it gives only a measure of the insanity, that is of the moral servitude, of England, and particularly of that stratum of the people that goes to public meetings and writes articles for the newspapers.

◈   ◈   ◈

And now there turns up a freak who simply tells them straight, and even with a kind of offensive naïveté, that all this is rubbish, that man is not at all a criminal *par le droit de naissance*, that he is as little responsible for himself as the other animals are and that, like them, he is not answerable to a court of law, *but to his upbringing—very much so.* And that is not all: before the faces of magistrates and parsons, who have as the only foundation, the only sufficient reason for their existence, the Fall, the punishment and the remission of sins, he announces publicly that a man does not create his character himself; that he has only to be put, from the day of his birth, in such an environment that it would be possible for him not to be a rogue, and he would be quite a decent fellow. But now society, with a

---

of Byron and Shelley) asked the Home Secretary in Parliament on 12th February what measures he proposed to take to set aside such refusals. The Minister answered, None. Similar cases have occurred more than once—with, for instance, the well known publicist Holyoake. To take a false oath is becoming a necessity.

[20] Shelley in 1817. The reasons for the Lord Chancellor's depriving him of the right to bring up his children were his illegal tie with Mary Godwin and the atheistical views that he uttered in his works. (*A.S.*)

pack of absurdities, steers him into crime, and people punish not the social system but the *individual*.

And did Owen really suppose that this was *easy* to understand?

Did he really not know that it was easier for us to imagine a cat hanged for muricide, and a dog awarded a collar of honour for zeal displayed in the capture of a concealed hare, than a child unpunished for a childish prank—to say nothing of a criminal? To reconcile oneself to the idea that to avenge the whole of society on a criminal is vile and stupid, to inflict on the criminal in full synod, in safety and cold blood, as much injury as he inflicted when he was frightened and in danger, is repellent and unavailing, horribly hard and uncongenial to our gills. It is too abrupt!

In the timorous obstinacy of the masses, in their narrow-minded bolstering up of what is old, in their tenacious conservatism there is a kind of recollection that the gallows and penance, capital punishment and the immortality of the soul, the fear of God and the fear of temporal authority, the criminal courts and the Last Judgment, the Tsar and the priest—all these were once huge steps ahead, huge strides upward, great *Errungenschaften*, scaffoldings on which men, straining themselves to the utmost, clambered up towards a tranquil life; canoes which, although they did not know the course, they paddled to harbours where they might rest from the hard struggle with the elements, from the labours of earth and from deeds of blood; where they might find leisure free from alarms, and a blessed idleness, these prerequisites for progress, liberty, art and consciousness.

In order to preserve their dearly won tranquillity, men surrounded their harbours with bugbears of all kinds and gave to their Tsar a rod in his hand to drive them on and to defend them, and to the priest the power to curse and bless.

A conquering tribe naturally enslaved the conquered, and on its slavery founded its own leisure, that is its development. Properly speaking, it was by means of slavery that there began the State, education, human liberty. The instinct of self-preservation led to ferocious laws, and unbridled phantasy completed the rest. Tradition, handed on from generation to generation, wrapped the origins more and more in a rosy cloud, and the oppressive ruler, just like the oppressed slave, bowed in terror before the decalogue, and believed that it had been dictated by Jehovah on Sinai to the flash of lightning and crash of thunder, or instilled into an elect man by some parasitical spirit dwelling in his brain.

If we reduce all the different corner-stones on which states have been built to the chief principles that liberate them from what is fantastic, what is childish, what appertains to their age, we shall see that they are constantly the very same, co-eternal with every church and every state: the forms and scenery alter but the principles are the same.

The savage punishment of the king of a hunting tribe in Africa, who with his own hands cuts the criminal's throat, is by no means so far away from the punishment of the judge who delegates the killing to another. The point is that neither the judge in ermine and a white wig, with a quill behind his ear, nor the naked African king, with a quill through his nose, and quite black, has any doubt that he is doing what he is doing for the salvation of society, and that in some cases he has not only the right to kill but a sacred duty to do so.

◈   ◈   ◈

Beside the fear of freedom—the fear that children feel when they begin to walk without leading-strings—beside the habituation to those mandates steeped in sweat and blood, to those boats which have become arks of salvation in which peoples have survived more than one rainy day, there are also strong buttresses supporting the dilapidated building. The backwardness of the masses on the one hand, who are incapable of understanding, and, on the other, self-interested fear, which prevents any comprehension of the minority's point of view—for a long time these will keep the old order on its feet. The educated classes are ready, against their convictions, to walk in a leash themselves if only the mob is not released from it.

This, in fact, would not be entirely without danger.

Below and above are different calendars. Above is the nineteenth century, and below perhaps the fifteenth: or even that is not at the very bottom—there are Hottentots and Kaffirs of different colours, breeds and climates.

If one does consider this civilisation, of which the sediment is the *lazzaroni* and the rabble of London, people who have turned back half-way and are returning to the condition of apes and lemurs, while on its peaks flourish the talentless Merovingians of all dynasties and the feeble Aztecs of all aristocracies—really, one's head begins to go round. Imagine this menagerie at liberty, without church, inquisition or lawcourt, without priest, Tsar or executioner!

The ancient strongholds of theology and jurisprudence Owen

considered to be a lie: that is, an obsolete truth; and this is comprehensible. But when under this plea he demanded that they should surrender, he had forgotten the gallant garrison defending the fortress.

There is nothing in the world more stubborn than a corpse: you can hit it, you can knock it to pieces, but you cannot convince it. Besides, on our Olympus there sit not the complaisant, rakish gods of Greece who, when a message came, according to Lucian, while they were trying to devise measures against atheism, that the game was lost, and that it had been proved at Athens that *they did not exist,* turned pale, volatilised and vanished.[21] The Greeks were simpler, both gods and men. The Greeks believed nonsense and played with marble dolls from a childish need for art; and we, for percentages, for profit, uphold the Jesuits and the old shop,[22] to keep the people curbed and safely exploited. What kind of logic could get a hold of this?

This brings us to the question, not whether Owen was right or wrong but *whether rational consciousness and moral independence are compatible with life in a State.*

History bears witness that societies are constantly attaining a rational autonomy, but testifies likewise that they remain in moral bondage. Whether these problems are soluble or not is hard to say; they are not to be solved in a plain, blunt manner, especially not by mere love for men, or by other noble, warm emotions.

In all spheres of life we strike against insoluble antinomies, against those asymptotes which are always striving towards their hyperbolas and never coinciding with them. These are the extreme limits between which life fluctuates, advances and ebbs, touching now one shore, now the other.

The emergence of people protesting against social bondage and the bondage of conscience is no new thing; they have appeared as accusers and prophets in all civilisations that have been at all mature, especially when these were growing old. This is the upper limit, the *arresting personality*, an exceptional and rare phenomenon, like genius, beauty or an extraordinary voice. Experience does not show that their Utopias were realised.

There is a frightening example before our eyes. Within the

---

[21] *The Dialogues of Lucian*: 'Zeus tragikos.' (*A.S.*)

[22] 'Old shop' (in English in the original) is H.'s version of 'the Old Firm,' *i.e.*, the Anglican Church. (*R.*)

memory of man there has never been encountered such a conflu-
ence of fortunate conditions for the rational, free development of
a State as in North America. Every impediment was absent
which existed on the exhausted soil of history, or on soil which
was quite untilled. The teaching of the great thinkers and
revolutionaries of the eighteenth century without the militarism
of France, English common law[23] without its caste system, lay
at the foundation of the life of their state. And what else? Everything that old Europe dreamt of: a republic, a democracy, a
federation, autonomy for each patch of land, the whole lightly
tied together by a common governmental girdle with an insecure
knot in the middle.

Now, what came of this?

Society, the majority, seized the powers of a dictator and of
the police; the people themselves fulfilled the function of a
Nicholas Pavlovich, of the Third Division and of the executioner; the people, who eighty years ago proclaimed the 'rights
of man,' is disintegrating because of the 'right to flog.' Persecution and victimisation in the Southern States (which have set
the word *Slavery* in their flag, as Nicholas once set the word
Autocracy in his) in the form of their thought and speech are
not inferior in vileness to what was done by the King of Naples
and the Emperor at Vienna.

In the Northern States 'slavery' has not been elevated into a
religious dogma; but what can be the standard of education and
of freedom of conscience in a country which throws aside its
account-book only to devote itself to tables that turn and spirits
that knock—a country which has kept in being all the intolerance of the Puritans and Quakers!

In milder forms we come across the same thing in England
and Sweden. The freer a country is from government interference, the more fully recognised its right to speak, to independence of conscience, the more intolerant grows the mob: public
opinion becomes a torture-chamber; your neighbour, your
butcher, your tailor, family, club, parish, keep you under supervision and perform the duties of a policeman. Can only a people
which is incapable of inner freedom achieve liberal institutions?
Or does not all this mean, after all, that a State continually
develops its requirements and ideals, which the better minds
fulfil by their activity, but the realisation of which is incompatible with life in a State?

We do not know the solution of this problem, but we have no

---

23 'Common law' is in English in the original. (*R.*)

right to consider it solved. Until now history has resolved it in one way, and certain thinkers—Robert Owen among them—in another. Owen *believes*, with the indestructible belief of the thinkers of the eighteenth century (called the age of unbelief), that humanity is on the eve of its solemn investiture with the *toga virilis*. We think, however, that all guardians and pastors, all pedagogues and wet-nurses may calmly eat and sleep at the expense of the backward child. Whatever rubbish peoples demand, *in our century* they will not demand the rights of a grown-up. For a long time to come humanity will still be wearing turn-down collars *à l'enfant*.

There is a mass of reasons for this. For a man to come to his senses and see reason he must be a giant; and after all not even colossal powers will help him to break through if the way of life of a society is so well and firmly established as it is in Japan or China. From the moment when the baby opens its eyes with a smile on its mother's breast until the time when, at peace with his conscience and his God, he shuts his eyes just as calmly, convinced that while he has a short nap he will be carried to an abode where there is neither weeping nor sighing, everything has been arranged in order that he shall not evolve a single simple conception, shall not run up against one simple, lucid thought. With his mother's milk he sucks in stramonium; no emotion is left undistorted, undiverted from its natural course. His education at school continues what has been done at home: it crystallises the optical illusion, consolidates it with book learning, theoretically legitimises the traditional trash and trains the children to *know without understanding* and to accept *denominations for definitions*.

Astray in his conceptions, entangled in words, man loses the flair for truth, the taste for nature. What a powerful intellect must you possess, to be suspicious of this moral carbon monoxide and, with your head swimming already, to hurl yourself out of it into the fresh air, with which, into the bargain, everyone round is trying to scare you! Owen's answer to this would have been that this was just why he was beginning his regeneration of society not with a Fourierist phalanstery, not with an Icaria,[24] but at school, at a school into which he would take children of two and less.

Owen was right and, what is more, he demonstrated in prac-

---

[24] *The Journal to Icaria*, by Etienne Cabet, a Utopian novel, depicts an imaginary country run on communist lines. (*A.S.*)

tice that he was: faced with New Lanark Owen's opponents were silent. That cursed New Lanark stuck in the throats of people who perpetually accused socialism of Utopianism and of inability to achieve anything in practice. 'What was done by Considérant and Brisbane, by the abbey of Cîteaux, by the tailors of Clichy and by Proudhon's *Banque du Peuple?*'[25] But against the brilliant success of New Lanark there was nothing to be said. Savants and ambassadors, ministers and dukes, merchants and lords, they all came out of the school with wonder and veneration. The Duke of Kent's doctor, a sceptic, spoke of New Lanark with a smile. The Duke, a friend of Owen's, advised him to visit New Lanark himself. In the evening the doctor wrote to the Duke: 'I am leaving a report until to-morrow. I am so much excited and touched by what I have seen that I can write no more; several times my eyes filled with tears.' I expect my old gentleman to make this solemn admission. So he demonstrated his conception in practice—he was right. Let us go farther.

New Lanark was at the height of its prosperity. The indefatigable Owen, in spite of his trips to London, the meetings he attended and the constant visits from all the celebrities of Europe—even, as we have seen, from Nicholas Pavlovich—applied himself with the same loving energy to his school-cum-factory and the well-being of his workers, among whom he was developing a communal life. And the whole thing blew up.

What do you think, then? That he went bankrupt? The instructors quarrelled, the children were spoilt, the parents took to drink? Forgive me: the factory prospered, the profits increased, the workers grew rich, the school flourished. But one fine morning there came into that school two buffoons in black wearing low-crowned hats and coats that were purposely badly cut: it was two Quakers,[26] who were just as much proprietors in

---

[25] Considérant, who emigrated to America in 1842, two years later organised, with the participation of Albert Brisbane,* the coloy of 'Réunion' in Texas. In the monastery at Cîteaux, after the revolution of 1848, there was founded one of the workers' productive associations. At Clichy, a small place not far from Paris, a great co-operative productive comradeship of tailors was organised in March 1848, to a plan of Louis Blanc's and with the support of the Luxemburg Committee. The 'People Bank,' founded by Proudhon in 1849, the object of which was the furnishing of workers with 'free credit.' All these undertakings proved to be failures. (*A.S.*)

[26] Quakers visited the school at New Lanark three times between 1814 and 1822 (Podmore, *op. cit.*, I, 158). (*R.*)

* (1809–90), father of the journalist Arthur Brisbane, who became William Randolph Hearst's columnist and adviser. (*D.M.*)

New Lanark as Owen himself was. They scowled at the sight of the merry children who were not grieving in the least over the Fall; they were horrified that the little boys wore no trousers,[27] and demanded that some catechism of theirs should be taught. Owen answered to start with by a stroke of genius: he gave them the figure of the rise in profits. Their jealousy for the Lord was quieted for a time; the sinful figure was so great.[28] But the conscience of the Quakers woke up again, and they began to demand even more insistently that the children should not be taught dancing nor *worldly* singing, but—peremptorily—their own schismatic catechism.

Owen, with whom choral singing, correct movements and dances played an important part in education, did not agree. There were long arguments; the Quakers decided this time to consolidate their places in paradise, and demanded the introduction of psalms, and of some sort of short trousers for the children who were going about *à l'écossaise*. Owen realised that the Quakers' crusade would not stop there. 'In that case,' he told them, 'run the place yourselves: I decline to do it.' He could not have acted otherwise.[29]

'The Quakers,' says a biographer of Owen, 'when they entered on the management of New Lanark, began by *lowering pay and increasing the hours of work*.'

New Lanark collapsed.

It must not be forgotten that Owen's success discloses one more great historical novelty, namely, that it is only at first that the poor, oppressed workman, denied an education, trained from childhood in drunkenness, deceit and war with society, opposes innovations, and this out of mistrust; but as soon as he is convinced that the change is not to his detriment, that in the course of it he, too, is not forgotten, he follows with submission, and then with confidence and love.

---

[27] They wore kilts. (*R.*)

[28] New Lanark produced £160,000 pure profit in the first five years, and after that the average yearly profit came to £15,000. (*A.S.*)

[29] The demands of the Quaker-companions were presented to Owen in January 1824; he put his signature to their conditions and agreed to continue temporarily with the conduct of the undertaking until a new manager could be found. Owen's break with his co-proprietors and his forced departure from New Lanark happened later in 1829. (*A.S.*) Podmore says (*op. cit.*, I, 158) that the schools at New Lanark continued to flourish . . . until the institution of Board Schools in Scotland in 1872. (*R.*)

The environment, which acted as a brake, is not here.

Gentz, the literary sycophant of Metternich, said to Robert Owen at a dinner in Frankfort:[30]

'Suppose you had been successful, what would have been the outcome of it?'

'It's very simple,' Owen answered. 'The outcome would have been that every man would have had enough to eat, would have been properly clothed and would have been given a sensible education.'

'But that's just what we don't want,' observed the Cicero of the Congress of Vienna. Gentz was frank, if nothing else.

From the moment that the shopkeepers realised, as the priests had, that those companies of 'play-workers' and teachers were something very much in earnest, the destruction of New Lanark was inevitable.

And it is for this reason that the failure of a small Scottish hamlet with its factory and school has the significance of a historical misfortune. The ruins of Owen's New Lanark inspire in us no less mournful thoughts than were once inspired in Marius by other ruins, with the difference that the Roman exile was sitting on the coffin of an old man and pondering the vanity of vanities, and we ponder the same thing, sitting at the fresh grave of a baby, a very promising one, killed by being badly looked after and through fear that *it would demand its inheritance!*

III

So, JUDGED BY REASON, Owen was right; his deductions were logical and, what is more, were justified in practice. All that they lacked was understanding in his hearers.

'It's a matter of time; people will understand one day.'

'I don't know.'

'One can't think, though, that people will never arrive at an understanding of their own interests.'

Yet it has been so till now; this lack of understanding has been made up by the Church and the State, that is, by the two chief obstacles to further development. This is a circular argument, from which it is very hard to get away. Owen imagined that it sufficed to point out to people their obsolete absurdities for

---

[30] A banquet arranged by Simon Moritz Bethmann, a banker, in 1818 in connection with a congress of the Holy Alliance then meeting at Aachen. (*A.S.*)

them to free themselves—and he was mistaken. Their absurdities, especially those of the Church, are obvious; but this does not hamper them in the least. Their indestructible solidity is based *not on reason but on the lack of it,* and therefore they are as little amenable to criticism as are hills, woods and cliffs. History has developed by means of absurdities; people have constantly set their hearts on chimeras, and have achieved very real results. In waking dreams they have gone after the rainbow, sought now paradise in heaven, now heaven on earth, and on the way have sung their everlasting songs, have decorated temples with their everlasting sculptures, have built Rome and Athens, Paris and London. One dream yields to another; the sleep *sometimes* becomes lighter, but is never quite gone. People will accept anything, believe in anything, submit to anything and are ready to sacrifice much; but they recoil in horror when through the gaping chink between two religions, which lets in the light of day, there blows upon them the cool wind of reason and criticism. If, for example, Owen had wished to reform the Church of England, he would have been just as successful as the Unitarians, the Quakers and I do not know who else. To reorganise the Church, to set up the altar behind a screen, or without one, to remove the images, or bring in more of them— all this is possible, and thousands would follow the reformer; but Owen wanted to lead people *out of* the Church, and here was the *sta, viator,* here was his Rubicon. It is easy to walk up to the frontier: the most difficult thing in every country is to cross it, especially when the people itself is on the side of the passport official.

In all the thousand and one nights of history, as soon as a little education has been amassed, there have been the same endeavours: a few men have woken up and protested against the sleepers, have announced that they themselves were awake, but have been unable to rouse those others. Their appearance demonstrates, without the slightest doubt, man's capacity to evolve a rational understanding. But this does not solve our problem: can this exceptional development become general? The guidance which the past gives us does not favour an affirmative verdict. Perhaps the future will go differently, will bring to bear different forces, other elements, unknown to us, which will change for the better or for the worse the destiny of humanity, or of a considerable part of it. The discovery of America is tantamount to a geological upheaval; railways and the electric telegraph have transformed all human relationships. What we do not know we have no right to introduce into our calculation;

but even if we have the best of luck we still cannot foresee that it will be soon that men will feel the need for *common sense*. The development of the brain needs and takes its time. There is no haste in nature: she could lie for thousands and thousands of years in a trance of stone, and for other thousands could twitter with the birds, scour the forests with the beasts or swim in the sea as a fish. The delirium of history will last her for a long time, and it will prolong magnificently the plasticity of nature, which in other spheres is exhausted.

People who have realised that this is a dream imagine that it is easy to wake up, and are angry with those who continue sleeping, not considering that the whole world that environs them does not permit them to wake. Life proceeds as a series of optical illusions, artificial needs and imaginary satisfactions.

Take at haphazard, without making a choice, any newspaper: cast your eye upon any family. What Robert Owen could help there? For absurdities people suffer with self-abnegation; for absurdities they go to their death; for absurdities they kill other men. Everlasting care and trouble, want, alarms, the sweat of his brow, toil without rest or end—man does not even enjoy them. If he has any leisure from his work he hastens to twist together the net of a family, he twines it quite casually, finds himself caught in it, pulls others in and, if he is not to escape from death by starvation by the never-ending toil of a galley slave, he starts upon a violent persecution of his wife, his children, his relations, or himself is persecuted by them. So people oppress each other in the name of family love, in the name of jealousy, in the name of marriage, and make hateful the most holy ties. When will man come to his senses? Will it be on the other side of the family, beyond its grave, when a man has lost everything—energy, freshness of intellect—and seeks only tranquillity?

Look at the troubles and cares of a whole ant-hill, or of a single ant: enter into its quests and purposes, its joys and sorrows, its conception of good and evil, *of honour and disgrace*, into everything that it does in the course of its whole life, from morning to night; see to what it devotes its last days and to what it sacrifices the best moments of its life—you will find yourself in a nursery, with its little horses on wheels, with gold foil and spangles, with dolls stood in one corner and the birch stood in another. In a baby's prattle a flash of sense can from time to time be perceived, but it is lost in childish distraction. You cannot stop and consider—you will confuse matters, fall behind, get stuck; everything has been too much compromised, and things move too quickly for it to be possible to stop, especially before a handful of people with no cannons, money or power, *protesting in the name of reason*, and not even warranting with miracles the truth of what they say.

A Rothschild or a Montefiore *must* be in his office in the morning, to begin the capitalisation of his hundredth million; in Brazil there is plague, and war in Italy, America is falling to pieces—everything is going *splendidly:* and, if someone talks to him then of man's exemption from responsibility and of a *different* distribution of wealth, of course he does not listen. Mac-Mahon spent days and nights considering how most surely, in the shortest time, to get the greatest number of people dressed in white uniforms destroyed by people in red trousers;[31] he destroyed more of them than he had thought he would; everyone congratulated him, even the Irish who, as papists, had been beaten by him—and then he is told that war is not only a repulsive absurdity but a crime too. Of course, instead of listening he sets himself to admiring the sword presented to him by Ireland.

To these people busy with military or civil service, stockbroking, family quarrels, cards, decorations, horses, Robert Owen advocated a different employment of their powers and pointed out the absurdity of their lives. Convince them he could not, but he exasperated them and drew down upon himself all the intolerance of incomprehension. Reason alone is long-suffering and merciful because it understands.

Owen's biographer judged very truly when he said that he destroyed his own influence when he repudiated religion. Really, when he bumped against the Church's fence, he should have stopped; but he climbed over to the other side and remained there all on his own, with the curses of the devout for company. But it seems to me that sooner or later he would have remained in just the same way with the wrong end of the shell—alone and an outlaw.[32]

The only reason why the mob did not flare up against him from the very outset was that the State and the lawcourt are not so popular as the Church and the altar. But the right to punish would *à la longue* have been upheld by people a trifle better grounded than God-crazed Quakers and newspaper hypocrites.

---

[31] Herzen is referring to the military expedition of 1830 for the seizure of Algeria. (*A.S.*)

[32] 'Outlaw' is in English. The reference is to ostracism in ancient Athens. (*R.*) For "shell," Americans would say "stick." (*D.M.*)

About the doctrine of the Church and the truths of the catechism no one argues who has any self-respect, for he knows
beforehand that they will not hold water at all. It is impossible
to be in earnest about proving the Immaculate Conception of the
Virgin Mary, or about affirming that the geological researches of
Moses conform to those of Murchison. The secular Churches of
civil and criminal law and the dogmas of the juridical catechism
stand much more firmly and enjoy, *pending scrutinisation,* the
rights of proven truths and unshakeable axioms.

Men who overturned altars dared not touch the mirror of
justice. Anarcharsis Clootz, the Hébertists, who called God by
the name of Reason, were just as certain of every *salus populi*
and other civic commandments as were mediaeval priests of the
canon law and the need to burn sorcerers.

It is not long since that one of the most powerful, daring
thinkers of our time,[33] in order to deal the Church a final blow,
secularised it, made of it a tribunal and, snatching from the
hands of the priests an Isaac who had been made ready to be
sacrificed to God, brought him before a court, that is, as a sacrifice to justice.

The eternal controversy, the controversy thousands of years
old, about free-will and predestination, is not over. It was not
only Owen in our time who doubted man's responsibility for his
actions. We shall find traces of this doubt in Bentham and
Fourier, in Kant and Schopenhauer, in the natural scientists and
physicians and, more important than all, in everyone who interests himself in the statistics of crime. The controversy is not
decided, in any case, *but that it is just to punish a criminal, and
this according to the degree of the crime, on that there is not
even any controversy:* that's something everyone knows for
himself!

On which side, then, is the lunatic asylum?

'Punishment is the inalienable right of the criminal,' said
Plato himself.

It is a pity that he himself uttered this quibble, but we at all
events are not obliged to keep repeating, with Addison's Cato,
'Plato, thou reasonest well,' even when he says that 'our soul
dieth not.'

If to be disembowelled or hanged constitutes the criminal's
right, let him bring a complaint himself if it has been violated.
There is no need to force people's rights upon them.

---

[33] P.-J. Proudhon. (*A.S.*)

Bentham calls the criminal a miscalculator, and of course, if someone has made a mistake in his reckoning, he must take the consequences of his mistake; but this is not his right, you know. No one says that, if you have bumped your forehead, you have a right to a bruise, and there is no special official who would send a surgeon's mate to raise a bruise if there is not one. Spinoza speaks still more simply of the possible necessity of killing a man, who prevents others from living, 'as a mad dog is killed.' That is comprehensible. But lawyers either are so disingenuous, or have so dammed up their intelligence, that they utterly refuse to recognise execution as a safeguard or as vengeance, and take it for some kind of moral recompense, 'a restoration of the equilibrium.' In war matters are more direct: the soldier does not speculate about the guilt of the enemy he kills; he does not even say that killing him is just: it is kill who kill can.

'But with these notions all the lawcourts will have to be shut.'

'Why? Basilicas were once made into parish churches; should we not try now to turn them into parish schools?'

'With these notions of impunity not a single government will be able to hold on.'

'Owen might have answered, *like the first brother in history*,[34] "Have I been bidden to strengthen governments?" '

'With governments he was very tractable, and could come to terms with crowned heads, Tory Ministers and the President of the American Republic.'

'But did he get on badly with Catholics or Protestants?'

'What? You think Owen was a republican?'

'I think that Robert Owen preferred that *form of government* which agreed best with the Church accepted by him.'

'What are you saying? He had no Church.'

'You see, then.'

'All the same, one cannot be without a government.'

'No doubt . . . however rotten it is, yet it's necessary. Hegel tells a story of a good old woman who said, "Well, what if it is bad weather? It's better than no weather at all." '

'All right: laugh; but the State will perish, you know, without a government.'

'And what business is that of mine?'

---

[34] Jesus Christ. (*A.S.*) Cain. (*R.*) Socrates. (*D.M.*)

IV

AT THE TIME of the Revolution the experiment was made of radically altering civic life while preserving the *powerful authority of the government*.[35]

Decrees of the government provided for have survived, with their heading:

ÉGALITÉ   LIBERTÉ
    BONHEUR COMMUN,

to which was sometimes added, by way of elucidation: '*Ou la mort!*'

The decrees, as indeed one ought to have expected, begin with the police decree.

§ 1. Persons who do nothing *for the fatherland* have no political rights: these are *foreigners* to whom the *republic* grants hospitality.

§ 2. Nothing is done *for the fatherland* by those who do not *serve it* with useful labour.

§ 3. *The law* considers useful labour:

Agriculture, stock-breeding, fishing, seafaring.
Mechanical and manual work.
Retail trade.
Carriers' and coachmen's work.
The military profession.
The sciences and instruction.

§ 4. However, *the sciences* and *instruction* will not be considered useful if the persons engaged in them do not present, within a given period, evidence of good citizenship (*civisme*) *written in the statutory form.*

§ 6. *Foreigners* are forbidden entry to public meetings.

§ 7. Foreigners are under the direct surveillance of the supreme administration, to which is reserved the right to eject them from their domicile and send them to places of correction.

In the decree 'of work' everything is assessed and assigned: at what time to do what; how many hours to work. Foremen give

---

[35] In 1796 Babeuf headed the revolutionary-communistic 'Agreement in the name of equality.' (*A.S.*)

'an example of zeal and activity,' others report to the authorities on everything done in the workshop. Workmen *are sent* from one place to another (as with us peasants are driven to work on the roads) according to the need for hands and labour.

> § 11. The supreme administration sends to forced labour (*travaux forcés*), under supervision of communes designated by it, persons of both sexes whose bad citizenship (*incivisme*), idleness, luxurious living and *bad behaviour* set a bad example to society. Their property will be confiscated.
> §14. Special officials will care for the maintenance and increase of cattle, for the clothing, removals and amenities of working citizens.

Decree of the distribution of property:

> § 1. No one member of a commune may make use of anything except that which is assigned to him by law and given through the instrumentality of an official (*magistrat*) invested with the power.
> § 2. A people's commune from the very beginning gives to its members quarters, clothes, laundry, light, heat, a sufficient quantity of bread, meat, poultry, fish, eggs, butter, wine and other beverages.
> § 3. In each commune, at fixed times, there will be communal meals, at which the members of the commune *are obliged* to be present.
> § 5. Every member taking payment for work, or keeping money by him, is punished.

Trade decree:

> § 1. Foreign trade *is forbidden* to private persons. The wares will be confiscated, the criminal punished.
> Trade will be carried on by officials. Subsequently money is abolished. It is forbidden to introduce gold and silver. The republic does not issue money; domestic private debts are cancelled, foreign ones discharged; and if anyone deceives or defrauds he is punished with *perpetual slavery* (*esclavage perpétuel*).

At the bottom of this you would expect to find: 'Peter. Tsarskoye Selo,' or 'Count Arakcheyev. Georgia'; but it is signed not by Peter I but by the first French socialist, Gracchus Babeuf![36]

---

[36] "Being an opponent of the centralized state, Herzen tries to present Babeuf's designs in an unfavorable light," note the savants of the

MY PAST AND THOUGHTS

It would be hard to complain that in this project there is not enough government. There is solicitude for everything, supervision of everything, custodianship of everything; everything is organised and set in order. Even the reproduction of animals is not left to their own weaknesses and coquetry but is regulated by superior authority.

And what, do you think, is the purpose of all this? For what are these *serfs* of well-being, these prisoners *adscripti* to equality, fed on 'poultry and fish, washed, clothed and *amused*'? Not simply for their own sakes: indeed, the decree says that all this shall be done *médiocrement*. 'The republic alone must be rich, splendid and omnipotent.'

This reminds one forcefully of our Iverskaya Mother of God: *sie hat Perlen und Diamanten*, a carriage and horses, regular priests to serve her, coachmen with unfreezable heads—in a word, she has everything—only she does not exist: she owns all this wealth *in effigie*.

The contrast between Robert Owen and Gracchus Babeuf is very remarkable. In a hundred years' time, when everything on this terrestrial globe will have changed, it will be possible by means of these two molar teeth to reconstruct the fossil skeletons of England and France down to the last little bone. The more these two mastodons of socialism belong in essence to one family, and proceed towards one goal and from the same stimuli, the clearer is the difference between them.

The one saw that, in spite of the execution of the King, of the proclamation of the Republic, the annihilation of the Federalists, and the democratic Terror, the people remained of no account; the other, that in spite of the huge development of industry, of capital, of machinery and of increased productivity, 'merry England' was more and more becoming 'sorry England,' and greedy England more and more hungry England. This led both of them to the necessity for change in the basic conditions of

---

Academy of Sciences of the U.S.S.R. Tries and, I'd say, succeeds. Their accusation that Herzen presents Babeuf's decrees—which must have had a most familiar ring to their ears—"in a form which is somewhat simplified and exaggerated" would be more impressive had they given examples. How they must have suffered, though, during their scholarly labors! Usually, to their credit, in silence. But Herzen's savage treatment of Babeuf's prematurely Leninist program was too much. Their protest that Herzen was prejudiced against Babeuf's left-totalitarian utopia because he was "an opponent of the centralized state," as indeed he was—this is a real *cri de coeur* from these ambivalent victims-cum-highpriests of Soviet ideology. (*D.M.*)

political and economic life. Why they (and many others) happened upon this way of thinking almost at the very same time is easily understood. The contradictions in the life of society had not become more numerous or worse than before, but by the end of the eighteenth century they stood out more sharply. Elements of social life, developing separately, destroyed the harmony which had formerly existed among them in less favourable circumstances.

Having been so close to each other at the point of departure, they both went off in opposite directions.

Owen sees, in the fact that social evil was being recognised, the last achievement, the last victory in the hard, complex, historic campaign; he greets the dawn of a *new* day, which had never existed or been able to exist in the past, and tries to persuade the children to cast away their swaddling-clothes and leading-strings as soon as possible and stand on their own feet. He has taken a look through the doors of the future and, like a traveller who has reached his destination, he no longer rages at the road or curses the posting-station masters or the broken-down horses.

But the constitution of 1793 thought differently, and Gracchus Babeuf,[37] too, thought differently along with it. It decreed *the restoration of the natural rights of man which had been forgotten and lost.* The way in which life was lived in a State was the criminal fruit of usurpation, the consequence of the wicked conspiracy of tyrants and their accomplices, the priests and aristocrats. They must be punished as enemies of their country, their property must be returned to its legal sovereign, who now had nothing and for that reason was called a *sansculotte*. The time had come to restore his ancient, *inalienable* rights. . . . Where were they? Why is the proletarian the sovereign? Why is it to him that all the property plundered by others belongs? Ah! you doubt—you are a suspect fellow: the nearest sovereign takes you off to the citizen judge, and he sends you to the citizen executioner, and you will not be doubting any more!

The practice of the *surgeon* Babeuf could not interfere with the practice of Owen, the *man-midwife*.

Babeuf wished by force, that is, by authority, to smash what had been created by force, to destroy what had been wrongfully acquired.

---

[37] The followers of Babeuf relied on the constitution accepted by the Convention of 24th June, 1793, which they considered a genuine expression of the will of the people. (*A.S.*)

With this purpose he laid a plot: if he had succeeded in making himself master of Paris, the insurrectionary committee would have *enjoined* his new system upon France, just as the victorious Osmanlis enjoined theirs upon Byzantium; he would have forced on the French his *slavery of general prosperity* and, of course, with such violence as would have provoked the most fearful reaction, in the struggle with which Babeuf and his committee would have perished, leaving to the world a great thought in an absurd form, a thought which even now glows under the ashes, and troubles the complacency of the complacent.

Owen, seeing that people of the educated countries were growing up towards a transition to a new epoch, had no thought of violence and simply wished to help this development. Just as consistently from his side as Babeuf from his, he set about the study of the embryo, the development of the cell. He began, like all natural scientists, with a particular instance: his microscope, his laboratory, was New Lanark; his study grew and came to puberty along with the cell and led him to the conclusion that the high road to the installation of a new order was *upbringing*.

For Owen a plot was unnecessary and a rebellion could only do him harm. He could get on not only with the best government in the world, the English government, but with any other. In a government he saw a superannuated, historical fact supported by people who were backward and undeveloped, and not a gang of bandits which must be caught unawares. While not seeking to overturn the government he also did not in the least seek to *amend it*. If the saintly shopkeepers had not put a spoke in his wheel, there would be in England and America now hundreds of New Lanarks and New Harmonies;[38] into them would have flowed the fresh vigour of the working population, and little by little they would have drawn off the best vital juices from the State's antiquated tanks. Why should he struggle with the moribund? He could let them have a natural death, knowing that each child brought into his schools, *c'est autant de pris* from Church and government!

Babeuf was guillotined. At the time of his trial he grew into

---

[38] By Owen's magic touch *co-operative workers' associations* began to be established in England; there are as many as 200 of them. The Rochdale society, which began modestly and in indigence fifteen years ago with a capital of 28 *livres*, is now building with the society's money a factory with two engines, each of 60 h.p., and each costing £30,000. The co-operative societies print a magazine, *The Co-operator*, which is published exclusively by working men.

one of those great personalities, those martyred and slaughtered prophets, before whom a man is compelled to bow. He was extinguished, and on his grave there grew and grew the all-devouring monster of *Centralisation*. Before this monster individuality withered and was effaced, personality paled and vanished. Never on European soil, from the time of the Thirty Tyrants at Athens to the Thirty Years War, and from that until the decline of the French Revolution, has man been so caught up in the spider's web of government, so enmeshed in the toils of administration, as in the most recent times in France.

V

ABOUT THE TIME that the heads of Babeuf and Dorthès fell into the fatal sack at Vendôme,[39] Owen was living in the same lodgings as another unrecognised genius and pauper, Fulton, and giving him his last shillings in order that he might make models of machines with which he would enrich and benefit the human race. It happened that a certain young officer was displaying his battery to some ladies. In order to show the proper attention he fired off—without the slightest necessity—a few cannon-balls (he tells this himself); the enemy replied: a few men fell dead and others were wounded. The ladies were left thoroughly content with the shock to their nerves. The officer felt some pangs of conscience: 'Those people,' he says, 'perished absolutely unnecessarily' . . . but they were at war and this feeling soon passed. *Cela promettait*, and subsequently the young man shed more blood than the whole of the Revolution, and demanded in one levy more soldiers than Owen would have needed pupils in order to transform the whole world.

Napoleon had no system, and for others he neither wished wealth nor promised it: wealth he desired only for himself, and by wealth he understood power. Now see how feeble Babeuf and Owen are compared with him! Thirty years after his death his name was enough to get his nephew recognised as Emperor.

What was his secret?

Babeuf wished to *enjoin prosperity* and a communist republic on people.

Owen wished to educate them to a different economic way of living, incomparably more profitable for them.

Napoleon wanted neither the one nor the other; he understood

---

[39] 27th May, 1797. (*A.S.*)

that Frenchmen did not in fact desire to feed on Spartan broth and to return to the morality of Brutus the Elder, that they were not very well satisfied that on feast-days 'citizens will assemble to discuss the laws and instruct their children in the civic virtues.' But—and this is a different thing—fighting and boasting of their own bravery they do like.

Instead of preventing them, or irritating them by preaching perpetual peace, Lacedaemonian fare, Roman virtues and crowns of myrtle Napoleon, seeing how passionately fond they were of bloody glory, began to egg them on against other peoples and himself to go hunting with them. There is no reason to blame him: the French would have been the same even without him; but this identity of tastes entirely explains his people's love for him: he was not a reproach to the mob, for he did not offend it by either his purity or his virtues nor did he offer it a lofty, transfigured ideal. He was neither a chastising prophet nor a sermonising genius. *He belonged himself to the mob* and he showed it its very self (with its deficiencies and sympathies, its passions and inclinations) elevated into a *genius* and covered with rags of glory. That is the answer to the enigma of his power and influence; that is why the mob wept for him, lovingly brought his coffin over and hung his portrait everywhere.

If he did fall, it was not at all because the mob abandoned him, because it discerned the emptiness of his designs, because it grew weary of surrendering its last son and of shedding human blood without reason. He provoked the other peoples to a ferocious resistance, and they began to fight desperately for their slavery and for their masters. Christian morality was satisfied: it would have been impossible to defend one's own enemies with a greater fury!

For this once, a military despotism was vanquished by a feudal one.

I cannot pass with indifference the engraving which shows the meeting of Wellington and Blücher at the moment of victory at Waterloo; I stand gazing at it every time, and every time my heart is chilled and frightened. That calm, British figure, which promises nothing brilliant, and that grey, roughly good-natured, German *condottiere*. The Irishman in the English service, a man without a fatherland, and the Prussian whose fatherland is in the barracks, greet each other gladly; and how should they not be glad? They have just turned history off the high road and up to the hubs in mud—mud out of which it will not be hauled in fifty years. It was dawn . . . Europe was still asleep in those days and did not know that her destinies had been altered—and how? Blücher hurried and Grouchy was too late! How many misfortunes, how many tears did that victory cost the nations! And how many misfortunes, how much blood would a victory of the opposing side have cost them?

Both nature and history *are going nowhere,* and therefore they are ready to go *anywhere* to which they are directed, *if this is possible,* that is, if nothing obstructs them. They are composed *au fur et à mesure* of an immense multitude of particles acting upon and meeting with each other, checking and attracting each other; but man is by no means lost because of this, like a grain of sand in a mountain; is not more subject to the elements nor more tightly bound down by necessity: he grows up, by reason of having understood his plight, into a helmsman who proudly ploughs the waves with his boat, making the bottomless abyss serve him as a path of communication.

Having neither programme, set theme nor unavoidable *dénouement,* the dishevelled improvisation of history is ready to walk with anyone; anyone can insert into it his line of verse and, if it is sonorous, it will remain *his* line until the poem is torn up, so long as the past ferments in its blood and memory. A multitude of possibilities, episodes, discoveries, in history and in nature, lies slumbering at every step. The rock had only to be touched with science and water flowed out of it—and what is water? Think what has been done by compressed steam, or by electricity, since man, not Jupiter, took them into his hands. Man's share in this is a great one and full of poetry: it is a kind of creation. The elements, matter, are indifferent: they can slumber for a thousand years and never wake up; but man sends them out to work for him, and they go. The sun had long been travelling across the sky: suddenly man intercepted its ray; he retained the trace of it, and the sun began to make portraits for him.

Nature never fights against man; this is a base, religious calumny. She is not intelligent enough to fight: she is indifferent. 'In proportion as a man knows her, so can he govern her,' said Bacon, and he was perfectly right. Nature cannot thwart man unless man thwarts her laws; she, as she goes on with her work, will unconsciously do his work for him. Men know this, and it is on this basis that they are masters of the seas and lands. But man has not the same respect for the objectivity of the historical world: here he is at home and does not stand on ceremony. In history it is easier for him to be carried passively along by the current of events, or to burst into it with a knife and a shout: 'General prosperity or death!' than to observe the flooding and ebbing of the waves on which he floats, to study the rhythm of their fluctuations, and by that same means to discover for himself unending fairways.

Of course, the position of man in history is more complicated: here he is at one time *boat, wave and pilot.*

'If only there were a chart!'

'But if Columbus had had a chart someone else would have discovered America.'

'Why?'

'Because it would have had to have been discovered to get on to the chart.'

It is only by depriving history of every predestined course that man and history become something earnest, effective and filled with profound interest. If events are stacked in advance, if the whole of history is the unfolding of some anti-historic *plot,* if the result of it all is one performance, one *mise en scène,* then at least let us too take up wooden swords and tin shields. Are we to shed real blood and real tears for the performance of a charade by providence? If there *is* a pre-ordained plan, history is reduced to an insertion of figures in an algebraical formula, and the future is mortgaged before its birth.

People who speak with horror of Owen's depriving man of free-will and moral splendour are reconciling predestination not only with freedom but also with the hangman!—except on the authority of the text that 'the son of man *must* be betrayed, but woe unto him who shall betray him.'[40]

Is it to be wondered at that with such elucidation the simplest everyday subjects become, thanks to scholastic interpretation, utterly incomprehensible? Can there be, for instance, a fact more

---

[40] Theologians, in general, are more courageous than doctrinaires; they say plainly that without the will of God a hair will not fall from the head, and the responsibility for every act, even for the intention, they leave with man. Scientific fatalism asserts that they do not even speak of persons, of *accidental* carriers of an idea . . . (that is, there is no mention of us, the ordinary man, and as for such persons as Alexander of Macedon or Peter I—our ears have been stunned with their universal, historical vocation). The doctrinaires, you see, are like great proprietors: they deal with the economy of history *en gros,* wholesale . . . but where is the boundary between individuals and the herd? At what point do a few grains, as my dear Athenian sophists used to ask, become a heap?

It goes without saying that we have never confused predestination with the theory of probabilities; we have the right to make deductions from the past to the future. When we perform an induction, we know what we

patent to everyone than the observation that the longer a man lives the more chance he has of making his fortune; the longer he looks at one object the better he sees it if nothing disturbs him and he does not go blind? And out of this fact they have contrived the idol of *progress*, a kind of golden calf, growing incessantly and promising to grow to infinity.

Is it not simpler to grasp that man lives not for the *fulfilment of his destiny*, not for the incarnation of an idea, not for progress, but solely because he was born; and he was born *for* (however bad a word that is) . . . for the present, which does not at all prevent his either receiving a heritage from the past or leaving something in his will. To idealists this seems humiliating and coarse: they will take absolutely no account of the fact that the great significance of us men, with all our unimportance, with the hardly discernible flicker of the life of each person, consists in just this: that while we are alive, until the knot held together by us has been resolved into its elements, *we are for all that ourselves*, and not dolls destined to suffer progress or embody some homeless idea. We must be proud of not being needles and thread in the hands of fate as it sews the motley stuff of history. . . . We know that this stuff is not sewn without us, but that is not the object of us, not our commission, not the lesson set us to learn, but the consequence of the complex reciprocal bond that links all existing things by their ends and beginnings, causes and effects.

And that is not all: we can *change the pattern of the carpet*. There is no master craftsman, no design, only a foundation, and we are quite, quite alone, too. The earlier weavers of fate, all those Vulcans and Neptunes, have taken leave of this world. Their executors conceal their testament from us—but the deceased bequeathed us their power.

'But if on the one hand you give a man's fate to him to do as he likes with, and on the other you deprive him of responsibility, then, if he accepts your teaching, he will fold his arms and do absolutely nothing at all.'

Then will people not stop eating and drinking, loving and

---

are doing, basing ourselves on the permanence of certain laws and phenomena, but admitting the possibility of their infringement. We see a man of thirty, and we have every right to suppose that after another thirty years he will be grey-haired or bald, somewhat stooped, and so on. This does not mean that it is ordained that he shall go grey or bald, or stoop—that this is his destiny. If he dies at thirty-nine, he will not go grey, but will turn 'to clay,' as Hamlet says, or into a salad.

producing children, delighting in music and the beauty of women, when they find out that they eat and listen, love and enjoy, for themselves alone, not for the fulfilment of higher designs, and not for the *soonest possible* attainment of an *endless* progress towards perfection?

If religion with its crushing fatalism, and doctrinairism with its chilly cheerlessness, have not made people fold their arms, then there is no reason to fear that this may be done by a view which rids them of these slabs of stone. A mere sniff of life and of its inconsistency was enough to rescue the Hebrew people from religious pranks like asceticism and quietism, which had constantly existed only in word and not in deed: is it possible that reason and consciousness will turn out to be feebler?

Moreover, a realistic view has a secret of its own; he who folds his arms in the face of it will not apprehend or embrace it; he belongs still to a different age of brain; he still needs spurs: the devil with his black tail on one side and on the other the angel with a white lily.

Men's aspiration towards a more harmonious way of living is perfectly natural; it cannot be stopped by anything, as hunger and thirst cannot be stopped. That is why we are not in the least afraid that people will fold their arms as a result of any teaching whatever. Whether, if better conditions of life are discovered, man will be successful in them, or will in one place go astray and in another commit follies, that is a different question. In saying that man will never get rid of hunger we are not saying whether there will always be victuals for everybody, and wholesome ones, too.

There are men who are content with little, who have meagre needs, narrow views and limited desires. There are also peoples with a small horizon and strange notions, who are content to be indigent, false and sometimes even vulgar. The Chinese and Japanese are without doubt two peoples who have found the most suitable social form for their way of living. That is why they remain so unalterably the same.

Europe, it seems to us, is also close to 'saturation' and aspires, tired as she is, to settle, to crystallise out, finding her stable social position in a *petty, mean mode of life.* She is prevented from composing herself at her ease by monarchico-feudal relics and the principle of conquest. A *petit bourgeois* system offers enormous improvement in comparison with the oligarchico-military—there is no doubt of that—but for Europe, and specially for Anglo-Germanic Europe, it offers improvement not only enormous but also sufficient. Holland is ahead: she was the

first to become quiescent, before the interruption of history. The
interruption of growth is the beginning of maturity. The life of
a student is more full of incidents and proceeds much more
stormily than the sober, workman-like life of the father of a
family. If England were not weighed down by the leaden shield
of feudal landlordship, if she did not, like Ugolino, constantly
tread on her children who are dying of hunger, if, like Holland,
she could achieve for everyone the prosperity of small shopkeepers and of *patrons* of moderate means, she would settle down
quietly in her pettiness. And along with that the level of intelligence, breadth of view and aesthetic taste would fall still lower,
and a life without incidents, sometimes diverted by external
impulses, would be reduced to a uniform rotation, to a faintly
varying *semper idem*. Parliament would assemble, the budget
would be presented, capable speeches delivered, forms improved
. . . and the next year it would be the same, and the same ten
years later; it would be the comfortable rut of a grown-up man,
his routine business days. Even in natural phenomena we see
how eccentric the beginnings are, and the settled continuation
goes noiselessly on; not like a tempestuous comet, its tresses
dishevelled, describing its unknown path, but like a tranquil
planet with its satellites like lamps, gliding along its beaten
track; small divagations attest even more the general order.
. . . The spring is somewhat wetter or somewhat drier, but after
every spring comes summer; but before every spring comes
winter.

'For goodness' sake! This means that the whole of humanity
will get as far as a system of pettiness and there get stuck?'

Not the whole of it, I think, but certain parts of it for sure.
The word 'humanity' is most repugnant; it expresses nothing
definite and only adds to the confusion of all the remaining
concepts a sort of piebald demi-god. What sort of unit is understood by the word 'humanity'? Is it what we understand by any
other collective denomination, like caviare, and so on? Who in
the world would dare say that there is any form of order that
would satisfy in an identical manner Iroquois and Irish, Arab
and Magyar, Kaffir and Slav? We may say only that to certain
peoples a petty order is repellent, and others are as much at
home in it as fish in water. The Spaniards and Poles, and in part
the Italians and Russians, contain very few petty elements; the
social order in which they would be well off is higher than that
which pettiness can give them. But it in no way follows from
this that they will *attain* this higher state or that they will not
turn aside on to the *bourgeois* road. Aspiration alone ensures

nothing; we are fearfully emphatic about the difference between the possible and the inevitable. It is not enough to know that such and such an order is repellent to us: we must know what order we want and whether its realisation is possible. There are many possibilities ahead: the *bourgeois* peoples may fly a quite different pitch; the most poetic peoples may turn shopkeepers.

Every man is supported by a huge genealogical tree whose roots go back almost to the paradise of Adam; at our backs, as behind the wave on the shore, is felt the pressure of the whole ocean—of the history of all the world; the thought of all the centuries is in our brain at this minute; there is no thought except in the brain, and with that thought we can be a power.

There is nothing extreme in anyone, but each person can be an irreplaceable reality; before every man the door is open. If a man *has something to say*, let him speak: he will be listened to; if he is tormented by a conviction, let him preach a sermon. People are not as submissive as the elements, but we are always dealing with the masses of our own time: they are not peculiar to themselves, nor are we independent of the common *background* of the picture, of identical antecedent influences; there is a common tie.

Now do you understand on whom the future of man, of peoples, depends?

'On whom?'

'What do you mean, on whom? Why, on you and me, for instance. How can we fold our arms after this?'

THE FREE
RUSSIAN
PRESS AND
THE BELL

(1858-1862)

Apogee and Perigee

ABOUT TEN O'CLOCK one morning I heard from downstairs a thick, discontented voice:

'*May dee comsa–colonel rioos ver vwar.*'

'*Monsieur ne reçoit jamais le matin et. . . .*'

'*Zhe par deman.*'

'*Et votre nom, monsieur?*'

'*May voo diray colonel rioos*'–and the colonel raised his voice.

Jules was in a very difficult situation. I went to the top of the stairs, and asked:

'*Qu'est-ce qu'il y a?*'

'*Say voo?*' asked the colonel.

'*Oui, c'est moi.*'

'Give orders for me to be admitted, my dear sir. Your man-servant won't let me in.'

'Be good enough to come up.'

The colonel's somewhat testy face became visible and, as he stepped with me into my study, he suddenly assumed an air of some dignity and said:

'I am Colonel So-and-so: I am passing through London and thought it my duty to call.'

I at once felt myself to be a general: I pointed to a chair and added:

'Sit down.'

The colonel sat down.

'Are you here for long?'

'Till to-morrow, sir.'

'Have you been here for a long time?'

'Three days, sir.'

'Why are you staying for such a short time?'

'You see, without speaking the language it's strange here, like being in a forest. I sincerely wanted to see you in person, to thank you for myself and many of my comrades. Your publications are very useful; there's a lot of truth in them, and some-times they make us split our sides.'

'I'm extremely grateful to you; this is the only acknowledg-ment we've received abroad. Are many of our issues received at home with you?'

'A great many, sir. And think how many people read each page: they read and re-read them till they're in holes, in rags;

there are devotees who even make copies of them. We meet sometimes to read them, and criticise: you know? I hope you will permit the frankness of a military man who has a sincere respect for you?'

'By all means. It hardly becomes *us* to oppose freedom of speech.'

'We often speak so among ourselves: there's much profit in your disclosures. You know yourself how much one can say over there about Sukhozanet, for instance: keep your tongue between your teeth, eh?; or about Adlerberg, let's say? But, you see, you left Russia a long time ago: you've forgotten *too much* about it, and we keep thinking you harp too much on the peasant question . . . it's not ripe yet . . .'

'Isn't it?'

'Yes, indeed, sir . . . I agree with you entirely; good gracious: the same soul, form, image of God . . . and all that, believe me, is seen by many people nowadays, but there mustn't be any hurry *prematurely*.'

'You think not?'

'I'm sure, sir. Our peasant is a fearful slacker, you know. He's a good chap, perhaps, but a drunkard and a slacker. Emancipate him at once, and he'll stop working, won't sow the fields and will simply die of hunger.'

'But why should you worry about that? Nobody has entrusted the feeding of the Russian people to you, Colonel, have they? . . .'

Of all possible and impossible rejoinders, this was the one that the colonel expected least.

'Of course, sir, on the one hand. . . .'

'Well, don't you be afraid about *on the other hand;* he won't really die of hunger, will he, because he will have sown wheat not for his master but for himself?'

'Excuse me: I thought it was my duty to say. . . . Besides, it seems to me I'm taking up too much of your valuable time. . . . Allow me to take my leave.'

'I thank you most humbly for calling.'

'Pray don't trouble. . . . *Oo ay mon kab?* You live a good way out, sir.'

'It's not close.'

I wanted, with this splendid scene, to begin the description of the period of our bloom and prosperity. Such scenes and similar ones were continually repeated. Neither the fearful distance at which I lived from the West End—at Putney or Fulham—nor the door that was permanently shut in the mornings—nothing helped. We were the fashion.[1]

Whom indeed did we not see at that time? How many people would now pay dearly to wipe out their visit from the memory, if not of themselves, then of humanity? But then, I repeat, *we were the fashion*, and in a tourist's guide-book I was mentioned as one of the curiosities of Putney.

So it was from 1857 to 1863, but it had not been so before. In proportion as reaction extended and strengthened itself in Europe after 1848, and Nicholas grew more savage not by the day but by the hour, Russians began to be rather frightened and to avoid me. Besides, it became known in 1851 that I had officially refused to go to Russia. At that time there were very few travellers. At long intervals one of my old acquaintances would appear, recount frightful, inconceivable things, speak with dread of his return and disappear, looking round to make sure there was no fellow-Russian there. When I was visited at Nice by A. I. Saburov, in a carriage with a body-servant, I looked on it as a feat of heroism. When I passed secretly through France in 1852 I met some of the Russians in Paris: these were the last. In London there was nobody. Weeks, months went by. . . .

'No Russian sound, nor Russian face.'[2]

No one wrote me any letters. M. S. Shchepkin was the first who was anything like a friend *from home* that I saw in London. I have told the story of our meeting in another place. His arrival for me was like an All Souls' Day. He and I held a general commemoration of the Muscovite dead, and our very mood was somehow sepulchral. The real dove from the ark with the olive leaf in its mouth was not Shchepkin but Dr Vensky.

He was the first Russian who came to see us, after the death of Nicholas, at Cholmondely Lodge, Richmond, and was perpetually amazed that it should be so spelt, but pronounced Chumly Lodge.[3] The news that Shchepkin brought was gloomy; he was in a mournful state of mind himself. Vensky used to laugh from morning till night, showing his white teeth; his news was full of the hope, the sanguineness, as the English say, that possessed

---

[1] The 'apogee' of *The Bell* was from 1857 to 1862. (*R.*)

[2] From A. S. Griboyedov: *Woe from Wit*, Act III, scene 22. (*A.S.*)

[3] Dear Vensky was always getting wonderfully stuck in the English language. 'Judging by the map,' he said to my son, 'Keff is not far away.' 'I haven't heard of such a place.' 'Oh, come: there's an enormous botanical garden there and the best orangery in Europe.' 'Let's ask the gardener.' They asked, and he did not know. Vensky unrolled the map. 'There it is, quite close to Richmond!' It was Kew.

Russia after the death of Nicholas and made a luminous band against the sullen background of Petersburg imperialism. True, he did bring a bad account of the health of Granovsky and Ogarëv, but even this disappeared in the glowing picture of an awakening society, of which he himself was a specimen.

How avidly I listened to his stories, cross-questioned him and ferreted out details. I do not know whether he knew then or appreciated afterwards the immeasurable good he did me.

Three years of life in London had fatigued me. It is a laborious business to work without seeing the fruit from close at hand; and as well as this I was too much cut off from any circle of my kin. Printing sheet after sheet with Chernetsky and piling up heaps of printed pamphlets in Trübner's cellars, I had hardly any opportunity to send anything across the frontier of Russia.[4] I could not give up: the Russian printing-press was my life's work, the plank from the paternal home that the ancient Germans used to take with them when they moved; with it I lived in the atmosphere of Russia; with it I was prepared and armed. But with all that, it wore one out that one's work was never heard of: one's hands sank to one's sides. Faith dwindled by the minute and sought after a sign, and not only was there no sign: there was not *one single* word of sympathy from home.

With the Crimean War, with the death of Nicholas, a new time came on; out of the continuous gloom there emerged new masses, new horizons; some movement could be sensed: it was hard to see well from a distance—there had to be an eye-witness. One appeared in the person of Vensky, who confirmed that these horizons were no mirage but reality, that the boat had moved and was under way. One had only to look at his glowing face to believe him. There had been no such faces at all in recent times in Russia.

Overwhelmed by a feeling so unusual for a Russian, I called to mind Kant taking off his velvet cap at the news of the proclamation of the republic in 1792 and repeating, 'Now lettest Thou Thy servant depart.' Yes, it is good to fall asleep at dawn after a long night of bad weather, fully believing that a marvellous day is coming!

Indeed, the *morning* was drawing near of the day for which I had been yearning since I was thirteen—a boy in a camlet jacket

---

[4] For how literature that was illegal in Russia was smuggled in from abroad, see Michael Futrell: *Northern Underground . . . 1865–1917* (Faber, 1963). (*R.*)

sitting with just such another 'malefactor' (only a year younger)
in a little room in the 'old house'; in the lecture-room at the
university, surrounded by an eager, lively brotherhood; in prison
and exile; in a foreign land, making my way through the havoc
of revolution and reaction; at the summit of domestic happiness,
and shattered, lost on the shores of England with my printed
monologue. The sun which had set, lighting up Moscow below
the Sparrow Hills and carrying with it a boyish vow . . . was
rising after a twenty-year-long night.

What was the use now of rest and sleep? . . . *To work!* And
to work I set myself with redoubled energy. The work no longer
went for nothing, no longer vanished in a dark expanse: loud
applause and burning sympathy were borne to us from Russia.
The Pole Star was bought up like hot cakes. The Russian ear,
unused to free speech, became reconciled to it, and looked
eagerly for its masculine solidity, its fearless frankness.

Ogarëv arrived in the spring of 1856 and a year later (1st
July, 1857) the first sheet of the *Kolokol* (*Bell*) came out. Without a fairly close periodicity there is no real bond between a
publication and its readership. A book remains, a magazine
disappears; but the book remains in the library and the magazine disappears in the reader's brain and is so appropriated by
him through repetition that it seems his very own thought; and,
if the reader begins to forget this thought, a new issue of the
magazine, never fearing to be repetitious, will prompt and
revive it.

In fact, for one year the influence of *The Bell* far outgrew *The
Pole Star*. *The Bell* was accepted in Russia as an answer to the
demand for a magazine not mutilated by the censorship. We
were fervently greeted by the young generation; there were
letters at which tears started to one's eyes . . . But it was not
only the young generation that supported us . . .

'*The Bell* is an authority,' I was told in London in 1859 by,
horribile dictu, Katkov, and he added that it lay on the table at
Rostovtsev's to be referred to about the peasant question. . . .
And before him the same thing had been repeated by Turgenev,
Aksakov, Samarin and Kavelin, by generals who were liberals,
liberals who were counsellors of state, ladies of the court with a
thirst for progress and aides-de-camp of literature; V. P. Botkin
himself, constant as a sunflower in his inclination towards any
manifestation of power, looked with tenderness on *The Bell* as
though it had been stuffed with truffles. All that was wanting for
a complete triumph was a sincere enemy. We were before the

Vehmgericht,[5] and we had not long to wait for him. The year 1858 was not yet over when there appeared the accusatory letter of Chicherin. With the haughty frigidity of an unbending doctrinaire, with the *roideur* of an incorruptible judge he summoned me to a reply and, like Biron, poured a bucket of cold water on my head in the month of December.[6] The behaviour of this Saint-Just of bureaucracy astonished me; but now, after seven years, Chicherin's letter seems to me the flower of politeness after the strong language and strong patriotism of the *Mikhaylovsky* time.[7] Yes, and the temper of society was different in those days; Chicherin's 'indictment' provoked an explosion of indignation and we had to try to calm down our exasperated friends. We received letters, articles, protests by dozens. To the accuser himself his former friends wrote letters singly and collectively, full of reproaches, one of them being signed by common friends of ours (three-quarters of them now are more friendly with Chicherin than with me); with the chivalry of bygone times he sent on this letter himself to be kept in our arsenal.

At the palace *The Bell* had received its rights of citizenship even earlier. Its articles led the Emperor to give orders for a review of the affair of 'Kochubey[8] the marksman' who winged his steward. The Empress wept over a letter to her about the upbringing of her children; and it is said that Butkov, the bold Secretary of State, repeated in a fit of arrogant self-sufficiency that he was afraid of nothing, 'Complain to the Tsar, do what you like, write to *The Bell*, if you must, it's all the same to me.' An officer passed over for promotion seriously asked us to print the fact, with a particular hint to the Emperor. The story of

---

5 The *Vehmgerichte* were mediaeval German tribunals which tried capital charges and were dreaded for their severity. (*Tr.*)

6 In the novel of I. I. Lazhechnikov (1792–1860), *The House of Ice*, it is described how Biron's servants, by pouring buckets of water over a disobedient Ukrainian, turned him into a statue of ice. (*A.S.*)

7 The era of the orgy of reaction, when part of liberal society turned to nationalism, chauvinism and a state of mind reminiscent of the Black Hundreds, is called by Herzen after two men who personified reaction— Mikhail Katkov and Mikhail Muravëv. (*A.S.*)

8 In 1853 Prince L. V. Kochubey shot at his steward, I. Saltzmann, and wounded him; yet not only did he remain unpunished but, by bribing the judges, he managed to get Saltzmann put in prison. H. devoted a series of notices in *The Bell* in 1858 and 1859 to the exposure of these abuses, with the result that the case was reviewed and Saltzmann was set free. (*A.S.*)

Shchepkin and Gedeonov I have told in another place—I could tell dozens of such stories.

. . . Gorchakov pointed with amazement to the account printed in *The Bell* of the secret session of the Council of State[9] to consider the peasant business. 'Now who,' he said 'can have told him the details so accurately, except one of those present?'

The Council was disquieted and there was a secret conversation once between 'Butkov and the Tsar' about how to muzzle *The Bell*. The *unmercenary* Muravëv advised that I should be bought off; Panin, the giraffe with the ribbon of St Andrew, preferred that I should be inveigled into the Civil Service. Gorchakov, who played between these two 'dead souls' the part of Mizhuyev,[10] had doubts about my venality and asked Panin:

'What position shall you offer him?'

'Assistant Secretary of State.'

'Well, he won't accept an assistant secretaryship of state,' answered Gorchakov, and the fate of *The Bell* was left to the will of God.

But the will of God evinced itself plainly in the flood of letters and correspondence from all parts of Russia. Each one wrote whatever came into his head: one to blow off steam, another to convince himself that he was a dangerous fellow . . . but there were letters written in a burst of indignation, passionate cries that revealed the everyday abominations. Letters like this compensated for dozens of 'exercises,' just as one visit made up for any number of *colonels rioos*.

Altogether the *bulk* of the letters could be divided into letters with no facts in them but with an abundance of heart and eloquence, letters with magisterial approval or magisterial rebukes, and finally letters with important communications from the provinces.

❖   ❖   ❖

1862

Again it was striking ten o'clock in the morning, and again I heard the voice of a stranger, not a military voice this time,

---

[9] The session was held on 28th January, 1861, and was reported in *The Bell* on 1st March. (*A.S.*)

[10] See N. V. Gogol: *Dead Souls*, Part I, chapter 4.

thick and stern, but a woman's, irritable, upset and sounding like tears:

'I must, I absolutely must see him. . . . I shan't go away till I have.'

And after that there came in a young Russian girl, or young lady, whom I had seen twice before.

She stopped in front of me and looked me steadily in the eyes: her features were sad, her cheeks on fire; she hastily excused herself, and then:

'I have only just come back from Russia, from Moscow; friends of yours, people who are fond of you, have commissioned me to tell you . . . to ask you . . .' Her voice failed her and she stopped.

I understood none of this.

'Can it be true that you—you that we were so passionately fond of—*you* . . . ?'

'But what is the matter?'

'Tell me, for God's sake, *yes or no*—did you have anything to do with the Petersburg fire?'[11]

'I?'

'Yes, yes, yes! They're accusing you . . . at any rate, they're saying you knew about the wicked scheme.'

'What madness! Can you take it seriously, this accusation?'

'Everyone's saying it!'

'Who's "everyone"? Some Nikolay Filippovich Pavlov?' (My imagination did not go any farther at that time!)

'No: people you know well, people who love you dearly; you must clear yourself for their sakes; they're suffering, they're waiting . . .'

'And do you believe it yourself?'

'*I don't know.* That's why I came, because I don't know: I expect you to explain. . . .'

'Let's begin by you calming yourself, and sitting down and listening to me. If I had secretly participated in this incendiarism, what makes you think that I should tell you so—like that, the first time I'm asked? You've no reason, no basis for believing me. You'd do better to say where in all that I've writ-

---

11 Great fires broke out in Petersburg on 28th May, 1862, and burned for several days. The Tsarist government took advantage of this to carry out a series of repressive measures against the revolutionary camp and endeavoured, by spreading rumours that the fires were the work of students incited by Herzen and Chernyshevsky, to produce a wave of hatred against the revolutionary young people and their leaders (*A.S.*)

ten there's anything, one single word, that could justify such an absurd accusation. We are not madmen, you know, to try to commend ourselves to the people of Russia by setting fire to the Rag Market.'

'Why do you keep silent? Why don't you clear yourself publicly?' she asked, and in her eyes there was irresolution and doubt. 'Brand these wicked men in print, say you're horrified by them, that you're not with them, or. . . .'

'Or what? Now, that's enough,' I said to her with a smile, 'of playing Charlotte Corday; you've no dagger and I'm not sitting in my bath. It's shameful of you, and twice as shameful of my friends, to believe such rot; but it would be shameful for us to try to clear ourselves of it, all the more if we tried to do so by way of trampling on and doing great harm to people quite unknown to us who now are in the hands of the secret police and who very likely had as much to do with the fires as you and I.'

'So you're determined not to clear yourself?'

'No, I won't.'

'Then what shall I write to them?'

'Write what you and I have been saying.'

She took the latest issue of *The Bell* out of her pocket and read out: ' "What fiery cup of suffering is passing us by? Is it the fire of senseless destruction, or punishment that purifies by flame? What has driven people to this, and what are these people? What painful moments are they for the absent one when gazing where all his love lies, all that a man lives by, he sees only the dull glow of a conflagration." '

'Dark, frightening lines, that say nothing against you and *nothing for you*. Believe me: clear yourself—or remember my words: *Your friends and supporters will abandon you.*'

Just as the *colonel rioos* had been the drum-major of our success, so the unmurderous Charlotte Corday was the prophetess of our collapse in public opinion—on both sides, too. At the same time as the reactionaries lifted their heads and called us monsters and incendiaries, some of the young people bade us farewell, as though we had fallen by the wayside. The former we despised, the latter we pitied, and we waited sadly for the rough waves of life to destroy those who had made too far out to sea, for we knew that only some of them would get back and make fast to the shore.

The slander grew and was quickly caught up by the press and spread over the whole of Russia. It was only then that the denunciatory era of our journalism began. I remember vividly the amazement of people who were simple and honourable, not in the least revolutionaries, before the printed denunciations—it was something quite new to them. The literature of disclosures quickly shifted its weapon and was twisted at once into a literature of police perquisitions and calumniation by informers.

There was a revolution in society itself. Some were sobered by the emancipation of the peasants; others were simply tired by political agitation; they wished for the former repose; they were satiated before a meal which had cost them so much trouble.

It cannot be denied: our breath is short and our endurance is long!

Seven years of liberalism had exhausted the whole reserve of radical aspirations. All that had been amassed and compressed in the mind since 1825 was expended in raptures of joy, in the foretaste of the good things to come. After the truncated emancipation of the peasants people with weak nerves thought that Russia had gone too far, was going too quickly.

At the same time the *radical* party, young, and for that very reason full of theories, began to announce its intentions more and more impulsively, frightening a society that was already frightened even before this. It set forth as its ostensible aim such extreme outcomes, that liberals and the champions of gradual progress crossed themselves and spat, and·ran away stopping their ears, to hide under the old, filthy but familiar blanket of the police. The headlong haste of the students and the landowners' want of practice in listening to other people could not help bringing them to blows.

The force of public opinion, hardly called to life, manifested itself as a savage conservatism. It declared its participation in public affairs by elbowing the government into the debauchery of terror and persecution.

Our position became more and more difficult. We could not stand up for the filth of reaction, but our *locus standi* outside it was lost. Like the knights-errant in the stories who have lost their way, we were hesitating at a cross-roads. Go to the right, and you will lose your horse, but you will be safe yourself; go to the left, and your horse will be safe but you will perish; go forward, and everyone will abandon you; go back—that was impossible: for us the road in that direction was overgrown with grass. If only a sorcerer or hermit would appear and relieve us of the burden of irresolution. . . .

Our acquaintances, and the Russian ones especially, used to meet at our house on Sunday evenings. In 1862 the number of the latter greatly increased: merchants and tourists, journalists and officials of all the departments, and of the Third Division [the Secret Police] in particular, were arriving for the Exhibition. It was impossible to make a strict selection; we warned our more intimate friends to come on a different day. The pious boredom of a London Sunday was too much for their discretion, and these Sundays did to some extent lead to disaster. But before I tell the story of that I must describe two or three specimens of our native fauna who made their appearance in the modest drawing-room of Orsett House.[12] Our gallery of living curiosities from Russia was, beyond all doubt, more remarkable and more interesting than the Russian Section at the Great Exhibition.

In 1860 I received from a hotel in the Haymarket a Russian letter in which some unknown persons informed me that they were Russians and were in the service of Prince Yury Nikolayevich Golitsyn, who had secretly left Russia: 'The prince himself has gone to Constantinople, but has sent us by another route. The prince bade us wait for him and gave us money enough for a few days. More than a fortnight has passed; there is no news of the prince; our money is spent, the hotel-keeper is angry. We do not know what to do. Not one of us speaks English.' Finding themselves in this helpless situation, they asked me to rescue them.

I went to them and arranged things. The hotel-keeper knew me, and consented to wait another week.

Five days later a sumptuous carriage with a pair of dapple-grey horses drove up to my front door. However much I explained to my servants that no one was to be admitted in the morning—even though he should arrive in a coach and six and call himself a duke—I could never overcome their respect for an aristocratic turn-out and title. On this occasion both these temptations to transgression were present, and so a moment later a huge man, stout and with the handsome face of an Assyrian bull-god, was embracing me and thanking me for my visit to his servants.

This was Prince Yury Nikolayevich Golitsyn. It was a long time since I had seen so solid and characteristic a fragment of All Russia, so choice a specimen from our fatherland.

He at once began telling me some incredible story, which all turned out to be true, of how he had given a pensioner's son an article from *The Bell* to copy, and how he had parted from his

---

[12] The house in London where Herzen lived from November 1860 'til June 1863. (*A.S.*)

wife; how the pensioner's son had informed against him, and how his wife did not send him money; how the Tsar had sent him into perpetual banishment at Kozlov, in consequence of which he had made up his mind to escape abroad, and therefore had brought off with him over the Moldavian frontier some young lady, a governess, a steward, a precentor and a maid-servant.

At Galatz he had picked up also a valet who spoke five languages after a fashion, and had proved to be a spy. Then he explained to me that he was passionately fond of music and was going to give concerts in London; and that therefore he wanted to make the acquaintance of Ogarëv.

'They d-do make you p-pay here in England at the C-Customs,' he said with a slight stammer, as he completed his course of universal history.

'For commercial goods, perhaps, they do,' I observed, 'but the Custom-house is very lenient to travellers.'

'I should not say so. I paid fifteen shillings for a c-crocodile.'

'Why, what do you mean?'

'What do I mean? Why, simply a c-crocodile.'

I opened my eyes wide and asked him:

'But what is the meaning of this, Prince? Do you take a crocodile about with you instead of a passport, in order to frighten the police on the frontier?'

'It happened like this. I was taking a walk in Alexandria, and I saw a little Arab offering a crocodile for sale. I liked it, so I bought it.'

'Oh, did you buy the little Arab too?'

'Ha-ha!—no.'

A week later the prince was already installed in Porchester Terrace, that is, in a large house in a very expensive part of the town. He began by ordering his gates to be for ever wide open, which is not the English custom, and a pair of dapple-grey horses to be for ever waiting in readiness at the door. He set up living in London as though he had been at Kozlov or Tambov.

He had no money of course, that is, he had a few thousand francs, enough to pay for the advertisement and title-page of a life in London; they were spent at once; but he threw dust in people's eyes, and succeeded for a few months in living free from care, thanks to the stupid trustfulness of the English, of which foreigners have not been able to break them to this day.

But the prince went ahead at full steam. The concerts began. London was impressed by the prince's title on the placards, and at the second concert the room (St James's Hall, Piccadilly) was full. The concert was magnificent. How Golitsyn had succeeded in training the chorus and the orchestra is his own secret, but the concert was absolutely first-rate. Russian songs and prayers, the *Kamarinskaya* and the Mass, fragments from an opera of Glinka's and from the Gospel (Our Father)—it all went splendidly.

The ladies could not sufficiently admire the colossal fleshy contours of the handsome Assyrian god, so majestically and gracefully wielding his ivory sceptre; the old ladies recalled the athletic figure of the Emperor Nicholas,[13] who had conquered the London ladies most of all by the tight elk *collants*, white as the Russian snows, of his Horse Guards' uniform.

Golitsyn found the means of making a loss out of this success. Intoxicated by the applause he sent at the end of the first half of the concert for a basket of bouquets (remember the London prices), and before the beginning of the second part of the programme he appeared on the stage; two liveried servants carried the basket, and the prince, thanking the singers and chorus, presented each with a bouquet. The audience received this act of gallantry on the part of the aristocratic conductor with a storm of applause. My prince, towering to his full height and beaming all over, invited *all* the musicians to supper at the end of the concert.

At this point not only London prices but also London habits must be considered. Unless previous notice is given in the morning, there is no place where one can find supper for fifty persons at eleven o'clock at night.

The Assyrian chief walked valiantly along Regent Street at the head of his musical army, knocking at the doors of various restaurants; and at last he knocked successfully. A restaurant-keeper, grasping the situation, rose to the occasion with cold meats and mulled wines.

After this there began a series of concerts of his with every possible trick, even with political tendencies. At each of them the orchestra struck up a Herzen waltz, an Ogarëv quadrille, and then the *Emancipation Symphony* . . . compositions with which the prince is very likely even now enchanting Moscow audiences, and which have probably lost nothing in the transfer from Albion, except their names; they could easily be altered to a Potapov waltz, a Mina waltz and Komissarov's *Partitur*.

With all this noise there was no money; he had nothing to pay

---

[13] The Tsar Nicholas I visited England in 1844. (*A.S.*)

with. His contractors began to murmur. And at home there began, little by little, Spartacus' revolt of the slaves.

One morning the prince's factotum came to me, that is, his steward who now styled himself his secretary, together with the precentor, a fair-haired, curly-headed Russian lad of two-and-twenty who directed the singers.

'We have come to see you, Alexander Ivanovich, sir.'

'What has happened?'

'Why, Yury Nikolayevich is treating us very badly. We want to go back to Russia, and we ask him to settle our account—do not betray your own gracious good nature: stand up for us.'

I felt myself surrounded by the atmosphere of 'Home,' which seemed to rise up like steam in a bath-house.

'Why do you come to me with this request? If you have serious grounds for complaining of the prince, there is a court of justice here for everyone, a court which will not behave crookedly in favour of any prince or any count.'

'We have heard of that indeed, but *why go to law?* Much better if you will sort it out.'

'What good will it be to you if I do? The prince will tell me to mind my own business; I shall look like a fool. If you do not want to go to law, go to the ambassador; the Russians in London are in his care, not in mine. . . .'

'But where should we be then? Once Russian gentlemen are sitting together, what chance can there be of settling with the prince? But you see, you are on the side of the people; so that is why we have come to you. Do be gracious, and take up our cause.'

'What fellows you are! But the prince won't accept my decision; what will you gain by it?'

'Allow me to report to you, sir,'[14] the secretary retorted eagerly, 'he will not venture on that, sir, since he has a very great respect for you; besides, he would be afraid. He would not be pleased to get into *The Bell*—he has his pride, sir.'

'Well, listen, to waste no more time; here is my decision. If the prince will consent to accept my mediation, I will undertake the matter; if not, you must go to law; and since you know neither the language nor the mode of proceeding here, if the prince really is treating you unfairly I shall send you a man who knows English and English ways and speaks Russian.'

'Allow me,' the secretary was beginning.

'No, I won't allow you, my dear fellow. Good-bye.'

---

[14] The formula used by soldiers when addressing an officer. (*R.*)

While they are on their way to the prince I shall say a word or two about them.

The precentor was in no way distinguished except by his musical abilities; he was a well-fed, soft, stupidly handsome, rosy servant-boy; his manner of speaking with a slight burr and his rather sleepy eyes called up before me a whole series, one reflection behind another in the looking-glass, when you are telling fortunes, of Sashkas, Senkas, Alëshkas and Miroshkas.

The secretary, too, was a purely Russian product, but a more striking specimen of his type. He was a man over forty, with an unshaven chin and hollow cheeks, in a greasy coat, unclean himself and soiled inwardly and outwardly, with small, crafty eyes and that peculiar smell of Russian drunkards, made up of the ever-persistent bouquet of corn-spirit fumes mixed with a flavour of onion and cloves to mask it. Every feature of his face encouraged and gave currency to every evil suggestion, which would doubtless have found response and appreciation in his heart, and would if profitable have received assistance from him. He was the prototype of the Russian petty official, the Russian extortioner, the pettifogging Russian clerk. When I asked him whether he was pleased at the approaching emancipation of the peasants, he answered:

'To be sure, sir—most certainly,' and added with a sigh: 'Good Lord, the lawsuits and examinations in the courts that there will be! And the prince has brought me here as though to make fun of me just at this time.'

Before Golitsyn arrived, this man had said to me with a show of genuine feeling:

'Don't you believe what people will tell you about the prince oppressing the peasants, or how he meant to set them free for a big redemption sum without any land. All that is a story spread by his enemies. It is true he is violent and extravagant, but to make up for that he has a good heart and has been a father to his peasants.'

As soon as he had quarrelled with the prince he had complained of him, cursed his own lot and lamented that he had trusted such a rogue. 'Why, he has done nothing all his life but debauch himself and ruin his peasants; you know he is just keeping up a pretence before you now—but he is really a beast, a plunderer. . . .'

'When were you telling lies: now, or when you praised him?' I asked him, smiling.

The secretary was overcome with confusion. I turned on my heel and went away. Had this man not been born in the servants' hall of the Prince Golitsyn, had he not been the son of some village clerk, he would long ago, with his abilities, have been a minister of state.

An hour later the precentor and his mentor appeared with a note from Golitsyn. He asked me, with apologies, whether I could go and see him to put an end to these petty squabbles. The prince promised beforehand to accept my decision without disputing it.

There was no getting out of it: I went.

Everything in the house indicated an unusual excitement; the French servant Picot hastily opened the door to me and, with the solemn fussiness with which a doctor is conducted to a consultation at the bedside of a dying man, showed me into the drawing-room. There I found Golitsyn's second wife, flustered and irritated. Golitsyn himself, with no cravat, his heroic chest bare, was pacing up and down the room with huge strides. He was furious, and so stammered twice as much as usual; his whole face betrayed his suffering from the blows, kicks and punches that were surging inwardly but could have no outlet into the actual world, though they would have been his answer to insurgents in the province of Tambov.

'For G-G-God's sake, forgive me for t-t-troubling you about these b-b-blackguards.'

'What is the matter?'

'P-p-please ask them yourself; I shall only listen.'

He summoned the precentor, and the following conversation took place between us:

'Are you dissatisfied in some way?'

'Yes, very much dissatisfied; that is just why I want to go back to Russia without fail.'

The prince, who had a voice as strong as Lablache's, emitted a leonine groan: another five blows in the face had to be stifled within him.

'The prince cannot keep you back; so tell us what it is you are dissatisfied with.'

'Everything, Alexander Ivanovich, sir.'

'Well, do speak more definitely.'

'What can I say? Ever since I came away from Russia I have been run off my legs with work, and had only two pounds of pay, and what the prince gave me the third time, in the evening, was more by way of a present.'

'And how much ought you to have received?'

'That I can't say, sir. . . .'

'Well, have you a definite salary?'

'No indeed, sir. The prince, when he was graciously pleased to escape abroad [this was said without the slightest malicious intention], said to me: "If you like to come with me, I'll make your future," says he, "and if I have luck, I'll give you a good salary; but if not, then you must be satisfied with a little"; so I took and came.'

He had come from Tambov to London on such terms. Oh, Russia!

'Well, and what do you think? has the prince been lucky or not?'

'Lucky? no, indeed! Though, to be sure, he might. . . .'

'That is a different question. If he has not been lucky, then you ought to be satisfied with a small salary.'

'But the prince himself told me that for my duties and my abilities, according to the rate of pay here, I ought not to get less than four pounds a month.'

'Prince, are you willing to pay him four pounds a month?'

'I shall be d-d-delighted.'

'That is capital; what more?'

'The prince promised that if I wanted to go back he would pay my return fare to Petersburg.'

The prince nodded and added: 'Yes, but only if I were satisfied with him!'

'What are you dissatisfied with him for?'

Now the dam burst; the prince leapt up. In a tragic bass, which gained weight from the quiver on some vowels and the little pauses between some of the consonants, he delivered the following speech:

'Could I be satisfied with that m-milksop, that p-p-pup? What enrages me is the foul ingratitude of the bandit. I took him into my service from the very poorest family of peasants, barefooted, devoured by lice; I trained the rascal. I have made a m-m-man of him, a m-musician, a precentor; I have trained the scoundrel's voice so that he could get a hundred roubles a month in Russia in the season.'

'All that is so, Yury Nikolayevich, but I can't share your view of it. Neither he nor his family asked you to make a Ronconi of him; so you can't expect any special gratitude on his part. You have trained him as one trains nightingales, and you have done a good thing, but that is the end of it. Besides, this is not the point.'

'You are right; but I meant to say, how can I put up with this? You know, I'll give the rascal. . . .'

'So you agree to pay his fare?'

'The devil take him. For your sake, only for your sake, I'll give it.'

'Well, the matter is settled, then: and do you know what the fare is?'

'I am told it is twenty pounds.'

'No, that is too much. A hundred silver roubles from here to Petersburg is more than enough. Will you give that?'

'Yes.'

I worked out the sum on paper and handed it to Golitsyn; he looked at the total . . . it amounted, I think, to just over £30. He handed me the money on the spot.

'You can read and write, of course?' I asked the precentor.

'Of course, sir.'

I wrote out a receipt for him in some such form as this: I have received from Prince Yury Nikolayevich Golitsyn £30 odd [so much in Russian money] being salary owing to me and my fare from London to Petersburg. With that I am satisfied, and have no other claims against him.

'Read it for yourself, and sign it.'

The young man read it, but made no movement to sign it.

'What is the matter?'

'I can't, sir.'

'Why can't you?'

'I am not satisfied.'

A restrained leonine roar—and, indeed, even I was on the point of raising my voice.

'What the devil is the matter? You said yourself what you claimed. The prince has paid you everything to the last farthing. What are you dissatisfied with?'

'Why, upon my word, sir, and the privations I've suffered since I've been here.'

It was clear that the ease with which he had obtained the money had whetted his appetite.

'For instance, sir, I ought to have something more for copying music.'

'You liar!' Golitsyn boomed, as even Lablache can never have boomed; the piano responded with a timid echo; Picot's pale face appeared at the crack of the door and vanished with the speed of a frightened lizard.

'Wasn't copying music a part of your definite duty? Why, what else would you have done all the time when there were no concerts?'

The prince was right, though he need not have frightened Picot with his *contre-bombardon* voice.

The precentor, being accustomed to sounds of all sorts, did not give way but dropped the music-copying and turned to me with the following absurdity:

'And then, too, there is something for clothes. I am quite threadbare.'

'But do you mean to tell me that Yury Nikolayevich undertook to clothe you, as well as to give you about £50 a year salary?'

'No, sir; but in old days the prince always did sometimes give me things, but now, I am ashamed to say it, I have come to going about without socks.'

'I am going about without s-s-socks myself,' roared the prince, and folding his arms across his chest he looked haughtily and contemptuously at the precentor. This outburst I had not expected, and I looked into his face with surprise; but, seeing that he did not intend to continue, and that the precentor certainly did, I said very gravely to the predatory singer:

'You came to me this morning to ask for my mediation: so you trusted me?'

'We know you very well, we have no doubt of you at all, you will not let us be wronged.'

'Excellent. Well, this is how I settle the matter: sign the receipt at once or give me back the money, and I shall give it back to the prince and at the same time decline to meddle any further.'

The precentor had no inclination to hand the money to the prince; he signed the receipt and thanked me.

I shall leave out of my tale how he converted his reckoning into roubles. I could not din into him that the rouble was not worth the same on the exchange as it had been when he left Russia.

'If you think that I want to cheat you of 30 shillings, this is what you had better do: go to our priest and ask him to reckon it for you.' He agreed to do so.

It seemed as though all was over, and Golitsyn's breast no longer heaved with such stormy menace; but as fate would have it the finale recalled our fatherland as the beginning had.

The precentor hesitated and hesitated, and suddenly, as though nothing had happened between them, turned to Golitsyn with the words:

'Your Excellency, since the steamer does not go from Hull for five days, be so gracious as to allow me to remain with you meanwhile.'

My Lablache will give it him, I thought, self-sacrificingly preparing myself for the shock of the sound.

'Of course you can stay. Where the devil could you go?'

The precentor thanked the prince and went away. Golitsyn said to me by way of explanation:

'You see he is a very good fellow; it is that b-b-blackguard, that thief, that vile pettifogger has put him up to it.'

Let Savigny and Mittermeyer do their best to formulate and classify the juridical concepts developed in our Orthodox father-land between the stables where the house-serfs were flogged and the master's study where the peasants were fleeced.

The second *cause célèbre*, the one with the pettifogger afore-said, was not successful. Golitsyn came in, and he suddenly shouted so loud, and the secretary shouted so loud, and after that there was nothing left but for them to go for each other, and then the prince, of course, would have smashed the stinking clerk. Since, however, everything in that household followed the laws of a peculiar logic, it was not the prince who fought with the secretary, but the secretary who fought with the door. Brimming over with spite and refreshed by another noggin of gin, he aimed a blow with his fist as he went out at the big glass window in the door, and broke it to bits. These windows are half an inch thick.

'Police!' roared Golitsyn. 'Burglary! Police!' and going into the drawing-room he fell fainting on the sofa. When he had recovered a little, he explained to me among other things what the ingratitude of the secretary consisted of. The man had been his brother's agent and had swindled him—I do not remember how—and must without fail have been brought to trial. Golitsyn was sorry for him; he put himself, as it were, so thoroughly in his place that he pawned his last watch to buy him off. And then, having complete proof that he was a rogue, he took him on as his steward!

There can be no doubt whatever that he had cheated Golitsyn at every turn.

I went away. A man who could smash a glass door with his fist could find justice and punishment for himself. Moreover, he told me afterwards himself, when he was asking me to get him a passport to return to Russia, that he had proudly offered Golitsyn a pistol and suggested casting lots which should fire.

If this was so, the pistol was certainly not loaded.

The prince spent his last penny in pacifying the Revolt of Spartacus, and none the less ended, as might have been expected, by being imprisoned for debt. Anyone else would have been clapped in prison, and that would have been the end of it; but even that could not happen to Golitsyn simply in the common way.

A policeman used to conduct him between seven and eight o'clock every evening to Cremorne Gardens; there he used to conduct a concert for the pleasure of the *lorettes* of all London, and with the last wave of his ivory sceptre a policeman, till then unobserved, would spring up out of the earth and escort the prince to the cab which took the captive in his black swallow-tail and white gloves to prison. There were tears in his eyes as he said 'Good-bye' to me in the Gardens. Poor prince! Another man might have laughed at it, but he took his incarceration to heart. His relations eventually redeemed him; then the government permitted him to return to Russia, and at first directed him to Yaroslavl to live, where he could conduct religious concerts, together with Felinski, the Bishop of Warsaw. The government was kinder to him than his father; as black a sheep as his son, he advised the latter *to go into a monastery*. The father knew the son well; and yet he was himself so good a musician that Beethoven dedicated a symphony[15] to him.

Next after the exuberant figure of the Assyrian god, of the fleshy ox-Apollo, a series of other Russian oddities must not be forgotten.

I am not speaking of flitting shades like the *colonel rioos,* but of those who, stranded by various vicissitudes of fate, have lingered for a long time in London; such as the clerk in the War Office who, having got into a mess with his files and debts, threw himself into the Neva, was drowned . . . and popped up in London, an *exile,* in a fur cap and a fur-lined coat, which he never abandoned, regardless of the muggy warmth of a London winter.

Or such as my friend Ivan Ivanovich Savich, whom the English called Savage and who, with antecedents and future and all, with raw skin on his head where there should have been hair, clamours for a place in my gallery of Russian rarities.[16] A retired officer of the Pavlovsky regiment of Life Guards, he lived

---

[15] The three string quartets, in E flat major, A minor and B major, were commissioned by Nikolay Borisovich Golitsyn, and were written in 1823. (*A.S.*)

[16] Savich, a retired officer, went abroad in 1844 for treatment. He became a permanent emigrant for fear of the police after the arrest of his brother, N. I. Savich, a member of the Cyril and Methodius secret society. I. I. Savich took no part in politics either at home or abroad. (*R.*)

in comfort in foreign parts, and so continued up to the revolution of February. Then he took fright, and began to look on himself as a criminal. Not that his conscience troubled him; what troubled him was the thought of the gendarmes who would meet him at the frontier, the thought of dungeons, of a troika, of the snow, and he resolved to postpone his return. Suddenly the news reached him that his brother had been arrested in connection with the Shevchenko case. There really was some risk for him, and he at once resolved to return. It was at that time that I made his acquaintance at Nice. Savich set off, having bought a minute phial of poison for the journey, which he intended as he crossed the frontier to insert in a hollow tooth and to bite if he should be arrested.

As he neared his native land his fright grew greater and greater, and by the time he arrived at Berlin it had become a suffocating anguish. However, Savich mastered himself and took his seat in a carriage. He remained there for the first five stations; farther than that he could not bear it. The engine stopped to take in water; on an entirely different pretext he left his carriage. The engine whistled and the train moved off without Savich; and that was just what he wanted. Leaving his trunk to the mercy of fate, he returned to Berlin by the first train going in the opposite direction. Thence he sent a telegram concerning his luggage, and went to get a *visa* for his passport to Hamburg. 'Yesterday you were going to Russia, and to-day you are going to Hamburg,' remarked the policeman, who had no intention of refusing the *visa*. The frightened Savich said: 'Letters—I have received letters,' and probably his expression as he said it was such that it was only by the Prussian official's neglect of his duty that he was not arrested. Thereupon Savich, like Louis-Philippe, escaping though pursued by no one, arrived in London. In London a hard life began for him, as for thousands and thousands of others; for years he maintained an honest and resolute struggle with poverty. But for him, too, destiny provided a comic trimming to all tragic events. He made up his mind to give lessons in mathematics, drawing and even French (for English people!). After consulting this man and that, he saw that it could not be done without an advertisement or visiting cards.

'But the trouble was this: how would the Russian government look at it? I thought and thought about it, and I had *anonymous* cards printed.'

It was a long time before I could get over my delight at this grand invention: it had never entered my head that it was possible to have a visiting-card without a name on it.

With the help of his anonymous cards, and with great perseverance and fearful self-denial (he used to live for days together on bread and potatoes), he succeeded in getting afloat, was employed in selling things on commission, and his fortunes began to mend.

And this was just at the time when the fortunes of another officer of the Pavlovsky bodyguard took a thoroughly bad turn; defeated, robbed, deceived, and made a fool of, the commanding officer of the Pavlovsky regiment[17] departed into eternity. Dispensations followed and amnesties; Savich too wished to take advantage of the Imperial mercies, so off he writes to Brunnov[18] and asks whether he comes under the amnesty. A month later Savich is invited to the Embassy. 'My case is not so simple,' he thought; 'they have been thinking it over for a month.'

'We have received an answer,' the senior secretary says to him; 'you have inadvertently put the Ministry in a difficult position; they have nothing about you. They have applied to the Ministry of Home Affairs, and they can find no file relating to you either. Tell us plainly what it was; it cannot have been anything of consequence.'

'Why, in 1849 my brother was arrested and afterwards exiled.'

'Well?'

'That was all.'

'No,' thought Nikolay, 'he is joking'; and he told Savich that if that was the case the Ministry would make further inquiries.

A couple of months went by. I can imagine what went on during these two months in Petersburg: references, reports, confidential inquiries, secret questions passed from the Ministry to the Third Division, from the Third Division to the Ministry, the reports of the Governor-General of Kharkov . . . reprimands, observations . . . but Savich's file could not be found.

The Ministry reported to London to that effect.

Brunnov himself sends for Savich.

'Here,' he says—'look at the answer: there is nothing anywhere concerning you. —Tell me, what business was it you were mixed up in?'

'My brother . . .'

---

[17] It was of the Izmaylovsky regiment that Nicholas I was Colonel-in-Chief. (*A.S.*)

[18] The Russian representative in London 1856–8 was not Brunnov but M. I. Khrebtovich. F. I. Brunnov was Russian plenipotentiary in England, 1840–54 and 1858–74, with the rank of ambassador from 1860. (*A.S.*)

'I have heard all that, but with what affair were you yourself connected?'

'There was nothing else.'

Brunnov, who had never been surprised at anything from his birth up, was surprised.

'Then what do you ask for a pardon for if you have done nothing?'

'I thought that it was better, anyway.'

'So quite simply you don't need to be amnestied: you need a passport,' and Brunnov ordered a passport to be given him.

In high delight Savich dashed off to us.

After describing in detail the whole story of how he had managed to be amnestied, he took Ogarëv by the arm and led him away into the garden.

'For God's sake, give me some advice,' he said to him. 'Alexander Ivanovich always laughs at me—that is his way; but you have a kind heart. Tell me candidly: do you think I can safely go through Vienna?'

Ogarëv did not justify this good opinion; he burst out laughing; but not only Ogarëv—I can imagine how the faces of Brunnov and Nikolay for two minutes lost the wrinkles traced by weighty affairs of State and smiled when Savich, amnestied, walked out of their office.

But with all his eccentricities Savich was an honest man. The other Russians who rose to the surface, God knows whence, strayed for a month or two about London, called on us with letters of introduction written by themselves and vanished God knows whither, were by no means so harmless.

The melancholy case which I am going to relate took place in the summer of 1862. The reaction was at that time in its incubation stage, and from its internal, hidden rottenness nothing had yet emerged into the open. No one was afraid to come and see us; no one was afraid to take copies of *The Bell* and other publications of ours away with him; many people boasted of the expert way in which they conveyed them over the frontier. When we advised them to be careful, they laughed at us. We hardly ever wrote letters to Russia: we had nothing to say to our old friends, for we were drifting ever farther and farther away from them; with our new, unknown friends we corresponded through *The Bell*.

In the spring Kelsiev returned from Moscow and Petersburg. His journey is undoubtedly one of the most remarkable episodes of that period. The man who had slipped under the noses of the police, scarcely concealing himself, who had been present at meetings of schismatics and drinking parties of comrades, with the stupidest Turkish passport in his pocket, and had returned safe and sound to London, had begun to champ the bit a good deal. He took it into his head to get up a subscription-dinner in our honour on the fifth anniversary of *The Bell* at Kühn's restaurant. I asked him to put off the celebration to another, happier time. He would not. The supper was not a success: there was no *entrain* about it, and there could not be. Among the participants were people whose interests were too extraneous to ours.

Talking of one thing and the other between toasts and anecdotes, it was mentioned as the simplest thing in the world that Kelsiev's friend, Vetoshnikov, was going to Petersburg and was ready to take something with him. The party broke up late. Many people said that they would be with us on Sunday. In fact, a regular crowd assembled, among whom were people whom we knew very little, and unfortunately Vetoshnikov himself; he came up to me and said that he was going next morning, and asked me whether I had not any letters or commissions. Bakunin had already given him two or three letters. Ogarëv went downstairs to his own room and wrote a few words of friendly greeting to Nikolay Serno-Solovyevich, to which I added a word of greeting and asked the latter to call the attention of Chernyshevsky (to whom I had never written) to our proposal in *The Bell* to print the *Sovremennik* (*Contemporary*) in London at our expense.

The guests began to leave about twelve o'clock. Two or three of them remained. Vetoshnikov came into my study and took the letter. It is very possible that even that might have remained unnoticed. But this is what happened. By way of thanking those who had taken part in the dinner, I asked them to choose any one of our publications or a big photograph of me by Levitsky as a souvenir. Vetoshnikov took the photograph; I advised him to cut off the margin and roll it up into a tube; he would not, and said he should put it at the bottom of his trunk, and so wrapped it in a sheet of *The Times* and went off. That could not escape notice.

Saying good-bye to him, the last of the party, I went calmly off to bed—so great is one's blindness at times—and of course never dreamed how dearly that minute would cost me and what sleepless nights it would bring me.

All put together it was stupid and careless in the extreme. We might have delayed Vetoshnikov until Tuesday: we might have sent him off on Saturday; why had he not come in the morning? . . . and, indeed, why had he come himself at all? . . . and, indeed, why did we write the letters?

It is said that one of our guests[19] telegraphed at once to Petersburg.

Vetoshnikov was arrested on the steamer; the rest is well known.[20]

◈ ◈ ◈

The Younger Emigrants: The Common Fund

KELSIEV[1] HAD HARDLY passed out of our door when fresh people, driven out by the severe cold of 1863, were knocking at it. These came not from the training-schools of the coming revolution but from the devastated stage on which they had already acted rôles. They were seeking shelter from the storm without and seeking nothing within; what they needed was a temporary haven until the weather improved, until a chance presented itself to return to the fray. These men, while still very young, had finished with ideas, with culture; theoretical questions did not interest them, partly because they had not yet arisen among them, partly because what they were concerned with was their application. Though they had been defeated physically, they had given proofs of their courage. They had furled their flag, and their task

---

[19] One of Herzen's guests was G. G. Peretts, an agent of the Third Division, who gave information of the return of P. A. Vetoshnikov with 'dangerous documents.' (A.S.)

[20] Mass arrests in Russia, the result of the seizure of the letters that Vetoshnikov was carrying, seriously weakened H.'s and Ogarëv's ties with the revolutionary movement in Russia. (A.S.)

[1] V. I. Kelsiev was temporarily a member of the circle of revolutionary emigrants and became one of the first renegades of the Russian liberation movement. (A.S.) The preceding chapter is devoted to his tragi-comic story; I regret space didn't permit including it, for it is a Chekhovian tale that displays both Herzen's novelistic talents and his humanity. (D.M.)

was to preserve its honour. Hence their dry tone, *cassant, raide,* abrupt and rather elevated. Hence their martial, impatient aversion for prolonged deliberation, for criticism, their somewhat elaborate contempt for all intellectual luxuries, among which they put Art in the foreground. What need had they of music? What need of poetry? 'The fatherland is in danger, *aux armes, citoyens!*' In certain cases they were theoretically right, but they did not take into account the complex, intricate process of balancing the ideal with the real, and, I need hardly say, they assumed that their views and theories were the views and theories of the whole of Russia. To blame for this our young pilots of the coming storm would be unjust. It is the common characteristic of youth; a year ago a Frenchman,[2] a follower of Comte, assured me that Catholicism did not exist in France, that it had *complètement perdu le terrain,* and he pointed among others to the medical faculty, to the professors and students who were not merely not Catholics but not even Deists.

'Well, but the part of France,' I observed, 'which neither gives nor hears medical lectures?'

'It, of course, keeps to religion and its rites—but more from habit and ignorance.'

'I can very well believe it, but what will you do with it?'

'What did they do in 1792?'

'Not much: at first the Revolution closed the churches, but afterwards opened them again. Do you remember Augereau's answer to Napoleon when they were celebrating the Concordat? "Do you like the ceremony?" the consul asked as they came out of Notre-Dame. The Jacobin general answered: "Very much. I am only sorry that the two hundred thousand men are not present who went to their graves to abolish such ceremonies!"'

'*Ah bah!* we have grown wiser, and we shall not open the church doors—or rather we shall not close them at all, but shall turn the temples of superstition into schools.'

'*L'infâme sera écrasée,*' I wound up, laughing.

'Yes, no doubt of it; that is certain!'

'But that you and I will not see it—that is even more certain.'

It is to this looking at the surrounding world through a prism coloured by personal sympathies that half the revolutionary

---

[2] G. N. Vyrubov, who had emigrated from Russia in 1864. Herzen was critical of his views and activities, calling him 'Frenchman' and 'doctrinaire' and censuring him for his complete break with his native country. (*A.S.*)

failures are due. The life of young people, spent in general in a noisy, closed seclusion of a sort, remote from the everyday, wholesale struggle for personal interests, though it clearly grasps general truths, nearly always comes to grief through a false understanding of their application to the needs of the day.

At first our new visitors cheered us with accounts of the movement in Petersburg, of the savage antics of the full-fledged reaction, of trials and persecutions, of university and literary parties. Then, when all this had been told with the rapidity with which in such cases men hasten to tell all they know, a pause, a hiatus would follow; our conversations became dull and monotonous.

'Can this,' I thought, 'actually be old age divorcing two generations? Is it the chill induced by years, by weariness, by ordeals?'

Whatever it might be due to, I felt that with the arrival of these new men our horizon was not widened but narrowed. The scope of our conversations was more limited. Sometimes we had nothing to say to one another. They were occupied with the details of their coteries, beyond which nothing interested them. Having once related everything of interest about them, there was nothing to do but to repeat it, and they did repeat it. They took little interest in learning or in public affairs; they even read little, and did not follow the newspapers regularly. Absorbed in memories and expectations, they did not care to step forth into other fields; while we had not air to breathe in that stifling atmosphere. We had been spoiled by different dimensions and were smothered.

Moreover, even if they did know a certain stratum in Petersburg, they did not know Russia at all and, though sincerely desirous of coming into contact with the people, they only approached them bookishly and theoretically.

What we had in common was too general. Advance together, *serve*, as the French say, take action together we might, but it was hard to stand still with arms folded and live together. It was useless even to think of a serious influence on them. A morbid and very unceremonious vanity had long ago taken the bit between its teeth.[3] Sometimes, it is true, they did ask for a

---

[3] Their vanity was not so much great as it was touchy and irritable, and above all, unrestrained in words. They could conceal neither their envy nor a special kind of punctilious insistence on respectful recognition of the position they ascribed to themselves. At the same time they looked down on everything and were perpetually jeering at one another, which was why their friendships never lasted longer than a month.

programme, for guidance, but for all their sincerity there was no reality about this. They expected us to formulate their own opinions, and only assented when what we said did not contradict them in the least. They looked upon us as respected veterans, as something past and over, and were naïvely surprised that we were not yet so very much behind themselves.

I have always and in everything feared 'above all sorrows,' *mésalliances;* I have always tolerated them, partly through humanity, partly through carelessness, and have always suffered from them.

It was not hard to foresee that our new ties would not last long, that sooner or later they would be broken and that, considering the churlish character of our new friends, this rupture would not come off without disagreeable consequences.

The question upon which our rickety relationship came to grief was just that old question through which acquaintances tacked together with rotten threads usually come apart. I mean money. Knowing absolutely nothing of my resources nor of my sacrifices, they made demands upon me which I did not think it right to satisfy. If I had been able, through all our reverses, without the slightest assistance, to conduct the Russian propaganda for fifteen years, it was only because I had put a careful limit to my other expenses. My new acquaintances considered that all I was doing was not enough, and looked with indignation at a man who gave himself out for a socialist and did not distribute his property in equal shares among people who wanted money without working. Obviously they had not advanced beyond the impractical point of view of Christian charity and voluntary poverty, and mistook that for practical socialism.

The attempts to collect a 'Common Fund' yielded no results of importance. Russians are not fond of giving money to any common cause, unless it includes the building of a church, a banquet, a drinking-party and the approval of the higher authorities.

When the impecuniosity of the exiles was at its height, a rumour circulated among them that I had a sum of money entrusted to me for the purposes of propaganda.

It seemed perfectly right to the young people to relieve me of it.

To make the position clear, I must relate a certain strange incident that occurred in the year 1857. One morning I received a very brief note from an unknown Russian; he wrote to me that he 'urgently needed to see me,' and asked me to fix a time.

I happened to be going to London at the time, and so instead of answering I went myself to the Sablonnière Hotel and inquired for him. He was at home. He was a young man who looked like a cadet, shy, very depressed, and with the peculiar rather rough-hewn appearance of the seventh or eighth son of a steppe landowner. Very uncommunicative, he was almost completely silent; it was evident that he had something on his mind, but he could not come to the point of putting it into words.

I went away, inviting him to dinner two or three days later. Before that date I met him in the street.

'May I walk with you?' he asked.

'Of course; there is no danger for me in being seen with you, though there is for you in being seen with me. But London is a big place.'

'I am not afraid'—and then all at once, taking the bit between his teeth, he hurriedly burst out: 'I shall never go back to Russia—no, no, I certainly shall not go back to Russia. . . .'

'Upon my word, and you so young?'

'I love Russia—I love it dearly; but there the people . . . I cannot live there. I want to found a colony on completely socialistic principles; I have thought it all over, and now I am going straight there.'

'Straight where?'

'To the Marquesas Islands.'

I looked at him in dumb amazement.

'Yes, yes; it is all settled. I am sailing by the next steamer, and so I am very glad that I have met you to-day—may I put an indiscreet question to you?'

'As many as you like.'

'Do you make any profit out of your publications?'

'Profit! I am glad to say that now the press pays its way.'

'Well, but what if it should not?'

'I shall make it up.'

'So that no sort of commercial aim enters into your propaganda?'

I laughed heartily.

'Well, but how are you going to pay it off alone? And your propaganda is essential. Please forgive me; I am not asking out of curiosity: when I left Russia for ever, I had the thought in my mind of doing something useful for our country, and I decided . . . well, I only wanted to know first from yourself about finances . . . yes, I decided to leave a small sum of money with you. Should your printing-press need it, or the Russian propaganda generally, then it would be at your disposal.'

Again I had to look at him in amazement.

'Neither the printing-press nor Russian propaganda nor I are in need of money; on the contrary, things are going swimmingly. Why should I take your money? But though I refuse to take it, allow me to thank you from the bottom of my heart for your kind intention.'

'No, sir, it is all decided. I have 50,000 francs. I shall take 30,000 with me to the Islands, and I shall leave 20,000 with you for propaganda.'

'What am I to do with it?'

'Well, if you don't need the money you can give it back to me if I return; but if I don't return within ten years, or if I die—use it for your propaganda efforts. Only,' he added, after a moment's thought, 'do what you like, but . . . but don't give anything to my heirs. Are you free to-morrow morning?'

'Certainly, if you like.'

'Do me the favour of taking me to the bank and to see Rothschild; I know nothing about these things, I can't speak English and I speak French very badly. I want to make haste to get rid of the 20,000 and be off.'

'Very well, I shall accept the money, but on these conditions: I shall give you a receipt.'

'I don't want any receipt.'

'No, but I must give you one, and I shan't take your money without it. Now listen. In the first place, it shall be stated in the receipt that your money is entrusted not to me alone, but to me and to Ogarëv. In the second, since you may get sick of the Marquesas Islands and begin to pine for your native country . . .' (he shook his head). 'How can one know what one does not know? . . . There is no need to specify the object with which you are giving us the capital: we will say that the money is put at the complete disposal of Ogarëv and myself; should we make no other use of it, we shall invest the whole sum for you in securities at five per cent. or thereabouts, guaranteed by the English government. Then I give you my word that we shall not touch your money except in case of extreme necessity for propaganda purposes; you may count upon it in any circumstances, except that of bankruptcy in England.'[4]

'If you insist on taking so much trouble, do so. And to-morrow let us go for the money!'

---

[4] Herzen's account corresponds exactly to the contents of a letter of 31st August, 1857, from P. A. Bakhmetev to H. After he left London B. was not seen in Europe and nothing is known of his further fortunes. In July 1869, at Ogarëv's request, H. gave him half the money in the fund, which was passed on to S. G. Nechayev. After H.'s death the other

The following day was an unusually amusing and busy one. It began with the bank and with Rothschild. The money was paid in notes. Bakhmetev at first conceived the guileless intention of changing them into Spanish gold or silver. Rothschild's clerks looked at him in amazement, but when suddenly, as though half awake, he said in very broken Franco-Russian: 'Well, then, *lettre crédit Ile Marquise*,' Kestner, the manager, turned on me an alarmed and anxious look, which said better than any words: 'He is not dangerous, is he?' Besides, never before in Rothschild's bank had anyone asked for a letter of credit to the Marquesas Islands.

We decided to take 30,000 francs in gold and go home; on the way we went into a café. I wrote the receipt; Bakhmetev for his part wrote for me that he put £800 at the complete disposal of myself and Ogarëv; then he went home to get something and I went off to a bookshop to wait for him; a quarter of an hour later he came in, white as a sheet, and announced that of his 30,000 francs 250, that is £10, were missing. He was utterly overcome. How the loss of 250 francs could so upset a man who had just given away 20,000 without any secure guarantee is another psychological riddle of human nature.

'Haven't you a note too much?' he asked me.

'I haven't the money with me. I gave it to Rothschild, and here is the receipt, precisely 800.' Bakhmetev, who had changed his French notes into sovereigns with no need to do so, scattered 30,000 on Tchorzewski's counter; he counted them and counted them over again; £10 were missing, and that was all about it. Seeing his despair, I said to Tchorzewski:

'I'll take that damned £10 on myself somehow; here he has done a good deed, and he is punished for it.

'It is no use grieving and discussing it,' I added to him, 'I propose going to Rothschild's at once.'

We drove there. By now it was after four and the bank was closed. I went in with the embarrassed Bakhmetev. Kestner

---

half, too, was given by Ogarëv to Nechayev. H.'s apprehension was realised and B.'s fund was squandered on adventurist enterprises of Bakunin and Nechayev. (*A.S.*) The Soviet Academicians are, for once, putting it mildly. For the facts on Nechayev's career, his sinister and masterful personality, and his exploitation of the aging Bakunin's idealism—and weakness—cf. Carr's The *Romantic Exiles*, chapter 14, "The 'Affaire Nechayev'; or the First Terrorist." For the fictional truth about him—as Verhovensky *fils*—and the political murder that landed him for the rest of his life in the Peter-Paul fortress, cf. Dostoevsky's *The Possessed.* (*D.M.*)

looked at him and smiled, took a £10 note from the table and handed it to me.

'When your friend changed the money he gave me two £10 notes instead of two £5 ones, and at first I did not notice it.'

Bakhmetev looked and looked, and commented:

'How stupid that £10 notes and £5 notes are the same colour; who would notice the difference? You see what a good thing it was that I changed the money into gold.'

His mind was at rest and he came to dine with me; I promised to go and say good-bye to him next day. He was quite ready to start. A little shabby, battered trunk such as cadets or students have, a greatcoat tied up with a strap, and . . . and . . . *30,000 francs in gold* wrapped up in a thick pocket-handkerchief, as people tie up a pound of gooseberries or nuts.

This was how the man was setting off for the Marquesas Islands.

'Upon my soul!' I said to him; 'why, you will be robbed and murdered before your ship casts off; you had better put your money in your trunk.'

'It is full.'

'I'll get you a bag.'

'Not on any account.'

And so he went off. During the first days I feared that he would be made away with and that I should incur the suspicion of having sent someone to kill him.

From that day there has been no sight nor sound of him. . . . I put his money in Consols with the firm intention of not touching it except in the case of the printing-press or propaganda being in the utmost straits.

For a long time no one in Russia knew of this; then there were vague rumours, for which we were indebted to two or three of our friends who had given their word to say nothing about it. At last it was learnt that the money really existed and was in my keeping.

This news fell like an apple of temptation, a chronic incitement and ferment. It turned out that everyone needed the money—and I did not give it to them. They could not forgive me for not having lost the whole of my own property, and here I had a deposit given me for the propaganda; and who were 'the propaganda' if not they? The sum quickly grew from modest francs to silver roubles, and was still more tantalising for those who desired to waste it privately for the common cause. They were indignant with Bakhmetev for having entrusted the money to me and not to someone else; the boldest among them declared that it was an error on his part; that he had really meant to give it not to me but to a certain political circle in Petersburg, and that, not knowing how to do this, he had given it to me in London. The audacity of these opinions was the more remarkable that Bakhmetev's surname was as unknown as was his very existence, and that he had not spoken to anyone else of his proposal before his departure, nor had anyone spoken to him since then.

Some needed the money in order to send emissaries; others for establishing centres on the Volga; others still for the publication of a journal. They were dissatisfied with *The Bell*, and did not readily respond to our invitation to work on it.

I absolutely refused to give the money; and let those who demanded it tell me themselves what would have become of it if I had.

'Bakhmetev may return without a farthing,' I said; 'it is not easy to make a fortune by founding a socialist colony in the Marquesas Islands.'

'He is dead for sure.'

'But what if he is alive to spite you?'

'Well, but he gave the money for the propaganda, you know.'

'So far I haven't needed it.'

'But we do.'

'What for precisely?'

'We must send someone to the Volga and someone to Odessa. . . .'

'I don't think that is very necessary.'

'So you don't believe in the indispensability of sending them?'

'I do not.'

'He is growing old and getting miserly,' the most resolute and ferocious said about me in different keys.

'But why mind him? Just take the money from him and have done with it,' the still more resolute and ferocious added, 'and if he resists, we will go for him in the papers and teach him to keep back other people's money.'

I did not give up the money.

They did not go for me in the papers. I was abused in the press much later, but that was over money too. . . .

These more ferocious ones of whom I have spoken were the clumsy and uncouth representatives of the 'New Generation,' who may be called the Sobakeviches and Nozdrëvs[5] of Nihilism.

However superfluous it may be to make a reservation, yet I

---

[5] Two characters in Gogol's *Dead Souls*. (*R*.)

shall do so, knowing the logic and the manners of our opponents. I have not the slightest desire in what I am saying to fling a stone at the younger generation or at Nihilism. Of the latter I have written many times. Our Sobakeviches of Nihilism do not constitute its most powerful expression, but only represent its exaggerated extremes.[6]

Who would judge of Christianity from the Flagellants of Origen or of the Revolution from the September butchers and the *tricoteuses* of Robespierre?

The arrogant lads of whom I am speaking are worth studying, because they are the expression of a temporary type, very definitely marked and very frequently repeated, a transitional form of the sickness of our development from our former stagnation.

For the most part they were lacking in the deportment which is given by breeding, and the staying power which is given by scientific studies. In the first fervour of emancipation they were in a hurry to cast off all the conventional forms and to push away all the rubber fenders which prevent rough collisions. This made difficult the simplest relations with them.

Removing everything to the last rag, our *enfants terribles* proudly appeared as their mothers bore them, and their mothers had not borne them well, not as simple, rather too plump lads but as inheritors of the evil, unhealthy life of our lower classes in Petersburg. Instead of athletic muscles and youthful nakedness, they displayed the melancholy traces of hereditary anaemia, the traces of old sores and of various fetters and collars. There were few among them who had come up from the people. The hall, the barrack-room, the seminary, the petty proprietor's farm survived in their blood and their brains, and lost none of their characteristic features though twisted in an opposite direction. So far as I know, this fact has attracted no serious attention.

On the one hand, the reaction against the old narrow, oppressive world was bound to throw the younger generation into antagonism and negation of their hostile surroundings; it was useless to expect moderation or justice in them. On the contrary, everything was done in defiance, everything was done in resentment. 'You are hypocrites, we shall be cynics; you have been moral in words, we will be wicked in words; you have been polite to your superiors and rude to your inferiors, we shall be

---

[6] At that very time in Petersburg and Moscow, and even in Kazan and Kharkov, there were circles being formed among the university youth who devoted themselves in earnest to the study of science, especially among the medical students. They worked honestly and conscientiously but, cut off from active participation in the questions of the day, they were not forced to leave Russia and we scarcely knew anything of them.

rude to everyone; you bow down to those whom you do not respect, we will jostle people without apologising; your feeling of personal dignity consisted in nothing but decorum and external honour, we make it our point of honour to flout every decorum and to scorn every *point d'honneur*.'

But on the other hand, though disowning all the ordinary forms of social life, their character was full of its own hereditary ailments and deformities. Casting off, as we have said, all veils, the most desperate played the dandy in the costume of Gogol's Petukh[7] and did not preserve the pose of the Medici Venus. Their nakedness did not conceal, but revealed, what they were. It revealed that their systematic uncouthness, their rude and insolent talk, had nothing in common with the inoffensive and simple-hearted coarseness of the peasant, but a great deal in common with the manners of the low-class pettifogger, the shop-boy and the flunkey. The people no more considered them as one of themselves than they did a Slavophil in a *murmolka*. To the people these men have remained alien, the lowest stratum of the enemies' camp, skinny young masters, scribblers out of a job, Russians turned Germans.

To be completely free, one must forget one's liberation and that from which one has been liberated, and cast off the habits of the environment out of which one has grown. Until this has been done we cannot help being conscious of the servants' hall, the barrack-room, the government office or the seminary in every gesture they make and every word they utter.

To hit a man in the phiz at the first objection he advances—if not with a fist then with a word of abuse—to call Stuart Mill a rascal,[8] forgetting all the service he has done, is not that the same as the Russian master's way of 'punching old Gavrilo in the snout for a crumpled cravat'?[9] In this and similar pranks do you not recognise the policeman, the district officer, the village constable dragging a bailiff by his grey beard? Do you not, in the insolent arrogance of their manners and answers, clearly recognise the insolence of the officers of the days of Nicholas? Do you not see, in men who talk haughtily and disdainfully of

---

[7] A character in Gogol's *Dead Souls*, who was naked when he met Chichikov, the hero of the story. (*Tr.*)

[8] N. V. Sokolov, the economist of *Russkoye Slovo*, applied the word 'rascal' in English, to John Stuart Mill in an article in the issue of July 1865. (*A.S.*)

[9] From D. V. Davydov's poem, 'A Contemporary Song.' (*A.S.*)

Shakespeare and Pushkin, the grandsons of Skalozub, reared in the house of their grandsire who wanted 'to make a Voltaire of his corporal'?[10]

The very leprosy of bribery has survived in high-handed importunity for money, by bias and threats under pretext of common causes, in the feeble impulse towards being fed at the expense of the service and towards avenging a refusal by slander and libel.

All this will be transformed and thrashed out with time. But there is no blinking the fact that a strange soil has been prepared by the Tsar's paternal government and imperial civilisation in our 'kingdom of darkness.' It is a soil on which seedlings of great promise have grown, on the one hand, into worshippers of the Muravëvs and the Katkovs and, on the other, into the bullies of Nihilism and the impudent Bazarov free-lances.

Our black earth needs a good deal of drainage!

M. Bakunin and the Cause of Poland

AT THE END of November we received the following letter from Bakunin:

San Francisco, October 15, 1861.

Friends,—I have succeeded in escaping from Siberia, and after long wanderings on the Amur, on the shores of the Gulf of Tartary and across Japan, I arrived to-day in San Francisco.

Friends, I long to come to you with my whole being, and as soon as I arrive I shall set to work; I shall work with you on the Polish-Slavonic question, which has been my *idée fixe* since 1846 and was in practice my speciality in 1848 and 1849.

The destruction, the complete destruction, of the Austrian empire will be my last word; I don't say deed: that

---

[10] A reference to A. S. Griboyedov: *Woe from Wit*, IV, 5. (*A.S.*)

would be too ambitious; to promote it I am ready to become a drummer-boy or even a scoundrel,[1] and if I should succeed in advancing it by one hair's-breadth I shall be satisfied. And beyond that there appears the glorious, free Slav Federation, the one way out for Russia, the Ukraine, Poland, and the Slavonic peoples generally. . . .

We had known of his intention to escape from Siberia some months before. By the New Year Bakunin in his own exuberant person was clasped in our arms.

Into our work, into our closed shop of two, a new element had entered, or rather an old element, perhaps a risen shade of the 'forties, and most of all of 1848. Bakunin was just the same; he had grown older in body only, his spirit was as young and enthusiastic as in the days of the all-night arguments with Khomyakov in Moscow. He was just as devoted to one idea, just as capable of being carried away by it, and seeing in everything the fulfilment of his desires and ideals, and even more ready for every experience, every sacrifice, feeling that he had not so much life before him, and that consequently he must make haste and not let slip a single chance. He was fretted by prolonged study, by the weighing of pros and cons and, confident and theoretical as ever, he longed for any action if only it were in the midst of the storms of revolution, in the midst of destruction and danger. Now, too, as in the articles signed 'Jules Elizard,'[2] he repeated: '*Die Lust der Zerstörung ist eine schaffende Lust.*' The fantasies and ideals with which he was imprisoned in Königstein[3] in 1849 he had preserved, and had carried them complete across Japan and California in 1861. Even his language recalled the finer articles of *La Réforme* and *La vraie République*, the striking speeches in *La Constituante* and at Blanqui's Club. The spirit of the parties of that period, their exclusiveness, their personal sympathies and antipathies, above all their faith in the second coming of the revolution—it was all here.

Strong characters, if not destroyed at once by prison and exile, are preserved by them in an extraordinary way; they come out of them as though out of a faint and go on with what they were

---

[1] The word used by Bakunin is '*prokhvost,*' which is the German '*Profoss*' (Eng. 'provost'), a military policeman; sometimes an executioner. (*R.*)

[2] Under this pseudonym Bakunin published articles on the reaction in Germany in the *Jahrbücher* of 1842, which were brought out under the editorship of Arnold Ruge. (*Tr.*)

[3] A fortress in Saxony where political offenders were imprisoned. (*A.S.*)

about when they lost consciousness. The Decembrists came back from being buried in the snows of Siberia more youthful than the young people who met them, who had been trampled down before ripening. While two generations of Frenchmen changed several times, turned red and white by turns, advancing with the flood and borne back by the ebb, Barbès and Blanqui remained steady beacons, recalling from behind prison bars and distant foreign lands the old ideals in all their purity.

'The Polish-Slavonic question . . . the destruction of the Austrian empire . . . the glorious free Slav Federation . . .' and all this is to happen straight off, as soon as he arrives in London! And it is written from San Francisco when he has one foot on the ship!

The European reaction did not exist for Bakunin, the bitter years from 1848 to 1858 did not exist for him either; of them he had but a brief, far-away, faint knowledge. He had read them in Siberia, just as he had read at Kaydanov about the Punic Wars and of the fall of the Roman Empire. Like a man who has returned after the plague, he heard who had died, and sighed for them all; but he had not sat by the bedside of the dying, had not hoped that they would be saved, had not followed them to the grave. The events of 1848, on the contrary, were all about him, near to his heart, vivid and in detail; the conversations with Caussidière, the speeches of the Slavs at the Prague Conference,[4] discussions with Arago or Ruge—to Bakunin all these were affairs of yesterday; they were all still ringing in his ears and flashing before his eyes.

There is nothing to wonder at in this, however, even over and above his imprisonment.

The first days after the February Revolution were the best days in Bakunin's life. Returning from Belgium, to which he had been driven by Guizot for his speech at the Polish anniversary of the 29th of November, 1847, he cast prudence to the winds and plunged head over ears into the revolutionary sea. He never left the barracks of the Montagnards, he slept with them, ate with them and preached, preached continually, communism and *l'égalité du salaire,* levelling-down in the name of equality, the emancipation of all the Slavs, the destruction of all the Austrias,

---

[4] 30th May–12th June, 1848. B. adhered to the radical Left. The leading part in the conference was played by the Czech Liberal *bourgeoisie* who put forward an idea for the transformation of the Austrian empire into a federation of Slav states under the aegis of the Habsburg monarchy. (*A.S.*)

the revolution *en permanence*, war to the death of the last foe. Caussidière, the Prefect from the barricades, who was making 'order out of disorder,' did not know how to get rid of the dear preacher, and planned with Flocon to send him off to the Slavs in earnest, with a brotherly *accolade* and a conviction that there he would break his neck and be no more trouble. '*Quel homme! quel homme!*' Caussidière used to say of Bakunin: 'On the first day of the revolution he is simply a treasure, but on the day after he ought to be shot!'[5]

When I arrived in Paris from Rome at the beginning of May 1848, Bakunin was already holding forth in Bohemia, surrounded by Old Believer monks, Czechs, Croats and democrats, and he continued haranguing them until Prince Windischgrätz put an end to his eloquence with cannon (and used this excellent opportunity to shoot his own wife by mistake on purpose).[6] Disappearing from Prague, Bakunin appeared again as military commandant of Dresden; the former artillery officer taught the art of war to the professors, musicians and chemists who had taken up arms, and advised them to hang Raphael's Madonna and Murillo's pictures on the city walls and with them protect themselves from the Prussians, who were *zu klassisch gebildet* to dare to fire on Raphael.[7]

Artillery, on the whole, was apt to excite him. On the way from Paris to Prague he knocked up against a revolt of peasants somewhere in Germany; they were shouting and making an uproar before a castle, unable to do anything. Bakunin got out of his vehicle and, not having time to find out what the matter was, formed the peasants up and instructed them so adroitly that by the time he went to get in again to continue his journey the castle was blazing on all four sides.

---

[5] 'Tell Caussidière,' I said in jest to his friends, 'that the difference between Bakunin and him is that Caussidière, too, is a splendid fellow, but it would be better to shoot him the day *before* the revolution.' Later on in London, in the year 1854, I reminded him of this. The Prefect in exile only smote with his huge fist upon his mighty chest with the force with which piles are driven into the earth, and said: 'I carry Bakunin's image here, here.'

[6] While Austrian troops under W. were putting down the rising in Prague in June 1848, W.'s wife went to the window of their house and was mortally wounded. (*A.S.*)

[7] A century later the Nazis mounted the "Baedeker bombings" against Coventry, Bath, central London (a special effort was made to destroy St. Paul's cathedral, which miraculously survived, but many Wren churches didn't), and other historic English beauty spots. The March of Progress has been swift and consistent—to the rear. (*D.M.*)

Some day Bakunin will conquer his sloth and keep his promise; some day he will tell the tale of the long martyrdom that began for him after the taking of Dresden. I recall here only the main points. Bakunin was sentenced to the scaffold. The Saxon king commuted the axe to imprisonment for life; and afterwards, with no ground for doing so, handed him over to Austria. The Austrian police thought to find out from him something about the intentions of the Slavs. They imprisoned Bakunin in the Hradcin, and getting nothing out of him they sent him to Olmütz. Bakunin was taken in fetters with a strong escort of dragoons; the officer who got into the conveyance with him loaded his pistol.

'What is that for?' Bakunin asked. 'Surely you don't think that I can escape under these conditions?'

'No, but your friends may try to rescue you; the government has heard rumours to that effect, and in that case . . .'

'What then?'

'I have orders to put a bullet into your head . . .'

And the companions galloped off.

At Olmütz Bakunin was chained to the wall, and in that situation he spent six months. At last Austria got tired of feeding a foreign criminal for nothing; she offered to give him up to Russia. Nicholas did not need Bakunin at all, but he had not the strength to refuse. At the Russian frontier Bakunin's fetters were removed. Of that act of clemency I have heard many times; the fetters were indeed taken off, but those who tell the tale have forgotten to add that others much heavier were put on instead. The Austrian officer who handed over the prisoner demanded the return of the fetters as being Imperial and Royal government property.

Nicholas praised Bakunin's brave conduct at Dresden, and put him into the Alexeyevsky ravelin. There he sent Orlov to him with orders to tell him that he (Nicholas) desired from him an account of the German and Slav movement (the monarch was not aware that every detail of this had been published in the newspapers). This account he 'required not as his Tsar, but as his spiritual father.' Bakunin asked Orlov in what sense the Tsar understood the words 'spiritual father': did it imply that everything told in confession must be a holy secret? Orlov did not know what to say: in general, these people are more accustomed to ask questions than to answer them. Bakunin wrote[8] a news-

---

[8] In the Peter-Paul Fortress, in the summer of 1851, B. wrote for Nicholas I his 'Confession,' in which his Pan-Slav tendencies found full expression.

paper 'leading article.' Nicholas was satisfied with this, too. 'He is a good, intelligent young fellow, but a dangerous man; he must be kept shut up,' and for *three whole years* after this approval from His Majesty, Bakunin was interred in the Alexey-evsky ravelin. His confinement must have been thorough, too, if even that giant was brought so low that he wanted to take his own life. In 1854 Bakunin was transferred to the Schlüsselburg. Nicholas was afraid that Charles Napier would liberate him; but Charles Napier and Co. did not liberate Bakunin from the ravelin but Russia from Nicholas. Alexander II, in spite of his fit of mercy and magnanimity, left Bakunin in the fortress till 1857, and then sent him to live in Eastern Siberia. In Irkutsk he found himself free after nine years of imprisonment. Fortunately for him the governor of the region was an original person—a demo-crat and a Tatar, a liberal and a despot, a relation of Mikhail Bakunin's and of Mikhail Muravëv's and himself a Muravëv, not yet called 'of the Amur.' He gave Bakunin a chance to breathe, an opportunity to live like a human being and to read the newspapers and magazines; he even shared his dreams of future revolutions and wars. In gratitude to Muravëv, Bakunin in his mind appointed him Commander-in-Chief of the future citizen army with which he proposed in his turn to annihilate Austria and found the Slav League.

In 1860 Bakunin's mother petitioned the Tsar for her son's return to Russia; the Tsar said that 'Bakunin should never be brought back from Siberia during his lifetime' but, that she might not be left without comfort and the Imperial clemency, he permitted her son to enter the civil service *as a copying clerk.*

Then Bakunin, taking into consideration the Tsar's ruddy cheeks and his mere forty years of age, made up his mind to escape; I completely approve of this decision. Recent years have shown, better than anything else could have, that he had noth-ing to expect in Siberia. Nine years in a fortress and several years of exile were more than enough. It was not, as was said, because of his escape that things became worse for the political exiles, but because the times had grown worse, men had grown worse. What influence had Bakunin's escape on the infamous

---

'I shall confess to You as to a spiritual father,' he wrote to the Tsar. In his 'Confession' B. admitted all his transgressions, and called his revolu-tionary activities mad and criminal, proceeding from immaturity of mind (M. A. Bakunin: *Sobr. soch. i pisem* . . . , IV, 104–206). He realised that his 'Confession' could only compromise him in the eyes of the revo-lutionaries, and therefore tried to conceal its actual contents. (*A.S.*)

persecution and death of Mikhaylov?[9] And as for the reprimand of a man like Korsakov[10]—that is not worth talking about. It is a pity it was not two.

Bakunin's escape is remarkable for the space it covered; it is the very longest escape in a geographical sense. After making his way to the Amur, on the pretext of commercial business, he succeeded in persuading an American skipper to take him to the shores of Japan. At Hakodate another American captain under-took to convey him to San Francisco. Bakunin went on board his ship and found the sea-captain busily fussing over a dinner; he was expecting an honoured guest, and invited Bakunin to join them. Bakunin accepted the invitation, and only when the visitor arrived found that it was the Russian Consul-General.

It was too late, too dangerous, too ridiculous to try to conceal himself: he entered at once into conversation with him and said that he had obtained leave to go on a pleasure-trip. A small Russian squadron under the command, if I remember right, of Admiral Popov was riding at anchor, about to sail for Nikolayev:

'You are not returning with our men?' inquired the Consul.

'I have only just arrived,' said Bakunin, 'and I want to see a little more of the country.'

After dining together they parted *en bons amis*. Next day he passed the Russian squadron in the American steamer: there were no more dangers, apart from those of the ocean.

As soon as Bakunin had looked about him and settled down in London, that is, had made the acquaintance of all the Poles and Russians who were there, he set to work. To a passion for propa-ganda, for agitation, for demagogy, if you like, to incessant activity in founding and organising plots and conspiracies and establishing relations and in ascribing immense significance to them, Bakunin added a readiness to be the first to carry out his ideas, a readiness to risk his life, and recklessness in accepting all the consequences. His nature was a heroic one, left out of work by the course of history. He sometimes wasted his powers on rubbish, as a lion wastes the pacing he does in his cage, always thinking that he will walk out of it. But Bakunin was not

[9] M. I. Mikhaylov was condemned at the end of 1861 to six years' forced labour and permanent residence in Siberia. He was put in irons and sent to extremely harsh forced labour in the Kandin mines, where he perished in 1865. (*A.S.*)

[10] M. S. Korsakov, Governor-General of Eastern Siberia, was severely reprimanded by Alexander II for allowing B. to escape. (*A.S.*)

a mere rhetorician, afraid to act upon his own words, or trying to evade carrying his theories into practice. . . .

Bakunin had many defects. But his defects were slight, and his strong qualities were great. . . . Is it not in itself a sign of greatness that, wherever he was cast up by fate, as soon as he had grasped two or three features of his surroundings, he singled out the revolutionary current and at once set to work to carry it farther, to expand it, making of it the burning question of life?

It is said that Turgenev meant to draw Bakunin's portrait in Rudin; but Rudin hardly recalls certain features of Bakunin. Turgenev, carried away by the biblical custom of God, created Rudin in his own image and semblance. Turgenev's Rudin, saturated in the jargon of philosophy, is Bakunin as a young man.

In London he first of all set about *revolutionising The Bell*, and in 1862 advanced against us almost all that in 1847 he had advanced against Belinsky. Propaganda was not enough; there ought to be immediate action; centres and committees ought to be organised; to have people closely and remotely associated with us was not enough, we ought to have 'dedicated and half-dedicated brethren,' organisations on the spot—a Slavonic organisation, a Polish organisation. Bakunin thought us too moderate, unable to take advantage of the situation of the moment, insufficiently fond of resolute measures. He did not lose heart, however, but was convinced that in a short time he would set us on the right path. While awaiting our conversion Bakunin gathered about him a regular circle of Slavs. Among them there were Czechs, from the writer Fritsch to a musician who was called Naperstok;[11] Serbs who were simply called after their father's names Ioanovic, Danilovic, Petrovic; there were Wallachians who did duty for Slavs, with the everlasting 'esco' at the end of their names; finally, there was a Bulgarian who had been a doctor in the Turkish army. And there were Poles of every diocese—the Bonapartist, the Mieroslawski, the Czartorysczki: democrats without socialist ideas but with a tinge of the officer; socialists, Catholics, anarchists, aristocrats and men who were simply soldiers, ready to fight anywhere in North or South America . . . and by preference in Poland.

With them Bakunin made up for his nine years' silence and solitude. He argued, lectured, made arrangements, shouted, decided, directed, organised and encouraged all day long, all night long, for days and nights together. In the brief minutes he had

---

[11] The word means 'thimble' in Russian. (*Tr.*)

free he rushed to his writing-table, cleared a little space from cigarette-ash, and set to work to write five, ten, fifteen letters to Semipalatinsk and Arad, to Belgrade and Tsargrad, to Bessarabia, Moldavia and Belokrinitsa. In the middle of a letter he would fling aside the pen and bring up to date the views of some old-fashioned Dalmatian, then, without finishing his exhortation, snatch up the pen and go on writing. This, however, was made easier for him by the fact that he was writing and talking about one and the same thing. His activity, his laziness, his appetite, and everything else, like his gigantic stature and the everlasting sweat he was in, everything, in fact, was on a superhuman scale, as he was himself; and he was himself a giant with his leonine head and tousled mane.

At fifty he was exactly the same wandering student from the Maroseyka, the same homeless *Bohémien* from the *Rue de Bourgogne,* with no thought for the morrow, careless of money, throwing it away when he had it, borrowing it indiscriminately right and left when he had not, as simply as children take from their parents, careless of repayment; as simply as he himself would give his last money to anyone, only keeping what he needed for cigarettes and tea. This manner of life did not worry him; he was born to be a great vagrant, a great nomad. If anyone had asked him once and for all what he thought of the right of property, he might have answered as Lalande answered Napoleon about God: 'Sire, in my pursuits I have not come upon any necessity for this right!' There was something child-like, simple and free from malice about him, and this gave him an unusual charm and attracted to him both the weak and the strong, repelling none but the affected *petit bourgeois.*[12] His striking personality, the eccentric and powerful appearance he made everywhere, in a coterie of young people in Moscow, in a lecture-room at Berlin University, among Weitling's Communists and Caussidière's Montagnards, his speeches in Prague, his command at Dresden, his trial, imprisonment, sentence to death, torture in Austria and surrender to Russia—where he vanished behind the fearful walls of the Alexeyevsky ravelin—make of

---

[12] When, carried away in argument, Bakunin poured on his opponent's head a noisy storm of abuse for which no one else would have been forgiven, Bakunin was forgiven, and I the first to do so. Martyanov would sometimes say: 'He is only a grown-up Liza,* Alexander Ivanovich; how could one be angry with her—a child?'

* H.'s daughter by Natalya Tuchkov-Ogarëv, born 1858. (*Tr.*)

him one of those individualists whom neither the contemporary world nor history can pass by.

That he ever came to marry, I can only put down to the boredom of Siberia. He had piously preserved all the habits and customs of his fatherland, that is of student-life in Moscow: heaps of tobacco lay on his table like stores of forage, cigar-ash covered his papers, together with half-finished glasses of tea; from morning onwards clouds of smoke hung about the room from a regular suite of smokers, who smoked as though they were racing each other, hurriedly blowing it out and drawing it in—as only Russians and Slavs do smoke, in fact. Many a time I enjoyed the amazement accompanied by a certain horror and perplexity, of the landlady's servant, Grace, when at dead of night she brought boiling water and a fifth basin of sugar into this hotbed of Slav emancipation.

Long after Bakunin left London, tales were told at No. 10 Paddington Green of the way he went on, which upset all the consolidated notions and religiously observed forms and degrees of English middle-class life. Note at the same time that both the maid and the landlady were madly devoted to him.

'Yesterday,' one of his friends told Bakunin, 'So-and-so arrived from Russia; he is a very fine man, formerly an officer.'

'I have heard about him; he is very well spoken of.'

'May I bring him?'

'Certainly; but why bring him, where is he? I'll go and see him. I'll go at once.'

'He seems to be rather a Constitutionalist.'

'Perhaps, but . . .'

'But I know he is a chivalrous, fearless and noble man.'

'And trustworthy?'

'He is much respected at Orsett House.'

'Let us go to him.'

'Why? He meant to come to you: that was what we agreed. I'll bring him.'

Bakunin rushes to his writing; he writes and scratches out something, writes it out again, and seals up a packet addressed to Jassy; in his restless expectation he begins walking about the room with a tread which sets the whole house—No. 10 Paddington Green—shaking with his step.

The officer makes his appearance quietly and modestly. Bakunin *le met à l'aise*, talks like a comrade, like a young man, fascinates him, scolds him for his constitutionalism and suddenly asks:

'I am sure you won't refuse to do something for the common cause.'

'Of course not.'

'There is nothing that detains you here?'

'Nothing; I have only just arrived, I. . . .'

'Can you go to-morrow or next day with this letter to Jassy?'

Such a thing had not happened to the officer either at the front in time of war or on the general staff in peace-time. However, accustomed to military obedience, he says, after a pause, in a voice that does not sound quite natural:

'Oh yes!'

'I knew you would. Here is the letter perfectly ready.'

'I am ready to set off at once . . . only . . .' (the officer is embarrassed). 'I had not at all reckoned on such a journey.'

'What? No money? Then say so; that's of no consequence. I'll get it for you from Herzen: you shall pay it back later on. Why, what is it? Only some £20 or so. I'll write to him at once. You will find money at Jassy. From there you can make your way to the Caucasus. We particularly need a trustworthy man there.'

The officer, amazed, dumbfounded, and his companion equally amazed and dumbfounded, take their leave. A little girl whom Bakunin employed on great diplomatic errands flies to me through the rain and sleet with a note. I used to keep chocolate *en losanges* expressly for her benefit, to comfort her for the climate of her native country, and so I give her a big handful and add:

'Tell the tall gentleman that I shall talk it over with him personally.'

The correspondence in fact turned out to be superfluous. Bakunin appeared for dinner, that is an hour later.

'Why £20 for X?'

'Not for him, for the cause; and I say, brother, isn't X a splendid fellow?'

'I have known him for some years. He has stayed in London before.'

'It is such a chance, it would be a sin to let it slip. I am sending him to Jassy, and then he'll have a look round in the Caucasus.'

'To Jassy? And from there to the Caucasus?'

'I see you are going to be funny,' said Bakunin. 'You won't prove anything by jokes.'

'But you know you don't want anything in Jassy.'

'How do you know?'

'I know, in the first place, because nobody does want anything in Jassy; and in the second place, if anything were wanted, you would have been telling me about it incessantly for the last week. You have simply come across a shy young man who wants to prove his devotion, and so you have taken it into your head to send him to Jassy. He wants to see the Exhibition and you will show him Moldo-Wallachia. Come, tell me what for?'

'What inquisitiveness! You never take part in these things with me: what right have you to ask?'

'That is true: in fact, I imagine that it is a secret you will keep from everyone; anyhow, I have not the slightest intention of giving money for couriers to Jassy and Bucharest.'

'But he will pay you back; he will have money.'

'Then let him make a wiser use of it. That's enough; you can send the letter by some Petresco-Manon-Lescaut; and now let's go and eat.'

And Bakunin, laughing himself, and shaking his head, which was always a little too heavy for him, set himself steadily and zealously to the work of eating his dinner, after which he would say each time: 'Now comes the happy moment,' and light a cigarette.

He used to receive everyone, at any time, everywhere. Often he would be still asleep like Onegin, or tossing on his bed, which creaked under him, and two or three Slavs would be in his bedroom smoking with desperate haste; he would get up heavily, souse himself with water, and at the same moment proceed to instruct them; he was never bored, never found them a burden; he could talk without being tired, with the same freshness of mind, to the cleverest or the stupidest man. This lack of discrimination sometimes led to very funny incidents.

Bakunin used to get up late; he could hardly have done otherwise, since he spent the night talking and drinking tea.

One morning some time after ten o'clock he heard someone moving about in his room. His bed stood curtained off in a large alcove.

'Who's there?' shouted Bakunin, waking up.

'A Russian.'

'What is your name?'

'So-and-so.'

'Delighted to see you.'

'Why is it you get up so late and you a democrat?'

Silence: the sounds of splashing water, cascades.

'Mikhail Alexandrovich!'

'Well?'

'I wanted to ask you, were you married in church?'

'Yes.'

'You did wrong. What an example of inconsistency; and here is Turgenev too, having his daughter legally married. You old men ought to set us an example.'

'What nonsense you are talking.'

'But tell me, did you marry for love?'

'What has that to do with you?'

'There was a rumour going about that you married because your bride was rich!'[13]

'Have you come here to cross-examine me? Go to the devil!'

'Well now, here you are angry, and I really meant no harm. Good-bye. But I shall come and see you again all the same.'

'All right, all right. Only be more sensible next time.'

Meanwhile the Polish storm was drawing nearer and nearer. In the autumn of 1862 Potebnya appeared in London for a few days. Melancholy, pure-hearted, devoted heart and soul to the hurricane, he came to talk to us for himself and his comrades, meaning in any case to go his own way. Poles began to arrive from their country more and more frequently; their language was sharper and more definite. They were moving directly and consciously towards the explosion. I felt with horror that they were going to unavoidable ruin.

'I am mortally sorry for Potebnya and his comrades,' I said to Bakunin, 'and the more so that I doubt whether their aims are the same as those of the Poles.'

'Oh yes they are, yes they are,' Bakunin retorted. 'We can't sit for ever with our arms folded, reflecting; we must take history as it presents itself, or else one will always be too far behind or too far in front.'

Bakunin grew younger; he was in his element: he loved not only the uproar of the revolt and the noise of the club, the market-place and the barricade; he loved the preparatory agitation, the excited and at the same time restrained life, spent among conspiracies, consultations, sleepless nights, conferences, agreements, corrections of cyphers, invisible inks and secret signs. Anyone who has taken part in rehearsals for private theatricals or in preparing a Christmas tree knows that the preparation is one of the best, most exquisite parts of it. But though he was carried away by the preparations of the Christmas tree I had a gnawing at my heart; I was continually

---

[13] Bakunin took no dowry with his wife.

arguing with him and reluctantly doing what I did not want to do.

Here I must stop to ask a sorrowful question. How, whence did I come by this readiness to give way, though with a murmur, this weak yielding, though after rebellion and a protest? I had, on the one hand, a conviction that I ought to act in one way, and, on the other, a readiness to act quite differently. This wavering, this dissonance, *dieses Zögernde* has done me infinite harm in my life, and has not even left me with the faint comfort of recognising that my mistake was involuntary, unconscious; I have made blunders *à contre-coeur;* I had all the arguments on the other side before my eyes. I have told in one of my earlier chapters of the part I took in the 13th of June, 1849. That is typical of what I am saying. I did not for one instant believe in the success of the 13th of June; I saw the absurdity of the movement and its impotence, the indifference of the people, the ferocity of the reaction, and the pettiness of the revolutionaries. (I had written about it already, and yet I went out into the square, laughing at the people who went with me.)

How many misfortunes, how many blows I should have been spared in my life, if at all the crises in it I had had the strength to listen to myself. I have been reproached for being easily carried away; I have been carried away, too, but that is not what matters most. Though I might be committed by my impressionable temper, I pulled myself up at once; thought, reflection and observation almost always gained the day in theory, but not in practice. That is just what is hard to explain: why I let myself be led *nolens volens.* . . .

The reason for my quick compliance was false shame, though sometimes it was the better influences of love, friendship and indulgence; but did all this overcome my power of reasoning?

After the funeral of Worcell on the 5th of February, 1857, when all the mourners had dispersed to their homes and I, returning to my room, sat down sadly at my writing-table, a melancholy question came into my mind. Had we not lowered into the ground with that just man, and had we not buried with him all our relations with the Polish emigrants?

The gentle character of the old man, which was a conciliating element in the misunderstandings that were constantly arising, had gone for ever, but the misunderstandings remained. Privately, personally, we might love one or another among the Poles and be friendly with them, but there was little common understanding between us in general, and that made our relations strained and conscientiously reserved; we made concessions to one another, that is, weakened ourselves and decreased in each other what was almost the best and strongest in us. It was impossible to come to a common understanding by open talk. We started from different points, and our paths only intersected in our common hatred for the autocracy of Petersburg. The ideal of the Poles was behind them: they strove towards their past, from which they had been cut off by violence and which was the only starting-point from which they could advance again. They had masses of holy relics, while we had empty cradles. In all their actions and in all their poetry there is as much of despair as there is of living faith.

They look for the resurrection of their dead, while we long to bury ours as soon as possible. Our lines of thought, our forms of inspiration are different; our whole genius, our whole constitution has nothing in common with theirs. Our association with them seemed to them alternately a *mésalliance* and a marriage of convenience. On our side there was more sincerity, but not more depth: we were conscious of our indirect guilt, we liked their daring and respected their indomitable protest. What could they like, what could they respect in us? They did violence to themselves in making friends with us; they made an honourable exception for a few Russians.

In that dark prison-house the reign of Nicholas locked us into as fellow-prisoners, we had more sympathy with than knowledge of each other. But as soon as the window was opened a little space, we divined that we had been brought by different paths and that we should disperse in different directions. After the Crimean War we heaved a sigh of relief, and our joy was an offence to them: the new atmosphere in Russia reminded them not of their hopes but of their losses. For us the new times began with presumptuous demands; we rushed forward ready to smash everything; with them it began with requiems and services for the dead. But for a second time the government welded us together. At the sound of firing at priests and children, at crucifixes and women, the sound of firing above the chanting of hymns and prayers, all questions were silenced, all differences were wiped out. With tears and lamentations, I wrote then a series of articles[14] which deeply touched the Poles.

From his deathbed old Adam Czartoryszki sent me by his son a warm word of greeting; a deputation of Poles in Paris presented me with an address signed by four hundred exiles, to

---

[14] 'Vivat Polonia,' '10th April and the Murders in Warsaw,' 'Mater Dolorosa' and others published in *The Bell*. (*A.S.*)

which signatures were sent from all parts of the world, even from Polish refugees living in Algiers and in America. It seemed as though in so much we were united; but one step farther in and the difference, the sharp difference, leaped to the eye.

One day Ksawery Branicki, Chojecki and one or two other Poles were sitting with me; they were all on a brief visit to London, and had come to shake hands with me for my articles. The talk fell on the shot fired at Constantine.[15]

'That shot,' I said, 'will do you terrible damage. The government might have made some concessions; now it will yield nothing, and will be twice as savage.'

'But that is just what we want!' Ch. E.[16] observed with heat; 'there could be no worse misfortune for us than concessions. We want a breach, an open conflict.'

'I hope most earnestly that you may not regret it.'

Ch. E. smiled ironically, and no one added a word. That was in the summer of 1861. And a year and a half later Padlewski said the same thing when he was on his way to Poland *through Petersburg.*

The die was cast! . . .

Bakunin believed in the possibility of a rising of the peasants and the army in Russia, and to some extent we believed in it too; and indeed the government itself believed in it, as was shown later on by a series of measures, of officially inspired articles, and of punishments by special decree. That men's minds were working and in a ferment was beyond dispute, and no one saw at the time that the popular excitement would be turned to ferocious patriotism.

Bakunin, not too much given to weighing every circumstance, looked only towards the ultimate goal, and took the second month of pregnancy for the ninth. He carried us away not by arguments but by his hopes. He longed to believe, and he believed, that Zhmud and the Volga, the Don and the Ukraine would rise as one man when they heard of Warsaw; he believed that the Old Believers would take advantage of the Catholic movement to obtain a legal standing for the Schism.

That the league among the officers of the troops stationed in Poland and Lithuania—the league to which Potebnya belonged

---

[15] The Grand Duke Constantine Nikolayevich was made viceroy of Poland in 1862. On the day of his arrival in Warsaw, in June of that year, an attempt was made on his life. (*A.S.*)

[16] Charles Edmond was the pseudonym of Chojecki. (*A.S.*)

—was growing and gathering strength was beyond all doubt; but it was very far from possessing the strength which the Poles through design and Bakunin through simplicity ascribed to it.

One day towards the end of September Bakunin came to me looking particularly preoccupied and somewhat solemn.

'The Warsaw Central Committee,' he said, 'has sent two members to negotiate with us. One of them you know—Padlewski; the other is Giller, a veteran warrior; he took a walk from Poland to the mines in fetters, and as soon as he was back he set to work again. This evening I will bring them to see you, and tomorrow we will meet in my room. We *must define our relations once for all.*'

My answer to the officers was being printed at that time.

'My programme is ready, I will read my letter aloud.'

'I agree with your letter, you know that; but I don't know whether they will altogether like it; in any case, I imagine that it won't be enough for them.'

In the evening Bakunin arrived with three visitors instead of two. I read them my letter. While we were talking and while I was reading, Bakunin sat looking alarmed, as relations are at an examination, or as lawyers are when they tremble lest their client should let something slip out and spoil the whole game of the defence that has been so well arranged, if not strictly in accordance with the truth, anyway for a successful finish.

I saw from their faces that Bakunin had guessed right, and that they were not particularly pleased by what I read them. 'First of all,' observed Giller, 'we shall read the letter to you from the Central Committee.' Milovicz read it; the document, with which readers of *The Bell* are familiar, was written *in Russian*, not quite correctly, but clearly. It has been said that I translated it from the French and altered the sense. That is *not true*. All three spoke Russian well.

The sense of the document was to tell the Russians through us that the provisional Polish government agreed with us and adopted as its basis for action: '*The recognition of the right of the peasantry to the land tilled by them, and the complete self-determination of every people, the right to determine its own destiny.*'

This manifesto, Milovicz said, bound me to soften the interrogative and hesitating form of my letter. I agreed to some changes, and suggested to them that they might accentuate and define more clearly the idea of the self-determination of provinces; they agreed. This dispute over words showed that our attitude towards the same questions was not identical.

Next day Bakunin was with me in the morning. He was dissatisfied with me, thought I had been too cold, as though I did not trust them.

'Whatever more do you want? The Poles have never made such concessions. They express themselves in other words which are accepted among them as an article of faith; they can't possibly at the first step, as they hoist the national flag, wound the sensitive popular feeling.'

'I fancy, all the same, that they really care very little about the land for the peasants and too much about the provinces.'

'My dear fellow, you will have a document in your hands corrected by you and signed in the presence of all of us; whatever more do you want?'

'I do want something else though!'

'How difficult every step is to you! You are not a practical man at all.'

'Sazonov used to say that before you did.'

Bakunin waved his hand in despair and went off to Ogarëv's room. I looked mournfully after him. I saw that he was in the middle of his revolutionary debauch, and that there would be no bringing him to reason now. With his seven-league boots he was striding over seas and mountains, over years and generations. Beyond the insurrection in Warsaw he was already seeing his 'Glorious and Slav Federation'[17] of which the Poles spoke with something between horror and repulsion; he already saw the red flag of 'Land and Freedom' waving on the Urals and the Volga, in the Ukraine and the Caucasus, possibly on the Winter Palace and the Peter-Paul fortress, and was in haste to smooth away all difficulties somehow, to conceal contradictions, not to fill up the gullies but to fling a skeleton bridge across them.

'There is no liberation without land.'

'You are like a diplomat at the Congress of Vienna,' Bakunin repeated to me with vexation, when we were talking afterwards with the representatives of the provisional Polish government in his room. 'You keep picking holes in words and expressions. This is not an article for a newspaper, it is not literature.'

'For my part,' observed Giller, 'I am not going to quarrel about words; change them as you like, so long as the main drift remains the same.'

'Bravo, Giller,' cried Bakunin gleefully.

'Well, that fellow,' I thought, 'has come with his horses shod

---

[17] *'Slava'* is the Russian for 'glory.' (*Tr.*)

for any season; he will not yield an inch in fact, and that is why he so readily yields in words.'

The manifesto was corrected, the members of the *Zhond*[18] signed it. I sent it off to the printing-press.

Giller and his companions were fully persuaded that we represented the focus abroad of a whole organisation which depended upon us and would at our command join them or not join them. For them what was essential lay not in words nor in theoretical agreements; they could always tone down their *profession de foi* by interpretations, so that its vivid colours would have altered, faded and vanished.

That the first nuclei of an organisation were being formed in Russia there was no doubt. The first fibrils, the first threads could be discerned with the naked eye; from these threads, these knots, a vast web might be woven, given time and tranquillity. All that was true, but it was not there yet, and every violent shock threatened to ruin the work for a whole generation and to tear asunder the first lacework of the spider's web.

That is just what, after sending the Committee's letter to the press, I said to Giller and his companions, telling them of the prematureness of their rising. Padlewski knew Petersburg too well to be surprised by my words—though he did assure me that the vigour and ramification of the League of Land and Freedom went much farther than we imagined; but Giller grew thoughtful. 'You thought,' I said to him, smiling, 'that we were stronger? You were right. We have great power and influence, but that power rests entirely on public opinion, that is, it may evaporate all in a minute; we are strong through the sympathy with us, through our harmony with our people. There is no organisation to which we could say, "Turn to the right or turn to the left." '

'But, my dear fellow, all the same . . .' Bakunin was beginning, walking about the room in excitement.

'Why, *is* there?' I asked him, and stopped.

'Well, that is as you like to call it; of course, if you go by the external form, it is not at all in the Russian character, but you see. . . .'

'Let me finish; I want to explain to Giller why I have been so insistent about words. If people in Russia do not see on your standard "Land for the Peasants" and "Freedom for the Provinces," then our sympathy *will do you no good at all but will*

---

[18] The Polish provisional government. (*R.*)

ruin us; because all our strength rests on their hearts beating in unison with ours. Our hearts may beat more strongly and so be one second ahead of our friends; but they are bound to us by sympathy and not by duty!'

'You will be satisfied with us,' said Giller and Padlewski.

Next day two of them went off to Warsaw, while the third went off to Paris.

The calm before the storm came on. It was a hard, dark time, in which it kept seeming as though the storm would pass over, but it drew nearer and nearer. Then came the *ukaz* 'juggling' with the levying of recruits;[19] this was the last straw; men who were still hesitating to take the final and irrevocable step dashed into the fray. Now even the *Whites* began to go over to the side of the rebellion.

Padlewski came again; the decree was not withdrawn. Padlewski went off to Poland.

Bakunin was going to Stockholm quite independently of Lapinski's expedition, of which no one thought at the time. Potebnya turned up for a brief moment and vanished after Bakunin. A plenipotentiary from 'Land and Freedom' came from Petersburg *via* Warsaw at the same time as Potebnya; he described with indignation how the Poles who had summoned him to Warsaw had done nothing. He was the first Russian who had seen the beginning of the rebellion; he told us about the murder of the soldiers, about the wounded officer who was a member of the Society. The soldiers thought that this was treachery and began exasperatedly to beat the Poles. Padlewski, who was the chief leader in Kovno, tore his hair, but was afraid to act openly in opposition to his followers.

The plenipotentiary was full of the importance of his mission and invited us to become the *agents* of the League of Land and Freedom. I declined this, to the extreme surprise not only of Bakunin but even of Ogarëv. I said that I did not like this hackneyed French term. The plenipotentiary was treating us as the *Commissaires* of the Convention of 1793 treated the generals in the distant armies. I did not like that either.

'And are there many of you?' I asked him.

---

[19] In the autumn of 1862 the Tsarist authorities issued an *ukaz* on the levying of recruits in the Kingdom of Poland, which was put into effect according to lists made up beforehand. The authorities tried by this means to put an end to the revolutionary movement in Poland. The conduct of the levy in January 1863, caused the start of the rising. (*A.S.*)

'That is hard to say: some hundreds in Petersburg and three thousand in the provinces.'

'Do you believe it?' I asked Ogarëv afterwards. He did not answer.

'Do you believe it?' I asked Bakunin.

'Of course; but,' he added, *'well, if there are not as many now there soon will be!'* and he burst into a roar of laughter.

'That is another matter.'

'The essence of it all is the giving support to feeble beginnings; if they were strong they would not need us,' observed Ogarëv, who was always dissatisfied with my scepticism on these occasions.

'Then they ought to come to us frankly admitting their weakness and asking for friendly help instead of proposing the stupid job of being agents.'

'That is youth,' Bakunin commented, and he went off to Sweden.

And after him Potebnya went off too. With heartfelt sorrow I said good-bye to him. I did not doubt for one second that he was going straight to destruction.[20]

A few days before Bakunin's departure Martyanov came in, paler than usual, gloomier than usual; he sat down in a corner and said nothing. He was pining for Russia and brooding over the thought of returning home. A discussion of the Polish rebellion sprang up. Martyanov listened in silence, then got up, preparing to go, and suddenly stopped in front of me, and said gloomily:

'You must not be angry with me, Alexander Ivanovich; that may be so or it may not, but, anyway, you have done for *The Bell*. What business had you to meddle in Polish affairs? The Poles may be in the right, but their cause is for their gentry, not for you. You have not spared us, God forgive you, Alexander Ivanovich; you will remember what I say. I shall not see it myself; I am going home. There is nothing for me to do here.'

'You are not going to Russia, and *The Bell* is not ruined,' I answered him.

He went out without another word, leaving me heavily weighed down by this second prediction and by a dim consciousness that a blunder had been made.

Martyanov did as he had said; he returned home in the spring of 1863 and went to die in penal servitude, exiled by his 'People's Tsar' for his love for Russia and his trust in him.

---

[20] A. A. Potebnya commanded a detachment which participated in the Polish rising; he died in battle, March 1863. (*A.S.*)

Towards the end of 1863 the circulation of *The Bell* dropped from two thousand or two thousand five hundred to five hundred, and never again rose above one thousand copies. The Charlotte Corday from Orlov and the Daniel from the peasants had been right.[21]

---

[21] The 'Charlotte Corday' was the young Russian woman who visited H. in London in 1862 and prophesied, 'Your friends and supporters will abandon you.' Daniel was Martyanov, who had warned H. of the decrease of *The Bell*'s influence in Russia because of his defence of the 1863 Polish revolt. (*A.S.*)

THE
LATER
YEARS

(1860-1868)

Fragments [1]

SWISS VIEWS

I REACHED FREIBURG at ten o'clock in the evening and went straight to the Zähringhof. The same landlord in a black velvet skull-cap who had received me in 1851, with the same regular features and superciliously polite face of a Russian master of the ceremonies, or an English hall-porter, came up to the omnibus and congratulated us on our arrival.

And the dining-room is the same, the same little rectangular folding sofas upholstered in red velvet.

Fourteen years have passed over Freiburg like fourteen days! There is the same pride in the cathedral organ, the same pride in their suspension bridge.

The breath of the new restless spirit, continually shifting and casting down barriers, that was raised by the equinoctial gales of 1848, scarcely touched towns which morally and physically stand apart, such as Jesuitical Freiburg and pietistic Neuchâtel. These towns, too, have advanced, though at the pace of a tortoise; they have improved, though to us they seem backward in their unfashionable, stony garb. . . . And of course much in the life of former days was not bad; it was more comfortable, more stable; it was better calculated for the small number of the chosen, and just for that reason it does not suit the huge number of the newly called, who are far from being spoiled or difficult to please.

Of course, in the present state of technical development, with the discoveries that are being made every day, with the facilitation of resources, it has been possible to organise modern life on a free and ample scale. But the Western European, as soon as he has a place of his own, is satisfied with little. In general, he has been falsely charged, and chiefly he has charged himself, with the passion for comfort and that self-indulgence of which people talk. All that, like everything else in him, is rhetoric and flourish. He has had free institutions without freedom, why not have a brilliant setting for a narrow and clumsy life? There are

---

[1] This is Herzen's title for the eighty-odd pages of "miscellaneous pieces" at the end of Volume III. They were written between 1865 and 1868. (*D.M.*)

exceptions. One may find all sorts of things among English aristocrats and French *camélias* and the Jewish princes of this world. . . . All that is personal and temporary; the lords and bankers have no future and the *camélias* have no heirs. We are talking about the whole world, about the golden mean, about the chorus and the *corps de ballet*, which now is on the stage and acting, leaving aside the father of Lord Stanley, who has 20,000 francs a day, and the father of that child of twelve who flung himself into the Thames the other day to ease for his parents the task of feeding him.

The old tradesman who has grown rich loves to talk of the conveniences of life. For him it is still a novelty that he is a gentleman, *qu'il a ses aises*, 'that he has the means to do this, and that doing that will not ruin him.' He marvels at money and knows its value and how quickly it flies, while his predecessors in wealth believed neither in its worth nor in its exhaustibility, and so have been ruined. But they ruined themselves with taste. The *bourgeois* has little notion of making ample use of his accumulated capital. The habit of the former narrow, hereditary, niggardly life remains. He may indeed spend a great deal of money, but he does not spend it on the right things.

A generation which has passed through the shop has absorbed standards and ambitions which are not those of spaciousness, and cannot get away from them. Everything with them is done as though for sale, and they naturally have in view the greatest possible benefit, profit and that end of the stuff that will make the best show. The *propriétaire* instinctively diminishes the size of his rooms and increases their number, not knowing why he makes the windows small and the ceilings low; he takes advantage of every corner to snatch it from his lodger or from his own family. That corner is of no use to him but, just in case, he will take it away from somebody. With peculiar satisfaction he builds two inconvenient kitchens instead of one decent one, and puts up a garret for his maid in which she can neither work nor turn round, but to make up for that it is damp. To compensate for this economy of light and space he paints the front of the house, packs the drawing-room with furniture, and lays out before the house a flower-bed with a fountain in it, which is a source of tribulation to children, nurses, dogs and tenants.

What is not spoilt by miserliness is finished off by sluggishness of intellect. Science, which cuts its way through the muddy pond of daily life without mingling with it, casts its wealth to right and left, but the puny boatmen do not know how to fish for it. All the profit goes to the wholesale dealers and for the others it is reckoned in scanty drops; the wholesale dealers are changing the face of the earth, while private life trails along beside their steam-engines in its old lumbering waggon with its broken-down nags. . . .

A fireplace which does not smoke is a dream. A landlord in Geneva said to me soothingly: 'This fireplace *only* smokes in the *bise*': that is just when one most needs a fire; and he says this as though the *bise* were an accident or a new invention, as though it had not blown before the birth of Calvin and would not blow after the death of Fazy. In all Europe, not excepting Spain or Italy, one must make one's will at the approach of winter, as men used to do formerly when they set off from Paris to Marseilles, and must hold a service to the Iversky Madonna in mid-April.

If these people tell me that they are not occupied with the vanity of vanities, and that they have many other things to do, I will forgive them their smoky chimneys, and the locks that open the door and your veins at the same time, and the stench in the passage, and so on; but I shall ask, what is their work, what are their higher interests? *They have none.* . . . They only make a display of them to cover the inconceivable emptiness and senselessness of their lives.

In the Middle Ages men lived in the very nastiest way and wasted their efforts on utterly unnecessary edifices which did not contribute to their comfort. But the Middle Ages did not talk about their passion for comfort; on the contrary, the more comfortless their life, the more nearly it approached their ideal; their luxury was in the splendour of the House of God and of their assembly hall, and there they were not niggardly, they grudged nothing. The knight in those days built a fortress, not a palace, and did not select a site with the most convenient road to it, but an inaccessible cliff. Nowadays there is no one to defend oneself against, and nobody believes in saving his soul by adorning a church; the peaceful and orderly citizen has dropped out of the forum and the *Rathaus*, out of the opposition and the club; passions and fanaticisms, religions and heroisms, have all given way to material prosperity: *and this has not been achieved.*

For me there is something melancholy, something tragic, in all this, as though this world were living somehow in expectation of the earth's giving way under its feet, and were seeking not orderliness but forgetfulness. I see this not only in the careworn, wrinkled faces but also in a fear of any serious thinking, in an aversion from any analysis of the situation, in a convulsive craving to be busy, and for external distractions. The old are ready to play with toys, 'if only to keep from thinking.'

The fashionable mustard-plaster is an International Exhibition. The remedy and the illness together form an intermittent fever centred first in one part and then in another. All are rushing about sailing, walking, flying, spending money, striving, staring and growing weary, living even more uncomfortably in order to run after *success*—what? Well, just that: successes. As though in three or four years there can be so much progress in everything; as though, when we have railways to travel by, there were such an extreme necessity to carry from place to place things like houses, machines, stables, cannon, even perhaps parks and kitchen gardens.

And when they are sick of exhibitions they will take to war and begin to be diverted by heaps of corpses—anything to avoid seeing certain *black spots* on the sky.

BEYOND THE ALPS

THE ARCHITECTURAL, monumental character of Italian towns, together with their neglected condition, eventually palls on one. A modern man is not at home in them, but in an uncomfortable box at a theatre on whose stage the scenery is magnificent.

Life in them has not become balanced, is not simple, and is not convenient. The tone is elevated, and in everything there is declamation—and Italian declamation too (anyone who has heard Dante read aloud knows what that is like). In everything there is the strained intensity which used to be the fashion among Moscow philosophers and German learned artists; everything is looked at from the highest point, *vom höhern Standpunkt*. This state of being constantly screwed up rejects all *abandon*, and is for ever prepared to give a rebuff and to deliver a homily in set phrases. Chronic enthusiasm is exhausting and irritating.

Man does not always want to be marvelling, to be spiritually exalted, to feel virtuous, to be moved and to be floating about mentally far back in the past; but Italy will never let him drop below a certain pitch and incessantly reminds him that her street is not simply a street but a monument, that he should not only walk through her squares but ought to study them.

At the same time everything in Italy that is particularly elegant and grand (possibly it is the same everywhere) borders upon insanity and absurdity—or at least is reminiscent of childhood. . . . The Piazza Signoria is the nursery of the Florentine people; grandfather Buonarroti and Uncle Cellini presented it with marble and bronze playthings, and it has planted them at random in the square where so often blood has been shed and its fate has been decided—without the slightest consideration for David or Perseus. . . . There is a town in the water so that pike and perch can stroll about the streets. . . . There is a town of stony chinks so that one must be a wood-louse or a lizard to creep and run along a narrow passage on the sea bottom left between the cliffs which are composed of palaces . . . and then there is a Belovezh Forest of marble. What brain dared create the draft of that stone forest called Milan Cathedral, that mountain of stalactites? What brain had the audacity to carry out that mad architect's dream? . . . And who gave the money for it, the huge, incredible sum of money?

People only make sacrifices for what is unnecessary. Their fantastic aims are always the dearest to them; dearer than daily bread, dearer than self-interest. In selfishness a man must be trained, just as he must in humaneness. But imagination carries him away without any training, enthrals him without argument. The ages of faith were the ages of miracles.

A town which is rather more modern but less historical and ornamental is Turin.

'It simply swamps one with its prosaicness.'

'Yes, but it is easier to live in, just because it is simply a town, a town that exists not only for its own memories but for everyday life, for the present; its streets are not archaeological museums, and do not remind us at every step: *memento mori;* but look at its working population, at their aspect, keen as the Alpine air, and you will see that they are a sturdier stamp of men than the Florentines or the Venetians, and have perhaps even more staying power than the Genoese.'

The Genoese, however, I do not know. It is very difficult to get a proper look at them, for they are always flitting before one's eyes, running, bustling, hurrying, scurrying. The lanes leading to the sea are swarming with people, but those who are standing still are not Genoese; they are sailors from all the seas and oceans, skippers and captains. A bell rings here, a bell rings there: *Partenza!—Partenza!*—and part of the ant-heap begins fussing about, some loading, others discharging.

ZU DEUTSCH

IT HAS BEEN POURING for three days. I cannot go out and I don't
feel like working. . . . In the bookshop window the two volumes of Heine's *Correspondance*[2] were displayed. Here was
salvation. I bought them and proceeded to read them till the sky
should clear.

Much water has flowed away since Heine was writing to
Moser, Immermann, and Varnhagen.

It is a strange thing: since 1848 we have kept backing and retreating; we have thrown everything overboard and curled
ourselves up like hedgehogs; and yet something has been done
and everything has gradually changed. We are nearer to the
earth, we stand on a lower, that is a firmer, level; the plough
cuts more deeply, our work is not so showy and it is more like
manual labour—perhaps because it really is work. The Don
Quixotes of the reaction have ripped open many of our balloons,
the smoky gases have evaporated, the airships have come down,
and we no longer move like the spirit of God over the waters
with reed-pipe and prophetic Psalm singing, but catch at the
trees, the roofs, and damp Mother Earth.

Where are those days when 'Young Germany' in its 'beautiful
sublime' was *theoretically* liberating the Fatherland, and in the
spheres of Pure Reason and Art was finishing with the world of
tradition and prejudice? Heine disliked the brightly lit, frosty
height upon which Goethe majestically slumbered in his old age,
dreaming the clever but not quite coherent dreams of the second
part of *Faust;* but even Heine never let himself sink below the
level of the bookshop; it was all still the *aula* of the university,
the literary circles, the journalistic parochial gatherings with
their tittle-tattle and squabbles, with their bookish Shylocks,
with their Göttingen high priests of philology and bishops of
jurisprudence at Halle or Bonn. Neither Heine nor his circle
knew the people, and the people did not know them. Neither the
sorrow nor the joy of the lowly fields rose up to those heights; to
understand the moan of humanity in the quaking-bogs of to-day
they had to transpose it into Latin manners and customs and to

---

[2] *Correspondance inédite de Henri Heine,* 2 vols. (Paris, 1866–67), containing the correspondence of Heine, not previously published, for the
years 1821–42. (*A.S.*)

arrive at their thought through the Gracchi and the proletariat of Rome.

The graduates of a *sublimated* world, they sometimes emerged into life, beginning like Faust with the beer-shop and always, like him, with a spirit of scholastic denial, which with its reflections prevented them as it did Faust from simply looking and seeing. That is why they immediately hastened back from living sources to the sources of history; there they felt more at home. Their pursuits were not only not *work* but were not *science* either, but rather erudition—and, above all, literature.

Heine at times revolted against the atmosphere of archives and of analytical enjoyment, for he wanted something different, but his letters are completely German letters of that German period, on the first page of which stands Bettina the child and on the last Rahel the Jewess.[3] We breathe more freely when we meet in his letters passionate outbursts of Judaism, for then Heine is genuinely carried away; but he quickly lost his warmth and turned cold towards Judaism, and was angry with it for his own by no means disinterested faithlessness.

The revolution of 1830 and Heine's moving afterwards to Paris did much for his progress. '*Der Pan ist gestorben!*' he says with enthusiasm, and hastens to the city to which I once hastened with so morbid a passion—to Paris; he wanted to see the 'great people' and 'grey-headed Lafayette' riding about on his grey horse. But literature soon gets the upper hand; his letters are filled, inside and on the envelope, with literary gossip and personalities alternating with complaining against fate about his health, his nerves, his low humour, through which there shines an immense, shocking vanity. And then Heine takes on a false note. His coldly inflated, rhetorical Bonapartism becomes as repulsive as the squeamish horror of the well-washed Hamburg Jew before the tribunes of the people when he meets them not in books but in real life. He could not stomach the fact that the workmen's meetings were not staged in the prim setting of the study and salon of Varnhagen, 'the fine-china' Varnhagen von Ense, as he himself called him.

His feeling of his own dignity, however, did not go beyond

---

[3] Bettina von Arnim, the author of a book well known in its time: *Goethes Briefwechsel mit einem Kinde*; Rahel Varnhagen von Ense, the author of *Galerie von Bildnissen aus Rahels Umgang und Briefwechsel*. Heine was a frequent visitor at the literary salon of Rahel, who took the young poet under her wing. (*A.S.*) See Hannah Arendt's book, *Rahel Varnhagen: The Life of a Jewess* (London, 1957). (*D.M.*)

having clean hands and being free from the smell of tobacco. It is hard to blame him for this. This feeling is not a German nor a Jewish one, and unhappily not a Russian one either.

Heine coquettes with the Prussian government, curries favour with it through the ambassador and through Varnhagen, and then abuses it.[4] He coquettes with the King of Bavaria and showers sarcasms on him; he more than coquettes with the 'high' German Diet, and tries to redeem his abject behaviour to it with biting taunts.

Does not all this explain why the scholastic and revolutionary flare-up in Germany so quickly came to grief in 1848? It, too, was merely a literary effort, and it vanished like a rocket let off in Krollgarden: it had its professor-leaders and its generals from the Faculty of Philology; it had its rank and file in Jack-boots and *bérets,* students who betrayed the revolutionary cause as soon as it passed from metaphysical valour and literary daring into the market-place.

Apart from a few working men who looked in for a moment, or were captivated, the people did not follow these pale *Führer,* but just held aloof from them.

'How can you put up with all Bismarck's insults?' I asked a year before the war of a deputy of the Left from Berlin at the very time when the count was getting his hand in, in order to knock out the teeth of Grabow and Co. more violently.

'We have done everything we could, *innerhalb* the Constitution.'

'Well, then, you should follow the example of the government and try *ausserhalb.*'

'How do you mean? Make an appeal to the people? Stop paying taxes? . . . That's a dream. . . . Not a single man would follow us or make a move to support us. . . . And we should provide a fresh triumph for Bismarck by ourselves giving evidence of our weakness.'

'Well, then, I shall say as your president does at each slap in the face: "Shout three times *Es lebe der König* and go home peaceably!" '

---

[4] Did not the *kept* genius of the Prussian King do the same? His twofold hypostasis drew down upon him a caustic remark. After 1848 the King of Hanover, an ultra-Conservative and Feudalist, arrived at Potsdam. On the palace staircase he was met by various courtiers, and among them Humboldt in a livery dress-coat. The malicious king stopped and said to him with a smile. *ume ̃elbe, immer Republikaner und immer im Vorzimmer des Palastes'* (Always the same—always republican and always in the antichamber of the palace).

LIVING FLOWERS—THE LAST
OF THE MOHICAN SQUAWS

'LET US GO to the *Bal de l'Opéra;* now is just the right time, half-past one,' I said, getting up from the table in a little room of the Café Anglais, to a Russian artist who was always coughing and never quite sober. I wanted some open air and noise; and besides I was rather afraid of a long *tête-à-tête* with my Claude Lorrain from the Neva.

'Let us go,' he said, and poured himself out another glass of brandy.

This was at the beginning of 1849, at the moment of delusive convalescence between two bouts of sickness when one still wanted, or thought that one wanted, to play the fool sometimes and be merry.

We wandered about the opera-hall and stopped before a particularly beautiful quadrille of powdered stevedores and pierrots with chalked faces. All the four girls were very young, about eighteen or nineteen, pretty and graceful, dancing and enjoying themselves with all their hearts, and imperceptibly passing from the quadrille to the *cancan.* We had not managed to admire them sufficiently when suddenly the quadrille was disturbed 'owing to circumstances in no way depending on the dancers,' as our journalists used to express it in the happy days of the censorship. One of the dancing girls, and alas! the most beautiful, so skilfully, or so unskilfully, lowered her shoulder that her bodice slipped down, displaying half her bosom and part of her back—a little more than is done by Englishwomen, especially elderly ones who have nothing with which they can attract except their shoulders, at the most decorous routs and in the most conspicuous boxes at Covent Garden (in consequence of which in the second tier it is absolutely impossible to listen to *Casta Diva* or *Sul Salice* with due modesty). I had scarcely had time to say to the becolded artist: 'If only Michelangelo or Titian were here! Pick up your brush or she will pull it up again,' when a huge black hand, not that of Michelangelo nor Titian, but of a *gardien de Paris,* seized her by the scruff of the neck, tore her away from the quadrille, and hauled her off. The girl tried not to go and dragged her feet as children do when they are to be washed in cold water, but order and human justice gained the upper hand and were satisfied. The other girls and their pierrots exchanged glances, found a fresh *stevedore*, and again began kicking above their heads and bouncing back from each other in order to advance with the more fury, paying hardly any attention to the rape of Proserpine.

'Let us go and see what the policeman does with her,' I said to my companion. 'I noticed the door he led her through.'

We went down by a side-staircase. Anyone who has seen and remembers a certain dog in bronze looking attentively and with some excitement at a tortoise can easily picture the scene which we came upon. The luckless girl in her light attire was sitting on a stone step in the piercing wind in floods of tears; facing her stood a lean, tall *municipal* in full uniform with a predatory and earnestly stupid air, with a comma of hair on his chin and half-grey moustaches. He was standing in a dignified attitude with folded arms, watching intently to see how these tears would end, and urging:

'*Allons, allons!*'

To complete the effect the girl was saying through her whining and tears:

'. . . *Et . . . et on dit . . . on dit que . . . que . . . nous sommes en République . . . et . . . on ne peut danser comme l'on veut! . . .*'

All this was so ludicrous, and so really pathetic, that I resolved to go to the rescue of the captive and to the restoration in her eyes of the republican honour of the form of government.

'*Mon brave,*' I said with calculated and insinuating courtesy to the policeman, 'what are you going to do with mademoiselle?'

'I shall put her *au violon* till to-morrow,' he answered grimly. The wails increased.

'To teach her to take off her bodice,' added the guardian of order and of public morality.

'It was an accident, *brigadier*, you might let her off.'

'I can't. *La consigne. . . .*'

'After all, at a fête. . . .'

'But what business is it of yours? *Etes-vous son réciproque?*'

'It is the first time I have seen her in my life, *parole d'honneur*. I don't know her name, ask her yourself. We are foreigners, and are surprised to see you in Paris so strict with a weak girl, *avec un être frêle*. In our country it's thought that the police here are so kind. . . . How is it that they are allowed to dance the *cancan* at all? For if it is allowed, *monsieur le brigadier*, sometimes without meaning it a foot will be kicked too high or a blouse will slip too low.'

'That may be so,' the *municipal* observed, impressed by my

eloquence, but chiefly hooked by my remark that foreigners have such a flattering opinion of the Parisian police.

'Besides,' I said, 'look what you are doing. You are giving her a cold—how can you bring the child, half-naked, out of that stifling dance-hall and sit her down in the piercing wind?'

'It is her own fault: she won't come. But here, I'll tell you what: if you will give me your word of honour that she shan't go back into the dance-hall to-night, I'll let her go.'

'Bravo! Though as a matter of fact I expected no less of you, *monsieur le brigadier*. I thank you with all my heart.'

I had now to enter into negotiations with the liberated victim.

'Excuse me interfering on your behalf without having the pleasure of being personally acquainted with you.'

She held out a hot, moist little hand to me and looked at me with still moister and hotter eyes.

'You heard how it is? I can't vouch for you if you won't give me your word, or better still if you won't come away at once. It is not a great sacrifice really; I expect it is half-past three by now.'

'I'm ready. I'll go and get my cloak.'

'No,' said the implacable guardian of order, 'not a step from here.'

'Where are your cloak and hat?'

'In *loge* so-and-so, row so-and-so.' The artist was rushing off, but he stopped to ask: 'But will they give them to me?'

'Only tell them what has happened and that you come from "Little Léontine". . . . What a ball that was!' she added with the air with which people say in a graveyard: 'Sleep in peace.'

'Would you like me to bring a *fiacre?*'

'I am not alone.'

'With whom then?'

'With a friend.'

The artist returned, his cold definitely very bad, with the hat and cloak and a young shop-assistant or *commis-voyageur*.

'Very much obliged,' he said to me, touching his hat, and then to her: 'Always making a scandal!' He seized her by the arm almost as roughly as the policeman had by the neck, and vanished into the big vestibule of the Opéra. . . . Poor girl . . . she will catch it . . . and what taste . . . she . . . and he!

I felt positively vexed. I suggested to the artist that we should have a drink. He did not refuse.

A month passed. Five of us, Tausenau, the Vienna agitator, General Haug, Müller-Strübing, and another gentleman and I arranged another time to go to a ball. Neither Haug nor Müller

had ever been to one. We stood together in a group. Suddenly a
masked figure pushed and broke a way through the crowd, came
straight up to me, almost threw herself on my neck, and said:

'I had not time to thank you then . . .'

'Ah, Mademoiselle Léontine . . . very, very glad to meet you.
I can just see before me your tear-stained face, your pouting
lips—you looked awfully nice; that does not mean that you don't
look nice now.'

The little rogue looked at me with a smile, knowing that this
was true.

'Didn't you catch cold then?'

'Not a bit.'

'In memory of your captivity, you ought, if you would be very,
very kind . . .'

'Well, what? *Soyez bref.*'

'You ought to have supper with us.'

'With pleasure, *ma parole*, only not now.'

'Where shall I look for you then?'

'Don't trouble. I'll come and look for you myself at four o'clock
exactly; but I say, I'm not here by myself. . . .'

'With your friend again . . . ?' and a shiver ran down my
back.

She burst out laughing.

'He's not very dangerous,' and she led up to me a blue-eyed
girl of seventeen with bright fair hair.

'Here's my friend.'

I invited her too.

At four o'clock Léontine ran up to me and gave me her hand,
and we set off to the Café Riche. Though that is not far from the
Opéra, yet Haug had time on the way to fall in love with the
Madonna of Andrea del Sarto, that is, with the fair girl. And at
the first course—indeed, we had hardly sat down—after long,
extravagant phrases about the Tintoretto charm of her hair and
eyes, Haug began a sermon on the aesthetic sin of dancing the
cancan with the face of a Madonna and the expression of an
angel of purity.

'*Armes, holdes Kind!*' he added, addressing us all.

'Why is it your friend talks such boring *fatras?*' Léontine said
in my ear, 'and why does he go to balls at the Opéra at all. He
should go to the Madeleine.'

'He is a German, and they all suffer from that complaint,' I
whispered to her.

'*Mais c'est qu'il est ennuyeux, votre ami avec son mal de
sermon. Mon petit saint, finiras-tu donc bientôt?*'

And while waiting for the end of the sermon Léontine, tired out, flung herself on to a sofa. Opposite her was a big looking-glass; she kept looking at herself in it, and at last could not refrain from pointing to herself and saying to me:

'Why, even with my hair so untidy and in this crumpled dress and this position, I really don't look bad.'

When she had said this, she suddenly dropped her eyes and blushed, frankly blushed up to her ears. To cover her confusion she began to sing the well known song which Heine has distorted in his translation, and which is terrible in its artless simplicity:

> *Et je mourrai dans mon hôtel,*
> *Ou à l'Hôtel-Dieu.*

A strange creature, elusive and full of life; the 'Lacerta'[5] of Goethe's Elegies, a child unconsciously overcome by fumes. Like a lizard she really could not sit still for one minute, and she could not keep silent either. When she had nothing to say, she was singing, making faces before the looking-glass, and all with the insouciance of a child and the grace of a woman. Her *frivolité* was naïve. Having started whirling by chance, she was still spinning, still hovering. . . . The shock which would have stopped her on the brink or finally thrust her into the abyss had not yet come. She had gone a good bit of the way, but she could still turn back. Her clear intelligence and innate grace were strong enough to save her.

This type, this coterie, this environment exist no more. She was '*la petite femme*' of the student-of-old days, the *grisette* who moved from the Quartier Latin to this side of the Seine, neither *faisant* the unhappy *trottoir* nor possessing the secure social position of the *camélia*. That type has passed away, just as conversations by the fireside, reading aloud at a round table, chatting over tea have gone. Other forms now, other sounds, other people, other words. . . . The present has its own scale, its own *crescendo*. The mischievous, rather wanton element of the 'thirties —*du leste, de l'espièglerie*—passed into *chic*; there was cayenne pepper in it, but it still retained a careless, exuberant grace, it still retained wit and intelligence. With the increase of business, commerce cast off everything superfluous, and sacrificed everything intellectual to the shop-front, the *étalage*. The type of Léontine, the lively Parisian *gamine*, stirring, intelligent, spoilt,

---

[5] *Lacertae* (lizards) is what Goethe called the young Venetian women of easy virtue in Nos. 67–72 of his *Epigrams* (Venice, 1790). (*A.S.*)

sparkling, liberal and, in case of need, proud, is not in demand, and *chic* has passed into *chienne*. What the Lovelace of the boulevards needs is the woman-*chienne*, and, above all, the *chienne* who has a master of her own. It is more economical and unmercenary—with her he can go hunting at someone else's expense, and pay only the extras. 'Parbleu,' an old man said to me, whose best years coincided with the beginning of the reign of Louis-Philippe, '*je ne me retrouve plus—où est le fion,*[6] *le chic, où est l'esprit? . . . Tout cela monsieur . . . ne parlez pas, monsieur—c'est bon, c'est beau, well-bred, mais . . . c'est de la charcuterie . . . c'est du Rubens.*'

That reminds me how in the 'fifties, nice, kind Talandier, with the vexation of a man in love with his France, explained her downfall to me with a musical illustration. 'When,' he said, 'we were great, in the early days after the revolution of February, nothing sounded but the "*Marseillaise*"—in the cafés, in the street-processions, always the "*Marseillaise*." Every theatre had its "*Marseillaise*," here with cannon, there with Rachel. When things grew duller and quieter, the monotonous sounds of "*Mourir pour la Patrie*"[7] took its place. That was no harm yet, but we sank lower. . . . "*Un sous-lieutenant accablé de besogne . . . drin, drin, din, din, din*" . . . the whole city, the capital of the world, the whole of France was singing that trash. That is not the end; after that, we began playing and singing "*Partant pour le Syrie*" at the top and "*Qu'aime donc Margot . . . Margot*" at the bottom: that is, senselessness and indecency. One can sink no lower.'

One can! Talandier did not foresee either '*Je suis la femme à barrrbe*' or '*The Sapper*'; he stopped short at *chic* and never reached the *chienne* stage.

Hasty, carnal debauchery got the upper hand of any embellishments. The body conquered the spirit and, as I said ten years ago, *Margot, la fille de marbre*, supplanted Béranger's Lisette and all the Léontines in the world. The latter had their humanity, their poetry, their conceptions of honour. They loved noise and spectacles better than wine and supper, and they loved their supper more for the sake of the setting, the candles, the sweets, the flowers. Without dancing and balls, without laughter and chatter they could not exist. In the most luxurious harem they

---

[6] '*Fion*' is a colloquial word about equivalent to '*esprit*.'(*Tr.*)

[7] By Rouget de Lisle and styled during the Revolution of February, 1848, 'the second *Marseillaise*.'(*R.*)

would have been stifled, would have withered away in a year. The finest representative was Déjazet—on the great stage of the world and in the little *Théâtre des Variétés*. She was the living embodiment of a song of Béranger, a saying of Voltaire, and was young at forty—Déjazet, who changed her adorers like a guard of honour, capriciously flung away packets of gold, and gave herself to the first-comer to get a friend out of trouble.

Nowadays it is all simplified, curtailed. One gets there sooner, as country gentlemen in the old days used to say who preferred vodka to wine. The woman of *fion* intrigued and interested, the woman of *chic* stung and amused, and both, as well as money, took up time. The *chienne* pounces straight away upon her victim, bites with her beauty, and pulls him by the coat-tail *sans phrases;* here there is no preface: here the epilogue comes at the beginning. Thanks to a paternal government and the medical faculty, even the two dangers of the past are gone; police and medicine have made great advances of late years.

And what will come after the *chienne?* Hugo's *pieuvre*[8] failed completely, perhaps because it is too much like a *pleutre*. Can we not stop at the *chienne?* However, let us leave prophesying. The designs of Providence are inscrutable.

What interests me is something else.

Which of the two prophecies of Cassandra has been fulfilled for Léontine? Is her once graceful little head resting on a lace-trimmed pillow in *her own hotel*, or has it declined on to a rough hospital-bolster to fall asleep for ever, or wake to poverty and woe? But perhaps neither the one nor the other has happened, and she is busy getting her daughter married or hoarding money to buy a substitute to go into the army in place of her son. She is no longer young now—and probably she is well over thirty.

---

[8] In 1866, after the appearance of *Les travailleurs de la mer*, by Victor Hugo, in which there is a brilliant and frightening description of an octopus, certain journalists began to compare beautiful women of light behaviour with the octopus: pictures appeared which depicted the octopus in the form of a charmer; frocks and hats *à la pieuvre* became fashionable and the word *pieuvre* soon acquired a new meaning—a woman of light behaviour who sucked out the substance of her admirer. (*A.S.*)

Cf. also A. C. Hilton's "Octopus," a parody of Swinburne's "Dolores":

Ah! thy red lips, lascivious and luscious,
    With death in their amorous kiss!
Cling round us and clasp us and crush us
    With bitings of agonized bliss! (etc.) (*D.M.*)

THE FLOWERS OF MINERVA

THIS PHALANX is the revolution in person, austere at seventeen.
. . . The fire of her eyes subdued by spectacles that only the
light of the mind may shine as it will; *sans-crinolines* advancing
to replace *sans-culottes*.

The girl-student and the young-lady-*Burschen* have nothing
in common with the Traviata ladies. The Bacchantes have
grown grey or bald, have grown old and retired, and the students have taken their place before they are out of their teens.
The Camélias and the Traviatas of the salons belonged to the
time of Nicholas. They were like the show-generals of the
same time, the strutting dandies whose victories were won over
their own soldiers, who knew every detail of military *toilette*, all
the foppishness of the parade, and never soiled their uniforms
with the blood of an enemy. The courtesan-generals, jauntily
faisant le trottoir on the Nevsky, were cut down at one blow by
the Crimean War; and 'the intoxicating glamour of the ball,' the
love-making of the boudoir and the noisy orgies of the generals'
ladies, were abruptly replaced by the academic lecture-hall and
the dissecting-room, where the cropped student in spectacles
studied the mysteries of nature. Then all the camellias and
magnolias had to be forgotten, it had to be forgotten that there
were two sexes. Before the truths of science, *im Reiche der
Wahrheit*, distinctions of sex are effaced.

Our Camélias stood for the Gironde, that is why they smack so
much of Faublas.[9]

Our young-lady students are the Jacobins, Saint-Justs in a
riding-habit—everything sharp-cut, pure, ruthless.

Our Camélias wore a mask, a *loup* from warm Venice.

Our students wear a mask too, but it is a mask of ice from the
Neva. The first may stick on, but the second will certainly melt
away; that, however, is in the future.

This is a real, conscious protest, a protest and breaking-point.
Ce n'est pas une émeute, c'est une révolution. Dissipation,
luxury, jeering and fine clothes are put aside. Love and passion
are in the far background. Aphrodite with her naked archer
sulked and has withdrawn; Pallas Athene has taken her place
with her spear and her owl. The Camélias were impelled by

---

[9] The reference is to Jean-Baptiste Louvet de Couvray: *Les aventures du
chevalier de Faublas* (Brussels, 1869). (*R.*)

vague emotion, indignation, insatiably languishing desire . . . and they went on 'til they reached satiety. In this case they are impelled by an idea in which they believe, by the declaration of 'the rights of woman,' and they are fulfilling a duty laid upon them by that belief. Some abandon themselves on principle, others are unfaithful from a sense of duty. Sometimes these students go too far, but they always remain children—disobedient and arrogant, but children. The earnestness of their radicalism shows that it is a matter of the head, of theory, not of the heart. They are passionate in general, but to particular encounters they bring no more 'pathos' (as it was called in old days) than any Léontine. Perhaps less. The Léontines play, they play with fire, and very often, ablaze from head to foot, seek safety from the conflagration in the Seine; drawn on by life before they have developed any power of reasoning, it is sometimes hard for them to conquer their hearts. Our students begin with criticism, with analysis; to them, too, a great deal may happen, but there will be no surprises, no downfalls; they fall with a parachute of theory in their hands. They throw themselves into the stream with a handbook on swimming, and intentionally swim against the current. Whether they will swim long *à livre ouvert* I do not know, but they will certainly take their place in history, and will deserve to do so.

The most short-sighted people in the world have guessed as much.

Our old gentlemen, senators and ministers, the fathers and grandfathers of their country, looked with a smile of indulgence and even encouragement at the aristocratic Camélias (so long as they were not their sons' wives). . . . But they did not like the students . . . so utterly different from the 'pretty rogues' with whom they had at one time liked to warm their old hearts with words.

For a long time the old gentlemen had been angry with the austere Nihilist girls and had sought an opportunity of overtrumping them.

And then, as though of design, Karakozov fired his pistol-shot.[10] . . . 'There it is, Your Majesty,' they began to whisper to him, 'that is what not dressing in uniform means . . . all these spectacles and shock-heads.' 'What? not in uniform-dress as approved?' says the Tsar. 'Prescribe it most strictly!' 'Lenience,

---

[10] D. V. Karakozov made an unsuccessful attempt on the life of Alexander II on 4th April, 1866. (*A.S.*)

lenience, Your Majesty! We have only been waiting for your gracious permission to save the sacred person of Your Majesty.'

It was no jesting matter; they set to work unanimously. The Privy Council, the Senate, the Synod, the ministers, the bishops, the military commanders, the town-governors and the other police took counsel together, thought, talked and decided in the first place to eject students of the female sex from the universities. During this, one of the bishops, fearing guile, recalled how once upon a time in the pseudo-Catholic Church a Pope Anna had been elected to the papacy, and would have offered his monks as inspectors . . . since 'there is no bodily shame before the eyes of the dead.' The living did not accept his suggestion: the generals, indeed, for their part supposed that such expert's duties could only be entrusted to an official of the highest rank, placed beyond temptation by his position and his monarch's confidence; there was an idea of offering the post to Adlerberg the Elder from the military department, and to Butkov from among the civilians. But this did not happen—it is said because the Grand Dukes were soliciting for the appointment.

After this the Privy Council, the Synod and the Senate gave orders that within twenty-four hours the girls were to grow their cropped hair, to remove their spectacles and to give a written undertaking to have sound eyes and to wear crinolines. Although there is nothing said in the *Book of Guidance*[11] about 'hooping of skirts' or 'widening of petticoats,' and it positively forbids the plaiting of the hair, the clergy agreed. For the moment the Tsar's life seemed secured till he should reach the Elysian Fields. It was not their fault that in Paris also there were Champs-Élysées, and with a Rond Point,[12] too.

These extreme measures were of enormous benefit, and this I say without the slightest irony: but to whom? To our Nihilist girls.

The one thing that they lacked was to cast aside their uniform, their formalism, and to develop in that broad freedom to which they have the fullest claim. It is terribly hard for one who

---

[11] A collection of ecclesiastical rules and laws of the State concerning religious observances. It appeared first in the sixth century at Constantinople under the name of *Nomokanon;* in the ninth century it was translated into Slavonic for the Bulgarian Church and in the eleventh century was accepted by the Russian Orthodox Church. Various amendments were made as time went on; it was last edited in 1787. (*A.S.*)

[12] Where on 6th June, 1867, the Polish *émigré* Anton Berezowski fired unsuccessfully at Alexander II. (*A.S.*)

is used to a uniform to cast it off of himself. The garment grows to the wearer. A bishop in a dress-coat would give over blessing and intoning.

Our girl-students and *Burschen* would have been a long time taking off their spectacles and their other emblems. They had them taken off at the expense of the government, which added to this good turn the aureole of a *toilette* martyrdom.

After that their business is to swim *au large*.

P.S.—Some are already coming back with the brilliant diploma of Doctor of Medicine, and all glory to them![13]

Nice, Summer 1867

VENEZIA LA BELLA[14]

FEBRUARY *1867*

THERE IS NO SUCH magnificent absurdity as Venice. To build a city where it is impossible to build a city is madness in itself; but to build there one of the most elegant and grandest of cities is the madness of genius. The water, the sea, their sparkle and glitter, call for a peculiar sumptuousness. Molluscs embellish their cabins with mother-of-pearl and pearls.

A single superficial look at Venice shows one that it is a city of strong will, of vigorous intellect—republican, commercial, oligarchical; that it is the knot that ties something together across the waters, a warehouse for merchandise under a military flag, a city with a noisy popular assembly and a soundless city of secret councils and measures; in its squares the whole population is jostling from morning 'til night, while the rivers of its streets flow silently to the sea. While the crowd clamours and shouts in St Mark's Square, a boat glides by and vanishes unobserved.

---

[13] The first Russian woman doctor, N. P. Suslova, was dismissed, together with other female students, from the Medico-Surgical Academy in Petersburg in 1864. In 1867 she completed the course at Zürich University with the degree of Doctor of Medicine. She had connections with revolutionary circles and in 1864 she worked for the *Contemporary*; when abroad she kept up her intercourse with several Russian revolutionary emigrants and was acquainted with Herzen. Her example strengthened the desire of the progressives among the young women for higher education and for work of benefit to society. (*A.S.*)

[14] This title may have been suggested either by a song that was very popular in Venice when Herzen was there, '*La bella Venezia*,' or by A. Grigorev's verses, '*Venezia la bella*.' (*A.S.*)

Who knows what is under its black awning? Was not this the very place to drown people, within hail of lovers' trysts.

The men who felt at home in the Palazzo Ducale must have been of an eccentric cast. They stuck at nothing. There is no earth, there are no trees, what does it matter? Let us have still more carved stones, more ornaments, gold, mosaics, sculptures, pictures and frescoes. Here an empty corner has been left; into the corner with a thin sea-god with a long, wet beard! Here is an empty recess; put in another lion with wings and a gospel of Saint Mark! There it is bare and empty; put down a carpet of marble and mosaic! and here, lacework of porphyry! Is there a victory over the Turks or over Genoa? does the Pope seek the friendship of the city? then more marble; cover a whole wall with a curtain of carving, and above all, more pictures. Let Paul Veronese, Tintoretto, Titian fetch their brushes and mount the scaffolding: every step in the triumphal progress of the Beauty of the Sea must be depicted for posterity in paint or sculpture. And so full of life was the spirit that dwelt in these stones that new routes and new seaports, Columbus and Vasco da Gama, were not enough to crush it. For its destruction the 'One and Indivisible Republic' had to rise up on the ruins of the French throne, and on the ruins of that republic the soldier who in Corsican fashion stabbed the lion with a stiletto poisoned by Austria.[15] But Venice has digested the poison and proves to be alive once more after half a century.

But is she alive? It is hard to say what has survived except the grand shell, and whether there is another future for Venice. . . . And, indeed, what future can there be for Italy at all? For Venice, perhaps, it lies in Constantinople, in the free federation of the rising Slav-Hellenic nationalities, which begins to stand out in vague outlines from the mists of the East.

And for Italy? . . . Of that later. There is a carnival in Venice now, the first carnival in freedom after seventy years' captivity.[16] The Square has been transformed into the hall of the Paris Opéra. Old Saint Mark gaily takes his part in the fête with his church paintings and his gilding, with his patriotic flags and his pagan horses. Only the pigeons, who appear in the Square at two o'clock every day to be fed, are bewildered and flutter from cornice to cornice to convince themselves that this really is their dining-room in such disorder.

---

[15] The treaty of Campo Formio, October 1797. (A.S.)
[16] In 1866, by an agreement concluded by Austria and Italy after the Austro–Prussian war, Venice became part of the Kingdom of Italy. (A.S.)

The crowd keeps growing, *le peuple s'amuse,* plays the fool
heartily with all its might, with great comic talent in words and
in their delivery of pronunciation and gesture, but without the
cantharidity of the Parisian pierrots, without the vulgar jokes of
the German, without our native filth. The absence of everything
indecent surprises one, though the significance of it is clear. This
is the frolic, the recreation, the fun of a whole people, and not a
dress-parade of brothels, of their *succursales,* whose inmates,
while they strip off so much else, put on a mask, like Bismarck's
needle,[17] to intensify their fire and make it irresistible. Here
they would be out of place; here the people is having its fun,
here sisters, wives and daughters are diverting themselves, and
woe to him who insults a mask. For the time of the carnival the
mask becomes for the woman what the Stanislaw ribbon in his
buttonhole used to be for a station-master.[18]

At first the carnival left me in peace, but it kept growing, and
with its elemental force it was bound to draw everyone in.

Nothing is too nonsensical to happen when St Vitus's Dance
takes hold of a whole population in fancy dress. Hundreds, perhaps more, of mauve dominoes were sitting in the big hall of a
restaurant; they had sailed across the Square in a gilded ship
drawn by oxen (everything that walks on dry land and with
four legs is a luxury and rarity in Venice), and now they were
eating and drinking. One of the guests suggested a curiosity to
entertain them, and undertook to furnish it; that curiosity was
myself.

The gentleman, who scarcely knew me, ran to me at the
Albergo Danieli, and begged and besought me to go with him
for a minute to the masqueraders. It was stupid to go, and stupid
to make a fuss. I went, and I was greeted with '*Evviva!*' and full
glasses. I bowed in all directions and talked nonsense, the
'*Evvivas*' were more hearty than ever; some shouted: '*Evviva*

---

[17] H. is thinking of the needle rifle with a firing-pin, invented by J. N.
von Dreyes (1787–1867), which was breech-loading. Although the needle
rifle was adopted as a weapon by the Prussian army in 1841, it was only
in Bismarck's time, in the middle of the 1860s, that it began to be widely
used. In the Austro–Prussian war of 1866 the needle rifle gave the
Prussian troops a decisive superiority over the Austrian army. (*A.S.*)

[18] A year ago I saw the carnival at Nice. What a fearful difference—
to say nothing of the soldiers fully armed and the gendarmes and the
commissaires of police with their scarves . . . the conduct of the people
themselves, not of the tourists, amazed me. Drunken masqueraders were
swearing and fighting with people standing at their gates, while pierrots
were violently knocked down into the mud.

l'amico di Garibaldi,' others drank to the *poeta russo!* Afraid
that the mauve masks would drink to me as the *pittore slavo,
scultore e maestro,* I withdrew to the Piazza San Marco.

In the Square there was a thick wall of people. I leaned
against a pilaster, proud of the title of poet; beside me stood my
conductor who had carried out the dominoes' *mandat d'amener.*
'My God, how lovely she is!' slipped out of my mouth as a very
young lady made her way through the crowd. My guide seized
me without a single word and at once set me before her. 'This is
that Russian,' my Polish count[19] began. 'Are you willing to give
me your hand after that?' I interrupted. She smiled, held out her
hand and said in Russian that she had long wanted to see me,
and looked at me so takingly that I pressed her hand once more
and followed her with my eyes so long as she was in sight.

'A blossom, torn away by the hurricane, washed by the tide of
blood from its Lithuanian fields!' I thought, looking after her.
'Your beauty shines for strangers now.'

I left the Square and went to meet Garibaldi. On the water
everything was still . . . the noise of the carnival came in discordant snatches. The stern, frowning masses of the houses
pressed closer and closer upon the boat and looked at it with
their lanterns; at an entry the rudder splashes, the steel boat-
hook gleams, the gondolier shouts: '*Apri—sia state*' . . . and
again the water draws us quietly into a by-lane, and suddenly
the houses move apart again, and we are in the Grand Canal
. . . '*Feyovia, Signoye,*' says the gondolier, mispronouncing his
r's, as all the town does. Garibaldi had stayed at Bologna and
had not arrived. The engine that was going to Florence groaned,
awaiting the whistle. 'I had better go too,' I thought; 'to-morrow
I shall be bored with the masks. To-morrow I shall not see my
Slav beauty. . . .'

The city gave Garibaldi a brilliant reception. The Grand
Canal was almost transformed into a continuous bridge; to get
into our boat when we set out we had to cross dozens of others.
The government and its hangers-on did everything possible to
show that they were cross with Garibaldi. If Prince Amadeo had
been ordered by his father to show all those petty indelicacies,
all that vulgar pique, how was it that the Italian boy's heart did
not speak out, that he did not for the moment reconcile the city
with the king and the king's son with his conscience? Why,
Garibaldi had made them a present of the crowns of the Two
Sicilies!

---

[19] Chotomski. (*A.S.*) The lady was a Pole, too. (*R.*)

I found Garibaldi neither ill nor any older since our meeting in London in 1864. But he was depressed, worried and not talkative with the Venetians who were presented to him next day. His real retinue was the masses of the people; he grew more lively at Chioggia, where the boatmen and fishermen were expecting him. Mingling with the crowd he said to those poor, simple people:

'How happy and at home I am with you, how deeply I feel that I was born of working folk and have been a working man; the misfortunes of our country tore me away from my peaceful occupations. I too grew up on the sea-coast and know the work of each one of you. . . .'

A murmur of delight drowned the words of the former boatman and the people rushed upon him.

'Give a name to my new-born child,' cried a woman.

'Bless mine.'

'And mine,' shouted the others.

BYZANTIUM

I HAVE DOUBTS about the *future of the Latin peoples*. I doubt their fertility in the future; they like the process of revolutions, but are bored by progress when they have attained it. They like to move headlong towards it without reaching it.

Of course, if the terrestrial globe does not crack, and if a comet does not pass too close and turn our atmosphere red-hot, Italy in the future too will be Italy, the land of blue sky and blue sea, of elegant contours, of a beautiful, attractive race of people, musical and artistic by nature. And of course, all the military and civilian *remue-ménage,* and glory and disgrace, fallen frontiers, and rising Assemblies will all be reflected in her life; she will change (and is changing) from clerical despotism to *bourgeois* parliamentarianism, from a cheap mode of living to an expensive one, from discomfort to comfort, and so on and so on. But that is not much, and it does not take one far. There is another fine country whose shores are washed by the same blue sea, the home of a fine breed of men, valiant and stern, living beyond the Pyrenees; it has no internal enemy, it has an Assembly, it has an outward unity . . . but for all that, what is Spain?

Nations are of strong vitality; they can lie fallow for ages, and again under favourable circumstances prove once more to be full of sap and vigour. But do they rise up the same as they were?

For how many centuries, I had almost said millennia, was the

Greek people wiped off the face of the earth as a nation, and still it remained alive, and at the very moment when the whole of Europe was suffocating in the fumes of the Restoration, Greece awoke and alarmed the whole world. But were the Greeks of Capodistria[20] like the Greeks of Pericles or the Greeks of Byzantium? All that was left of them was the name and a far-fetched memory. Italy, too, may be renewed, but then she will have to begin a new history. Her emancipation is no more than a right to exist.

The example of Greece is very apt; it is so far away from us that it awakens fewer passions. The Greece of Athens, of Macedon, deprived of independence by Rome, appears again politically independent in the Byzantine period. What does she do in it? Nothing, or worse than nothing: theological controversy, seraglio revolutions *par anticipation*. The Turks come to the help of stick-in-the-mud nature and add the brilliance of a conflagration to her violent death. Ancient Greece *had lived out her life* when the Roman Empire covered and preserved her as the lava and ashes of the volcano preserved Pompeii and Herculaneum. The Byzantine period raised the coffin-lid, and the dead remained dead, controlled by priests and monks as every tomb is, administered by eunuchs who were perfectly in place as representatives of barrenness. Who does not know the tales of crusaders in Byzantium? Incomparably inferior in culture, in refinement of manners, these savage men-at-arms, these rude swash-bucklers, were yet full of strength, daring and impetuosity; they were advancing, and the *god of history* was with them. He likes men, not for their good qualities but for their sturdy vigour and for their coming upon the stage *à propos*. That is why as we read the tedious chronicles we rejoice when the Varangians sweep down from their northern snows, and the Slavs float down in cockleshells and leave the mark of their targets on the proud walls of Byzantium. As a schoolboy I was overjoyed at the savage in his shirt[21] paddling his canoe alone and going with a gold ear-ring in his ear to an interview with the effeminate, luxurious, scholarly Emperor,[22] John Tsimisces.

Think a little about Byzantium. Until our Slavophils bring

---

[20] Capodistria, Ioannis Antonios, Count of, was President of the Greek Republic from 1828 to 1831, when he was assassinated. (*Tr.*)

[21] Svyatoslav, Prince of Kiev, is meant. (*Tr.*)

[22] John Tsimisces became Emperor in 969 by marriage with Theophania, the widow of Romanus II, and reigned till 976. He was, in fact, victorious over the Russians. (*Tr.*)

into the world a new chronicle adorned with old ikon paintings, and until it receives the sanction of the government, Byzantium will explain a great deal of what it is hard to put into words.

Byzantium could *live*, but there was nothing for her to *do*; and nations in general only take a place in history while they are on the stage, that is, while they are doing something.

I think I have mentioned the answer Thomas Carlyle gave to me when I spoke to him of the severities of the Parisian censorship.

'But why are you so angry with it?' he said. 'In compelling the French to keep quiet Napoleon has done them the greatest service. They have nothing to say, but they want to talk. . . . Napoleon has given them an official justification. . . .'

I do not say how far I agree with Carlyle, but I do ask myself: Will Italy have anything to say and do on the day after the taking of Rome? And sometimes, without finding an answer, I begin to wish that Rome may long remain a quickening *desideratum*.

Until Rome is taken everything will go fairly well; there will be energy and strength enough, if only there is money enough. . . .'Til then, Italy will put up with a great deal: taxes, the Piedmontese struggle for precedence, an extortionate administration and a quarrelsome and importunate bureaucracy; while waiting for Rome, everything seems unimportant. In order to have it people will put up with constraints and they must stand together. Rome is the boundary line, the flag; it is there before their eyes, it stops them sleeping, it prevents their attending to business, it keeps up the fever. In Rome everything will be changed, everything will snap. . . . There, they fancy, is the conclusion, the crown; not at all . . . there is the *beginning*.

Nations that are trying to redeem their independence never know (and it is a very good thing too) that independence of itself gives them nothing except the rights of their majority, a place among their peers, and the recognition of their capability as citizens to *pass acts*, and that is all.

FRANCE, GERMANY...
AND AMERICA

In the midst of these reflections I happened to come across Quinet's pamphlet, *France and Germany*. I was fearfully pleased with it—not that I specially depended upon the judgments of the celebrated historical thinker, though I have a great respect for him personally, but it was not on my own account that I rejoiced.

In old days in Petersburg a friend of mine well known for his humour, finding on my table a book of the Berlin Michelet,[23] *On the Immortality of the Soul*, left me a note which read as follows: 'Dear friend, when you have read this book, be so good as to tell me briefly whether there is an immortality of the soul or not. It does not matter for me, but I should like to know in order to set at rest the minds of my relations.' Well, it is for the sake of my relations that I am glad I have come upon Quinet. In spite of the supercilious attitude many of them have taken up in regard to European authorities, our friends still pay more attention to them than to the likes of us. That is why I have tried when I could to put my own thoughts under the protection of a European nurse. Availing myself of Proudhon, I said that not Catiline but death was at the doors of France; hanging on to the coat-tails of Stuart Mill, I learnt by heart what he said about the Chineseness of the English; and I am very glad that I can take Quinet by the hand and say: 'Here my honoured friend Quinet says in 1867 about Latin Europe what I said about the whole of it in 1847 and all the following years.'

Quinet sees with horror and grief the degradation of France, the softening of her brain, her increasing shallowness. He does not understand the cause; he seeks it in her deviation from the principles of 1789 and in her loss of political liberty, and so through his grief there is a hint in his words of a hidden hope of recovery by a return to a genuine parliamentary régime, to the great principles of the Revolution.

Quinet does not observe that the great principles of which he speaks, and the political ideas of the Latin world generally, have lost their significance, their musical-box spring has played as much as it could and has almost snapped. *Les principes de* 1789 were not mere words, but now they have become mere words, like the liturgy and the words of a prayer. Their service has been enormous: by them, through them, France has accomplished her revolution, she has raised the veil of the future and has sprung back in dismay.

A dilemma has presented itself.

Either free institutions will once more set their hands to the

---

[23] Karl Ludwig Michelet (1801–93), a professor at the University of Berlin. (*A.S.*)

sacred veil, or there will be government tutelage, external order and internal slavery.

If in the life of the peoples of Europe there had been one single aim, one single aspiration, one side or the other would have gained the upper hand long ago. But as the history of Western Europe is constituted, it has led to everlasting struggle. In the fundamental fact of its everyday life, that its culture is twofold, lies the organic obstacle to consistent development. To live in two civilisations, on two levels, in two worlds, at two stages of development, to live not as a whole organism but as one part of it, while using the other for food and fuel, and to be always talking about liberty and equality, is becoming more and more difficult.

Attempts to reach a more harmonious, better-balanced system have not been successful. But if they have failed in any given place, that rather proves the unsuitability of the place than the falsity of the principle.

The whole gist of the matter lies in that.

The States of North America with their unity of civilisation will easily outstrip Europe; their situation is simpler. The standard of their civilisation is lower than that of Western Europe, but they have *one* standard and *all* attain to it: in that is their fearful strength.

Twenty years ago France burst like a Titan into another life, struggling in the dark, meaninglessly, without plan and with no other knowledge than of her insufferable agony. She was beaten 'by order and civilisation,' but it was the victor who retreated. The *bourgeoisie* have had to pay for their melancholy victory with all they had gained by ages of effort, of sacrifice, of wars and revolutions, with the best fruits of their culture.

The centres of power, the paths of development—all have changed; the hidden activity and suppressed work of social reconstruction have passed to other lands beyond the borders of France.

As soon as the Germans were convinced that the French tide had ebbed, that its frightening revolutionary ideas had fallen into decay, that there was no need to fear her, the Prussian helmet appeared behind the walls of the fortresses on the Rhine.

France still fell back, the helmet still moved forward. Bismarck has never thought much of his own people, he has kept both ears cocked towards France, he has sniffed the air coming from there, and, convinced of the permanent degradation of that country, he understood that Prussia's day was at hand. Having understood this he ordered a plan from Moltke, he ordered needles from the gun-smiths, and systematically, with unmannerly German churlishness, gathered the ripe German pears and poured them into the apron of the ridiculous Friedrich Wilhelm, assuring him that he was a hero by a special miracle of the Lutheran god.

I do not believe that the destinies of the world will be left for a long time in the hands of the Germans and the Hohenzollerns. This is impossible, it is contrary to the good sense of humanity, repugnant to the aesthetic of history. I shall say, as Kent said to Lear, only the other way about: 'In thee, oh Prussia, there is nothing that I could call a king.' But nevertheless, Prussia has thrust France into the background and herself taken the front seat. But nevertheless, having painted the motley rags of the German fatherland all one colour, she will lay down the law to Europe so long as her laws are laid down by the bayonet and carried out by grape-shot, for the very simple reason that she has more bayonets and more grape-shot.

Behind the Prussian wave there will arise another that will not trouble itself much whether the old men with their classical principles like it or not.

England craftily preserves the appearance of strength, standing on one side, as though proud of her pretended non-participation. . . . She has felt in the depth of her innards the same social ache that she cured so easily in 1848 with policemen's staves; but the throes are more violent . . . and she is drawing in her far-reaching tentacles to meet the conflict at home.

France, amazed, embarrassed by her changed condition, threatens to make war not on Prussia but on Italy if the latter touches the temporal possessions of the eternal father, and she collects money for a monument to Voltaire.

Will the ear-splitting Prussian trumpet of the *last* judgment by battle bring Latin Europe to life? Will the approach of the *learned* barbarians awaken her?

Chi lo sa?

I arrived at Genoa with some Americans who had only just crossed the ocean. They were impressed by Genoa. Everything they had read in books about the Old World they now saw with their own eyes, and they were never tired of gazing at the precipitous, narrow, black, mediaeval streets, the singular height of the houses, the half-ruined passages, fortifications and so on.

We went into the vestibule of some palace. A cry of delight broke from one of the Americans: 'How these people did live! How they did live! What dimensions, what elegance! No, you

will find nothing like it among us.' And he was ready to blush
for his America. We peeped inside a huge salon. The portraits of
former owners, the pictures, the faded walls, the old furniture,
the old coats of arms, the unlived-in air, the emptiness, and the
old custodian in a black, knitted skull-cap and a threadbare,
black frock-coat, with his bunch of keys . . . all said as plainly
as words that this was not a house but a curiosity, a sarcophagus,
a sumptuous relic of past life.

'Yes,' I said to the Americans as we went out, 'you are perfectly right, these people *did* live well.'

March 1867

The Superfluous and the Jaundiced [1] *(1860)*

> *The Onegins and the Pechorins* [2] *were perfectly true to life;
> they expressed the real sorrow and breakdown of Russian
> life at that time. The melancholy type of the man who was
> superfluous, lost merely because he had developed into a
> man, was to be seen in those days not only in poems and
> novels but in the streets and the villages, in the hotels and
> the towns. . . . But the day of the Onegins and the Pe-
> chorins is over. There are no superfluous men now in Rus-
> sia: on the contrary, now there are not hands enough to till
> the vast fields of ours that need ploughing. One who does
> not find work now has no one else to blame for it. He must
> be really a hollow man, a worm-eaten waster or a sluggard.*
>
> *The Bell,* 1859.

THESE two classes of superfluous men,[3] between whom Nature
herself raised up a mountain chain of Oblomovs,[4] and History,

---

[1] First published in *The Bell*, 15th October, 1860. (*A.S.*)

[2] Pechorin, the hero of Lermontov's *A Hero of Our Time*. (*Tr.*)

[3] Cf. William E. Harkins: *Dictionary of Russian Literature*. (*R.*)

[4] Oblomov, the hero of I. A. Goncharov's novel of that name. (*Tr.*) His
problem was ennui in general and, in particular, getting out of bed in
the morning—or at all. "Oblomovism" was an upperclass Russian socio-
political complaint of the period. (*D.M.*)

marking out its boundaries, dug a frontier ditch—the very one in which Nicholas is buried—are continually mixed up. And therefore we want, with a partiality like that of Cato for the cause of the vanquished, to champion the older generation. Superfluous men were in those days as essential as it is essential now that there should be none.

Nothing is more lamentable than, in the midst of the growing activity, as yet unorganised and awkward but full of enterprise and initiative, to meet those gaping, unnerved lads who lose their heads before the toughness of practical work, and expect a gratuitous solution of their difficulties and answers to problems which they have never been able to state clearly.

We will lay aside these volunteers who have appointed themselves superfluous men and, just as the French only recognise as real grenadiers *les vieux de la vieille,* so we will recognise as honourable and truly superfluous men only those of the reign of Nicholas. We ourselves belonged to that unhappy generation and, grasping many years ago that we were superfluous on the banks of the Neva, we very practically made off as soon as the rope was untied.

There is no need for us to defend ourselves, but we are sorry for our former comrades and want to protect them from the batch of the sick that followed them after being discharged from Nicholas's infirmary.

One cannot but share the healthy, realistic attitude of one of the best Russian reviews in attacking recently the flimsy moral point of view which in the French style seeks personal responsibility for public events. Historical strata can no more be judged by a criminal court than geological ones. And men who say that one ought not to bring down one's thunders and lightnings on bribe-takers and embezzlers of government funds, but on the environment which makes bribes a zoological characteristic of a whole tribe, of the *beardless* Russians, for instance, are perfectly right. All we desire is that the superfluous men of Nicholas's reign should have the rights of bribe-takers and enjoy the privileges granted to the embezzlers of public funds. They are the more deserving of this in that they are not only superfluous but almost all dead; and the bribe-takers and embezzlers are alive, and not only prosperous but historically justified.

With whom are we to fight here? Whom have we to ridicule? On the one hand, men who have fallen from exhaustion; on the other, men crushed by the machine; to blame them for it is as ungenerous as to blame scrofulous and lymphatic children for the poorness of their parents' blood.

There can be only one serious question; were these morbid phenomena really due to the conditions of their environment, to their circumstances? . . .

I think it can hardly be doubted.

There is no need to repeat how cramped, how painful, was the development of Russia. We were kept in ignorance by the knout and the Tatars: we were civilised by the axe and by Germans: and in both cases our nostrils were slit and we were branded with irons. Peter I drove civilisation into us with such a wedge that Russia could not stand it and split into two layers. We are hardly beginning now, after a hundred and fifty years, to understand how this split diverged. There was nothing in common between the two parts; on the one side, there was robbery and contempt; on the other, suffering and mistrust; on the one side, the liveried lackey, proud of his social position and haughtily displaying it; on the other, the plundered peasant, hating him and concealing his hatred. Never did Turk, slaughtering men and carrying off women to his harem, oppress so systematically, nor disdain the Frank and the Greek so insolently, as did the Russia of the nobility despise the Russia of the peasant. There is no other instance in history of a caste of the same race getting the upper hand so thoroughly and becoming so completely alien as our class of upper government servants.

A renegade always goes to the extreme, to the absurd and the revolting, to the point at last of clapping a man in prison because, being a writer, he wears Russian dress, refusing to let him enter an eating-house because he is wearing a caftan and is girt with a sash. This is colossal and reminds one of Indian Asia.

On the borders of these savagely opposed worlds strange phenomena developed, whose very distortion points to latent forces, ill at ease and seeking something different. The *Raskolniki* and Decembrists stand foremost among them, and they are followed by all the Westerners and Easterners, the Onegins and the Lenskys, superfluous and jaundiced men. All of them, like Old Testament prophets, were at once a protest and a hope. By them Russia was exerting itself to escape from the Petrine period, or to digest it to her real body and her healthy flesh. These pathological formations called forth by the conditions of the life of the period pass away without fail when the conditions are changed, just as now superfluous men have already passed away; but it does not follow that they deserved judgment and condemnation unless from their younger comrades in the Service. And this is on the same principle on which one of the inmates of Bedlam pointed with indignation at a patient who called himself the Apostle Paul, while he, who was Christ himself, knew for certain that the other was not the Apostle Paul but simply a shopkeeper from Fleet Street.

Let us recall how superfluous men were evolved.

The executions of 13th July, 1826, at the Kronverk curtain-wall[5] could not at once check or change the current of ideas of that time, and as a fact the traditions of the reign of Alexander and the Decembrists persisted through the first half of Nicholas's thirty years' reign, though disappearing from sight and turning inwards. Children caught in the schools dared to hold their heads erect, for they did not yet know that they were the prisoners of education.

They were the same when they left school.

These were far different from the serene, self-confident, enthusiastic lads, open to every impression, that Pushkin and Pushchin[6] appear to us to have been when they were leaving the Lycée. They have neither the proud, unbending, overwhelming daring of a Lunin,[7] nor the dissolute profligacy of a Polezhayev,[8] nor the melancholy serenity of Venevitinov.[9] But yet they kept the faith inherited from their fathers and elder brothers, the faith that 'It will rise—the dawn of enchanting happiness,'[10] the faith in Western liberalism in which all then believed—Lafayette, Godefroy Cavaignac, Börne and Heine. Frightened and disconsolate, they dreamed of escaping from their false and unhappy situation. This was that last hope which every one of us has felt before the death of one we love. Only doctrinaires (red or parti-coloured—it makes no difference) readily accept the most terrible conclusions because properly speaking they accept them *in effigie*, on paper.

Meanwhile every event, every year, confirmed for them the frightful truth that not only the government was against them, with gallows and spies, with the iron hoop with which the hangman compressed Pestel's head, and with Nicholas putting this hoop on all Russia, but that the people, too, were not with them,

---

[5] At this place in the Peter-Paul Fortress P. I. Pestel, K. F. Ryleyev, S. I. Muravëv-Apostol, M. P. Bestuzhev-Ryumin and P. G. Kakhovsky, 'Decembrists,' were hanged on the night of 12th–13th July, 1826. (*A.S.*)
[6] Ivan Ivanovich Pushchin (1798–1859), was a great friend of the poet Pushkin. (*Tr.*)
[7] Mikhail Sergeyevich, one of the Decembrists. (*Tr.*)
[8] See pp. 117–20 above. (*D.M.*)
[9] Dmitri Vladimirovich (1805–27), a young poet of the greatest promise who died in 1827 at the age of twenty-two. (*Tr.*)
[10] From Pushkin's lines 'To Chaadayev.' (*A.S.*)

or at least were completely strangers to them. If the people were discontented, the objects of their discontent were different. Together with this crushing recognition they suffered, on the other hand, from growing doubt of the most fundamental, unshakeable principles of Western European opinion. The ground was giving way under their feet; and in this perplexity they were forced actually to enter the Service or to fold their arms and become superfluous, idle. We venture to assert that this is one of the most tragic situations in the world. Now these superfluous men are an anachronism, but of course Royer-Collard or Benjamin Constant would also be an anachronism now. However, one must not cast a stone at them for that.

While men's minds were kept in distress and painful irresolution, not knowing where to find an escape or in what direction to move, Nicholas went his way with dull, elemental obstinacy, trampling down the cornfields and every sign of growth. A master of his craft, he began from the year 1831 to make war on the children; he grasped that he must erode everything human in the years of childhood in order to make faithful subjects in his own image and after his likeness. The upbringing of which he dreamed was organised. A simple word, a simple gesture was reckoned as much an insolence and a crime as an open neck or an unbuttoned collar. And this massacre of the souls of innocents went on for thirty years!

Nicholas—reflected in every inspector, every school director, every tutor and guardian—confronted the boy at school, in the street, in church, even to some extent in the parental home, stood and gazed at him with pewtery, unloving eyes, and the child's heart ached and grew faint with fear that those eyes might detect some budding of free thought, some human feeling.

And who knows what chemical change in the composition of a child's blood and nervous system is caused by intimidation, by the checking or dissimulation of speech, by the repression of feeling?

The terrified parents helped Nicholas in his task; to save their children by ignorance, they concealed from them their one noble memory. The younger generation grew up without traditions, without a future, except a career in the Service. The government office and the barracks little by little conquered the drawing-room and society, aristocrats turned gendarmes. Kleinmikhels turned aristocrats; the narrow-minded personality of Nicholas was gradually imprinted on everything, vulgarising everything and giving everything an official, governmental aspect.

Of course, in all this unhappiness, not everything perished. No one plague, not even the Thirty Years' War, exterminated every-one. Man is a tough creature. The demand for humane progress, the striving for independent initiative, survived, and most of all in the two Macedonian phalanxes of our civilisation, Moscow University and the Tsarskoye Selo Lycée. On their youthful shoulders they carried across the whole kingdom of dead souls the Ark in which lay the Russia of the future; they carried her living thought, her living faith in what was to come.

History will not forget them.

But in this conflict they too lost, for the most part, the youth-fulness of their early years: they were over-strained, grew over-ripe too soon. Old age was on them before their legal coming of age. These were not idle, not superfluous men; these were exas-perated men, sick in body and soul, men wasted by the affronts they had endured, who looked at everything askance, and were unable to rid themselves of the bile and venom accumulated more than five years before. They offer a manifest step forward, but still it is a sickly step; this is no longer a heavy, chronic lethargy, but an acute suffering which must be followed by recovery or the grave.

The superfluous men have left the stage, and the jaundiced, who are more angry with the superfluous than any, will follow them. Indeed, they will be gone very soon. They are too morose, and they get too much on one's nerves, to stand their ground long. The world, in spite of eighteen centuries of Christian contrition, is in a very heathen fashion devoted to epicureanism and *à la longue* cannot put up with the depressing face of the Daniels of the Neva, who gloomily reproach men for dining without gnashing their teeth, and for enjoying pictures or music without remembering the misfortunes of this world.

Their relief is on its way; already we see men of quite a different stamp, with untried powers and stalwart muscles, appearing from remote universities, from the sturdy Ukraine, from the sturdy north-east, and perhaps we old folks may yet have the luck to hold out a hand across the sickly generation to the fresh stock, who will briefly bid us farewell and go on their broad road.

We have studied the type of jaundiced men, not on the spot, and not from books; we have studied it in specimens who have crossed the Neman and sometimes even the Rhine since 1850.

The first thing that struck us in them was the ease with which they despaired of everything, the vindictive pleasure of their renunciation, and their terrible ruthlessness. After the events of 1848 they were at once set on a height from which they saw the defeat of the republic and the revolution, the regression of civilisation, and the insulting of banners—and they could feel no compassion for the unknown fighters. Where the likes of us stopped short, tried to restore animation, and looked to see if there was no spark of life, they went farther through the desert of logical deduction and easily arrived at those final, abrupt conclusions which are alarming in their radical audacity but which, like the spirits of the dead, are but the essence gone out of life, not life itself. In these conclusions the Russian on the whole enjoys a terrific advantage over the European; he has in this no tradition, no habit, nothing germane to him to lose. The man who has no property of his own or of others passes most safely along dangerous roads.

This emancipation from everything traditional fell to the lot not of healthy, youthful characters but of men whose heart and soul had been strained in every fibre. After 1848 there was no living in Petersburg. The autocracy had reached the Hercules' Pillars of absurdity; they had reached the instructions issued to teachers at the military academies, Buturlin's scheme for closing the universities and the signature of the censor Yelagin on patterns for stencils. Can one wonder that the young men who broke out of this catacomb were crazy and sick?

Then they faded before their summer, knowing no free scope, nothing of frank speech. They bore on their countenances deep traces of a soul roughly handled and wounded. Every one of them had some tic, and apart from that personal tic they all had one in common, a devouring, irritable and distorted vanity. The denial of every personal right, the insults, the humiliations they had endured evolved a secret claim to admiration; these undeveloped prodigies, these unsuccessful geniuses, concealed themselves under a mask of humility and modesty. All of them were hypochondriacs and physically ill, did not drink wine, and were afraid of open windows; all looked with studied despair at the present; they reminded one of monks who from love for their neighbour came to hating all humanity and cursed everything in the world from desire to bless something.

One half of them were constantly repenting, the other half constantly chastising.

Yes, deep scars had been left on their souls. The world of Petersburg in which they had lived was reflected in themselves; it was thence they took their restless tone, their language—*saccadé*, yet suddenly deliquescing into bureaucratic twaddle—their shuffling meekness and haughty fault-finding, their intentional aridity and readiness on any occasion to blackguard one, their offensive acceptance of accusations in front of everyone, and the uneasy intolerance of the director of a department.

This knack of administering a reprimand in the style of a director, uttered contemptuously with eyes screwed up, is more repugnant to us than the husky shout of a general, which is like the deep bark of a steady old dog, who growls in deference to his social position rather than from spite.

Tone is not a matter of no importance.

Das was innen—das ist draussen!

Extremely kind at heart and noble in tendency, they—I mean our jaundiced men—might by their tone drive an angel to fighting and a saint to cursing. Moreover, they exaggerate everything in the world with such *aplomb*—and not to amuse but to mortify—that there is simply no bearing it. Every time anyone mentions a mole-hill they will start talking darkly about mountains.

'Why do you defend these sluggards' (a jaundiced friend, *sehr ausgeziechnet in seine Fache,* said to us lately), 'parasites, drones, white-handed spongers *à la Onéghine*? . . . They were formed differently, please observe, and the world surrounding them is too dirty for them, not polished enough; they will dirty their hands, they will dirty their feet. It was much nicer to go on moaning over their unhappy situation and at the same time eat and drink in comfort.'

We put in a word for our classification of the superfluous men into those of the Old Dispensation and those of the New. But our Daniel would not hear of a distinction: he would have nothing to say to the Oblomovs nor to the fact that Nicholas cast in bronze had been gathered to his fathers, and just for that reason had been cast in bronze. On the contrary, he attacked us for our defence and, shrugging his shoulders, said that he looked upon us as on the fine skeleton of a mammoth, as at an interesting bone that had been dug up and belonged to a world with a different sun and different trees.

'Allow me on that ground and in the character of a *Homo Benckendorfi testis* to defend my fellow-fossils. Surely you do not really think that these men did nothing, or did something absurd, of their own choice?'

'Without any doubt; they were romantics and aristocrats; they hated work, they would have thought themselves degraded if they had taken up an axe or an awl, and it is true they would not have known how to use them.'

'In that case I will quote names: for instance, Chaadayev. He did not know how to use an axe but he knew how to write an article which jolted the whole of Russia, and was a turning-point in our understanding of ourselves.[11] That article was his first step in the literary career. You know what came of it. A German, Wiegel, took offence on behalf of Russia, the Protestant and future Catholic Benckendorf took offence on behalf of Orthodoxy, and by the lie of the Most High, Chaadayev was declared mad and forced to sign an undertaking not to write. Nadezhdin, who published the article in the *Telescope,* was banished to Ust-Sysolsk; Boldyrev, the old rector, was dismissed: Chaadayev became an idle man. I grant that Ivan Kireyevsky could not make boots, yet he could publish a magazine; he published two numbers and the magazine was forbidden; he contributed an article to the *Dennitsa,* and the censor, Glinka, was put in custody: Kireyevsky became a superfluous man. N. Polevoy cannot, of course, be charged with idleness; he was a resourceful man, and yet the wings of the *Telegraph* were clipped, and, I confess my feebleness, when I read how Polevoy told Panayev that he, as a married man, handicapped by a family, was afraid of the police, I did not laugh but almost cried.'

'But Belinsky could write and Granovsky could give lectures; they did not sit idle.'

'If there were men of such energy that they could write or give lectures within sight of the police-troika and the fortress, is it not clear that there were many others of less strength who were paralysed and suffered deeply from it?'

'Why did they not actually take to making boots or splitting logs? It would have been better than nothing.'

'Probably because they had money enough not to be obliged to do such dull work; I have never heard of anyone taking to cobbling for pleasure. Louis XVI is the only example of a king by trade and a locksmith for the love of it. However, you are not the first to observe this lack of practical labour in superfluous men; in order to correct it, our watchful government sent them to hard labour.'

'My fossil friend, I see that you still look down upon work.'

'As on a far from gay necessity.'

'Why should they not have shared in the general necessity?'

'No doubt they should, but in the first place they were born not in North America but in Russia, and unluckily were not brought up to it.'

'Why were they not brought up to it?'

---

[11] For H.'s appraisal of P. Ya. Chaadayev's 'Philosophical Letter,' which appeared in the *Telescope,* 1836, No. 15, see pp. 292–8. (*R.*)

'Because they were born not in the tax-paying classes of Russia but in the gentry; perhaps that really is reprehensible, but being at that period in the inexperienced condition of *cercaria* they cannot, owing to their tender years, be responsible for their conduct. And having once made this mistake in the choice of their parents, they were bound to submit to the education of the time. By the way, what right have you to demand of men that they should do one thing or another? This is some new compulsory organisation of labour; something in the style of socialism transferred to the methods of the Ministry of State Property.'

'I don't compel anyone to work; I simply state the fact that they were idle, futile aristocrats who led an easy and comfortable life, and I see no reason for sympathising with them.'

'Whether they deserve sympathy or not let each person decide for himself. All human suffering, especially if it is inevitable, awakens our sympathy, and there is no sort of suffering to which one could refuse it. The martyrs of the early centuries of Christendom believed in redemption and in a future life. The Roman Mukhanovs, Timashevs and Luzhins tried to compel the Christians to bow down in the dust before the august image of the Caesar; the Christians would not make this trivial concession and they were hunted down by beasts. They were mad; the Romans were half-witted, and there is no place here for sympathy or surprise. . . . But then farewell, not only to Thermopylae and Golgotha but also to Sophocles and Shakespeare, and incidentally to the whole long, endless epic poem which is continually ending in frenzied tragedies and continually going on again under the title of history.'

Bazarov Once More (1868)

LETTER 1[1]

INSTEAD OF A LETTER, dear friend,[2] I am sending you a dissertation, and an unfinished one too. After our conversation I read over again Pisarev's article on Bazarov, which I had quite forgotten, and I am very glad I did—that is, not that I had forgot-

---

[1] Published in *The Pole Star*, 1868. (*A.S.*)
[2] N. P. Ogarëv. (*A.S.*)

ten it, but that I read it again. The article confirms my point of view. In its one-sidedness it is more true and more remarkable than its opponents have supposed. Whether Pisarev has correctly grasped the character of Bazarov as Turgenev meant it, does not concern me. What does matter is that he has recognised himself and his comrades in Bazarov, and has added to the portrait what was lacking in the book. The less Pisarev has kept to the stocks into which the exasperated father has tried to thrust the obstinate son, the more freely has he been able to treat him as the expression of his ideal.[3]

'But what interest can Mr Pisarev's ideal have for us? Pisarev is a smart critic, he has written a great deal, he has written about everything, sometimes about subjects of which he had knowledge, but all that does not give his ideal any claim on the attention of the public.'

The point is that it is not his own personal ideal but the ideal which both before and since the appearance of Turgenev's Bazarov has haunted the younger generation, has been embodied

---

[3] Dmitry Ivanovich Pisarev (1840–68) was one of those tough-minded young Russian radicals who despised the aging Herzen (the feeling was mutual) as liberal, or "soft," politically, and conservative, or "bourgeois," culturally—accusations that were true enough, in their terms. (Herzen's friend, Turgenev, in *Fathers and Sons* had given them a name that stuck, "Nihilists," and a personality type in the anti-hero, Bazarov.) In this essay disguised as a letter to Ogarëv—always a personal writer, Herzen felt freer in such informal dress—Pisarev is taken as the type of revolutionary youth who were then modeling themselves on Bazarov with a perversity that must have distressed his inventor: "living persons who have tried to take Bazarovism as the basis of their words and actions." Herzen's life-imitates-art point would have been stronger a year or so later: like Bazarov, Pisarev died young, at twenty-eight.

The similarities of our "New Left" to the nineteenth-century Russian Nihilists—and, in its more benign aspect, to the later "Narodniki," or "Back-to-the-People," idealists—have often been remarked on, usually with more heat than light, by elderly (*i.e.*, over thirty) critics of the American radical youth movement in the sixties. As a "critical supporter" of the quondam New Left, who was, like Herzen a century earlier, uneasily divided between hope and skepticism, I wish certain undivided elderly Cassandras, most of them younger than me, had read his last volume before they made their deadly historical parallels (the other was with Hitler's youth movement). His cool treatment of the painful subject of the Nihilists (see also "The Superfluous and Jaundiced" in this volume), which was unsparing and yet infused with comradely sympathy, might have been useful to them. Nor would his humor have come amiss: it brought his sternest philippics down to human scale. But, as noted in my Preface, Americans don't seem to have read him much. (*D.M.*)

not only in various heroes in novels and stories but in living persons who have tried to take Bazarovism as the basis of their words and actions. What Pisarev says I have seen and heard myself a dozen times; in the simplicity of his heart, he has let out the cherished thought of a whole circle and, focusing the scattered rays on one centre, has shed a light on the typical Bazarov.

To Turgenev, Bazarov is more than alien; to Pisarev, more than a comrade. To study the type, of course, one must take the view which sees in Bazarov the desideratum.

Pisarev's opponents were frightened by his lack of caution; while renouncing Turgenev's Bazarov as a caricature, they repudiated even more violently his transfigured double; they were displeased at Pisarev's having put his foot in it, but it does not follow from this that he was wrong in his interpretation.

Pisarev knows the heart of his Bazarov through and through; he makes a confession for his hero. 'Perhaps,' he says, 'at the bottom of his heart Bazarov does accept a great deal of what he denies in words, and perhaps it is just what is accepted and concealed that saves him from moral decline and from moral nothingness.'

We regard this indiscreet utterance, which looks so deeply into another's soul, as very important.

Farther on Pisarev describes his hero's character thus: 'Bazarov is extremely proud, but his pride is not noticeable' [clearly this is not Turgenev's Bazarov] 'just because it is so great. Nothing would satisfy Bazarov but an *eternity of ever-widening activity and ever-increasing enjoyment.*'[4]

Bazarov acts everywhere and in everything only as he wishes, or as he thinks advantageous and convenient; he is guided only by his personal desire or personal calculation. He acknowledges no Mentor above him, without himself or within himself. Before him is no lofty aim, in his mind is no lofty notion, and with all this his powers are enormous. If Bazarovism is a malady, it is a malady of our time, and will have to be suffered to the end in spite of any amputations or palliatives.

Bazarov looks down on people, and even rarely gives himself the trouble to conceal his half-contemptuous and half-patronising attitude to those who hate and to those who obey him. He loves no one. He thinks it quite superfluous to put any constraint

---

[4] Youth is fond of expressing itself in all sorts of incommensurables and striking the imagination by images of infinite magnitude. The last sentence reminds me vividly of Karl Moor, Ferdinand and Don Carlos.

on himself whatever. There are two sides to his cynicism, an internal and an external, the cynicism of thought and feeling and the cynicism of manner and expression. The essence of his inner cynicism lies in an ironical attitude to emotion of every sort, to dreaminess, to poetical enthusiasm. The crude expression of this irony, the causeless and aimless roughness of manner, are part of his external cynicism. Bazarov is not merely an empiricist; he is also an unkempt *Bursch*. Among the admirers of Bazarov there will doubtless be some who will be delighted with his boorish manners, the vestiges left by his rough student life, and will imitate those manners, which are in any case a defect and not a merit.[5] Such people are most often evolved in the grey environment of laborious work: rough work coarsens the hands, coarsens the manners, coarsens the feelings; the man is toughened, casts off youthful dreaminess and gets rid of tearful sentimentality; there is no possibility of dreaming at work; the hard-working man looks upon idealism as a folly peculiar to the idleness and effeminacy of the well-to-do; he reckons moral sufferings as imaginary, moral impulses and exploits as far-fetched and absurd. He feels a repulsion for high-flown talk.

Then Pisarev draws the genealogical tree of Bazarov: the Onegins and Pechorins begot the Rudins and the Beltovs,[6] the Rudins and the Beltovs begot Bazarov. (Whether the Decembrists are omitted intentionally or unintentionally, I do not know.) The tired and the bored are succeeded by men who strive to act; life rejects them both as worthless and incomplete. 'It is sometimes their lot to suffer, but they never succeed in getting anything done. Society is deaf and inexorable to them. They are incapable of adapting themselves to its conditions, not one of them has ever risen so high as head-clerk of a government office. Some are consoled by becoming professors and working for a future generation.' Their negative usefulness is incontestable.

---

[5] The prophecy has now been fulfilled. This mutual interaction of men on books, and books on men, is a curious thing. A book takes its whole stamp from the society in which it is conceived; it generalises, it makes it more vivid and sharp, and afterwards is outdone by reality. The originals caricature their sharply shaded portraits, and actual persons grow into their literary shadows. At the end of the last century all young Germans were a little after the style of Werther, while all their young ladies resembled Charlotte; at the beginning of the present century the university Werthers had begun to change into 'Robbers,' not real ones but Schilleresque robbers. The young Russians who have come on the scene since 1862 are almost all derived from Chernyshevsky's *What Is to Be Done?* with the addition of a few Bazarov features.

[6] The hero of Herzen's novel, *Who Is at Fault?* (*Tr.*)

They increase the numbers of men incapable of practical activity, in consequence of which practical activity itself, or more precisely the forms in which it usually finds expression now, slowly but steadily sink lower in public esteem.

'It seemed (after the Crimean War) that Rudinism was over, that the period of fruitless ideals and yearnings was being succeeded by a period of seething and useful activity. But the mirage was dissipated. The Rudins did not become practical workers, and a new generation has come forward from behind them and taken up a reproachful and mocking attitude towards its predecessors. "What are you whining about, what are you seeking, what are you asking from life? You want happiness, I suppose? I daresay you do! Happiness has to be conquered. If you are strong, take it. If you are weak, hold your tongue; we feel sick enough without your whining!" A sombre, concentrated energy was expressed in this unfriendly attitude of the younger generation to their Mentors. In their conceptions of good and evil the young generation and the best men of the preceding one were alike, the sympathies and antipathies of both are the same; they desired the same thing, but the men of the past generation fussed and fretted. The men of to-day are not in a fuss, they are not trying to find anything, they will not submit to any compromise and they hope for nothing. They are as powerless as the Rudins, but they recognise their impotence.

' "I cannot act now," each of these new men thinks, "and I am not going to try. I despise everything that surrounds me, and I shan't try to conceal my contempt. I shall enter on the battle with evil when I feel myself strong." Having no possibility of acting, men begin to reflect and investigate. Superstitions and authorities are torn to shreds, and the philosophy of life is completely cleared of all sorts of fantastic conceptions. It is nothing to them whether the public is following in their footsteps. They are full of themselves, of their own inner life. In short, the Pechorins had will without knowledge, the Rudins knowledge without will, the Bazarovs both knowledge and will. Thought and action are blended in one firm whole.'

As you see there is everything here (if there is no mistake), both character-drawing and classification. All is brief and clear, the sum is added up, the bill is presented, and perfectly correctly from the point of view from which the author attacked the question.

But we do not accept this bill, and we protest against it from our premature coffins which have not yet arrived. We are not Charles V, and have no desire to be buried alive.

How strange has been the fate of *Fathers and Sons*! That Turgenev brought out Bazarov with no idea of patting him on the head is clear; that he meant to do something for the 'Fathers' is clear too. But when he came to deal with such pitiful and worthless 'Fathers' as the Kirsanovs, Turgenev was carried away by Bazarov in spite of his harshness, and instead of thrashing the sons he chastised the fathers.

And so it has come to pass that some of the younger generation have recognised themselves in Bazarov. But we entirely fail to recognise ourselves in the Kirsanovs, just as we did not recognise ourselves in the Manilovs nor the Sobakeviches, although Manilovs and Sobakeviches existed all over the place in the days of our youth, and exist now.

Whole herds of moral abortions live at the same time in different layers of society and in its different currents; undoubtedly they represent more or less general types, but they do not represent the most striking and characteristic side of their generation, the side which most fully expresses its force. Pisarev's Bazarov is, in a one-sided sense, to a certain extent the extreme type of what Turgenev called the 'Sons'; while the Kirsanovs are the most trite and trivial representatives of the 'Fathers.'

Turgenev was more of an artist in his novel than it is thought, and that is why he turned out of his course, and to my thinking he did well in so doing—he meant to go into one room, and he found himself in another and a better one.

He might just as well have sent his Bazarov to London. That nasty fellow, Pisemsky, was not afraid of the travelling expenses for his sorely tried freaks. We could perhaps have proved to him on the banks of the Thames that, without rising to the post of head-clerk of an office, one might do quite as much good as any head of a department; that society is not always deaf and inexorable when the protest finds a response; that action does sometimes succeed; that the Rudins and the Beltovs sometimes have will and perseverance; and that, seeing the impossibility of carrying on the activity to which they were urged by their inner impulse, they have abandoned many things, gone abroad, and without 'fussing and fretting' have set up a Russian printing-press, and are carrying on Russian propaganda. The influence of the London press from 1856 to the end of 1863 is not merely a practical fact but a fact of history. It cannot be effaced, it has to be accepted. In London Bazarov would have seen that it was only from a distance that we seemed to be merely brandishing our arms, and that in reality we were keeping our hands at work. Perhaps his wrath would have been changed to loving kindness, and he would have given up treating us with 'reproach and mockery.'

I frankly confess this throwing of stones at one's predecessors is very distasteful to me. I repeat what I have said already: 'I should like to save the younger generation from historical ingratitude, and even from historical error. It is time for the fathers not to devour their children like Saturn, but it is time for the children, too, to cease following the example of those natives of Kamchatka who kill off their old people.' Surely it is not right that only in natural science the phases and degrees of development, the declinations and deviations, even the *avortements*, should be studied, accepted, considered *sine ira et studio*, but as soon as one approaches history the physiological method is abandoned at once, and in its place methods of the criminal court and the police station are adopted.

The Onegins and Pechorins have passed away.

The Rudins and the Beltovs are passing.

The Bazarovs will pass . . . and very quickly, as a matter of fact. It is a too far-fetched, bookish, over-strained type to persist for long.

A type has already tried to thrust himself forward to replace him, one rotten in the spring of his days, the type of the Orthodox student, the Conservative patriot educated at government expense in whom everything loathsome in Imperial Russia was regurgitated, though even he felt embarrassed after serenading the Iversky Madonna and singing a thanksgiving service to Katkov.[7]

All the types that arise will pass, and all, in virtue of the law of the conservation of energy which we have learnt to recognise in the physical world, will persist and will spring up in different forms in the future progress of Russia and in its future organisation.

And so would it not be more interesting, instead of pitting Bazarov against Rudin, to analyse what constitutes the 'red threads' connecting them, and the reasons of their appearing and their transformation? Why have precisely these forms of development been called forth by our life, and why have they passed one into the other in this way? Their dissimilarity is obvious, but in some respects they are alike.

Typical characters readily seize on distinctions, exaggerate the

---

[7] H. is referring to the public thanksgiving for the escape of Alexander II from the attempt of D. V. Karakozov to assassinate him in 1866. (*A.S.*)

angles and prominent features for the sake of emphasising them, paint the barriers in vivid colours and tear apart the bonds. The play of colours is lost and unity is left far away, hidden in mist, like the plain that joins the foot of the mountains, whose tops, far apart from each other, are brightly lighted up. Moreover, we load on the shoulders of these types more than they can bear and ascribe to them in life a significance that they have not had, or had only in a limited sense. To take Onegin as the *positive* type of the intellectual life of the 1820s, as the integral of all the aspirations and activities of the class then awakening, would be quite mistaken, although he does represent one of the aspects of the life of that time.

The type of that time, one of the most splendid types of modern history, was the Decembrist and not Onegin. He could not be dealt with by Russian literature for all of forty years, but he is not the less for that.

How is it that the younger generation had not the clearness of vision, the judgment or the heart to grasp all the grandeur, all the vigour of those brilliant young men who emerged from the ranks of the Guards, those spoilt darlings of wealth and eminence who left their drawing-rooms and their piles of gold to demand the rights of man, to protest, to make a statement for which—and they knew it—the hangman's rope and penal servitude awaited them? It is a melancholy and puzzling question.

To resent the fact that these men appeared in the one class in which there was some degree of culture, of leisure and of security, is senseless. If these 'princes, boyars, *voyevodas*,' these Secretaries of State and colonels, had not been the first to wake up from moral hunger but had waited to be aroused by bodily hunger, there would have been no whining and restless Rudins nor Bazarovs resting on their 'unity of will and knowledge': there would have been a regimental doctor who would have done the soldiers to death, robbing them of their rations and medicines, and have sold a certificate of natural death to a Kirsanov's bailiff when he had flogged peasants to death; or there would have been a court clerk taking bribes, for ever drunk, fleecing the peasants of their quarter-roubles and handing overcoat and galoshes to his Excellency, a Kirsanov and governor of the province; and what is more, serfdom would not have received its death-blow, nor would there have been any of that underground activity beneath the heavy crust of authority, gnawing away the imperial ermine and the quilted dressing-gown of the landowners.

It was fortunate that, side by side with men who found their gentlemanly pastimes in the kennels and the serfs' quarters, in violating and flogging at home and in cringing servility in Petersburg, there were some whose 'pastime' it was to tear the rod out of their hands and fight for liberty, not for licence in some remote field but for liberty of mind, for human life. Whether this pastime of theirs was their serious business, their passion, they proved on the gallows and in prison . . . they proved it, too, when they came back after thirty years in Siberia.

If the type of the Decembrist has been reflected at all in literature, it is—faintly but with kindred features—in Chatsky.[8]

In his exasperated, jaundiced thoughts, his youthful indignation, one can detect a healthy impulse to action; he feels what it is he is dissatisfied with, he beats his head against the stone wall of social prejudices and tests whether the prison bars are strong. Chatsky was on the straight road for penal servitude, and if he survived the 14th December he certainly did not turn into a passively suffering or proudly contemptuous person. He would have been more likely to rush into some indignant extreme to become a Catholic, like Chaadayev, a Slav-hater or a Slavophil, but he would not in any case have abandoned his propaganda, which he did not abandon either in the drawing-room of Famusov or in his entrance-hall, and he would not have confronted himself with the thought that 'his hour had not yet come.' He had that restless turbulence which cannot endure to be out of harmony with what surrounds it, and must either break it or be broken. This is the ferment which makes stagnation in history impossible and clears away the scum on its flowing but dilatory wave.

If Chatsky had survived the generation that followed the 14th December in fear and trembling and grew up flattened out by terror, humiliated and crushed, he would have stretched across it a warm hand of greeting to us. With us Chatsky would have come back to his own soil. These *rimes croisées* across the generations are not uncommon even in zoology. And it is my profound conviction that we shall meet Bazarov's children with sympathy and they us 'without exasperation and mockery.' Chatsky could not have lived with his arms folded, neither in capricious peevishness nor in haughty self-deification; he was not old enough to find satisfaction in grumbling sulkiness, nor young enough to enjoy the self-sufficiency of adolescence. The whole essence of the man lies in this restless ferment, this working yeast. But it is just this aspect that displeases Bazarov, it is

---

[8] The hero of *Woe from Wit*. (*Tr.*)

that that incenses his proud stoicism. 'Keep quiet in your corner if you have not the strength to do anything; it is sickening enough as it is without your whining,' he says; 'if you are beaten, well, stay beaten. . . . You have enough to eat; as for your weeping, that's only a thing the masters go in for' . . . and so on.

Pisarev was bound to speak in that way for Bazarov; the part he played required it.

It is hard not to play a part so long as it is liked. Take off Bazarov's uniform, make him forget the jargon he uses, let him be free to utter one word simply, without posing (he so hates affectation!), let him for one minute forget the iron hand of duty, his artificially frigid language, his role of castigator, and within an hour we should understand each other in all the rest.

In their conceptions of good and evil the new generation were like the old. Their sympathies and antipathies, says Pisarev, were the same; what they desired is the same thing . . . at the bottom of their hearts the younger generation accept much that they reject in words. It would be quite easy then to come to terms. But until he is stripped of his ceremonial trappings Bazarov consistently demands from men who are crushed under every burden on earth, outraged, tortured, deprived both of sleep and of all possibility of action when awake, that they shall not speak of their pain; there is more than a smack of Arakcheyev about this.

What reason is there to deprive Lermontov, for instance, of his bitter complaint, his upbraidings of his own generation which sent a shock of horror through so many? Would the prison-house of Nicholas have been really any better if the gaolers had been as irritably nervous and carping as Bazarov and had suppressed those voices?

'But what are they for? What is the use of them?'

'Why does a stone make a sound when it is hit with a hammer?'

'It cannot help it.'

'And why do these gentlemen suppose that men can suffer for whole generations without speech, complaint, indignation, cursing, protest? If complaint is not necessary for others, it is for those who complain; the expression of sorrow eases the pain. "*Ihm*," says Goethe, "*gab ein Gott zu sagen, was er leidet.*" '

'But what has it to do with us?'

Nothing to do with you, perhaps, but perhaps it has something to do with others; but you must not lose sight of the fact that every generation lives for itself also. From the point of view of history it is a transition, but in relation to itself it is the goal, and it cannot, it ought not to endure without a murmur the afflictions that befall it, especially when it has not even the consolation which Israel had in the expectation of the Messiah, and has no idea that from the seed of the Onegins and the Rudins will be born a Bazarov. In reality what drives our young people to fury is that in our generation *our* demand for activity, *our* protest against the existing order of things was *differently* expressed from theirs, and that the motive of both was not always and completely dependent on cold and hunger.

Is not this passion for uniformity another example of the same irritable spirit which has made of formality and routine the one thing of consequence and reduced military evolutions to the goose-step? That side of the Russian character is responsible for the development of Arakcheyevism, civil and military. Every personal, individual manifestation or deviation was regarded as disobedience, and excited persecution and incessant bullying. Bazarov leaves no one in peace; he galls everyone with his haughtiness. Every word of his is a reprimand from a superior to a subordinate. There is no future for that.

'If,' says Pisarev, 'Bazarovism is the malady of our age, it will have to run its course.'

By all means. This malady is in place only until the end of the university course; like teething, it is quite unseemly in the grown-up.

The worst service Turgenev did Bazarov was in putting him to death by typhus because he did not know how to manage him. That is an *ultima ratio* which no one can withstand; had Bazarov escaped from typhus, he would certainly have developed out of Bazarovism, at any rate into a man of science, which in physiology he loved and prized, and which does not change in methods, whether frog or man, embryology or history, is its subject.

Bazarov drove every sort of prejudice out of his head, and even after that he remained an extremely uncultured man. He had heard something about poetry, something about art and, without troubling himself to think, abruptly passed sentence on a subject of which he knew nothing. This conceit is characteristic of us Russians in general; it has its good points, such as intellectual daring, but in return for that it leads us at times into crude errors.

Science would have saved Bazarov; he would have ceased to look down on people with profound and unconcealed contempt.

Science even more than the Gospel teaches us humility. She cannot look down on anything, she does not know what superiority means, she despises nothing, never lies for the sake of a pose, and conceals nothing out of coquetry. She stops before the facts as an investigator, sometimes as a physician, never as an executioner, and still less with hostility and irony.

Science—I anyhow am not bound to keep some words hidden in the silence of the spirit—science is love, as Spinoza said of thought and cognisance.

LETTER 2

WHAT HAS BEEN leaves in history an imprint by means of which science sooner or later restores the past in its basic features. All that is lost is the accidental illumination, from one or another angle, under which it occurred. Apotheoses and calumnies, partialities and envies, all this is weathered and blown away. The light footstep on the sand vanishes; the imprint which has force and insistence stamps itself on the rock and will be brought to light by the honest labourer.

Connections, degrees of kinship, testators and heirs and their mutual rights, will all be revealed by the heraldry of science.

Only goddesses are born without predecessors, like Venus from the foam of the sea. Minerva, more intelligent, sprang from the ready head of Jupiter.

The Decembrists are our great fathers, the Bazarovs our prodigal sons.

The heritage we received from the Decembrists was the awakened feeling of human dignity, the striving for independence, the hatred of slavery, the respect for Western Europe and for the Revolution, the faith in the possibility of an upheaval in Russia, the passionate desire to take part in it, our youth and the integrity of our energies.

All that has been recast and moulded into new forms, but the foundations are untouched.

What has our generation bequeathed to the coming one?

Nihilism.

Let us recall the course of affairs a little.

About the 1840s our life began to force its way out more violently, like steam from under tightly shut valves. A scarcely perceptible change passed all over Russia, the change by which the doctor discerns, before he can fully account for it, that the malady has taken a turn for the better, that the patient's strength, though very weak, is reviving—there is a different *tone*. Somewhere within, in the morally microscopic world, there is the breath of a different air, more irritant, but healthier. Outwardly everything was death-like under the ice of Nicholas's government, but something was stirring in the consciousness and the conscience—a feeling of uneasiness, of dissatisfaction. The horror had lost its edge, and men were sick of the twilight of that dark reign.

I saw that change with my own eyes when I came back from banishment, first in Moscow and afterwards in Petersburg. But I saw it in the literary and learned circles. Another man,[9] whose Baltic antipathy for the Russian movement places him beyond the suspicion of partiality, told not so long ago how, returning in the 'forties to the Petersburg aristocracy of the barracks after an absence of some years, he was puzzled at the weakening of discipline. Aides-de-camp of the Tsar and colonels of the Guards were murmuring, were criticising the measures taken by the government, and were dissatisfied with Nicholas himself. He was so stupefied, distressed and alarmed for the future of the autocracy that in perplexity of spirit he felt, when dining with the aide-de-camp B., almost in the presence of Dubelt himself, that *Nihilism* had been born between the cheese and the pears. He did not recognise the new-born baby, but the new-born baby was there. The machine screwed down by Nicholas had begun to give way; he gave the screw another turn and everyone felt it; some spoke, others kept silent, speech was forbidden; but everyone understood that things were really going wrong, that everyone was distressed, and that this distress would bring no good to anyone.

Laughter intervened in the affair; laughter, which is a bad companion for any religion, and autocracy is a religion. The abomination and desolation of the lower ranks of the officials had reached such a pitch that the government left them to be insulted. Nicholas, roaring with laughter[10] in his box at the Mayor and his Derzhimorda, helped the propaganda, not guessing that after the approval of His Majesty the mockery would quickly go higher up the Table of Ranks.

It is difficult to apply Pisarev's rubrics to this period in all their sharpness. Everything in life consists of *nuances*, fluctuations, cross-currents, ebbing and flowing, and not of disconnected

---

[9] H. here refers to a book by D. K. Schédo-Ferrotti (Baron F. I. Firks): *Études sur l'avenir de la Russie. Nihilisme en Russie* (Berlin and Brussels, 1867), Chapter 2. (*A.S.*)

[10] Two contemporary diaries record that Nicholas was pleased with the play, Gogol's *The Government Inspector*. (*R.*)

fragments. At what point did the men of will without knowledge cease to be and the men of knowledge without will begin?

Nature resolutely eludes classification, even classification by age. Lermontov was in years a contemporary of Belinsky; he was at the university when we were, but he died in the hopeless pessimism of the Pechorin tendency, against which the Slavophils and ourselves had already risen in opposition.

And by the way I have mentioned the Slavophils. Where are Khomyakov and his 'brethren' to be put? What had they—will without knowledge, or knowledge without will? Yet the position they filled was no trifling one in the modern development of Russia, and their thought left a deep imprint on the current of life of that time. Or in what levy of recruits shall we put Gogol, and by what standard? He had not knowledge; whether he had will I don't know, but I doubt it; but he had genius, and his influence was colossal.

And so, leaving aside the *lapides crescunt, plantae crescunt et vivunt* . . . of Pisarev, let us pass on.

There were no secret societies, but the secret agreement of those who understood was very extensive. Circles consisting of men who had, more or less, felt the bear's claw of the government on their own persons kept a vigilant watch on their membership. Any action was impossible, even a word must be masked, but, to make up for this, great was the power of speech, not only of the printed but even more of the spoken word, less easily detected by the police.

Two batteries were quickly moved forward. Journalism became propaganda. At the head of it, in the full flush of his youthful powers, stood Belinsky. University chairs were transformed into pulpits, lectures into the preaching of humanisation; the personality of Granovsky, surrounded by young instructors, became more and more prominent.

Then suddenly another outburst of laughter. Strange laughter, frightening laughter, the laughter of hysteria, in which were mingled shame and pangs of conscience, and perhaps not the tears that follow laughter but the laughter that follows tears. The absurd, monstrous, narrow world of *Dead Souls* could not endure it; it subsided and began to withdraw. And the preaching went on gathering strength . . . always the same preaching; tears and laughter and books and speech and Hegel[11] and history—all roused men to the consciousness of their condition, to a feeling of horror for serfdom and for their own lack of rights,

----

[11] Hegel's dialectic is a fearful battering-ram in spite of its double-facedness and its badge of Prussian Protestantism; it vaporised every-

everything pointed them on to science and culture, to the purging of thought from all the litter of tradition, to the liberty of conscience and reason.

This period saw the first dawn of *Nihilism*—that most perfect freedom from all ready-made conceptions, from all the inherited obstructions and barriers which hinder the Western European mind from going forward, with the cannon-ball of history chained to its legs.

The silent work of the 'forties was cut short all at once. A time even blacker and more oppressive than the beginning of Nicholas's reign followed upon the Revolution of February. Belinsky died before the beginning of the persecution. Granovsky envied him and wanted to leave Russia.

A dark, seven-years-long night fell upon Russia, and in it that cast of thought, the manner of reflecting that was called *Nihilism*, took shape, developed and gained a firm hold on the Russian mind.

Nihilism (I repeat what I said lately in *The Bell*) is logic without structure, it is science without dogmas, it is the unconditional submission to experience and the resigned acceptance of all consequences, whatever they may be, if they follow from observation, or are required by reason. Nihilism does not transform something into nothing, but shows that a nothing which has been taken for a something is an optical illusion, and that every truth, however it contradicts our fantastic imaginings, is more wholesome than they are, and is in any case what we are in duty bound to accept.

Whether the name is appropriate or not does not matter. We are accustomed to it; it is accepted by friend and foe, it has become a police label, it has become a denunciation, an insult with some, a word of praise with others. Of course, if by Nihilism we are to understand destructive creativeness, that is, the turning of facts and thoughts into nothing, into barren scepticism, into haughty folding of the arms, into the despair which leads to inaction, then true Nihilists are the last people to be included in the definition, and one of the greatest Nihilists will be Turgenev, who flung the first stone at them, and another will be perhaps his favourite philosopher, Schopenhauer. When Belinsky, after listening to one of his friends, who explained at length that the *spirit* attains self-consciousness in man, answered indignantly: 'So, I am not conscious for my own sake, but for the

---

thing that existed and dissipated everything that was a check on reason. Moreover, this was the time of Feuerbach, *der kritischen Kritik*.

spirit's? . . . Why should I be its fool? I had better not think at all; what do I care for its consciousness? . . .' He was a Nihilist.

When Bakunin convicted the Berlin professors of being afraid of negation, and the Parisian revolutionaries of 1848 of conservatism, he was a Nihilist in the fullest sense.

All these discriminations and jealous reservations lead as a rule to nothing but violent antagonism.

When the Petrashevsky group were sent to penal servitude for 'trying to overthrow all laws, human and divine, and to destroy the foundations of society,' in the words of their sentence, the terms of which were stolen from the inquisitorial notes of Liprandi, they were Nihilists.

Since then Nihilism has broadened out, has recognised itself more clearly, has to some extent become doctrinaire, has absorbed a great deal from science, and has produced leaders of enormous force and enormous talent. All that is beyond dispute.

But it has brought forth no new principles.

Or if it has, where are they? I await an answer to this question from you, or perhaps from someone else, and then I shall continue.

A Relevant Chrestomathy from the Later Years

(Selected by the Abridger)

ABRIDGER'S NOTE: The above, unlike the other chapter titles, is not Herzen's but mine. I've chosen the following excerpts from the heterogeneous fourth volume partly because I couldn't bear to omit them but lacked space for the long articles in which they occur, partly as specimens of Herzen's mature prose—his style became more flexibly varied in the last decade, sometimes more conversationally open and sometimes more rhetorically dense and allusive—but mostly because they struck me as relevant to some of our own problems today.

ON STYLE: Cf. I, as an epiphany of Herzen's feelings about his people—and their rulers; in II, the formal wit (in the eighteenth-century sense) of a paragraph like "The Peterhof fête is over, the Court masque in fancy dress is played out, the lamps are smoking and going out, the fountains have almost run dry—let us go home"; the long footnote 5 on the same page, as an example of his use of historical anecdotes that are both entertaining and profound as metaphors. As for his colloquial style, easy and spontaneous but never trivial, cf. especially V and VI.

ON RELEVANCE: See II, on the difficulties of "raising up the people" from above, du haut en bas, with the best liberal (or radical) intentions. "So long as we take people for clay and ourselves as sculptors, we shall encounter nothing but stubborn resistance or offensively passive obedience. The pedagogic method of our civilising reformers is a bad one. It starts from the fundamental principle that we know everything and the people know nothing. . . . We cannot set them free that way."

III begins with reflections on the importance (and the alienation) of the intelligentsia in a backward country like Tsarist Russia (or Nixonian America) and ends with a long credo of Russian separatism that could be transposed into a black separatist credo in America today. Thus: "The past of you Western European peoples serves us as a lesson and nothing more; we do not regard ourselves as the executors of your historic testament. . . . Your faith doesn't rouse us. . . . We do not respect what you respect. . . . All our memories are filled with bitterness and resentment. Civilization and learning were held out to us at the end of a knout."

IV explores the problem of the avant-garde artist or intellectual in that massified petty-bourgeois culture that has spread like a fungus over Europe and America since the eighteenth century. He sees the necessity, and justification, for it socially: 'The crowds of holiday-makers in the Champs-Elysées or Kensington Gardens depress one with their vulgar faces, their dull expressions, but . . . what is important to them is that their fathers were not in a position to go holiday-making and they are: that their elders sometimes sat on the box of carriages while they drive about in cabs." But he also understands the cost: "The crowd is without ignorance and also without education. . . . Those who are in advance live in tiny cliques like secular monasteries."

The last pages of V, on "the monks of knowledge," remind me of our UN sentimentalists like Norman Cousins, our Marxian believers. "Pedantry and scholasticism prevent men from grasping things with simple, lively enthusiasm more than do superstition and ignorance."

Toward the end of VI there is a curious adumbration of Trotsky's "law of combined development": that new nations

*don't necessarily have to go through all the evolutionary stages
but may sometimes "combine" them—as he and Lenin (always a
bold experimenter) did, unfortunately, when they flouted orthodox Marxist theory and aimed their October* coup d'état *not at
the next stage, bourgeois democracy, but at the one after, a one-
party "dictatorship of the Proletariat" which would immediately
begin to "build socialism." It built something even worse than
bourgeois democracy. But it's an interesting idea, and it's also
interesting that Herzen, long before Trotsky, was asking
whether the Russian people needed to go through a bourgeois
period after Tsarism. "Why should we put on a European
blouse when we have our own shirt with the collar buttoning
on one side?" That the "European blouse," cut on loose Menshevik, Social-Democratic lines, would have fitted the historical neck (and needs) of the Russian people in 1917 better than
the Bolshevik straitjacket seems to me hardly worth arguing
now,* pace *Lenin, Trotsky, Stalin—and Herzen.*

I

In 1789 the following incident took place. A young man[1] of no
importance, after supping with his friends in Petersburg, drove
to Moscow in a post-chaise. The first station he slept through. At
the second, Sofia, he spent a long time trying to get horses, and
consequently must have been so thoroughly woken up that when
the three fresh horses set off with him, their bells ringing, instead of sleeping he listened to the driver's song in the fresh
morning air. Strange thoughts came into the head of the young
man of no importance. Here are his words:

'My driver struck up a song, a plaintive one, as usual. Anyone
who knows the sounds of the songs of the Russian people will
admit that there is something in them that expresses a sadness of
the spirit. Almost every tune of these songs is in a minor key.
The government should be founded on this musical inclination
of the people's ear. In it one will find the formation of the soul of
our people. Look at the Russian and you will find him pensive. If
he wants to shake off tedium or, as he calls it himself, if he
wants to have a good time, he goes to the pot-house. . . . The
barge-hauler going with hanging head to the pot-house and
coming back bloody from blows in the face may provide the

---

[1] Alexander Nikolayevich Radishchev (1749–1802) is meant, the author
of the famous *Journey from Petersburg to Moscow.* (*Tr.*)

solution of much that has hitherto been enigmatic in the history of Russia.'

The driver went on wailing his song: the traveller went on thinking his thoughts, and before he had reached Chudovo he suddenly remembered how once in Petersburg he had struck his Petrushka for being drunk; and he burst out crying like a child, and, without blushing for his honours as a gentleman, he had the shamelessness to write: 'Oh, if only, drunk as he was, he had come to his senses, enough to answer me in the same way!'

This song, these tears, these words, scattered between two stations on the post-road, must be regarded as one of the first signs of the turning tide. The conception always happens quietly, and the trace of it is usually lost to begin with.

The Empress Catherine understood the point of it, and was graciously pleased 'with warmth and feeling' to say to Khrapovitsky: 'Radishchev is a worse rebel than Pugachëv!'[2]

To be surprised that she sent him in chains to Ilimsky prison is absurd. It is much more surprising that Paul brought him back; but he did that to spite his dead mother—he had no other purpose.

—from *The Emperor Alexander I and V. N. Karazin* (1862)

II

WHEN IN 1826 Yakubovich saw Prince Obolensky with a beard and wearing the coarse uniform of a soldier, he could not help exclaiming: 'Well, Obolensky, if I am like Stenka Razin,[3] you must be like Vanka Kain[4] and no mistake!' . . . Then the officer commanding the escort came up; the prisoners were put in fetters and sent to penal servitude in Siberia.

The common people did not recognise this resemblance, and dense crowds of them looked on indifferently in Nizhny Novgorod as the fettered prisoners were conveyed through it at the very time of the fair. Perhaps they were thinking: 'Our poor dears have to walk there *on foot*, but here the gentry are driven by the gendarmes in carts!'

---

[2] Pugachëv led the great rebellion of the serfs in 1775. (*D.M.*)

[3] Legendary Cossack bandit who led a large-scale peasant uprising in 1670. (*D.M.*)

[4] 'Vanka Kain' (equivalent to Jack Cain—from Cain of the Bible) is a slang term of abuse for a desperate fellow ready for anything. (*Tr.*)

But on the other side of the Ural Range comes a mournful equality in the face of penal servitude and hopeless misfortune. Everything changes. The petty official whom we were accustomed to know as a heartless, dirty taker of bribes, in a voice trembling with tears beseeches the exiles at Irkutsk to accept a gift of money from him; the rude Cossacks escorting them leave them in peace and freedom so far as they can; the merchants entertain them as they pass through. On the farther side of Lake Baikal some of them stopped at the ford at Verkhne-Udinsk; the inhabitants learnt who they were, and an old man at once sent them by his grandson a basket of white bread and rolls, and the grandfather dragged himself out to tell them about the country beyond the Baikal and ask them questions about the great world.

While Prince Obolensky was still at the Usolsky Works he went out early one morning to the place where he had been told to chop down trees. While he was at work a man appeared out of the forest, looked at him intently with a friendly air and then went on his way. In the evening, as he was going home, Obolensky met him again; he made signs to him and pointed to the forest. Next morning he came out of a thicket and made signs to Obolensky to follow him. Obolensky went. Leading him deeper into the forest, the man stopped and said to him solemnly: 'We have long known of your coming. It is told of you in the prophecy of Ezekiel. We have been expecting you. There are many of us here; rely upon us, for we shall not betray you!' It was a banished Dukhobor.

Obolensky had for a long time been tormented by his desire to have news of his own people through Princess Trubetskoy, who had come to Irkutsk. He had no means of getting a letter to her so he asked the schismatic for help. The man did not waste time thinking. 'At dusk to-morrow,' he said, 'I shall be at such and such a place. Bring the letter, and it shall be delivered. . . .' Obolensky gave him the letter, and the same night the man set off for Irkutsk; two days later the answer was in Obolensky's hands.

What would have happened if he had been caught?

'One's own people do not regard dangers. . . .'

The Dukhobor paid the people's debt for Radishchev.

And so in the forests and mines of Siberia, the Russia of Peter, of the landowner, of the public official, of the officer, and the 'black' Russia of the peasants and the village, both banished and fettered, both with an axe in the belt, both leaning on the spade and wiping the sweat from their faces, looked at each other for the first time and recognised the long-forgotten traits of kinship.

It is time that this should take place in the light of day, loudly, openly, everywhere.

It is time that the nobility, artificially raised above the common level in a reservoir of their own by German engineers, should mingle with the surrounding sea. We have become accustomed to seeing fountains, and Samson's column of water from the lion's jaws is no wonder to us beside the infinity of the surging sea.

The Peterhof fête is over, the Court masque in fancy dress is played out, the lamps are smoking and going out, the fountains have almost run dry—let us go home.

'All that is so, but . . . but . . . would it not be better to raise the people?' Perhaps; only one must know that to make them really bristle up there is one sure method—the method of the torture-chamber, the method of Peter I, of Biron, of Arakcheyev. That is why the Emperor Alexander accomplished nothing with his Karazins and Speranskys—but when he got to Arakcheyev that was where he stayed.

There are too many ordinary common people for it to be possible actually to raise them all to the Fourteenth Rank,[5] and in

---

[5] The Old Believers of the English school, who are bound by their doctrine to maintain all the age-old gains of their historical life, even when these do not exist or when they are pernicious, do not agree with this. They think that every sort of right, however wrongly acquired, must be kept, and others united to it. For instance, instead of depriving the nobles of the right to flog and beat the peasants, the peasants should be given the same right. In the old days they used to say that it would be a good thing to promote all the people into the Fourteenth Rank,* in order that they should not be flogged: would it not be better to promote them directly to be captains in the Guards or hereditary noblemen, seeing that heredity with us is reckoned in the opposite direction?† Yet the Ukrainians in the seventeenth century did not reason like this when there was a plan to ennoble them—a plan suggested not by bookish scholars but by the brilliant, magnificent, exuberant nobility of the Free Kingdom of Poland and Lithuania. They thought it better to go on being Cossacks. There is something like that Cossack principle in organic development generally (which our doctrinaires are very fond of taking as an example). One side of an organism can under certain circumstances develop especially, and get the upper hand, always to the detriment of the rest. In itself this organ may be well developed, but in the organism it constitutes a deformity, which one cannot get rid of in the organism by artificially developing the remaining parts to the point of grotesqueness.

* The Fourteenth was the lowest rank in the Table of Ranks. (*Tr.*)

† In Russia a 'hereditary nobleman' was not one who had inherited his rank but one whose heirs would inherit it. (*Tr.*)

general, every people has a strongly defined physiological character which even foreign conquests rarely alter. So long as we take the people for clay and ourselves for sculptors, and from our sublime height mould it into a statue *à l'antique,* in the French style, in the English manner, or on a German last, we shall encounter nothing in the people except stubborn indifference or offensively passive obedience.

The pedagogic method of our civilising reformers is a bad one. It starts from the fundamental principle that we know everything and the people know nothing: as though we had taught the peasant his right to the land, his communal ownership, his system, the *artel*[6] and the *mir*.[7]

It goes without saying that we can teach the people a great deal, but there is a great deal that we have to learn from them and to study among them. We have theories, adopted by us and representing the worked-up discoveries of European culture. To determine which suits our national way of living, it is not enough to translate word for word; a lexicon is not enough. One must do with it in the first place what theoretical authorities are trying to do in the West with the way of living of the European peoples—introduce it into their consciousness.

The people cling obstinately to their way of living—for they believe in it; but we, too, cling obstinately to our theories and we believe in them and, what is more, we think that we know them, that the reality is so. Passing on after a fashion in conventional language what we have learnt out of books, we see with despair that the people do not understand us, and we complain of the stupidity of the people, just as a schoolboy blushes for his poor relations, because they do not know where to put 'i' and

---

This reminds me of a remarkable case from the religio-surgical practice of Prince Hohenlohe, who was one of the last mortals endowed with miraculous powers. This was in that blessed epoch in our century when everything feudal and clerical was rising again with power and incense on the ruins of the French Revolution. The Prince was summoned to a patient, one of whose legs was too short; his relations had not realised that properly speaking the other leg was too long. The miracle-working Prince betook himself to his prayers . . . the leg grew longer, but the Prince was not sufficiently careful and prayed very immoderately: the short leg got overgrown—vexatious. He began praying for the other and then that outgrew the former: back to the former . . . and it ended in the Prince's leaving his patient still with legs of unequal lengths and both of them as long as live stilts.

6 An association, for a longer or shorter time, of a group of men for communal work. (*R.*)

7 The village community in pre-revolutionary times. (*R.*)

where 'y,' but never considers why there should be two different letters for one sound.

Genuinely desirous of the good of the people, we seek remedies for their ailments in foreign pharmacopoeias; there the herbs are foreign, but it is easier to look for them in a book than in the fields. We easily and consistently become liberals, constitutionalists, democrats, Jacobins, but not members of the Russian people. All these political *nuances* one can acquire from books: all this is understood, explained, written, printed, bound. . . . But here one must go wholly by oneself. . . . The life of Russia is like the forest in which Dante lost his way, and the wild beasts that are in it are even worse than the Florentine ones, but there is no Vergil to show the way; there were some Moscow Susanins,[8] but even those led one to the cemetery shrine instead of to the peasants' cottage. . . .

Without knowing the people we may oppress the people, we may enslave them, we may conquer them, but we cannot set them free.

Without the help of the people they will be liberated neither by the Tsar with his clerks, nor by the nobility with the Tsar nor by the nobility without the Tsar.

What is now happening in Russia ought to open the eyes of the blind. The people endured the frightful burden of serfdom without ever admitting the legality of it; seeing the force opposed to them they remained silent. But as soon as others wished to set them free in their own way, they passed from murmuring, from passive resistance, almost to open revolt. And yet they are obviously better off now. What new signs do the reformers expect?

Only the man who, when summoned to action, understands the life of the people, while not losing what science has given him; only the man who voices its aspirations, and founds on the realisation of them his participation in the common cause of the people of the soil, will be the bridegroom that is to come.

This lesson is repeated to us alike by the mournful figure of Alexander with his crown; by Radishchev[9] with his glass of

---

[8] Ivan Susanin, a peasant, saved the elected Tsar Mikhail Romanov from the Poles, who sought to assassinate him. Susanin undertook to lead them to the monastery in which the Tsar was concealed, but led them instead into the forest, where they killed him but were themselves frozen to death. It is the subject of Glinka's opera, *A Life for the Tsar*. (*Tr.*)

[9] *I.e.*, his *Journey from St. Petersburg to Moscow*, cited by Herzen above, which slipped past the censors in 1790 and so enraged Catherine the Great that she condemned him to death, later relenting to ten years'

poison; by Karazin[10] darting through the Winter Palace like a burning meteor; by Speransky[11] who shone for years together with a glimmer like moonshine, with no warmth, no colour; and by our holy martyrs of the Fourteenth of December.[12]

Who will be the destined man?

Will it be an emperor who, renouncing the Petrine tradition, combines in himself Tsar and Stenka Razin? Will it be a new Pestel?[13] Or another Yemelyan Pugachëv, Cossack, Tsar and schismatic? Or will it be a prophet and a peasant, like Antony Bezdninsky?

It is hard to tell: these are *des détails*, as the French say. Whoever it may be, it is our task to go to meet him with bread and salt!

—from *The Emperor Alexander I and V. N. Karazin* (1862)

III

NEXT TO THE COMMUNISM of the peasants nothing is more characteristic of Russia, nothing is such an earnest of her future, as her literary movement.

Between the peasantry and literature there looms the monster of official Russia, of 'Russia the lie,' or 'Russia the cholera,' as you call her. This Russia extends from the Emperor and passes from soldier to soldier, from petty clerk to petty clerk, down to the smallest assistant to a commissary of police in the remotest corner of the Empire. So it unfolds and so, at every step of the ladder, as in Dante's Malebolge, it gains a new power for evil, a new degree of corruption and tyranny. This living pyramid of crimes, abuses and extortions, of the batons of policemen, of heartless German administrators everlastingly famished, igno-

---

exile in Siberia. It was the first important liberal-humanitarian protest in Russian history. (*D.M.*)

[10] A social reformer encouraged by Alexander I when he was young and idealistic. "In my early youth I saw Karazin two or three times," Herzen writes. "I remember my father used to tell of his letter to Alexander I, of his close association with the Tsar, and of his rapid fall." (*D.M.*)

[11] On Speransky, see p. 186, fn. 1. (*D.M.*)

[12] The small group of liberal army officers whose unsuccessful conspiracy to prevent Nicholas I from succeeding to the throne he punished by execution or banishment to Siberia. (*D.M.*)

[13] One of the five "Decembrists" executed by Nicholas I in 1826. (*D.M.*)

rant judges everlastingly drunk and aristocrats everlastingly
servile; all this is soldered together by complicity, by the sharing
of the plunder and gain, and supported at its base on six hundred
thousand animated machines with bayonets. The peasant is
never defiled by contact with this world of governing cynicism;
he endures it—that is the only way in which he is an accessory.

The camp opposed to official Russia consists of a handful of
men who are ready to face anything, who protest against it, fight
it, expose and undermine it. From time to time these isolated
champions are thrown into dungeons, tortured, relegated to
Siberia, but their place does not long remain empty, for fresh
combatants come forward; it is our tradition, the inheritance
entailed upon us.

The terrible consequences of human speech in Russia necessarily give it added power. The voice of a free man is welcomed
with sympathy and reverence, because with us to lift it up one
absolutely must have something to say. One does not so lightly
decide to publish one's thoughts when at the end of every page
one sees looming a gendarme, a troika, a *kibitka* and, in prospect,
Tobolsk or Irkutsk.

❖   ❖   ❖

The Russian people do not read. You know, Monsieur,[14] that it
was not the country-folk, either, who read the Voltaires and
Diderots: it was the nobility and part of the Third Estate. In
Russia the enlightened part of the Third Estate belongs to the
nobility and gentry, which consists of all that has ceased to be
the peasantry. There is even a proletariat of the nobility which
partly merges into the peasantry, and another, an emancipated
proletariat, mounts on high and is ennobled. This fluctuation,
this continual exchange, stamps the Russian nobility with a
character which you will not find in the privileged classes in the
rest of Europe. In a word the whole history of Russia, since the
time of Peter I, is only the history of the nobility and gentry and
of the influence on them of European civilisation. I shall add
here that the Russian nobility and gentry equal in numbers at
least half the electorate of France established by the law of 31st
May, 1850.

During the eighteenth century the neo-Russian literature
continued to elaborate the rich, sonorous, magnificent language
that we write to-day: a supple, powerful language capable of

---

[14] Herzen characteristically wrote this major essay, *The Russian People
and Socialism*, as a letter to the French historian Jules Michelet. (*D.M.*)

expressing the most abstract ideas of German metaphysics and the light sparkling wit of French conversation. This literature, which flowered under the inspiration of the genius of Peter I, bore, it is true, the impress of the government—but in those days 'government' meant reform, almost revolution.

Till the moment of the great Revolution of 1789 the Imperial throne complacently draped itself in the finest vestments of European civilisation and philosophy. Catherine II deserved to be shown cardboard villages and palaces of boards freshly distempered; no one knew better than she did the art of stage-effect.[15] In the Hermitage there was continual talk about Voltaire, Montesquieu and Beccaria. You, Monsieur, know the medal's reverse.

Yet the triumphal concert of the Pindaric *apologiae* of the Court began to be disturbed by a strange, unexpected note. This was a sound vibrant with irony and sarcasm, with a strong tendency towards criticism and scepticism, and this sound, I say, was the only one susceptible of vitality, of external development. The rest, the temporary and exotic, had necessarily to perish.

The true character of Russian thought, poetical or speculative, develops in its full force after the accession of Nicholas to the throne. Its distinguishing feature is a tragic emancipation of conscience, an implacable negation, a bitter irony, a painful self-analysis. Sometimes this all breaks into insane laughter, but there is no gaiety in that laughter.

Cast into oppressive surroundings and endowed with great sagacity and a fatal logic, the Russian frees himself abruptly from the religion and morals of his fathers. The emancipated Russian is the most independent man in Europe. What could stop him? Respect for his past? . . . But what serves as a starting point of the modern history of Russia if not an absolute denial of nationalism and tradition?

Could it be that other 'past indefinite,' the Petersburg period perhaps? That tradition lays no obligation on us; on the contrary, that 'fifth act of the bloody drama staged in a brothel'[15] sets us free, but it imposes on us no belief.

On the other hand, the past of you Western European peoples serves us as a lesson and nothing more; we do not regard ourselves as the executors of your historic testament.

Your doubts we accept, but your faith does not rouse us. For us

---

[15] Herzen refers to the "Potemkin Villages" her minister and lover, Count Potemkin, rigged up to impress her with the prosperity of her subjects. This hoax, by now proverbial, has kept the count's memory green—with an assist from Eisenstein's movie. (*D.M.*)

you are too religious. We share your hatreds, but we do not understand your devotion to what your forefathers have bequeathed to you: we are too downtrodden, too wretched, to be satisfied with a half-freedom. You are restrained by scruples, and held back by reservations. We have neither reservations nor scruples; all we lack at the moment is strength. . . .

It is from this, Monsieur, that we get the irony, the fury which exasperates us, which preys upon us, which drives us forward, which sometimes brings us to Siberia, torture, banishment, premature death. We sacrifice ourselves with no hope, from distaste, from tedium. . . . There is indeed something irrational in our life, but there is nothing vulgar, nothing stagnant, nothing *bourgeois*.

Do not accuse us of immorality because we do not respect what you respect. Since when has it been possible to reproach foundlings for not venerating their parents? We are independent because we are beginning from our own efforts. We have no tradition but our structure, our national character; they are inherent in our being, they are our blood, our instinct, but by no means a binding authority. We are independent because we possess nothing. We have hardly anything to love. All our memories are filled with bitterness and resentment. Civilisation and learning were held out to us at the end of a knout.

What have we to do with your traditional duties, we younger brothers robbed of our heritage? And how could we honestly accept your faded morality, unchristian and inhuman, existing only in rhetorical exercises and indictments of the prosecution? What respect can be inspired in us by your Roman-barbaric system of law, those heavy, crushing vaults, without light or air, repaired in the Middle Ages and whitewashed by the newly enfranchised Third Estate? I admit that the tricks of the Russian lawcourts are even worse, but who could prove to us that your system is just?

We see clearly that the distinction between your laws and our *ukazy* lies principally in the formula with which they begin. *Ukazy* begin with a crushing truth: 'The Tsar commands'; your laws are headed with the insulting lie of the threefold republican motto and the ironical invocation of the name of the French people. The code of Nicholas is directed exclusively against men and in favour of authority. The Code Napoléon does not seem to us to have any other quality. We are dragging about too many chains that violence has fastened on us to increase the weight of them with others of our choice. In this respect we stand precisely on a level with our peasants. We submit to brute force. We are slaves because we have no means of freeing ourselves; from the enemy camp, none the less, we accept nothing.

Russia will never be Protestant. Russia will never be *juste-milieu.*

Russia will not make a revolution with the sole object of getting rid of the Tsar Nicholas and gaining, as the prize of victory, other Tsars: parliamentary representatives, judges, police officials and laws. We are asking for too much, perhaps, and shall achieve nothing. That may be so, but yet we do not despair; before the year 1848 Russia could not, and should not, have entered the phase of revolution; she had only her education to get, and she is getting it at this moment. The Tsar himself perceives it, so he bludgeons the universities, ideas, the sciences; he is striving to isolate Russia from Europe, to kill culture. He is practising his vocation.

Will he succeed? As I have said elsewhere, we must not have blind faith in the future; every foetus has its claim to development, but for all that not every foetus does develop. The future of Russia does not depend on her alone but is bound up with the future of the whole of Europe. Who can foretell what the fate of the Slav world will be when reaction and absolutism shall have vanquished the revolution in Europe?

Perhaps it will perish: who knows?

But in that case Europe too will perish. . . .

And history will continue in America.[16]

—from *The Russian People and Socialism* (1851)

IV

THERE WAS A TIME when you defended the ideas of Western Europe, and you did well; the only pity is that it was entirely

---

[16] This famous "letter" to Michelet is severely critical of the French historian's judgments about Russia but is also infused with a deep respect for Michelet's work and thought in general, a respect which was reciprocated. In his *Democratic Legends of the North,* Michelet, the target of Herzen's polemic, pays an extravagant tribute to his adversary: "The author [of *The Russian People and Socialism*] writes our language with heroic vigor. [Herzen seems to have addressed Michelet in French, a language he was as much at home in, like many nineteenth-century aristocrats, as in his own.] Methought I saw one of the ancient heroes of the north tracing with a merciless rod of iron the sentence on this miserable world. . . . Alas! It is not the condemnation of Russia only; it is that of France and Europe also. 'We flee from Russia,' he says,

unnecessary.[17] The ideas of Western Europe, that is, scientific ideas, have long been recognised by all as the entailed estate of humanity. Science is entirely free of meridian and equator; it is like Goethe's *Diwan—westöstlich.*

Now you want to maintain that the actual forms of Western European life are also the heritage of mankind, and you believe that the manner of life of the European upper classes, as evolved in the historic past, is alone in harmony with the aesthetic needs of human development, that it alone furnishes the conditions essential for intellectual and artistic life; that in Western Europe art was born and grew up, and to Western Europe it belongs; and finally, that there is no other art at all. Let us pause first at this point.

Pray do not think that I shall from the point of view of civic austerity and ascetic demagogy object to the place which you give to art in life. I am in agreement with you on that point. Art—*c'est autant de prix;* together with the summer lightning of personal happiness, it is our one undoubted blessing. In everything else we are either toiling or drawing water in a sieve for humanity, for our country, for fame, for our children, for money, and at the same time for trying to solve an endless problem. In art we find enjoyment, in it the goal is attained; it, too, is an 'End' in itself.

And so, giving to Diana of Ephesus what is due to Diana, I shall ask you of what exactly you are speaking, of the present or the past? Of the fact that art has developed in Western Europe, that Dante and Michelangelo, Shakespeare and Rembrandt, Mozart and Goethe, were by birth and opinion 'Westerners'? But no one disputes this. Or do you mean that a long historical life has prepared both a better stage for art and a finer framework for it, that museums are more sumptuous in Europe than anywhere else, galleries and schools richer, students more numerous, teachers more gifted, theatres better appointed and so on? And that, too, is true; or nearly so, for ever since the great opera has returned to its primitive state of performers strolling from town to town, only grand opera is *überall und nirgends.* In the whole

---

'but Russia is everywhere—Europe is one great prison.' So long, however, as Europe possesses such men as the author, everything may be hoped." (*D.M.*)

[17] "You" is the novelist Turgenev, an old friend of Herzen's (*D.M.*) Turgenev came to England in May 1862, and the discussions which took place between the two friends were continued by Herzen in *Ends and Beginnings.* (*A.S.*)

of America there is no such Campo Santo as in Pisa, but still the
Campo Santo is a grave-yard. It is quite natural, indeed, that
where there have been most corals there should be most coral-
reefs, too. . . . But in all this where is the new living, creative
art, where is the artistic element in life itself? To be continually
calling up the dead, to be repeating Beethoven, to be playing
Phèdre and Athalie, is all very well, but it says nothing for
creativeness. In the dullest periods of Byzantium Homer was
read and Sophocles recited at literary evenings; in Rome the
statues of Pheidias were preserved, and the best sculpture collected on the eve of the Genserics and the Alarics. Where is the
new art, where is the artistic initiative? Is it to be found in
Wagner's 'music of the future'?

Art is not fastidious; it can depict anything, setting upon
everything the indelible imprint of the gift of the spirit of
beauty, and disinterestedly raising to the level of the madonnas
and demigods every casual incident of life, every sound and
every form, the slumbering pool under the tree, the fluttering
bird, the horse at the drinking-trough, the sunburnt beggar-boy.
From the savage, menacing phantasy of Hell and the Day of
Judgment to the Flemish tavern with its peasant with his back
turned, all lie within the domain of art. . . . But even art has
its limit. There is a stumbling-block which neither the violinist's
bow nor the painter's brush nor the sculptor's chisel can deal
with; art to conceal its impotence mocks at it and turns it into
caricature. That stumbling-block is *petit bourgeois* vulgarity.
The artist who excellently portrays a man completely naked,
covered with rags, or so completely dressed that nothing is to be
seen but armour or a monk's cassock, is reduced to despair before
the *bourgeois* in a swallow-tail coat. Hence the extravagance of
casting a Roman toga upon Robert Peel; hence a banker is
stripped of his coat and his cravat, and his shirt is pulled
straight, so that if he could see his bust after death he would be
covered with blushes before his own wife. . . . Robert Macaire
and Prudhomme are great caricatures. Sometimes great caricatures are works of genius; in Dickens they are tragically true to
life, but still they are caricatures. Beyond Hogarth this *genre*
cannot go. The Van Dyck and Rembrandt of *petite bourgeoisie*
are Punch and Charivari, they are its portrait gallery and
scaffold; they are the family records and the pillory.

The fact is that the whole *petit bourgeois* character, both in its
good and bad qualities, is opposed to art and cramping to it; art
withers in it like a green leaf in chlorine, and only the passions

inherent in all humanity can at times, by breaking into *bour-geois* life or, even better, breaking out of its decorum, raise it to artistic significance.

Decorum, that is the real word. The *petit bourgeois* has two talents, and he has the same ones, Moderation and Punctuality. The life of the middle class is full of small defects and small virtues; it is self-restrained, often niggardly, and shuns what is extreme and what is superfluous. The garden is transformed into a kitchen garden; the thatched cottage into a little country-town house with an escutcheon painted on the shutters; but every day they drink tea and every day they eat meat in it. It is an *immense step* forward, but not at all artistic. Art is more at home with poverty and luxury than with crude prosperity or with comfort when it is an end in itself; if it comes to that, it is more at home with the harlot selling herself than with the respectable woman selling at three times the cost the work of the starving seamstress. Art is not at ease in the stiff, over-neat, thrifty house of the *petit bourgeois*, and his house is bound to be such; art feels instinctively that in that life it is reduced to the level of external decoration such as wall-paper and furniture, to the level of a hurdy-gurdy; if the hurdy-gurdy man is a nuisance he is kicked out, if they want to listen they give him a halfpenny and that's that. . . . Art which is pre-eminently elegance of proportion cannot endure the yard-measure; a life self-satisfied with its narrow mediocrity is stigmatised in the eyes of art by the worst of blots—vulgarity.

But that does not in the least prevent the whole cultured world from passing into *petite bourgeoisie*, and the vanguard has arrived there already. *Petite bourgeoisie* is the ideal to which Europe is striving, and rising from every point on the ground. It is the 'chicken in the cabbage soup,' about which Henri Quatre dreamt. A little house with little windows looking into the street, a school for the son, a dress for the daughter, a servant for the hard work—all that makes up indeed a haven of refuge—*Havre de Grâce!* The man driven off the soil which he had tilled for ages for his master; the descendant of the villager broken in the struggle, doomed to everlasting toil and hunger, the home-less day-labourer, the journey-man, born a beggar and dying a beggar—can only wipe the sweat from his brow and look without horror at his children by becoming a property owner, a master, *bourgeois;* his son will not be handed over to life-long bondage for his bread, his daughter will not be condemned to the factory or the brothel. How should he not strive to be *bourgeois?* The bright image of the shopkeeper—the knight and the priest for the middle classes—hovers as the ideal before the eyes of the casual labourer, until his tired, horny hands drop on his sunken chest, and he looks at life with that Irish peace of despair which precludes every vision, every expectation, except the vision of a whole bottle of whisky next Sunday.

Bourgeoisie, the last word of civilisation, founded on the absolute despotism of property, is the 'democratisation' of aristocracy, the 'aristocratisation' of democracy. In this environment Almaviva is the equal of Figaro—from below everything is straining up into *bourgeoisie,* from above everything is sinking down into it through the impossibility of maintaining itself. The American States present the spectacle of one class—the middle class—with nothing below it and nothing above it, the *petit bourgeois* manners and morals have remained. The German peasant is the *petit bourgeois* of agriculture; the working man of every country is the *petit bourgeois* of the future. Italy, the most poetical land in Europe, was not able to hold out, but at once forsook her fanatical lover, Mazzini, and betrayed her husband, the Hercules Garibaldi, as soon as Cavour, the *petit bourgeois* of genius, the little fat man in spectacles, offered to keep her as his mistress.

With the coming of *bourgeoisie,* individual characters are effaced, but these effaced persons are better fed; clothes are made by the dozen, not to measure or to order, but there are more people who wear them. With the coming of *bourgeoisie,* the beauty of the race is effaced, but its prosperity increases; the classic-looking beggar from Trastevere is used for manual labour by the bald shopkeeper of the Via del Corso. The crowds of holiday-makers in the Champs-Elysées or Kensington Gardens, or the audiences in churches or theatres, depress one with their vulgar faces, their dull expressions; but the holiday-makers in the Champs-Elysées are not concerned at that, they do not notice it. But what is very important to them and very striking is that their fathers and elder brothers were not in a position to go holiday-making or to the theatre, and they are: that their elders sometimes sat as coachmen on the box of carriages while they drive about in cabs, and very often too.

It is in the name of this that *bourgeoisie* is triumphing and is bound to triumph. One cannot say to a hungry man, 'You look better when you are hungry; don't look for food.' The sway of *bourgeoisie* is the answer to emancipation without land, to the freeing of men from bondage while the soil is left in bondage to a few of the elect. The crowds that have earned their halfpence have come to the top and are enjoying themselves in their own way and possessing the world. They have no need of strongly marked characters or original minds. Science cannot help stumbling upon the discoveries that lie closest at hand. Photography—that barrel-organ version of painting—replaces the artist; if a creative artist does appear he is welcome, but there is no crying need of him. Beauty and talent are altogether out of the normal; they are the exceptions, the luxury of Nature, its highest limit or the result of great effort, of whole generations. The voice of Mario,[18] the points of the winner of the Derby, are rarities, but a good lodging and a dinner are indispensable. There is a great deal that is *bourgeois* in Nature herself, one may say; she very often stops short in the middle, half-way, and evidently has not the spirit to go farther. Who has told you that Europe will have it?

Europe has been through a bad quarter of an hour. The *bourgeois* were all but losing the fruits of a long life-time, of prolonged efforts, of hard work. An undefined but frightening protest has arisen in the conscience of humanity. The *petits bourgeois* have remembered their wars for their rights, their heroic age and biblical traditions. Abel, Remus, Thomas Münster have been subdued once more, and long will the grass grow upon their tombs as a warning how the autocratic *bourgeoisie* punishes its enemies. Since then all has returned to its normal routine, which seems durable and based on reason and strong and growing, but has no artistic sense, no aesthetic chord: it does not even seek to have them, for it is too practical; it agrees with Catherine II that it is not becoming for a serious man to play the piano well; the Empress, too, regarded men from a practical point of view. The gardens are too heavily manured for flowers to grow; flowers are too unprofitable for the *petit bourgeois'* garden; if he does sometimes grow them, it is for sale.

In the spring of 1850 I was looking for lodgings in Paris. By that time I had got used to so much from living in Europe that I had grown to hate the crowding and crush of civilisation, which at first we Russians like very much. I already looked with horror mixed with disgust at the continually moving, swarming crowd, foreseeing how it would take up half the room that was my due at the theatre and in the *diligence,* how it would dash like a wild beast into the railway carriages, how it would heat and saturate the air—and for that reason I was looking for a flat, not

---

[18] Mario, Giuseppe, Marchese di Candia (1810–83), an Italian tenor. (*A.S.*)

in a crowded place, and to some extent free from the snug vulgarity and deadly sameness of the lodgings *à trois chambres à coucher de maître.*[19]

Someone suggested to me the lodge of a big, old house on the farther side of the Seine in the Faubourg St Germain, or close by. I went there. The old wife of the concierge took the keys and led me by way of the yard. The house and the lodge stood behind a fence; within the courtyard behind the house there were green trees. The lodge was untidy and neglected; probably no one had been living there for many years. The somewhat old-fashioned furniture was of the period of the First Empire, with Roman straight lines and blackened gilt. The lodge was by no means large or sumptuous, but the furniture and the arrangement of the rooms all pointed to a different idea of the conveniences of life. Near the little drawing-room, to one side, next the bedroom, was a tiny study with cupboards for books and a big writing-table. I walked about the rooms, and it seemed to me that after long wanderings I had come again upon a dwelling for a man, *un chez soi,* not a hotel room nor a human stall.

This remark may be applied to everything—the theatre, holiday-making, inns, books, pictures, clothes: everything has gone down in quality and gone up fearfully in numbers. The crowd of which I was speaking is the best proof of success, of strength, of growth; it is bursting through all the dams, flooding and overflowing everything; it is content with anything, and can never have enough. London is crowded, Paris is cramped. A hundred railway carriages coupled on are insufficient; there are forty theatres and not a seat free; a play has to be running for three months for the London public to be able to see it.

'Why are your cigars so bad?' I asked one of the leading London tobacconists.[20]

'It is hard to get them, and, indeed, it is not worth taking trouble; there are few connoisseurs and still fewer well-to-do ones.'

'Not worth-while? You charge eightpence each for them.'

'That hardly brings us out even. While you and a dozen like

---

[19] A very intelligent man, Count Oskar Reichenbach, said to me once, speaking of the better-class houses in London: 'Tell me the rent and the storey, and I will undertake to go on a dark night without a candle and fetch a clock, a vase, a decanter . . . whatever you like of the things that are invariably standing in every middle-class dwelling.'
[20] Carreras.

you will buy them, is there much profit in that? In one day I sell more twopenny and threepenny cigars than I do of these in a year. I am not going to order any more of them.'

Here was a man who had grasped the spirit of the age. All trade, especially in England, is based now on quantity and cheapness, and not at all on quality, as old-fashioned Russians imagine when they reverently buy Tula penknives with an English trademark on them. Everything receives wholesale, herd-like, rank and file consideration; everything is within the reach of almost everyone, but does not allow of aesthetic finish or personal taste. Everywhere the hundred-thousand-headed hydra waits expectantly close at hand round a corner, ready to listen to everything, to look at everything indiscriminately, to be dressed in anything, to gorge itself on anything—this is the autocratic crowd of 'conglomerated mediocrity' (to use Stuart Mill's expression) which purchases everything, and therefore owns everything. The crowd is without ignorance, but also without education. To please it art shouts, gesticulates, lies and exaggerates, or in despair turns away from human beings and paints dramatic scenes of animals and portraits of cattle, like Landseer and Rosa Bonheur.

Have you seen in the last fifteen years in Europe an actor, a single actor, who is not a mountebank, a buffoon of sentimentality, or a buffoon of burlesque? Name him!

Many blessings may have been ordained by fate for the epoch of which the last expression is to be found in the notes of Verdi, but the artistic vocation was certainly not among them. Its own creation—the *café chantant*—an amphibious product, half-way between the beer-cellar and the boulevard theatre, fits it perfectly. I have nothing against *cafés chantants*, but I cannot give them serious artistic significance; they satisfy the 'average customer,' as the English say, the average consumer, the average bidder, the hundred-headed hydra of the middle class, and there is nothing more to be said.

The way out of this situation is still far in the distance. Behind the multitude now ruling stands an even greater multitude of candidates for it, to whom the manners, ideas and habits of life of the middle class appear as the one goal to strive for. There are enough to fill their places ten times over. A world without land, a world dominated by town life, with the right of property carried to the extreme, has no other way of salvation, and it will all pass through *petite bourgeoisie*, which in our eyes is inferior, but in the eyes of the agricultural population and the proletariat stands for culture and progress. Those who are in advance live in tiny cliques like secular monasteries, taking no interest in what is being done by the world outside their walls.

The same thing has happened before, but on a smaller scale and less consciously; moreover, in the past there were ideals and beliefs, words which set beating both the simple heart of the poor citizen and the heart of the haughty knight; they had holy things in common, to which all men bowed down as before the blessed sacrament. Where is there a hymn which could be sung nowadays with faith and enthusiasm in every storey of the house from the cellar to the garret? Where is our *'Ein feste Burg ist unser Gott'* or our *'Marseillaise'*?

When Ivanov was in London he used to say with despair that he was looking for a new religious type, and could find it nowhere in the world about him. A pure artist, fearing to lie with his brush as if it had been perjury, penetrating rather by imagination than by analysis, he required us to show him where were the picturesque features in which a new Redemption would shine forth. We did not show them to him. 'Perhaps Mazzini will,' he thought.

Mazzini would have pointed out to him 'the unity of Italy,' or perhaps Garibaldi in 1861, as the *forerunner, the last of the great men*.

Ivanov died still knocking; the door was not opened to him.

> Isle of Wight, 10th June, 1862

—from Letter 1 of *Ends and Beginnings: Letters to I. S. Turgenev* (1862–3)

V [21]

LAST SUMMER a friend, a Saratov landowner, and a great Fourierist, came to see me in Devonshire.

Please don't be angry with me (it was not the landowner who

---

[21] This fourth "letter" to Turgenev is here uncut, as is the following eighth letter, both examples of the remarkable political prose Herzen was writing toward the end of his life. I know little else comparable in its unusual combination of an easy, spontaneous, flexibly varied style with original insights drawn from a lifetime of experience as an activist in radical politics—and, more important, one who reflected on his actions. . . . Also I couldn't bear to cut them, wildly digressive as they are—indeed, for that very reason, since even more than in the rest of the memoirs, which is saying a lot, the detours are obviously the main road. (*D.M.*)

said this to me, but I who say it to you) for so continually wandering from the point. Parentheses are my joy and my misfortune. A French literary man of the days of the Restoration, a classic and a purist, more than once said to me, taking a pinch of snuff in the prolonged Academy fashion which will soon have passed away altogether: *'Notre ami abuse de la parenthèse avec intempérance!'* It is for the sake of digressions and parentheses that I prefer writing in the form of letters, that is, letters to friends; one can then write without embarrassment whatever comes into one's head.

Well, so my Saratov Fourierist is in Devonshire and says to me: 'Do you know what is odd? I have just been in Paris for the first time. Well—of course . . . there's no denying . . . but, if you look a bit deeper, Paris is a dull place—really dull!'

'What next!' I said to him.

'Upon my soul, it is.'

'But why did you think it was gay there?'

'Upon my word, after the wilds of Saratov!'

'Perhaps it is just because of that. But really, weren't you bored in Paris just because it's so excessively gay there?'

'You are playing the fool, just as you always did.'

'Not at all. London, that always looks like September, is more to our taste; though the boredom here, too, is frightful.'

'Where is it better, then? It seems the old proverb is right: It is where we are not!'

'I don't know; but it must be supposed that it is not very nice there either.'

This conversation, though apparently it was not very long nor particularly important, stirred in me a whole series of old notions concerning the fact that the brain of modern man is short of a sort of fish-glue; that is why his mind does not settle, and is thick with sediment—new theories, old practice, new practice, old theories.

And what logic was that? I say it is dull in Paris and London, and he answers, 'Where is it better, then?' not noticing that this was the line of argument employed by our house-serfs of the old style: in reply to the remark, 'I fancy you are drunk, my lad,' they usually answered, 'Well, did you stand treat?'

What grounds are there for the idea that men are happy anywhere? That they can or ought to be happy? And what men? And happy in what? Let us assume that men do have a better life in one place than another. Why are Paris and London the upper limits of this better life?

Is it so according to Reichardt's guide-book?

Paris and London are closing a volume of world history—a volume in which few pages remain uncut. People, trying with all their might to turn them as quickly as possible, are surprised that as they approach the end there is more in the past than in the present, and are vexed that the two most complete representatives of Western Europe are declining along with it. The audacity and recklessness in general conversations which float, as the Spirit of God before, over the waters, are terrific, but as soon as it comes to action, or even to a critical appreciation of events, all is forgotten and the old weights and measures are hauled out of grandmother's store-room. Decayed forms can only be restored by a complete rebirth: Western Europe must rise up like the Phoenix in a baptism of fire.

'Oh well, in God's name, into the flames with it.'

What if it does not rise up again, but singes its beautiful feathers, or perhaps is burnt to ashes?

In that case continue to baptise it with water, and do not be bored in Paris. Take my father, for example: he spent eight years in Paris and was never bored. Thirty years afterwards he loved to tell of the fêtes given by the *maréchaux* and by Napoleon himself, the suppers at the Palais Royal in company with actresses and opera dancers decked in diamonds that had been plucked out of conquered royal crowns, of the Yusupovs, the Tyufyakins and other *princes russes* who staked there more souls of peasants than fell at Borodino. With various changes and *un peu plus canaille* the same thing exists even now. The generals of finance give banquets as good as those of the generals of the army. The suppers have moved from the Rue St Honoré to the Champs-Elysées and the Bois de Boulogne. But you are a serious person; you prefer to look behind the scenes of world history rather than behind the scenes of the Opera. . . . Here you have a parliament, even two. What more do you want? . . . With what envy and heart-ache I used to listen to people who had come home from Europe in the 'thirties, as though they had robbed me of everything that they had seen and I had not. They, too, had not been bored, but had great hopes, some of Odilon Barrot, some of Cobden. You, too, must learn not to be bored; and in any case be a little consistent; and if you still feel dull, try to find the cause. You may find that your demands are trivial—then you must take treatment for this; it is the boredom of idleness, of emptiness, of not knowing how to find your real self. And perhaps you will find something else: that you are bored because Paris and London have no answer to make to the yearnings that are growing stronger and stronger in the heart and brain of the man of to-day—which does not in the least prevent their standing for the highest development and most brilliant result of the past, and being rich conclusions to a rich period.

I have said this a dozen times, but it is impossible to avoid repetitions. Persons of experience know this. I once spoke to Proudhon of the fact that there often appeared in his journal articles which were almost identical, with only slight variations.

'And do you imagine,' Proudhon answered, 'that once a thing has been said, it is enough? That a new idea will be accepted straight off? You are mistaken. It has to be dinned into people, it has to be repeated, repeated over and over again, in order that the mind may no longer be surprised by it, that it may be not merely understood, but assimilated, and obtain real rights of citizenship in the brain.'

Proudhon was perfectly right. There are two or three ideas which are particularly dear to me; I have been repeating them for about fifteen years; fact upon fact confirms them with unnecessary abundance. Part of what I expected has come to pass and the other part is coming to pass before our eyes; yet these ideas are as outrageous and unaccepted as they were before.

And, what is most mortifying, people seem to understand you; they agree, but your ideas remain like aliens in their heads, always irrelevant, never passing into that spontaneous part of consciousness and the moral being which as a rule lies at the undisputed foundation of our acts and opinions.

It is owing to this duality that people who apparently are highly developed are constantly startled by the unexpected, are caught unawares, rebel against the inevitable, struggle with the irresistible, pass by what is springing into life, and apply all sorts of allopathies and homeopathies to those who are at their last gasp. They know that their watch was properly set but, like the late 'unlamented' Kleinmikhel,[22] cannot grasp that the meridian is not the same.

Pedantry and scholasticism prevent men from grasping things with simple, lively understanding more than do superstition and ignorance. With the latter the instincts are left, hardly realised, but trustworthy; moreover, ignorance does not exclude passionate enthusiasm, nor does superstition exclude inconsistency. But pedantry is always true to itself.

At the time of the Italian war a decent, worthy professor

---

[22] Kleinmikhel, Count Pëtr Andreyevich (1793–1869), Senator and member of the Council of State. His dismissal in October 1855 was received with great satisfaction in broad circles of the Russian public. (*A.S.*)

lectured on the great triumphs of 'international law,' describing
how the principles once sketched big by Hugo Grotius had
developed and entered into the consciousness of nations and
governments, how questions which had in old times been decided by rivers of blood and the miseries of entire provinces, of
whole generations, were now settled, like civil disputes between
private persons, on the principles of national conscience.

Who, apart from some old professional *condottieri*, would not
agree with the professor that this is one of the greatest victories
of humanity and culture over brute violence? The trouble is not
that the lecturer's judgment is wrong, but that humanity is very
far from having gained this victory.

While the professor in eloquent words was inspiring his young
audience to these *Weltanschauungen*, very different commentaries on international law were taking place on the fields of
Magenta and Solferino. It would have been all the harder for
any Amphictyonic Councils to avert the Italian war because
there was no international cause for it—since there was no subject in dispute. Napoleon waged this war as a remedial measure
to calm down the French by the gymnastics of liberation and the
shocks of victory. What Grotius or Vattel[23] could have solved
such a problem? How was it possible to avert a war which was
essential for domestic interests? If it had not been Austria the
French would have had to beat somebody else. One can only
rejoice that it was just Austrians who incurred it.

Then, India, Pekin—war waged by democrats to maintain the
slavery of the blacks, war waged by republicans to obtain the
slavery of political unity. And the professor goes on lecturing;
his audience are touched; they fancy that they have heard the
last creak of the church gates in the cathedral of Janus, that the
warriors have laid down their weapons, put on crowns of myrtle
and taken up the distaff, that the armies are demobilised and are
tilling the fields. . . . And all this at the very time when England was covered with volunteers, when at every step you met a
uniform, when every shopkeeper had a fire-arm, when the
French and Austrian armies stood with lighted matches, and
even a prince—I think it was of Hesse Cassel—placed on a military footing and armed with revolvers the two hussars who had
from the time of the Congress of Vienna ridden peacefully and
unarmed behind his carriage.

If war blazed up again—and that depends on a thousand

---

[23] Vattel, Emmerich de (1714–67), a Swiss writer, author of *Traité du
Droit des Gens.* (*Tr.*)

accidents, on one well-timed shot—in Rome or on the frontier of Lombardy, it would spill over in a sea of blood from Warsaw to London. The professor would be surprised; the professor would be pained. But one would have thought he should not be surprised nor pained. The trend of history is not a hole and corner business! The misfortune of the doctrinaires is that they shut their eyes when arguing so that they may not see their opponent is Nature itself, history itself.

To complete the absurdity we ought not to lose sight of the fact that in abstract logic the professor is right, and that if not a hundred but a hundred million men had grasped the principles of Grotius and Vattel, they would not slaughter each other either for the sake of exercise or for the sake of a bit of land. But the misfortune is that under the present political régime only a hundred and not a hundred million men can understand the principles of Grotius and Vattel.

That is why neither lectures nor sermons have any effect; that is why neither the learned fathers nor the spiritual fathers can bring us any relief; the monks of knowledge, like the monks of ignorance, know nothing outside the walls of their monasteries and do not test their theories or their deductions by events, and while men are perishing from the eruption of the volcano they are blissfully beating time, listening to the music of the heavenly spheres and marvelling at its harmony.

Lord Verulam, Bacon, ages ago divided the learned into spiders and bees. There are epochs in which the spiders are decidedly in the ascendant, and then masses of spiders' webs are spun, but little honey is gathered. There are conditions of life which are particularly favourable to spiders. Lime groves, flowering meadows and, above all, wings and a social form of life, are necessary for the production of honey. For spiders' webs a quiet corner is enough, with untroubled leisure, plenty of dust and indifference towards everything except the internal process.

At ordinary times it is still possible to plod drowsily along a dusty, smooth road without breaking the spiders' webs, but as soon as it comes to crossing rough ground and tussocks there is trouble.

There was a really good, quiet belt of European history beginning with Waterloo and lasting till the year 1848. There was no war then but plenty of international law and standing armies. The governments openly encouraged 'true enlightenment' and quietly suppressed the *false;* there was not much freedom but there was not much slavery either. Even the despotic rulers were all good-natured in the style of the patriarchal

Francis II, the pietist Friedrich Wilhelm, and Alexander the friend of Arakcheyev. The king of Naples and Nicholas came by way of dessert. Industry flourished, trade flourished even more, factories worked, masses of books were written; it was the golden age for all cobwebs; in academic *aulae* and in the studies of the learned endless webs were woven! . . .

History, criminal and civil law, international law, and religion itself were all brought into the field of pure science and thence they dropped like the lacy fringes of a spider's web. The spiders swung at their own sweet will by their filaments, never touching the earth. Which was very fortunate, however, since the earth was covered with other crawling insects, who represented the great idea of the State *armed for self-defence*, and clapped over-bold spiders into Spandau and other fortresses. The doctrinaires understood everything most perfectly *à vol d'araignée*. The progress of humanity was as certain in those days as the route mapped out for His Imperial Majesty when he travelled incognito—from stage to stage with horses ready at the stations. And then came—February the 24th, June the 24th, the 25th, the 26th and December the 2nd.

These flies were too big for a spider's web.

Even the comparatively slight shock of the July revolution fairly killed such giants as Niebuhr and Hegel. But the triumph was still to the advantage of the doctrinaires; the journalists, the Collège de France, the political economists sat on the top steps of the throne together with the Orléans dynasty; those who remained alive recovered and adapted themselves somehow to 1830; they would have probably got on all right even with the republic of the troubadour, Lamartine.

But how could they cope with the days of June?

And the 2nd of December?

Of course, Gervinus[24] teaches us that a democratic revolution is followed by an epoch of centralisation and despotism, but yet something was amiss. Some began asking whether we should not go back to the Middle Ages; others quite simply urged a return to Catholicism. The Stylites of the Revolution pointed with undeviating finger along the whole railway line of time to the year 1793; the Jews of doctrinairism went on lecturing regardless of facts, in the expectation that mankind would have had its fling and return to Solomon's temple of wisdom.

---

[24] Gervinus, Georg Gottfried (1805–71), a German historian. (*R.*)

Ten years have passed.

Nothing of all that has come off. England has not become Catholic, as Donoso Cortés[25] desired; the nineteenth century has not become the thirteenth, as certain Germans desired; the peoples resolutely refuse French fraternity (or death!), international law after the pattern of the Peace Society, honourable poverty after Proudhon and a Kirgiz diet of milk and honey.

While the Catholics . . .

The mediaevalists . . .

The Stylites of 1793 . . .

And all the doctrinaires harp on the same strings. . . .

Where is humanity going since it despises such authorities?

Perhaps it does not know itself.

But we ought to know for it.

Apparently not where we expected it to go. And, indeed, it is hard to tell where one will get to, travelling on a globe which a few months ago only just missed a comet and may crack any day, as I informed you in my last letter.

1st September, 1862

—Letter 4 of *Ends and Beginnings: Letters to I. S. Turgenev* (1862–3)

VI [26]

Be a man, stop and make answer!. .

'*Halte-là! Stop!*' was said to me this time not by a lunatic but, quite the contrary, by a very well-adjusted gentleman who walked into my room with *The Bell* in his hand. 'I have come,' he said, 'to have it out with you. Your *Ends and Beginnings* have exceeded all bounds; it is time to know when to stop, and really put an end to them, with regrets for having begun.'

'Has it really come to that?'

'It has. You know I'm fond of you, I respect your talent. . . .'

'Well,' I thought, 'it's a bad look-out; it is clear that this "well-

---

[25] Juan Francisco Donoso Cortés, Marqués Valdegamas (1803–53), a Spaniard, was a moderate liberal until the revolution of 1848 and after that an extreme reactionary. (*R.*)

[26] This is the eighth, and last, of Herzen's "letters" to Turgenev, which he ran as a series titled *Ends and Beginnings* in his magazine *The Bell*, 1862–3. It is uncut. (*D.M.*)

adjusted man" means to abuse me in earnest, or he wouldn't have attacked me with such flattering approaches.'

'Here is my breast,' I said; 'strike.'

My resignation, together with the classical allusion, had a happy effect on my irritated friend, and with a more good-natured air he said: 'Hear me out calmly, laying aside the vanity of the author and the narrow exclusiveness of the exile: with what object are you writing all this?'

'There are many reasons for it; in the first place, I believe what I write to be the truth, and every man who is not indifferent to the truth has a weakness for spreading it abroad. Secondly . . . but I imagine the first reason is sufficient.'

'No. You ought to know the public whom you are addressing, the stage of development it has reached, and the circumstances in which it is placed. I'll tell you straight: you have the most pernicious influence on our young people, who are learning from you disrespect for Europe and her civilisation, and consequently do not care to study it seriously but are satisfied with a smattering and think that the breadth of their own nature is enough.'

'Ugh! how you have aged since I saw you last! you abuse the young and want to rear them on falsehoods, like nurses who tell children that the midwife brings the babies, and the difference between a boy and a girl is the cut of their clothes. You had better consider for how many centuries men have been telling godless lies, with a moral purpose, and morality has been none the better. Why not try speaking the truth? If the truth turns out to be bad, it will be a good precedent. As to my bad influence on the young—I've long been resigned to that, remembering how all who have been of any use to the younger generation have invariably been accused of corrupting it, from Socrates to Voltaire, from Voltaire to Shelley and Belinsky. Besides, I am comforted by the fact that it is very difficult to corrupt our young Russians. Brought up on the estates of slave-owners by Nicholas's officials and officers, completing their studies in army barracks, government offices or the houses of the gentry, they are either incapable of being corrupted, or their corruption is already so complete that it would be hard to add to it by any bitter truth about Western Europe.'

'Truth! . . . But allow me to ask you whether your truth really is the truth?'

'I can't answer for that. You may be sure of one thing, that I say conscientiously what I think. If I am mistaken, without being aware of it, what can I do? It is more your job to open my eyes.'

'There's no convincing you—and you know why; it's because you are partly right; you are a good prosecutor, as you say yourself, and a bad *accoucheur*.'

'But you know I am not living in a maternity hospital, but in a clinic and an anatomy theatre.'

'And you are writing for nursery-schools. Children must be taught that they may not eat each other's porridge and pull each other's hair. But you regale them with the subtleties of your pathological anatomy, and keep on adding besides: Look here, how nasty the entrails of these old Europeans are! What is more, you use two standards of weight and two of measure. If you have taken up the scalpel, you should be uniform in your dissection.'

'What, am I cutting up the living too? How awful! And children too! Do I seem to you to be a Herod?'

'You may joke as you like; you won't put me off with that. With great insight you diagnose the malady of modern man, but when you have made out all the symptoms of a chronic disease, you say that it is all due to the patient's being French or German. And our people at home actually imagine that they have youth and a future. Everything that is dear to us in the traditions, the civilisation and the history of the Western nations you cut open relentlessly and mercilessly, exposing frightful sores, and in that you are performing your task as a demonstrator. But you are sick of messing about for ever with corpses. And so, abandoning every ideal in the world, you are creating for yourself a new idol, not a golden calf but a woolly sheepskin, and you set to bowing down to it and glorifying it as "The Absolute Sheepskin, the Sheepskin of the Future, the Sheepskin of Communism, of Socialism!" You who have made for yourself a duty and a profession of scepticism, expect from a people, which has done nothing so far, a new and original form of society in the future and every other blessing; and, in the excess of your fanatical ecstasy, you stop up your ears and squeeze your eyes shut that you may not see that your god is as crude and hideous as any Japanese idol, with its three-tiered belly and nose flattened onto its cheekbones and moustaches like the King of Sardinia. Whatever you are told, whatever facts are brought forward, you talk in "ardent ecstasy" of the freshness of spring, of beneficent tempests, of rainbows and sprouts full of promise! It is no wonder that our young people, after drinking deep of your still fermenting brew of Slavophil socialism, are staggering, drunk and dizzy, till they break their necks or knock their noses against our *real* reality. Of course, it is as hard to sober them as it is to sober you—history, philology, statistics, incontestable facts, go for nothing with both of you.'

'But allow me; I, in my turn, shall tell you that you must keep within bounds. What are these indubitable facts?'

'There are scores of them.'

'Such as?'

'Such as the fact that we Russians belong both by race and language to the European family, *genus europaeum*, and consequently by the most immutable laws of physiology we are bound to follow the same path. I have never heard of a duck, belonging to the breed of ducks, breathing with gills. . . .'

'Only fancy, I haven't either.'

I pause at this agreeable moment of complete agreement with my opponent to turn to you again and submit to your judgment such censure of the honour and virtue of my epistles.

My whole sin lies in avoiding dogmatic statement and perhaps relying too much on my readers; this has led many into temptation and given my *practical* opponents a weapon against me—of various temper and not always of equal purity. I shall try to condense into a series of aphorisms the grounds of the theory on the basis of which I thought myself entitled to draw the conclusions, which I have passed on like apples I had picked without mentioning the ladder which I had put up to the tree, nor the shears with which I cut them off. But before I proceed to do this I want to show you by one example that my stern judges cannot be said to be on very firm ground. The learned friend who came to trouble the peace of my retreat takes it as you see for an indubitable fact, for an invariable physiological law, that if the Russians belong to the European family the same line of development awaits them as that followed by the Latin and Germanic peoples. But there is no such paragraph in the code of laws of physiology. It reminds me of the typically Muscovite invention of various institutions and regulations in which everyone believes, which everyone repeats, and which in fact have never existed. One friend of mine and of yours used to call them the laws of the English Club.

The general plan of development admits of endless unforeseen deviations, such as the trunk of the elephant and the hump of the camel. There are any number of variations on the same theme: dogs, wolves, foxes, harriers, borzois, water-spaniels and pugs. . . . A common origin by no means conditions an identical biography. Cain and Abel, Romulus and Remus, were brothers, but what different careers they had! It is the same in all spiritual societies or communities. Every form of Christianity has similarities in the organisation of the family, of the Church and so on, but it cannot be said that the history of the English Protestants has been very similar to that of the Abyssinian Christians, or that the most Catholic Austrian army has much in common with the extremely Orthodox monks of Mount Athos. That the duck does not breathe through gills is true; it is even truer that quartz does not fly like a humming-bird. You certainly know, however, though my learned friend does not, that there was a moment's hesitation in the duck's life when its aorta had not turned its stalk downwards, but branched out with pretensions to gills; but having a physiological tradition, the habit and possibility of development, the duck did not stop short at the inferior form of respiratory organ, but passed on to lungs.

It simply and plainly comes to this, that the fish has become adapted to the conditions of aquatic life and does not advance beyond gills, while the duck does. But why the fish's breathing should blow away my view, I do not understand. It seems to me, on the contrary, to explain it. In the *genus europaeum* there are peoples that have grown old without fully developing a *bourgeoisie* (the Celts, some parts of Spain, of Southern Italy and so on), while there are others whom the *bourgeois* system suits as water suits gills. So why should not there be a nation for whom the *bourgeois* system will be a transitory and unsatisfactory condition, like gills for a duck?

Why is it a wicked heresy, a defection from my own principles, and from the immutable laws of creation and the rules and doctrines, human and divine, that I do not regard the *bourgeois* system as the final form of Russian society, the organisation towards which Russia is striving and to attain which she will probably pass through a *bourgeois* period? Possibly the European peoples will themselves pass to another order of life, and perhaps Russia will not develop at all; but just because this is possible, there are other possibilities too: the more so that in the order in which problems arise, in the accidents of time and place and development, in the conditions and habits of life and the permanent traits of character, there is a multitude of indications and directions.

The Russian people, extended so widely between Europe and Asia, and standing to the general family of European peoples somewhat in the relationship of a cousin, has taken scarcely any part in the family chronicle of Western Europe. Having been combined late and with difficulty, it must either show a complete incapacity for progress, or must develop something of its own under the influence of the past and of borrowings, of its neighbours' examples and of its own angle of reflection.

Up till our day Russia has developed nothing of her own, but has preserved something; like a river, she has reflected things truly but superficially. The Byzantine influence has perhaps been the deepest; the rest went according to Peter: beards were shaved, heads were cropped, the skirts of caftans were cut off, the people were silent and submissive, the minority changed their dress and went into the Service, and the State, after receiving the general European outline, grew and grew. . . . This is the usual history of childhood. It is finished: that no one doubts, neither the Winter Palace nor Young Russia. It is time to stand on our own feet: why is it absolutely necessary to take to wooden legs because they are of foreign make? Why should we put on a European blouse when we have our own shirt with the collar buttoning on one side?

We are vexed at the feebleness, at the narrow outlook of the government, which in its sterility tries to improve our life by putting on us the tricolour *camisole de force* cut on the Parisian pattern, instead of the yellow and black *Zwangsjacke*, in which we have been herded for a hundred and fifty years. But here we have not the government but the mandarins of literature, the senators of journalism, the university professors preaching to us that such is the immutable law of physiology, that we belong to the *genus europaeum*, and must therefore cut all the old capers to a new tune, that we must trip like sheep over the same rut, fall into the same gully, and afterwards settle down as an everlasting shopkeeper selling vegetables to other sheep. Away with their physiological law! And why is it that Europe has been more fortunate? No one has made her play the part of Greece and Rome *da capo*.

There are in life and nature no monopolies, no measures for preventing and suppressing new biological species, new historical destinies and political systems—they are only limited by practical possibility. The future is a variation improvised on a theme of the past. Not only do the phases of development, and the forms of life vary but new nations are created, new nationalities whose destinies go different ways. Before our eyes, so to speak, a new breed has been formed, a variety European by free choice and elemental composition. The manners, morals and habits of the Americans have developed a peculiar character of their own; the Anglo-Saxon and the Celtic physical types have so changed beyond the Atlantic that you can nearly always tell an American. If a fresh soil is enough to make an individual, characteristic nation out of old peoples, why should a nation that has developed in its own way under completely different conditions from those of the West European States, with different elements in its life, live through the European past, and that, too, when it knows perfectly well what that past leads to?

Yes, but what do those elements consist of?

I have said what they consist of many times, and not once have I heard a *serious* objection; but every time I hear again *the same* objections, and not from foreigners only, but from Russians. . . . There is no help for it; we must repeat our arguments again, too.

15th January, 1863

—from Letter 8 of *Ends and Beginnings: Letters to I. S. Turgenev*

APPENDIX:
MARX V. HERZEN

The lengthy note in the recent Soviet edition of Herzen (Volume XI, 1957, pp. 678–80) on the hostility between Marx and Herzen was omitted by Mr. Higgens from his edition for scholarly reasons—little information, much ideologese—but I think it worth including, with cuts, in this more topically oriented version because of the later historical importance of Marx. Also because the Herzen–Marx antagonism had much deeper roots— in personal style as well as political ideas—than the Soviet scholars seem to realize. The stereotyped Marxistic formulae they use to obscure it merely reveal how unbridgeable is the chasm. I have felt it necessary, and pleasurable, to add some lengthy glosses which may throw some light on the political psychology of Marx and his epigones. (D.M.)

For a correct understanding of Herzen's chapter on 'The German Emigrants'—in particular, of how he could arrive at such a gross distortion of the activity and role of Marx—one must consider the reasons for the estrangement, indeed, the hostility, which separated them.

The roots of Herzen's activity were in a social environment sharply different from the one in which Marx, the proletarian [*sic*] revolutionary, functioned. Herzen came from a backward country of serfdom in which capitalism was poorly developed and the revolutionary proletariat had not manifested itself at all. The spiritual bankruptcy which followed the defeat of the 1848 revolution; the profound doubts whether, after the 'June Days,' the European proletariat could recover new strength for the struggle; and the 'halt' before historical materialism—all these likewise prevented Herzen's receiving any correct notion of the great revolutionary and scientific role of Marx and Engels.

There was no personal acquaintance between Herzen and the founder of scientific socialism. The persons Herzen met in the late 1840s had already become opponents (Proudhon, Bakunin) of the founder of scientific socialism or were their ignorant pupils (Sazonov, Moses Hess). Information from such sources Herzen can have found only confusing.

[The stiff-starched uniform of official rhetoric which these Moscow scholars put on (do they ever take it off? in bed?) as they try to explain (away) why Herzen couldn't stand Marx and vice versa is as confining intellectually as were physically the uniforms Herzen found so absurd and repulsive on the persons of the Tsar's bureaucrats. Both are too tight to allow any freedom of individual (*i.e.*, human) expression. (*D.M.*)]

On the other hand, Marx and Engels in the late forties and early fifties had not at their disposal the objective, indisputable data which would have made it possible for them to judge of the good aspects of the revolutionary activity of Iskander (Herzen's pen-name) and how profoundly he was related to the development of progressive thought in Russia and the revolutionary stimulus he exerted on the Russian intelligentsia.

However, certain aspects of Herzen's activity could not but provoke in Marx and Engels extreme caution and even hostility: his pessimistic view of the revolutionary movement in the West and, following from this, certain erroneous predictions about the future of the Slavs and of Western Europe which caused Marx to charge that, in Herzen's view, 'the old, rotten Europe must be revivified by the victory of Panslavism,' although in fact Herzen often denounced 'imperialistic Panslavism.'

Marx criticized Herzen's populist views, seeing in his hopes for the Russian commune merely Panslavism and noting that Herzen 'had discovered the Russian commune not in Russia but in the book of a Prussian *Regierungsrat* named Haxthausen.'

[This crack is typical of the kind of polemical infighting Marx often went in for. It is defective (a) epistemologically and (b) factually. (a) The provenance of a fact or idea doesn't affect its validity: worse men than Haxthausen have told the truth and added to wisdom. As for (b), see pp. 310–12 of Martin Malia's *Herzen and the Birth of Russian Socialism*, which state that while (1) *"Herzen's first reference to the socialist possibilities of the Russian peasant commune* [or *mir*] *occurs in his Diary in 1843 apropos of a visit to Russia of the Prussian ethnologist, Baron Haxthausen* [the baron, *Regierungsrat* though he was, whatever that is— sounds terrible, which is why Marx uses it—was a perfectly serious scholar. *D.M.*] *with whom he had a long conversation*," the fact is also (2) that he had written about the *mir* in an 1836 essay and was by then *"aware that the absence of private property in the commune distinguished Russia from the West.*" Then (3) Malia proceeds to pull what's left of the Haxthausen rug from under Marx's polemical stance: "*It is virtually certain, however, that Herzen first heard the idea of the 'socialist' character of the commune not from Haxthausen but from the Slavophiles.*" For another page and a half he patiently untangles the Gordian knot, a pleasant contrast to Marx's method which was more in the style of Alexander the Great, as was his accusation that Herzen was a Panslavist (maybe he got "Panslav" mixed up with "Slavophile"—which Herzen wasn't either). In any case, see Malia *passim* for a non-Alexandrian unraveling of both questions. (*D.M.*)]

It followed from this that Marx and Engels, who, like Herzen, were living in London in the 1850s and 1860s, considered it impossible to make political speeches on the same platform with him.

[How "it followed from this"—unless one accepts sectarian spite and ignorance as a reasonable justification—I don't understand. The platform referred to was that of the 1855 meeting organized by the Chartist Ernest Jones to commemorate "The Great Revolutionary Movement of 1848." Marx first accepted, then withdrew when he learned Herzen was going to speak. See pp. 482–3 above, for Herzen's account of the incident, which is not objected to there (or here) by the Soviet academicians. (*D.M.*)]

Herzen was inclined to attach to Marx as well his criticism of the German petty-bourgeois emigrants for their nationalism, narrow-mindedness and sectarianism. He could not understand the place in history that belonged to him.

[Possibly because Marx didn't then have much of a "place in history." If Herzen had foreseen how big it would be, he would have been even more depressed than after 1848. Still, if only out of touristic curiosity—he was a masterful tourist —he had made a social effort (even Marx might have thawed if they'd ever met), what an interesting portrait we might have had! Not all unflattering, either: Herzen was as generous as he was perceptive. He wouldn't have confused Marx, once he'd met him, with the other German emigrants. Maybe worse, maybe better, but certainly not petty-bourgeois. (*D.M.*)]

This was aggravated by the conflicts that arose because of Herzen's friendly relations with Bakunin and Karl Vogt.

[They might have added Proudhon, to whose demolishment Marx devoted a whole book, *The Poverty of Philosophy*. He also wrote a much smaller book, *Herr Vogt*, attacking the Swiss naturalist as the wrong kind of materialist—the undialectical, or philistine, kind. "Herr Vogt"—Marx never let up—was a close friend of and an influence on Herzen. Naturally. Sometimes the Herzen–Marx antagonism seems so perfect as to suggest instinct, like cat–dog or mongoose–cobra. *(D.M.)*]

Plekhanov was right when, in 'Herzen the Emigré,' he wrote: 'Only with Marx and his small circle—with the "Marxids" as Herzen called them—was he on bad terms. This was the result of a series of unhappy misunderstandings. It was as if some evil fate had prevented *rapprochement* between the founder of scientific socialism and the Russian publicist who was exerting himself to set socialism on a scientific basis.'

[That Plekhanov, most steadfast of Marxids, was driven to so un-Marxian a formulation as "an evil fate" to bridge the chasm, shows its depth. But isn't there a less mystical explanation: wasn't it simply Marx's temperament—reclusive, exclusive with more than a bit of paranoiac suspicion: a reverse negative of Herzen's—that made "rapprochement" impossible? Herzen's relations with his fellow exiles in London were as ecumenical as Marx's were parochial. As Plekhanov notes and as the memoirs show, Herzen was on human terms—friendly, critical, ironical but always sociable terms, seeing them and sharing platforms with them whether he agreed or disagreed—with the big, and small, fry of every national group except for "Marx and his small circle." While Marx seems to have disliked, despised, and kept aloof from everybody outside his *cénacle:* Ledru-Rollin, Louis Blanc, Mazzini, Garibaldi, Robert Owen (Engels dealt with *him* in *Socialism—Scientific and Utopian*), Worcell and his Poles, Kossuth and his Hungarians—the whole menagerie. "The only company he could easily stand," writes J. Hampden Jackson in *Marx, Proudhon and European Socialism*, "was that of Germans." And even there he had no use for outsiders like Ruge and Kinkel or, later, that "nigger Jewboy" Lassalle (to telescope the racial epithets he showered, privately, on his pan-flashy rival in the German Social Democratic movement). Marx was quite a different type from Herzen, and their "misunderstandings" were not really misunderstandings. (*D.M.*)]

However, by the end of the 1860s, as Lenin has shown, Herzen had come to recognize the power of the First International. In 1868, rebuking 'our enemies'—the reactionaries headed by Katkov who proclaimed that 'socialism is now a dead cause'—Herzen pointed to the Brussels congress of the First International, the 'movement' of the German working class, and other signs of revolutionary enthusiasm.

[The First International was founded in London in 1864 and Marx soon became its ideological leader. But from the beginning his dominance was challenged strongly by French, Swiss, Spanish, and Italian affiliates whose membership followed the anarchistic ideas of Proudhon and, especially, Bakunin. Maybe Herzen's "other signs of revolutionary enthusiasm" referred to such followers of his old friends —I haven't looked it up. Or maybe not. But it is a fact that at the Hague congress in 1872, two years after Herzen's death, the anarchists were so strong, and so on the rise (after the 1870 Paris Commune, which was a Proudhon–Bakunin, not a Marxist, show) that Marx used his last voting muscle to transfer the headquarters of the First International to New York City, where it died, as he expected, of pernicious anemia in a few years, after which he planned and structured the Second International along more sensible, power-practical lines. (*D.M.*)]

And in a letter to Ogarëv (September 29, 1869) he writes: 'All the enmity between myself and the Marxids is over Bakunin.' Note also that Herzen did not publish his chapter on 'The German Emigrants' during his lifetime.

[I don't know why in his last year Herzen came to think his enmity with the "Marxids" was only due to Bakunin. Maybe he was irritated with Bakunin, as he often was, and relieved his feelings to the ever-sympathetic Ogarëv with no idea of their being engraved by the muse of History, or the Soviet Academy, as the final summary of his relations to Bakunin and Marx. As for Herzen's not publishing his chapter on "The German Emigrants" during his lifetime: Isaiah Berlin's Introduction (page xxxi) explains this not as due to a rapprochement with Marx but to Herzen's distaste (which Marx didn't share) for "washing the revolutionaries' dirty linen in public." (*D.M.*)

On Marx's attitude to Herzen in the sixties, cf. his letter of February 13, 1863, on the Polish risings: '. . . now Herzen & Co. have a chance to prove their revolutionary honour.' And Herzen, as is known, did prove it. When he came out for the Polish insurgents, Lenin writes, 'Herzen saved the honor of Russian democracy.' (V. I. Lenin: *Works*, V. 18, p. 13.) In the second edition of *Das Kapital* (1873) Marx deleted a sharp, ironical remark aimed at Herzen which had appeared in the first edition (1866). However, it is hard to judge to what extent this represents a change in Marx's estimation of Herzen—see his 1877 'Letter to the Editor of *Notes of the Fatherland*.'

[I haven't seen it but the implication is that Marx was still denigrating Herzen in 1877. Nor do I know why Marx deleted that "sharp, ironical" remark about Herzen in the second edition (maybe space?), but I do notice that Marx, after challenging "Herzen & Co." (the "Co." by that time was reduced to Ogarëv—and Bakunin) to "prove their revolutionary honor" when the Polish revolt began, wasn't generous enough to concede that Herzen *had* proved it (unless the Soviet scholars, incredibly, overlooked some such expression, private or public, in their laborious search for every straw of "rapprochement"). That tribute Marx left for Lenin to pay—posthumously. (*D.M.*)]

Finally, the interest Marx took in Herzen's writings may be gathered from the fact that in studying the Russian language he made use of *My Past and Thoughts*.

[On this gracious dying fall, the Academy of Sciences ends its apologetic chronicle. Gracious, but even an amateur detects a certain desperation. ("Well, anyway, he was good to his mother.") For Herzen's memoirs were, even in his, let alone Marx's, lifetime, recognized as a literary classic, and Marx dug classics, old or new. He admired Balzac's novels despite their retrograde politics and is said to have reread Aeschylus, in Greek, every year. So, of course he would dig Herzen stylistically as a language text. But there is no evidence he ever dug him politically. Quite the contrary, as the Soviet scholars and I have between us demonstrated. (*D.M.*)]

POSTSCRIPT: *In Martin Malia's* Herzen and the Birth of Russian Socialism *there is an explanation (footnote 5, pp. 429–30) of the grandeurs and miseries of Herzen as a subject for Soviet scholarship which may be illuminating to readers puzzled by the above learned egg-dance. Or by the even more bewildering fact from which it proceeds: that so un-Marxist and unsovietsimpatico a political writer has lately had his complete works collected, annotated, and published by the Academy of Sciences of the U.S.S.R. (Moscow, 1954–65, 30 volumes). True, Volume 1 appeared just after Stalin's death—though they must have been preparing—but still . . .*

It's all due, according to Professor Malia, to Lenin's having dashed off three casual appreciations of Herzen as the founder of Russian socialism. "Short journalistic efforts of no great value as historical analysis unlike some of Lenin's longer and more pondered works" is his description. But one of them was decisive in establishing Herzen's place in Soviet iconography as a precursive "voice crying in the wilderness." Namely "Parmiati Gertsena" ("To the Memory of Herzen") in the April 25, 1912, issue of the newspaper Sotsial-Demokrat.

"This article," Professor Malia writes, "was written to commemorate the hundredth anniversary of Herzen's birth. It is no more than an attempt to annex Herzen to the tradition of Lenin's own party against the claims of the Socialist Revolutionaries, which in reality were more substantial. Yet this chance article has been the basis for Herzen's great fortune in Soviet historiography. Without it, Herzen might well have been spurned as an aristocrat, an anarchist, and Marx's foe—which was the fate of Bakunin. But Lenin's blessing has not been an unmixed one, for the same 're-markable' article (as it is inevitably described) has also been the strait-jacket into which all Soviet scholarship on Herzen has had to fit since the 1930s, and it is a narrow one indeed."

An item in The New York Times, *March 16, 1947, is relevant here: "At the Lenin Library, where Moscow University students represent a formidable section of readers, Alexander Herzen was mentioned as among the most widely read authors. His works are required reading in courses on the literature and history of the revolutionary movement in Russia." One wonders what (silent) conclusions some of the Lenin Library readers may have drawn, for Herzen's notion of revolution was basically "soft"—Menshevik—rather than "hard"—Bolshevik: "I do not believe that people are serious when they prefer destruction and rude force to evolution and compromise. Men must be preached to, incessantly preached to, workmen as well as masters." (D.M.)*

INDEX OF PERSONS

VINTAGE BIOGRAPHY AND AUTOBIOGRAPHY

VINTAGE CRITICISM,
LITERATURE, MUSIC, AND ART